IMMANUEL KANT'S
CRITIQUE OF PURE REASON

By Norman Kemp Smith

★

THE PHILOSOPHY OF DAVID HUME
NEW STUDIES IN THE PHILOSOPHY OF DESCARTES

sophie yetton

IMMANUEL KANT'S
CRITIQUE OF PURE REASON

TRANSLATED BY

NORMAN KEMP SMITH

FORMERLY PROFESSOR OF LOGIC AND METAPHYSICS IN THE UNIVERSITY OF EDINBURGH

MACMILLAN

First published 1929 by
MACMILLAN PRESS LTD
Houndmills, Basingstoke, Hampshire RG21 2XS
and London
Companies and representatives
throughout the world

ISBN 0-333-01994-6 hardcover
ISBN 0-333-05713-9 paperback

36 35 34 33 32 31 30
04 03 02 01 00 99

Printed in Hong Kong

TRANSLATOR'S PREFACE

THE present translation was begun in 1913, when I was completing my *Commentary to Kant's 'Critique of Pure Reason.'*
Owing, however, to various causes, I was unable at that time to do more than prepare a rough translation of about a third of the whole ; and it was not until 1927 that I found leisure to revise and continue it. In this task I have greatly profited by the work of my two predecessors, J. M. D. Meiklejohn and Max Müller. Meiklejohn's work, a translation of the second edition of the *Critique*, was published in 1855. Max Müller's translation, which is based on the first edition of the *Critique*, with the second edition passages in appendices, was published in 1881. Meiklejohn has a happy gift—which only those who attempt to follow in his steps can, I think, fully appreciate—of making Kant speak in language that reasonably approximates to English idiom. Max Müller's main merit, as he has very justly claimed, is his greater accuracy in rendering passages in which a specially exact appreciation of the niceties of German idiom happens to be important for the sense. Both Meiklejohn and Max Müller laboured, however, under the disadvantage of not having made any very thorough study of the Critical Philosophy; and the shortcomings in their translations can usually be traced to this cause.

In the past fifty years, also, much has been done in the study and interpretation of the text. In particular, my task has been facilitated by the quite invaluable edition of the *Critique* edited by Dr. Raymund Schmidt. Indeed, the appearance of this edition in 1926 was the immediate occasion of my resuming the work of translation. Dr Schmidt's restora-

tion of the original texts of the first and second editions of the
Critique, and especially of Kant's own punctuation—so very
helpful in many difficult and doubtful passages—and his citation of alternative readings, have largely relieved me of the
time-consuming task of collating texts, and of assembling the
emendations suggested by Kantian scholars in their editions
of the *Critique* or in their writings upon it.

The text which I have followed is that of the second
edition (1787) ; and I have in all cases indicated any departure
from it. I have also given a translation of all first edition
passages which in the second edition have been either
altered or omitted. Wherever possible, this original first edition
text is given in the lower part of the page. In the two
sections, however, which Kant completely recast in the second
edition—*The Transcendental Deduction of the Categories* and
The Paralogisms of Pure Reason—this cannot conveniently
be done ; and I have therefore given the two versions in
immediate succession, in the main text. For this somewhat
unusual procedure there is a twofold justification; first, that
the *Critique* is already, in itself, a composite work, the different
parts of which record the successive stages in the development
of Kant's views; and secondly, that the first edition versions
are, as a matter of fact, indispensable for an adequate understanding of the versions which were substituted for them. The
pagings of both the first and the second edition are given
throughout, on the margins—the first edition being referred
to as A, the second edition as B.

Kant's German, even when judged by German standards,
makes difficult reading. The difficulties are not due merely to
the abstruseness of the doctrines which Kant is endeavouring
to expound, or to his frequent alternation between conflicting
points of view. Many of the difficulties are due simply to his
manner of writing. He crowds so much into each sentence,
that he is constrained to make undue use of parentheses, and,
what is still more troublesome to the reader, to rely upon
particles, pronouns and genders to indicate the connections

between the parts of the sentence. Sometimes, when our main
clue is a gender, we find more than one preceding substantive
with which it may agree. Sometimes, also, Kant uses terms
in a gender which is obsolete. Certain terms, indeed, he uses
in more than one gender. Thus, even in regard to so important
a philosophical term as *Verhältniss*, he alternates between
the feminine and the neuter. But even when these and other
difficulties, inherent in the original German, have been overcome, there remains for the translator the task, from which
there is no escape, of restating the content of each of the more
complex sentences in a number of separate sentences. To do
this without distortion of meaning is probably in most cases
possible; and indeed I have found that, by patient and careful handling, even the most cumbrous sentences can generally
be satisfactorily resolved.

Certain sentences, however, occurring not infrequently,
present the translator with another type of problem: how far
he ought to sacrifice part of what is said, or at least suggested,
to gain smoothness in the translation. There are sentences
which, to judge by their irregular structure and by the character of their constituents, must have owed their origin to the
combination of passages independently written and later combined. In the "four to five months" in which Kant prepared
the *Critique* for publication, utilising, in the final version,
manuscripts written at various dates throughout the period
1769–1780, he had, it would seem, in collating different statements of the same argument, inserted clauses into sentences
that were by no means suited for their reception. In such cases
I have not attempted to translate the sentences just as they
stand. Were the irregularities retained, they would hinder, not
aid, the reader in the understanding of Kant's argument. The
reader would not, indeed, be able to distinguish between them
and possible faultiness in the translator's English. Nor would
it be practicable to retain them, with the addition of explana-
tory notes; the notes would have to be too numerous, and
would be concerned with quite trivial points. The irregularities

that are thus smoothed out may, it is true, be of considerable importance in the detailed study of the composite origins of the *Critique*, and of the stages in the development of Kant's views. But even in this connection, they are valueless save when studied in the *ipsissima verba* of the original German. In the translation itself nothing is being sacrificed that is materially worth retaining.

My chief personal obligations are to Dr. A. C. Ewing. In 1927, while I was still hesitating whether I could find time and energy to complete the translation single-handed, he kindly consented, upon my appealing to him, to try the experiment of collaborating in a joint-translation. We soon found, however, that to arrive at a uniform translation involved so much mutual consultation as hardly to be practicable. But though I am alone responsible for this translation, Dr. Ewing has very generously given me assistance at every stage in the work. He has read the whole translation both in manuscript and in proof; and I have greatly benefited by his comments and criticisms. I am also indebted to him for preparing the index.

My friends Dr. R. A. Lillie, Mr. R. D. Maclennan, and Mr. W. G. Maclagan have done me the service of reading the proofs. To Dr. Lillie I am especially indebted for the kindly rigour with which he has refused to accept excuses when my sentences would seem to be needlessly cumbrous.

In a careful final revision of the translation I have found a number of errors, major and minor; and I fear that others must have remained undetected. Should students of the *Critique*, in using this translation, discover any, I shall be grateful if they will report them to me.

NORMAN KEMP SMITH.

EDINBURGH, *October* 1929.

In revising the translation for this impression I have been aided by some very helpful criticisms from Professor H. H. Joachim and Professor H. J. Paton.   N. K. S.

EDINBURGH, *March* 1933.

TABLE OF CONTENTS[1]

[1] [This table of contents, with a few additions referring to Sections omitted, altered, or added in B, is the table given in B. The briefer table of A is given below on p. 39.]

TABLE OF CONTENTS

TABLE OF CONTENTS

II. TRANSCENDENTAL DOCTRINE OF METHOD

Critik

der

reinen Vernunft

***

von

Immanuel Kant

Professor in Königsberg.

Riga,
verlegts Johann Friedrich Hartknoch
1781

Kritik

der

reinen Vernunft

von

Immanuel Kant

Professor in Königsberg
der Königl. Akademie der Wissenschaften in Berlin Mitglied

Zweite hin und wieder verbesserte Auflage

Riga
bei Johann Friedrich Hartknoch
1787

BACO DE VERULAMIO

INSTAURATIO MAGNA. PRAEFATIO.

DE nobis ipsis silemus: De re autem, quae agitur, petimus: ut homines eam non Opinionem, sed Opus esse cogitent; ac pro certo habeant, non Sectae nos alicujus, aut Placiti, sed utilitatis et amplitudinis humanae fundamenta moliri. Deinde ut suis commodis aequi . . . in commune consulant, . . . et ipsi in partem veniant. Praeterea ut bene sperent, neque Instaurationem nostram ut quiddam infinitum et ultra mortale fingant, et animo concipiant; quum revera sit infiniti erroris finis et terminus legitimus [1]

---

* [This motto added in B.]

To his Excellency
  The Royal Minister of State
    Baron von Zedlitz

HONOURED SIR,

To further, so far as in us lies, the growth of the sciences is to work along the lines of your Excellency's own interests, which are closely bound up with the sciences, not only in virtue of your exalted position as a patron, but through your more intimate relation to them as lover and enlightened judge. I therefore avail myself of the only means that is in any degree in my power, of expressing my gratitude for the gracious confidence with which your Excellency honours me, if that I could perhaps be of assistance in this respect.

To [1] the same gracious attention with which your Excellency has honoured the first edition of this work I now dedicate this second edition, and therewith I crave the protection [2] of all the other concerns of my literary mission, and remain with the most profound reverence,

Your Excellency's

Humble, most obedient servant,

IMMANUEL KANT

---

[1] [In A, in place of this closing paragraph, there are the two paragraphs:]
Whoever limiting his worldly ambitions finds satisfaction in the speculative life, has in the approval of an enlightened and competent judge a powerful incentive to labours, the benefits of which are great but remote, and therefore such as the vulgar altogether fail to recognise.

To such a judge and to his gracious attention I now dedicate this work, and to his protection all the other . . .

[2] [Reading *zugleich seinem Schutze*.]

PREFACE TO FIRST EDITION

HUMAN reason has this peculiar fate that in one species of its knowledge it is burdened by questions which, as prescribed by the very nature of reason itself, it is not able to ignore, but which, as transcending all its powers, it is also not able to answer.

The perplexity into which it thus falls is not due to any fault of its own. It begins with principles which it has no option save to employ in the course of experience, and which this experience at the same time abundantly justifies it in using. Rising with their aid (since it is determined to this also by its own nature) to ever higher, ever more remote, conditions, it soon becomes aware that in this way—the questions never ceasing—its work must always remain incomplete; and it therefore finds itself compelled to resort to principles which overstep all possible empirical employment, and which yet seem so unobjectionable that even ordinary consciousness readily accepts them. But by this procedure human reason precipitates itself into darkness and contradictions; and while it may indeed conjecture that these must be in some way due to concealed errors, it is not in a position to be able to detect them. For since the principles of which it is making use transcend the limits of experience, they are no longer subject to any empirical test. The battle-field of these endless controversies is called metaphysics.

Time was when metaphysics was entitled the Queen of all the sciences; and if the will be taken for the deed, the pre-eminent importance of her accepted tasks gives her every right to this title of honour. Now, however, the changed fashion of the time brings her only scorn; a matron outcast

and forsaken, she mourns like Hecuba: *Modo maxima rerum,*
A ix. *tot generis natisque potens—nunc trahor exul, inops.*[a]

Her government, under the administration of the *dogmatists*, was at first *despotic*. But inasmuch as the legislation still bore traces of the ancient barbarism, her empire gradually through intestine wars gave way to complete anarchy; and the *sceptics*, a species of nomads, despising all settled modes of life, broke up from time to time all civil society. Happily they were few in number, and were unable to prevent its being established ever anew, although on no uniform and self-consistent plan. In more recent times, it has seemed as if an end might be put to all these controversies and the claims of metaphysics receive final judgment, through a certain *physiology* of the human understanding—that of the celebrated Locke. But it has turned out quite otherwise. For however the attempt be made to cast doubt upon the pretensions of the supposed Queen by tracing her lineage to vulgar origins in common experience, this genealogy has, as a matter of fact, been fictitiously invented, and she has
A x. still continued to uphold her claims. Metaphysics has accordingly lapsed back into the ancient time-worn dogmatism, and so again suffers that depreciation from which it was to have been rescued. And now, after all methods, so it is believed, have been tried and found wanting, the prevailing mood is that of weariness and complete *indifferentism*—the mother, in all sciences, of chaos and night, but happily in this case the source, or at least the prelude, of their approaching reform and restoration. For it at least puts an end to that ill-applied industry which has rendered them thus dark, confused, and unserviceable.

But it is idle to feign indifference to such enquiries, the object of which can never be indifferent to our human nature. Indeed these pretended *indifferentists*, however they may try to disguise themselves by substituting a popular tone for the language of the Schools, inevitably fall back, in so far as they think at all, into those very metaphysical assertions which they profess so greatly to despise. None the less this indifference, showing itself in the midst of flourishing sciences, and affecting precisely those

[a] Ovid, *Metam.* [xiii. 508-510].

sciences, the knowledge of which, if attainable, we should
least of all care to dispense with, is a phenomenon that A xi.
calls for attention and reflection. It is obviously the effect
not of levity but of the matured judgment[a] of the age, which
refuses to be any longer put off with illusory knowledge. It is
a call to reason to undertake anew the most difficult of all
its tasks, namely, that of self-knowledge, and to institute
a tribunal which will assure to reason its lawful claims, and
dismiss all groundless pretensions, not by despotic decrees, A xii.
but in accordance with its own eternal and unalterable
laws. This tribunal is no other than the *critique of pure
reason*.

I do not mean by this a critique of books and systems,
but of the faculty of reason in general, in respect of all knowledge after which it[1] may strive *independently of all experience*. It will therefore decide as to the possibility or impossibility of metaphysics in general, and determine its sources,
its extent, and its limits—all in accordance with principles.

I have entered upon this path—the only one that has remained unexplored—and flatter myself that in following it I
have found a way of guarding against all those errors which
have hitherto set reason, in its non-empirical employment, at

[a] We often hear complaints of shallowness of thought in our age
and of the consequent decline of sound science. But I do not see
that the sciences which rest upon a secure foundation, such as mathematics, physics, etc., in the least deserve this reproach. On the contrary, they merit their old reputation for solidity, and, in the case
of physics, even surpass it. The same spirit would have become
active in other kinds of knowledge, if only attention had first been
directed to the determination of their principles. Till this is done, indifference, doubt, and, in the final issue, severe criticism, are themselves proofs of a profound habit of thought. Our age is, in especial
degree, the age of criticism,[2] and to criticism everything must submit. Religion through its sanctity, and law-giving through its majesty,
may seek to exempt themselves from it. But they then awaken just
suspicion, and cannot claim the sincere respect which reason accords
only to that which has been able to sustain the test of free and open
examination.

[1] [Reading, with Adickes, *es* for *sie*.]
[2] [*Kritik*. This term I have sometimes translated 'criticism' and sometimes
'critique'.]

variance with itself. I have not evaded its questions by pleading the insufficiency of human reason. On the contrary, I have specified these questions exhaustively, according to principles; and after locating the point at which, through misunderstanding, reason comes into conflict with itself, I have A xiii solved them to its complete satisfaction. The answer to these questions has not, indeed, been such as a dogmatic and visionary insistence upon knowledge might lead us to expect— that can be catered for only through magical devices, in which I am no adept. Such ways of answering them are, indeed, not within the intention of the natural constitution of our reason; and inasmuch as they have their source in misunderstanding, it is the duty of philosophy to counteract their deceptive influence, no matter what prized and cherished dreams may have to be disowned. In this enquiry I have made completeness my chief aim, and I venture to assert that there is not a single metaphysical problem which has not been solved, or for the solution of which the key at least has not been supplied. Pure reason is, indeed, so perfect a unity that if its principle were insufficient for the solution of even a single one of all the questions to which it itself gives birth we should have no alternative but to reject the principle, since we should then no longer be able to place implicit reliance upon it in dealing with any one of the other questions.

While I am saying this I can fancy that I detect in the face A xiv. of the reader an expression of indignation, mingled with contempt, at pretensions seemingly so arrogant and vain-glorious. Yet they are incomparably more moderate than the claims of all those writers who on the lines of the usual programme profess to prove the simple nature of the soul or the necessity of a first beginning of the world. For while such writers pledge themselves to extend human knowledge beyond all limits of possible experience, I humbly confess that this is entirely beyond my power. I have to deal with nothing save reason itself and its pure thinking; and to obtain complete knowledge of these, there is no need to go far afield, since I come upon them in my own self. Common logic itself supplies an example, how all the simple acts of reason can be enumerated completely and systematically. The subject of the present enquiry is the [kindred] question, how much we can hope to achieve by reason, when all the material and assistance of experience are taken away.

So much as regards *completeness* in our determination of each question, and *exhaustiveness* in our determination of all the questions with which we have to deal. These questions are not arbitrarily selected; they are prescribed to us, by the very nature of knowledge itself, as being the subject-matter of our critical enquiry.

As regards the *form* of our enquiry, *certainty* and *clearness* A xv. are two essential requirements, rightly to be exacted from any-one who ventures upon so delicate an undertaking.

As to *certainty*, I have prescribed to myself the maxim, that in this kind of investigation it is in no wise permissible to hold *opinions*. Everything, therefore, which bears any manner of resemblance to an hypothesis is to be treated as contraband; it is not to be put up for sale even at the lowest price, but forthwith confiscated, immediately upon detection. Any knowledge that professes to hold *a priori* lays claim to be regarded as absolutely necessary. This applies still more to any *determination* of all pure *a priori* knowledge, since such determination has to serve as the measure, and therefore as the [supreme] example, of all apodeictic (philosophical) certainty. Whether I have succeeded in what I have undertaken must be left altogether to the reader's judgment; the author's task is solely to adduce grounds, not to speak as to the effect which they should have upon those who are sitting in judgment. But the author, in order that he may not himself, innocently, be A xvi. the cause of any weakening of his arguments, may be permitted to draw attention to certain passages, which, although merely incidental, may yet occasion some mistrust. Such timely intervention may serve to counteract the influence which even quite undefined doubts as to these minor matters might otherwise exercise upon the reader's attitude in regard to the main issue.

I know no enquiries which are more important for exploring the faculty which we entitle understanding, and for determining the rules and limits of its employment, than those which I have instituted in the second chapter of the Transcendental Analytic under the title *Deduction of the Pure Concepts of Understanding*. They are also those which have

cost me the greatest labour—labour, as I hope, not unre-
warded. This enquiry, which is somewhat deeply grounded,
has two sides. The one refers to the objects of pure understanding, and is intended to expound and render intelligible
the objective validity of its *a priori* concepts. It is therefore
essential to my purposes. The other seeks to investigate the
pure understanding itself, its possibility and the cognitive
A xvii. faculties upon which it rests; and so deals with it in its subjective aspect. Although this latter exposition is of great
importance for my chief purpose, it does not form an essential
part of it. For the chief question is always simply this:—what
and how much can the understanding and reason know apart
from all experience? not:—how is the faculty of thought itself
possible? The latter is, as it were, the search for the cause of
a given effect, and to that extent is somewhat hypothetical
in character (though, as I shall show elsewhere, it is not really
so); and I would appear to be taking the liberty simply of
expressing an *opinion*, in which case the reader would be free
to express a different *opinion*. For this reason I must forestall
the reader's criticism by pointing out that the objective deduction with which I am here chiefly concerned retains its full
force even if my subjective deduction should fail to produce
that complete conviction for which I hope. On this matter,
what has been said on pp. 92-93[1] should in any case suffice
by itself.

As regards *clearness*, the reader has a right to demand, in
the first place, a *discursive* (logical) clearness, through *con-*
A xviii. *cepts*, and secondly, an *intuitive* (aesthetic) clearness, through
intuitions, that is, through examples and other concrete
illustrations. For the first I have sufficiently provided. That
was essential to my purpose; but it has also been the incidental
cause of my not being in a position to do justice to the second
demand, which, if not so pressing, is yet still quite reasonable.
I have been almost continuously at a loss, during the progress
of my work, how I should proceed in this matter. Examples
and illustrations seemed always to be necessary, and so took
their place, as required, in my first draft. But I very soon
became aware of the magnitude of my task and of the multiplicity of matters with which I should have to deal; and as

[1] [Paging in A.]

I perceived that even if treated in dry, purely *scholastic* fashion, the outcome would by itself be already quite sufficiently large in bulk, I found it inadvisable to enlarge it yet further through examples and illustrations. These are necessary only from a *popular* point of view; and this work can never be made suitable for popular consumption. Such assistance is not required by genuine students of the science, and, though always pleasing, might very well in this case have been self-defeating in its effects. Abbot Terrasson [1] has remarked that if the size of a volume be measured not by the A xix. number of its pages but by the time required for mastering it, it can be said of many a book, *that it would be much shorter if it were not so short.* On the other hand, if we have in view the comprehensibility of a whole of speculative knowledge, which, though wide-ranging, has the coherence that follows from unity of principle, we can say with equal justice *that many a book would have been much clearer if it had not made such an effort to be clear.* For the aids to clearness, though they may be of assistance [2] in regard to details, often interfere with our grasp of the whole. The reader is not allowed to arrive sufficiently quickly at a conspectus of the whole; the bright colouring of the illustrative material intervenes to cover over and conceal the articulation and organisation of the system, which, if we are to be able to judge of its unity and solidity, are what chiefly concern us.

The reader, I should judge, will feel it to be no small inducement to yield his willing co-operation, when the author is thus endeavouring, according to the plan here proposed, to carry through a large and important work in a complete and lasting manner. Metaphysics, on the view which we are adopt- A xx. ing, is the only one of all the sciences which dare promise that through a small but concentrated effort it will attain, and this in a short time, such completion as will leave no task to our successors save that of adapting it in a *didactic* manner according to their own preferences, without their

---

[1] [The reference is to a posthumous work of Abbot Terrasson, which appeared in 1754. Kant was probably acquainted with it in the German translation, published in 1762, under the title, *Philosophie nach ihrem allgemeinen Einflusse auf alle Gegenstände des Geistes und der Sitten.* The passage cited is on p. 117 of that translation.]

[2] [Reading, with Rosenkranz, *helfen* for *fehlen.*]

being able to add anything whatsoever to its content. For it is nothing but the *inventory* of all our possessions through *pure* reason, systematically arranged. In this field nothing can escape us. What reason produces entirely out of itself cannot be concealed, but is brought to light by reason itself immediately the common principle has been discovered. The complete unity of this kind of knowledge, and the fact that it is derived solely from pure concepts, entirely uninfluenced by any experience or by *special* intuition, such as might lead to any determinate experience that would enlarge and increase it, make this unconditioned completeness not only practicable but also necessary. *Tecum habita, et noris quam sit tibi curta supellex.*[a]

A xxi. Such a system of pure (speculative) reason I hope myself to produce under the title *Metaphysics of Nature*. It will be not half as large, yet incomparably richer in content than this present *Critique*, which has as its first task to discover the sources and conditions of the possibility of such criticism, clearing, as it were, and levelling what has hitherto been wasteground. In this present enterprise I look to my reader for the patience and impartiality of a *judge*; whereas in the other I shall look for the benevolent assistance of a *fellow-worker*. For however completely all the *principles* of the system are presented in this *Critique*, the completeness of the system itself likewise requires that none of the *derivative* concepts be lacking. These cannot be enumerated by any *a priori* computation, but must be discovered gradually. Whereas, therefore, in this *Critique* the entire *synthesis* of the concepts has been exhausted, there will still remain the further work of making their *analysis* similarly complete, a task which is rather an amusement than a labour.

I have only a few remarks to add of a typographical character. As the beginning of the printing was delayed, I
A xxii. was not able to see more than about half of the proof-sheets, and I now find some misprints, which do not, however, affect the sense except on p. 379, line 4 from the bottom,[1] where specific has to be read in place of sceptical. The antinomy

---

[a] Persius [*Sat.* iv. 52].

[1] [Paging in A]

of pure reason, from p. 425 to p. 461,[1] has been so arranged, in tabular form, that all that belongs to the thesis stands on the left and what belongs to the antithesis on the right. This I have done in order that proposition and counter-proposition may be the more easily compared with one another.

[1] [Paging in A.]

PREFACE TO SECOND EDITION B vii

WHETHER the treatment of such knowledge as lies within the province of reason does or does not follow the secure path of a science, is easily to be determined from the outcome. For if after elaborate preparations, frequently renewed, it is brought to a stop immediately it nears its goal; if often it is compelled to retrace its steps and strike into some new line of approach; or again, if the various participants are unable to agree in any common plan of procedure, then we may rest assured that it is very far from having entered upon the secure path of a science, and is indeed a merely random groping. In these circumstances, we shall be rendering a service to reason should we succeed in discovering the path upon which it can securely travel, even if, as a result of so doing, much that is comprised in our original aims, adopted without reflection, may have to be abandoned as fruitless.

That logic has already, from the earliest times, proceeded B viii. upon this sure path is evidenced by the fact that since Aristotle it has not required to retrace a single step, unless, indeed, we care to count as improvements the removal of certain needless subtleties or the clearer exposition of its recognised teaching, features which concern the elegance rather than the certainty of the science. It is remarkable also that to the present day this logic has not been able to advance a single step, and is thus to all appearance a closed and completed body of doctrine. If some of the moderns have thought to enlarge it by introducing *psychological* chapters on the different faculties of knowledge (imagination, wit, etc.), *metaphysical* chapters on the origin of knowledge or on the different kinds of certainty according to difference in the objects (idealism, scepticism, etc.), or *anthropological* chapters on prejudices, their causes and remedies, this could only arise from their ignorance of the

17

peculiar nature of logical science. We do not enlarge but disfigure sciences, if we allow them to trespass upon one another's territory. The sphere of logic is quite precisely delimited; its sole concern is to give an exhaustive exposition and a strict proof of the formal rules of all thought, whether it be *a priori* or empirical, whatever be its origin or its object, and whatever hindrances, accidental or natural, it may encounter in our minds.

B ix.

That logic should have been thus successful is an advantage which it owes entirely to its limitations, whereby it is justified in abstracting—indeed, it is under obligation to do so—from all objects of knowledge and their differences, leaving the understanding nothing to deal with save itself and its form. But for reason to enter on the sure path of science is, of course, much more difficult, since it has to deal not with itself alone but also with objects. Logic, therefore, as a propaedeutic, forms, as it were, only the vestibule of the sciences; and when we are concerned with specific modes of knowledge, while logic is indeed presupposed in any critical estimate of them, yet for the actual acquiring of them we have to look to the sciences properly and objectively so called.

Now if reason is to be a factor in these sciences, something in them must be known *a priori*, and this knowledge may be related to its object in one or other of two ways, either as merely *determining* it and its concept (which must be supplied from elsewhere) or as also *making it actual*. The former is *theoretical*, the latter *practical* knowledge of reason. In both, that part in which reason determines its object completely *a priori*, namely, the *pure* part—however much or little this part may contain—must be first and separately dealt with, in case it be confounded with what comes from other sources. For it is bad management if we blindly pay out what comes in, and are not able, when the income falls into arrears, to distinguish which part of it can justify expenditure, and in which[1] line we must make reductions.

B x.

Mathematics and physics, the two sciences in which reason yields theoretical knowledge, have to determine their objects *a priori*, the former doing so quite purely, the latter having

[1] [Reading, with Erdmann, *von welchem* for *von welcher*.]

to reckon, at least partially, with sources of knowledge other than reason.

In the earliest times to which the history of human reason extends, *mathematics*, among that wonderful people, the Greeks, had already entered upon the sure path of science. But it must not be supposed that it was as easy for mathematics as it was for logic—in which reason has to deal with itself alone—to light upon, or rather to construct for itself, that royal road. B xi. On the contrary, I believe that it long remained, especially among the Egyptians, in the groping stage, and that the transformation must have been due to a *revolution* brought about by the happy thought of a single man, the experiment which he devised marking out the path upon which the science must enter, and by following which, secure progress throughout all time and in endless expansion is infallibly secured. The history of this intellectual revolution—far more important than the discovery of the passage round the celebrated Cape of Good Hope—and of its fortunate author, has not been preserved. But the fact that Diogenes Laertius, in handing down an account of these matters, names the reputed author of even the least important among the geometrical demonstrations, even of those which, for ordinary consciousness, stand in need of no such proof, does at least show that the memory of the revolution, brought about by the first glimpse of this new path, must have seemed to mathematicians of such outstanding importance as to cause it to survive the tide of oblivion. A new light flashed upon the mind of the first man (be he Thales or some other) who demonstrated the properties of the isosceles triangle. The true method, so he found, was not to inspect what he dis- B xii. cerned either in the figure, or in the bare concept of it, and from this, as it were, to read off its properties; but to bring out what [1] was necessarily implied in the concepts that he had himself formed *a priori*, and had put into the figure in the construction by which he presented it to himself. If he is to know anything with *a priori* certainty he must not ascribe to the figure anything save what necessarily follows from what he has himself set into it in accordance with his concept.

Natural science was very much longer in entering upon the highway of science. It is, indeed, only about a century and a

---

[1] [Reading, with Adickes, *sondern das* for *sondern durch das*.]

half since Bacon, by his ingenious proposals, partly initiated this discovery, partly inspired fresh vigour in those who were already on the way to it. In this case also the discovery can be explained as being the sudden outcome of an intellectual revolution. In my present remarks I am referring to natural science only in so far as it is founded on *empirical* principles.

When Galileo caused balls, the weights of which he had himself previously determined, to roll down an inclined plane; when Torricelli made the air carry a weight which he had calculated beforehand to be equal to that of a definite volume of water; or in more recent times, when Stahl changed metals B xiii. into oxides, and oxides back into metal, by withdrawing something and then restoring it,[a] a light broke upon all students of nature. They learned that reason has insight only into that which it produces after a plan of its own, and that it must not allow itself to be kept, as it were, in nature's leading-strings, but must itself show the way with principles of judgment based upon fixed laws, constraining nature to give answer to questions of reason's own determining. Accidental observations, made in obedience to no previously thought-out plan, can never be made to yield a necessary law, which alone reason is concerned to discover. Reason, holding in one hand its principles, according to which alone concordant appearances can be admitted as equivalent to laws, and in the other hand the experiment which it has devised in conformity with these principles, must approach nature in order to be taught by it. It must not, however, do so in the character of a pupil who listens to everything that the teacher chooses to say, but of an appointed judge who compels the witnesses to answer questions which he has himself formulated. Even physics, therefore, owes the beneficent revolution in its point of view B xiv. entirely to the happy thought, that while reason must seek in nature, not fictitiously ascribe to it, whatever as not being knowable through reason's own resources has to be learnt, if learnt at all, only from nature, it must adopt as its guide, in so seeking, that which it has itself put into nature. It is thus that the study of nature has entered on the secure path of a

---

[a] I am not, in my choice of examples, tracing the exact course of the history of the experimental method; we have indeed no very precise knowledge of its first beginnings.

science, after having for so many centuries been nothing but a process of merely random groping.

Metaphysics is a completely isolated speculative science of reason, which soars far above the teachings of experience, and in which reason is indeed meant to be its own pupil. Metaphysics rests on concepts alone—not, like mathematics, on their application to intuition. But though it is older than all other sciences, and would survive even if all the rest were swallowed up in the abyss of an all-destroying barbarism, it has not yet had the good fortune to enter upon the secure path of a science. For in it reason is perpetually being brought to a stand, even when the laws into which it is seeking to have, as it professes, an *a priori* insight are those that are confirmed by our most common experiences. Ever and again we have to retrace our steps, as not leading us in the direction in which we desire to go. So far, too, are the students of metaphysics from exhibiting any B xv. kind of unanimity in their contentions, that metaphysics has rather to be regarded as a battle-ground quite peculiarly suited for those who desire to exercise themselves in mock combats, and in which no participant has ever yet succeeded in gaining even so much as an inch of territory, not at least in such manner as to secure him in its permanent possession. This shows, beyond all questioning, that the procedure of metaphysics has hitherto been a merely random groping, and, what is worst of all, a groping among mere concepts.

What, then, is the reason why, in this field, the sure road to science has not hitherto been found? Is it, perhaps, impossible of discovery? Why, in that case, should nature have visited our reason with the restless endeavour whereby it is ever searching for such a path, as if this were one of its most important concerns? Nay, more, how little cause have we to place trust in our reason, if, in one of the most important domains of which we would fain have knowledge, it does not merely fail us, but lures us on by deceitful promises, and in the end betrays us! Or if it be only that we have thus far failed to find the true path, are there any indications to justify the hope that by renewed efforts we may have better fortune than has fallen to our predecessors?

The examples of mathematics and natural science, which by a single and sudden revolution have become what they B xvi.

now are, seem to me sufficiently remarkable to suggest our considering what may have been the essential features in the changed point of view by which they have so greatly benefited. Their success should incline us, at least by way of experiment, to imitate their procedure, so far as the analogy which, as species of rational knowledge, they bear to metaphysics may permit. Hitherto it has been assumed that all our knowledge must conform to objects. But all attempts to extend our knowledge of objects by establishing something in regard to them *a priori*, by means of concepts, have, on this assumption, ended in failure. We must therefore make trial whether we may not have more success in the tasks of metaphysics, if we suppose that objects must conform to our knowledge. This would agree better with what is desired, namely, that it should be possible to have knowledge of objects *a priori*, determining something in regard to them prior to their being given. We should then be proceeding precisely on the lines of Copernicus' primary hypothesis.[1] Failing of satisfactory progress in explaining the movements of the heavenly bodies on the supposition that they all revolved round the spectator, he tried whether he might not have better success if he made the spectator B xvii. to revolve and the stars to remain at rest. A similar experiment can be tried in metaphysics, as regards the *intuition* of objects. If intuition must conform to the constitution of the objects, I do not see how we could know anything of the latter *a priori*; but if the object (as object of the senses) must conform to the constitution of our faculty of intuition, I have no difficulty in conceiving such a possibility. Since I cannot rest in these intuitions if they are to become known, but must relate them as representations to something as their object, and determine this latter through them, either I must assume that the *concepts*, by means of which I obtain this determination, conform to the object, or else I assume that the objects, or what is the same thing, that the *experience* in which alone, as given objects, they can be known, conform to the concepts. In the former case, I am again in the same perplexity as to how I can know anything *a priori* in regard to the objects. In the latter case the outlook is more hopeful. For experience is itself a species of knowledge which involves

[1] [*mit den ersten Gedanken des Kopernikus.*]

understanding; and understanding has rules which I must pre-suppose as being in me prior to objects being given to me, and therefore as being *a priori*. They find expression in *a priori* concepts to which all objects of experience necessarily con-   B xviii. form, and with which they must agree. As regards objects which are thought solely through reason, and indeed as necessary, but which can never—at least not in the manner in which reason thinks them—be given in experience, the attempts at thinking them (for they must admit of being thought) will furnish an excellent touchstone of what we are adopting as our new method of thought, namely, that we can know *a priori* of things only what we ourselves put into them.[a]

This experiment succeeds as well as could be desired, and promises to metaphysics, in its first part—the part that is occupied with those concepts *a priori* to which the correspond-ing objects, commensurate with them, can be given in ex-perience—the secure path of a science. For the new point of B xix. view enables us to explain how there can be knowledge *a priori*; and, in addition, to furnish satisfactory proofs of the laws which form the *a priori* basis of nature, regarded as the sum of the objects of experience—neither achievement being possible on the procedure hitherto followed. But this deduction of our power of knowing *a priori*, in the first part of metaphysics, has a consequence which is startling, and which has the appear-

[a] This method, modelled on that of the student of nature, con-sists in looking for the elements of pure reason in *what admits of con-firmation or refutation by experiment*. Now the propositions of pure reason, especially if they venture out beyond all limits of possible experience, cannot be brought to the test through any experiment with their *objects*, as in natural science. In dealing with those *con-cepts* and *principles* which we adopt *a priori*, all that we can do is to contrive that they be used for viewing objects from two different points of view—on the one hand, in connection with experience, as B xix. objects of the senses and of the understanding, and on the other hand, for the isolated reason that strives to transcend all[1] limits of experience, as objects which are thought merely. If, when things are viewed from this twofold standpoint, we find that there is agreement with the principle of pure reason, but that when we regard them only from a single point of view reason is involved in unavoidable self-conflict, the experiment decides in favour of the correctness of this distinction.

[1] [Reading, with Adickes, *über alle* for *über*.]

ance of being highly prejudicial to the whole purpose of metaphysics, as dealt with in the second part. For we are brought to the conclusion that we can never transcend the limits of possible experience, though that is precisely what this science is concerned, above all else, to achieve. This situation yields, however, just the very experiment by which, indirectly, we are enabled to prove the truth of this first estimate of our *a priori* knowledge of reason, namely, that such knowledge has to do only with appearances, and must leave the thing in itself[1] as indeed real *per se*, but as not known by us. For what necessarily forces us to transcend the limits of experience and of all appearances is the *unconditioned*, which reason, by necessity and by right, demands in things in themselves, as required to complete the series of conditions. If, then, on the supposition that our empirical knowledge conforms to objects as things in themselves, we find that the unconditioned *cannot be thought without contradiction*, and that when, on the other hand, we suppose that our representation of things, as they are given to us, does not conform to these things as they are in themselves, but that these objects, as appearances, conform to our mode of representation, *the contradiction vanishes*; and if, therefore, we thus find that the unconditioned is not to be met with in things, so far as we know them, that is, so far as they are given to us, but only so far as we do not know them, that is, so far as they are things in themselves, we are justified in concluding that what we at first assumed for the purposes of experiment is now definitely confirmed.[a] But when all progress in the field of the supersensible has thus been denied to speculative reason, it is still open to us to enquire whether, in the practical

B xx.

B xxi.

---

[a] This experiment of pure reason bears a great similarity to what in chemistry is sometimes entitled the experiment of *reduction*, or more usually the *synthetic* process. The *analysis of the metaphysician* separates pure *a priori* knowledge into two very heterogeneous elements, namely, the knowledge of things as appearances, and the knowledge of things in themselves; his *dialectic* combines these two again, in *harmony* with the necessary idea of the *unconditioned* demanded by reason, and finds that this harmony can never be obtained except through the above distinction, which must therefore be accepted.

[1] [*die Sache an sich selbst.*]

knowledge of reason, data may not be found sufficient to determine reason's transcendent concept of the unconditioned, and so to enable us, in accordance with the wish of metaphysics, and by means of knowledge that is possible *a priori*, though only from a practical point of view, to pass beyond the limits of all possible experience. Speculative reason has thus at least made room for such an extension; and if it must at the same time leave it empty, yet none the less we are at B xxii liberty, indeed we are summoned, to take occupation of it, if we can, by practical data of reason.[a]

This attempt to alter the procedure which has hitherto prevailed in metaphysics, by completely revolutionising it in accordance with the example set by the geometers and physicists, forms indeed the main purpose of this critique of pure speculative reason. It is a treatise on the method, not a system of the science itself. But at the same time it marks out the whole plan of the science, both as regards its limits and as regards its entire internal structure. For pure speculative reason B xxiii has this peculiarity, that it can measure its powers according to the different ways in which it chooses the objects of its thinking, and can also give an exhaustive enumeration of the various ways in which it propounds its problems, and so is able, nay bound, to trace the complete outline of a system of metaphysics. As regards the first point, nothing in *a priori* knowledge can be ascribed to objects save what the thinking subject derives from itself; as regards the second point, pure reason, so far as the principles of its knowledge are concerned,

---

[a] Similarly, the fundamental laws of the motions of the heavenly bodies gave established certainty to what Copernicus had at first assumed only as an hypothesis, and at the same time yielded proof of the invisible force (the Newtonian attraction) which holds the universe together. The latter would have remained for ever undiscovered if Copernicus had not dared, in a manner contradictory of the senses, but yet true, to seek the observed movements, not in the heavenly bodies, but in the spectator. The change in point of view, analogous to this hypothesis, which is expounded in the *Critique*, I put forward in this preface as an hypothesis only, in order to draw attention to the character of these first attempts at such a change, which are always hypothetical. But in the *Critique* itself it will be proved, apodeictically not hypothetically, from the nature of our representations of space and time and from the elementary concepts of the understanding.

is a quite separate self-subsistent unity, in which, as in an
organised body, every member exists for every other, and
all for the sake of each, so that no principle can safely be
taken in *any one* relation, unless it has been investigated in
the *entirety* of its relations to the whole employment of pure
reason. Consequently, metaphysics has also this singular
advantage, such as falls to the lot of no other science which
deals with objects (for *logic* is concerned only with the form
of thought in general), that should it, through this critique,
be set upon the secure path of a science, it is capable of ac-
B xxiv. quiring exhaustive knowledge of its entire field. Metaphysics
has to deal only with principles, and with the limits of their
employment as determined by these principles themselves,
and it can therefore finish its work and bequeath it to posterity
as a capital to which no addition can be made. Since it is
a fundamental science, it is under obligation to achieve this
completeness. We must be able to say of it: *nil actum re-
putans, si quid superesset agendum.*

But, it will be asked, what sort of a treasure is this that
we propose to bequeath to posterity? What is the value of
the metaphysics that is alleged to be thus purified by criticism and established once for all? On a cursory view of the
present work it may seem that its results are merely *negative,*
warning us that we must never venture with speculative reason
beyond the limits of experience. Such is in fact its primary use.
But such teaching at once acquires a *positive* value when we
recognise that the principles with which speculative reason
ventures out beyond its proper limits do not in effect *extend*
the employment of reason, but, as we find on closer scrutiny,
inevitably *narrow* it. These principles properly belong [not
to reason but] to sensibility, and when thus employed they
B xxv. threaten to make the bounds of sensibility coextensive with
the real, and so to supplant reason in its pure (practical) employment. So far, therefore, as our Critique limits speculative
reason, it is indeed *negative*; but since it thereby removes an
obstacle which stands in the way of the employment of practical reason, nay threatens to destroy it, it has in reality a *positive* and very important use. At least this is so, immediately
we are convinced that there is an absolutely necessary *practical* employment of pure reason—the *moral*—in which it

inevitably goes beyond the limits of sensibility. Though [practical] reason, in thus proceeding, requires no assistance from speculative reason, it must yet be assured against its opposition, that reason may not be brought into conflict with itself. To deny that the service which the Critique renders is *positive* in character, would thus be like saying that the police are of no positive benefit, inasmuch as their main business is merely to prevent the violence of which citizens stand in mutual fear, in order that each may pursue his vocation in peace and security. That space and time are only forms of sensible intuition, and so only conditions of the existence of things as appearances; that, moreover, we have no concepts of understanding, and consequently no elements for the knowledge of things, save in so far as intuition can be given corresponding B xxvi. to these concepts; and that we can therefore have no knowledge of any object as thing in itself, but only in so far as it[1] is an object of sensible intuition, that is, an appearance—all this is proved in the analytical part of the Critique. Thus it does indeed follow that all possible speculative knowledge of reason is limited to mere objects of *experience*. But our further contention must also be duly borne in mind, namely, that though we cannot *know* these objects as things in themselves, we must yet be in position at least to *think* them as things in themselves;[a] otherwise we should be landed in the absurd conclusion that there can be appearance without anything that appears B xxvii. Now let us suppose that the distinction, which our Critique has shown to be necessary, between things as objects of experience and those same things as things in themselves, had not been made. In that case all things in general, as far as they are

---

[a] To *know* an object I must be able to prove its possibility, either from its actuality as attested by experience, or *a priori* by means of reason. But I can *think* whatever I please, provided only that I do not contradict myself, that is, provided my concept is a possible thought. This suffices for the possibility of the concept, even though I may not be able to answer for there being, in the sum of all possibilities, an object corresponding to it. But something more is required before I can ascribe to such a concept objective validity, that is, real possibility; the former possibility is merely logical. This something more need not, however, be sought in the theoretical sources of knowledge; it may lie in those that are practical.

[1] [Reading, with Erdmann, *er* for *es*.]

efficient causes, would be determined by the principle of causality, and consequently by the mechanism of nature. I could
not, therefore, without palpable contradiction, say of one and
the same being, for instance the human soul, that its will is free
and yet is subject to natural necessity, that is, is not free. For
I have taken the soul in both propositions *in one and the same
sense*, namely as a thing in general, that is, as a thing[1] in itself;
and save by means of a preceding critique, could not have done
otherwise. But if our Critique is not in error in teaching that
the object is to be taken *in a twofold sense*, namely as appearance and as thing in itself; if the deduction of the concepts of
understanding is valid, and the principle of causality therefore applies only to things taken in the former sense, namely,
in so far as they are objects of experience—these same objects,
taken in the other sense, not being subject to the principle—
then there is no contradiction in supposing that one and the
B xxviii. same will is, in the appearance, that is, in its visible acts,
necessarily subject to the law of nature, and so far *not free*,
while yet, as belonging to a thing in itself, it is not subject
to that law, and is therefore *free*. My soul, viewed from the
latter standpoint, cannot indeed be known by means of speculative reason (and still less through empirical observation);
and freedom as a property of a being to which I attribute effects
in the sensible world, is therefore also not knowable in any
such fashion. For I should then have to know such a being as
determined in its existence, and yet as not determined in time—
which is impossible, since I cannot support my concept by any
intuition. But though I cannot *know*, I can yet *think* freedom;
that is to say, the representation of it is at least not self-contradictory, provided due account be taken of our critical distinction between the two modes of representation, the sensible
and the intellectual, and of the resulting limitation of the pure
concepts of understanding and of the principles which flow
from them.

   If we grant that morality necessarily presupposes freedom
(in the strictest sense) as a property of our will; if, that is to
say, we grant that it yields practical principles—original principles, proper to our reason—as *a priori data* of reason, and
B xxix. that this would be absolutely impossible save on the assump-

----

¹ [*Sache.*]

tion of freedom; and if at the same time we grant that speculative reason has proved that such freedom does not allow of being thought, then the former supposition—that made on behalf of morality—would have to give way to this other contention, the opposite of which involves a palpable contradiction. For since it is only on the assumption of freedom that the negation of morality contains any contradiction, freedom, and with it morality, would have to yield to the mechanism of nature.

Morality does not, indeed, require that freedom should be understood, but only that it should not contradict itself, and so should at least allow of being thought, and that as thus thought it should place no obstacle in the way of a free act (viewed in another relation) likewise conforming to the mechanism of nature. The doctrine of morality and the doctrine of nature may each, therefore, make good its position. This, however, is only possible in so far as criticism has previously established our unavoidable ignorance of things in themselves, and has limited all that we can theoretically *know* to mere appearances.

This discussion as to the positive advantage of critical principles of pure reason can be similarly developed in regard to the concept of *God* and of the *simple nature* of our *soul*; but for the sake of brevity such further discussion may be omitted. [From what has already been said, it is evident that] even the *assumption*—as made on behalf of the necessary practical em- B xxx. ployment of my reason—of *God, freedom*, and *immortality* is not permissible unless at the same time speculative reason be deprived of its pretensions to transcendent insight. For in order to arrive at such insight it must make use of principles which, in fact, extend only to objects of possible experience, and which, if also applied to what cannot be an object of experience, always really change this into an appearance, thus rendering all *practical extension* of pure reason impossible. I have therefore found it necessary to deny *knowledge*, in order to make room for *faith*.[1] The dogmatism of metaphysics, that is, the preconception that it is possible to make headway in metaphysics without a previous criticism of pure reason, is the source of all that unbelief,[2] always very dogmatic, which wars against morality.

---

[1] [*Glaube.*]   [2] [*Unglaube.*]

Though it may not, then, be very difficult to leave to posterity the bequest of a systematic metaphysic, constructed in conformity with a critique of pure reason, yet such a gift is not to be valued lightly. For not only will reason be enabled to follow the secure path of a science, instead of, as hitherto, B xxxi. groping at random, without circumspection or self-criticism; our enquiring youth will also be in a position to spend their time more profitably than in the ordinary dogmatism by which they are so early and so greatly encouraged to indulge in easy speculation about things of which they understand nothing, and into which neither they nor anyone else will ever have any insight—encouraged, indeed, to invent new ideas and opinions, while neglecting the study of the better-established sciences. But, above all, there is the inestimable benefit, that all objections to morality and religion will be for ever silenced, and this in Socratic fashion, namely, by the clearest proof of the ignorance of the objectors. There has always existed in the world, and there will always continue to exist, some kind of metaphysics, and with it the dialectic that is natural to pure reason. It is therefore the first and most important task of philosophy to deprive metaphysics, once and for all, of its injurious influence, by attacking its errors at their very source.

Notwithstanding this important change in the field of the sciences, and the *loss* of its fancied possessions which specula- B xxxii. tive reason must suffer, general human interests remain in the same privileged position as hitherto, and the advantages which the world has hitherto derived from the teachings of pure reason are in no way diminished. The loss affects only the *monopoly of the schools*, in no respect the *interests of humanity*. I appeal to the most rigid dogmatist, whether the proof of the continued existence of our soul after death, derived from the simplicity of substance, or of the freedom of the will as opposed to a universal mechanism, arrived at through the subtle but ineffectual distinctions between subjective and objective practical necessity, or of the existence of God as deduced from the concept of an *ens realissimum* (of the contingency of the changeable and of the necessity of a prime mover), have ever, upon passing out from the schools, succeeded in reaching the public mind or in exercising the slightest influence on its convictions? That has never been found to occur, and in view of the unfitness of the common human understanding for such subtle speculation, ought never to have been expected. Such widely held convictions, so far as they rest on rational grounds, are due to quite other considerations. The hope of a *future life* has its source in that notable characteristic of our nature, never to be capable of being satisfied by what is temporal (as insufficient for the capacities of its whole destination); the consciousness of *freedom* rests exclusively on the clear ex- B xxxiii. hibition of duties, in opposition to all claims of the inclinations; the belief in a wise and great *Author of the world* is generated solely by the glorious order, beauty, and providential care everywhere displayed in nature. When the Schools have been brought to recognise that they can lay no claim to higher and fuller insight in a matter of universal human concern than that which is equally within the reach of the great mass of men (ever to be held by us in the highest esteem), and that, as Schools of philosophy, they should limit themselves to the study of those universally comprehensible, and, for moral purposes, sufficient grounds of proof, then not only do these latter possessions remain undisturbed, but through this very fact they acquire yet greater authority. The change affects only the arrogant pretensions of the Schools, which would fain be counted the sole authors and possessors of such truths (as, indeed, they can justly claim to be in many other branches of knowledge), reserving the key to themselves, and communicating to the public their use only—*quod mecum nescit, solus vult scire videri.* At the same time due regard is paid to the more moderate claims of the speculative philosopher. B xxxiv. He still remains the sole authority in regard to a science which benefits the public without their knowing it, namely, the critique of reason. That critique can never become popular, and indeed there is no need that it should. For just as fine-spun arguments in favour of useful truths make no appeal to the general mind, so neither do the subtle objections that can be raised against them. On the other hand, both inevitably present themselves to everyone who rises to the height of speculation; and it is therefore the duty of the Schools, by means of a thorough investigation of the rights of speculative reason, once for all to prevent the scandal which, sooner or later, is sure to break out even among the masses, as the result of the disputes in which metaphysicians (and, as such, finally also the clergy) inevitably become involved to the consequent perversion of their teaching. Criticism alone can sever the root of *materialism, fatalism, atheism, free-thinking, fanaticism,* and *superstition,* which can be injurious universally; as well as of *idealism* and *scepticism,* which are dangerous chiefly to the Schools, and hardly allow of being handed on to the

B xxxv. public. If governments think proper to interfere with the affairs of the learned, it would be more consistent with a wise regard for science as well as for mankind, to favour the freedom of such criticism, by which alone the labours of reason can be established on a firm basis, than to support the ridiculous despotism of the Schools, which raise a loud cry of public danger over the destruction of cobwebs to which the public has never paid any attention, and the loss of which it can therefore never feel.

This critique is not opposed to the *dogmatic procedure* of reason in its pure knowledge, as science, for that must always be dogmatic, that is, yield strict proof from sure principles *a priori.* It is opposed only to *dogmatism,* that is, to the presumption that it is possible to make progress with pure knowledge, according to principles, from concepts alone (those that are philosophical), as reason has long been in the habit of doing; and that it is possible to do this without having first investigated in what way and by what right reason has come into possession of these concepts. Dogmatism is thus the dogmatic procedure of pure reason, *without previous criticism of its own powers.* In withstanding dogmatism we must not allow ourselves to give free rein to that loquacious shallowness, which assumes

B xxxvi. for itself the name of popularity, nor yet to scepticism, which makes short work with all metaphysics. On the contrary, such criticism is the necessary preparation for a thoroughly grounded metaphysics, which, as science, must necessarily be developed dogmatically, according to the strictest demands of system, in such manner as to satisfy not the general public but the requirements of the Schools. For that is a demand to which it stands pledged, and which it may not neglect, namely, that it carry out its work entirely *a priori,* to the complete satisfaction of speculative reason. In the execution of the plan prescribed by the critique, that is, in the future system of metaphysics, we have therefore to follow the strict method of the celebrated Wolff, the greatest of all the dogmatic philosophers. He was the first to show by example (and by his example he awakened that spirit of thoroughness which is not extinct in Germany) how the secure progress of a science is to be attained only through orderly establishment of principles, clear determination of concepts, insistence upon strictness of proof, and avoidance of venturesome, non-consecutive steps in our inferences. He was thus peculiarly well fitted to raise metaphysics to the dignity of a science, if only it had occurred to him to prepare the ground beforehand by a critique of the organ, that is, of pure reason itself. The blame for his having failed to do so B xxxvii. lies not so much with himself as with the dogmatic way of thinking prevalent in his day, and with which the philosophers of his time, and of all previous times, have no right to reproach one another. Those who reject both the method of Wolff and the procedure of a critique of pure reason can have no other aim than to shake off the fetters of *science* altogether, and thus to change work into play, certainty into opinion, philosophy into philodoxy.

Now, *as regards this second edition*, I have, as is fitting, endeavoured to profit by the opportunity, in order to remove, wherever possible, difficulties and obscurity which, not perhaps without my fault, may have given rise to the many misunderstandings into which even acute thinkers have fallen in passing judgment upon my book. In the propositions themselves and their proofs, and also in the form and completeness of the [architectonic] plan, I have found nothing to alter. This is due partly to the long examination to which I have subjected them, before offering them [1] to the public, partly to the nature of the subject-matter with which we are dealing. For pure speculative reason has a structure wherein everything is an *organ*, the whole being for the sake of every part, and every part for the sake of all the others, so that even the B xxxviii. smallest imperfection, be it a fault (error) or a deficiency, must inevitably betray itself in use. This system will, as I hope, maintain, throughout the future, this unchangeableness. It is not self-conceit which justifies me in this confidence, but

[1] [Reading, with Erdmann, *sie* for *es*.]

the evidence experimentally obtained through the parity of the result, whether we proceed from the smallest elements to the whole of pure reason or reverse-wise from the whole (for this also is presented to reason through its final end in the sphere of the practical) to each part. Any attempt to change even the smallest part at once gives rise to contradictions, not merely in the system, but in human reason in general. As to the mode of *exposition*, on the other hand, much still remains to be done; and in this edition I have sought to make improvements which should help in removing, first, the misunderstanding in regard to the Aesthetic, especially concerning the concept of time; secondly, the obscurity of the deduction of the concepts of understanding; thirdly, a supposed want of sufficient evidence in the proofs of the principles of pure understanding; and finally, the false interpretation placed upon the paralogisms charged against rational psychology. Beyond this point, that is, beyond the end of the

B xxxix. first chapter of the Transcendental Dialectic, I have made no
B xl. changes in the mode of exposition.* Time was too short to

* The only addition, strictly so called, though one affecting the method of proof only, is the new refutation of psychological *idealism* (cf. below, p. 244), and a strict (also, as I believe, the only possible) proof of the objective reality of outer intuition. However harmless idealism may be considered in respect of the essential aims of metaphysics (though, in fact, it is not thus harmless), it still remains a scandal to philosophy and to human reason in general that the existence of things outside us (from which we derive the whole material of knowledge, even for our inner sense) must be accepted merely on *faith*, and that if anyone thinks good to doubt their existence, we are unable to counter his doubts by any satisfactory proof. Since there is some obscurity in the expressions used in the proof, from the third line to the sixth line, I beg to alter the passage as follows: "*But this permanent cannot be an intuition in me. For all grounds of determination of my existence which are to be met with in me are representations; and as representations themselves require a permanent distinct from them, in relation to which their change, and so my existence in the time wherein they change, may be determined.*" To this proof it will probably be objected, that I am immediately conscious only of that which is in me, that is, of my *representation* of outer things; and consequently that it must still remain uncertain whether outside me there is anything corresponding to it,

B xl or not. But through inner *experience* I am conscious of *my existence*

allow of further changes; and besides, I have not found among B xli.
competent and impartial critics any misapprehension in regard
to the remaining sections. Though I shall not venture to name
these critics with the praise that is their due, the attention B xlii.
which I have paid to their comments will easily be recognised
in the [new] passages [above mentioned]. These improvements
involve, however, a small loss, not to be prevented save by
making the book too voluminous, namely, that I have had
to omit or abridge certain passages, which, though not
indeed essential to the completeness of the whole, may yet
be missed by many readers as otherwise helpful. Only so
could I obtain space for what, as I hope, is now a more
intelligible exposition, which, though altering absolutely
nothing in the fundamentals of the propositions put forward or even in their proofs, yet here and there departs
so far from the previous method of treatment, that mere in-
terpolations could not be made to suffice. This loss, which is
small and can be remedied by consulting the first edition, will,
I hope, be compensated by the greater clearness of the new

---

in time (consequently also of its determinability in time), and this is
more than to be conscious merely of my representation. It is identical
with the *empirical consciousness of my existence*, which is determinable only through relation to something which, while bound up with
my existence, is outside me. This consciousness of my existence in
time is bound up in the way of identity [1] with the consciousness of a
relation to something outside me, and it is therefore experience not
invention, sense not imagination, which inseparably connects this
outside something with my inner sense. For outer sense is already
in itself a relation of intuition to something actual outside me, and
the reality of outer sense, in its distinction from imagination, rests
simply on that which is here found to take place, namely, its being
inseparably bound up with inner experience, as the condition of its
possibility. If, with the *intellectual consciousness* of my existence, in
the representation 'I am', which accompanies all my judgments and
acts of understanding, I could at the same time connect a determination of my existence through *intellectual intuition*, the consciousness of a relation to something outside me would not be required.
But though that intellectual consciousness does indeed come first,[2]
the inner intuition, in which my existence can alone be determined,
is sensible and is bound up with the condition of time. This determination, however, and therefore the inner experience itself, depends

[1] [*identisch verbunden.*]   [2] [*vorangeht.*]

text. I have observed, with pleasure and thankfulness, in
various published works—alike in critical reviews and in independent treatises—that the spirit of thoroughness is not
extinct in Germany, but has only been temporarily over-
B xliii. shadowed by the prevalence of a pretentiously free manner of
thinking; and that the thorny paths of the Critique have not
discouraged courageous and clear heads from setting themselves to master my book—a work which leads to a methodical, and as such alone enduring, and therefore most necessary,
science of pure reason. To these worthy men, who so happily
combine thoroughness of insight with a talent for lucid exposition — which I cannot regard myself as possessing — I
leave the task of perfecting what, here and there, in its
exposition, is still somewhat defective; for in this regard
the danger is not that of being refuted, but of not being

---

upon something permanent which is not in me, and consequently
B xli. can be only in something outside me, to which I must regard myself as standing in relation. The reality of outer sense is thus necessarily bound up with inner sense, if experience in general is to be
possible at all; that is, I am just as certainly conscious that there are
things outside me, which are in relation to my sense, as I am conscious that I myself exist as determined in time. In order to determine to which given intuitions objects outside me actually correspond, and which therefore belong to outer *sense* (to which, and not
to the faculty of imagination, they are to be ascribed), we must in
each single case appeal to the rules according to which experience
in general, even inner experience, is distinguished from imagination
—the proposition that there is such a thing as outer experience being
always presupposed. This further remark may be added. The representation of something *permanent* in existence is not the same as
permanent representation. For though the representation of [some-
thing permanent] [1] may be very transitory and variable like all our
other representations, not excepting those of matter, it yet refers to
something permanent. This latter must therefore be an external
thing distinct from all my representations, and its existence must be
included in the *determination* of my own existence, constituting with
it but a single experience such as would not take place even inwardly
if it were not also at the same time, in part, outer. How this should
be possible we are as little capable of explaining further as we are of
accounting for our being able to think the abiding in time, the coexistence of which with the changing generates the concept of alteration.

[1] [Reading, with Wille, *jene* for *diese*.]

understood From now on, though I cannot allow myself to
enter into controversy, I shall take careful note of all suggestions, be they from friends or from opponents, for use, in
accordance with this propaedeutic, in the further elaboration
of the system. In the course of these labours I have advanced
somewhat far in years (this month I reach my sixty-fourth
year), and I must be careful with my time if I am to succeed
in my proposed scheme of providing a metaphysic of nature
and of morals which will confirm the truth of my Critique in
the two fields, of speculative and of practical reason. The
clearing up of the obscurities in the present work—they are B xliv.
hardly to be avoided in a new enterprise—and the defence
of it as a whole, I must therefore leave to those worthy men
who have made my teaching their own. A philosophical work
cannot be armed at all points, like a mathematical treatise,
and may therefore be open to objection in this or that respect,
while yet the structure of the system, taken in its unity, is not
in the least endangered. Few have the versatility of mind to
familiarise themselves with a new system; and owing to the
general distaste for all innovation, still fewer have the inclination to do so. If we take single passages, torn from their
contexts, and compare them with one another, apparent contradictions are not likely to be lacking, especially in a work
that is written with any freedom of expression. In the eyes of
those who rely on the judgment of others, such contradictions have the effect of placing the work in an unfavourable
light; but they are easily resolved by those who have mastered
the idea of the whole. If a theory has in itself stability, the
stresses and strains which may at first have seemed very
threatening to it serve only, in the course of time, to smooth
away its inequalities; and if men of impartiality, insight, and
true popularity devote themselves to its exposition, it may also,
in a short time, secure for itself the necessary elegance of
statement

KÖNIGSBERG, *April* 1787.

TABLE OF CONTENTS[1]

[1] [This is the table of contents in A. The table of contents in B is, with minor changes, given above, pp. ix-xiii.]

INTRODUCTION

* I. The Distinction between Pure and Empirical Knowledge

THERE can be no doubt that all our knowledge begins with experience. For how should our faculty of knowledge be awakened into action did not objects affecting our senses partly of themselves produce representations, partly arouse the activity of our understanding to compare these representations, and, by combining or separating them, work up the raw material of the sensible impressions into that knowledge of objects which is entitled experience? In the order of time, therefore, we have no knowledge antecedent to experience, and with experience all our knowledge begins.

But though all our knowledge begins with experience, it does not follow that it all arises out of experience. For it

---

* [In B the Introduction is divided into five sections, in place of the two sections of the original Introduction. The new sections I. and II. (with their headings) are substituted in B for the original two opening paragraphs (with their heading), which are as follows:]

I. The Idea of Transcendental Philosophy　　A I

Experience is, beyond all doubt, the first product to which our understanding gives rise, in working up the raw material of sensible impressions.[1] Experience is therefore our first instruction, and in its progress is so inexhaustible in new information, that in the interconnected lives of all future generations there will never be any lack of new knowledge that can be thus ingathered. Nevertheless, it is by no means

[1] [*sinnliche Empfindungen.*]

41

may well be that even our empirical knowledge is made up of what we receive through impressions and of what our own faculty of knowledge (sensible impressions serving merely as the occasion) supplies from itself. If our faculty of knowledge makes any such addition, it may be that we are not in a posi-

B 2 tion to distinguish it from the raw material, until with long practice of attention we have become skilled in separating it.

This, then, is a question which at least calls for closer examination, and does not allow of any off-hand answer:— whether there is any knowledge that is thus independent of experience and even of all impressions of the senses. Such knowledge is entitled *a priori*, and distinguished from the

---

the sole field to which our understanding is confined. Experience tells us, indeed, what is, but not that it must necessarily be so, and not otherwise. It therefore gives us no true universality; and reason, which is so insistent upon this

A 2 kind of knowledge, is therefore more stimulated by it than satisfied. Such universal modes of knowledge,[1] which at the same time possess the character of inner necessity, must in themselves, independently of experience, be clear and certain. They are therefore entitled knowledge *a priori*; whereas, on the other hand, that which is borrowed solely from experience is, as we say, known only *a posteriori*, or empirically.

Now we find, what is especially noteworthy, that even into our experiences there enter modes of knowledge which must have their origin *a priori*, and which perhaps serve only to give coherence to our sense-representations.[2] For if we eliminate from our experiences everything which belongs to the senses, there still remain certain original concepts and certain judgments derived from them, which must have arisen completely *a priori*, independently of experience, inasmuch as they enable us to say, or at least lead us to believe that we can say, in regard to the objects which appear to the senses, more than mere experience would teach—giving to assertions true universality and strict necessity, such as mere empirical knowledge cannot supply.

---

[1] [As the term 'knowledge' cannot be used in the plural, I have usually trans-lated *Erkenntnisse* 'modes of knowledge'.]

[2] [*Vorstellungen der Sinne.*]

empirical, which has its sources *a posteriori*, that is, in experience.

The expression '*a priori*' does not, however, indicate with sufficient precision the full meaning of our question. For it has been customary to say, even of much knowledge that is derived from empirical sources, that we have it or are capable of having it *a priori*, meaning thereby that we do not derive it immediately from experience, but from a universal rule—a rule which is itself, however, borrowed by us from experience. Thus we would say of a man who undermined the foundations of his house, that he might have known *a priori* that it would fall, that is, that he need not have waited for the experience of its actual falling. But still he could not know this completely *a priori*. For he had first to learn through experience that bodies are heavy, and therefore fall when their supports are withdrawn.

In what follows, therefore, we shall understand by *a priori* knowledge, not knowledge independent of this or that experience, but knowledge absolutely independent of all experience. B 3 Opposed to it is empirical knowledge, which is knowledge possible only *a posteriori*, that is, through experience. *A priori* modes of knowledge are entitled pure when there is no admixture of anything empirical. Thus, for instance, the proposition, 'every alteration has its cause', while an *a priori* proposition, is not a pure proposition, because alteration is a concept which can be derived only from experience.[1]

II. We are in Possession of certain Modes of *A Priori* Knowledge, and even the Common Understanding is never without them

What we here require is a criterion[2] by which to distinguish with certainty between pure and empirical knowledge. Experience teaches us that a thing is so and so, but not that it cannot be otherwise. First, then, if we have a proposition which in being thought is thought as *necessary*, it is an *a priori* judgment; and if, besides, it is not derived from any proposition except one which also has the validity of a necessary judgment, it is an absolutely *a priori* judgment. Secondly,

---

[1] [Cf. below, pp. 44, 76, 216-7.]   [2] [*Merkmal.*]

experience never confers on its judgments true or strict, but
only assumed and comparative *universality*, through induction. We can properly only say, therefore, that, so far as
B 4 we have hitherto observed, there is no exception to this or
that rule. If, then, a judgment is thought with strict universality, that is, in such manner that no exception is allowed as
possible, it is not derived from experience, but is valid absolutely *a priori*. Empirical universality is only an arbitrary extension of a validity holding in most cases to one which holds
in all, for instance, in the proposition, 'all bodies are heavy'.
When, on the other hand, strict universality is essential to a
a judgment, this indicates a special source of knowledge,
namely, a faculty of *a priori* knowledge. Necessity and strict
universality are thus sure criteria of *a priori* knowledge, and
are inseparable from one another. But since in the employment of these criteria the contingency of judgments is sometimes more easily shown than their empirical limitation,[1] or,
as sometimes also happens, their unlimited universality can
be more convincingly proved than their necessity, it is advisable to use the two criteria separately, each by itself being
infallible.

Now it is easy to show that there actually are in human
knowledge judgments which are necessary and in the strictest
sense universal, and which are therefore pure *a priori* judgments. If an example from the sciences be desired, we have
only to look to any of the propositions of mathematics; if we
seek an example from the understanding in its quite ordinary
B 5 employment, the proposition, 'every alteration must have a
cause', will serve our purpose. In the latter case, indeed, the
very concept of a cause so manifestly contains the concept of
a necessity of connection with an effect and of the strict universality of the rule, that the concept would be altogether lost if
we attempted to derive it, as Hume has done, from a repeated
association of that which happens with that which precedes,
and from a custom of connecting representations, a custom
originating in this repeated association, and constituting
therefore a merely subjective necessity. Even without appeal-

---

[1] [Reading, with Vaihinger, *die Zufälligkeit in den Urteilen als die empirische
Beschränktheit derselben* for *die empirische Beschränktheit derselben als die
Zufälligkeit in den Urteilen.*]

ing to such examples, it is possible to show that pure *a priori* principles are indispensable for the possibility of experience, and so to prove their existence *a priori*. For whence could experience derive its certainty, if all the rules, according to which it proceeds, were always themselves empirical, and therefore contingent? Such rules could hardly be regarded as first principles. At present, however, we may be content to have established the fact that our faculty of knowledge does have a pure employment, and to have shown what are the criteria of such an employment.

Such *a priori* origin is manifest in certain concepts, no less than in judgments. If we remove from our empirical concept of a body, one by one, every feature in it which is [merely] empirical, the colour, the hardness or softness, the weight, even[1] the impenetrability, there still remains the space which the body (now entirely vanished) occupied, and this cannot be removed. Again, if we remove from our em- B 6 pirical concept of any object, corporeal or incorporeal, all properties which experience has taught us, we yet cannot take away that property through which the object is thought as substance or as inhering in a substance (although this concept of substance is more determinate than that of an object in general). Owing, therefore, to the necessity with which this concept of substance forces itself upon us, we have no option save to admit that it has its seat in our faculty of *a priori* knowledge.

III. PHILOSOPHY STANDS IN NEED OF A SCIENCE WHICH SHALL DETERMINE THE POSSIBILITY, THE PRINCIPLES, AND THE EXTENT OF ALL *A PRIORI* KNOWLEDGE

But what is still more extraordinary than all the preceding[2] is this, that certain modes of knowledge leave the field of all possible experiences and have the appearance of extending A 3 the scope of our judgments beyond all limits of experience, and this by means of concepts to which no corresponding object can ever be given in experience.

It is precisely by means of the latter modes of knowledge, in a realm beyond the world of the senses, where experience

---

1 [*selbst* omitted in the 4th edition.]   2 [*als alle vorige* added in B.]

can yield neither guidance nor correction, that our reason
carries on those enquiries which owing to their importance
B 7 we consider to be far more excellent, and in their purpose
far more lofty, than all that the understanding can learn in
the field of appearances. Indeed we prefer to run every risk
of error rather than desist from such urgent enquiries, on the
ground of their dubious character, or from disdain and indifference. [1]These unavoidable problems set by pure reason
itself are *God, freedom*, and *immortality*. The science which,
with all its preparations, is in its final intention directed
solely to their solution is metaphysics; and its procedure
is at first dogmatic, that is, it confidently sets itself to this
task without any previous examination of the capacity or
incapacity of reason for so great an undertaking.

Now it does indeed seem natural that, as soon as we have
left the ground of experience, we should, through careful enquiries, assure ourselves as to the foundations of any building
that we propose to erect, not making use of any knowledge
that we possess without first determining whence it has come,
and not trusting to principles without knowing their origin.
It is natural, that is to say, that the question should first be
considered, how the understanding can arrive at all this knowledge *a priori*, and what extent, validity, and worth it may
A 4 have. Nothing, indeed, could be more natural, if by the term
B 8 'natural' [2] we signify what fittingly and reasonably ought to
happen. But if we mean by 'natural' what ordinarily happens,
then on the contrary nothing is more natural and more intelligible than the fact that this enquiry has been so long neg-
lected. For one part of this knowledge, the mathematical, has
long been of established reliability, and so gives rise to a favourable presumption as regards the other part, which may yet be of
quite different nature. Besides, once we are outside the circle
of experience, we can be sure of not being *contradicted* by
experience. The charm of extending our knowledge is so
great that nothing short of encountering a direct contradiction can suffice to arrest us in our course; and this can be
avoided, if we are careful in our fabrications—which none the
less will still remain fabrications. Mathematics gives us a shin-

---

[1] ["These unavoidable . . ." to end of paragraph added in B.]
[2] [In A *unter diesem Wort*: in B *unter dem Worte natürlich*.]

ing example of how far, independently of experience, we can progress in *a priori* knowledge. It does, indeed, occupy itself with objects and with knowledge solely in so far as they allow of being exhibited in intuition. But this circumstance is easily overlooked, since this intuition can itself be given *a priori*, and is therefore hardly to be distinguished from a bare and pure concept. Misled[1] by such a proof of the power of reason, the demand for the extension of knowledge recog- A 5
nises no limits. The light dove, cleaving the air in her free flight, and feeling its resistance, might imagine that its flight would be still easier in empty space. It was thus that Plato B 9
left the world of the senses, as setting too narrow limits to[2] the understanding, and ventured out beyond it on the wings of the ideas, in the empty space of the pure understanding. He did not observe that with all his efforts he made no ad-vance—meeting no resistance that might, as it were, serve as a support upon which he could take a stand, to which he could apply his powers, and so set his understanding in motion. It is, indeed, the common fate of human reason to complete its speculative structures as speedily as may be, and only afterwards to enquire whether the foundations are reliable. All sorts of excuses will then be appealed to, in order to reassure us of their solidity, or rather indeed[3] to enable us to dispense altogether with so late and so dangerous an enquiry. But what keeps us, during the actual building, free from all apprehension and suspicion, and flatters us with a seeming thoroughness, is this other circumstance, namely, that a great, perhaps the greatest, part of the business of our reason consists in analysis[4] of the concepts which we already have of objects. This analysis supplies us with a consider-able body of knowledge, which, while nothing but explanation or elucidation of what has already been thought in our con- A 6
cepts, though in a confused manner, is yet prized as being, at least as regards its form, new insight. But so far as the matter or content is concerned, there has been no extension of our previously possessed concepts, but only an analysis of them. Since this procedure yields real knowledge *a priori*, which B 10

---

[1] [In A: Encouraged.]
[2] [In A: placing such manifold hindrances in the way of.]
[3] [*lieber gar* added in B.]
[4] [Reading, with the 5th edition. *Zergliederung* for *Zergliederungen*.]

progresses in an assured and useful fashion, reason is so far
misled as surreptitiously to introduce, without itself being
aware of so doing, assertions of an entirely different order, in
which it attaches to given concepts others completely foreign
to them, and moreover attaches them *a priori*.[1] And yet it is
not known how reason can be in position to do this. Such a
question[2] is never so much as thought of. I shall therefore
at once proceed to deal with the difference between these two
kinds of knowledge.

[3]IV. THE DISTINCTION BETWEEN ANALYTIC AND SYNTHETIC JUDGMENTS

In all judgments in which the relation of a subject to the
predicate is thought (I take into consideration affirmative
judgments only, the subsequent[4] application to negative judgments being easily made), this relation is possible in two
different ways. Either the predicate B belongs to the subject
A, as something which is (covertly) contained in this concept
A; or B lies outside the concept A, although it does indeed
stand in connection with it. In the one case I entitle the judgment analytic, in the other synthetic. Analytic judgments
(affirmative) are therefore those in which the connection of the
predicate with the subject is thought through identity; those
in which this connection is thought without identity should
be entitled synthetic. The former, as adding nothing through
the predicate to the concept of the subject, but merely break-
ing it up into those constituent concepts that have all along
been thought in it, although confusedly, can also be entitled
explicative. The latter, on the other hand, add to the concept
of the subject a predicate which has not been in any wise thought
in it, and which no analysis could possibly extract from it; and
they may therefore be entitled ampliative. If I say, for instance,
'All bodies are extended', this is an analytic judgment. For I
do not require to go beyond the concept which I connect with
'body'[5] in order to find extension as bound up with it. To

A 7

B 11

---

[1] [In A: attaches *a priori* to given concepts others completely foreign to
them.]
[2] [In A: This question.]   [3] ["IV" added in B.]   [4] [*nachher* added in B.]
[5] [In A: outside the concept which I connect with the word body.]

meet with this predicate, I have merely to analyse the concept, that is, to become conscious to myself[1] of the manifold which I always think in that concept. The judgment is therefore analytic. But when I say, 'All bodies are heavy', the predicate is something quite different from anything that I think in the mere concept of body in general; and the addition of such a predicate therefore yields a synthetic judgment.

* Judgments of experience, as such, are one and all synthetic. For it would be absurd to found an analytic judgment on experience. Since, in framing the judgment, I must not go outside my concept, there is no need to appeal to the testimony of experience in its support. That a body is extended is a proposition that holds *a priori* and is not empirical. For, before **B 12** appealing to experience, I have already in the concept of body all the conditions required for my judgment. I have only to extract from it, in accordance with the principle of contradiction, the required predicate, and in so doing can at the same time become conscious of the necessity of the judgment—and that is what experience could never have taught me. On the other hand, though I do not include in the concept of a body in general the predicate 'weight', none the less this concept indicates an object of experience through one of its parts, and I can add to that part other parts of this same experience, as in this way belonging together with the concept. From the start

---

* ["Judgments of experience" to end of paragraph substituted in B in place of the following:]

Thus it is evident: 1. that through analytic judgments our knowledge is not in any way extended, and that the concept **A 8** which I already have is merely set forth and made intelligible to me; 2. that in synthetic judgments I must have besides the concept of the subject something else (X), upon which the understanding may rely, if it is to know that a predicate, not contained in this concept, nevertheless belongs to it.

In the case of empirical judgments, judgments of experience, there is no difficulty whatsoever in meeting this demand. This X is the complete experience of the object which I think through the concept A—a concept which forms only one part of this experience. For though I do not include in the concept

[1] [*mir* added in B.]

I can apprehend the concept of body analytically through the characters of extension, impenetrability, figure, etc., all of which are thought in the concept. Now, however, looking back on the experience from which I have derived this concept of body, and finding weight to be invariably connected with the above characters, I attach it as a predicate to the concept; and in doing so I attach it synthetically, and am therefore extending my knowledge. The possibility of the synthesis of the predicate 'weight' with the concept of 'body' thus rests upon experience. While the one concept is not contained in the other, they yet belong to one another, though only contingently, as parts of a whole, namely, of an experience which is itself a synthetic combination of intuitions.

A 9   But in *a priori* synthetic judgments this help is entirely
B 13   lacking. [I do not here have the advantage of looking around in the field of experience.] Upon what, then, am I to rely, when I seek to go beyond[1] the concept A, and to know that another concept B is connected with it? Through what is the synthesis made possible? Let us take the proposition, 'Everything which happens has its cause' In the concept of 'something which happens', I do indeed think an existence which is preceded by a time, etc., and from this concept analytic judgments may be obtained. But the concept of a 'cause' lies entirely outside the other concept, and[2] signifies something different

---

of a body in general the predicate 'weight', the concept none the less indicates the complete experience through one of its parts; and to this part, as belonging to it, I can therefore add other parts of the same experience. By prior analysis I can apprehend the concept of body through the characters of extension, impenetrability, figure, etc., all of which are thought in this concept. To extend my knowledge, I then look back to the experience from which I have derived this concept of body, and find that weight is always connected with the above characters. Experience is thus the X which lies outside the concept A, and on which rests the possibility of the synthesis of the predicate 'weight' (B) with the concept (A).

[1] [In A: outside.]
[2] [*liegt ganz ausser jenem Begriffe, und* added in B.]

from 'that which happens', and is not therefore[1] in any way contained in this latter representation. How come I then to predicate of that which happens something quite different, and to apprehend that the concept of cause, though not contained in it, yet belongs, and indeed necessarily belongs,[2] to it? What is here the unknown[3] $= X$ which gives support to the understanding when it believes that it can discover outside the concept A a predicate B foreign to this concept, which it yet at the same time considers to be connected with it?[4] It cannot be experience, because the suggested principle has connected the second representation[5] with the first, not only with greater universality,[6] but also with the character of necessity, and therefore completely *a priori* and on the basis of mere concepts. Upon such synthetic, that is, ampliative principles, all our *a priori* speculative knowledge must ultimately rest; analytic judgments[7] are very important, and indeed necessary, but only for obtaining that clearness in the concepts which is requisite for such a sure and wide synthesis as will lead to a genuinely new addition[8] to all previous knowledge.*

A 10

B 14

---

* [In A there follows the passage, omitted in B:]

A certain mystery lies here concealed;[a] and only upon its solution can the advance into the limitless field of the knowledge yielded by pure understanding be made sure and trustworthy. What we must do is to discover, in all its proper universality, the ground of the possibility of *a priori* synthetic judgments, to obtain insight into the conditions which make

[a] If it had occurred to any of the ancients even to raise this question, this by itself would, up to our own time, have been a powerful influence against all systems of pure reason, and would have saved us so many of those vain attempts, which have been blindly undertaken without knowledge of what it is that requires to be done.

[1] [*ist also* substituted in B for *und ist.*]
[2] [*und sogar notwendig* added in B.]
[3] [*das Unbekannte* $= X$ substituted in B for *das X.*]
[4] [In A: and yet at the same time connected with it.]
[5] [Reading, with Grillo, *Vorstellung* for *Vorstellungen.*]
[6] [In A: with greater universality than experience can yield, but . . .]
[7] [Adding, with Erdmann, *Urteile.*]
[8] [In B *Erwerb* substituted for *Anbau.*]

¹V. In all Theoretical Sciences of Reason Synthetic *A Priori* Judgments are contained as Principles

1. *All mathematical judgments, without exception, are synthetic.* This fact, though incontestably certain and in its consequences very important, has hitherto escaped the notice of those who are engaged in the analysis of human reason, and is, indeed, directly opposed to all their conjectures. For as it was found that all mathematical inferences proceed in accordance with the principle of contradiction (which the nature of all apodeictic certainty requires), it was supposed that the fundamental propositions of the science can themselves be known to be true² through that principle. This is an erroneous view. For though a synthetic proposition can indeed be discerned in accordance with the principle of contradiction, this can only be if another synthetic proposition is presupposed, and if it can then be apprehended as following from this other proposition; it can never be so discerned in and by itself.

First of all, it has to be noted that mathematical propositions, strictly so called, are always judgments a priori, not empirical; because they carry with them necessity, which B 15 cannot be derived from experience. If this be demurred to, I am willing to limit my statement to *pure* mathematics, the very concept of which implies that it does not contain empirical, but only pure *a priori* knowledge.

We might, indeed, at first suppose that the proposition $7 + 5 = 12$ is a merely analytic proposition, and follows by the principle of contradiction from the concept of a sum of 7 and 5. But if we look more closely we find that the concept of the sum of 7 and 5 contains nothing save the union of the two numbers into one, and in this no thought is being taken

---

each kind of such judgments possible, and to mark out all this knowledge, which forms a genus by itself, not in any cursory outline, but in a system, with completeness and in a manner sufficient for any use, according to its original sources, divisions, extent, and limits. So much, meantime, as regards what is peculiar in synthetic judgments.

¹ [Sections V. and VI. added in B.]
² [In 4th edition *erkannt* changed to *anerkannt*.]

as to what that single number may be which combines both. The concept of 12 is by no means already thought in merely thinking this union of 7 and 5; and I may analyse my concept of such a possible sum as long as I please, still I shall never find the 12 in it. We have to go outside these concepts, and call in the aid of the intuition which corresponds to one of them, our five fingers, for instance, or, as Segner[1] does in his *Arithmetic*, five points, adding to the concept of 7, unit by unit, the five given in intuition. For starting with the number 7, and for the concept of 5 calling in the aid of the fingers of my hand as intuition, I now add one by one to the number 7 the units which I previously took together to form the number 5, and with the aid of that figure[2] [the hand] see the number 12 come into being. That 5 should be added to 7,[3] I have indeed already thought in the concept of a sum = 7 + 5, but not that this sum is equivalent to the number 12. Arithmetical propositions are therefore always synthetic. This is still more evident if we take larger numbers. For it is then obvious that, however we might turn and twist our concepts, we could never, by the mere analysis of them, and without the aid of intuition, discover what [the number is that] is the sum.

B 16

Just as little is any fundamental proposition of pure geometry analytic. That the straight line between two points is the shortest, is a synthetic proposition. For my concept of *straight* contains nothing of quantity, but only of quality. The concept of the shortest is wholly an addition, and cannot be derived, through any process of analysis, from the concept of the straight line. Intuition, therefore, must here be called in; only by its aid is the synthesis possible. What here[4] causes us commonly to believe that the predicate of such apodeictic judgments is already contained in our concept, and that the judgment is therefore analytic, is merely the ambiguous character of the terms used. We are required to join in thought a certain predicate to a given concept, and this neces-

B 17

---

[1] [*Anfangsgründe der Arithmetik*, translated from the Latin, second edition, Halle, 1773, pp. 27, 79.]

[2] [*an jenem meinem Bilde*.]

[3] [Reading, with Erdmann, 5 *zu* 7.]

[4] [As Vaihinger has pointed out (*Commentar*, i. pp. 303-4), this passage, which in both A and B is made to follow "Some few fundamental propositions . . . exhibited in intuition", is quite obviously displaced. In the above translation the necessary rearrangement has been made.]

sity is inherent in the concepts themselves. But the question is not what we *ought* to join in thought to the given concept, but what we *actually* think in it, even if only obscurely; and it is then manifest that, while the predicate is indeed attached necessarily to the concept,[1] it is so in virtue of an intuition which must be added to the concept, not as thought in the concept itself.

B 16   Some few fundamental propositions, presupposed by the geometrician, are, indeed, really analytic, and rest on the principle of contradiction. But, as identical propositions, they
B 17 serve only as links in the chain of method and not as principles; for instance, $a = a$; the whole is equal to itself; or $(a + b) > a$, that is, the whole is greater than its part. And even these propositions, though they are valid according to pure concepts, are only admitted in mathematics because they can be exhibited in intuition.

2. *Natural science (physics) contains* a priori *synthetic judgments as principles.* I need cite only two such judgments: that in all changes of the material world the quantity of matter remains unchanged; and that in all communication of motion, action and reaction must always be equal. Both propositions, it is evident, are not only necessary, and therefore in their origin
B 18 *a priori*, but also synthetic. For in the concept of matter I do not think its permanence, but only its presence in the space which it occupies. I go outside and beyond the concept of matter, joining to it *a priori* in thought something which I have not thought *in* it. The proposition is not, therefore, analytic, but synthetic, and yet is thought *a priori*; and so likewise are the other propositions of the pure part of natural science.

3. *Metaphysics*, even if we look upon it as having hitherto failed in all its endeavours, is yet, owing to the nature of human reason, a quite indispensable science, and *ought to contain* a priori *synthetic knowledge*. For its business is not merely to analyse concepts which we make for ourselves *a priori* of things, and thereby to clarify them analytically, but to extend our *a priori* knowledge. And for this purpose we must employ principles which add to the given concept something that was not contained in it, and through *a priori* synthetic judgments venture out so far that experience is quite

---

[1] [Reading, with Erdmann, *jenem Begriffe* for *jenen Begriffen*.]

unable to follow us, as, for instance, in the proposition, that
the world must have a first beginning, and such like. Thus
metaphysics consists, at least *in intention*, entirely of *a priori*
synthetic propositions.

VI. THE GENERAL PROBLEM OF PURE REASON   B 19

Much is already gained if we can bring a number of investigations under the formula of a single problem. For we
not only lighten our own task, by defining it accurately, but
make it easier for others, who would test our results, to judge
whether or not we have succeeded in what we set out to do.
Now the proper problem of pure reason is contained in the
question: How are *a priori* synthetic judgments possible?

That metaphysics has hitherto remained in so vacillating
a state of uncertainty and contradiction, is entirely due to the
fact that this problem, and perhaps even the distinction between analytic and synthetic judgments, has never previously
been considered. Upon the solution of this problem, or upon
a sufficient proof that the possibility which it desires to have
explained does in fact not exist at all, depends the success or
failure of metaphysics. Among philosophers, David Hume
came nearest to envisaging this problem, but still was very far
from conceiving it with sufficient definiteness and universality.
He occupied himself exclusively with the synthetic proposition regarding the connection of an effect with its cause
(*principium causalitatis*), and he believed himself to have   B 20
shown that such an *a priori* proposition is entirely impossible. If we accept his conclusions, then all that we call
metaphysics is a mere delusion whereby we fancy ourselves to
have rational insight into what, in actual fact, is borrowed
solely from experience, and under the influence of custom has
taken the illusory semblance of necessity. If he had envisaged
our problem in all its universality, he would never have been
guilty of this statement, so destructive of all pure philosophy.
For he would then have recognised that, according to his own
argument, pure mathematics, as certainly containing *a priori*
synthetic propositions, would also not be possible; and from
such an assertion his good sense would have saved him.

In the solution of the above problem, we are at the same

time deciding as to the possibility of the employment of pure reason in establishing and developing all those sciences which contain a theoretical *a priori* knowledge of objects, and have therefore to answer the questions:

> How is pure mathematics possible?
> How is pure science of nature possible?

Since these sciences actually exist, it is quite proper to ask *how* they are possible; for that they must be possible is proved

B 21   by the fact that they exist.[a] But the poor progress which has hitherto been made in metaphysics, and the fact that no system yet propounded can, in view of the essential purpose of metaphysics, be said really to exist, leaves everyone sufficient ground for doubting as to its possibility.

Yet, in a certain sense, this *kind of knowledge* is to be looked upon as given; that is to say, metaphysics actually exists, if not as a science, yet still as natural disposition (*metaphysica naturalis*). For human reason, without being moved merely by the idle desire for extent and variety of knowledge, proceeds impetuously, driven on by an inward need, to questions such as cannot be answered by any empirical employment of reason, or by principles thence derived. Thus in all men, as soon as their reason has become ripe for speculation, there has always existed and will always continue to exist some kind of metaphysics. And so we have the question:

B 22   *How is metaphysics, as natural disposition, possible?*

that is, how from the nature of universal human reason do those questions arise which pure reason propounds to itself, and which it is impelled by its own need to answer as best it can?

But since all attempts which have hitherto been made to answer these natural questions—for instance, whether the

---

[a] Many may still have doubts as regards pure natural science. We have only, however, to consider the various propositions that are to be found at the beginning of (empirical) physics, properly so called, those, for instance, relating to the permanence in the quantity of matter, to inertia, to the equality of action and reaction, etc., in order to be soon convinced that they constitute a *physica pura*, or *rationalis*, which well deserves, as an independent science, to be separately dealt with in its whole extent, be that narrow or wide.

world has a beginning or is from eternity—have always met
with unavoidable contradictions, we cannot rest satisfied with
the mere natural disposition to metaphysics, that is, with the
pure faculty of reason itself, from which, indeed, some sort of
metaphysics (be it what it may) always arises. It must be
possible for reason to attain to certainty whether we know or
do not know the objects of metaphysics, that is, to come to
a decision either in regard to the objects of its enquiries or in
regard to the capacity or incapacity of reason to pass any
judgment upon them, so that we may either with confidence
extend our pure reason or set to it sure and determinate
limits. This last question, which arises out of the previous
general problem, may, rightly stated, take the form:

How is metaphysics, as science, possible?

Thus the critique of reason, in the end, necessarily leads to
scientific knowledge; while its dogmatic employment, on the
other hand, lands us in dogmatic assertions to which other B 23
assertions, equally specious, can always be opposed—that is,
in *scepticism*.

This science cannot be of any very formidable prolixity,
since it has to deal not with the objects of reason, the variety
of which is inexhaustible, but only with itself and the problems which arise entirely from within itself, and which are
imposed upon it by its own nature, not by the nature of things
which are distinct from it. When once reason has learnt completely to understand its own power in respect of objects which
can be presented to it in experience, it should easily be able to
determine, with completeness and certainty, the extent and
the limits of its attempted employment beyond the bounds of
all experience.

We may, then, and indeed we must, regard as abortive all
attempts, hitherto made, to establish a metaphysic *dogmatically*. For the analytic part in any such attempted system,
namely, the mere analysis of the concepts that inhere in our
reason *a priori*, is by no means the aim of, but only a preparation for, metaphysics proper, that is, the extension of its *a
priori* synthetic knowledge. For such a purpose, the analysis
of concepts is useless, since it merely shows what is contained
in these concepts, not how we arrive at them *a priori*. A solution

of this latter problem is required, that we may be able to de-
B 24 termine the valid employment of such concepts in regard to
the objects of all knowledge in general. Nor is much self-denial
needed to give up these claims, seeing that the undeniable,
and in the dogmatic procedure of reason also unavoidable,
contradictions of reason with itself have long since undermined
the authority of every metaphysical system yet propounded.
Greater firmness will be required if we are not to be deterred
by inward difficulties and outward opposition from endeavouring, through application of a method entirely different from
any hitherto employed, at last to bring to a prosperous and
fruitful growth a science indispensable to human reason—a
science whose every branch may be cut away but whose root
cannot be destroyed.[1]

VII. The Idea and Division of a Special Science, under the Title "Critique of Pure Reason"[2]

In view of all these considerations, we arrive at the idea of
a special science which can be entitled [3] the Critique of Pure
A 11 Reason.* For reason is the faculty which supplies the principles
of *a priori* knowledge. Pure reason is, therefore, that which
contains the principles whereby we know anything absolutely
a priori. An organon of pure reason would be the sum-total of
B 25 those principles according to which all modes of pure *a priori*
knowledge can be acquired and actually brought into being.
The exhaustive application of such an organon would give
rise to a system of pure reason. But as this would be asking
rather much, and as it is still doubtful whether, and in what
cases, any [4] extension of our knowledge be here [5] possible, we

---

* [In A follow two sentences, omitted in B]:
Any knowledge is entitled pure, if it be not mixed with anything extraneous. But knowledge is more particularly to be
called absolutely pure, if no experience or sensation whatsoever be mingled with it, and if it be therefore possible completely *a priori*.

[1] [End of the new sections added in B.]   [2] [Heading added in B.]
[3] [In A: *dienen könne* for *heissen kann*.]   [4] [In A: *eine solche*.]
[5] [*hier* added in B.]

can regard a science of the mere examination of pure reason, of its sources and limits, as the *propaedeutic* to the system of pure reason. As such, it should be called a critique, not a doctrine, of pure reason. Its utility, in speculation,[1] ought properly to be only negative, not to extend, but only to clarify our reason, and keep it free from errors—which is already a very great gain. I entitle *transcendental* all knowledge which is occupied not so much with objects as with the mode of our knowledge of objects in so far as this mode of knowledge is to be possible *a priori*.[2] A system of such concepts might be entitled transcendental philosophy. But that is still,[3] at this stage, too large an undertaking. For since such a science must contain, with completeness, both kinds of *a priori* knowledge, the analytic no less than the synthetic, it is, so far as our present purpose is concerned, much too comprehensive. We have to carry the analysis so far only as is indispensably necessary in order to comprehend, in their whole extent, the principles of *a priori* synthesis, with which alone we are called upon to deal. It is upon this enquiry, which should be entitled not a doctrine, but only a transcendental critique, that we are now engaged. Its purpose is not to extend knowledge, but only to correct it, and to supply a touchstone of the value, or lack of value, of all *a priori* knowledge. Such a critique is therefore a preparation, so far as may be possible, for an organon; and should this turn out not to be possible, then at least for a canon, according to which, in due course, the complete system of the philosophy of pure reason—be it in extension or merely in limitation of its knowledge—may be carried into execution, analytically as well as synthetically. That such a system is possible, and indeed that it may not be of such great extent as to cut us off from the hope of entirely completing it, may already be gathered from the fact that what here constitutes our subject-matter is not the nature of things, which is inexhaustible, but the understanding which passes judgment upon the nature of things; and this understanding, again, only in respect of its *a priori* knowledge. These *a priori* possessions of the understanding, since they

A 12

B 26

A 13

1 [*in Ansehung der Spekulation* added in B.]
2 [In A: as with our *a priori* concepts of objects in general.]
3 [*noch* added in B.]

have not to be sought for without, cannot remain hidden from us, and in all probability are sufficiently small in extent to allow of our apprehending them in their completeness, of judging B 27 as to their value or lack of value, and so of rightly appraising them. Still less[1] may the reader here expect a critique of books and systems of pure reason; we are concerned only with the critique of the faculty of pure reason itself. Only in so far as we build upon this foundation do we have a reliable touchstone for estimating the philosophical value of old and new works in this field. Otherwise the unqualified historian or critic is passing judgments upon the groundless assertions of others by means of his own, which are equally groundless.

[2] Transcendental philosophy is only the idea of a science,[3] for which the critique of pure reason has to lay down the complete architectonic plan. That is to say, it has to guarantee, as following from principles, the completeness and certainty of the structure in all its parts. It is the system of all principles of pure reason.[4] And if this critique is not itself to be entitled a transcendental philosophy, it is solely because, to be a complete system, it would also have to contain an exhaustive analysis of the whole of *a priori* human knowledge. Our critique must, indeed, supply a complete enumeration of all the fundamental concepts that go to constitute such pure knowledge. But it is not required to give an exhaustive analysis of these concepts, nor a complete review of those that can be derived from them. Such a demand would be A 14 unreasonable, partly because this analysis would not be B 28 appropriate to our main purpose, inasmuch as there is no such uncertainty in regard to analysis as we encounter in the case of synthesis, for the sake of which alone our whole critique is undertaken; and partly because it would be inconsistent with the unity of our plan to assume responsibility for the completeness of such an analysis and derivation, when in view of our purpose we can be excused from doing so. The analysis of these *a priori* concepts, which later we shall have to enumerate, and the derivation of other concepts from them, can easily, how-

---

[1] ["Still less . . ." to end of paragraph added in B.]
[2] [In A this paragraph is preceded by the heading: *The Division of Trans cendental Philosophy*.]
[3] [In A: as here referred to, is only an idea.]
[4] [This sentence added in B.]

ever, be made complete when once they have been established as exhausting the principles of synthesis, and if in this essential respect nothing be lacking in them.

The critique of pure reason therefore will contain all that is essential in transcendental philosophy. While it is the complete idea of transcendental philosophy, it is not equivalent to that latter science; for it carries the analysis only so far as is requisite for the complete examination of knowledge which is *a priori* and synthetic.

What has chiefly to be kept in view in the division of such a science, is that no concepts be allowed to enter which contain in themselves anything empirical, or, in other words, that it consist in knowledge wholly *a priori*. Accordingly, although the highest principles and fundamental concepts of morality are *a priori* knowledge, they have no place in tran- A 15 scendental philosophy, because,[1] although they do not lay at B 29 the foundation of their precepts the concepts of pleasure and pain, of the desires and inclinations, etc., all of which are of empirical origin, yet in the construction of a system of pure morality these empirical concepts must necessarily be brought into the concept of duty, as representing either a hindrance, which we have to overcome, or an allurement, which must not be made into a motive. Transcendental philosophy is therefore a philosophy of pure and merely speculative reason. All that is practical, so far as it contains motives, relates to feelings, and these belong to the empirical sources of knowledge.

If we are to make a systematic division of the science which we are engaged in presenting, it must have first a *doctrine of the elements*, and secondly, a *doctrine of the method of pure reason*. Each of these chief divisions will have its subdivisions, but the grounds of these we are not yet in a position to explain. By way of introduction or anticipation we need only say that there are two stems of human knowledge, namely, *sensibility* and *understanding*, which perhaps spring from a common, but to us unknown, root. Through the former, objects are given to us; through the latter, they are

[1] ["Because, although they . . . made into a motive" substituted in B for: since the concepts of pleasure and pain, of the desires and inclinations, of free-will, etc., have to be presupposed.]

thought.. Now in so far as sensibility may be found to contain
B 30 *a priori* representations constituting the condition[1] under
which objects are given to us, it will belong to transcendental
A 16 philosophy. And since the conditions under which alone the
objects of human knowledge are given must precede those
under which they are thought, the transcendental doctrine
of sensibility will constitute the first part of the science of the
elements.

[1] [In A: conditions.]

CRITIQUE OF PURE REASON $\left\{{{\rm A}\,17 \atop {\rm B}\,31}\right.$

I

TRANSCENDENTAL DOCTRINE OF ELEMENTS

TRANSCENDENTAL DOCTRINE OF ELEMENTS

FIRST PART

TRANSCENDENTAL AESTHETIC

§ 1[1]

IN whatever manner and by whatever means a mode of knowledge[2] may relate to objects, *intuition* is that through which it is in immediate relation to them, and to which all thought as a means is directed. But intuition takes place only in so far as the object is given to us. This again is only possible, to man at least,[3] in so far as the mind is affected in a certain way. The capacity (receptivity) for receiving representations through the mode in which we are affected by objects, is entitled *sensibility*. Objects are *given* to us by means of sensibility, and it alone yields us *intuitions*; they are *thought* through the understanding, and from the understanding arise *concepts*. But all thought must, directly or indirectly, by way of certain characters,[4] relate ultimately to intuitions, and therefore, with us, to sensibility, because in no other way can an object be given to us.

The effect of an object upon the faculty of representation, so far as we are affected by it, is *sensation*. That intuition which is in relation to the object through sensation, is entitled *empirical*. The undetermined object of an empirical intuition is entitled *appearance*.

That in the appearance which corresponds to sensation

---

[1] [In A the sub-sections are not numbered.]   [2] [*eine Erkenntnis.*]
[3] [*uns Menschen wenigstens* added in B.]
[4] [*vermittelst gewisser Merkmale* added in B. Cf. Kant's *Nachträge zur Kritik* (edited by B. Erdmann, 1881), xi: " if the representation is not in itself the cause of the object."]

I term its *matter*; but that which so determines[1] the manifold of appearance that it allows of being ordered[2] in certain relations, I term the *form* of appearance. That in which alone the sensations can be posited and ordered in a certain form, cannot itself be sensation; and therefore, while the matter of all appearance is given to us *a posteriori* only, its form must lie ready for the sensations *a priori* in the mind, and so must allow of being considered apart from all sensation.

I term all representations *pure* (in the transcendental sense) in which there is nothing that belongs to sensation. The pure form of sensible intuitions in general, in which all the manifold of intuition is intuited in certain relations, must be found in the mind *a priori*. This pure form of sensibility may

B 35 also itself be called *pure intuition*. Thus, if I take away from the representation of a body that which the understanding thinks in regard to it, substance, force, divisibility, etc., and

A 21 likewise what belongs to sensation, impenetrability, hardness, colour, etc., something still remains over from this empirical intuition, namely, extension and figure. These belong to pure intuition, which, even without any actual object of the senses or of sensation, exists in the mind *a priori* as a mere form of sensibility.

The science of all principles of *a priori* sensibility I call *transcendental aesthetic*.[a] There must be such a science, form-

---

[a] The Germans are the only people who currently make use of the word 'aesthetic' in order to signify what others call the critique of taste. This usage originated in the abortive attempt made by Baumgarten,[3] that admirable analytical thinker, to bring the critical treatment of the beautiful under rational principles, and so to raise its rules to the rank of a science. But such endeavours are fruitless. The said rules or criteria are, as regards their chief [4] sources, merely empirical, and consequently can never serve as determinate [5] *a priori* laws by which our judgment of taste must be directed. On the contrary, our judgment is the proper test of the correctness

B 36 of the rules. For this reason it is advisable either [6] to give up using the name in this sense of critique of taste, and to reserve it for that doctrine of sensibility which is true science—thus ap-

[1] [*das jenige welches macht dass.*]
[2] [In B: *geordnet werden kann* for *geordnet angeschaut wird.*]
[3] [A. G. Baumgarten (1714–62): *Aesthetica* (1750).]
[4] [*vornehmsten* added in B.]   [5] [*bestimmten* added in B.]
[6] [*entweder* added in B.]

ing the first part of the transcendental doctrine of elements, B 36
in distinction from that part which deals with the principles
of pure thought, and which is called transcendental logic.

In the transcendental aesthetic we shall, therefore, first A 22
isolate sensibility, by taking away from it everything which the
understanding thinks through its concepts, so that nothing
may be left save empirical intuition. Secondly, we shall also
separate off from it everything which belongs to sensation, so
that nothing may remain save pure intuition and the mere
form of appearances, which is all that sensibility can supply
a priori. In the course of this investigation it will be found
that there are two pure forms of sensible intuition, serving as
principles of *a priori* knowledge, namely, space and time. To
the consideration of these we shall now proceed.

THE TRANSCENDENTAL AESTHETIC   B 37

Section I

SPACE

§ 2

Metaphysical Exposition of this Concept [1]

By means of outer sense, a property of our mind, we represent to ourselves objects as outside us, and all without exception in space. In space their shape, magnitude, and relation to
one another are determined or determinable. Inner sense,
by means of which the mind intuits itself or its inner state,
yields indeed no intuition of the soul itself as an object; but
there is nevertheless a determinate form [namely, time] in A 23
which alone the intuition of inner states is possible, and everything which belongs to inner determinations is therefore

---

proximating to the language and sense of the ancients, in their
far-famed division of knowledge into αἰσθητὰ καὶ νοητά—or else
to share the name with speculative philosophy, employing it partly
in the transcendental and partly in the psychological sense.[2]

   [1] ["§ 2" and sub-heading added in B.]
   [2] ["or else . . ." to end of sentence added in B.]

represented in relations of time. Time cannot be outwardly
intuited, any more than space can be intuited as something
in us. What, then, are space and time? Are they real existences? Are they only determinations or relations of things, yet
such as would belong to things even if they were not intuited?
Or are space and time such that they belong only to the form
B 38 of intuition, and therefore to the subjective constitution of our
mind, apart from which they could not be ascribed to anything
whatsoever? In order to obtain light upon these questions,
let us first give an exposition of the concept of space.[1] By
exposition[2] *(expositio)* I mean the clear, though not necessarily
exhaustive, representation of that which belongs to a concept:
the exposition is *metaphysical* when it contains that which
exhibits the concept *as given a priori*.

1. Space is not an empirical concept which has been derived from outer experiences. For in order that certain sensations be referred to something outside me (that is, to something
in another region of space from that in which I find myself),
and similarly in order that I may be able to represent them as
outside and alongside [3] one another, and accordingly as not
only different but as in different places, the representation of
space must be presupposed. The representation of space cannot, therefore, be empirically obtained from the relations of
outer appearance. On the contrary, this outer experience is
itself possible at all only through that representation.

A 24   2. Space is a necessary *a priori* representation, which
underlies all outer intuitions. We can never represent to ourselves the absence of space, though we can quite well think it
B 39 as empty of objects. It must therefore be regarded as the condition of the possibility of appearances, and not as a determination dependent upon them. It is an *a priori* representation,
which necessarily underlies outer appearances.*

* [In A there is here inserted the following argument:]
3. The apodeictic certainty of all geometrical propositions,
and the possibility of their *a priori* construction, is grounded
in this *a priori* necessity of space. Were this representation of

[1] [In B: *den Begriff des Raumes erörtern* substituted for *zuerst den Raum
betrachten.*]
[2] ["By *exposition* . . ." to end of sentence added in B.]
[3] [*und neben* added in B.]

3.[1] Space is not a discursive or, as we say, general concept of relations of things in general, but a pure intuition. For, in the A 25 first place, we can represent to ourselves only one space; and if we speak of diverse spaces, we mean thereby only parts of one and the same unique space. Secondly, these parts cannot precede the one all-embracing space, as being, as it were, constituents out of which it can be composed; on the contrary, they can be thought only as *in* it. Space is essentially one; the manifold in it, and therefore the general concept of spaces, depends solely on [the introduction of] limitations. Hence it follows that an *a priori*, and not an empirical, intuition underlies all concepts of space. For kindred reasons, geometrical propositions, that, for instance, in a triangle two sides together are greater than the third, can never be derived from the general concepts of line and triangle, but only from intuition, and this indeed *a priori*, with apodeictic certainty.

4.* Space is represented as an infinite *given* magnitude. Now every concept must be thought as a representation B 40 which is contained in an infinite number of different possible

---

space a concept acquired *a posteriori*, and derived from outer experience in general, the first principles of mathematical determination would be nothing but perceptions. They would therefore all share in the contingent character of perception; that there should be only one straight line between two points would not be necessary, but only what experience always teaches. What is derived from experience has only comparative universality, namely, that which is obtained through induction. We should therefore only be able to say that, so far as hitherto observed, no space has been found which has more than three dimensions.

* [In A this paragraph runs:]

5. Space is represented as an infinite given magnitude. A general concept of space, which is found alike in a foot and in an ell, cannot determine anything in regard to magnitude. If there were no limitlessness in the progression of intuition, no concept of relations could yield a principle of their infinitude.

[1] [In A: "4".]

representations (as their common character), and which therefore contains these *under* itself; but no concept, as such, can be thought as containing an infinite number of representations *within* itself. It is in this latter way, however, that space is thought; for all the parts of space coexist *ad infinitum*. Consequently, the original representation of space is an *a priori* intuition, not a concept.

§ 3[1]

The Transcendental Exposition of the Concept of Space

I understand by a transcendental exposition the explanation of a concept, as a principle from which the possibility of other *a priori* synthetic knowledge can be understood. For this purpose it is required (1) that such knowledge does really flow from the given concept, (2) that this knowledge is possible only on the assumption of a given mode of explaining the concept.

Geometry is a science which determines the properties of space synthetically, and yet *a priori*. What, then, must be our representation of space, in order that such knowledge of it may be possible? It must in its origin be intuition; for

B 41 from a mere concept no propositions can be obtained which go beyond the concept—as happens in geometry (Introduction, V).[2] Further, this intuition must be *a priori*, that is, it must be found in us prior to any perception of an object, and must therefore be pure, not empirical, intuition. For geometrical propositions are one and all apodeictic, that is, are bound up with the consciousness of their necessity ; for instance, that space has only three dimensions. Such propositions cannot be empirical or, in other words, judgments of experience, nor can they be derived from any such judgments (Introduction, II).[3]

How, then, can there exist in the mind an outer intuition which precedes the objects themselves, and in which the concept of these objects can be determined *a priori*? Manifestly, not otherwise than in so far as the intuition has **its** seat in the subject only, as the formal character of the

---

[1] [This whole sub-section added in B.]
[2] [Above, p. 52.]   [3] [Above, p. 43.]

subject, in virtue of which, in being affected by objects, it obtains *immediate representation*, that is, *intuition*, of them; and only in so far, therefore, as it is merely the form of outer *sense* in general.

Our explanation is thus the only explanation that makes intelligible the *possibility* of geometry, as a body of *a priori* synthetic knowledge. Any mode of explanation which fails to do this, although it may otherwise seem to be somewhat similar, can by this criterion[1] be distinguished from it with the greatest certainty.

Conclusions from the above Concepts   {A 26 / B 42}

(*a*) Space does not represent any property of things in themselves, nor does it represent them in their relation to one another. That is to say, space does not represent any determination that attaches to the objects themselves, and which remains even when abstraction has been made of all the subjective conditions of intuition. For no determinations, whether absolute or relative, can be intuited prior to the existence of the things to which they belong, and none, therefore, can be intuited *a priori*.

(*b*) Space is nothing but the form of all appearances of outer sense. It is the subjective condition of sensibility, under which alone outer intuition is possible for us. Since, then, the receptivity of the subject, its capacity to be affected by objects, must necessarily precede all intuitions of these objects, it can readily be understood how the form of all appearances can be given prior to all actual perceptions, and so exist in the mind *a priori*, and how, as a pure intuition, in which all objects must be determined, it can contain, prior to all experience, principles which determine the relations of these objects.

It is, therefore, solely from the human standpoint that we can speak of space, of extended things, etc. If we depart from the subjective condition under which alone we can have outer intuition, namely, liability to be affected by objects, the representation of space stands for nothing whatsoever. B 43

1 [End of the sub-section added in B.]

A 27   This predicate can be ascribed to things only in so far as they
appear to us, that is, only to objects of sensibility. The constant form of this receptivity, which we term sensibility, is a
necessary condition of all the relations in which objects can
be intuited as outside us; and if we abstract from these
objects, it is a pure intuition, and bears the name of space.
Since we cannot treat the special conditions of sensibility as
conditions of the possibility of things, but only of their appearances, we can indeed say that space comprehends all things
that appèar to us as external, but not all things in themselves,
by whatever subject they are intuited, or whether they be
intuited or not. For we cannot judge in regard to the intuitions of other thinking beings, whether they are bound by
the same conditions as those which limit our intuition and
which for us are universally valid. If we add to the concept of
the subject of a judgment the limitation under which the judgment is made, the judgment is then unconditionally valid.
The proposition, that all things are side by side in space, is
valid under[1] the limitation that these things are viewed as
objects of our sensible intuition. If, now, I add the condition
to the concept, and say that all things, as outer appearances,
are side by side in space, the rule is valid universally and
B 44   without limitation. Our exposition[2] therefore establishes the
A 28   *reality*, that is, the objective validity, of space in respect of
whatever can be presented to us outwardly as object, but also
at the same time the *ideality* of space in respect of things when
they are considered in themselves through reason, that is,
without regard to the constitution of our sensibility. We
assert, then, the *empirical reality* of space, as regards all
possible outer experience; and yet at the same time we
assert its *transcendental ideality*—in other words, that it
is nothing at all, immediately we withdraw the above condition, namely, its limitation to possible experience, and so
look upon it as something that underlies things in themselves.

   With the sole exception of space there is no subjective
representation, referring to something *outer*, which could be

---

   [1] [In A: valid only under.]
   [2] [Following the 4th edition substitution of *Erörterung lehrt* for *Erörterungen
lehren.*]

entitled [at once] objective [and] *a priori*. For* there is no other
subjective representation from which we can derive *a priori*
synthetic propositions, as we can from intuition in space (§ 3 [1]).
Strictly speaking, therefore, these other representations have no
ideality, although they agree with the representation of space in
this respect, that they belong merely to the subjective constitution of our manner of sensibility, for instance, of sight, hearing,
touch,[2] as in the case of the sensations of colours, sounds, and
heat, which, since they are mere sensations and not intuitions,
do not of themselves yield knowledge of any object, least of
all any *a priori* knowledge.

The above remark is intended only to guard anyone from   B 45
supposing that the ideality of space as here asserted can be
illustrated by examples so altogether insufficient as colours,
taste, etc. For these cannot rightly be regarded as properties
of things, but only as changes in the subject, changes which
may, indeed, be different for different men. In such examples
as these, that which originally is itself only appearance, for
instance, a rose, is being treated by the empirical understanding as a thing in itself, which, nevertheless, in respect of its   A 30
colour, can appear differently to every observer. The transcendental concept of appearances in space, on the other hand,
is a critical reminder that nothing intuited in space is a thing
in itself, that space is not a form inhering in things in them-

---

* ["For there is . . ." to end of paragraph, substituted in B for
the following:]

This subjective condition of all outer appearances cannot,
therefore, be compared to any other. The taste of a wine does
not belong to the objective determinations of the wine, not
even if by the wine as an object we mean the wine as appearance, but to the special constitution of sense in the subject that
tastes it. Colours are not properties of the bodies to the intuition of which they are attached, but only modifications of
the sense of sight, which is affected in a certain manner by
light. Space, on the other hand, as condition of outer objects,
necessarily belongs to their appearance or intuition. Taste and
colours are not necessary conditions under which alone objects   A 29
can be for us objects of the senses. They are connected with

[1] [Above, p. 70.]   [2] [*Gefühls*, cf. below, p. 74.]

selves as their intrinsic property, that objects in themselves are quite unknown to us, and that what we call outer objects are nothing but mere representations of our sensibility, the form of which is space. The true correlate of sensibility, the thing in itself, is not known, and cannot be known, through these representations; and in experience no question is ever asked in regard to it.

B 46

TRANSCENDENTAL AESTHETIC

SECTION II

TIME

§ 4

Metaphysical Exposition of the Concept of Time[1]

1. Time is not an empirical concept that has been derived from any experience. For neither coexistence nor succession would ever come within our perception, if the representation of time were not presupposed as underlying them *a priori*. Only on the presupposition of time can we represent to ourselves a number of things as existing at one and the same time (simultaneously) or at different times (successively).

A 31

2. Time is a necessary representation that underlies all

the appearances only as effects accidentally added by the particular constitution of the sense organs. Accordingly, they are not *a priori* representations, but are grounded in sensation, and, indeed, in the case of taste, even upon feeling[2] (pleasure and pain), as an effect of sensation. Further, no one can have *a priori* a representation of a colour or of any taste; whereas, since space concerns only the pure form of intuition, and therefore involves no sensation whatsoever, and nothing empirical, all kinds and determinations of space can and must be represented *a priori*, if concepts of figures and of their relations are to arise. Through space alone is it possible that things should be outer objects to us.

[1] ["§ 4" and sub-title added in B.]   [2] [*Gefühl*, cf. above, p. 73.]

intuitions. We cannot, in respect of appearances in general, remove time itself, though we can quite well think time as void of appearances. Time is, therefore, given *a priori*. In it alone is actuality of appearances possible at all. Appearances may, one and all, vanish; but time (as the universal condition of their possibility)[1] cannot itself be removed.

3. The possibility of apodeictic principles concerning the B 47 relations of time, or of axioms of time in general, is also grounded upon this *a priori* necessity. Time has only one dimension; different times are not simultaneous but successive (just as different spaces are not successive but simultaneous). These principles cannot be derived from experience, for experience would give neither strict universality nor apodeictic certainty. We should only be able to say that common experience teaches us that it is so; not that it must be so. These principles are valid as rules under which alone experiences are possible; and they instruct us in regard to[2] the experiences, not by means of them.

4. Time is not a discursive, or what is called a general concept, but a pure form of sensible intuition. Different times are but parts of one and the same time; and the representation A 32 which can be given only through a single object is intuition. Moreover, the proposition that different times cannot be simultaneous is not to be derived from a general concept. The proposition is synthetic, and cannot have its origin in concepts alone. It is immediately contained in the intuition and representation of time.

5. The infinitude of time signifies nothing more than that every determinate magnitude of time is possible only through B 48 limitations of one single time that underlies it. The original representation, *time*, must therefore be given as unlimited. But when an object is so given that its parts, and every quantity of it, can be determinately represented only through limitation, the whole representation cannot be given through concepts, since they contain only partial representations;[3] on the contrary, such concepts must themselves rest on immediate intuition.

---

[1] [Brackets added in B.]
[2] [Taking the 3rd edition reading of *von* for *vor*.]
[3] [In A: since in their case the partial representations come first.]

D 2

§ 5[1]

The Transcendental Exposition of the Concept of Time

I may here refer to No. 3,[2] where, for the sake of brevity, I have placed under the title of metaphysical exposition what is properly transcendental. Here I may add that the concept of alteration,[3] and with it the concept of motion, as alteration of place, is possible only through and in the representation of time; and that if this representation were not an *a priori* (inner) intuition, no concept, no matter what it might be, could render comprehensible the possibility of an alteration, that is, of a combination of contradictorily opposed predicates in one and the same object, for instance, the being and the not-being of one and the same thing in one and the same place. Only in time can two contradictorily opposed predicates meet in one and the same object, namely, *one after the other*. Thus our concept of time explains the possibility of that body of *a priori* synthetic knowledge which is exhibited in the general doctrine of motion, and which is by no means unfruitful.

B 49

§ 6[4]

Conclusions from these Concepts

(*a*) Time is not something which exists of itself, or which inheres in things as an objective determination, and it does not, therefore, remain when abstraction is made of all subjective conditions of its intuition. Were it self-subsistent, it would be something which would be actual and yet not an actual object. Were it a determination or order inhering in things themselves, it could not precede the objects as their condition, and be known and intuited *a priori* by means of synthetic propositions. But this[5] last is quite possible if time is nothing but the subjective condition under which alone[6] intuition can take place in us. For that being so, this form of inner intuition can be represented prior to the objects, and therefore *a priori*.

A 33

---

[1] [The whole of sub-section 5 is added in B.]
[3] [*Veränderung.* Cf. below, pp. 216-17.]
[5] [Reading, with Grillo, *Dieses* for *Diese.*]
[6] [Reading, with Erdmann, *allein* for *alle.*]

[2] [*I.e.* to § 4, No. 3.]
[4] ["§ 6" added in B.]

(*b*) Time is nothing but the form of inner sense, that is, of the intuition of ourselves and of our inner state. It cannot be a determination of outer appearances; it has to do neither with shape nor position, but with the relation of representations in B 50 our inner state. And just because this inner intuition yields no shape, we endeavour to make up for this want by analogies. We represent the time-sequence by a line progressing to infinity, in which the manifold constitutes a series of one dimension only; and we reason from the properties of this line to all the properties of time, with this one exception, that while the parts of the line are simultaneous the parts of time are always successive. From this fact also, that all the relations of time allow of being expressed in an outer intuition, it is evident that the representation is itself an intuition.

(*c*) Time is the formal *a priori* condition of all appearances A 34 whatsoever. Space, as the pure form of all *outer* intuition, is so far limited; it serves as the *a priori* condition only of outer appearances. But since all representations, whether they have for their objects outer things or not, belong, in themselves, as determinations of the mind, to our inner state; and since this inner state stands under the formal condition of inner intuition, and so belongs to time, time is an *a priori* condition of all appearance whatsoever. It is the immediate condition of inner appearances (of our souls), and thereby the mediate condition of outer appearances. Just as I can say *a priori* that B 51 all outer appearances are in space, and are determined *a priori* in conformity with the relations of space, I can also say, from the principle of inner sense, that all appearances whatsoever, that is, all objects of the senses, are in time, and necessarily stand in time-relations.

If we abstract from *our* mode of inwardly intuiting ourselves—the mode of intuition in terms of which we likewise take up into our faculty of representation[1] all outer intuitions— and so take objects as they may be in themselves, then time is nothing. It has objective validity only in respect of appearances, these being things which we take *as objects of our senses*. It is no longer objective, if we abstract from the sensi- A 35 bility of our intuition, that is, from that mode of representation which is peculiar to us, and speak of *things in general*. Time is

[1] [*in der Vorstellungskraft zu befassen.*]

therefore a purely subjective condition of our (human) intuition (which is always sensible, that is, so far as we are affected by objects), and in itself, apart from the subject, is nothing. Nevertheless, in respect of all appearances, and therefore of all the things which can enter into our experience, it is necessarily objective. We cannot say that all things are in time, be-

B 52 cause in this concept of things in general we are abstracting from every mode of their intuition and therefore from that condition under which alone objects can be represented as being in time. If, however, the condition be added to the concept, and we say that all things as appearances, that is, as objects of sensible intuition, are in time, then the proposition has legitimate objective validity and universality *a priori*.

What we are maintaining is, therefore, the *empirical reality* of time, that is, its objective validity in respect of all objects which allow of ever being given to our senses. And since our intuition is always sensible, no object can ever be given to us in experience which does not conform to the condition of time. On the other hand, we deny to time all claim to absolute reality; that is to say, we deny that it belongs

A 36 to things absolutely, as their condition or property, independently of any reference to the form of our sensible intuition; properties that belong to things in themselves can never be given to us through the senses. This, then, is what constitutes the *transcendental ideality* of time. What we mean by this phrase is that if we abstract from the subjective conditions of sensible intuition, time is nothing, and cannot be ascribed to the objects in themselves (apart from their relation to our intuition) in the way either of subsistence or of inherence. This

B 53 ideality, like that of space, must not, however, be illustrated by false analogies with sensation,[1] because it is then assumed that the appearance, in which the sensible predicates inhere, itself has objective reality. In the case of time, such objective reality falls entirely away, save in so far as it is merely empirical, that is, save in so far as we regard the object itself merely as appearance. On this subject, the reader may refer to what has been said at the close of the preceding section.[2]

[1] [*mit den Subreptionen der Empfindung in Vergleichung zu stellen, i.e.* the ideality of time and space must not be confused with the ideality ascribed to sensations.]

[2] [Above, pp. 73-4.]

§ 7 [1]

Elucidation

Against this theory, which admits the empirical reality of time, but denies its absolute and transcendental reality, I have heard men of intelligence so unanimously voicing an objection, that I must suppose it to occur spontaneously to every reader to whom this way of thinking is unfamiliar. The objection is this. Alterations [2] are real,[3] this being proved by change [4] of our A 37 own representations—even if all outer appearances, together with their alterations, be denied. Now alterations are possible only in time, and time is therefore something real. There is no difficulty in meeting this objection. I grant the whole argument. Certainly time is something real, namely, the real form of inner intuition. It has therefore subjective reality in respect of inner experience; that is, I really have the representation of time and B 54 of my determinations in it. Time is therefore to be regarded as real, not indeed as object but as the mode of representation of myself as object. If without this condition of sensibility I could intuit myself, or be intuited by another being, the very same determinations which we now represent to ourselves as alterations would yield knowledge into which the representation of time, and therefore also of alteration, would in no way enter. Thus empirical reality has to be allowed to time, as the condition of all our experiences; on our theory, it is only its absolute reality that has to be denied. It is nothing but the form of our inner intuition.[a] If we take away from our inner intuition the peculiar condition of our sensibility, the concept of time likewise vanishes; it does not inhere in the objects, but A 38 merely in the subject which intuits them.

But the reason why this objection is so unanimously urged,

[a] I can indeed say that my representations follow one another; but this is only to say that we are conscious of them as in a time-sequence, that is, in conformity with the form of inner sense. Time is not, therefore, something in itself, nor is it an objective determination inherent in things.

[1] ["§ 7" added in B.]   [2] [*Veränderungen.*]
[3] [*Wirklich* here, as often elsewhere, is used by Kant as the adjective corresponding to the substantive *Realität*, and in such cases it is more suitably translated by 'real' than by 'actual'.]   [4] [*Wechsel.*]

B 55 and that too by those who have nothing very convincing to say against the doctrine of the ideality of space, is this. They have no expectation of being able to prove apodeictically the absolute reality of space; for they are confronted by idealism, which teaches that the reality of outer objects does not allow of strict proof. On the other hand, the reality of the object of our inner sense (the reality of myself and my state) is, [they argue,] immediately evident through consciousness. The former may be merely an illusion; the latter is, on their view, undeniably something real. What they have failed, however, to recognise is that both are in the same position; in neither case can their reality as representations be questioned, and in both cases they belong only to appearance, which always has two sides, the one by which the object is viewed in and by itself (without regard to the mode of intuiting it—its nature therefore remaining always problematic), the other by which the form of the intuition of this object is taken into account. This form is not to be looked for in the object in itself, but in the subject to which the object appears; nevertheless, it belongs really and necessarily to the appearance of this object.

Time and space are, therefore, two sources of knowledge, from which bodies of *a priori* synthetic knowledge can be
A 39 derived. (Pure mathematics is a brilliant example of such knowledge, especially as regards space and its relations.)
B 56 Time and space, taken together, are the pure forms of all sensible intuition, and so are what make *a priori* synthetic propositions possible. But these *a priori* sources of knowledge, being merely conditions of our sensibility, just by this very fact determine their own limits, namely, that they apply to objects only in so far as objects are viewed as appearances, and do not present things as they are in themselves. This is the sole field of their validity; should we pass beyond it, no objective use can be made of them. This ideality[1] of space and time leaves, however, the certainty of empirical knowledge unaffected, for we are equally sure of it, whether these forms necessarily inhere in things in themselves or only in our intuition of them. Those, on the other hand, who maintain the absolute reality of space and time, whether as

[1] [Reading, with Laas, Adickes, and Vaihinger, *Idealität* for *Realität*.]

subsistent[1] or only as inherent, must come into conflict with the principles of experience itself. For if they decide for the former alternative (which is generally the view taken by mathematical students of nature), they have to admit two eternal and infinite self-subsistent[2] non-entities[3] (space and time), which are there (yet without there being anything real) only in order to contain in themselves all that is real. If they adopt the latter alternative (as advocated by certain meta-   A 40 physical students of nature), and regard space and time as relations of appearances, alongside or in succession to one   B 57 another—relations abstracted from experience, and in this isolation confusedly represented—they are obliged to deny that *a priori* mathematical doctrines have any validity in respect of real things (for instance, in space), or at least to deny their apodeictic certainty. For such certainty is not to be found in the *a posteriori*. On this view, indeed, the *a priori* concepts of space and time are merely creatures of the imagination, whose source must really be sought in experience, the imagination framing out of the relations abstracted from experience something that does indeed contain what is general in these relations, but which cannot exist without the restrictions which nature has attached to them. The former thinkers obtain at least this advantage, that they keep the field of appearances open for mathematical propositions. On the other hand, they have greatly embarrassed themselves by those very conditions [space and time, eternal, infinite, and self-subsistent], when with the understanding they endeavour to go out beyond this field. The latter have indeed an advantage, in that the representations of space and time do not stand in their way if they seek to judge of objects, not as appearances but merely in their relation to the understanding. But since they are unable to appeal to a true and objectively valid *a priori* intuition, they can neither account for the possibility of *a priori* mathematical know-ledge, nor bring the propositions of experience into necessary   A 41 agreement with it. On our theory of the true character of   B 58 these two original forms of sensibility, both difficulties are removed.

Lastly, transcendental aesthetic cannot contain more than

----

[1] [*subsistierend.*]   [2] [*für sich bestehende.*]   [3] [*Undinge.*]

these two elements, space and time. This is evident from the fact that all other concepts belonging to sensibility, even that of motion, in which both elements are united, presuppose something empirical. Motion presupposes the perception of something movable. But in space, considered in itself, there is nothing movable; consequently the movable must be something that is found *in space only through experience*, and must therefore be an empirical datum. For the same reason, transcendental aesthetic cannot count the concept of alteration among its *a priori* data. Time itself does not alter, but only something which is in time. The concept of alteration thus presupposes the perception of something existing and of the succession of its determinations; that is to say, it presupposes experience.

§ 8[1]

General Observations on Transcendental Aesthetic

I.[1] To avoid all misapprehension, it is necessary to explain, as clearly as possible, what our view is regarding the fundamental constitution of sensible knowledge in general.

What we have meant to say is that all our intuition is nothing but the representation of appearance; that the things which we intuit are not in themselves what we intuit them as being, nor their relations so constituted in themselves as they appear to us, and that if the subject, or even only the subjective constitution of the senses in general, be removed, the whole constitution and all the relations of objects in space and time, nay space and time themselves, would vanish. As appearances, they cannot exist in themselves, but only in us. What objects may be in themselves, and apart from all this receptivity of our sensibility, remains completely unknown to us. We know nothing but our mode of perceiving them—a mode which is peculiar to us, and not necessarily shared in by every being, though, certainly, by every human being. With this alone have we any concern. Space and time are its pure forms, and sensation in general its matter. The former alone can we know *a priori*, that is, prior to all actual perception; and such knowledge is therefore called pure

---

[1] ["§ 8" and "I" added in B.]

intuition. The latter is that in our knowledge which leads to its being called *a posteriori* knowledge, that is, empirical intuition. The former inhere in our sensibility with absolute necessity, no matter of what kind our sensations may be; the latter can exist in varying modes. Even if we could bring our A 43 intuition to the highest degree of clearness, we should not thereby come any nearer to the constitution of objects in themselves. We should still know only our mode of intuition, that is, our sensibility. We should, indeed, know it completely, but always only under the conditions of space and time— conditions which are originally inherent in the subject. What the objects may be in themselves would never become known to us even through the most enlightened knowledge of that which is alone given us, namely, their appearance.

The concept of sensibility and of appearance would be falsified, and our whole teaching in regard to them would be rendered empty and useless, if we were to accept the view that our entire sensibility is nothing but a confused representation of things, containing only what belongs to them in themselves, but doing so under an aggregation of characters and partial representations that we do not consciously distinguish. For the difference between a confused and a clear representation B 61 is merely logical, and does not concern the content. No doubt the concept of 'right',[1] in its common-sense usage, contains all that the subtlest speculation can develop out of it, though in its ordinary and practical use we are not conscious of the manifold representations comprised in this [2] thought But we cannot say that the common concept is therefore sensible, containing a mere appearance. For 'right' can never be an appear- A 44 ance; it is a concept in the understanding, and represents a property (the moral property) of actions, which belongs to them in themselves. The representation of a body in intuition, on the other hand, contains nothing that can belong to an object in itself, but merely the appearance of something, and the mode in which we are affected by that something; and this receptivity of our faculty of knowledge is termed sensibility. Even if that appearance could become completely transparent

---

[1] [*Recht.*]
[2] [Reading, with 4th edition, *diesem* for *diesen.*]

to us, such knowledge would remain *toto coelo* different from knowledge of the object in itself.

The philosophy of Leibniz and Wolff, in thus treating the difference between the sensible and the intelligible as merely logical, has given a completely wrong direction to all investigations into the nature and origin of our knowledge. This difference is quite evidently transcendental. It does not merely B 62 concern their [logical] form, as being either clear or confused. It concerns their origin and content. It is not that by our sensibility we cannot know the nature of things in themselves in any save a confused fashion; we do not apprehend them in any fashion whatsoever. If our subjective constitution be removed, the represented object, with the qualities which sensible intuition bestows upon it, is nowhere to be found, and cannot possibly be found. For it is this subjective constitution which determines its form as appearance.

A 45   We commonly distinguish in appearances that which is essentially inherent in their intuition and holds for sense in all human beings, from that which belongs to their intuition accidentally only, and is valid not in relation to sensibility in general but only in relation to a particular standpoint or to a peculiarity of structure in this or that sense. The former kind of knowledge is then declared to represent the object in itself, the latter its appearance only. But this distinction is merely empirical. If, as generally happens, we stop short at this point, and do not proceed, as we ought, to treat the empirical intuition as itself mere appearance, in which nothing that belongs to a thing in itself can be found, our transcendental distinction is lost. We then believe that we know things in themselves, and this in spite of the fact that in the world of sense, however B 63 ever deeply we enquire into its objects, we have to do with nothing but appearances. The rainbow in a sunny shower may be called a mere appearance, and the rain the thing in itself. This is correct, if the latter concept be taken in a merely physical sense. Rain will then be viewed only as that which, in all experience and in all its various positions relative to the senses, is determined thus, and not otherwise, in our intuition. But if we take this empirical object in its general character, A 46 and ask, without considering whether or not it is the same for all human sense, whether it represents an object in

itself (and by that we cannot mean the drops of rain, for these
are already, as appearances, empirical objects), the question
as to the relation of the representation to the object at once
becomes transcendental. We then realise that not only are the
drops of rain mere appearances, but that even their round
shape, nay even the space in which they fall, are nothing in
themselves, but merely modifications or fundamental forms of
our sensible intuition, and that the transcendental object
remains unknown to us.

The second important concern of our Transcendental Aesthetic is that it should not obtain favour merely as a plausible
hypothesis, but should have that certainty and freedom from
doubt which is required of any theory that is to serve as an
organon. To make this certainty completely convincing, we
shall select a case by which the validity of the position adopted
will be rendered obvious, and which will serve to set what has   B 64
been said in § 3 in a clearer light.

Let us suppose that space and time are in themselves
objective, and are conditions of the possibility of things in
themselves. In the first place, it is evident that in regard to
both there is a large number of *a priori* apodeictic and synthetic propositions. This is especially true of space, to which
our chief attention will therefore be directed in this enquiry.
Since the propositions of geometry are synthetic *a priori*, and
are known with apodeictic certainty, I raise the question,   A 47
whence do you obtain such propositions, and upon what does
the understanding rely in its endeavour to achieve such absolutely necessary and universally valid truths? There is no
other way than through concepts or through intuitions; and
these are given either *a priori* or *a posteriori*. In their latter
form, namely, as *empirical* concepts, and also as that upon
which these are grounded, the *empirical* intuition, neither the
concepts nor the intuitions can yield any synthetic proposition
except such as is itself also merely empirical (that is, a proposition of experience), and which for that very reason can
never possess the necessity and absolute universality which are
characteristic of all geometrical propositions. As regards the
first and sole means of arriving at such knowledge, namely,
in *a priori* fashion through mere concepts or through intuitions, it is evident that from mere concepts only analytic

B 65 knowledge, not synthetic knowledge, is to be obtained. Take, for instance, the proposition, "Two straight lines cannot enclose a space, and with them alone no figure is possible", and try to derive it from the concept of straight lines and of the number two. Or take the proposition, "Given three straight lines, a figure is possible", and try, in like manner, to derive it from the concepts involved. All your labour is vain; and you find that you are constrained to have recourse to intuition, as is always done in geometry. You therefore give yourself an object

A 48 in intuition. But of what kind is this intuition? Is it a pure *a priori* intuition or an empirical intuition? Were it the latter, no universally valid proposition could ever arise out of it—still less an apodeictic proposition—for experience can never yield such. You must therefore give yourself an object *a priori* in intuition, and ground upon this your synthetic proposition. If there did not exist in you a power of *a priori* intuition; and if that subjective condition were not also at the same time, as regards its form, the universal *a priori* condition under which alone the object of this outer intuition is itself possible; if the object (the triangle) were something in itself, apart from any relation to you, the subject, how could you say that what necessarily exist in you as subjective conditions for the construction of a triangle, must of necessity belong to the triangle itself? You could not then add anything new (the figure) to

B 66 your concepts (of three lines) as something which must necessarily be met with in the object, since this object is [on that view] given antecedently to your knowledge, and not by means of it. If, therefore, space (and the same is true of time) were not merely a form of your intuition, containing conditions *a priori*, under which alone things can be outer objects to you, and without which subjective conditions outer objects are in themselves [1] nothing, you could not in regard to outer objects determine anything whatsoever in an *a priori* and synthetic manner. It is, therefore, not merely possible or probable, but

A 49 indubitably certain, that space and time, as the necessary conditions of all outer and inner experience, are merely subjective conditions of all our intuition, and that in relation to these conditions all objects are therefore mere appearances, and not given us as things in themselves which exist in this

[1] [*an sich*, meaning *as outer objects.*]

manner. For this reason also, while much can be said *a priori* as regards the form of appearances, nothing whatsoever can be asserted of the thing in itself, which may underlie these appearances.

II.[1] In confirmation of this theory of the ideality of both outer and inner sense, and therefore of all objects of the senses, as mere appearances, it is especially relevant to observe that everything in our knowledge which belongs to intuition— feeling of pleasure and pain, and the will, not being knowledge, are excluded—contains nothing but mere relations; namely, of locations in an intuition (extension), of change of location (motion), and of laws according to which this change is determined (moving forces). What it is that is present in this or that location, or what it is that is operative[2] in the things themselves apart from change of location, is not given through intuition. Now a thing in itself[3] cannot be known through mere relations; and we may therefore conclude that since outer sense gives us nothing but mere relations, this sense can contain in its representation only the relation of an object to the subject, and not the inner properties of the object in itself. This also holds true of inner sense, not only because the representations of the *outer senses* constitute the proper material with which we occupy our mind, but because the time in which we set these representations, which is itself antecedent to the consciousness of them in experience, and which underlies them as the formal condition of the mode in which we posit[4] them in the mind, itself contains [only] relations of succession, coexistence, and of that which is coexistent with succession, the enduring. Now that which, as representation, can be antecedent to any and every act of thinking anything, is intuition; and if it contains nothing but relations, it is the form of intuition. Since this form does not represent anything save in so far as something is posited in the mind, it can be nothing but the mode in which the mind is affected through its own activity (namely, through this positing of its[5] representation), and so is affected by itself; in other words, it is

B 67

B 68

----

1 [Sub-sections II., III., IV. and Conclusion to the Transcendental Aesthetic added in B.]
2 [*wirke.*]   3 [*eine Sache an sich.*]   4 [*setzen.*]
5 [Reading, with Kehrbach, *seiner* for *ihrer.*]

nothing but an inner sense in respect of the form of that sense. Everything that is represented through a sense is so far always appearance, and consequently we must either refuse to admit that there is an inner sense, or we must recognise that the subject, which is the object of the sense, can be represented through it only as appearance, not as that subject would judge of itself if its intuition were self-activity only, that is, were intellectual. The whole difficulty is as to how a subject can inwardly intuit itself; and this is a difficulty common to every theory. The consciousness of self (apperception) is the simple representation of the 'I', and if all that is manifold in the subject were given by the *activity of the self*, the inner intuition would be intellectual. In man this consciousness demands inner perception of the manifold which is antecedently given in the subject, and the mode in which this manifold is given in the mind must, as non-spontaneous, be entitled sensibility. If the faculty of coming to consciousness of oneself is to seek out (to apprehend) that which lies in the mind, it must affect the mind, and only in this way can it give rise to an intuition of itself. But the form of this intuition, which exists antecedently in the

B 69   mind, determines, in the representation of time, the mode in which the manifold is together in the mind, since it then intuits itself not as it would represent itself if immediately self-active, but as it is affected by itself, and therefore as it appears to itself, not as it is.

III. When I say that the intuition of outer objects and the self-intuition of the mind alike represent the objects and the mind, in space and in time, as they affect our senses, that is, as they appear, I do not mean to say that these objects are a mere *illusion*.[1] For in an appearance the objects, nay even the properties that we ascribe to them, are always regarded as something actually given. Since, however, in the relation of the given object to the subject, such properties depend upon the mode of intuition of the subject, this object as *appearance*[2] is to be distinguished from itself as object *in itself*. Thus when I maintain that the quality of space and of time, in conformity with which, as a condition of their existence, I posit both bodies and my own soul, lies in my mode of intuition and not in those objects in themselves, I am not saying that bodies merely *seem*[3]

[1] [*Schein.*]   [2] [*Erscheinung.*]   [3] [*scheinen.*]

to be outside me, or that my soul only *seems* to be given in my self-consciousness. It would be my own fault, if out of that which I ought to reckon as appearance, I made mere illusion.^a That does not follow as a consequence of our principle of the ideality B 70 of all our sensible intuitions—quite the contrary. It is only if we ascribe *objective reality* to these forms of representation, that it becomes impossible for us to prevent everything being thereby transformed into mere *illusion*. For if we regard space and time as properties which, if they are to be possible at all,[1] must be found in things in themselves, and if we reflect on the absurdities in which we are then involved, in that two infinite things, which are not substances, nor anything actually inhering in substances, must yet have existence, nay, must be the necessary condition of the existence of all things, and B 71 moreover must continue to exist, even although all existing things be removed,—we cannot blame the good Berkeley for degrading bodies to mere illusion. Nay, even our own existence, in being made thus dependent upon the self-subsistent reality of a non-entity, such as time, would necessarily be changed with it into sheer illusion—an absurdity of which no one has yet been guilty.

IV. In natural theology, in thinking an object [God], who not only can never be an object of intuition to us but

  ^a The predicates of the appearance can be ascribed to the object itself, in relation to our sense, for instance, the red colour or the B 70 scent to the rose. [But what is illusory can never be ascribed as predicate to an object (for the sufficient reason that we then attribute to the object, taken by itself, what belongs to it only in relation to the senses, or in general to the subject), for instance, the two handles which were formerly ascribed to Saturn].[2] That which, while inseparable from the representation of the object, is not to be met with in the object in itself, but always in its relation to the subject, is appearance. Accordingly the predicates of space and time are rightly ascribed to the objects of the senses, as such; and in this there is no illusion. On the other hand, if I ascribe redness to the rose *in itself* [handles to Saturn],[2] or extension to all outer objects *in themselves*, without paying regard to the determinate relation of these objects to the subject, and without limiting my judgment to that relation, illusion then first arises.

  [1] [*ihrer Möglichkeit nach*.]
  [2] [The passage which I have enclosed in brackets conflicts with the main argument, and is probably a later addition carelessly inserted.]

cannot be an object of sensible intuition even to himself, we are careful to remove the conditions of time and space from his intuition—for all his knowledge must be intuition, and not *thought*, which always involves limitations. But with what right can we do this if we have previously made time and space forms of things in themselves, and such as would remain, as *a priori* conditions of the existence of things, even though the things themselves were removed? As conditions of all existence in general, they must also be conditions of the existence of God. If we do not thus treat them as objective forms of all B 72 things, the only alternative is to view them as subjective forms of our inner and outer intuition, which is termed sensible, for the very reason that it is *not original*, that is, is not such as can itself give us the existence of its object—a mode of intuition which, so far as we can judge, can belong only to the primordial being.[1] Our mode of intuition is dependent upon the existence of the object, and is therefore possible only if the subject's faculty of representation is affected by that object.

This mode of intuiting in space and time need not be limited to human sensibility. It may be that all finite, thinking beings necessarily agree with man in this respect, although we are not in a position to judge whether this is actually so. But however universal this mode of sensibility may be, it does not therefore cease to be sensibility. It is derivative (*intuitus derivativus*), not original (*intuitus originarius*), and therefore not an intellectual intuition. For the reason stated above, such intellectual intuition seems to belong solely to the primordial being, and can never be ascribed to a dependent being, dependent in its existence as well as in its intuition, and which through that intuition determines its existence solely in relation to given objects.[2] This latter remark, however, must be taken only as an illustration of our aesthetic theory, not as forming part of the proof.

B 73   *Conclusion of the Transcendental Aesthetic*

Here, then, in pure *a priori* intuitions, space and time, we have one of the factors required for solution of the general

---

[1] [*nur dem Urwesen.*]

[2] [May be more freely translated as: "through that intuition is conscious of its own existence only in relation to given objects".]

problem of transcendental philosophy: *how are synthetic a priori judgments possible?* When in *a priori* judgment we seek to go out beyond the given concept, we come in the *a priori* intuitions upon that which cannot be discovered in the concept but which is certainly found *a priori* in the intuition corresponding to the concept, and can be connected with it synthetically. Such judgments, however, thus based on intuition, can never extend beyond objects of the senses; they are valid only for objects of possible experience.

TRANSCENDENTAL DOCTRINE OF ELEMENTS

SECOND PART

TRANSCENDENTAL LOGIC

INTRODUCTION
IDEA OF A TRANSCENDENTAL LOGIC

I

LOGIC IN GENERAL

OUR knowledge springs from two fundamental sources of the mind; the first is the capacity of receiving representations (receptivity for impressions), the second is the power of knowing an object through these representations (spontaneity [in the production] of concepts). Through the first an object is *given* to us, through the second the object is *thought* in relation to that [given] representation (which is a mere determination of the mind). Intuition and concepts constitute, therefore, the elements of all our knowledge, so that neither concepts without an intuition in some way corresponding to them, nor intuition without concepts, can yield knowledge. Both may be either pure or empirical. When they contain sensation (which presupposes the actual presence of the object), they are empirical. When there is no mingling of sensation with the representation, they are pure. Sensation may be entitled the material of sensible knowledge.

B 75 Pure intuition, therefore, contains only the form under which
A 51 something is intuited; the pure concept only the form of the thought of an object in general. Pure intuitions or pure concepts alone are possible *a priori*, empirical intuitions and empirical concepts only *a posteriori*.

If the *receptivity* of our mind, its power of receiving representations in so far as it is in any wise affected, is to be entitled sensibility, then the mind's power of producing representations from itself, the *spontaneity* of knowledge, should be called the understanding. Our nature is so constituted that our *intuition* can never be other than sensible; that is, it contains only the mode in which we are affected by objects. The faculty, on the other hand, which enables us to *think* the object of sensible intuition is the understanding. To neither of these powers may a preference be given over the other. Without sensibility no object would be given to us, without understanding no object would be thought. Thoughts without content are empty, intuitions without concepts are blind. It is, therefore, just as necessary to make our concepts sensible, that is, to add the object to them in intuition, as to make our intuitions intelligible, that is, to bring them under concepts. These two powers or capacities cannot exchange their functions. The understanding can intuit nothing, the senses can think nothing. Only through their union can knowledge arise. But that is no reason for confounding the B 76 contribution of either with that of the other; rather is it a strong reason for carefully separating and distinguishing A 52 the one from the other. We therefore distinguish the science of the rules of sensibility in general, that is, aesthetic, from the science of the rules of the understanding in general, that is, logic.

Logic, again, can be treated in a twofold manner, either as logic of the general or as logic of the special employment of the understanding. The former contains the absolutely necessary rules of thought without which there can be no employment whatsoever of the understanding. It therefore treats of understanding without any regard to difference in the objects to which the understanding may be directed. The logic of the special employment of the understanding contains the rules of correct thinking as regards a certain kind of objects. The former may be called the logic of elements, the latter the organon of this or that science. The latter is commonly taught in the schools as a propaedeutic to the sciences, though, according to the actual procedure of human reason, it is what is obtained last of all, when the particular science

under question has been already brought to such completion
that it requires only a few finishing touches to correct and
perfect it. For the objects under consideration must already
be known fairly completely before it can be possible to pre-
B 77 scribe the rules according to which a science of them is to
be obtained.

General logic is either pure or applied. In the former we
A 53 abstract from all empirical conditions under which our understanding is exercised, *i.e.* from the influence of the senses, the
play of imagination, the laws of memory, the force of habit,
inclination, etc., and so from all sources of prejudice, indeed
from all causes from which this or that knowledge may arise
or seem to arise. For they concern the understanding only in
so far as it is being employed under certain circumstances,
and to become acquainted with these circumstances experience is required. Pure general logic has to do, therefore, only
with principles *a priori*, and is a *canon of understanding* and
of reason, but only in respect of what is formal in their employment, be the content what it may, empirical or transcendental. General logic is called applied, when it is directed
to the rules of the employment of understanding under the
subjective empirical conditions dealt with by psychology.
Applied logic has therefore empirical principles, although it
is still indeed in so far general that it refers to the employment of the understanding without regard to difference in the
objects. Consequently it is neither a canon of the under-
B 78 standing in general nor an organon of special sciences, but
merely a cathartic of the common understanding.

In general logic, therefore, that part which is to constitute
the pure doctrine of reason must be entirely separated from
A 54 that which constitutes applied (though always still general)
logic. The former alone is, properly speaking, a science,
though indeed concise and dry, as the methodical exposition
of a doctrine of the elements of the understanding is bound
to be. There are therefore two rules which logicians must
always bear in mind, in dealing with pure general logic:

1. As general logic, it abstracts from all content of the
knowledge of understanding and from all differences in its
objects, and deals with nothing but the mere form of
thought.

2. As pure logic, it has nothing to do with empirical principles, and does not, as has sometimes been supposed, borrow
anything from psychology, which therefore has no influence
whatever on the canon of the understanding. Pure logic is a
body of demonstrated doctrine, and everything in it must be
certain entirely *a priori*.

What I call applied logic (contrary to the usual meaning
of this title, according to which it should contain certain
exercises for which pure logic gives the rules) is a representation of the understanding and of the rules of its necessary
employment *in concreto*, that is, under the accidental subjective conditions which may hinder or help its application,   B 79
and which are all given only empirically. It treats of attention,
its impediments [1] and consequences, of the source of error, of
the state of doubt, hesitation, and conviction, etc. Pure general
logic stands to it in the same relation as pure ethics, which
contains only the necessary moral laws of a free will in general,   A 55
stands to the doctrine of the virtues strictly so called—the
doctrine which considers these laws under the limitations of
the feelings, inclinations, and passions to which men are
more or less subject. Such a doctrine can never furnish a
true and demonstrated science, because, like applied logic,
it depends on empirical and psychological principles.

II

TRANSCENDENTAL LOGIC

General logic, as we have shown, abstracts from all content of knowledge, that is, from all relation of knowledge to
the object, and considers only the logical form in the relation of
any knowledge to other knowledge; that is, it treats of the form
of thought in general. But since, as the Transcendental Aesthetic has shown, there are pure as well as empirical intuitions,
a distinction might likewise be drawn between pure and empirical thought of objects. In that case we should have a logic   B 80
in which we do not abstract from the entire content of knowledge. This other logic, which should contain solely the rules
of the pure thought of an object, would exclude only those

_____
[1] [Reading, with Erdmann, *Hindernissen* for *Hindernis*.]

modes of knowledge[1] which have empirical content. It would also treat of the origin of the modes in which we know objects, in so far as that origin cannot be attributed to the objects. General logic, on the other hand, has nothing to do with the origin of knowledge, but only considers representations, be they originally *a priori* in ourselves or only empirically given, according to the laws which the understanding employs when, in thinking, it relates them to one another. It deals therefore only with that form which the understanding is able to impart to the representations, from whatever source they may have arisen.

And here I make a remark which the reader must bear well in mind, as it extends its influence over all that follows. Not every kind of knowledge *a priori* should be called transcendental, but that only by which we know that—and how—certain representations (intuitions or concepts) can be employed or are possible purely *a priori*. The term 'transcendental', that is to say, signifies such knowledge as concerns the *a priori* possibility of knowledge, or its *a priori* employment. Neither space nor any *a priori* geometrical determination of it is a transcendental representation; what can alone be entitled transcendental is the knowledge that these representations are not of empirical origin, and the possibility that they can[2] yet relate *a priori* to objects of experience. The application of space to objects in general would likewise be transcendental, but, if restricted solely to objects of sense, it is empirical. The distinction between the transcendental and the empirical belongs therefore only to the critique of knowledge; it does not concern the relation of that knowledge to its objects.

In the expectation, therefore, that there may perhaps be concepts which relate *a priori* to objects, not as pure or sensible intuitions, but solely as acts of pure thought—that is, as concepts which are neither of empirical nor of aesthetic origin—we form for ourselves by anticipation the idea of a science of the knowledge which belongs to pure understanding[3] and reason, whereby we think objects entirely *a priori*. Such a science, which should determine the origin, the scope, and

---

[1] [Reading, with Adickes, *bloss alle* for *alle*.]
[2] [Reading, with Erdmann, *können* for *könne*.]
[3] [Reading, with Erdmann, *Verstandes-* for *Verstandes*.]

the objective validity of such knowledge, would have to be called *transcendental logic*, because, unlike general logic, B 82 which has to deal with both empirical and pure knowledge of reason, it concerns itself with the laws of understanding and of reason solely in so far as they relate *a priori* to objects.

III

THE DIVISION OF GENERAL LOGIC INTO ANALYTIC AND DIALECTIC

The question, famed of old, by which logicians were supposed to be driven into a corner, obliged either to have recourse to a pitiful sophism, or to confess their ignorance and consequently the emptiness of their whole art, is the A 58 question: What is truth? The nominal definition of truth, that it is the agreement of knowledge with its object, is assumed as granted; the question asked is as to what is the general and sure criterion of the truth of any and every knowledge.

To know what questions may reasonably be asked is already a great and necessary proof of sagacity and insight. For if a question is absurd in itself and calls for an answer where none is required, it not only brings shame on the propounder of the question, but may betray an incautious listener into absurd answers, thus presenting, as the ancients said, the B 83 ludicrous spectacle of one man milking a he-goat and the other holding a sieve underneath.

If truth consists in the agreement of knowledge with its object, that object must thereby be distinguished from other objects; for knowledge is false, if it does not agree with the object to which it is related, even although it contains something which may be valid of other objects. Now a general criterion of truth must be such as would be valid in each and every instance of knowledge, however their objects may vary. It is obvious however that such a criterion [being general] cannot take account of the [varying] content of knowledge (relation to its [specific] object). But since truth concerns just this very A 59 content, it is quite impossible, and indeed absurd, to ask for a general test of the truth of such content. A sufficient and at the same time general criterion of truth cannot possibly be given. Since we have already entitled the content of knowledge its matter, we must be prepared to recognise that of the truth of knowledge, so far as its matter is concerned, no general criterion can be demanded. Such a criterion would by its very nature be self-contradictory.

But, on the other hand, as regards knowledge in respect of its mere form (leaving aside all content), it is evident that logic, in so far as it expounds the universal and necessary rules of the understanding, must in these rules furnish criteria of truth. Whatever contradicts these rules is false. For the understanding would thereby be made to contradict its own general rules of thought, and so to contradict itself. These criteria, however, concern only the form of truth, that is, of thought in general; and in so far they are quite correct, but are not by themselves sufficient. For although our knowledge may be in complete accordance with logical demands, that is, may not contradict itself, it is still possible that it may be in contradiction with its object. The purely logical criterion of truth, namely, the agreement of knowledge with the general and formal laws of the understanding and reason, is a *conditio sine qua non*, and is therefore the negative condition of all truth. But further than this logic cannot go. It has no touchstone for the discovery of such error as concerns not the form but the content.

General logic resolves the whole formal procedure of the understanding and reason into its elements, and exhibits them as principles of all logical criticism of our knowledge. This part of logic, which may therefore be entitled *analytic*, yields what is at least the negative touchstone of truth. Its rules must be applied in the examination and appraising of the form of all knowledge before we proceed to determine whether their content contains positive truth in respect to their object. But since the mere form of knowledge, however completely it may be in agreement with logical laws, is far from being sufficient to determine the material (objective) truth of knowledge, no one can venture with the help of logic alone to judge regarding objects, or to make any assertion. We must first, independently of logic, obtain reliable information; only

B 84

A 60

B 85

then are we in a position to enquire, in accordance with logical laws, into the use of this information and its connection in a coherent whole, or rather to test it by these laws. There is, however, something so tempting in the possession of an art so specious, through which we give to all our knowledge, however uninstructed we may be in regard to its content, the form of understanding, that general logic, which is merely a *canon* of judgment, has been employed as if it were an *organon* for the actual production of at least the semblance of [1] objective assertions, and has thus been misapplied. General logic, when thus treated as an organon, is called *dialectic*. A 61

However various were the significations in which the ancients used 'dialectic' as the title for a science or art, we can safely conclude from their actual employment of it that with them it was never anything else than the *logic of illusion*. It was a sophistical art of giving to ignorance, and indeed to intentional sophistries, the appearance of truth, by the device of [2] imitating the methodical thoroughness which logic prescribes, and of using its 'topic' to conceal the emptiness of its pretensions. Now it may be noted as a sure and useful warning, that general logic, if viewed as an organon, is always a logic of illusion, that is, dialectical. For logic teaches us nothing whatsoever regarding the content of knowledge, but lays down only the formal conditions of agreement with the understanding; and since these conditions can tell us nothing at all as to the objects concerned, any attempt to use this logic as an instrument (organon) that professes to extend and enlarge our knowledge can end in nothing but mere talk—in which, with a certain plausibility, we maintain, or, if such be our choice, attack, any and every possible assertion. B 86

Such instruction is quite unbecoming the dignity of philosophy. The title 'dialectic' has therefore come to be otherwise employed, and has been assigned to logic, as a *critique of dialectical illusion*. This is the sense in which it is to be understood in this work. A 62

[1] [Reading, with Kehrbach, *des Blendwerks*.]
[2] [Reading, with Erdmann, *dadurch dass*.]

IV

B 87   THE DIVISION OF TRANSCENDENTAL LOGIC INTO
TRANSCENDENTAL ANALYTIC AND DIALECTIC

In a transcendental logic we isolate the understanding—
as above, in the Transcendental Aesthetic, the sensibility—
separating out from our knowledge that part of thought which
has its origin solely in the understanding. The employment of
this pure knowledge depends upon the condition that objects
to which it can be applied be given to us in intuition. In the
absence of intuition all our knowledge is without objects,
and therefore remains entirely empty. That part of transcendental logic which deals with the elements of the pure knowledge yielded by understanding, and the principles without
which no object can be thought, is transcendental analytic. It
is a logic of truth. For no knowledge can contradict it without
A 63   at once losing all content, that is, all relation to any object, and
therefore all truth. But since it is very tempting to use these
pure modes of knowledge of the understanding and these principles by themselves, and even beyond the limits of experience,
B 88   which alone can yield the matter (objects) to which those pure
concepts of understanding can be applied, the understanding is
led to incur the risk of making, with a mere show of rationality,
a material use of its pure and merely formal principles, and of
passing judgments upon objects without distinction—upon
objects which are not given to us, nay, perhaps cannot in any
way be given. Since, properly, this transcendental analytic
should be used only as a canon for passing judgment upon the
empirical employment of the understanding, it is misapplied
if appealed to as an organon of its general and unlimited
application, and if consequently we venture, with the pure
understanding alone, to judge synthetically, to affirm, and to
decide regarding objects in general. The employment of the
pure understanding then becomes dialectical. The second part
of transcendental logic must therefore form a critique of this
dialectical illusion, and is called transcendental dialectic, not
as an art of producing such illusion dogmatically (an art unfortunately very commonly practised by metaphysical jugglers),
but as a critique of understanding and reason in respect of

their hyperphysical employment. It will expose the false, illusory character of those groundless pretensions, and in place A 64 of the high claims to discover and to extend knowledge merely by means of transcendental principles, it will substitute what is no more than a critical treatment of the pure understanding, for the guarding of it against sophistical illusion.

TRANSCENDENTAL LOGIC

TRANSCENDENTAL ANALYTIC

TRANSCENDENTAL analytic consists in the dissection of all our *a priori* knowledge into the elements that pure understanding by itself yields. In so doing, the following are the points of chief concern: (1) that the concepts be pure and not empirical; (2) that they belong, not to intuition and sensibility, but to thought and understanding; (3) that they be fundamental and be carefully distinguished from those which are derivative or composite; (4) that our table of concepts be complete, covering the whole field of the pure understanding. When a science is an aggregate brought into existence in a merely experimental manner, such completeness can never be guaranteed by any kind of mere estimate. It is possible only by means of *an idea of the totality* of the *a priori* knowledge yielded by the understanding; such an idea can furnish an exact classification of the concepts which compose
A 65 that totality, exhibiting their *interconnection in a system*. Pure understanding distinguishes itself not merely from all that is empirical but completely also from all sensibility. It
B 90 is a unity self-subsistent, self-sufficient, and not to be increased by any additions from without. The sum of its knowledge thus constitutes a system, comprehended and determined by one idea. The completeness and articulation of this system can at the same time yield a criterion of the correctness and genuineness of all its components. This part of transcendental logic requires, however, for its complete exposition, two books, the one containing the *concepts*, the other the *principles* of pure understanding.

TRANSCENDENTAL ANALYTIC

BOOK I

ANALYTIC OF CONCEPTS

By 'analytic of concepts' I do not understand their analysis, or the procedure usual in philosophical investigations, that of dissecting the content of such concepts as may present themselves, and so of rendering them more distinct; but the hitherto rarely attempted *dissection of the faculty of the understanding* itself, in order to investigate the possibility of concepts *a priori* by looking for them in the understanding alone, as their birthplace, and by analysing the pure use of this faculty. This is the proper task of a transcendental philosophy; anything beyond this belongs to the logical treatment of concepts in philosophy in general. We shall therefore follow up the pure concepts to their first seeds and dispositions in the human understanding, in which they lie prepared, till at last, on the occasion of experience, they are developed, and by the same understanding are exhibited in their purity, freed from the empirical conditions attaching to them.

ANALYTIC OF CONCEPTS

CHAPTER I

THE CLUE TO THE DISCOVERY OF ALL PURE CONCEPTS OF THE UNDERSTANDING

WHEN we call a faculty of knowledge into play, then, as the occasioning circumstances differ, various concepts stand forth and make the faculty known, and allow of their being collected with more or less completeness, in proportion as observation has been made of them over a longer time or with greater acuteness. But when the enquiry is carried on in this mechanical fashion, we can never be sure whether it has been brought to completion. Further, the concepts which we thus discover only as opportunity offers, exhibit no order and systematic unity, but are in the end merely arranged in pairs according to similarities, and in series according to the amount of their contents, from the simple on to the more composite—an arrangement which is anything but systematic, although to a certain extent methodically instituted.

Transcendental philosophy, in seeking for its concepts, has the advantage and also the duty of proceeding according to a single principle. For these concepts spring, pure and unmixed, out of the understanding which is an absolute unity; and must therefore be connected with each other according to one concept or idea. Such a connection supplies us with a rule, by which we are enabled to assign its proper place to each pure concept of the understanding, and by which we can determine in an *a priori* manner their systematic completeness. Otherwise we should be dependent in these matters on our own discretionary judgment or merely on chance.

A 67
B 92

104

THE TRANSCENDENTAL CLUE TO THE DISCOVERY OF ALL PURE CONCEPTS OF THE UNDERSTANDING

Section 1

THE LOGICAL EMPLOYMENT OF THE UNDERSTANDING

The understanding has thus far been explained merely negatively, as a non-sensible faculty of knowledge. Now since without sensibility we cannot have any intuition, understand- A 68 ing cannot be a faculty of intuition. But besides intuition there is no other mode of knowledge except by means of concepts. B 93 The knowledge yielded by understanding, or at least by the human understanding, must therefore be by means of concepts, and so is not intuitive, but discursive. Whereas [1] all intuitions, as sensible, rest on affections,[2] concepts rest on functions. By 'function' I mean the unity of the act of bringing various representations under one common representation. Concepts are based on the spontaneity of thought, sensible intuitions on the receptivity of impressions. Now the only use which the understanding can make of these concepts is to judge by means of them. Since no representation, save when it is an intuition, is in immediate relation to an object, no concept is ever related to an object immediately, but to some other representation of it, be that other representation an intuition, or itself a concept. Judgment is therefore the mediate knowledge of an object, that is, the representation of a representation of it. In every judgment there is a concept which holds of many representations, and among them of a given representation that is immediately related to an object. Thus in the judgment, 'all bodies are divisible',[3] the concept of the divisible applies to various other concepts, but is here applied in particular to the concept of body, and this concept again to certain appear- A 69 ances that present themselves to us. These objects, therefore, are mediately represented through the concept of divisibility. Accordingly, all judgments are functions of unity among our

[1] [Reading, with Adickes, *aber* for *also*.]
[2] [*Affektionen*.]
[3] [In the 4th edition *veränderlich* is corrected to *teilbar*.]

B 94   representations; instead of an immediate representation, a
higher representation, which comprises the immediate representation and various others, is used in knowing the object,
and thereby much possible knowledge is collected into one.
Now we can reduce all acts of the understanding to judgments, and the *understanding* may therefore be represented
as a *faculty of judgment*. For, as stated above, the understanding is a faculty of thought. Thought is knowledge by
means of concepts. But concepts, as predicates of possible
judgments, relate to some representation of a not *yet* determined object. Thus the concept of body means something, for
instance, metal, which can be known by means of that concept. It is therefore a concept solely in virtue of its comprehending other representations, by means of which it can
relate to objects. It is therefore the predicate of a possible
judgment, for instance, 'every metal is a body'. The functions
of the understanding can, therefore, be discovered if we can
give an exhaustive statement of the functions of unity in
judgments. That this can quite easily be done will be shown
in the next section.

A 70⎫
B 95⎭   THE CLUE TO THE DISCOVERY OF ALL PURE
CONCEPTS OF THE UNDERSTANDING

Section 2

§ 9[1]

The Logical Function of the Understanding in
Judgments

If we abstract from all content of a judgment, and consider only the mere form of understanding, we find that the
function of thought in judgment can be brought under four
heads, each of which contains three moments.[2] They may be
conveniently represented in the following table:

---

¹ ["§ 9" added in B.]
² [*Momente.*]

I
Quantity of Judgments
Universal
Particular
Singular

II
Quality
Affirmative
Negative
Infinite

III
Relation
Categorical
Hypothetical
Disjunctive

IV
Modality
Problematic
Assertoric
Apodeictic

As this division appears to depart in some, though not in any essential respects, from the technical distinctions ordinarily recognised by logicians, the following observations may serve to guard against any possible misunderstanding. B 96 A 71

1. Logicians are justified in saying that, in the employment of judgments in syllogisms, singular judgments can be treated like those that are universal. For, since they have no extension at all, the predicate cannot relate to part only of that which is contained in the concept of the subject, and be excluded from the rest. The predicate is valid of that concept, without any such exception, just as if it were a general concept and had an extension to the whole of which the predicate applied. If, on the other hand, we compare a singular with a universal judgment, merely as knowledge, in respect of quantity, the singular stands to the universal as unity to infinity, and is therefore in itself essentially different from the universal. If, therefore, we estimate a singular judgment (*judicium singulare*), not only according to its own inner validity, but as knowledge in general, according to its quantity in comparison with other knowledge, it is certainly different from general judgments (*judicia communia*), and in a complete table of the moments of thought in general deserves a separate place—though not, indeed, in a logic limited to the use of judgments in reference to each other. B 97

2. In like manner *infinite judgments* must, in transcendental logic, be distinguished from those that are *affirm-*
A 72 *ative*, although in general logic they are rightly classed with
them, and do not constitute a separate member of the division.
General logic abstracts from all content of the predicate (even
though it be negative); it enquires only whether the predicate
be ascribed to the subject or opposed to it. But transcendental
logic also considers what may be the worth or content of a
logical affirmation that is thus made by means of a merely
negative predicate, and what is thereby achieved in the way
of addition to our total knowledge. If I should say of the soul,
'It is not mortal', by this negative judgment I should at least
have warded off error. Now by the proposition, 'The soul
is non-mortal',[1] I have, so far as the logical form is concerned,
really made an affirmation. I locate the soul in the unlimited
sphere of non-mortal beings. Since the mortal constitutes
one part of the whole extension of possible beings, and the
non-mortal the other, nothing more is said by my proposition
than that the soul is one of the infinite number of things which
remain over when I take away all that is mortal. The infinite
sphere of all that is possible is thereby only so far limited that
B 98 the mortal is excluded from it, and that the soul is located
in the remaining part of its extension.[2] But, even allowing
for such exclusion, this extension[3] still remains infinite, and
several more parts of it may be taken away without the con-
A 73 cept of the soul being thereby in the least increased, or determined in an affirmative manner. These judgments, though
infinite in respect of their logical extension, are thus, in respect
of the content of their knowledge, limitative only, and cannot
therefore be passed over in a transcendental table of all
moments of thought in judgments, since the function of the
understanding thereby expressed may perhaps be of importance in the field of its pure *a priori* knowledge.

3. All relations of thought in judgments are (*a*) of the
predicate to the subject, (*b*) of the ground to its consequence,
(*c*) of the divided knowledge and of the members of the
division, taken together,[4] to each other.   In the first kind of

---

[1] [Reading, with Erdmann, *nichtsterblich* for *nicht sterblich*.]
[2] [*Umfang ihres Raums*.]
[3] [*Raum*.]   [4] [*gesammelten*.]

judgments we consider only two concepts, in the second two judgments, in the third several judgments in their relation to each other. The hypothetical proposition, 'If there is a perfect justice, the obstinately wicked are punished', really contains the relation of two propositions, namely, 'There is a perfect justice', and 'The obstinately wicked are punished'. Whether both these propositions are in themselves true, here remains undetermined. It is only the logical sequence which is thought by this judgment. Finally, the disjunctive judgment B 99 contains a relation of two or more propositions to each other, a relation not, however, of logical sequence, but of logical opposition, in so far as the sphere of the one excludes the sphere of the other, and yet at the same time of community, in so far as the propositions taken together occupy the whole sphere of the knowledge in question. The disjunctive judgment expresses, therefore, a relation of the parts of the sphere A 74 of such knowledge, since the sphere of each part is a complement of the sphere of the others, yielding together the sum-total of the divided knowledge. Take, for instance, the judgment, 'The world exists either through blind chance, or through inner necessity, or through an external cause'. Each of these propositions occupies a part of the sphere of the possible knowledge concerning the existence of a world in general; all of them together occupy the whole sphere To take the knowledge out of one of these spheres means placing it in one of the other spheres, and to place it in one sphere means taking it out of the others. There is, therefore, in a disjunctive judgment a certain community of the known constituents, such that they mutually exclude each other, and yet thereby determine *in their totality* the true knowledge. For, when taken together, they constitute the whole content of one given knowledge. This is all that need here be considered, so far as concerns what follows.

4. The *modality* of judgments is a quite peculiar function. Its distinguishing characteristic is that it contributes nothing B 100 to the content of the judgment (for, besides quantity, quality, and relation, there is nothing that constitutes the content of a judgment), but concerns only the value of the copula in relation to thought in general. Problematic judgments are those in which affirmation or negation is taken as merely

A 75 possible (optional). In assertoric judgments affirmation or negation is viewed as real (true), and in apodeictic judgments as necessary.[a] Thus the two judgments, the relation of which constitutes the hypothetical judgment (*antecedens et consequens*), and likewise the judgments the reciprocal relation of which forms the disjunctive judgment (members of the division), are one and all problematic only. In the above example, the proposition, 'There is a perfect justice', is not stated assertorically, but is thought only as an optional judgment, which it is possible to assume; it is only the logical sequence which is assertoric. Such judgments may therefore be obviously false, and yet, taken problematically, may be conditions of the knowledge of truth. Thus the judgment, 'The world exists by blind chance', has in the disjunctive judgment only problematic meaning, namely, as a proposition that may

B 101 for a moment be assumed. At the same time, like the indication of a false road among the number of all those roads that can be taken, it aids in the discovery of the true proposition. The problematic proposition is therefore that which expresses only logical (which is not objective) possibility—a free choice of admitting such a proposition, and a purely optional admission of it into the understanding. The assertoric proposition deals with logical reality or truth. Thus, for instance,

A 76 in a hypothetical syllogism the antecedent is in the major premiss problematic, in the minor assertoric, and what the syllogism shows is that the consequence follows in accordance with the laws of the understanding. The apodeictic proposition thinks the assertoric as determined by these laws of the understanding, and therefore as affirming *a priori*; and in this manner it expresses logical necessity. Since everything is thus incorporated in the understanding step by step—inasmuch as we first judge something problematically, then maintain its truth assertorically, and finally affirm it as inseparably united with the understanding, that is, as necessary and apodeictic—we are justified in regarding these three functions of modality as so many moments of thought.

[a] Just as if thought were in the problematic a function of the understanding; in the assertoric, of the faculty of judgment; in the apodeictic, of reason. This is a remark which will be explained in the sequel.

THE CLUE TO THE DISCOVERY OF ALL PURE CONCEPTS OF THE UNDERSTANDING

B 102

Section 3

§ 10[1]

THE PURE CONCEPTS OF THE UNDERSTANDING, OR CATEGORIES

General logic, as has been repeatedly said, abstracts from all content of knowledge, and looks to some other source, whatever that may be, for the representations which it is to transform into concepts by process of analysis. Transcendental logic, on the other hand, has lying before it a manifold of *a priori* sensibility, presented by transcendental aesthetic, as material for the concepts of pure understanding. In the absence of this material those concepts would be[2] without any content, therefore entirely empty. Space and time contain a manifold of pure *a priori* intuition, but at the same time are conditions of the receptivity of our mind—conditions under which alone it can receive representations of objects, and which therefore must also always affect the concept of these objects. But if this manifold is to be known, the spontaneity of our thought requires that it be gone through in a certain way, taken up, and connected. This act I name *synthesis*.

A 77

By *synthesis*, in its most general sense, I understand the act of putting different representations together, and of grasping[3] what is manifold in them in one [act of] knowledge. Such a synthesis is *pure*, if the manifold is not empirical but is given *a priori*, as is the manifold in space and time. Before we can analyse our representations, the representations must themselves be given, and therefore as regards *content* no concepts can first arise by way of analysis. Synthesis of a manifold (be it given empirically or *a priori*) is what first gives rise to knowledge. This knowledge may, indeed, at first, be crude and confused, and therefore in need of analysis. Still the synthesis is that which gathers the elements for knowledge, and unites them to [form] a certain content.[4] It is to synthesis, therefore,

B 103

A 78

---

[1] ["§ 10" added in B.]   [2] [Reading, with v. Leclair, *würden* for *würde*.]
[3] [*begreifen.*]   [4] [*und zu einem gewissen Inhalte vereinigt.*]

that we must first direct our attention, if we would determine the first origin of our knowledge.

Synthesis in general, as we shall hereafter see, is the mere result of the power of imagination, a blind but indispensable function of the soul, without which we should have no knowledge whatsoever, but of which we are scarcely ever conscious. To bring this synthesis *to concepts* is a function which belongs to the understanding, and it is through this function of the understanding that we first obtain knowledge properly so called.

B 104   Pure synthesis, *represented in its most general aspect*, gives us the pure concept of the understanding. By this pure synthesis I understand that which rests upon a basis of *a priori* synthetic unity. Thus our counting, as is easily seen in the case of larger numbers, is a synthesis according to concepts, because it is executed according to a common ground of unity, as, for instance, the decade. In terms of this concept, the unity of the synthesis of the manifold is rendered necessary.

By means of analysis different representations are brought under one concept—a procedure treated of in general logic. What transcendental logic, on the other hand, teaches, is how we bring to concepts, not representations, but the *pure synthesis* of representations. What must first be given—with a view to the *a priori* knowledge of all objects—is the *manifold*
A 79   of pure intuition; the second factor involved is the *synthesis* of this manifold by means of the imagination. But even this does not yet yield knowledge. The concepts which give *unity* to this pure synthesis, and which consist solely in the representation of this necessary synthetic unity, furnish the third requisite for the knowledge of an object; and they rest on the understanding.

The same function which gives unity to the various representations *in a judgment* also gives unity to the mere synB 105   thesis of various representations *in an intuition*; and this unity, in its most general expression, we entitle the pure concept of the understanding. The same understanding, through the same operations by which in concepts, by means of analytical unity, it produced the logical form of a judgment, also introduces a transcendental content into its representations, by means of the synthetic unity of the manifold in intuition in general. On this account we are entitled to call these representations pure concepts of the understanding, and to regard them as applying *a priori* to objects—a conclusion which general logic is not in a position to establish.

In this manner there arise precisely the same number of pure concepts of the understanding which apply *a priori* to objects of intuition in general, as, in the preceding table, there have been found to be logical functions in all possible judgments. For these functions specify the understanding completely, and yield an exhaustive inventory of its powers. These concepts we shall, with Aristotle, call *categories*, for our A 80 primary purpose is the same as his, although widely diverging from it in manner of execution.

TABLE OF CATEGORIES   B 106

I

Of Quantity

Unity
Plurality
Totality

II	III
Of Quality	*Of Relation*
Reality	Of Inherence and Subsistence
Negation	(*substantia et accidens*)
Limitation	Of Causality and Dependence
	(*cause and effect*)
	Of Community (reciprocity between agent and patient)

IV

Of Modality

Possibility—Impossibility
Existence—Non-existence
Necessity—Contingency

This then is the list of all original pure concepts of synthesis that the understanding contains within itself *a priori*.

Indeed, it is because it contains these concepts that it is called pure understanding; for by them alone can it *understand* anything in the manifold of intuition, that is, think an object of intuition. This division is developed systematically A 81 from a common principle, namely, the faculty of judgment (which is the same as the faculty of thought). It has not arisen rhapsodically, as the result of a haphazard search after pure concepts, the complete enumeration of which, as based on B 107 induction only, could never be guaranteed. Nor could we, if this were our procedure, discover why just these concepts, and no others, have their seat in the pure understanding. It was an enterprise worthy of an acute thinker like Aristotle to make search for these fundamental concepts. But as he did so on no principle, he merely picked them up as they came his way, and at first procured ten of them, which he called *categories* (predicaments). Afterwards he believed that he had discovered five others, which he added under the name of post-predicaments. But his table still remained defective. Besides, there are to be found in it some modes of pure sensibility (*quando*, *ubi*, *situs*, also *prius*, *simul*), and an empirical concept (*motus*), none of which have any place in a table of the concepts that trace their origin to the understanding. Aristotle's list also enumerates among the original concepts some derivative concepts (*actio*, *passio*); and of the original concepts some are entirely lacking.

In this connection, it is to be remarked that the categories, as the true primary concepts of the pure understanding, have also their pure derivative concepts. These could not be passed over in a complete system of transcendental philosophy, but A 82 in a merely critical essay the simple mention of the fact may suffice.

B 108   I beg permission to entitle these pure but derivative concepts of the understanding the *predicables* of the pure understanding—to distinguish them from the predicaments [*i.e* the categories]. If we have the original and primitive concepts, it is easy to add the derivative and subsidiary, and so to give a complete picture of the family tree of the [concepts of] pure understanding. Since at present we are concerned not with the completeness of the system, but only with the principles to be followed in its construction, I reserve this supplementary work for another occasion. It can easily be carried out, with the aid of the ontological manuals—for instance, by placing under the category of causality the predicables of force, action, passion; under the category of community the predicables of presence, resistance; under the predicaments of modality the predicables of coming to be, ceasing to be, change, etc. The categories, when combined with the modes of pure sensibility, or with one another, yield a large number of derivative *a priori* concepts. To note, and, where possible, to give a complete inventory of these concepts, would be a useful and not unpleasant task, but it is a task from which we can here be absolved.

In this treatise, I purposely omit the definitions of the categories, although I may be in possession of them. I shall proceed to analyse these concepts only so far as is necessary in connection with the doctrine of method which I am propounding. In a system of pure reason, definitions of the categories would rightly be demanded, but in this treatise they would merely divert attention from the main object of the enquiry, arousing doubts and objections which, without detriment to what is essential to our purposes, can very well be reserved for another occasion. Meanwhile, from the little that I have said, it will be obvious that a complete glossary, with all the requisite explanations, is not only a possible, but an easy task. The divisions are provided; all that is required is to fill them; and a systematic 'topic', such as that here given, affords sufficient guidance as to the proper location of each concept, while at the same time indicating which divisions are still empty.

A 83

B 109

§ 11 [1]

This table of categories suggests some nice points, which may perhaps have important consequences in regard to the scientific form of all modes of knowledge obtainable by reason. For that this table is extremely useful in the theoretical part of philosophy, and indeed is indispensable as supplying the *complete plan of a whole science*, so far as that science rests on *a priori* concepts, and as dividing it systematically [2] *according to*

---

[1] [The whole of sections 11 and 12 added in B.]
[2] [Reading, with Vaihinger, *systematisch* for *mathematisch*.]

determinate principles, is already evident from the fact that the table contains all the elementary concepts of the understanding in their completeness, nay, even the form of a system
B 110 of them in the human understanding, and accordingly indicates all the *momenta* of a projected speculative science, and even their *order*, as I have elsewhere * shown.

The first of the considerations suggested by the table is that while it contains four classes of the concepts of understanding, it may, in the first instance, be divided into two groups; those in the first group being concerned with objects of intuition, pure as well as empirical, those in the second group with the existence of these objects, in their relation either to each other or to the understanding.

The categories in the first group I would entitle the *mathematical*, those in the second group the *dynamical*. The former have no correlates; these are to be met with only in the second group. This distinction must have some ground in the nature of the understanding.

Secondly, in view of the fact that all *a priori* division of concepts must be by dichotomy, it is significant that in each class the number of the categories is always the same, namely, three. Further, it may be observed that the third category in each class always arises from the combination of the second category with the first.

B 111   Thus *allness* or *totality* is just plurality considered as unity; *limitation* is simply reality combined with negation; *community* is the causality of substances reciprocally determining one another; lastly, *necessity* is just the existence which is given through possibility itself. It must not be supposed, however, that the third category is therefore merely a derivative, and not a primary, concept of the pure understanding. For the combination of the first and second concepts, in order that the third may be produced, requires a special act of the understanding, which is not identical with that which is exercised in the case of the first and the second. Thus the concept of a *number* (which belongs to the category of totality) is not always possible simply upon the presence of concepts of plurality and unity

---

* *Metaphysical First Principles of Natural Science.* [In the Introduction by which Kant prefaces this treatise.]

(for instance, in the representation of the infinite); nor can I, by simply combining the concept of a cause and that of a substance, at once have understanding of *influence*, that is, how a substance can be the cause of something in another substance. Obviously in these cases, a separate act of the understanding is demanded; and similarly in the others.

Thirdly, in the case of one category, namely, that of *community*, which is found in the third group, its accordance with the form of a disjunctive judgment—the form which corresponds to it in the table of logical functions—is not as evident as in the case of the others. B 112

To gain assurance that they do actually accord, we must observe that in all disjunctive judgments the sphere (that is, the multiplicity which is contained in any one judgment) is represented as a whole divided into parts (the subordinate concepts), and that since no one of them can be contained under any other, they are thought as co-ordinated with, not subordinated to, each other, and so as determining each other, not in one direction only, as in a series, but reciprocally, as in an aggregate[1]—if one member of the division is posited, all the rest are excluded, and conversely.

Now in a *whole* which is made up of *things*, a similar combination is being thought; for one thing is not subordinated, as effect, to another, as cause of its existence, but, simultaneously and reciprocally, is co-ordinated with it, as cause of the determination of the other (as, for instance, in a body the parts of which reciprocally attract and repel each other). This is a quite different kind of connection from that which is found in the mere relation of cause to effect (of ground to consequence), for in the latter relation the consequence does not in its turn reciprocally determine the ground, and therefore does not constitute with it a whole—thus the world, for instance, does not with its Creator serve to constitute a whole.[2] The procedure which the understanding follows in representing to B 113 itself the sphere of a divided concept it likewise follows when it thinks a thing as divisible; and just as, in the former case, the members of a division exclude each other, and yet are com-

---

[1] [*Aggregat*].
[2] [Reading, with Vaihinger, *die Welt mit dem Weltschöpfer* for *der Weltschöpfer mit der Welt*.]

tined in one sphere, so the understanding represents to itself the parts of the latter as existing (as substances) in such a way that, while each exists independently of the others, they are yet combined together in one whole.

§ 12

In the transcendental philosophy of the ancients there is included yet another chapter containing pure concepts of the understanding which, though not enumerated among the categories, must, on their view, be ranked as *a priori* concepts of objects. This, however, would amount to an increase in the number of the categories, and is therefore not feasible. They are propounded in the proposition, so famous among the Schoolmen, *quodlibet ens est unum, verum, bonum*. Now, although the application of this principle has proved very meagre in consequences, and has indeed yielded only propositions that are tautological, and therefore in recent times has retained its place in metaphysics almost by courtesy only, yet, on the other hand, it represents a view which, however empty it may seem to be, has maintained itself over this very long period. It therefore deserves to be investigated in respect of its origin, and we are justified in conjecturing that it has its ground in some rule of the understanding which, as often happens, has only been wrongly interpreted. These supposedly transcendental predicates of *things* are, in fact, nothing but logical requirements and criteria of all *knowledge* of things in general, and prescribe for such knowledge the categories of quantity, namely, *unity, plurality*, and *totality*. But these categories, which, properly regarded, must be taken as material, belonging to the possibility of the things themselves [empirical objects], have, in this further application, been used only in their formal meaning, as being of the nature of logical requisites of all knowledge, and yet at the same time have been incautiously converted from being criteria of thought to be properties of things in themselves. In all knowledge of an object there is *unity* of concept, which may be entitled *qualitative unity*, so far as we think by it only the unity in the combination of the manifold of our knowledge: as, for example, the unity of the theme in a play, a speech, or a story. Secondly, there is

B 114

truth, in respect of its consequences. The greater the number of true consequences that follow from a given concept, the more criteria are there of its objective reality. This might be entitled the *qualitative plurality* of characters, which belong to a concept as to a common ground (but are not thought in it, as quantity). Thirdly, and lastly, there is *perfection*, which consists in this, that the plurality together leads back to the unity of the concept, and accords completely with this and with no other concept. This may be entitled the *qualitative completeness* (totality). Hence it is evident that these logical criteria of B 115 the possibility of knowledge in general are the three categories of quantity, in which the unity in the production of the quantum has to be taken as homogeneous throughout; and that these categories are here being transformed so as also to yield connection of *heterogeneous* knowledge in one consciousness, by means of the quality of the knowledge as the principle of the connection. Thus the criterion of the possibility of a concept (not of an object) is the definition of it, in which the *unity* of the concept, the *truth* of all that may be immediately deduced from it, and finally, the *completeness* of what has been thus deduced from it, yield all that is required for the construction of the whole concept. Similarly, the criterion of an hypothesis consists in the intelligibility of the assumed ground of explanation, that is,[1] in its *unity* (without any auxiliary hypothesis); in the *truth* of the consequences that can be deduced from it (their accordance with themselves and with experience); and finally, in the *completeness* of the ground of explanation of these consequences, which carry us back to neither more nor less than was assumed in the hypothesis, and so in an *a posteriori* analytic manner give us back and accord with what has previously been thought in a synthetic *a priori* manner. We have not, therefore, in the concepts of unity, truth, and perfection, made any addition to the transcendental table of the categories, as if it were in any respect imperfect. All that we have done is to bring the employment of these concepts under general logical rules, for the agreement of knowledge with itself—the question of their relation to objects not being in any B 116 way under discussion.

1 [Taking *oder* as equivalent to 'that is', and not as expressing an alternative.]

ANALYTIC OF CONCEPTS[1]

CHAPTER II

THE DEDUCTION OF THE PURE CONCEPTS OF
UNDERSTANDING

Section 1

§ 13[2]

THE PRINCIPLES OF ANY TRANSCENDENTAL DEDUCTION

JURISTS, when speaking of rights and claims, distinguish in a
legal action the question of right (*quid juris*) from the question
of fact (*quid facti*); and they demand that both be proved.
Proof of the former, which has to state the right or the legal
claim, they entitle the *deduction*. Many empirical concepts are
employed without question from anyone. Since experience is
always available for the proof of their objective reality, we believe ourselves, even without a deduction, to be justified in ap-
B 117 propriating to them a meaning, an ascribed[3] significance. But
there are also usurpatory concepts, such as *fortune, fate*,
which, though allowed to circulate by almost universal indul-
gence, are yet from time to time challenged by the question:
quid juris. This demand for a deduction involves us in con-
A 85 siderable perplexity, no clear legal title, sufficient to justify
their[4] employment, being obtainable either from experience or
from reason.

Now among the manifold concepts which form the highly

¹ [Following Michaelis, in substituting this heading for the heading in A
and B, *Der transzcendentalen Analytik.* Cf. above p. 104.]
² ["§ 13" added in B.]
³ [Reading, as in A and B, *eingebildete.* Vaihinger suggests instead *eine
giltige.*]
⁴ [Reading, with Erdmann, *ihres* for *seines.*]

complicated web of human knowledge, there are some which are marked out for pure *a priori* employment, in complete independence of all experience; and their right to be so employed always demands a deduction. For since empirical proofs do not suffice to justify this kind of employment, we are faced by the problem how these concepts can relate to objects which they yet do not obtain from any experience. The explanation of the manner in which concepts can thus relate *a priori* to objects I entitle their transcendental deduction; and from it I distinguish empirical deduction, which shows the manner in which a concept is acquired through experience and through reflection upon experience, and which therefore concerns, not its legitimacy, but only its *de facto* mode of origination.

We are already in possession of concepts which are of two quite different kinds, and which yet agree in that they relate to objects in a completely *a priori* manner, namely, the concepts of space and time as forms of sensibility, and the categories as concepts of understanding. To seek an empirical deduction of either of these types of concept would be labour entirely lost. For their distinguishing feature consists just in this, that they relate to their objects without having borrowed from experience anything that can serve in the representation of these objects. If, therefore, a deduction of such concepts is indispensable, it must in any case be transcendental.

We can, however, with regard to these concepts, as with regard to all knowledge, seek to discover in experience, if not the principle of their possibility, at least the occasioning causes [1] of their production. The impressions of the senses supplying the first stimulus,[2] the whole faculty of knowledge opens out to them, and experience is brought into existence. That experience contains two very dissimilar elements, namely, the *matter* of knowledge [obtained] from the senses, and a certain *form* for the ordering of this matter, [obtained] from the inner source[3] of the pure intuition and thought which, on occasion of the sense-impressions, are first brought into action and yield concepts. Such an investigation of the first strivings of our faculty of knowledge, whereby it advances from particular perceptions to universal concepts, is undoubtedly of great service. We are indebted to the celebrated

B 118

A 86

B 119

---

[1] [*Gelegenheitsursachen.*]   [2] [*Anlass.*]   [3] [*aus dem inneren Quell.*]

Locke for opening out this new line of enquiry. But a *deduction* of the pure *a priori* concepts can never be obtained in this manner; it is not to be looked for in any such direction. For in view of their subsequent employment, which has to be entirely independent of experience, they must be in a position to show a certificate of birth quite other than that of descent A 87 from experiences. Since this attempted physiological derivation concerns a *quaestio facti*, it cannot strictly be called deduction; and I shall therefore entitle it the explanation of the *possession* of pure knowledge. Plainly the only deduction that can be given of this[1] knowledge is one that is transcendental, not empirical. In respect to pure *a priori* concepts the latter type of deduction is an utterly useless enterprise which can be engaged in only by those who have failed to grasp the quite peculiar nature of these modes of knowledge.

But although it may be admitted that the only kind of deduction of pure *a priori* knowledge which is possible is on transcendental lines, it is not at once obvious that a deduction is indispensably necessary We have already, by means of a transcendental deduction, traced the concepts of space and time to their sources, and have explained and determined B 120 their *a priori* objective validity. Geometry, however, proceeds with security in knowledge that is completely *a priori*, and has no need to beseech philosophy for any certificate of the pure and legitimate descent of its fundamental concept of space. But the concept is employed in this science only in its reference to the outer sensible world—of the intuition of which space is the pure form—where all geometrical knowledge, grounded as it is in *a priori* intuition, possesses immediate evidence. The objects, so far as their form is concerned, are given, A 88 through the very knowledge of them, *a priori* in intuition. In the case of the *pure concepts of understanding*, it is quite otherwise; it is with them that the unavoidable demand for a transcendental deduction, not only of themselves, but also of the concept of space, first originates. For since they speak of [2] objects through predicates not of intuition and sensibility but of pure *a priori* thought, they relate to objects universally,

---

[1] [Reading, with Erdmann, *dieser es allein* for *diesen allein es.*]
[2] [Reading, with Hartenstein, *reden* for *redet.*]

that is, apart from all conditions of sensibility. Also,[1] not being grounded in experience, they cannot, in *a priori* intuition, exhibit any object such as might, prior to all experience, serve as ground for their synthesis. For these reasons, they arouse suspicion not merely in regard to the objective validity and the limits of their own employment, but owing to their tendency to employ the *concept of space* beyond the conditions of sensible intuition, that concept also they render ambiguous; and this, indeed, is why we have already found B 121 a transcendental deduction of it necessary. The reader must therefore be convinced of the unavoidable necessity of such a transcendental deduction before he has taken a single step in the field of pure reason. Otherwise he proceeds blindly, and after manifold wanderings must come back to the same ignorance from which he started. At the same time, if he is not to lament over obscurity in matters which are by their very nature deeply veiled, or to be too easily discouraged[2] in the removal of obstacles, he must have a clear foreknowledge of the inevitable difficulty of the undertaking. For we must A 89 either completely surrender all claims to make judgments of pure reason in[3] the most highly esteemed of all fields, that which transcends the limits of all possible experience, or else bring this critical enquiry to completion.

We have already been able with but little difficulty to explain how the concepts of space and time, although *a priori* modes of knowledge, must necessarily relate to objects, and how independently of all experience they make[4] possible a synthetic knowledge of objects. For since only by means of such pure forms of sensibility can an object appear to us, and so be an object of empirical intuition, space and time are pure intuitions which contain *a priori* the condition of the possibility of objects as appearances, and the synthesis which B 122 takes place in them has objective validity.

The categories of understanding, on the other hand, do not represent the conditions under which objects are given in intuition. Objects may, therefore, appear to us without

1 [Reading, with Erdmann, *und sie, da sie* for *und die, da sie.*]
2 [Reading, with Hartenstein, *werde* for *werden.*]
3 [Reading, with Erdmann, *als auf das* for *als das.*]
4 [Reading, with Erdmann, *machen* for *machten.*]

their being under the necessity of being related to the functions of understanding; and understanding need not, therefore, contain their *a priori* conditions. Thus a difficulty such as we did not meet with in the field of sensibility is here presented, namely, how *subjective conditions of thought* can have *objective validity*, that is, can furnish conditions of the A 90 possibility of all knowledge of objects. For appearances can certainly be given in intuition independently of functions of the understanding. Let us take, for instance, the concept of cause, which signifies a special kind of synthesis, whereby upon something, A, there is posited something quite different, B, according to a rule. It is not manifest *a priori* why appearances should contain anything of this kind (experiences cannot be cited in its proof, for what has to be established is the objective validity of a concept that is *a priori*); and it is therefore *a priori* doubtful whether such a concept be not perhaps altogether empty, and have no object anywhere among appearances. That objects of sensible intuition must B 123 conform to the formal conditions of sensibility which lie *a priori* in the mind is evident, because otherwise they would not be objects for us. But that they must likewise conform to the conditions which the understanding requires for the synthetic unity[1] of thought, is a conclusion the grounds of which are by no means so obvious. Appearances might very well be so constituted that the understanding should not find them to be in accordance with the conditions of its unity. Everything might be in such confusion that, for instance, in the series of appearances nothing presented itself which might yield a rule of synthesis and so answer to the concept of cause and effect. This concept would then be altogether empty, null, and meaningless. But since intuition stands in A 91 no need whatsoever of the functions of thought, appearances would none the less present objects to our intuition.

   If we thought to escape these toilsome enquiries by saying that experience continually presents examples of such regularity among appearances and so affords abundant opportunity of abstracting the concept of cause, and at the same time of verifying the objective validity of such a concept, we should be overlooking the fact that the concept of cause can

   [1] [Reading, with v. Leclair, *Einheit* for *Einsicht.*]

never arise in this manner. It must either be grounded completely *a priori* in the understanding, or must be entirely given up as a mere phantom of the brain. For this concept makes B 124 strict demand that something, A, should be such that something else, B, follows from it *necessarily and in accordance with an absolutely universal rule*. Appearances do indeed present cases from which a rule can be obtained according to which something usually happens, but they never prove the sequence[1] to be *necessary*. To the synthesis of cause and effect there belongs a dignity which cannot be empirically expressed, namely, that the effect not only succeeds upon the cause, but that it is posited *through* it and arises *out of* it.[2] This strict universality of the rule is never a characteristic of empirical rules; they can acquire through induction only comparative universality, that is, extensive applicability. If we A 92 were to treat pure concepts of understanding as merely empirical products, we should be making a complete change in [the manner of] their employment.

§ 14[3]

Transition to the Transcendental Deduction of the Categories

There are only two possible ways in which synthetic representations[4] and their objects[5] can establish connection, obtain necessary relation to one another, and, as it were, meet one another. Either the object alone must make the representation possible, or the representation alone must make the object possible. In the former case, this relation is only empirical, and the representation is never possible *a priori*. This B 125 is true of appearances,[6] as regards that [element] in them which belongs to sensation. In the latter case, representation in itself does not produce its object in so far as *existence* is concerned, for we are not here speaking of its causality by means of the will. None the less the representation is *a priori* determinant of the object, if it be the case that only through

---

[1] [*Erfolg.*]   [2] [*aus ihr erfolge.*]
[3] ["§ 14", inadvertently omitted in B, added in 3rd edition.]
[4] [Reading, with Erdmann, *Vorstellungen* for *Vorstellung.*]
[5] [*Gegenstände.*]
[6] [Reading, with Grillo, *Erscheinungen* for *Erscheinung.*]

the representation is it possible to *know* anything *as an object*. Now there are two conditions under which alone the knowledge of an object is possible, first, *intuition*, through which it is given, though only as appearance; secondly, *concept*, **A 93** through which an object is thought corresponding to this intuition. It is evident from the above that the first condition, namely, that under which alone objects can be intuited, does actually lie[1] *a priori* in the mind as the formal ground of the objects.[2] All appearances necessarily agree with this formal condition of sensibility, since only through it can they appear, that is, be empirically intuited and given. The question now arises whether *a priori* concepts do not also serve as antecedent conditions under which alone anything can be, if not intuited, yet thought as object in general. In that case all empirical **B 126** knowledge of objects would necessarily conform to such concepts, because only as thus presupposing them is anything possible as *object of experience*. Now all experience does indeed contain, in addition to the intuition of the senses through which something is given, a *concept* of an object as being thereby given, that is to say, as appearing. Concepts of objects in general thus underlie all empirical knowledge as its *a priori* conditions. The objective validity of the categories as *a priori* concepts rests, therefore, on the fact that, so far as the form of thought is concerned, through them alone does experience become possible. They relate of necessity and *a priori* to objects of experience, for the reason that only by means of them can any object whatsoever of experience be thought.

A 94 The transcendental deduction of all *a priori* concepts has thus a principle according to which the whole enquiry must be directed, namely, that they must be recognised as *a priori* conditions of the possibility of experience,[3] whether of the intuition which is to be met with in it or of the thought. Concepts which yield the objective ground of the possibility of experience are for this very reason necessary. But the unfolding[4] of the experience wherein they are encountered is not their deduction; it is only their illustration. For on any such

---

[1] [Reading, with Kehrbach, *liegt* for *liegen*.]
[2] [*Objekten*. Here, as elsewhere, Kant employs *Objekt* and *Gegenstand* as equivalent terms.]
[3] [Reading, with Erdmann, *Erfahrung* for *Erfahrungen*.]
[4] [*Entwicklung*.]

exposition they would be merely accidental. Save through their original relation to possible experience, in which all B 127 objects of knowledge are found,[1] their relation to any one object would be quite incomprehensible.

* The illustrious Locke, failing to take account of these considerations, and meeting with pure concepts of the understanding in experience, deduced them also from experience, and yet proceeded so *inconsequently* that he attempted with their aid to obtain knowledge which far transcends all limits of experience. David Hume recognised that, in order to be able to do this, it was necessary that these concepts should have an *a priori* origin. But since he could not explain how it can be possible that the understanding must think concepts, which are not in themselves connected in the understanding, as being necessarily connected in the object, and since it never occurred to him that the understanding might itself, perhaps, through these concepts, be the author of the experience in which its objects are found, he was constrained to derive them from experience, namely, from a subjective necessity (that is, from *custom*), which arises from repeated association in experience, and which comes mistakenly to be regarded as objective. But from these premises he argued quite consistently. It is impossible, he declared, with these concepts and the principles to which they give rise, to pass beyond the limits of experience.

---

* [The next three paragraphs are substituted in B for the following:]

There are three original sources (capacities or faculties of the soul) which contain the conditions of the possibility of all experience, and cannot themselves be derived from any other faculty of the mind, namely, *sense, imagination*, and *apperception*. Upon them are grounded (1) the *synopsis* of the manifold *a priori* through sense; (2) the *synthesis* of this manifold through imagination; finally (3) the *unity* of this synthesis through original apperception. All these *faculties* have a transcendental (as well as an empirical) employment which concerns the form alone, and is possible *a priori*. As regards sense,[2] we have treated of this above in the first part; we shall A 95 now endeavour to comprehend the nature of the other two.

---

[1] [*vorkommen*.]   [2] [*in Ansehung der Sinne*.]

B 128 Now this *empirical* derivation, in which both philosophers agree, cannot be reconciled with the scientific *a priori* knowledge which we do actually possess, namely, *pure mathematics* and *general science of nature*; and this fact therefore suffices to disprove such derivation.

While the former of these two illustrious men opened a wide door to *enthusiasm*[1]—for if reason once be allowed such rights, it will no longer allow itself to be kept within bounds by vaguely defined recommendations of moderation—the other gave himself over entirely to *scepticism*, having, as he believed, discovered that what had hitherto been regarded as reason was but an all-prevalent illusion infecting our faculty of knowledge. We now propose to make trial whether it be not possible to find for human reason safe conduct between these two rocks, assigning to her determinate limits, and yet keeping open for her the whole field of her appropriate activities.

But first I shall introduce a word of explanation in regard to the categories. They are concepts of an object in general, by means of which the intuition of an object is regarded as determined in respect of one of the logical functions of judgment. Thus the function of the categorical judgment is that of the relation of subject to predicate; for example, 'All bodies are divisible'. But as regards the merely logical employment of the understanding, it remains undetermined to which[2] of the two concepts the function of the subject, and to which the

B 129 function of predicate, is to be assigned. For we can also say, 'Something divisible is a body'. But when the concept of body is brought under the category of substance, it is thereby determined that its empirical intuition in experience must always be considered as subject and never as mere predicate. Similarly with all the other categories.

[1] [*Schwärmerei.*]
[2] [Reading, with Grillo, *welchem* for *welcher*.]

THE DEDUCTION OF THE PURE CONCEPTS OF
UNDERSTANDING[1]

[as in 1st edition]

Section 2

THE *A PRIORI* GROUNDS OF THE POSSIBILITY OF
EXPERIENCE

THAT a concept, although itself neither contained in the concept of possible experience nor consisting of elements of a possible experience, should be produced completely *a priori* and should relate to an object, is altogether contradictory and impossible. For it would tnen have no content, since no intuition corresponds to it; and intuitions in general, through which objects can be given to us, constitute the field, the whole object, of possible experience. An *a priori* concept which did not relate to experience would be only the logical form of a concept, not the concept itself through which something is thought.

Pure *a priori* concepts, if such exist, cannot indeed contain anything empirical; yet, none the less, they can serve solely as *a priori* conditions of a possible experience. Upon this ground alone can their objective reality rest.

If, therefore, we seek to discover how pure concepts of understanding are possible, we must enquire what are the *a priori* conditions upon which the possibility of experience A 96 rests, and which remain as its underlying grounds when everything empirical is abstracted from appearances. A concept which universally and adequately expresses such a formal and

---

[1] [The Deduction, as here given, up to p. 150, was omitted in B. The Deduction, as restated in B, is given below, pp. 151 to 175.]

objective condition of experience would be entitled a pure concept of understanding. Certainly, once I am in possession of
pure concepts of understanding, I can think objects which may
be impossible, or which, though perhaps in themselves possible,
cannot be given in any experience. For in the connecting of
these concepts something may be omitted which yet necessarily belongs to the condition of a possible experience (as in
the concept of a spirit). Or, it may be, pure concepts are extended further than experience can follow (as with the concept
of God). But the *elements* of all modes of *a priori* knowledge,
even of capricious and incongruous fictions, though they
cannot, indeed, be derived from experience, since in that case
they would not be knowledge *a priori*, must none the less
always contain the pure *a priori* conditions of a possible experience and of an empirical object. Otherwise nothing would
be thought through them, and they themselves, being without
data, could never arise even in thought.

The concepts which thus contain *a priori* the pure thought
involved in every experience, we find in the categories. If we
A 97 can prove that by their means alone an object can be thought,
this will be a sufficient deduction of them, and will justify their
objective validity. But since in such a thought more than simply
the faculty of thought, the understanding, is brought into play,
and since this faculty itself, as a faculty of *knowledge* that is
meant to relate to objects, calls for explanation in regard to the
possibility of such relation, we must first of all consider, not in
their empirical but in their transcendental constitution, the
subjective sources which form the *a priori* foundation of the
possibility of experience.

If each representation were completely foreign to every
other, standing apart in isolation, no such thing as knowledge
would ever arise. For knowledge is [essentially] a whole in
which representations stand compared and connected. As sense
contains a manifold in its intuition, I ascribe to it a synopsis.
But to such synopsis a synthesis must always correspond; receptivity can make knowledge possible only when combined
with spontaneity. Now this spontaneity is the ground of a
threefold synthesis which must necessarily be found in all
knowledge; namely, the *apprehension* of representations as
modifications of the mind in intuition, their *reproduction* in

imagination, and their *recognition* in a concept. These point to three subjective sources of knowledge which make possible the understanding itself—and consequently all experience as A 98 its empirical product.

Preliminary Remark

The deduction of the categories is a matter of such extreme difficulty, compelling us to penetrate so deeply into the first grounds of the possibility of our knowledge in general, that in order to avoid the elaborateness of a complete theory, and yet at the same time to omit nothing in so indispensable an enquiry, I have found it advisable in the four following passages rather to prepare than to instruct the reader. Systematic exposition of these elements of the understanding is first given in Section 3, immediately following. The reader must not therefore be deterred by obscurities in these earlier sections. They are unavoidable in an enterprise never before attempted. They will, as I trust, in the section referred to, finally give way to complete insight.

1. *The Synthesis of Apprehension in Intuition*

Whatever the origin of our representations, whether they are due to the influence of outer things, or are produced through inner causes, whether they arise *a priori*, or being appearances have an empirical origin, they must all, as modifications of the mind, belong to inner sense. All our know- A 99 ledge is thus finally subject to time, the formal condition of inner sense. In it they must all be ordered, connected, and brought into relation. This is a general observation which, throughout what follows, must be borne in mind as being quite fundamental.

Every intuition contains in itself a manifold which can be represented as a manifold only in so far as the mind distinguishes the time in the sequence of one impression upon another; for each representation, *in so far as it is contained in a single moment*, can never be anything but absolute unity. In order that unity of intuition may arise out of this manifold (as is required in the representation of space) it must first be run through, and held together. This act I name the *synthesis of apprehension*, because it is directed immediately upon intuition, which does indeed offer a manifold, but a manifold which can never be represented[1] as a manifold, and as contained *in a single representation*, save in virtue of such a synthesis.

This synthesis of apprehension must also be exercised *a priori*, that is, in respect of representations which are not empirical. For without it we should never have *a priori* the representations either of space or of time. They can be pro-
A 100   duced only through the synthesis of the manifold which sensibility presents in its original receptivity We have thus a pure synthesis of apprehension.

2. *The Synthesis of Reproduction in Imagination*

It is a merely empirical law, that representations which have often followed or accompanied one another finally become associated, and so are set in a relation whereby, even in the absence of the object, one of these representations can, in accordance with a fixed rule, bring about a transition of the mind to the other. But this law of reproduction presupposes that appearances are themselves actually subject to such a rule, and that in the manifold of these[2] representations a co-existence or sequence takes place in conformity with certain rules. Otherwise our empirical imagination would never find opportunity for exercise appropriate to its powers, and so would remain concealed within the mind as a dead and to us unknown faculty. If cinnabar were sometimes red, sometimes black, sometimes light, sometimes heavy, if a man changed sometimes into this and sometimes into that animal form, if the country on the longest day were sometimes covered with
A 101   fruit, sometimes with ice and snow, my empirical imagination would never find opportunity when representing red colour to bring to mind heavy cinnabar. Nor could there be an empirical synthesis of reproduction, if a certain name were sometimes given to this, sometimes to that object, or were one and the same thing named sometimes in one way, sometimes in another, independently of any rule to which appearances are in themselves subject.

There must then be something which, as the *a priori* ground of a necessary synthetic unity of appearances, makes their reproduction possible. What that something is we

---

[1] [Adding, with Vaihinger, *vorzustellen* after *enthalten*.]
[2] [*ihrer*.]

soon discover, when we reflect that appearances are not things in themselves, but are the mere play of our representations, and in the end reduce to determinations of inner sense. For if we can show that even our purest *a priori* intuitions yield no knowledge, save in so far as they contain a combination of the manifold such as renders a thoroughgoing synthesis of reproduction possible, then this synthesis of imagination is likewise grounded, antecedently to all experience, upon *a priori* principles; and we must assume a pure transcendental synthesis of imagination as conditioning the very possibility of all experience. For experience as such necessarily presupposes the reproducibility of appearances. When A 102 I seek to draw[1] a line in thought, or to think of the time from one noon to another, or even to represent to myself some particular number, obviously the various manifold representations that are involved must be apprehended by me in thought one after the other. But if I were always to drop out of thought the preceding representations (the first parts of the line, the antecedent parts of the time period, or the units in the order represented), and did not reproduce them while advancing to those that follow, a complete representation would never be obtained: none of the above-mentioned thoughts, not even the purest and most elementary representations of space and time, could arise.

The synthesis of apprehension is thus inseparably bound up with the synthesis of reproduction. And as the former constitutes the transcendental ground of the possibility of all modes of knowledge whatsoever—of those that are pure *a priori* no less than of those that are empirical—the reproductive synthesis of the imagination is to be counted among the transcendental acts of the mind. We shall therefore entitle this faculty the transcendental faculty of imagination.

3. *The Synthesis of Recognition in a Concept*   A 103

If we were not conscious that what we think is the same as what we thought a moment before, all reproduction in the series of representations would be useless. For it would in its present state be a new representation which would not in any way belong to the act whereby it was to be gradually gener-

[1] [Reading, with Erdmann, *ziehen* for *ziehe*.]

ated. The manifold of the representation would never, therefore, form a whole, since it would lack that unity which only
consciousness can impart to it. If, in counting, I forget that
the units, which now hover before me,[1] have been added to
one another in succession, I should never know that a total
is being produced through this successive addition of unit to
unit, and so would remain ignorant of the number. For the
concept of the number is nothing but the consciousness of
this unity of synthesis.

The word 'concept'[2] might of itself suggest this remark.
For this unitary consciousness[3] is what combines the manifold, successively intuited, and thereupon also reproduced,
into one representation. This consciousness may often be only
faint, so that we do not connect it with[4] the act itself, that
is, not in any direct manner with the *generation* of the representation, but only with the outcome [that which is thereby
represented]. But notwithstanding these variations, such consciousness, however indistinct, must always be present; without it, concepts, and therewith knowledge of objects, are
altogether impossible.

At this point we must make clear to ourselves what we
mean by the expression 'an object of representations'. We
have stated above that appearances are themselves nothing
but sensible representations, which, as such and in themselves,
must not be taken as objects capable of existing outside our
power of representation. What, then, is to be understood when
we speak of an object corresponding to, and consequently
also distinct from, our knowledge? It is easily seen that this
object must be thought only as something in general = x, since
outside our knowledge we have nothing which we could set
over against this knowledge as corresponding to it.

Now we find that our thought of the relation of all knowledge to its object carries with it an element of necessity; the
object is viewed as that which prevents our modes of knowledge from being haphazard or arbitrary, and which determines them *a priori* in some definite fashion. For in so far
as they are to relate to an object, they must necessarily agree

A 104

---

[1] [*die mir jetzt vor Sinnen schweben.*]
[2] [*Begriff.*]   [3] [*dieses eine Bewusstsein.*]
[4] [Reading, with Adickes, *mit der . . . mit dem* for *in der . . . in dem.*]

with one another, that is, must possess that unity which constitutes the concept of an object.

But it is clear that, since we have to deal only with the
manifold of our representations, and since that x (the object)
which corresponds to them is nothing to us—being, as it is,
something that has to be distinct from all our representations
—the unity which the object makes necessary can be nothing
else than the formal unity of consciousness in the synthesis of
the manifold of representations. It is only when we have thus
produced synthetic unity in the manifold of intuition that we
are in a position to say that we know the object. But this unity
is impossible if the intuition cannot be generated in accordance with a rule by means of such a function of synthesis as
makes the reproduction of the manifold *a priori* necessary,
and renders possible a concept in which it is united. Thus we
think a triangle as an object, in that we are conscious of the
combination of three straight lines according to a rule by
which such an intuition can always be represented. This *unity
of rule* determines all the manifold, and limits it to conditions
which make unity of apperception possible. The concept of
this unity is the representation of the object = x, which I
think through the predicates, above mentioned, of a triangle.

All knowledge demands a concept, though that concept
may, indeed, be quite imperfect or obscure. But a concept
is always, as regards its form, something universal which
serves as a rule. The concept of body, for instance, as the
unity of the manifold which is thought through it, serves as
a rule in our knowledge of outer appearances. But it can be
a rule for intuitions only in so far as it represents in any given
appearances the necessary reproduction of their manifold,
and thereby the synthetic unity in our consciousness of them.
The concept of body, in the perception of something outside
us, necessitates the representation of extension, and therewith representations of impenetrability, shape, etc.

All necessity, without exception, is grounded in a transcendental condition. There must, therefore, be a transcendental ground of the unity of consciousness in the synthesis
of the manifold of all our intuitions, and consequently also
of the concepts of objects in general, and so of all objects
of experience, a ground without which it would be impossible

to think any object for our intuitions; for this object is no more than that something, the concept of which expresses such a necessity of synthesis.

A 107 This original and transcendental condition is no other than *transcendental apperception*. Consciousness of self according to the determinations of our state in inner perception is merely empirical, and always changing. No fixed and abiding self can present itself in this flux of inner appearances. Such consciousness is usually named *inner sense*, or *empirical apperception*. What has *necessarily* to be represented as numerically identical cannot be thought as such through empirical data. To render such a transcendental presupposition valid, there must be a condition which precedes all experience, and which makes experience itself possible.

There can be in us no modes of knowledge, no connection or unity of one mode of knowledge with another, without that unity of consciousness which precedes all data of intuitions, and by relation to which representation of objects is alone possible. This pure original unchangeable consciousness I shall name *transcendental apperception*. That it deserves this name is clear from the fact that even the purest objective unity, namely, that of the *a priori* concepts (space and time), is[1] only possible through relation of the intuitions to such unity of consciousness. The numerical unity of this apperception is thus the *a priori* ground of all concepts, just as the manifoldness of space and time is the *a priori* ground of the intuitions of sensibility.

A 108 This transcendental unity of apperception forms out of[2] all possible appearances, which can stand alongside one another in one experience, a connection of all these representations according to laws. For this unity of consciousness would be impossible if the mind in knowledge of the manifold could not become conscious of the identity of function whereby it[3] synthetically combines it in one knowledge. The original and necessary consciousness of the identity of the self is thus at the same time a consciousness of an equally necessary unity of the synthesis of all appearances according to concepts, that

---

[1] [Reading, with Erdmann, *sei* for *sein*.]   [2] [*macht aus.*]
[3] [Reading, with Wille, *es* for *sie*.]

is, according to rules, which not only make them necessarily reproducible but also in so doing determine an object for their intuition, that is, the concept of something wherein they are necessarily interconnected. For the mind could never think its identity in the manifoldness of its representations, and indeed think this identity *a priori*, if it did not have before its eyes the identity of its act, whereby it subordinates all synthesis of apprehension (which is empirical) to a transcendental unity, thereby rendering possible their interconnection according to *a priori* rules.

Now, also, we are in a position to determine more adequately our concept[1] of an *object* in general. All representations have, as representations, their object, and can themselves in turn become objects of other representations. Appearances are the sole objects which can be given to us immediately, and A 109 that in them which relates immediately to the object is called intuition. But these appearances are not things in themselves; they are only representations, which in turn have their object —an object which cannot itself be intuited by us, and which may, therefore, be named the non-empirical, that is, transcendental object = x.

The pure concept of this transcendental object, which in reality throughout all our knowledge is always one and the same, is what can alone confer upon all[2] our empirical concepts in general relation to an object, that is, objective reality. This concept cannot contain any determinate intuition, and therefore refers only to that unity which must be met with in any manifold of knowledge which stands in relation to an object. This relation is nothing but the necessary unity of consciousness, and therefore also of the synthesis of the manifold, through a common function of the mind, which combines it in one representation. Since this unity must be regarded as necessary *a priori*—otherwise knowledge would be without an object—the relation to a transcendental object, that is, the objective reality of our empirical knowledge, rests A 110 on the transcendental law, that all appearances, in so far as through them objects are to be given to us, must stand under those *a priori* rules of synthetical unity whereby the inter-

---

[1] [Reading, with Adickes, *unseren Begriff* for *unsere Begriffe*.]
[2] [Reading, with Erdmann, *was allen* for *was in allen*.]

relating of these appearances in empirical intuition is alone possible. In other words, appearances in experience must stand under the conditions of the necessary unity of apperception, just as in mere intuition they must be subject to the formal conditions of space and of time. Only thus can any knowledge become possible at all.

4. Preliminary Explanation of the Possibility of the Categories, as Knowledge a priori

There is one single experience in which all perceptions are represented as in thoroughgoing and orderly connection, just as there is only one space and one time in which all modes[1] of appearance and all relation of being or not being occur. When we speak of different experiences, we can refer only to the various perceptions, all of which, as such, belong to one and the same general experience. This thoroughgoing synthetic unity of perceptions is indeed the form of experience; it is nothing else than the synthetic unity of appearances in accordance with concepts.

A III   Unity of synthesis according to empirical concepts would be altogether accidental, if these latter were not based on a transcendental ground of unity. Otherwise it would be possible for appearances to crowd in upon the soul, and yet to be such as would never allow of experience. Since connection in accordance with universal and necessary laws would be lacking, all relation of knowledge to objects would fall away. The appearances might, indeed, constitute intuition without thought,[2] but not knowledge; and consequently would be for us as good as nothing.

The a priori conditions of a possible experience in general are at the same time conditions of the possibility of objects of experience. Now I maintain that the categories, above[3] cited, are nothing but the conditions of thought in a possible experience, just as space and time are[4] the conditions of intuition for that same experience. They are fundamental concepts by which we think objects in general for appearances, and have therefore a priori objective validity. This is exactly what we desired to prove.

----

¹ [Formen.]   ² [gedankenlose Anschauung.]
³ [Reading, with Erdmann, oben for eben.]   ⁴ [enthalten.]

But the possibility, indeed the necessity, of these categories rests on the relation in which our entire sensibility, and with it all possible appearances, stand to original apperception. In original apperception everything must necessarily conform to the conditions of the thoroughgoing unity of self-consciousness, that is, to the universal functions of synthesis,   A 112
namely, of that synthesis according to concepts in which alone apperception can demonstrate *a priori* its complete and necessary identity. Thus the concept of a cause is nothing but a synthesis (of that which follows in the time-series, with other appearances) *according to concepts*; and without such unity, which has its *a priori* rule, and which subjects the appearances to itself, no thoroughgoing, universal, and therefore necessary, unity of consciousness would be met with in the manifold of perceptions. These perceptions would not then belong to any experience, consequently would be without an object, merely a blind play of representations, less even than a dream.

All attempts to derive these pure concepts of understanding from experience, and so to ascribe to them a merely empirical origin, are entirely vain and useless. I need not insist upon the fact that, for instance, the concept of a cause involves the character of necessity, which no experience can yield. Experience does indeed show that one appearance customarily follows upon another, but not that this sequence is necessary, nor that we can argue *a priori* and with complete universality from the antecedent, viewed as a condition, to the consequent. But as regards the empirical rule of *association*, which we must postulate throughout when we assert that everything in the series of events is so subject to rule that nothing ever   A 113
happens save in so far as something precedes it on which it universally follows—upon what, I ask, does this rule, as a law of nature, rest? How is this association itself possible? The ground of the possibility of the association of the manifold, so far as it lies in the object, is named the *affinity* of the manifold. I therefore ask, how are we to make comprehensible to ourselves the thoroughgoing affinity of appearances, whereby they stand and *must* stand under unchanging laws?

On my principles it is easily explicable. All possible appearances, as representations, belong to the totality of a possible self-consciousness.[1] But as self-consciousness is a transcendental representation, numerical identity is inseparable from it, and is *a priori* certain. For nothing can come to our knowledge save in terms of this original apperception. Now, since this identity must necessarily enter into the synthesis of all the manifold of appearances, so far as the synthesis is to yield empirical knowledge, the appearances are subject to *a priori* conditions, with which the synthesis of their apprehension must be in complete accordance. The representation of a universal condition according to which a certain manifold can be posited in uniform fashion is called a *rule*, and, when it *must* be so posited, a *law*. Thus all appearances stand in thoroughgoing connection according to necessary laws, and therefore in a transcendental affinity, of which the empirical is a mere consequence.

A 114

That nature should direct itself according to our subjective ground of apperception, and should indeed depend upon it in respect of its conformity to law, sounds very strange and absurd. But when we consider that this nature is not a thing in itself but is merely an aggregate of appearances, so many representations of the mind, we shall not be surprised that we can discover it only in the radical faculty of all our knowledge, namely, in transcendental apperception, in that unity on account of which alone it can be entitled object of all possible experience, that is, nature. Nor shall we be surprised that just for this very reason this unity can be known *a priori*, and therefore as necessary. Were the unity given in itself independently of the first sources of our thought, this would never be possible. We should not then know of any source from which we could obtain the synthetic propositions asserting such a universal unity of nature. For they would then have to be derived from the objects of nature themselves; and as this could take place only empirically, none but a merely accidental unity could be obtained, which would fall far short of the necessary interconnection that we have in mind when we speak of nature.

[1] [*zu dem ganzen möglichen Selbstbewusstsein.*]

DEDUCTION OF THE PURE CONCEPTS OF UNDERSTANDING

Section 3

THE RELATION OF THE UNDERSTANDING TO OBJECTS IN GENERAL, AND THE POSSIBILITY OF KNOWING THEM *A PRIORI*

What we have expounded separately and singly in the preceding section, we shall now present in systematic interconnection. There are three subjective sources of knowledge upon which rests the possibility of experience in general and of knowledge of its objects—*sense, imagination*, and *apperception*. Each of these can be viewed as empirical, namely, in its application to given appearances. But all of them are likewise *a priori* elements or foundations, which make this empirical employment itself possible. *Sense* represents appearances empirically in *perception, imagination* in *association* (and reproduction), *apperception* in the *empirical consciousness* of the identity of the reproduced representations with the appearances whereby they were given, that is, in recognition.

But all perceptions are grounded *a priori* in pure intuition (in time, the form of their inner intuition as representations), association in pure synthesis of imagination, and empirical A 116 consciousness in pure apperception, that is, in the thoroughgoing identity of the self in all possible representations.

If, now, we desire to follow up the inner ground of this connection of the representations to the point upon which they have all to converge in order that they may therein for the first time acquire the unity of knowledge necessary for a possible experience, we must begin with pure apperception. Intuitions are nothing to us, and do not in the least concern us if they cannot be taken up into consciousness, in which they may participate either directly or indirectly. In this way alone is any knowledge possible. We are conscious *a priori* of the complete identity of the self in respect of all representations which can ever belong to our knowledge, as being a necessary condition of the possibility of all representations. For in me they can represent something only in so far as they belong with all others[1] to one consciousness, and therefore must be at least capable of being so connected. This principle holds *a priori*, and may be called the transcendental principle of the *unity* of all that is manifold in our representations, and consequently also in intuition. Since this unity of the manifold in one subject is synthetic, pure apperception supplies a principle of the synthetic unity of the manifold in all possible intuition.[a]

This synthetic unity presupposes or includes a synthesis, and if the former is to be *a priori* necessary, the synthesis must also be *a priori*. The transcendental unity of apperception thus relates to the pure synthesis of imagination, as an *a priori* condition of the possibility of all combination of the manifold in one knowledge. But only the *productive* synthesis of the

A 117

A 118

[a] This proposition is of great importance and calls for careful consideration. All representations have a necessary relation to a *possible* empirical consciousness. For if they did not have this, and if it were altogether impossible to become conscious of them, this would practically amount to the admission of their non-existence. But all empirical consciousness has a necessary relation to a transcendental consciousness which precedes all special experience, namely, the consciousness of myself as original apperception. It is therefore absolutely necessary that in my knowledge all consciousness should belong to a single consciousness, that of myself. Here, then, is a synthetic unity of the manifold (of consciousness), which is known *a priori*, and so yields the ground for synthetic *a priori* propositions which concern pure thought, just as do space and time for the propositions which refer to the form of pure intuition. The synthetic proposition, that all the variety of *empirical consciousness* must be combined in one single[2] self-consciousness, is the *absolutely* first and synthetic principle of our thought in general. But it must not be forgotten that the bare representation 'I' in relation to all other representations (the collective unity of which it makes possible) is transcendental consciousness. Whether this representation is clear (empirical consciousness)[3] or obscure, or even whether it ever actually occurs, does not here concern us. But the possibility of the logical form of all knowledge is necessarily conditioned by relation to this apperception *as a faculty*.

[1] [Reading, with Erdmann, *allen andern* for *allem anderen*.]
[2] [Reading, with Vorländer, *in einem einzigen* for *in einem einigen*.]
[3] [Vorländer would omit, as being meaningless, the parenthesis: (*empirisches Bewusstsein*).]

imagination can take place *a priori*; the reproductive rests upon empirical conditions. Thus the principle of the necessary unity of pure (productive) synthesis of imagination, prior to apperception, is the ground of the possibility of all knowledge, especially of experience.

We entitle the synthesis of the manifold in imagination transcendental, if without distinction of intuitions it is directed exclusively to the *a priori* combination of the manifold; and the unity of this synthesis is called transcendental, if it is represented as *a priori* necessary in relation to the original unity of apperception. Since this unity of apperception underlies the possibility of all knowledge, the transcendental unity of the synthesis of imagination is the pure form of all possible knowledge; and by means of it all objects of possible experience must be represented *a priori*.

The unity of apperception in relation to the synthesis of A 119
imagination is the *understanding*; and this same unity, with reference to the *transcendental synthesis* of the imagination, the *pure understanding*. In the understanding there are then pure *a priori* modes of knowledge[1] which contain the necessary unity of the pure synthesis of imagination in respect of all possible appearances. These are the *categories*, that is, the pure concepts of understanding. The empirical faculty of knowledge in man must therefore contain an understanding which relates to all objects of the senses, although only by means of intuition and of its synthesis through imagination. All appearances, as data[2] for a possible experience, are subject to this understanding. This relation of appearances to possible experience is indeed necessary, for otherwise they would yield no knowledge and would not in any way concern us. We have, therefore, to recognise that pure understanding, by means of the categories, is a formal and synthetic principle of all experiences, and that appearances have *a necessary relation to the understanding*.

We will now, starting from below, namely, with the empirical, strive to make clear the necessary connection in which understanding, by means of the categories, stands to appearances. What is first given to us is appearance. When combined A 120
with consciousness, it is called perception. (Save through its

---

[1] [*Erkenntnisse.*]   [2] [*Data.*]

relation to a consciousness that is at least possible, appearance could never be for us an object of knowledge, and so would be nothing to us; and since it has in itself no objective reality, but exists only in being known, it would be nothing at all.) Now, since every appearance contains a manifold, and since different perceptions therefore occur in the mind separately and singly, a combination of them, such as they cannot have in sense itself, is demanded. There must therefore exist in us an active faculty for the synthesis of this manifold. To this faculty I give the title, imagination. Its action, when immediately directed upon perceptions, I entitle apprehension.ᵃ Since imagination has to bring the manifold of intuition into the form of an image, it must previously have taken the impressions up into its activity, that is, have apprehended them.

A 121   But it is clear that even this apprehension of the manifold would not by itself produce an image and a connection of the impressions, were it not that there exists a subjective ground which leads the mind to reinstate a preceding perception alongside the subsequent perception to which it has passed, and so to form whole series of perceptions. This is the reproductive faculty of imagination, which is merely empirical.

If, however, representations reproduced one another in any order, just as they happened to come together, this would not lead to any determinate connection of them, but only to accidental collocations;¹ and so would not give rise to any knowledge. Their reproduction must, therefore, conform to a rule, in accordance with which a representation connects in the imagination with some one representation in preference to another. This subjective and *empirical* ground of reproduction according to rules is what is called the *association* of representations.

Now if this unity of association had not also an objective

ᵃ Psychologists have hitherto failed to realise that imagination is a necessary ingredient of perception itself. This is due partly to the fact that that faculty has been limited to reproduction, partly to the belief that the senses not only supply impressions but also combine them so as to generate images of objects. For that purpose something more than the mere receptivity of impressions is undoubtedly required, namely, ₽ function for the synthesis of them.

¹ [*Haufen.*]

ground which makes it impossible that appearances should be apprehended by the imagination otherwise than under the condition of a possible synthetic unity of this apprehension, it would be entirely accidental that appearances should fit into a connected whole of human knowledge. For even though we should have the power of associating perceptions, it would remain entirely undetermined and accidental whether they A 122 would themselves be associable; and should they not be associable, there might exist a multitude of perceptions, and indeed an entire sensibility, in which much empirical consciousness would arise in my mind, but in a state of separation, and without belonging to a consciousness of myself. This, however, is impossible. For it is only because I ascribe all perceptions to one consciousness (original apperception) that I can say of all perceptions that I am conscious of them. There must, therefore, be an objective ground (that is, one that can be comprehended *a priori*, antecedently to all empirical laws of the imagination) upon which rests the possibility, nay, the necessity, of a law that extends to all appearances—a ground, namely, which constrains us to regard all appearances as data of the senses that must be associable in themselves and subject to universal rules of a thoroughgoing connection in their reproduction. This objective ground of all association of appearances I entitle their *affinity*. It is nowhere to be found save in the principle of the unity of apperception, in respect of all knowledge which is to belong to me. According to this principle all appearances, without exception, must so enter the mind or be apprehended, that they conform to the unity of apperception. Without synthetic unity in their connection, this would be impossible; and such synthetic unity is itself, therefore, objectively necessary.

The objective unity of all empirical consciousness in one A 123 consciousness, that of original apperception, is thus the necessary condition of all possible perception; and [this being recognised we can prove that] the affinity of all appearances, near or remote, is a necessary consequence of a synthesis in imagination which is grounded *a priori* on rules.

Since the imagination is itself a faculty of *a priori* synthesis, we assign to it the title, productive imagination. In so far as it aims at nothing but necessary unity in the synthesis of what is manifold in appearance, it may be entitled the transcendental function of imagination. That the affinity of appearances, and with it their association, and through this, in turn, their reproduction according to laws, and so [as involving these various factors] experience itself, should only be possible by means of this transcendental function of imagination, is indeed strange, but is none the less an obvious consequence of the preceding argument. For without this transcendental function no concepts of objects would together make up a unitary experience.

The abiding and unchanging 'I'[1] (pure apperception) forms the correlate of all our representations in so far as it is to be at all possible that we should become conscious of them. All consciousness as truly belongs to an all-comprehensive pure apperception, as all sensible intuition, as representation, does to a pure inner intuition, namely, to time. It is this apperception which must be added to pure imagination, in order to render its function intellectual. For since the synthesis of imagination connects the manifold only as it *appears* in intuition, as, for instance, in the shape of a triangle, it is, though exercised *a priori*, always in itself sensible. And while concepts, which belong to the understanding, are brought into play[2] through relation of the manifold to the unity of apperception, it is only by means of the imagination that they can be brought into relation to sensible intuition.

A pure imagination, which conditions all *a priori* knowledge, is thus one of the fundamental faculties of the human soul. By its means we bring the manifold of intuition on the one side, into connection with the condition of the necessary unity of pure apperception on the other. The two extremes, namely sensibility and understanding, must stand in necessary connection with each other through the mediation of this transcendental function of imagination, because otherwise the former, though indeed yielding appearances, would supply no objects of empirical knowledge, and consequently no experience. Actual experience, which is constituted by apprehension, association (reproduction), and finally recognition of appearances, contains in recognition, the last and highest of these

A 124

A 125

---

[1] [*das stehende und bleibende Ich.*]
[2] [Reading, with Vaihinger, *werden Begriffe ins Spiel gebracht.*]

merely empirical elements of experience, certain concepts which render possible the formal unity of experience, and therewith all objective validity (truth) of empirical knowledge. These grounds of the recognition of the manifold, so far as they concern *solely the form of an experience in general,* are the *categories.* Upon them is based not only all formal unity in the [transcendental] synthesis of imagination, but also, thanks to that synthesis, all its empirical employment[1] (in recognition, reproduction, association, apprehension) in connection with[2] the appearances. For only by means of these fundamental concepts[3] can appearances belong to knowledge or even to our consciousness, and so to ourselves.

Thus the order and regularity in the appearances, which we entitle *nature,* we ourselves introduce. We could never find them in appearances, had not we ourselves, or the nature of our mind, originally set them there. For this unity of nature has to be a necessary one, that is, has to be an *a priori* certain unity of the connection of appearances; and such synthetic unity could not be established *a priori* if there were not subjective grounds of such unity contained *a priori* in the original cognitive powers of our mind, and if these subjective conditions, inasmuch as they are the grounds of the possibility of knowing any object whatsoever in experience, were not at the same time objectively valid. A 126

We have already defined the understanding in various different ways: as a spontaneity of knowledge (in distinction from the receptivity of sensibility), as a power of thought, as a faculty of concepts, or again of judgments. All these definitions, when they are adequately understood, are identical. We may now characterise it as the *faculty of rules.* This distinguishing mark is more fruitful, and approximates more closely to its essential nature. Sensibility gives us forms (of intuition), but understanding gives us rules. The latter is always occupied in investigating appearances, in order to detect some rule in them. Rules, so far as they are objective, and therefore necessarily depend upon the knowledge of the object, are called laws. Although we learn many laws through

---

[1] [Reading, with Adickes, *aller empirische Gebrauch* for *alles empirischen Gebrauchs.*]
[2] [*bis herunter zu.*]   [3] [*Elemente.*]

experience, they are only special determinations of still higher laws, and the highest of these, under which the others all[1] stand, issue *a priori* from the understanding itself. They are not borrowed from experience; on the contrary, they have to confer upon appearances their conformity to law, and so to make experience possible. Thus the understanding is something more than a power of formulating rules through comparison of appearances; it is itself the lawgiver of nature. Save through it, nature, that is, synthetic unity of the manifold of appearances according to rules, would not exist at all (for appearances, as such, cannot exist outside us—they exist only in our sensibility); and this[2] nature, as object of knowledge in an experience, with everything which it may contain, is only possible in the unity of apperception. The unity of apperception is thus[3] the transcendental ground of the necessary conformity to law of all appearances in one experience. This same unity of apperception in respect to a manifold of representations (determining it out of a unity)[4] acts as the rule, and the faculty of these rules is the understanding. All appearances, as possible experiences, thus lie *a priori* in the understanding, and receive from it their formal possibility, just as, in so far as they are mere intuitions, they lie in the sensibility, and are, as regards their form, only possible through it.

However exaggerated and absurd it may sound, to say that the understanding is itself the source of the laws of nature, and so of its formal unity, such an assertion is none the less correct, and is in keeping with the object to which it refers, namely, experience. Certainly, empirical laws, as such, can never derive their origin from pure understanding. That is as little possible as to understand completely the inexhaustible multiplicity of appearances merely by reference to the pure form of sensible intuition. But all empirical laws are only special determinations of the pure laws of understanding, under which, and according to the norm of which, they first become possible. Through them appearances take on an orderly character, just as these same appearances, despite

A 127

A 128

---

[1] [Reading, with Erdmann, *die andern alle* for *andere alle*.]
[2] [Reading, with Vaihinger, *Jene* for *Diese*.]
[3] [Reading, with Erdmann, *also* for *aber*.]   [4] [*aus einer einzigen*.]

the differences of their empirical form,[1] must none the less always be in harmony with the pure form of sensibility.

Pure understanding is thus in the categories the law of the synthetic unity of all appearances, and thereby first and originally makes experience, as regards its form, possible. This is all that we were called upon to establish in the transcendental deduction of the categories, namely, to render comprehensible this relation of understanding to sensibility, and, by means of sensibility, to all objects of experience. The objective validity of the pure *a priori* concepts is thereby made intelligible, and their origin and truth determined.

Summary Representation of the Correctness of this Deduction of the pure Concepts of Understanding, and of its being the only Deduction possible

If the objects with which our knowledge has to deal were things in themselves, we could have no *a priori* concepts of them. For from what source could we obtain the concepts? If we derived them from the object (leaving aside the question how the object could become known to us), our concepts would A 129 be merely empirical, not *a priori*. And if we derived them from the self, that which is merely in us could not determine the character of an object distinct from our representations, that is, could not be a ground why a thing should exist characterised by that which we have in our thought, and why such a representation should not, rather, be altogether empty. But if, on the other hand, we have to deal only with appearances, it is not merely possible, but necessary, that certain *a priori* concepts should precede empirical knowledge of objects. For since a mere modification of our sensibility can never be met with outside us, the objects, as appearances, constitute an object which is merely in us. Now to assert in this manner, that all these appearances, and consequently all objects with which we can occupy ourselves, are one and all in me, that is, are determinations of my identical self, is only another way of saying that there must be a complete unity of them in one and the same apperception. But this unity of possible consciousness also constitutes the form of all knowledge of objects; through it the manifold is thought as belonging to a

[1] [*unerachtet der Verschiedenheit ihrer empirischen Form.*]

single object. Thus the mode in which the manifold of sensible representation (intuition) belongs to one consciousness precedes all knowledge of the object as the intellectual form of such knowledge, and itself constitutes a formal *a priori* knowledge of all objects, so far as they are thought (categories). The synthesis of the manifold[1] through pure imagination, the unity of all representations in relation to original apperception, precede all empirical knowledge. Pure concepts of understanding are thus *a priori* possible, and, in relation to experience, are indeed necessary; and this for the reason that our knowledge has to deal solely with appearances, the possibility of which lies in ourselves, and the connection and unity of which (in the representation of an object) are to be met with only in ourselves. Such connection and unity must therefore precede all experience, and are required for the very possibility of it in its formal aspect. From this point of view, the only feasible one, our deduction of the categories has been developed.

A 130

---

[1] [Reading *desselben* for *derselben*.]

DEDUCTION OF THE PURE CONCEPTS OF THE UNDERSTANDING[1]

[*As restated in 2nd edition*]

Section 2

TRANSCENDENTAL DEDUCTION OF THE PURE CONCEPTS OF THE UNDERSTANDING

§ 15

The Possibility of Combination in General

THE manifold of representations can be given in an intuition which is purely sensible, that is, nothing but receptivity; and the form of this intuition can lie *a priori* in our faculty of representation, without being anything more than the mode in which the subject is affected. But the combination (*conjunctio*) of a manifold in general can never come to us through the senses, and cannot, therefore, be already contained in the pure form of sensible intuition. For it is an act of spontaneity of the B 130 faculty of representation; and since this faculty, to distinguish it from sensibility, must be entitled understanding, all combination—be we conscious of it or not, be it a combination of the manifold of intuition, empirical or non-empirical,[2] or of various concepts—is an act of the understanding. To this act the general title 'synthesis' may be assigned, as indicating that we cannot represent to ourselves anything as combined in the object which we have not ourselves previously combined, and that of all representations *combination* is the only one which

---

[1] [What follows, up to p. 175, is Kant's restatement of the Transcendental Deduction, in B.]
[2] [Reading, with Mellin, *empirischen oder nicht empirischen* for *sinnlichen oder nicht sinnlichen*.]

cannot be given through objects. Being an act of the self-activity of the subject, it cannot be executed save by the subject itself. It will easily be observed that this action is originally one and is equipollent¹ for all combination, and that its dissolution, namely, *analysis*, which appears to be its opposite, yet always presupposes it. For where the understanding has not previously combined, it cannot dissolve, since only as having been combined *by the understanding* can anything that allows of analysis be given to the faculty of representation.

But the concept of combination includes, besides the concept of the manifold and of its synthesis, also the concept of the unity of the manifold. Combination is representation of the synthetic unity of the manifold.ᵃ The representation of this unity cannot, therefore, arise out of the combination. On the contrary, it is what, by adding itself to the representation of the manifold, first makes possible the concept of the combination. This unity, which precedes *a priori* all concepts of combination, is not the category of unity (§ 10); for all categories are grounded in logical functions of judgment, and in these functions combination, and therefore unity of given concepts, is already thought. Thus the category already presupposes combination. We must therefore look yet higher for this unity (as qualitative, § 12), namely in that which itself contains the ground of the unity of diverse concepts in judgment, and therefore of the possibility of the understanding, even as regards its logical employment

B 131

§ 16

The Original Synthetic Unity of Apperception

It must be possible for the 'I think' to accompany all my representations; for otherwise something would be represented

ᵃ Whether the representations are in themselves identical, and whether, therefore, one can be analytically thought through the other, is not a question that here arises. The *consciousness* of the one, when the manifold is under consideration, has always to be distinguished from the consciousness of the other; and it is with the synthesis of this (possible) consciousness that we are here alone concerned.

¹ [*gleichgeltend.*]

in me which could not be thought at all, and that is equivalent B 132
to saying that the representation would be impossible, or at
least would be nothing to me. That representation which can
be given prior to all thought is entitled intuition. All the
manifold of intuition has, therefore, a necessary relation to the
'I think' in the same subject in which this manifold is found.
But this representation is an act of *spontaneity*, that is, it
cannot be regarded as belonging to sensibility. I call it *pure
apperception*, to distinguish it from empirical apperception, or,
again, *original*[1] *apperception*, because it is that self-consciousness which, while generating the representation '*I think*' (a
representation which must be capable of accompanying all
other representations, and which in all consciousness is one and
the same), cannot itself be accompanied by any further representation. The unity of this apperception I likewise entitle the
transcendental unity of self-consciousness, in order to indicate
the possibility of *a priori* knowledge arising from it. For the
manifold representations, which are given in an intuition,
would not be one and all *my* representations, if they did
not all belong to one self-consciousness. As *my* representations (even if I am not conscious of them as such) they
must conform to the condition under which alone they *can*
stand together in one universal self-consciousness, because
otherwise they would not all without exception belong to B 133
me. From this original combination many consequences
follow.

This thoroughgoing identity of the apperception of a
manifold which is given in intuition contains a synthesis of
representations, and is possible only through the consciousness of this synthesis. For the empirical consciousness, which
accompanies different representations, is in itself diverse and
without relation to the identity of the subject. That relation
comes about, not simply through my accompanying each representation with consciousness, but only in so far as I *conjoin*
one representation with another, and am conscious of the synthesis of them. Only in so far, therefore, as I can unite a
manifold of given representations in *one consciousness*, is it
possible for me to represent to myself the *identity of the consciousness in* [*i.e. throughout*] *these representations*. In other

[1] [*ursprüngliche.*]

words, the *analytic* unity of apperception is possible only under
the presupposition of a certain *synthetic* unity.^a

B 134   The thought that the reʃres ʾntations given in intuition one
and all belong to me, is therefore equivalent to the thought
that I unite them in one self-consciousness, or can at least
so unite them; and although this thought is not itself the
consciousness of the *synthesis* of the representations, it presupposes the possibility of that synthesis. In other words, only
in so far as I can grasp the manifold of the representations in
one consciousness, do I call them one and ʾll *mine*. For otherwise I should have as many-coloured and diverse a self as I
have representations of which I am conscious to myself. Synthetic unity of the manifold of intuitions, as generated[1] *a
priori*, is thus the ground of the identity of apperception itself,
which precedes *a priori* all *my* determinate thought. Combination does not, however, lie in the objects, and cannot be
borrowed from them, and so, through perception, first taken up
into the understanding. On the contrary, it is an affair of the
B 135 understanding alone, which itself is nothing but the faculty
of combining *a priori*, and of bringing the manifold of given
representations under the unity of apperception. The principle
of apperception is the highest principle in the whole sphere of
human knowledge.

     This principle of the necessary unity of apperception is

---

^a The analytic unity of consciousness belongs to all general con-
cepts, as such. If, for instance, I think red in general, I thereby represent to myself a property which (as a characteristic) can be found in
something, or can be combined with other representations; that is,
only by means of a presupposed possible synthetic unity can I represent to myself the analytic unity. A representation which is to be
thought as common to *different* representations is regarded as be-
B 134 longing to such as have, in addition to it, also something *different*.
Consequently it must previously be thought in synthetic unity with
other (though, it may be, only possible) representations, before I can
think in it the analytic unity of consciousness, which makes it a *conceptus communis*. The synthetic unity of apperception is therefore
that highest point, to which we must ascribe all employment of the
understanding, even the whole of logic, and conformably therewith,
transcendental philosophy. Indeed this faculty of apperception is the
understanding itself.

---

¹ [Reading, with Vaihinger, *hervorgebracht* for *gegeben*.]

itself, indeed, an identical, and therefore analytic, proposition; nevertheless it reveals the necessity of a synthesis of the manifold given in intuition, without which the thoroughgoing identity of self-consciousness cannot be thought. For through the 'I', as simple representation, nothing manifold is given; only in intuition, which is distinct from the 'I', can a manifold be given; and only through *combination* in one consciousness can it be thought. An understanding in which through self-consciousness all the manifold would *eo ipso* be given, would be *intuitive*; our understanding can only *think*, and for intuition must look to the senses. I am conscious of the self as identical in respect of the manifold of representations that are given to me in an intuition, because I call them one and all *my* representations, and so apprehend them as constituting *one* intuition. This amounts to saying, that I am conscious to myself *a priori* of a necessary synthesis of representations—to be entitled the original synthetic unity of apperception—under which all representations that are given to me must stand, but under which they have also first to be brought by means of a synthesis.   B 136

§ 17

The Principle of the Synthetic Unity is the Supreme Principle of all Employment of the Understanding

The supreme principle of the possibility of all intuition in its relation to sensibility is, according to the Transcendental Aesthetic, that all the manifold of intuition should be subject to the formal conditions of space and time. The supreme principle of the same possibility, in its relation to understanding, is that all the manifold of intuition should be subject to conditions of the original synthetic unity of apperception.[a] In so

[a] Space and time, and all their parts, are *intuitions*, and are, therefore, with the manifold which they contain, singular representations (*vide* the Transcendental Aesthetic). Consequently they are not mere concepts through which one and the same consciousness is found to be contained in a number of representations. On the contrary, through them many representations are found to be contained in one representation, and in the consciousness of that representation; and they are thus composite. The unity of that consciousness

far as the manifold representations of intuition are *given* to us, they are subject to the former of these two principles; in so far as they must allow of being *combined* in one consciousness, they are subject to the latter. For without such combination nothing can be thought or known, since the given representations would not have in common the act of the apperception 'I think', and so could not be apprehended together in one self-consciousness.

Understanding is, to use general terms, *the faculty of knowledge*. This knowledge consists in the determinate relation of given representations to an object; and an *object* is that in the concept of which the manifold of a given intuition is *united*. Now all unification of representations demands unity of consciousness in the synthesis of them. Consequently it is the unity of consciousness that alone constitutes the relation of representations to an object, and therefore their objective validity and the fact that they are modes of knowledge; and upon it therefore rests the very possibility of the understanding

The first pure knowledge of understanding, then, upon which all the rest of its employment is based, and which also at the same time is completely independent of all conditions of sensible intuition, is the principle of the original *synthetic* unity of apperception. Thus the mere form of outer sensible intuition, space, is not yet [by itself] knowledge; it supplies only the manifold of *a priori* intuition for a possible knowledge. To know anything in space (for instance, a line), I must *draw* it, and thus synthetically bring into being a determinate combination of the given manifold, so that the unity of this act is at the same time the unity of consciousness (as in the concept of a line); and it is through this unity of consciousness that an object (a determinate space) is first known. The synthetic unity of consciousness is, therefore, an objective condition of all knowledge. It is not merely a condition that I myself require in knowing an object, but is a condition under which every intuition must stand in order *to become an object for me*. For otherwise, in the absence of this

---

is therefore synthetic and yet is also original. The *singularity* of such intuitions is found to have important consequences (*vide* § 25).

synthesis, the manifold would *not* be united in one consciousness.

Although this proposition makes synthetic unity a condition of all thought, it is, as already stated, itself analytic.
For it says no more than that all *my* representations in any
given intuition must be subject to that condition under which
alone I can ascribe them to the identical self as *my* representations, and so can comprehend them as synthetically combined in one apperception through the general expression,[1]
'*I think*'

This principle is not, however, to be taken as applying
to every possible understanding, but only to that understanding through whose pure apperception, in the representation
'I am', nothing manifold is given. An understanding which
through its self-consciousness could supply to itself the manifold of intuition—an understanding, that is to say, through   B 139
whose representation the objects of the representation should
at the same time exist—would not require, for the unity of
consciousness, a special act of synthesis of the manifold. For
the human understanding, however, which thinks only, and
does not intuit, that act is necessary. It is indeed the first
principle of the human understanding, and is so indispensable
to it that we cannot form the least conception of any other
possible understanding, either of such as is itself intuitive or
of any that may possess an underlying mode of sensible intuition which is different in kind from that in space and time.

§ 18

The Objective Unity of Self-Consciousness

The transcendental unity of apperception is that unity
through which all the manifold given in an intuition is united
in a concept of the object. It is therefore entitled *objective*,
and must be distinguished from the *subjective* unity of consciousness, which is a *determination* of *inner sense*—through
which the manifold of intuition for such [objective] combination is empirically given. Whether I can become *empirically*
conscious of the manifold as simultaneous or as successive
depends on circumstances or empirical conditions. Therefore

[1] [*allgemeinen Ausdruck.*]

B 140   the empirical unity of consciousness, through association of representations, itself concerns an appearance, and is wholly contingent. But the pure form of intuition in time, merely as intuition in general, which contains a given manifold, is subject to the original unity of consciousness, simply through the necessary relation of the manifold of the intuition to the one '*I think*', and so through the pure synthesis of understanding which is the *a priori* underlying ground of the empirical synthesis. Only the original unity is objectively valid; the empirical unity of apperception, upon which we are not here dwelling, and which besides is merely derived from the former under given conditions *in concreto*, has only subjective validity. To one man, for instance, a certain word suggests one thing, to another some other thing; the unity of consciousness in that which is empirical is not, as regards what is given, necessarily and universally valid.

§ 19

The Logical Form of all Judgments consists in the Objective Unity of the Apperception of the Concepts which they contain

I have never been able to accept the interpretation which logicians give of judgment in general. It is, they declare, the representation of a relation between two concepts. I do B 141   not here dispute with them as to what is defective in this interpretation—that in any case it applies only to *categorical*, not to hypothetical and disjunctive judgments (the two latter containing a relation not of concepts but of judgments), an oversight from which many troublesome consequences have followed.[a] I need only point out that the definition does not determine in what the asserted *relation* consists.

[a] The lengthy doctrine of the four syllogistic figures concerns categorical syllogisms only; and although it is indeed nothing more than an artificial method of securing, through the surreptitious introduction of immediate inferences (*consequentiae immediatae*) among the premisses of a pure syllogism, the appearance that there are more kinds of inference than that of the first figure, this would hardly have met with such remarkable acceptance, had not its authors succeeded in bringing categorical judgments into such ex-

But if I investigate more precisely the relation of the given modes of knowledge[1] in any judgment, and distinguish it, as belonging to the understanding, from the relation according to laws of the reproductive imagination, which has only subjective validity, I find that a judgment is nothing but the manner in which given modes of knowledge are brought to the objective unity of apperception. This is what is intended by the copula[2] 'is'. It is employed to distinguish B 142 the objective unity of given representations from the subjective. It indicates their relation to original apperception, and its *necessary unity*. It holds good even if the judgment is itself empirical, and therefore contingent, as, for example, in the judgment, 'Bodies are heavy'. I do not here assert that these representations *necessarily* belong *to one another* in the empirical intuition, but that they belong to one another *in virtue of the necessary unity* of apperception in the synthesis of intuitions, that is, according to principles of the objective determination of all representations, in so far as knowledge can be acquired by means of these representations—principles which are all derived from the fundamental principle of the transcendental unity of apperception. Only in this way does there arise from this relation a *judgment*, that is, a relation which is *objectively valid*, and so can be adequately distinguished from a relation of the same representations that would have only subjective validity—as when they are connected according to laws of association. In the latter case, all that I could say would be, 'If I support a body, I feel an impression of weight'; I could not say, 'It, the body, is heavy'. Thus to say 'The body is heavy' is not merely to state that the two representations have always been conjoined in my perception, however often that perception be repeated; what we are asserting is that they are combined *in the object*, no matter what the state of the subject may be.

---

clusive respect, as being those to which all others must allow of being reduced—teaching which, as indicated in § 9, is none the less erroneous.

[1] [*Erkenntnisse.*]   [2] [*Verhältniswörtchen.*]

§ 20

All Sensible Intuitions are subject to the Categories, as Conditions under which alone their Manifold can come together in one Consciousness

The manifold given in a sensible intuition is necessarily subject to the original synthetic unity of apperception, because in no other way is the *unity* of intuition possible (§ 17). But that act of understanding by which the manifold of given representations (be they intuitions or concepts) is brought under one apperception, is the logical function of judgment (cf. § 19). All the manifold, therefore, so far as it is given in a single empirical intuition, is *determined* in respect of one of the logical functions of judgment, and is thereby brought into one consciousness. Now the *categories* are just these functions of judgment, in so far as they are employed in determination of the manifold of a given intuition (cf. § 13). Consequently, the manifold in a given intuition is necessarily subject to the categories.

§ 21

Observation

A manifold, contained in an intuition which I call mine, is represented, by means of the synthesis of the understanding, as belonging to the *necessary* unity of self-consciousness; and this is effected by means of the category.[a] This [requirement of a] category therefore shows that the empirical consciousness of a given manifold in a single intuition is subject to a pure self-consciousness *a priori*, just as is empirical intuition to a pure sensible intuition, which likewise takes place *a priori*. Thus in the above proposition a beginning is made of a *deduction* of the pure concepts of understanding; and in this deduction, since the categories have their source in the understanding alone, *independently of sensibility*, I must abstract from the

---

[a] The proof of this rests on the represented *unity of intuition*, by which an object is given. This unity of intuition always includes in itself a synthesis of the manifold given for an intuition, and so already contains the relation of this manifold to the unity of apperception.

mode in which the manifold for an empirical intuition is given, and must direct attention solely to the unity which, in terms of the category, and by means of the understanding, enters into the intuition. In what follows (cf. § 26) it will be shown, from the mode in which the empirical intuition is given in sensibility, that its unity is no other than that which the category B 145 (according to § 20) prescribes to the manifold of a given intuition in general. Only thus, by demonstration of the *a priori* validity of the categories in respect of all objects of our senses, will the purpose of the deduction be fully attained.

But in the above proof there is one feature from which I could not abstract, the feature, namely, that the manifold to be intuited must be given prior to the synthesis of understanding, and independently of it. How this takes place, remains here undetermined. For were I to think an understanding which is itself intuitive (as, for example, a divine understanding which should not represent to itself given objects, but through whose representation the objects should themselves be given or produced), the categories would have no meaning whatsoever in respect of such a mode of knowledge. They are merely rules for an understanding whose whole power consists in thought, consists, that is, in the act whereby it brings the synthesis of a manifold, given to it from elsewhere in intuition, to the unity of apperception—a faculty, therefore, which by itself knows nothing whatsoever, but merely combines and arranges the material of knowledge, that is, the intuition, which must be given to it by the object. This peculiarity of our understanding, that it can produce *a priori* unity of apperception solely by means of the categories, and only by such and so many, is as little capable B 146 of further explanation as why we have just these and no other functions of judgment, or why space and time are the only forms of our possible intuition.

§ 22

The Category has no other Application in Knowledge than to Objects of Experience

To *think* an object and to *know* an object are thus by no means the same thing Knowledge involves two factors: first, the concept, through which an object in general is thought (the category); and secondly, the intuition, through which it is given. For if no intuition could be given corresponding to the concept, the concept would still indeed be a thought, so far as its form is concerned, but would be without any object, and no knowledge of anything would be possible by means of it. So far as I could know, there would be nothing, and could be nothing, to which my thought could be applied. Now, as the Aesthetic has shown, the only intuition possible to us is sensible; consequently, the thought of an object in general, by means of a pure concept of understanding, can become knowledge for us only in so far as the concept is related to objects

B 147 of the senses. Sensible intuition is either pure intuition (space and time) or empirical intuition of that which is immediately represented, through sensation, as actual in space and time. Through the determination of pure intuition we can acquire *a priori* knowledge of objects, as in mathematics, but only in regard to their form, as appearances; whether there can be things which must be intuited in this form, is still left undecided. Mathematical concepts are not, therefore, by themselves knowledge, except on the supposition that there are things which allow of being presented to us only in accordance with the form of that pure sensible intuition. Now *things in space and time* are given only in so far as they are perceptions (that is, representations accompanied by sensation)—therefore only through empirical representation. Consequently, the pure concepts of understanding, even when they are applied to *a priori* intuitions, as in mathematics, yield knowledge only in so far as these intuitions—and therefore indirectly by their means the pure concepts also—can be applied to empirical intuitions. Even, therefore, with the aid of [pure] intuition, the categories do not afford us any knowledge of things; they do so only through their possible application to *empirical intuition*. In other words, they serve only for the possibility of *empirical knowledge*; and such knowledge is what we entitle experience. Our conclusion is therefore this: the categories, as yielding knowledge of *things*, have no kind of application,

B 148 save only in regard to things which may be objects of possible experience.

§ 23

The above proposition is of the greatest importance; for it determines the limits of the employment of the pure concepts of understanding in regard to objects, just as the Transcendental Aesthetic determined the limits of the employment of the pure form of our sensible intuition. Space and time, as conditions under which alone objects can possibly be given to us, are valid no further than for objects of the senses, and therefore only for experience Beyond these limits they represent nothing; for they are only in the senses, and beyond them have no reality. The pure concepts of understanding are free from this limitation, and extend to objects of intuition in general, be the intuition like or unlike ours, if only it be sensible and not intellectual. But this extension of concepts beyond *our* sensible intuition is of no advantage to us. For as concepts of objects they are then empty, and do not even enable us to judge of their objects whether or not they are possible. They are mere forms of thought, without objective reality, since we have no intuition at hand to which the synthetic unity of apperception, which constitutes the whole content of these forms, could be applied, and in being so applied determine an object. Only *our* sensible and empirical intuition can give B 149 to them body and meaning.[1]

If we suppose an object of a *non-sensible* intuition to be given, we can indeed represent it through all the predicates which are implied in the presupposition that it has none of the characteristics proper to sensible intuition; that it is not extended or in space, that its duration is not a time, that no change (succession of determinations in time) is to be met with in it, etc. But there is no proper knowledge if I thus merely indicate what the intuition of an object is *not*, without being able to say what it is that is contained in the intuition. For I have not then shown that the object which I am thinking through my pure concept is even so much as possible, not being in a position to give any intuition corresponding to the concept, and being able only to say that our intuition is not applicable to it. But what has chiefly to be noted is this, that to such a something [in general] not a single one of all the categories could

[1] [*Sinn und Bedeutung*.]

be applied. We could not, for instance, apply to it the concept of substance, meaning something which can exist as subject and never as mere predicate. For save in so far as empirical intuition provides the instance to which to apply it, I do not know whether there can be anything that corresponds to such a form of thought. But of this more hereafter.

B 150

§ 24

The Application of the Categories to Objects of the Senses in General

The pure concepts of understanding relate, through the mere understanding, to objects of intuition in general, whether that intuition be our own or any other, provided only it be sensible. The concepts are, however, for this very reason, mere *forms of thought,* through which alone no determinate object is known. The synthesis or combination of the manifold in them relates only to the unity of apperception, and is thereby the ground of the possibility of *a priori* knowledge, so far as such knowledge rests on the understanding. This synthesis, there-fore, is at once transcendental and also purely intellectual. But since there lies in us a certain form of *a priori* sensible intui-tion, which depends on the receptivity of the faculty of repre-sentation (sensibility), the understanding, as spontaneity, is able to determine inner sense through the manifold of given repre-sentations, in accordance with the synthetic unity of apper-ception, and so to think synthetic unity of the apperception of the manifold of *a priori sensible intuition*—that being the condition under which all objects of our human intuition must necessarily stand. In this way the categories, in themselves mere forms of thought, obtain objective reality, that is, ap-
B 151 plication to objects which can be given us in intuition. These objects, however, are only appearances, for it is solely of appearances that we can have *a priori* intuition.

This synthesis of the manifold of sensible intuition, which is possible and necessary *a priori,* may be entitled *figurative* synthesis (*synthesis speciosa*), to distinguish it from the syn-thesis which is thought in the mere category in respect of the manifold of an intuition in general, and which is entitled combination through the understanding (*synthesis intellectua-*

lis). Both are *transcendental*, not merely as taking place [1] *a priori*, but also as conditioning the possibility of other *a priori* knowledge.

But the figurative synthesis, if it be directed merely to the original synthetic unity of apperception, that is, to the transcendental unity which is thought in the categories, must, in order to be distinguished from the merely intellectual combination, be called the *transcendental synthesis of imagination. Imagination* is the faculty of representing in intuition an object that is *not itself present*. Now since all our intuition is sensible, the imagination, owing to the subjective condition under which alone it can give to the concepts of understanding a corresponding intuition, belongs to *sensibility*. But inasmuch as its synthesis is an expression of spontaneity, which is determinative and not, like sense, determinable merely, and which is therefore able to determine sense *a priori* in respect of its form in accordance with the unity of apperception, imagination is to that extent a faculty which determines the sensibility *a priori*; and its synthesis of intuitions, conforming as it does to the *categories*, must be the transcendental synthesis of *imagination*. This synthesis is an action [2] of the understanding on the sensibility; and is its first application—and thereby the ground of all its other applications—to the objects of our possible intuition. As figurative, it is distinguished from the intellectual synthesis, which is carried out by the understanding alone, without the aid of the imagination. In so far as imagination is spontaneity, I sometimes also entitle it the *productive* imagination, to distinguish it from the *reproductive* imagination, whose synthesis is entirely subject to empirical laws, the laws, namely, of association, and which therefore contributes nothing to the explanation of the possibility of *a priori* knowledge. The reproductive synthesis falls within the domain, not of transcendental philosophy, but of psychology.

B 152

*   *   *

This is a suitable place for explaining the paradox which must have been obvious to everyone in our exposition of the

---

[1] [Reading, with Erdmann, *stattfinden* for *vorgehen*.]
[2] [*Wirkung*.]

form of inner sense (§ 6): namely, that this sense represents
B 153 to consciousness even our own selves only as we appear to
ourselves, not as we are in ourselves. For we intuit ourselves
only as we are inwardly *affected*, and this would seem to be
contradictory, since we should then have to be in a passive
relation [of active affection] to ourselves. It is to avoid this
contradiction that in systems of psychology *inner sense*,
which we have carefully distinguished from the faculty
of *apperception*, is commonly regarded as being identical
with it.

What determines inner sense is the understanding and its
original power of combining the manifold of intuition, that is,
of bringing it under an apperception, upon which the possibility of understanding itself rests. Now the understanding
in us men is not itself a faculty of intuitions, and cannot,
even if intuitions be given[1] in sensibility, take them up *into
itself* in such manner as to combine them as the manifold of
its *own* intuition. Its synthesis, therefore, if the synthesis be
viewed by itself alone, is nothing but the unity of the act,
of which, as an act, it is conscious to itself, even without
[the aid of] sensibility, but through which it is yet able to
determine the sensibility. The understanding, that is to say,
in respect of the manifold which may be given to it in accordance with the form of sensible intuition, is able to determine sensibility inwardly. Thus the understanding, under
the title of a *transcendental synthesis of imagination*, performs
this act upon the *passive* subject, whose *faculty* it is, and we
B 154 are therefore justified in saying that inner sense is affected
thereby. Apperception and its synthetic unity is, indeed, very
far from being identical with inner sense. The former, as the
source of all *combination*, applies to the manifold of *intuitions in general*, and in the guise of[2] the *categories*, prior
to all sensible intuition, to *objects in general*. Inner sense,
on the other hand, contains the mere form of intuition, but
without combination of the manifold in it, and therefore so
far contains no *determinate* intuition, which is possible only
through the consciousness of the determination of the manifold
by the transcendental act of imagination (synthetic influence

---

[1] [Reading, with Vaihinger, *wären* for *wäre*.]
[2] [*unter dem Namen*. And reading, with Görland, *und unter* for *unter*.]

of the understanding upon inner sense), which I have entitled figurative synthesis.

This we can always perceive in ourselves. We cannot think a line without *drawing* it in thought, or a circle without *describing* it. We cannot represent the three dimensions of space save by *setting* three lines at right angles to one another from the same point. Even time itself we cannot represent, save in so far as we attend, in the *drawing* of a straight line (which has to serve as the outer figurative representation of time), merely to the act of the synthesis of the manifold whereby we successively determine inner sense, and in so doing attend to the succession of this determination in inner sense. Motion, as an act of the subject (not as a determination of an object),[a] and therefore the synthesis of the manifold in space, first produces the concept of succession—if we abstract from this manifold and attend solely to the act through which we determine the *inner* sense according to its form. The understanding does not, therefore, find in inner sense such a combination of the manifold, but *produces* it, in that it *affects* that sense.

How the 'I' that thinks[1] can be distinct from the 'I' that intuits itself (for I can represent still other modes of intuition as at least possible), and yet, as being the same subject, can be identical with the latter; and how, therefore, I can say: "I, as intelligence and *thinking*[2] subject, know myself as an object that is *thought*,[3] in so far as I am given to myself [as something other or] beyond that [I] which is [given to myself] in intuition, and yet know myself, like other phenomena, only as I appear to myself, not as I am to the understanding"— these are questions that raise no greater nor less difficulty than how I can be an object to myself at all, and, more particularly, an object of intuition and of inner perceptions

B 155

B 156

[a] Motion of an object in space does not belong to a pure science, and consequently not to geometry. For the fact that something is movable cannot be known *a priori*, but only through experience. Motion, however, considered as the describing of a space, is a pure act of the successive synthesis of the manifold in outer intuition in general by means of the productive imagination, and belongs not only to geometry, but even to transcendental philosophy.

[1] [Reading, with Vaihinger, *das Ich, das denkt* for *das Ich, der ich denke.*]
[2] [*denkend.*]
[3] [*gedachtes.*]

Indeed, that this is how it must be, is easily shown—if we admit that space is merely a pure form of the appearances of outer sense—by the fact that we cannot obtain for ourselves a representation of time, which is not an object of outer intuition, except under the image of a line, which we draw, and that by this mode of depicting it alone could we know the singleness[1] of its dimension; and similarly by the fact that for all inner perceptions we must derive the determination of lengths of time or of points of time from the changes which are exhibited to us in outer things, and that the determinations of inner sense have therefore to be arranged as appearances in time in precisely the same manner in which we arrange those of outer sense in space. If, then, as regards the latter, we admit that we know objects only in so far as we are externally affected, we must also recognise, as regards inner sense, that by means of it we intuit ourselves only as we are inwardly affected *by ourselves*; in other words, that, so far as inner intuition is concerned, we know our own subject only as appearance, not as it is in itself.[a]

B 157

§ 25

On the other hand, in the transcendental synthesis of the manifold of representations in general, and therefore in the synthetic original unity of apperception, I am conscious of myself, not as I appear to myself, nor as I am in myself, but only that I am. This *representation* is a *thought*, not an *intuition*. Now in order to *know* ourselves, there is required in addition to the act of thought, which brings the manifold of every possible intuition to the unity of apperception, a determinate mode of intuition, whereby this manifold is given; it therefore follows that although my existence is not indeed

[a] I do not see why so much difficulty should be found in admitting that our inner sense is affected by ourselves. Such affection finds
B 157 exemplification in each and every act of *attention*. In every act of attention the understanding determines inner sense, in accordance with the combination which it thinks, to that inner intuition which corresponds to the manifold in the synthesis of the understanding. How much the mind is usually thereby affected, everyone will be able to perceive in himself.

[1] [*Einheit.*]

appearance (still less mere illusion), the determination of my existence^a can take place only in conformity with the form of B 158 inner sense, according to the special mode in which the manifold, which I combine, is given in inner intuition. Accordingly I have no *knowledge* of myself as I am but merely as I appear to myself. The consciousness of self is thus very far from being a knowledge of the self, notwithstanding all the categories which [are being employed to] constitute the thought of an *object in general*, through combination of the manifold in one apperception. Just as for knowledge of an object distinct from me I require, besides the thought of an object in general (in the category), an intuition by which I determine that general concept, so for knowledge of myself I require, besides the consciousness, that is, besides the thought of myself, an intuition of the manifold in me, by which I determine this thought. I exist as an intelligence which is conscious solely of its power of combination; but in respect of the manifold B 159 which it has to combine I am subjected to a limiting condition (entitled inner sense), namely, that this combination can be made intuitable only according to relations of time, which lie entirely outside the concepts of understanding, strictly regarded. Such an intelligence, therefore, can know itself only as it appears to itself in respect of an intuition which is not intellectual and cannot be given by the understanding itself, not as it would know itself if its *intuition* were intellectual.

^a The 'I think' expresses the act of determining my existence. Existence is already given thereby, but the mode in which I am to determine this existence, that is, the manifold belonging to it, is not thereby given. In order that it be given, self-intuition is required; and such intuition is conditioned by a given *a priori* form, namely, time, which is sensible and belongs to the receptivity of the determinable [in me]. Now since I do not have another self-intuition B 158 which gives the *determining* in me (I am conscious only of the spontaneity of it) prior to the act of *determination*,[1] as time does in the case of the determinable, I cannot determine my existence as that of a self-active being; all that I can do is to represent to myself the spontaneity of my thought, that is, of the determination; and my existence is still only determinable sensibly, that is, as the existence of an appearance. But it is owing to this spontaneity that I entitle myself an *intelligence*.

[1] [*vor dem Aktus des Bestimmens.*]

§ 26

Transcendental Deduction of the Universally Possible Employment in Experience of the Pure Concepts of the Understanding

In the *metaphysical deduction* the *a priori* origin of the categories has been proved through their complete agreement with the general logical functions of thought; in the *transcendental deduction* we have shown their possibility as *a priori* modes of knowledge of objects of an intuition in general (cf. §§ 20, 21). We have now to explain the possibility of knowing *a priori*, by means of *categories*, whatever objects may *present themselves to our senses*, not indeed in respect of the form of their intuition, but in respect of the laws of their combination, and so, as it were, of prescribing laws to
B 160   nature, and even of making nature possible. For unless the categories discharged this function, there could be no explaining why everything that can be presented to our senses must be subject to laws which have their origin *a priori* in the understanding alone.

First of all, I may draw attention to the fact that by *synthesis of apprehension* I understand that combination of the manifold in an empirical intuition, whereby perception, that is, empirical consciousness of the intuition (as appearance), is possible.

In the representations of space and time we have *a priori forms* of outer and inner sensible intuition; and to these the synthesis of apprehension of the manifold of appearance must always conform, because in no other way can the synthesis take place at all. But space and time are represented *a priori* not merely as *forms* of sensible intuition, but as themselves *intuitions* which contain a manifold [of their own], and therefore are represented with the determination of the *unity* of this manifold (*vide* the Transcendental Aesthetic).[a] Thus

[a] Space, represented as *object* (as we are required to do in geometry), contains more than mere form of intuition; it also contains *combination* of the manifold, given according to the form of sensibility, in an *intuitive* representation, so that the *form of intuition* gives only a manifold, the *formal intuition* gives unity of representation. In the Aesthetic I have treated this unity as belonging merely

unity of the synthesis of the manifold, without or within us,   B 161
and consequently also a *combination* to which everything that
is to be represented as determined in space or in time must
conform, is given *a priori* as the condition of the synthesis
of all *apprehension*—not indeed in, but with these intuitions.
This synthetic unity can be no other than the unity of the
combination of the manifold of a given *intuition in general*
in an original[1] consciousness, in accordance with the categories, in so far as the combination is applied to our *sensible
intuition*. All synthesis, therefore, even that which renders
perception possible, is subject to the categories; and since
experience is knowledge by means of connected perceptions,
the categories are conditions of the possibility of experience,
and are therefore valid *a priori* for all objects of experience.

*   *   *

When, for instance, by apprehension[2] of the manifold of a   B 162
house I make the empirical intuition of it into a perception,
the *necessary unity* of space and of outer sensible intuition in
general lies at the basis of my apprehension, and I draw as it
were the outline of the house in conformity with this synthetic
unity of the manifold in space. But if I abstract from the form
of space, this same synthetic unity has its seat in the understanding, and is the category of the synthesis of the homogeneous in an intuition in general, that is, the category of *quantity*.
To this category, therefore, the synthesis of apprehension, that
is to say, the perception, must completely conform.[b]

---

to sensibility, simply in order to emphasise that it precedes any con-   B 161
cept, although, as a matter of fact, it presupposes a synthesis which
does not belong to the senses but through which all concepts of
space and time first become possible. For since by its means (in that
the understanding determines the sensibility) space and time are
first *given* as intuitions, the unity of this *a priori* intuition belongs to
space and time, and not to the concept of the understanding (cf.
§ 24).
    [b] In this manner it is proved that the synthesis of apprehension,
which is empirical, must necessarily be in conformity with the synthesis of apperception, which is intellectual and is contained in the
category completely *a priori*. It is one and the same spontaneity,

[1] [*ursprünglichen*.]
[g] [Changed, in 4th edition, to *apperception*.]

When, to take another example, I perceive the freezing of water, I apprehend two states, fluidity and solidity, and these as standing to one another in a relation of time. But in time, B 163 which I place at the basis of the appearance [in so far] as [it is] inner *intuition*, I necessarily represent to myself synthetic *unity* of the manifold, without which that relation of time could not be given in an intuition as being *determined* in respect of time-sequence. Now this synthetic unity, as a condition *a priori* under which I combine the manifold of an *intuition in general*, is—if I abstract from the constant form of *my* inner intuition, namely, time—the category of *cause*, by means of which, when I apply it to my sensibility, I determine *everything that happens* in accordance with the relation which it prescribes, and I do so *in time in general*. Thus my apprehension of such an event, and therefore the event itself, considered as a possible perception, is subject to the concept of the *relation* of *effects* and *causes*, and so in all other cases.

Categories are concepts which prescribe laws *a priori* to appearances, and therefore to nature, the sum of all appearances (*natura materialiter spectata*). The question therefore arises, how it can be conceivable that nature should have to proceed in accordance with categories which yet are not derived from it, and do not model themselves upon its pattern; that is, how they can determine *a priori* the combination of the manifold of nature, while yet they are not derived from it. The solution of this seeming enigma is as follows.

B 164   That the *laws* of appearances in nature must agree with the understanding and its *a priori* form, that is, with its faculty of *combining* the manifold in general, is no more surprising than that the appearances themselves must agree with the form of *a priori* sensible intuition. For just as appearances do not exist in themselves but only relatively to the subject in which, so far as it has senses, they inhere, so the laws do not exist in the appearances but only relatively to this same being, so far as it has understanding. Things in themselves would necessarily,

---

which in the one case, under the title of imagination, and in the other case, under the title of understanding, brings combination into the manifold of intuition.

apart from any understanding that knows them, conform to laws of their own. But appearances are only representations of things which are unknown as regards what they may be in themselves. As mere representations, they are subject to no law of connection save that which the connecting faculty prescribes. Now it is imagination that connects the manifold of sensible intuition; and imagination is dependent for the unity of its intellectual synthesis upon the understanding, and for the manifoldness of its apprehension upon sensibility. All possible perception is thus dependent upon synthesis of apprehension, and this empirical synthesis in turn upon transcendental synthesis, and therefore upon the categories. Consequently, all possible perceptions, and therefore everything that can come to empirical consciousness, that is, all appearances of nature, must, so far as their connection is concerned, be subject to the categories. Nature, considered merely as nature in general, is dependent upon these categories as the original ground of its necessary conformity to law (*natura formaliter spectata*). Pure understanding is not, however, in a position, through mere categories, to prescribe to appearances any *a priori* laws other than those which are involved in a *nature in general*, that is, in the conformity to law of all appearances in space and time. Special laws, as concerning those appearances which are empirically determined, cannot in their specific character be *derived* from the categories, although they are one and all subject to them. To obtain any knowledge whatsoever of these special laws, we must resort to experience; but it is the *a priori* laws that alone can instruct us in regard to experience in general, and as to what it is that can be known as an object of experience.

B 165

§ 27

Outcome of this Deduction of the Concepts of Understanding

We cannot think an object save through categories; we cannot *know* an object so thought save through intuitions corresponding to these concepts. Now all our intuitions are sensible; and this knowledge, in so far as its object is given, is empirical. But empirical knowledge is experience. *Conse-*

B 166

quently, there can be no a priori *knowledge, except of objects of possible experience.*[a]

But although this knowledge is limited to objects of experience, it is not therefore all derived from experience. The pure intuitions [of receptivity] and the pure concepts of understanding are elements in knowledge, and both are found in us *a priori*. There are only two ways in which we can account for a *necessary* agreement of experience with the concepts of its objects: either experience makes these concepts possible or these concepts make experience possible. The former supposition B 167 does not hold in respect of the categories (nor of pure sensible intuition); for since they are *a priori* concepts, and therefore independent of experience, the ascription to them of an empirical origin would be a sort of *generatio aequivoca*. There remains, therefore, only the second supposition—a system, as it were, of the *epigenesis* of pure reason—namely, that the categories contain, on the side of the understanding, the grounds of the possibility of all experience in general. How they make experience possible, and what are the principles of the possibility of experience that they supply in their application to appearances, will be shown more fully in the following chapter on the transcendental employment of the faculty of judgment.

A middle course may be proposed between the two above mentioned, namely, that the categories are neither *self-thought*[1] first principles *a priori* of our knowledge nor derived from experience, but subjective dispositions of thought, implanted in us from the first moment of our existence, and so ordered by our Creator that their employment is in complete harmony with the laws of nature in accordance with which experience

[a] Lest my readers should stumble at the alarming evil consequences which may over-hastily be inferred from this statement, I may remind them that *for thought* the categories are not limited by the conditions of our sensible intuition, but have an unlimited field. It is only the *knowledge* of that which we think, the determining of the object, that requires intuition. In the absence of intuition, the thought of the object may still have its true and useful consequences, as regards the subject's *employment of reason*. The use of reason is not always directed to the determination of the object, that is, to knowledge, but also to the determination of the subject and of its volition —a use which cannot therefore be here dealt with.

[1] [*selbstgedachte.*]

proceeds—a kind of *preformation-system* of pure reason. Apart, however, from the objection that on such an hypothesis we can set no limit to the assumption of predetermined dispositions to future judgments, there is this decisive objection against the suggested middle course, that the *necessity*   B 168 of the categories, which belongs to their very conception, would then have to be sacrificed. The concept of cause, for instance, which expresses the necessity of an event under a presupposed condition, would be false if it rested only on an arbitrary subjective necessity, implanted in us, of connecting certain empirical representations according to the rule of causal relation. I would not then be able to say that the effect is connected with the cause in the object, that is to say, necessarily, but only that I am so constituted that I cannot think this representation otherwise than as thus connected. This is exactly what the sceptic most desires. For if this be the situation, all our insight, resting on the supposed objective validity of our judgments, is nothing but sheer illusion; nor would there be wanting people who would refuse to admit this subjective necessity, a necessity which can only be felt. Certainly a man cannot dispute with anyone regarding that which depends merely on the mode in which he is himself organised.

Brief Outline of this Deduction

The deduction is the exposition[1] of the pure concepts of the understanding, and therewith of all theoretical *a priori* knowledge, as principles of the possibility of experience—the principles being here taken as the *determination* of appearances in space and time *in general*, and this determination, in turn, as   B 169 ultimately following from the *original* synthetic unity of apperception, as the form of the understanding in its relation to space and time, the original forms of sensibility.

*   *   *

I consider the division by numbered paragraphs as necessary up to this point, because thus far we have had to treat of the elementary concepts. We have now to give an account of their employment, and the exposition may therefore proceed in continuous fashion, without such numbering.

[1] [*Darstellung.*]

TRANSCENDENTAL ANALYTIC

Book II

THE ANALYTIC OF PRINCIPLES

GENERAL logic is constructed upon a ground plan which exactly coincides with the division of the higher faculties of knowledge. These are: *understanding, judgment,*[1] and *reason.*

A 131   In accordance with the functions and order of these mental powers, which in current speech are comprehended under the general title of understanding, logic in its analytic deals with *concepts, judgments,* and *inferences.*

B 170   Since this merely formal logic abstracts from all content of knowledge, whether pure or empirical, and deals solely with the form of thought in general (that is, of discursive knowledge), it can comprehend the canon of reason in its analytic portion. For the form of reason possesses its established rules, which can be discovered *a priori,* simply by analysing the actions of reason into their components,[2] without our requiring to take account of the special nature of the knowledge involved.

As transcendental logic is limited to a certain determinate content, namely, to the content of those modes of knowledge which are pure and *a priori,* it cannot follow general logic in this division. For the transcendental employment of reason is not, it would seem, objectively valid, and consequently does not belong to the *logic of truth, i.e.* to the Analytic. As a *logic of illusion,* it calls for separate location in the scholastic edifice, under the title of Transcendental Dialectic.

---

[1] [Here, and throughout the subsequent sections, judgment, when thus used in the singular, is to be understood as a translation of the term *Urteilskraft,* and so as signifying 'faculty of judgment'.]
[2] [*in ihre Momente.*].

Understanding and judgment find, therefore, in transcendental logic their canon of objectively valid and correct employment; they belong to its analytic portion. Reason, on the other hand, in its endeavours to determine something *a priori* in regard to objects and so to extend knowledge beyond the limits of possible experience, is altogether *dialectical*. Its illusory assertions cannot find place in a canon such as the analytic is intended to contain.

B 171

A 132

The *Analytic of Principles* will therefore be a canon solely for *judgment*, instructing it how to apply to appearances the concepts of understanding, which contain the condition for *a priori* rules. For this reason, while adopting as my theme the *principles of the understanding*, strictly so called, I shall employ the title *doctrine of judgment*, as more accurately indicating the nature of our task.

INTRODUCTION

TRANSCENDENTAL JUDGMENT IN GENERAL

If understanding in general is to be viewed as the faculty of rules, judgment will be the faculty of subsuming under rules; that is, of distinguishing whether something does or does not stand under a given rule (*casus datae legis*). General logic contains, and can contain, no rules for judgment. For since general logic abstracts from all content of knowledge, the sole task that remains to it is to give an analytical exposition of the form of knowledge [as expressed] in concepts, in judgments, and in inferences, and so to obtain formal rules for all employment of understanding. If it sought to give general instructions how we are to subsume under these rules, that is, to distinguish whether something does or does not come under them, that could only be by means of another rule. This in turn, for the very reason that it is a rule, again demands guidance from judgment. And thus it appears that, though understanding is capable of being instructed, and of being equipped with rules, judgment is a peculiar talent which can be practised only, and cannot be taught. It is the specific quality of so-called mother-wit; and its lack no school can make good. For although an abundance of rules borrowed from the insight of others may

{ A 133
{ B 172

indeed be proffered to, and as it were grafted upon, a limited understanding, the power of rightly employing them must belong to the learner himself; and in the absence of such a natural gift no rule that may be prescribed to him for this pur- pose can ensure against misuse.[a] A physician, a judge, or a ruler may have at command many excellent pathological, legal, or political rules, even to the degree that he may become a profound teacher of them, and yet, none the less, may easily stumble in their application. For, although admirable in understanding, he may be wanting in natural power of judgment. He may comprehend the universal *in abstracto*, and yet not be able to distinguish whether a case *in concreto* comes under it. Or the error may be due to his not having received, through examples and actual practice, adequate training for this particular act of judgment. Such sharpening of the judgment is indeed the one great benefit of examples. Correctness and precision of intellectual insight, on the other hand, they more usually somewhat impair. For only very seldom do they adequately fulfil the requirements of the rule (as *casus in terminis*). Besides, they often weaken that effort which is required of the understanding to comprehend properly the rules in their universality, in independence of the particular circumstances of experience, and so accustom us to use rules rather as formulas than as principles. Examples are thus the go-cart of judgment; and those who are lacking in the natural talent can never dispense with them.

But although general logic can supply no rules for judgment, the situation is entirely different in transcendental logic. The latter would seem to have as its peculiar task the correcting and securing of judgment, by means of determinate rules, in the use of the pure understanding. For as a doctrine, that is,

A 134
B 173

B 174

A 135

---

[a] Deficiency in judgment is just what is ordinarily called stupidity, and for such a failing there is no remedy. An obtuse or narrow-minded person to whom nothing is wanting save a proper degree of understanding and the concepts appropriate thereto, may indeed be trained through study, even to the extent of becoming learned. But as such people are commonly still lacking in judgment (*secunda Petri*), it is not unusual to meet learned men who in the application of their scientific knowledge betray that original want, which can never be made good.

B 173

as an attempt to enlarge the sphere of the understanding in the field of pure *a priori* knowledge, philosophy is by no means necessary, and is indeed ill-suited for any such purpose, since in all attempts hitherto made, little or no ground has been won. On the other hand, if what is designed be a critique to guard against errors of judgment (*lapsus judicii*) in the employment of the few pure concepts of understanding that we possess, the task, merely negative as its advantages must then be, is one to which philosophy is called upon to devote all its resources of acuteness and penetration.

Transcendental philosophy has the peculiarity that besides the rule (or rather the universal condition of rules), which is given in the pure concept of understanding, it can also specify *a priori* the instance to which the rule[1] is to be applied. The B 175 advantage which in this respect it possesses over all other didactical sciences, with the exception of mathematics, is due to the fact that it deals with concepts which have to relate to objects *a priori*, and the objective validity of which cannot therefore be demonstrated *a posteriori*, since that would mean A 136 the complete ignoring[2] of their peculiar dignity. It must formulate by means of universal but sufficient marks the conditions under which objects can be given in harmony with these concepts. Otherwise the concepts would be void of all content, and therefore mere logical forms, not pure concepts of the understanding.

This transcendental doctrine of judgment will consist of two chapters. The first will treat of the sensible condition under which alone pure concepts of understanding can be employed, that is, of the schematism of pure understanding. The second will deal with the synthetic judgments which under these conditions follow *a priori* from pure concepts of understanding, and which lie *a priori* at the foundation of all other modes of knowledge—that is, with the principles of pure understanding.

[1] [Reading, with Erdmann, *soll* for *sollen*.]
[2] [Reading, with Vaihinger, *unberücksichtigt* for *unberührt*.]

TRANSCENDENTAL DOCTRINE OF JUDGMENT

(OR ANALYTIC OF PRINCIPLES)

CHAPTER I

THE SCHEMATISM OF THE PURE CONCEPTS OF
UNDERSTANDING

IN all subsumptions of an object under a concept the representation of the object must be *homogeneous* with the concept; in other words, the concept must contain something which is represented in the object that is to be subsumed under it. This, in fact, is what is meant by the expression, 'an object is contained under a concept'. Thus the empirical concept of a *plate* is homogeneous with the pure geometrical concept of a *circle*. The roundness which is thought in the latter can be intuited in the former.[1]

But pure concepts of understanding being quite heterogeneous from empirical intuitions, and indeed from all sensible intuitions, can never be met with in any intuition.

B 177⎱
A 138⎰ For no one will say that a category, such as that of causality, can be intuited through sense and is itself contained in appearance. How, then, is the *subsumption* of intuitions under pure concepts, the *application* of a category to appearances, possible? A transcendental doctrine of judgment is necessary just because of this natural and important question. We must be able to show how pure concepts can be applicable to appearances. In none of the other sciences is this necessary. For since in these sciences the concepts through which the object is thought in [its] general [aspects] are not so utterly distinct and heterogeneous from those which represent it *in concreto*,

---

[1] [Reading, with Vaihinger, *in dem letzteren* . . . *im ersteren* for *in dem ersteren* . . . *im letzteren*.]

as given, no special discussion of the applicability of the[1]
former to the latter is required.

Obviously there must be some third thing, which is homogeneous on the one hand with the category, and on the other
hand with the appearance, and which thus makes the application of the former to the latter possible. This mediating
representation must be pure, that is, void of all empirical
content, and yet at the same time, while it must in one
respect be *intellectual*, it must in another be *sensible*. Such a
representation is the *transcendental schema*.

The concept of understanding contains pure synthetic
unity of the manifold in general. Time, as the formal condition of the manifold of inner sense, and therefore of the
connection of all representations, contains an *a priori* manifold
in pure intuition. Now a transcendental determination of
time is so far homogeneous with the category, which constitutes its unity, in that it is universal and rests upon an B 178
a priori rule. But, on the other hand, it is so far homogeneous A 139
with appearance, in that time is contained in every empirical
representation of the manifold. Thus an application of the
category to appearances becomes possible by means of the
transcendental determination of time, which, as the schema
of the concepts of understanding, mediates the subsumption
of the appearances under the category.

After what has been proved in the deduction of the categories, no one, I trust, will remain undecided in regard to
the question whether these pure concepts of understanding
are of merely empirical or also of transcendental employment; that is, whether as conditions of a possible experience
they relate *a priori* solely to appearances, or whether, as
conditions of the possibility of things in general, they can be
extended to objects in themselves, without any restriction
to our sensibility. For we have seen that concepts are altogether impossible,[2] and can have no meaning, if no object
is given for them, or at least for the elements of which they
are composed. They cannot, therefore, be viewed as applicable to things in themselves, independent of all question
as to whether and how these may be given to us. We

[1] [Reading, with Vorländer, *der* for *des*.]
[2] [Altered by Kant (*Nachträge* lviii) to: "are for us without meaning."]

have also proved that the only manner in which objects
can be given to us is by modification of our sensibility; and
B 179 finally, that pure *a priori* concepts, in addition to the function
A 140 of understanding expressed in the category, must contain
a priori certain formal conditions of sensibility, namely, those
of inner sense. These conditions of sensibility constitute the
universal condition under which alone the category can be
applied to any object. This formal and pure condition of
sensibility to which the employment of the concept of understanding is restricted, we shall entitle the *schema* of the
concept. The procedure of understanding in these schemata
we shall entitle the *schematism* of pure understanding.

The schema is in itself always a product of imagination.
Since, however, the synthesis of imagination aims at no
special intuition, but only at unity in the determination of
sensibility, the schema has to be distinguished from the image.
If five points be set alongside one another, thus, ..., I
have an image of the number five. But if, on the other hand,
I think only a number in general, whether it be five or a
hundred, this thought is rather the representation of a method
whereby a multiplicity, for instance a thousand, may be represented in an image in conformity with a certain concept,
than the image itself. For with such a number as a thousand
the image can hardly be surveyed and compared with the
concept. This representation of a universal procedure of
B 180 imagination in providing an image for a concept, I entitle the
schema of this concept.

Indeed it is schemata, not images of objects, which underlie
A 141 our pure sensible concepts. No image could ever be adequate
to the concept of a triangle in general. It would never attain
that universality of the concept which renders it valid of all
triangles, whether right-angled, obtuse-angled, or acute-
angled; it would always be limited to a part only of this
sphere. The schema of the triangle can exist nowhere but in
thought. It is a rule of synthesis of the imagination, in respect
to pure figures in space. Still less is an object of experience or
its image ever adequate to the empirical concept; for this latter
always stands in immediate relation to the schema of imagination, as a rule for the determination of our intuition, in accordance with some specific universal concept. The concept 'dog'

signifies a rule according to which my imagination can delineate the figure of a four-footed animal in a general manner, without limitation to any single determinate figure such as experience, or any possible image that I can represent *in concreto*, actually presents. This schematism of our understanding, in its application to appearances and their mere form, is an art concealed in the depths of the human soul, whose real modes of activity nature is hardly likely ever B 181 to allow us to discover, and to have open to our gaze. This much only we can assert: the *image* is a product of the empirical faculty of reproductive[1] imagination; the *schema* of sensible concepts, such as of figures in space, is a product and, A 142 as it were, a monogram, of pure *a priori* imagination, through which, and in accordance with which, images themselves first become possible. These images can be connected with the concept only by means of the schema to which they belong.[2] In themselves they are never completely congruent with the concept. On the other hand, the schema of a *pure* concept of understanding can never be brought into any image whatsoever. It is simply the pure synthesis, determined by a rule of that unity, in accordance with concepts, to which the category gives expression. It is a transcendental product of imagination, a product which concerns the determination of inner sense in general according to conditions of its form (time), in respect of all representations, so far as these representations are to be connected *a priori* in one concept in conformity with the unity of apperception.

That we may not be further delayed by a dry and tedious analysis of the conditions demanded by transcendental schemata of the pure concepts of understanding in general, we shall now expound them according to the order of the categories and in connection with them.

The pure image of all magnitudes (*quantorum*) for[3] outer B 182 sense is space; that of all objects of the senses in general is time. But the pure *schema* of magnitude (*quantitatis*), as a concept of the understanding, is *number*, a representation which comprises the successive addition of homogeneous

---

[1] [Reading, with Vaihinger, *reproduktiven* for *produktiven*.]
[2] [*welches sie bezeichnen.*]
[3] [Reading, with Grillo, *für den* for *vor dem.*]

A 143   units. Number is therefore simply the unity of the synthesis of the manifold of a homogeneous intuition in general, a unity due to my generating time itself in the apprehension of the intuition.

Reality, in the pure concept of understanding, is that which corresponds to a sensation in general; it is that, therefore, the concept of which in itself points to being (in time). Negation is that the concept of which represents not-being (in time). The opposition of these two thus rests upon the distinction of one and the same time as filled and as empty. Since time is merely the form of intuition, and so of objects as appearances, that in the objects which corresponds to sensation is not[1] the transcendental matter of all objects as things in themselves (thinghood,[2] reality). Now every sensation has a degree or magnitude whereby, in respect of its representation of an object otherwise remaining the same, it can fill out one and the same time, that is, occupy inner sense more or less completely, down to its cessation in nothingness ($=0=negatio$). There therefore exists a relation and connection between reality and negation, or rather a

B 183   transition from the one to the other, which makes every reality representable as a quantum. The schema of a reality, as the quantity of something in so far as it fills time, is just this continuous and uniform production of that reality in time as we successively descend from a sensation which has a certain degree to its vanishing point, or progressively ascend from its negation to some magnitude of it.

The schema of substance is permanence of the real in time, that is, the representation of the real as a substrate of empirical determination of time in general, and so as abiding while all else changes. (The existence of what is transitory[3] passes away in time but not time itself. To time, itself non-transitory[4] and abiding, there corresponds in the [field of] appearance what is non-transitory in its existence, that is, substance. Only in [relation to] substance can the succession and coexistence of appearances be determined in time.)

---

[1] [Reading, with Wille, *nicht die* for *die*. This seems, on the whole, preferable to taking, with Erdmann, the second part of the sentence as: "that in the objects [as things in themselves] which corresponds to sensation is the transcendental matter . . ."]

[2] [*Sachheit.*]   [3] [*des Wandelbaren.*]   [4] [*unwandelbar.*]

The schema of cause,[1] and of the causality[2] of a thing in A 144
general, is the real upon which, whenever posited, something
else always follows. It consists, therefore, in the succession
of the manifold, in so far as that succession is subject to a
rule.

The schema of community or reciprocity, the reciprocal
causality of substances in respect of their accidents, is the coexistence, according to a universal rule, of the determinations B 184
of the one substance with those of the other.

The schema of possibility is the agreement of the synthesis
of different representations with the conditions of time in
general. Opposites, for instance, cannot exist in the same thing
at the same time, but only the one after the other. The schema
is therefore the determination of the representation of a thing
at some time or other.

The schema of actuality is existence in some determinate A 145
time.

The schema of necessity is existence of an object at all
times.

We thus find that the schema of each category contains and
makes capable of representation only a determination of time.[3]
The schema of magnitude is the generation (synthesis) of
time itself in the successive apprehension of an object. The
schema of quality is the synthesis of sensation or perception
with the representation of time; it is the filling of time. The
schema of relation is the connecting of perceptions with one
another at all times according to a rule of time-determination.
Finally the schema of modality and of its categories is time
itself as the correlate of the determination whether and how
an object belongs to time. The schemata are thus nothing
but *a priori* determinations of time in accordance with rules.
These rules relate in the order of the categories to the *time-
series*, the *time-content*, the *time-order*, and lastly to the *scope
of time*[4] in respect of all possible objects. B 185

It is evident, therefore, that what the schematism of understanding effects by means of the transcendental synthesis of

---

1 [*Ursache.*]   2 [*Kausalität.*]
3 [Reading, with Adickes, *einer jeden Kategorie nur eine Zeitbestimmung,
als* for *einer jeden Kategorie, als.*]
4 [*Zeitinbegriff.*]

imagination is simply the unity of all the manifold of intuition in inner sense, and so indirectly the unity of apperception which as a function corresponds to the receptivity of inner sense.

A 146 The schemata of the pure concepts of understanding are thus the true and sole conditions under which these concepts obtain relation to objects and so possess *significance*. In the end, therefore, the categories have no other possible employment than the empirical. As the grounds of an *a priori* necessary unity that has its source in the necessary combination of all consciousness in one original apperception, they serve only to subordinate appearances to universal rules of synthesis, and thus to fit them for thoroughgoing connection in one experience.

All our knowledge falls within the bounds of possible experience, and just in this universal relation to possible experience consists that transcendental truth which precedes all empirical truth and makes it possible.

But it is also evident that although the schemata of sensi-
B 186 bility first realise the categories, they at the same time restrict them, that is, limit them to conditions which lie outside the understanding, and are due to sensibility. The schema is, properly, only the phenomenon, or sensible concept, of an object in agreement with the category. (Numerus *est quantitas phaeno-menon*, sensatio *realitas phaenomenon*, constans et perdurabile rerum *substantia phaenomenon*, aeternitas *necessitas phaeno-menon*,[1] etc.) If we omit a restricting condition, we would seem
A 147 to extend the scope of the concept that was previously limited. Arguing from this assumed fact, we conclude that the categories in their pure significance, apart from all conditions of sensibility, ought to apply to things in general, *as they are*, and not, like the schemata, represent them only *as they appear*. They ought, we conclude, to possess a meaning independent of all schemata, and of much wider application. Now there certainly does remain in the pure concepts of understanding, even after elimination of every sensible condition, a meaning; but it is purely logical, signifying only the bare unity of the representations. The pure concepts can find no object, and so

---

[1] In the text the words *et perdurabile rerum* are in italics, and there are commas after aeternitas and *necessitas*. I also read, with Erdmann, *phaenomenon* for *phaenomena*.]

can acquire no meaning which might yield a concept[1] of some object. Substance, for instance, when the sensible determination of permanence is omitted, would mean simply a something which can be thought only as subject, never as a predicate of something else. Such a representation I can put to no use, for it tells me nothing as to the nature of that which is thus to B 187 be viewed as a primary subject. The categories, therefore, without schemata, are merely functions of the understanding for concepts; and represent no object. This [objective] meaning they acquire from sensibility, which realises the understanding in the very process of restricting it.

[1] [Altered by Kant (*Nachträge* lxi) to: *eine Erkenntnis*.]

TRANSCENDENTAL DOCTRINE OF JUDGMENT

(OR ANALYTIC OF PRINCIPLES)

CHAPTER II

SYSTEM OF ALL PRINCIPLES OF PURE UNDERSTANDING

IN the preceding chapter we have considered transcendental judgment with reference merely to the universal conditions under which it is alone justified in employing pure concepts of understanding for synthetic judgments. Our task now is to exhibit, in systematic connection, the judgments which understanding, under this critical provision, actually achieves *a priori*. There can be no question that in this enquiry our table of categories is the natural and the safe guide. For since it is through the relation of the categories to possible experience that all pure *a priori* knowledge of understanding has to be constituted, their relation to sensibility in general will exhibit completely and systematically all the transcendental principles of the use of the understanding.

Principles *a priori* are so named not merely because they contain in themselves the grounds of other judgments, but also because they are not themselves grounded in higher and more universal modes of knowledge. But this characteristic does not remove them beyond the sphere of proof. This proof cannot, indeed, be carried out in any objective fashion, since such principles [do not rest on objective considerations but] lie at the foundation of all *knowledge* of objects.[1] This does not, however, prevent our attempting a proof, from the subjective sources of the possibility of knowledge of an object in general. Such proof is, indeed, indispensable, if the propositions are not to incur the suspicion of being merely surreptitious assertions.

[1] [This sentence has been variously emended. In the main, I follow Wille.]

Secondly, we shall limit ourselves merely to those principles which stand in relation to the categories. The principles of the Transcendental Aesthetic, according to which space and time are the conditions of the possibility of all things as appearances, and likewise the restriction of these principles, namely, that they cannot be applied to things in themselves, are matters which do not come within the range of our present enquiry. For similar reasons mathematical principles form no part of this system. They are derived solely from intuition, not from the pure concept of understanding. Nevertheless, since they too are synthetic *a priori* judgments, their possi- B 189 bility must receive recognition in this chapter. For though their correctness and apodeictic certainty do not indeed require to be established, their possibility, as cases of evident *a priori* knowledge, has to be rendered conceivable, and to be deduced.

We shall also have to treat of the principle of analytic judgments, in so far as it stands in contrast with that[1] of syn- A 150 thetic judgments with which alone strictly we have to deal. For by thus contrasting them we free the theory of synthetic judgments from all misunderstanding, and have them in their own peculiar nature clearly before us.

THE SYSTEM OF THE PRINCIPLES OF PURE UNDERSTANDING

Section 1

THE HIGHEST PRINCIPLE OF ALL ANALYTIC JUDGMENTS

The universal, though merely negative, condition of all our judgments in general, whatever be the content of our knowledge, and however it may relate to the object, is that they be not self-contradictory; for if self-contradictory, these judgments are in themselves, even without reference to the object, null and void. But even if our judgment contains no contradiction, it may B 190 connect concepts in a manner not borne out by the object, or else in a manner for which no ground is given, either *a priori* or *a posteriori*, sufficient to justify such judgment, and so may

---

[1] [Reading, with Mellin, *mit dem der* for *mit der*.]

still, in spite of being free from all inner contradiction, be
either false or groundless.

A 151   The proposition that no predicate contradictory of a thing
can belong to it, is entitled the principle of contradiction, and
is a universal, though merely negative, criterion of all truth.
For this reason it belongs only to logic. It holds of knowledge,
merely as knowledge in general, irrespective of content; and
asserts that the contradiction completely cancels and in-
validates it.

But it also allows of a positive employment, not merely,
that is, to dispel falsehood and error (so far as they rest on
contradiction), but also for the knowing of truth. For, *if
the judgment is analytic*, whether negative or affirmative, its
truth can always be adequately known in accordance with the
principle of contradiction. The reverse [1] of that which as concept is contained and is thought in the knowledge of the object,
B 191   is always rightly denied. But since the opposite of the concept
would contradict the object, the concept itself must necessarily be affirmed of it.

The principle of contradiction must therefore be recognised
as being the universal and completely sufficient *principle of
all analytic knowledge*; but beyond the sphere of analytic
knowledge it has, as a *sufficient* criterion of truth, no authority
and no field of application. The fact that no knowledge can
be contrary to it without self-nullification, makes this prin-
A 152   ciple a *conditio sine qua non*, but not a determining ground,
of the truth of our [non-analytic] knowledge. Now in our
critical enquiry it is only with the synthetic portion of our
knowledge that we are concerned; and in regard to the truth
of this kind of knowledge we can never look to the above
principle for any positive information, though, of course, since
it is inviolable, we must always be careful to conform to it.

Although this famous principle is thus without content and
merely formal, it has sometimes been carelessly formulated in
a manner which involves the quite unnecessary admixture of
a synthetic element. The formula runs: It is impossible that
something should *at one and the same time* both be and not be.
Apart from the fact that the apodeictic certainty, expressed
through the word 'impossible', is superfluously added—since

[1] [*Widerspiel.*]

it is evident of itself from the [very nature of the] proposition
—the proposition is modified by the condition of time. It then,
as it were, asserts: A thing = A, which is something = B, can- B 192
not at the same time be not-B, but may very well in succession
be both B and not-B. For instance, a man who is young cannot
at the same time be old, but may very well at one time be young
and at another time not-young, that is, old. The principle of
contradiction, however, as a merely logical principle, must not
in any way limit its assertions to time-relations. The above
formula is therefore completely contrary to the intention of the A 153
principle. The misunderstanding results from our first of all
separating a predicate of a thing from the concept of that
thing, and afterwards connecting this predicate with its opposite—a procedure which never occasions a contradiction with
the subject but only with the predicate which has been synthetically connected with that subject, and even then only
when both predicates are affirmed at one and the same time.
If I say that a man who is unlearned is not learned, the condition, *at one and the same time*, must be added; for he who
is at one time unlearned can very well at another be learned.
But if I say, no unlearned man is learned, the proposition is
analytic, since the property, unlearnedness, now goes to make
up the concept of the subject, and the truth of the negative
judgment then becomes evident as an immediate consequence
of the principle of contradiction, without requiring the supplementary condition, *at one and the same time*. This, then, is
the reason why I have altered its formulation, namely, in order B 193
that the nature of an analytic proposition be clearly expressed
through it.

THE SYSTEM OF THE PRINCIPLES OF PURE   A 154
UNDERSTANDING

Section 2

THE HIGHEST PRINCIPLE OF ALL SYNTHETIC JUDGMENTS

The explanation of the possibility of synthetic judgments
is a problem with which general logic has nothing to do. It
need not even so much as know the problem by name. But in

transcendental logic it is the most important of all questions; and indeed, if in treating of the possibility of synthetic *a priori* judgments we also take account of the conditions and scope of their validity, it is the only question with which it is concerned. For upon completion of this enquiry, transcendental logic is in a position completely to fulfil its ultimate purpose, that of determining the scope and limits of pure understanding.

In the analytic judgment we keep to the given concept, and seek to extract something from it. If it is to be affirmative, I ascribe to it only what is already thought in it. If it is to be negative i exclude from it only its opposite. But in synthetic judgments I have to advance beyond the given concept,

B 194   viewing as in relation with the concept something altogether different from what was thought in it. This relation is consequently never a relation either of identity or of contradiction;

A 155   and from the judgment, taken in and by itself, the truth or falsity of the relation can never be discovered.

Granted, then, that we must advance beyond a given concept in order to compare it synthetically with another, a third something[1] is necessary, as that wherein alone the synthesis of two concepts can be achieved. What, now, is this third something that is to be the medium of all synthetic judgments? There is only one[2] whole[3] in which all our representations are contained, namely, inner sense and its *a priori* form, time. The synthesis of representations rests on imagination; and their synthetic unity, which is required for judgment, on the unity of apperception. In these, therefore, [in inner sense, imagination, and apperception], we must look for the possibility of synthetic judgments; and since all three contain the sources of *a priori* representations, they must also account for the possibility of *pure* synthetic judgments. For these reasons they are, indeed, indispensably necessary for any knowledge of objects, which rests entirely on the synthesis of representations.

If knowledge is to have objective reality, that is, to relate to an object, and is to acquire meaning and significance in respect to it, the object must be capable of being in some

---

[1] [*ein Drittes.*]
[2] [Reading, with Mellin, *Es gibt nur einen* for *Es ist nur ein.*]
[3] [*Inbegriff.*]

manner given. Otherwise the concepts are empty; through them we have indeed thought, but in this thinking we have B 195 really known nothing; we have merely played with representations. That an object be given (if this expression be A 156 taken, not as referring to some merely mediate process, but as signifying immediate presentation in intuition), means simply that the representation through which the object is thought relates to actual or possible experience. Even space and time, however free[1] their concepts are from everything empirical, and however certain it is that they are represented in the mind completely *a priori*, would yet be without objective validity, senseless and meaningless, if their necessary application to the objects of experience were not established. Their representation is a mere schema which always stands in relation to the reproductive imagination that calls up and assembles the objects of experience. Apart from these objects of experience, they would be devoid of meaning. And so it is with concepts of every kind.

The *possibility of experience* is, then, what gives objective reality to all our *a priori* modes of knowledge. Experience, however, rests on the synthetic unity of appearances, that is, on a synthesis according to concepts of an[2] object of appearances in general. Apart from such synthesis it would not be knowledge, but a rhapsody of perceptions that would not fit into any context according to rules of a completely interconnected (possible) consciousness, and so would not conform to the transcendental and necessary unity of apperception. Ex- B 196 perience depends, therefore, upon *a priori* principles of its form, that is, upon universal rules of unity in the synthesis of A 157 appearances. Their objective reality, as necessary conditions of experience, and indeed of its very possibility, can always be shown in experience. Apart from this relation synthetic *a priori* principles are completely impossible. For they have then no third something, that is, no[3] object, in which the synthetic unity can exhibit the objective reality of its concepts.[4]

Although we know *a priori* in synthetic judgments a great deal regarding space in general and the figures which produc-

---

[1] [*rein*.]   [2] [Reading, with Vaihinger, *von einem* for *vom*.]
[3] [Reading, with Grillo, *keinen* for *reinen*.]
[4] [Reading, with Vaihinger, *Einheit die objektive Realität ihrer Begriffe* for *Einheit ihrer Begriffe objektive Realität*.]

tive imagination describes in it, and can obtain such judgments without actually requiring any experience, yet even this
knowledge would be nothing but a playing with a mere fig-
ment of the brain, were it not that space has to be regarded as
a condition of the appearances which constitute the material
for outer experience. Those pure synthetic judgments therefore relate, though only mediately, to possible experience, or
rather to the possibility of experience; and upon that alone is
founded the objective validity of their synthesis.

Accordingly, since experience, as empirical synthesis, is,
in so far as such experience is possible, the one species of
knowledge which is capable of imparting reality to any non-
empirical synthesis,[1] this latter [type of synthesis], as know-
B 197 ledge *a priori*, can possess truth, that is, agreement with the
object, only in so far as it contains nothing save what is
A 158 necessary to synthetic unity of experience in general.

The highest principle of all synthetic judgments is therefore this: every object stands under the necessary conditions of
synthetic unity of the manifold of intuition in a possible experience.

Synthetic *a priori* judgments are thus possible when we relate the formal conditions of *a priori* intuition, the synthesis of
imagination and the necessary unity of this synthesis in a transcendental apperception, to a possible empirical knowledge in
general. We then assert that the conditions of the *possibility
of experience* in general are likewise conditions of the *possibility of the objects of experience*, and that for this reason they
have objective validity in a synthetic *a priori* judgment.

THE SYSTEM OF THE PRINCIPLES OF PURE
UNDERSTANDING

Section 3

SYSTEMATIC REPRESENTATION OF ALL THE SYNTHETIC
PRINCIPLES OF PURE UNDERSTANDING

That there should be principles at all is entirely due to the
pure understanding. Not only is it the faculty of rules in re-

---

[1] [*aller anderen Synthesis.*]

spect of that which happens, but is itself the source of principles
according to which[1] everything that can be presented to us as
an object must conform to rules. For without such rules appearances would never yield knowledge of an object corresponding to them. Even natural laws, viewed as principles of the empirical employment of understanding, carry with them an expression of necessity, and so contain at least the suggestion of a determination from grounds which are valid *a priori* and antecedently to all experience. The laws of nature, indeed, one and all, without exception, stand under higher principles of understanding. They simply apply the latter to special cases [in the field] of appearance. These principles alone supply the concept which contains the condition, and as it were the exponent, of a rule in general. What experience gives is the instance which stands under the rule.

There can be no real danger of our regarding merely empirical principles as principles of pure understanding, or conversely. For the necessity according to concepts which distinguishes the principles of pure understanding, and the lack of which is evident in every empirical proposition, however general its application, suffices to make this confusion easily preventable. But there are pure *a priori* principles that we may not properly ascribe to the pure understanding, which is the faculty of concepts. For though they are mediated by the
understanding, they are not derived from pure concepts but
from pure intuitions. We find such principles in mathematics. The question, however, of their application to experience, that is, of their objective validity, nay, even the deduction of the possibility of such synthetic *a priori* knowledge, must always carry us back to the pure understanding.

While, therefore, I leave aside the principles of mathematics, I shall none the less include those [more fundamental] principles upon which the possibility and *a priori* objective validity of mathematics are grounded. These latter must be regarded as the foundation[2] of all mathematical principles. They proceed from concepts to intuition, not from intuition to concepts.

In the application of pure concepts of understanding to

---

[1] [Reading, with Erdmann, *welchen* for *welchem*.]
[2] [*Principium*.]

possible experience, the employment of their synthesis[1] is either *mathematical* or *dynamical*; for it is concerned partly with the mere *intuition* of an appearance in general, partly with its *existence*. The *a priori* conditions of intuition are absolutely necessary conditions of any possible experience; those of the existence of the objects of a possible empirical intuition are in themselves only accidental. The principles of mathematical employment will therefore be unconditionally necessary, that is, apodeictic. Those of dynamical employment will also indeed possess the character of *a priori* necessity, but only under the condition of empirical thought in some experience, therefore only mediately and indirectly. Notwithstanding their undoubted certainty throughout experience, they will not contain that immediate evidence which is peculiar to the former. But of this we shall be better able to judge at the conclusion of this system of principles.

B 200

A 161

The table of categories is quite naturally our guide in the construction of the table of principles. For the latter are simply rules for the objective employment of the former. All principles of pure understanding are therefore—

1
Axioms
of intuition.

2
Anticipations
of perception.

3
Analogies
of experience.

4
Postulates
of empirical thought in general.

These titles I have intentionally chosen in order to give prominence to differences in the evidence and in the application of the principles. It will soon become clear that the principles involved in the *a priori* determination of appearances according to the categories of quantity and of quality (only the formal aspect of quantity and quality being considered) allow of intuitive certainty, alike as regards their evidential force[2] and as regards their *a priori* application to

B 201

---

[1] [*der Gebrauch ihrer Synthesis.*]   [2] [*Evidenz.*]

appearances. They are thereby distinguished from those of A 162
the other two groups, which are capable only of a merely
discursive certainty. This distinction holds even while we
recognise that the certainty is in both cases complete. I shall
therefore entitle the former principles *mathematical,* and
· the latter *dynamical.*[a] But it should be noted that we are as
little concerned in the one case with the principles of mathe- B 202
matics as in the other with the principles of general physical
dynamics. We treat only of the principles of pure understanding in their relation to inner sense (all differences among the
given representations being ignored). It is through these
principles of pure understanding that the special principles of
mathematics and of dynamics become possible. I have named
them, therefore, on account rather of their application than
of their content. I now proceed to discuss them in the order
in which they are given in the above table.

I

AXIOMS OF INTUITION *

Their principle is: All intuitions are extensive magnitudes.

Proof[1]

Appearances, in their formal aspect,[2] contain an intuition
in space and time, which conditions them, one and all, *a*

---

* [In A:]

The Axioms of Intuition.

Principle of the pure understanding: All appearances
are, in their intuition, extensive magnitudes.

[a] [Note added in B.] All combination (*conjunctio*) is either composition (*compositio*) or connection (*nexus*). The former is the synthesis of the manifold where its constituents do not necessarily belong to one another. For example, the two triangles into which a
square is divided by its diagonal do not necessarily belong to one
another. Such also is the synthesis of the *homogeneous* in everything
which can be *mathematically* treated. This synthesis can itself be
divided into that of *aggregation* and that of *coalition,* the former

1 [This heading and the first paragraph added in B.]
2 [der Form nach.]

priori. They cannot be apprehended, that is, taken up into empirical consciousness, save through that synthesis of the manifold whereby the representations of a determinate space or time are generated, that is, through combination of the

B 203 homogeneous manifold and consciousness of its synthetic unity. Consciousness of the synthetic unity[1] of the manifold [and] homogeneous in intuition in general, in so far as the representation of an object first becomes possible by means of it, is, however, the concept of a magnitude (*quantum*). Thus even the perception of an object, as appearance, is only possible through the same synthetic unity of the manifold of the given sensible intuition as that whereby the unity of the combination of the manifold [and] homogeneous is thought in the concept of a *magnitude*. In other words, appearances are all without exception *magnitudes*, indeed *extensive magnitudes*. As intuitions in space or time, they must be represented through the same synthesis whereby space and time in general are determined.

I entitle a magnitude extensive when the representation of the parts makes possible, and therefore necessarily precedes, the representation of the whole. I cannot represent to myself a line, however small, without drawing it in thought, that

A 163 is, generating from a point all its parts one after another. Only in this way can the intuition be obtained Similarly with all times, however small. In these I think to myself only that successive advance from one moment to another, whereby through the parts of time and their addition a determinate time-magnitude is generated. As the [element of]

---

applying to *extensive* and the latter to *intensive* quantities. The second mode of combination (*nexus*) is the synthesis of the manifold so far as its constituents *necessarily belong to one another*, as, for example, the accident to some substance, or the effect to the cause. It is therefore synthesis of that which, though *heterogeneous*, is yet represented as combined *a priori*. This combination, as not being arbitrary and as concerning the connection of the *existence* of the

B 202 manifold, I entitle *dynamical*. Such connection can itself, in turn, be divided into the *physical* connection of the appearances with one another, and their *metaphysical* connection in the *a priori* faculty of knowledge.

[1] [Adding, with Vaihinger, *der synthetischen Einheit*].

pure intuition in all appearances is either space or time, every
appearance is as intuition an extensive magnitude; only   B 204
through successive synthesis of part to part in [the process of]
its apprehension can it come to be known. All appearances
are consequently intuited as aggregates, as complexes of
previously given parts. This is not the case with magnitudes
of every kind, but only with those magnitudes which are
represented and apprehended by us in this *extensive* fashion.

The mathematics of space[1] (geometry) is based upon this
successive synthesis of the productive imagination in the
generation of figures. This is the basis of the axioms which
formulate the conditions of sensible *a priori* intuition under
which alone the schema of a pure concept of outer appearance can arise—for instance, that between two points only
one straight line is possible, or that two straight lines cannot
enclose a space, etc. These are the axioms which, strictly,
relate only to magnitudes (*quanta*) as such.

As regards magnitude (*quantitas*), that is, as regards
the answer to be given to the question, 'What is the magnitude
of a thing?' there are no axioms in the strict meaning of the   A 164
term, although there are a number of propositions which are
synthetic and immediately certain (*indemonstrabilia*). The
propositions, that if equals be added to equals the wholes
are equal, and if equals be taken from equals the remainders
are equal, are analytic propositions; for I am immediately
conscious of the identity of the production of the one magnitude with the production of the other. [Consequently, they   B 205
are not] axioms, [for these] have to be *a priori synthetic* propositions. On the other hand, the evident propositions of
numerical relation are indeed synthetic, but are not general
like those of geometry, and cannot, therefore, be called axioms
but only numerical formulas. The assertion that 7 + 5 is equal
to 12 is not an analytic proposition. For neither in the representation of 7, nor in that of 5, nor in the representation of the
combination of both, do I think the number 12. (That I must
do so in the *addition* of the two numbers is not to the point,
since in the analytic proposition the question is only whether
I actually think the predicate in the representation of the
subject.) But although the proposition is synthetic, it is also

[1] [*Ausdehnung.*]

only singular. So far as we are here attending merely to the
synthesis of the homogeneous (of units), that synthesis can
take place only in one way, although the *employment* of
these numbers is general. If I assert that through three
lines, two of which taken together are greater than the
third, a triangle can be described, I have expressed merely
A 165 the function of productive imagination whereby the lines
can be drawn greater or smaller, and so can be made to
meet at any and every possible angle. The number 7, on the
other hand, is possible only in one way. So also is the
number 12, as thus generated through the synthesis of 7
with 5. Such propositions must not, therefore, be called
B 206 axioms (that would involve recognition of an infinite number
of axioms), but numerical formulas.

This transcendental principle of the mathematics of appearances greatly enlarges our *a priori* knowledge. For it alone
can make pure mathematics, in its complete precision, applicable to objects of experience. Without this principle, such
application would not be thus self-evident; and there has indeed
been much confusion of thought in regard to it. Appearances are not things in themselves. Empirical intuition is
possible only by means of the pure intuition of space and of
time. What geometry asserts of pure intuition is therefore
undeniably valid of empirical intuition. The idle objections,
that objects of the senses may not conform to such rules of
construction in space as that of the infinite divisibility of lines
or angles, must[1] be given up. For if these objections hold good,
we deny the objective validity of space, and consequently of
all mathematics, and no longer know why and how far
mathematics can be applicable to appearances. The synthesis
of spaces and times, being a synthesis of the essential forms[2]
A 166 of all intuition, is what makes possible the apprehension of
appearance, and consequently every outer experience and all
knowledge of the objects of such experience. Whatever pure
mathematics establishes in regard to the synthesis of the form
of apprehension is also necessarily valid of the objects apprehended. All objections are only the chicanery of a falsely

[1] [Reading, with Kehrbach, *dürfen, mussen* for *dürfe, muss*.]
[2] [Reading, with Erdmann, *der wesentlichen Formen* for *der wesentlichen
Form*.]

instructed reason, which, erroneously professing to isolate the B 207
objects of the senses from the formal condition of our sensibility, represents them, in spite of the fact that they are mere
appearances, as objects in themselves, given to the understanding. Certainly, on that assumption, no synthetic knowledge
of any kind could be obtained of them *a priori*, and nothing
therefore could be known of them synthetically through pure
concepts of space. Indeed, the science which determines these
concepts, namely geometry, would not itself be possible.

2
ANTICIPATIONS OF PERCEPTION *

In all appearances, the real that is an object of sensation
has intensive magnitude, that is, a degree.

Proof[1]

Perception is empirical consciousness, that is, a consciousness in which sensation is to be found. Appearances, as objects
of perception, are not pure, merely formal, intuitions, like space
and time. For in and by themselves these latter cannot be perceived. Appearances contain in addition to intuition the matter
for some object in general (whereby something existing in space
or time is represented); they contain, that is to say, the real
of sensation as merely subjective representation, which gives
us only the consciousness that the subject is affected, and
which we relate to an object in general. Now from empirical B 208
consciousness to pure consciousness **a** graduated transition
is possible, the real in the former completely vanishing and a
merely formal *a priori* consciousness of the manifold in space
and time remaining. Consequently there is also possible a

---

* [In A:]
The Anticipations of Perception

The principle which anticipates all perceptions, as such, is
as follows: In all appearances sensation, and the *real* which
corresponds to it in the object (*realitas phaenomenon*), has an
intensive magnitude, that is, a degree.

[1] [This heading and the first paragraph added in B.]

synthesis in the process of generating the magnitude of a sensation from its beginning in pure intuition = 0, up to any
required magnitude. Since, however, sensation is not in itself
an objective representation, and since neither the intuition
of space nor that of time is to be met with in it, its magnitude is not extensive but *intensive*. This magnitude is
generated in the act of apprehension whereby the empirical
consciousness of it can in a certain time increase from nothing
= 0 to the[1] given measure. Corresponding to this intensity
of sensation, an *intensive magnitude*, that is, a degree of
influence on the sense [*i.e.* on the special sense involved],
must be ascribed to all objects of perception, in so far as
the perception contains sensation.

All knowledge by means of which I am enabled to know
and determine *a priori* what belongs to empirical knowledge
may be entitled an anticipation; and this is undoubtedly the
sense in which Epicurus employed the term πρόληψις. But as
there is an element in the appearances (namely, sensation, the
matter of perception) which can never be known *a priori*, and
which therefore constitutes the distinctive difference between
empirical and *a priori* knowledge, it follows that sensation is
just that element which cannot be anticipated. On the other
hand, we might very well entitle the pure determinations in
space and time, in respect of shape as well as of magnitude,
anticipations of appearances, since they represent *a priori* that
which may always be given *a posteriori* in experience. If,
however, there is in every sensation, as sensation in general
(that is, without a particular sensation having to be given),
something that can be known *a priori*, this will, in a quite
especial sense, deserve to be named anticipation. For it does
indeed seem surprising that we should forestall experience,
precisely in that which concerns what is only to be obtained
through it, namely, its matter. Yet, none the less, such is
actually the case.

Apprehension by means merely of sensation occupies only
an instant,[2] if, that is, I do not take into account the succession of different sensations. As sensation is that element in

---

[1] [Taking, with Erdmann, *ihrem* as referring, not to *Bewusstsein*, but to
Empfindung.]
[2] [*Augenblick*.]

the [field of] appearance the apprehension of which does not involve a successive synthesis proceeding from parts to the whole representation, it has no extensive magnitude. The absence of sensation at that instant would involve the representation of the instant as empty, therefore as = 0. Now A 168 what corresponds in empirical intuition to sensation is reality (*realitas phaenomenon*); what corresponds to its absence is negation = 0. Every sensation, however, is capable of diminu- B 210 tion, so that it can decrease and gradually vanish. Between reality in the [field of] appearance and negation there is therefore a continuity[1] of many possible intermediate sensations, the difference between any two of which is always smaller than the difference between the given sensation and zero or complete negation. In other words, the real in the [field of] appearance has always a magnitude. But since its apprehension by means of mere sensation takes place in an instant and not through successive synthesis of different sensations, and therefore does not proceed from the parts to the whole, the magnitude is to be met with only in the apprehension.[2] The real has therefore magnitude, but not extensive magnitude.

A magnitude which is apprehended only as unity, and in which multiplicity can be represented only through approximation to negation = 0, I entitle an *intensive* magnitude. Every reality in the [field of] appearance has therefore intensive magnitude or degree. If this reality is viewed as cause, either of sensation or of some other reality in the [field of] appearance, such as change, the degree of the reality as cause is then entitled a moment,[3] the moment of gravity. It is so named for the reason that degree signifies only that magnitude A 169 the apprehension of which is not successive, but instantaneous.[4] This, however, I touch on only in passing; for with causality I am not at present dealing.

Every sensation, therefore, and likewise every reality in B 211 the [field of] appearance, however small it may be, has a degree, that is, an intensive magnitude which can always be diminished. Between reality and negation there is a continuity of possible realities and of possible smaller perceptions.

---

[1] [*ein kontinuierlicher Zusammenhang.*]
[2] [Reading, with Wille, *welche aber nur in der Apprehension* for *welche aber nicht in der Apprehension*. Cf. proof added in B, 207-8.]
[3] [*ein Moment.*]   [4] [*augenblicklich.*]

H 2

Every colour, as for instance red, has a degree which, however small it may be, is never the smallest; and so with heat, the moment of gravity, etc.

The property of magnitudes by which no part of them is the smallest possible, that is, by which no part is simple, is called their continuity. Space and time are *quanta continua*, because no part of them can be given save as enclosed between limits (points or instants), and therefore only in such fashion that this part is itself again a space or a time. Space therefore consists solely of spaces, time solely of times. Points and instants are only limits, that is, mere positions which limit space and time. But positions always presuppose the intuitions which they limit or are intended to limit; and out of mere positions, A 170 viewed as constituents capable of being given prior to space or time, neither space nor time can be constructed. Such magnitudes may also be called *flowing*, since the synthesis of productive imagination involved in their production is a pro- B 212 gression in time, and the continuity of time is ordinarily designated by the term flowing or flowing away.

All appearances, then, are continuous magnitudes, alike in their intuition, as extensive, and in their mere perception (sensation, and with it reality) as intensive. If the synthesis of the manifold of appearance is interrupted, we have an aggregate of different appearances, and not appearance as a genuine quantum. Such an aggregate[1] is not generated by continuing without break productive synthesis of a certain kind, but through repetition of an ever-ceasing synthesis. If I called thirteen thalers a quantum of money, I should be correct, provided my intention is to state the value of a mark of fine silver. For this is a continuous magnitude, in which no part is the smallest, and in which every part can constitute a piece of coin that always contains material for still smaller pieces. But if I understand by the phrase thirteen round thalers, so many coins, quite apart from the question of what their silver standard may be, I then use the phrase, quantum of thalers, inappropriately. It ought to be entitled an aggregate, that is, A 171 a number of pieces of money. But as unity must be presupposed in all number, appearance as unity is a quantum, and as a quantum is always a continuum.

---

[1] [Reading, with Kehrbach, *welches Aggregat* for *welches*.]

Since all appearances, alike in their extensive and in their intensive aspect, are thus continuous magnitudes, it might seem to be an easy matter to prove with mathematical conclusiveness the proposition that all alteration (transition of a B 213 thing from one state to another), is continuous. But the causality of an alteration in general, presupposing, as it does, empirical principles, lies altogether outside the limits of a transcendental philosophy. For upon the question as to whether a cause capable of altering the state of a thing, that is, of determining it to the opposite of a certain given state, may be possible, the *a priori* understanding casts no light; and this not merely because it has no insight into its possibility (such insight is lacking to us in many other cases of *a priori* knowledge), but because alterableness is to be met with only in certain determinations of appearances, and because, whereas [in fact] the cause of these determinations lies in the unalterable, experience alone can teach what they are. Since in our present enquiry we have no data of which we can make use save only the pure fundamental concepts of all possible experience, in which there must be absolutely nothing that is empirical, we cannot, without destroying the unity of our system, anticipate general natural science, which is based A 172 on certain primary experiences.[1]

At the same time, there is no lack of proofs of the great value of our principle in enabling us to anticipate perceptions, and even to some extent to make good their absence, by placing a check upon all false inferences which might be drawn from their absence.

If all reality in perception has a degree, between which B 214 and negation there exists an infinite gradation of ever smaller degrees, and if every sense must likewise[2] possess some particular degree[3] of receptivity of sensations, no perception, and consequently no experience, is possible that could prove, either immediately or mediately (no matter how far-ranging the reasoning may be), a complete absence of all reality in the [field of] appearance. In other words, the proof of an empty space or of an empty time can never be derived from experience. For, in the first place, the complete absence of reality

---

[1] [*Grunderfahrungen.*]
[2] [Reading, with Erdmann, *ebensowohl* for *gleichwohl.*]   [3] [*i.e.* limit.]

from a sensible intuition can never be itself perceived; and, secondly, there is no appearance whatsoever and no difference in the degree of reality of any appearance from which it can be inferred. It is not even legitimate to postulate it in order to explain any difference. For even if the whole intuition of a certain determinate space or time is real through and through, that is, though no part of it is empty, none the less, since every A 173 reality has its degree, which can diminish to nothing (the void) through infinite gradations without in any way altering the extensive magnitude of the appearance, there must be infinite different degrees in which space and time may be filled. Intensive magnitude can in different appearances be smaller or greater, although the extensive magnitude of the intuition remains one and the same.

B 215   Let us give an example. Almost all natural philosophers, observing—partly by means of the moment of gravity or weight, partly by means of the moment of opposition to other matter in motion—a great difference in the quantity of various kinds of matter in bodies that have the same volume, unanimously conclude that this volume, which constitutes the extensive magnitude of the appearance, must in all material bodies be empty in varying degrees. Who would ever have dreamt of believing that these students of nature, most of whom are occupied with problems in mathematics and mechanics, would base such an inference solely on a metaphysical presupposition—the sort of assumption they so stoutly profess to avoid? They assume that the real in space (I may not here name it impenetrability or weight, since these are empirical concepts) is everywhere uniform and varies only in extensive magnitude, that is, in amount. Now to this presupposition, for which they could find no support in experi-
A 174 ence, and which is therefore purely metaphysical, I oppose a transcendental proof, which does not indeed explain the difference in the filling of spaces, but completely destroys the supposed necessity of the above presupposition, that the difference is only to be explained on the assumption of empty space. My proof has the merit at least of freeing the understanding, so that it is at liberty to think this difference in
B 216 some other manner, should it be found that some other hypothesis is required for the explanation of the natural

appearances. For we then recognise that although two equal spaces can be completely filled with different kinds of matter, so that there is no point in either where matter is not present, nevertheless every reality has, while keeping its quality unchanged, some specific degree (of resistance or weight) which can, without diminution of its extensive magnitude or amount, become smaller and smaller *in infinitum*, before it passes into the void and [so] vanishes [out of existence]. Thus a radiation which fills a space, as for instance heat, and similarly every other reality in the [field of] appearance, can diminish in its degree *in infinitum*, without leaving the smallest part of this space in the least empty. It may fill the space just as completely with these smaller degrees as another appearance does with greater degrees. I do not at all intend to assert that this is what actually occurs when material bodies differ in specific gravity, but only to establish from a principle of pure understanding that the nature of our per- A 175 ceptions allows of such a mode of explanation, that we are not justified in assuming the real in appearances to be uniform in degree, differing only in aggregation and extensive magnitude, and that we are especially in error when we claim that such interpretation can be based on an *a priori* principle of the understanding.

This anticipation of perception must always, however, B 217 appear somewhat strange to anyone trained in transcendental reflection,[1] and to any student of nature who by such teaching has been trained to circumspection. The assertion that the understanding anticipates[2] such a synthetic principle, ascribing a degree to all that is real in the appearances, and so asserting the possibility of an internal distinction in sensation itself (abstraction being made of its empirical quality), awakens doubts and difficulties. It is therefore a question not unworthy of solution, how the understanding can thus in *a priori* fashion pronounce synthetically upon appearances, and can indeed anticipate in that which in itself is merely empirical and concerns only sensation.

The *quality* of sensation, as for instance in colours, taste, etc., is always merely empirical, and cannot be represented

[1] [Adding, with Erdmann, *Überlegung.*]
[2] [Adding, with Hartenstein, *antizipiert.*]

a priori. But the real, which corresponds to sensations in general, as opposed to negation = o, represents only that something the very concept of which includes being, and A 176 signifies nothing but the synthesis in an empirical consciousness in general. Empirical consciousness can in inner sense be raised from o to any higher degree, so that a certain extensive magnitude of intuition, as for instance of illuminated surface, may excite as great a sensation as the combined aggregate of many[1] such surfaces less illuminated. [Since the extensive magnitude of the appearance thus varies independ- B 218 ently], we can completely abstract from it, and still represent in the mere sensation in any one of its moments a synthesis that advances uniformly from o to the given empirical consciousness. Consequently, though all sensations as such are given only *a posteriori*,[2] their property of possessing a degree can be known *a priori*. It is remarkable that of magnitudes in general we can know *a priori* only a single *quality*, namely, that of continuity, and that in all quality (the real in appearances) we can know *a priori* nothing save [in regard to] their intensive *quantity*, namely that they have degree. Everything else has to be left to experience.

3

ANALOGIES OF EXPERIENCE *

The principle of the analogies is: Experience is possible only through the representation of a necessary connection of perceptions.

Proof[3]

Experience is an empirical knowledge, that is, a knowledge which determines an object through perceptions. It

---

* [In A:]

The Analogies of Experience

The general principle of the analogies is: All appearances A 177 are, as regards their existence, subject *a priori* to rules determining their relation to one another in one time.

[1] [Reading, with Erdmann, *vielen* for *vielem*.]
[2] [Reading, with Mellin, *a posteriori* for *a priori*.]
[3] [This heading and the first paragraph added in B.]

is a synthesis of perceptions, not contained in perception but itself containing in one consciousness the synthetic unity of the manifold of perceptions. This synthetic unity constitutes the essential in any knowledge of *objects* of the senses, that is, in experience as distinguished from mere intuition or sensa- B 219 tion of the senses. In experience, however, perceptions come together only in accidental order, so that no necessity determining their connection is or can be revealed in the perceptions themselves. For apprehension is only a placing together of the manifold of empirical intuition; and we can find in it no representation of any necessity which determines the appearances thus combined to have connected existence in space and time. But since experience is a knowledge of objects through perceptions, the relation [involved] in the existence of the manifold has to be represented in experience, not as it comes to be constructed[1] in time but as it exists objectively in time. Since time, however, cannot itself be perceived, the determination of the existence of objects in time can take place only through their relation in time in general, and therefore only through concepts that connect them *a priori*. Since these always carry necessity with them, it follows that experience is only possible through a representation of necessary connection of perceptions.

The three modes of time are *duration, succession,* and *coexistence.* There will, therefore, be three rules of all relations of appearances in time, and these rules will be prior to all experience, and indeed make it possible. By means of these rules the existence of every appearance can be determined in respect of the unity of all time.

The general principle of the three analogies rests on the B 220 necessary *unity* of apperception, in respect of all possible empirical consciousness, that is, of all perception, *at every* [*instant of*] *time.* And since this unity lies *a priori* at the foundation of empirical consciousness, it follows that the above principle rests on the synthetic unity of all appearances as regards their relation in time. For the original apperception stands in relation to inner sense (the sum of all representations), and indeed *a priori* to its form, that is, to the time-order of the manifold empirical consciousness. All this manifold must, as regards its time-relations, be united in the original apperception. This

¹ [*wie es in der Zeit zusammengestellt ist.*]

is demanded by the *a priori* transcendental unity of apperception, to which everything that is to belong to my knowledge
(that is, to my unified [1] knowledge), and so can be an object for
me, has to conform. This *synthetic unity* in the time-relations
of all perceptions, as thus determined *a priori*, is the law, that
A 178 all empirical time-determinations must stand under rules of
universal time-determination. The analogies of experience, with
which we are now to deal, must be rules of this description.

These principles have this peculiarity, that they are not
concerned with appearances and the synthesis of their empirical intuition, but only with the *existence* of such appearances
and their *relation* to one another in respect of their existence.
B 221 The manner in which something is apprehended in appearance can be so determined *a priori* that the rule of its synthesis
can at once give, that is to say, can bring into being, this
[element of] *a priori* intuition in every example that comes
before us empirically. The *existence* of appearances cannot,
however, be thus known *a priori*; and even granting that we
could in any such manner contrive to infer that something
exists, we could not know it determinately, could not, that is,
anticipate the features through which its empirical intuition is
distinguished from other intuitions.

The two previous principles, which, as justifying [2] the application of mathematics to appearances, I entitled the mathematical, referred to the possibility of appearances, and taught
how, alike as regards their intuition and the real in their perception, they can be generated according to rules of a mathematical synthesis. Both principles justify us in employing
numerical magnitudes, and so enable us to determine appear-
A 179 ance as magnitude. For instance, I can determine *a priori*, that
is, can construct, the degree of sensations of sunlight by combining some 200,000 illuminations of the moon. These first
principles may therefore be called constitutive.

It stands quite otherwise with those principles which seek
B 222 to bring the *existence* of appearances under rules *a priori*.
For since existence cannot be constructed, the principles can
apply only to the relations of existence, and can yield only *regulative* principles. We cannot, therefore, expect either axioms

[1] [*meinem einigen.*]
[2] [Reading, with Erdmann, *berechtigen* for *berechtigten.*]

or anticipations. If, however, a perception is given in a time-relation to some other perception, then even although this latter is indeterminate, and we consequently cannot decide *what* it is, or what its *magnitude* may be, we may none the less assert that in its existence it is necessarily connected with the former in this mode of time. In philosophy analogies signify something very different from what they represent in mathematics. In the latter they are formulas which express the equality of two quantitative relations, and are always *constitutive*; so that if three [1] members of the proportion are given, the fourth [2] is likewise given, that is, can be constructed. But in philosophy the analogy is not the equality of two *quantitative* but of two *qualitative* relations; and from three given members we can obtain *a priori* knowledge only of the relation to a   A 180 fourth, not of the fourth member itself. The relation yields, however, a rule for seeking the fourth member in experience, and a mark whereby it can be detected. An analogy of experience is, therefore, only a rule according to which a unity of experience may arise from perception. It does not tell us how mere perception or empirical intuition in general itself comes about. It is not a principle *constitutive* of the objects, that is, of the appearances, but only *regulative*. The same can be asserted of   B 223 the postulates of empirical thought in general, which concern the synthesis of mere intuition (that is, of the form of appearance), of perception (that is, of the matter of perception), and of experience (that is, of the relation of these perceptions). They are merely regulative principles, and are distinguished from the mathematical, which are constitutive, not indeed in certainty—both have certainty *a priori*—but in the nature of their evidence, that is, as regards the character of the intuitive (and consequently of the demonstrative) factors peculiar to the latter.

In this connection what has been said of all principles that are synthetic must be specially emphasised, namely, that these analogies have significance and validity only as principles of the empirical, not of the transcendental, employment of understanding; that only as such can they be established; and that   A 181 appearances have therefore to be subsumed, not simply [3] under

---

[1] [Reading, with Mellin, *drei* for *zwei*.]
[2] [Reading, with Mellin, *vierte* for *dritte*.]   [3] [*schlechthin*.]

the categories, but under their schemata. For if the objects to which these principles are to be related were things in themselves, it would be altogether impossible to know anything of them synthetically *a priori*. They are, however, nothing but appearances; and complete knowledge of them, in the furtherance of which the sole function of *a priori* principles must ultimately consist, is simply our possible experience of them. The principles can therefore have no other purpose save that

B 224 of being the conditions of the unity of *empirical* knowledge in the synthesis of *appearances*. But such unity can be thought only in the *schema* of the pure concept of understanding. The category expresses a function which is restricted by no sensible condition, and contains the unity of this schema,[1] [in so far only] as [it is the schema] of a synthesis in general. By these principles, then, we are justified in combining appearances only according to what is no more than an analogy with the logical and universal unity of concepts. In the principle itself we do indeed make use of the category, but in applying it to appearances we substitute for it[2] its schema as the key to its employment, or rather set it alongside the category, as its restricting condition, and as being what may be called its formula.

A 182

A

FIRST ANALOGY

Principle of Permanence of Substance[3]

In all change of appearances substance is permanent; its quantum in nature is neither increased nor diminished.*

---

* [In A:]

All appearances contain the permanent (substance) as the object itself, and the transitory[4] as its mere determination that is, as a way[5] in which the object exists.

[1] [Reading, with Kehrbach, *dessen* for *deren*.]
[2] [Reading, with Max Müller, *den ... der ersteren* for *dessen ... des ersteren*.]
[3] ['of substance' added in **B.**]
[4] [*das Wandelbare*.]
[5] [*eine Art*.]

Proof *

All appearances are in time; and in it alone, as substratum
(as permanent form of inner intuition), can either coexistence
or succession be represented. Thus the time in which all
change of appearances has to be thought, remains and does B 225
not change. For it is that in which, and as determinations of
which, succession or coexistence can alone be represented
Now time cannot by itself be perceived. Consequently there
must be found in the objects of perception, that is, in the
appearances, the substratum which represents time in general;
and all change or coexistence must, in being apprehended,
be perceived in this substratum, and through relation of the
appearances to it. But the substratum of all that is real, that is,
of all that belongs to the existence of things, is *substance*;
and all that belongs to existence can be thought only as a
determination of substance. Consequently the permanent, in
relation to which alone all time-relations of appearances can
be determined, is substance in the [field of] appearance, that
is, the real in appearance, and as the substrate of all change
remains ever the same. And as it is thus unchangeable in
its existence, its quantity in nature can be neither increased nor
diminished.

Our *apprehension* of the manifold of appearance is always
successive, and is therefore always changing. Through it alone
we can never determine whether this manifold, as object of experience, is coexistent or in sequence. For such determination
we require an underlying ground which exists *at all times*, that
is, something *abiding* and *permanent*, of which all change B 226
and coexistence are only so many ways (modes of time) in
which the permanent exists. And simultaneity and succes-

---

* [This heading and the first paragraph substituted in B for:]

Proof of this first Analogy

All appearances are in time. Time can determine them as
existing in a twofold manner, either as in succession to one
another or as coexisting. Time, in respect of the former, is
viewed as time-series, in respect of the latter as time-volume [1]

[1] [*Zeitumfang.*]

sion being the only relations in time, it follows that only in
A 183 the permanent are relations of time possible. In other words,
the permanent is the *substratum* of the empirical representation of time itself; in it alone is any determination of time
possible. Permanence, as the abiding correlate of all existence
of appearances, of all change and of all concomitance, expresses time in general. For change does not affect time itself,
but only appearances in time. (Coexistence is not a mode of
time itself; for none of the parts of time coexist; they are all
in succession to one another.) If we ascribe succession to time
itself, we must think yet another time, in which the sequence
would be possible. Only through the permanent does existence
in different parts of the time-series acquire a magnitude which
can be entitled duration. For in bare succession existence is
always vanishing and recommencing, and never has the least
magnitude. Without the permanent there is therefore no time-
relation. Now time cannot be perceived in itself; the permanent
in the appearances is therefore the substratum of all determination of time, and, as likewise follows, is also the condition
of the possibility of all synthetic unity of perceptions, that is,
B 227 of experience. All existence and all change in time have thus
to be viewed as simply a mode of the existence of that which
remains and persists. In all appearances the permanent is the
object itself, that is, substance as phenomenon; everything, on
A 184 the other hand, which changes or can change belongs only to
the way in which substance or substances exist, and therefore
to their determinations.

I find that in all ages, not only philosophers, but even the
common understanding, have recognised this permanence
as a substratum of all change of appearances, and always
assume it to be indubitable. The only difference in this matter
between the common understanding and the philosopher is
that the latter expresses himself somewhat more definitely,
asserting that throughout all changes in the world *substance*
remains, and that only the *accidents* change. But I nowhere
find even the attempt at a proof of this obviously synthetic
proposition. Indeed, it is very seldom placed, where it truly
belongs, at the head of those laws of nature which are pure
and completely *a priori*. Certainly the proposition, that substance is permanent, is tautological. For this permanence is

our sole ground for applying the category of substance to appearance; and we ought first to have proved that in all appearances there is something permanent, and that the transitory is nothing but determination of its existence. But such a proof cannot be developed dogmatically, that is, from concepts, since it concerns a synthetic *a priori* proposition. Yet as it never occurred to anyone that such propositions are valid only in relation to possible experience, and can therefore be proved only through a deduction of the possibility of experience, we need not be surprised that though the above principle is always postulated as lying at the basis of experience (for in empirical knowledge the need of it is *felt*), it has never itself been proved.

A philosopher, on being asked how much smoke weighs, made reply: "Subtract from the weight of the wood burnt the weight of the ashes which are left over, and you have the weight of the smoke". He thus presupposed as undeniable that even in fire the matter (substance) does not vanish, but only suffers an alteration of form. The proposition, that nothing arises out of nothing, is still another consequence of the principle of permanence, or rather of the ever-abiding existence, in the appearances, of the subject proper. For if that in the [field of] appearance which we name substance is to be the substratum proper of all time-determination, it must follow that all existence, whether in past or in future time, can be determined solely in and by it. We can therefore give an appearance the title 'substance' just for the reason that we presuppose its existence throughout all time, and that this is not adequately expressed by the word permanence, a term which applies chiefly to future time. But since the inner necessity of persisting is inseparably bound up with the necessity of always having existed, the expression [principle of permanence] may be allowed to stand. *Gigni de nihilo nihil, in nihilum nil posse reverti*, were two propositions which the ancients always connected together, but which are now sometimes mistakenly separated owing to the belief that they apply to things in themselves, and that the first would run counter to the dependence of the world—even in respect of its substance—upon a supreme cause. But such apprehension is unnecessary. For we have here to deal only with appearances in the

B 228

A 185

B 229

A 186

field of experience;[1] and the unity of experience would never be possible if we were willing to allow that new things, that is, new *substances*, could come into existence. For we should then lose that which alone can represent the unity of time, namely, the identity of the substratum, wherein alone all change has thoroughgoing unity. This permanence is, however, simply the mode in which we represent to ourselves the existence of things in the [field of] appearance.

The determinations of a substance, which are nothing but special ways in which it exists, are called *accidents*. They are always real, because they concern the existence of substance. (Negations are only determinations which assert[2] the non-existence of something in substance.) If we ascribe a special [kind of] existence to this real in substance (for instance, to motion, as an accident of matter), this existence is entitled inherence, in distinction from the existence of substance which is entitled subsistence. But this occasions many misunderstandings; it is more exact and more correct to describe an accident as being simply the way in which the existence of a substance is positively determined. But since it is unavoidable, owing to the conditions of the logical employment of our understanding, to separate off, as it were, that which in the existence of a substance can change while the substance still remains, and to view this variable element in relation to the truly permanent and radical,[3] this category has to be assigned a place among the categories of relation, but rather as the condition of relations than as itself containing a relation

The correct understanding of the concept of *alteration*[4] is also grounded upon [recognition of] this permanence. Coming to be and ceasing to be are not alterations of that which comes to be or ceases to be. Alteration is a way of existing which follows upon another way of existing of the same object. All that alters[5] *persists*, and only its *state changes*.[6] Since this change thus concerns only the determinations, which can cease to be or begin to be, we can say, using what may seem a somewhat paradoxical expression, that only the permanent

B 230

A 187

---

[1] [This is one of the few instances in which Kant employs the phrase *im Felde der Erfahrung* in place of the more usual *in der Erfahrung*.]
[2] [*ausdrücken*.]
[3] [*auf das eigentliche Beharrliche und Radikale*.]
[4] [*Veränderung*.]   [5] [*sich verändert*.]   [6] [*wechselt*.]

(substance) is altered, and that the transitory suffers no   B 231
alteration but only a *change*, inasmuch as certain determinations cease to be and others begin to be.

Alteration can therefore be perceived only in substances. A   A 188
coming to be or ceasing to be that is not simply a determination
of the permanent but is absolute, can never be a possible perception. For this permanent is what alone makes possible the
representation of the transition from one state to another, and
from not-being to being. These transitions can be empirically
known only as changing determinations of that which is permanent. If we assume that something absolutely begins to be,
we must have a point of time in which it was not. But to what
are we to attach this point, if not to that which already exists?
For a preceding empty time is not an object of perception.
But if we connect the coming to be with things which previously existed, and which persist in existence up to the
moment of this coming to be, this latter must be simply a determination of what is permanent in that which precedes it.[1]
Similarly also with ceasing to be; it presupposes the empirical
representation of a time in which an appearance no longer
exists.

Substances, in the [field of] appearance, are the substrata
of all determinations of time. If some of these substances could
come into being and others cease to be, the one condition of
the empirical unity of time would be removed. The appearances would then relate to two different times, and existence   B 232
would flow in two parallel streams—which is absurd. There
is only one time in which all different times must be located,   A 189
not as coexistent but as in succession to one another.

Permanence is thus a necessary condition under which
alone appearances are determinable as things or objects in a
possible experience. We shall have occasion in what follows
to make such observations as may seem necessary in regard
to the empirical criterion of this necessary permanence—the
criterion, consequently, of the substantiality of appearances.

---

[1] [Literally: of the former, as of the permanent.]

B

SECOND ANALOGY

Principle of Succession in Time, in accordance with the Law of Causality *

All alterations take place in conformity with the law of the connection of cause and effect.

Proof

² (The preceding principle has shown that all appearances of succession in time are one and all only *alterations*, that is, a successive being and not-being of the determinations of substance which abides; and therefore that the being of substance as following on its not-being, or its not-being as

B 233 following upon its being cannot be admitted—in other words, that there is no coming into being or passing away of substance itself. Still otherwise expressed the principle is, that *all change (succession) of appearances is merely alteration.* Coming into being and passing away of substance are not alterations of it, since the concept of alteration presupposes one and the same subject as existing with two opposite determinations, and therefore as abiding. With this preliminary reminder, we pass to the proof.)

I perceive that appearances follow one another, that is, that there is a state of things at one time the opposite of which was in the preceding time.³ Thus I am really connecting two perceptions in time. Now connection is not the work ⁴ of mere sense and intuition, but is here the product of a synthetic faculty of imagination, which determines inner sense in respect of the time-relation. But imagination can connect these two states

---

* [In A:]

Principle of Production ¹

Everything that happens, that is, begins to be, presupposes something upon which it follows according to a rule.

¹ [*Erzeugung*.]   ² [The first two paragraphs added in B.]
³ [Reading, with Wille, *in voriger Zeit* for *im vorigen Zustande.*]
⁴ [*Werk.*]

in two ways, so that either the one or the other precedes in time. For time cannot be perceived in itself, and what precedes and what follows cannot, therefore, by relation to it, be empirically determined in the object. I am conscious only that my imagination sets the one state before and the other after, not that the one state precedes the other in the object. In other words, the *objective relation* of appearances that follow upon B 234 one another is not to be determined through mere perception. In order that this relation be known as determined, the relation between the two states must be so thought that it is thereby determined as necessary which of them must be placed before, and which of them after, and that they cannot be placed in the reverse relation. But the concept which carries with it a necessity of synthetic unity can only be a pure concept that lies in the understanding, not in perception; and in this case it is the concept of the *relation of cause and effect*, the former of which determines the latter in time, as its consequence[1]—not as in a sequence that may occur solely in the imagination (or that may not be perceived at all). Experience itself—in other words, empirical knowledge of appearances--is thus possible only in so far as we subject the succession of appearances, and therefore all alteration, to the law of causality; and, as likewise follows, the appearances, as objects of experience, are themselves possible only in conformity with the law

The apprehension of the manifold of appearance is always successive. The representations of the parts follow upon one another. Whether they also follow one another in the object is a point which calls for further reflection, and which is not decided by the above statement. Everything, every representation even, in so far as we are conscious of it, may be entitled object. But it is a question for deeper enquiry what B 235 the word ' object ' ought to signify in respect of appearances A 190 when these are viewed not in so far as they are (as representations) objects, but only in so far as they stand for[2] an object. The appearances, in so far as they are objects of consciousness simply in virtue of being representations, are not in any way distinct from their apprehension, that is, from their reception in the synthesis of imagination; and we must therefore

---

[1] [*als die Folge.*]   [2] [*bezeichnen.*]

agree that the manifold of appearances is always generated in the mind successively. Now if appearances were things in themselves, then since we have to deal solely with our representations, we could never determine from the succession of the representations how their manifold may be connected in the object. How things may be in themselves, apart from the representations through which they affect us, is entirely outside our sphere of knowledge. In spite, however, of the fact that the appearances are not things in themselves, and yet are what alone can be given to us to know, in spite also of the fact that their representation in apprehension is always successive, I have to show what sort of a connection in time belongs to the manifold in the appearances themselves. For instance, the apprehension of the manifold in the appearance of a house which stands before me is successive. The question then arises, whether the manifold of the house is also in itself successive. This, however, is what no one will grant. Now immediately I unfold the transcendental meaning of my concepts of an object, I realise that the house is not a thing in itself, but only an appearance, that is, a representation, the transcendental object of which is unknown. What, then, am I to understand by the question: how the manifold may be connected in the appearance itself, which yet is nothing in itself? That which lies in the successive apprehension is here viewed as representation, while the appearance which is given to me, notwithstanding that it is nothing but the sum of these representations, is viewed as their object; and my concept, which I derive from the representations of apprehension, has to agree with it. Since truth consists in the agreement of knowledge with the object, it will at once be seen that we can here enquire only regarding the formal conditions of empirical truth, and that appearance, in contradistinction to the representations of apprehension, can be represented as an object distinct from them only if it stands under a rule which distinguishes it from every other apprehension and necessitates some one particular mode of connection of the manifold. The object is *that* in the appearance which contains the condition of this necessary rule of apprehension.

Let us now proceed to our problem. That something happens, *i.e.* that something, or some state which did not pre-

B 236

A 191

viously exist, comes to be, cannot be perceived[1] unless it is
preceded by an appearance which does not contain in itself this
state. For an event[2] which should follow upon an empty time,
that is, a coming to be preceded by no state of things, is as
little capable of being apprehended as empty time itself. Every
apprehension of an event[3] is therefore a perception that follows upon another perception. But since, as I have above
illustrated by reference to the appearance of a house, this likewise happens in all synthesis of apprehension, the apprehension of an event is not yet thereby distinguished from other
apprehensions. But, as I also note, in an appearance which
contains a happening (the preceding state of the perception we may entitle A, and the succeeding B) B can be
apprehended only as following upon A; the perception A
cannot follow upon B but only precede it. For instance, I
see a ship move down stream. My perception of its lower
position follows upon the perception of its position higher
up in the stream, and it is impossible that in the apprehension of this appearance the ship should first be perceived lower down in the stream and afterwards higher up.
The order in which the perceptions succeed one another in
apprehension is in this instance determined, and to this order
apprehension is bound down. In the previous example of a
house my perceptions could begin with the apprehension of
the roof and end with the basement, or could begin from below
and end above; and I could similarly apprehend the manifold
of the empirical intuition either from right to left or from left
to right. In the series of these perceptions there was thus no
determinate order specifying at what point[4] I must begin in
order to connect the manifold empirically. But in the perception of an event there is always a rule that makes the order in
which the perceptions (in the apprehension of this appearance)
follow upon one another a *necessary* order.

In this case, therefore, we must derive the *subjective succession* of apprehension from the *objective succession* of appearances. Otherwise the order of apprehension is entirely
undetermined, and does not distinguish one appearance from
another. Since the subjective succession by itself is altogether

---

[1] [Omitting, with Mellin, *empirisch*.]   [2] [*eine Wirklichkeit*.]
[3] [*einer Begebenheit*.]   [4] [Reading, with Mellin, *wo* for *wenn*.]

arbitrary, it does not prove anything as to the manner in which the manifold is connected in the object. The objective succession will therefore consist in that order of the manifold of appearance according to which, *in conformity with a rule*, the apprehension of that which happens follows upon the apprehension of that which precedes. Thus only can I be justified in asserting, not merely of my apprehension, but of appearance itself, that a succession is to be met with in it. This is only another way of saying that I cannot arrange the apprehension otherwise than in this very succession.

In conformity with such a rule there must lie in that which precedes an event the condition of a rule according to which this event invariably and necessarily follows. I cannot reverse this order, proceeding back from the event to determine through apprehension that which precedes. For appearance never goes back from the succeeding to the preceding point of time, though it does indeed stand in relation to *some* preceding point of time. The advance, on the other hand, from a given time to the determinate time that follows is a necessary advance. Therefore, since there certainly is something that follows [*i.e.* that is *apprehended* as following], I must refer it necessarily to something else which precedes it and upon which it follows in conformity with a rule, that is, of necessity. The event, as the conditioned, thus affords reliable evidence of some condition, and this condition is what determines the event.

Let us suppose that there is nothing antecedent to an event, upon which it must follow according to rule. All succession of perception would then be only in the apprehension, that is, would be merely subjective, and would never enable us to determine objectively which perceptions are those that really precede and which are those that follow. We should then have only a play of representations, relating to no object; that is to say, it would not be possible through our perception to distinguish one appearance from another as regards relations of time. For the succession in our apprehension would always be one and the same, and there would be nothing in the appearance which so determines it that a certain sequence is rendered objectively necessary. I could[1] not then assert that two states follow upon one another in the [field of]

B 239

A 194

B 240

A 195

---

[1] [Reading, with Vaihinger, *sagen können* for *sagen*.]

appearance, but only that one apprehension follows upon the other. That is something merely subjective, determining no object; and may not, therefore, be regarded as[1] knowledge of any object, not even of an object in the [field of] appearance.

If, then, we experience that something happens, we in so doing always presuppose that something precedes it, on which it follows according to a rule. Otherwise I should not say of the object that it follows. For mere succession in my apprehension, if there be no rule determining the succession in relation to something that precedes, does not justify me in assuming[2] any succession in the object. I render my subjective synthesis of apprehension objective only by reference to a rule in accordance with which the appearances in their succession, that is, as they happen, are determined by the preceding state. The experience of an event[3] [i.e. of anything as *happening*] is itself possible only on this assumption.

This may seem to contradict all that has hitherto been taught in regard to the procedure of our understanding. The accepted view is that only through the perception and comparison of events repeatedly following in a uniform manner upon preceding appearances are we enabled to discover a rule according to which certain events always follow upon certain B 241 appearances, and that this is the way in which we are first led to construct for ourselves the concept of cause. Now the con- A 196 cept, if thus formed, would be merely empirical, and the rule which it supplies, that everything which happens has a cause, would be as contingent as the experience upon which it is based. Since the universality and necessity of the rule would not be grounded *a priori*, but only on induction, they would be merely fictitious and without genuinely universal validity. It is with these, as with other pure *a priori* representations— for instance, space and time. We can extract clear concepts of them from experience, only because we have put them into experience, and because experience is thus itself brought about only by their means. Certainly, the logical clearness of this representation of a rule determining the series of events is possible only after we have employed it in experience. Never-

1 [Reading, with Hartenstein, *für* for *vor*.]
2 [Adding, with Erdmann, *anzunehmen*.]
3 [*von etwas, was geschieht*.]

theless, recognition of the rule, as a condition of the synthetic unity of appearances in time, has been the ground of experience itself, and has therefore preceded it *a priori*.

We have, then, to show, in the case under consideration, that we never, even in experience, ascribe succession (that is, the happening of some event which previously did not exist) to the object, and so distinguish it from subjective sequence in our apprehension, except when there is an underlying rule which compels us to observe this order of perceptions rather than any other; nay, that this compulsion is really what first makes possible the representation of a succession in the object.

We have representations in us, and can become conscious of them. But however far this consciousness may extend, and however careful and accurate it may be, they still remain mere representations, that is, inner determinations of our mind in this or that relation of time. How, then, does it come about that we posit an object for these representations, and so, in addition to their subjective reality, as modifications, ascribe to them some mysterious kind of[1] objective reality. Objective meaning cannot consist in the relation to another representation (of that which we desire to entitle object[2]), for in that case the question again arises, how this latter representation goes out beyond itself, acquiring objective meaning in addition to the subjective meaning which belongs to it as determination of the mental state. If we enquire what new character *relation to an object* confers upon our representations, what dignity they thereby acquire, we find that it results only in subjecting the representations to a rule, and so in necessitating us to connect them in some one specific manner; and conversely, that only in so far as our representations are necessitated in a certain order as regards their time-relations do they acquire objective meaning.

In the synthesis of appearances the manifold of representations is always successive. Now no object is hereby represented, since through this succession, which is common to all apprehensions, nothing is distinguished from anything else. But immediately I perceive or assume that in this succession there is a relation to the preceding state, from which the representa-

B 242

A 197

B 243

A 198

---

[1] [*ich weiss nicht, was für eine.*]

[2] [Reading, with Mellin, *Gegenstand* for *vom Gegenstande.*]

tion follows in conformity with a rule, I represent[1] something as an event, as something that happens; that is to say, I apprehend[2] an object to which I must ascribe a certain determinate position in time—a position which, in view of the preceding state, cannot be otherwise assigned. When, therefore, I perceive that something happens, this representation first of all contains [the consciousness] that there is something preceding, because only by reference to what precedes does the appearance acquire its time-relation, namely, that of existing after a preceding time in which it itself was not. But it can acquire this determinate position in this relation of time only in so far as something is presupposed in the preceding state upon which it follows invariably, that is, in accordance with a rule. From this there results a twofold consequence. In the first place, I cannot reverse the series, placing that which happens prior to that upon which it follows. And secondly, if the state which precedes is posited, this determinate event follows inevitably and necessarily. The situation, then, is this: there is an order in our representations in which the present, so far as it has come to be, refers us to some preceding state as a correlate of the event which is given; and though this correlate is, indeed, indeterminate, it none the less stands in a determining relation to the event as its consequence, connecting the event in necessary relation with itself in the time-series.

B 244

A 199

If, then, it is a necessary law of our sensibility, and therefore a *formal condition* of all perceptions, that the preceding time necessarily determines the succeeding (since I cannot advance to the succeeding time save through the preceding), it is also an indispensable law of *empirical representation* of the time-series that the appearances of past time determine all existences in the succeeding time, and that these latter, as events, can take place only in so far as the appearances of past time determine their existence in time, that is, determine them according to a rule. *For only in appearances can we empirically apprehend[3] this continuity in the connection of times.*

Understanding is required for all experience and for its possibility. Its primary contribution does not consist in making the representation of objects distinct, but in making the repre-

---

[1] [Reading, with Erdmann, *stelle ich* for *stellt sich.*]
[2] [*erkenne.*] [3] [*erkennen.*]

sentation of an object possible at all. This it does by carrying B 245 the time-order over into the appearances and their existence. For to each of them, [viewed] as [a] consequent, it assigns, through relation to the preceding appearances, a position determined *a priori* in time. Otherwise, they would not accord A 200 with time itself, which [in] *a priori* [fashion] determines the position of all its parts. Now since absolute time is not an object of perception, this determination of position cannot be derived from the relation of appearances to it. On the contrary, the appearances must determine for one another their position in time, and make their[1] time-order a necessary order. In other words, that which follows or happens must follow in conformity with a universal rule upon that which was contained in the preceding state. A series of appearances thus arises which, with the aid of[2] the understanding, produces and makes necessary the same order and continuous connection in the series of possible perceptions as is met with *a priori* in time—the form of inner intuition wherein all perceptions must have a position.

That something happens is, therefore, a perception which belongs to a possible experience. This experience becomes actual when I regard the appearance as determined in its position in time, and therefore as an object that can always be found in the connection of perceptions in accordance with a B 246 rule. This rule, by which we determine something according to succession of time, is, that the condition under which an event invariably and necessarily follows is to be found in what A 201 precedes the event. The principle of sufficient reason is thus the ground of possible experience, that is, of objective knowledge of appearances in respect of their relation in the order of time.

The proof of this principle rests on the following considerations.[3] All empirical knowledge involves the synthesis of the manifold by the imagination. This synthesis is always successive, that is, the representations in it are always sequent upon one another. In the imagination this sequence is not in any way determined in its order, as to what must precede and what must follow, and the series of sequent representations

---

[1] [Reading, with Görland, *dieselben* for *dieselbe*.]
[2] [*vermittelst*.]   [3] [*Momenten*.]

can indifferently be taken either in backward or in forward order. But if this synthesis is a synthesis of apprehension[1] of the manifold of a given appearance, the order is determined in the object, or, to speak more correctly, is an order of successive synthesis that determines an object. In accordance with this order something must necessarily precede, and when this antecedent is posited, something else must necessarily follow. If, then, my perception is to contain knowledge of an event, of something as actually happening, it must be an empirical judgment in which we think the sequence as determined; that is, it presupposes another appearance in time, B 247 upon which it follows necessarily, according to a rule. Were it not so, were I to posit the antecedent and the event were not to follow necessarily thereupon, I should have to regard the succession as a merely subjective play of my fancy; and if I still represented it to myself as something objective, I should A 202 have to call it a mere dream. Thus the relation of appearances (as possible perceptions) according to which the subsequent event, that which happens, is, as to its existence, necessarily determined in time by something preceding in conformity with a rule—in other words, the relation of cause to effect—is the condition of the objective validity of our empirical judgments, in respect of the series of perceptions, and so of their empirical truth; that is to say, it is the condition of experience. The principle of the causal relation in the sequence of appearances is therefore also valid of[2] all objects of experience ([in so far as they are] under the conditions of succession), as being itself the ground of the possibility of such experience.

At this point a difficulty arises with which we must at once deal. The principle of the causal connection among appearances is limited in our formula to their serial succession, whereas it applies also to their coexistence, when cause and effect are simultaneous. For instance, a room is warm while the outer air is cool. I look around for the cause, and find a B 248 heated stove. Now the stove, as cause, is simultaneous with its effect, the heat of the room. Here there is no serial succession in time between cause and effect. They are simultaneous, and

---

[1] [Wille may possibly be right in suggesting that in place of *Apprehension* we should read *Apperzeption*.]

[2] [Reading, with Hartenstein, *von* for *vor*.]

A 203 yet the law is valid. The great majority of efficient natural causes are simultaneous with their effects, and the sequence in time of the latter is due only to the fact that the cause cannot achieve its complete effect in one moment. But in the moment in which the effect first comes to be, it is invariably simultaneous with the causality of its cause. If the cause should have ceased to exist a moment before, the effect would never have come to be. Now we must not fail to note that it is the *order* of time, not the *lapse* of time, with which we have to reckon; the relation remains even if no time has elapsed. The time between the causality of the cause and its immediate effect may be [a] *vanishing* [quantity], and they may thus be simultaneous; but the relation of the one to the other will always still remain determinable in time. If I view as a cause a ball which impresses a hollow as it lies on a stuffed cushion, the cause is simultaneous with the effect. But I still distinguish the two through the time-relation of their dynamical connection. For if I lay the ball on the cushion, a hollow follows upon the previous flat smooth shape; but B 249 if (for any reason) there previously exists a hollow in the cushion, a leaden ball does not follow upon it.

The sequence in time is thus the sole empirical criterion of an effect in its relation to the causality of the cause which A 204 precedes it. A glass [filled with water] is the cause of the rising of the water above its horizontal surface, although both appearances are simultaneous. For immediately I draw off water from a larger vessel into the glass, something follows, namely, the alteration from the horizontal position which the water then had to the concave form which it assumes in the glass.

Causality leads to the concept of action, this in turn to the concept of force, and thereby to the concept of substance. As my critical scheme, which is concerned solely with the sources of synthetic *a priori* knowledge, must not be complicated through the introduction of analyses, which aim only at the clarification, not at the extension, of concepts, I leave detailed exposition of my concepts to a future system of pure reason. Such an analysis has already, indeed, been developed in considerable detail in the existing text-books. But I must not leave unconsidered the empirical criterion of a substance, in so far as substance appears to manifest itself not through permanence of appearance, but more adequately and easily through action.

Wherever there is action—and therefore activity and force B 250 —there is also substance, and it is in substance alone that the seat of this fruitful source of appearances must be sought. This is, so far, well said; but when we seek to explain what is to be understood by substance, and in so doing are careful to avoid the fallacy of reasoning in a circle, the discovery of an answer is no easy task. How are we to conclude directly A 205 from the action to the *permanence* of that which acts? For that is an essential and quite peculiar characteristic of substance (as phenomenon). But while according to the usual procedure, which deals with concepts in purely analytic fashion, this question would be completely insoluble, it presents no such difficulty from the standpoint which we have been formulating Action signifies the relation of the subject of causality to its effect. Since, now, every effect consists in that which happens, and therefore in the transitory,[1] which signifies time in its character of succession, its ultimate subject, as the substratum of everything that changes, is the *permanent*, that is, substance. For according to the principle of causality actions are always the first ground of all change of appearances, and cannot therefore be found in a subject which itself changes, because in that case other actions and another subject would be required to determine this change. For this reason action is a sufficient empirical criterion to establish the substantiality of a subject,[2] without my requiring first to go in quest of its B 251 permanence through the comparison of perceptions. Besides, by such method [of comparison] we could not achieve the completeness required for the magnitude and strict universality of the concept. That the first subject of the causality of all coming to be and ceasing to be cannot itself, in the field of appearances, come to be and cease to be, is an assured A 206 conclusion which leads to [the concept of] empirical necessity and permanence in existence, and so to the concept of a substance as appearance.

When something happens, the mere coming to be, apart from all question of what it is that has come to be, is already in

---

[1] [*im Wandelbaren.*]   [2] [Adding, with Wille, *eines Subjektes.*]

230 KANT'S CRITIQUE OF PURE REASON

itself a matter for enquiry. The transition from the not-being of a state to this state, even supposing that this state [as it occurs] in the [field of] appearance exhibited no quality, of itself demands investigation. This coming to be, as was shown above in the *First Analogy*, does not concern substance, which does not come to be, but its state. It is, therefore, only alteration, not a coming to be out of nothing. For if coming to be out of nothing is regarded as effect of a foreign[1] cause, it has to be entitled creation, and that cannot be admitted as an event among appearances, since its mere possibility would destroy the unity of experience. On the other hand, when I view all things not as phenomena but as things in themselves, and

B 252 as objects of the mere understanding, then despite their being substances they can be regarded, in respect of their existence, as depending upon a foreign cause. But our terms would then carry with them quite other meanings, and would not apply to appearances as possible objects of experience.

How anything can be altered, and how it should be possible

A 207 that upon one state in a given moment an opposite state may follow in the next moment—of this we have not, *a priori*, the least conception. For that we require knowledge of actual forces, which can only be given empirically, as, for instance, of the moving forces, or what amounts to the same thing, of certain successive appearances, as motions, which indicate [the presence of] such forces. But apart from all question of what the content of the alteration, that is, what the state which is altered, may be, the form of every alteration, the condition under which, as a coming to be of another state, it can alone take place, and so the succession of the states themselves (the happening[2]), can still be considered *a priori* according to the law of causality and the conditions of time.[a]

B 253 If a substance passes from one state, *a*, to another, *b*, the point of time of the second is distinct from that of the first, and

---

[a] It should be carefully noted that I speak not of the alteration of certain relations in general, but of alteration of state. Thus, when a body moves uniformly, it does not in any way alter its state (of motion); that occurs only when its motion increases or diminishes.

[1] [*fremden.*]
[2] [Reading, with Vaihinger, *das Geschehen* for *das Geschehene.*]

follows upon it. Similarly, the second state as reality in the [field of] appearance differs from the first wherein it did not exist, as b from zero. That is to say, even[1] if the state b differed from the state a only in magnitude, the alteration would be a coming to be of $b-a$, which did not exist in the A 208 previous state, and in respect of which it = 0.

The question therefore arises how a thing passes from one state = a to another = b. Between two instants[2] there is always a time, and between any two states in the two instants there is always a difference which has magnitude. For all parts of appearances are always themselves magnitudes. All transition from one state to another therefore occurs in a time which is contained between two instants, of which the first determines the state from which the thing arises, and the second that into which it passes. Both instants, then, are limits of the time of a change, and so of the intermediate state between the two states, and therefore as such form part of the total alteration. Now every alteration has a cause which evinces[3] its causality in the whole time in which the alteration takes place. This cause, therefore, does not engender the alteration suddenly, that is, at once or in one instant, but in a time; so that, as the time in- B 254 creases from the initial instant a to its completion in b, the magnitude of the reality ($b-a$) is in like manner generated through all smaller degrees which are contained between the first and the last. All alteration is thus only possible through a continuous action of the causality which, so far as it is uniform, is entitled a moment.[4] The alteration does not consist of these moments, but is generated by them as their effect. A 209

That is the law of the continuity of all alteration. Its ground is this: that neither time nor appearance in time consists of parts which are the smallest [possible], and that, nevertheless, the state of a thing passes in its alteration through all these parts, as elements, to its second state. In the [field of] appearance there is no difference of the real that is the smallest, just as in the magnitude of times there is no time that is the smallest; and the new state of reality accordingly proceeds from the first wherein this reality was not, through all the infinite degrees, the differences of which from one another are all smaller than that between 0 and a.

[1] [auch.]   [2] [Augenblicken.]   [3] [beweist.]   [4] [Moment.]

While we are not concerned to enquire what utility this principle may have in the investigation of nature, what does imperatively call for investigation is the question how such a principle, which seems to extend our knowledge of nature, can be possible completely *a priori*. Such an enquiry cannot be dispensed with, even though direct inspection may show the principle to be true and [empirically] real, and though the question, how it should be possible, may therefore be considered superfluous. For there are so many ungrounded claims to the extension of our knowledge through pure reason, that we must take it as a universal principle that any such pretension is of itself a ground for being always mistrustful, and that, in the absence of evidence afforded by a thoroughgoing deduction, we may not believe and assume the justice of such claims, no matter how clear the *dogmatic* proof of them may appear to be.

B 255

A 210

All increase in empirical knowledge, and every advance of perception, no matter what the objects may be, whether appearances or pure intuitions, is nothing but an extension of the determination of inner sense, that is, an advance in time. This advance in time determines everything, and is not in itself determined through anything further. That is to say, its parts are given only in time, and only through the synthesis of time; they are[1] not given antecedently to the synthesis. For this reason every transition in perception to something which follows in time is a determination of time through the generation of this perception, and since time is always and in all its parts a magnitude, is likewise the generation of a perception as a magnitude through all degrees of which no one is the smallest, from zero up to its determinate degree. This reveals the possibility of knowing *a priori* a law of alterations, in respect of their form. We are merely anticipating our own apprehension, the formal condition of which, since it dwells in us prior to all appearance that is given, must certainly be capable of being known *a priori*.

B 256

In the same manner, therefore, in which time contains the sensible *a priori* condition of the possibility of a continuous advance of the existing to what follows, the understanding, by virtue of[2] the unity of apperception, is the *a priori* condition of the possibility of a continuous determination of all positions for the appearances in this time, through the series of

A 211

---

[1] [Reading, with Vaihinger, *sind* for *sie*.]   [2] [*vermittelst*.]

causes and effects, the former of which inevitably lead to the existence of the latter, and so render the empirical knowledge of the time-relations valid universally for all time, and therefore objectively valid.

C

THIRD ANALOGY

Principle of Coexistence, in accordance with the Law of Reciprocity or Community

All substances, in so far as they can be perceived to coexist in space, are in thoroughgoing reciprocity *

Proof

[1]Things are coexistent when in empirical intuition the perceptions of them can follow upon one another recipro- B 257 cally, which, as has been shown in the proof of the second principle, cannot occur in the succession of appearances. Thus I can direct my perception first to the moon and then to the earth, or, conversely, first to the earth and then to the moon; and because the perceptions of these objects can follow each other reciprocally, I say that they are coexistent. Now coexistence is the existence of the manifold in one and the same time. But time itself cannot be perceived, and we are not, therefore, in a position to gather, simply from things being set in the same time, that their perceptions can follow each other reciprocally. The synthesis of imagination in apprehension would only reveal that the one perception is in the subject when the other is not there, and *vice versa*, but not that the objects are coexistent, that is, that if the one exists the other exists at the same time, and that it is only because they thus coexist that the perceptions are able to

---

* [In A:]
Principle of Community
All substances, so far as they coexist, stand in thoroughgoing community, that is, in mutual interaction.

[1] [This paragraph added in B.]

234 KANT'S CRITIQUE OF PURE REASON

follow one another reciprocally. Consequently, in the case of things which coexist externally to one another, a pure concept of the reciprocal sequence of their determinations is required, if we are to be able to say that the reciprocal sequence of the perceptions is grounded in the object, and so to represent the coexistence as objective. But the relation of substances in which the one contains determinations the ground of which is contained in the other is the relation of influence; and when each substance[1] reciprocally contains the ground of the determinations in the other, the relation is that of community or reciprocity. Thus the coexistence of substances in space cannot be known in experience save on the assumption of their reciprocal interaction. This is therefore the condition of the possibility of the things themselves as objects of experience.

Things are coexistent so far as they exist in one and the same time. But how do we know that they are in one and the same time? We do so when the order in the synthesis of apprehension of the manifold is a matter of indifference, that is, whether it be from A through B, C, D to E, or reversewise from E to A. For if they were[2] in succession to one another in time, in the order, say, which begins with A and ends in E, it is impossible that we should begin the apprehension in the perception of E and proceed backwards to A, since A belongs to past time and can no longer be an object of apprehension.

Now assuming that in a manifold of substances, as appearances, each of them is completely isolated, that is, that no one acts on[3] any other and receives reciprocal influences in return, I maintain that their *coexistence* would not be an object of a possible perception and that the existence of one could not lead by any path of empirical synthesis to the existence of another. For if we bear in mind that they would be separated by a completely empty space, the perception which advances from one to another in time would indeed, by means of a succeeding perception, determine the existence of the latter, but would not be able to distinguish whether it follows object-

---

[1] [Reading, with Wille, *jede* (*Substanz*) for *dieses*.]
[2] [Reading, with Wille, *wären* for *wäre*.]
[3] [Reading, with Vorländer, *auf* for *in*.]

ively upon the first or whether it is not rather coexistent
with it.

There must, therefore, besides the mere existence of A and
B, be something through which A determines for B, and also
reversewise B determines for A, its position in time, because
only on this condition can these substances be empirically
represented as *coexisting*. Now only that which is the cause of
another, or of its determinations, determines the position of the
other in time. Each substance (inasmuch as only in respect of
its determinations can it be an effect[1]) must therefore contain
in itself the causality of certain determinations in the other
substance, and at the same time the effects of the causality of
that other; that is, the substances must stand, immediately or
mediately, in dynamical community, if their coexistence is to A 213
be known in any possible experience. Now, in respect to the
objects of experience, everything without which the experience of these objects would not itself be possible is necessary. B 260
It is therefore necessary that all substances in the [field of]
appearance, so far as they coexist, should stand in thoroughgoing community of mutual interaction.

The word community is in the German language ambiguous. It may mean either *communio* or *commercium* We here
employ it in the latter sense, as signifying a dynamical community, without which even local community (*communio spatii*)
could never be empirically known. We may easily recognise
from our experiences that only the continuous influences in all
parts of space can lead our senses from one object to another.
The light, which plays between our eye and the celestial bodies,
produces a mediate community between us and them, and
thereby shows[2] us that they coexist. We cannot empirically
change our position, and perceive the change, unless matter
in all parts of space makes perception of our position possible
to us. For only thus by means of their reciprocal influence can
the parts of matter establish their simultaneous existence, and
thereby, though only mediately, their coexistence, even to
the most remote objects. Without community each perception of an appearance in space is broken off from every other, A 214
and the chain of empirical representations, that is, experience,

---

[1] [*Folge.*]
[2] [Reading, with Adickes, *bewirke ... beweise* for *bewirken ... beweisen.*]

I 2

would have to begin entirely anew with each new object,
B 261 without the least connection with the preceding representation,
and without standing to it in any relation of time. I do not by
this argument at all profess to disprove void space, for it may
exist where perceptions cannot reach, and where there is,
therefore, no empirical knowledge of coexistence. But such a
space is not for us an object of any possible experience.

The following remarks may be helpful in [further] elucidation [of my argument]. In our mind, all appearances, since
they are contained in a possible experience, must stand in
community (*communio*) of apperception, and in so far as the
objects are to be represented as coexisting in connection with
each other, they must mutually determine their position in
one time, and thereby constitute a whole. If this subjective
community is to rest on an objective ground, or is to hold of
appearances as substances, the perception of the one must
as ground make possible the perception of the other, and
reversewise—in order that the succession which is always
found in the perceptions, as apprehensions, may not be ascribed to the objects, and in order that, on the contrary, these
objects may be represented as coexisting. But this is a reciprocal influence, that is, a real community (*commercium*) of
A 215 substances; without it the empirical relation of coexistence
could not be met with[1] in experience. Through this *com-*
mercium the appearances, so far as they stand outside one
B 262 another and yet in connection, constitute a composite (*com-*
positum reale), and such composites are possible in many
different ways. The three dynamical relations, from which
all others spring, are therefore inherence, consequence,[2] and
composition

*   *   *

These, then, are the three analogies of experience. They are
simply principles of the determination of the existence of appearances in time, according to all its three modes, viz. the relation to time itself as a magnitude (the magnitude of existence,
that is, *duration*), the relation in time as a *successive* series, and
finally the relation in time as a sum of all *simultaneous* existence. This unity of time-determination is altogether dynamical.

---

[1] [*stattfinden.*]   [2] [*Konsequenz.*]

For time is not viewed as that wherein experience immediately determines position for every existence. Such determination is impossible, inasmuch as absolute time is not an object of perception with which appearances could be confronted. What determines for each appearance its position in time is the rule of the understanding through which alone the existence of appearances can acquire synthetic unity as regards relations of time; and that rule consequently determines the position [in a manner that is] *a priori* and valid for each and every time.

By nature, in the empirical sense, we understand the connection of appearances as regards their existence according to necessary rules, that is, according to laws. There are certain laws which first make a nature possible, and these laws are *a priori*. Empirical laws can exist and be discovered only through experience, and indeed in consequence of those original laws through which experience itself first becomes possible. Our analogies therefore really portray the unity of nature in the connection of all appearances under certain exponents[1] which express nothing save the relation of time (in so far as time comprehends all existence) to the unity of apperception —such unity being possible only in synthesis according to rules. Taken together, the analogies thus declare that all appearances lie, and must lie, in *one* nature, because without this *a priori* unity no unity of experience, and therefore no determination of objects in it, would be possible.

As to the mode of proof of which we have made use in these transcendental laws of nature, and as to their peculiar character, an observation has to be made which must likewise be of very great importance as supplying a rule to be followed in every other attempt to prove *a priori* propositions that are intellectual and at the same time synthetic. Had we attempted to prove these analogies dogmatically; had we, that is to say, attempted to show from concepts that everything which exists is to be met with only in that which is permanent, that every event presupposes something in the preceding state upon which it[2] follows in conformity with a rule; and finally, that in the manifold which is coexistent the states coexist in relation to one another in conformity with a rule and so stand in

{A 216
{B 263

B 264
A 217

---

[1] [*Exponenten*.]   [2] [Reading, with Hartenstein, *sie* for *es*.]

community, all our labour would have been wasted. For through mere concepts of these things, analyse them as we may, we can never advance from one object and its existence to the existence of another or to its mode of existence. But there is an alternative method, namely, to investigate the possibility of experience as a knowledge wherein all objects—if their representation is to have objective reality for us—must finally be capable of being given to us. In this third [medium],[1] the essential form of which consists in the synthetic unity of the apperception of all appearances, we have found *a priori* conditions of complete and necessary determination of time for all existence in the [field of] appearance, without which even empirical determination of time would be impossible. In it we have also found rules of synthetic unity *a priori*, by means of which we can anticipate experience. For lack of this method, and owing to the erroneous assumption that synthetic propositions, which the empirical employment of the understanding recommends as being its principles, may be proved dogmatically, the attempt has, time and again, been made, though always vainly, to obtain a proof of the principle of sufficient reason.[2] And since the guiding-thread of the categories, which alone can reveal and make noticeable every gap in the understanding, alike in regard to concepts and to principles, has hitherto been lacking, no one has so much as thought of the other two analogies, although use has always tacitly been made of them.[a]

B 265
A 218

[a] The unity of the world-whole, in which all appearances have to be connected, is evidently a mere consequence of the tacitly assumed principle of the community of all substances which are coexistent. For if they were isolated, they would not as parts constitute a whole. And if their connection (the reciprocal action of the manifold) were not already necessary because of their coexistence, we could not argue from this latter, which is a merely ideal relation, to the former, which is a real relation. We have, however, in the proper context, shown that community is really the ground of the possibility of an empirical knowledge of coexistence, and that the inference, rightly regarded, is simply from this empirical knowledge to community as its condition.

[1] [*In diesem Dritten.*]
[2] [*des zureichenden Grundes.*]

4

THE POSTULATES OF EMPIRICAL THOUGHT IN GENERAL

1. That which agrees with the formal conditions of experience, that is, with the conditions of intuition and of concepts, is *possible*.

2. That which is bound up with the material conditions B 266 of experience, that is, with sensation, is *actual*.

3. That which in its connection with the actual is determined in accordance with universal conditions of experience, is (that is, exists as) *necessary*.

Explanation

The categories of modality have the peculiarity that, in A 219 determining an object, they do not in the least enlarge the concept to which they are attached as predicates. They only express the relation of the concept to the faculty of knowledge. Even when the concept of a thing is quite complete, I can still enquire whether this object is merely possible or is also actual, or if actual, whether it is not also necessary. No additional determinations are thereby thought in the object itself; the question is only how the object, together with all its determinations, is related to understanding and its empirical employment, to empirical judgment,[1] and to reason in its application to experience.

Just on this account also the principles of modality are nothing but explanations of the concepts of possibility, actuality, and necessity, in their empirical employment; at the same time they restrict all categories to their merely empirical employment, and do not approve or allow their transcendental B 267 employment. For if they are not to have a purely logical significance, analytically expressing the form of *thought*, but are to refer to the possibility, actuality, or necessity of *things*, they must concern possible experience and its synthetic unity, in which alone objects of knowledge can be given.

The postulate of the *possibility* of things requires that A 220 the concept of the things should agree with the formal conditions of an experience in general. But this, the objective form of experience in general, contains all synthesis that is

[1] [*Urteilskraft.*]

required for knowledge of objects. A concept which contains a synthesis is to be regarded as empty and as not related to any object, if this synthesis does not belong to experience either as being derived from it, in which case it is an *empirical concept*, or as being an *a priori* condition upon which experience in general in its formal aspect rests, in which case it is a *pure concept*. In the latter case it still belongs to experience, inasmuch as its object is to be met with only in experience. For whence shall we derive the character of the possibility of an object which is thought through a synthetic *a priori* concept, if not from the synthesis which constitutes the form of B 268 the empirical knowledge of objects? It is, indeed, a necessary logical condition that a concept of the possible must not contain any contradiction; but this is not by any means sufficient to determine the objective reality of the concept, that is, the possibility of such an object as is thought through the concept. Thus there is no contradiction in the concept of a figure which is enclosed within two straight lines, since the concepts of two straight lines and of their coming together contain no negation A 221 of a figure. The impossibility arises not from the concept in itself, but in connection with its construction in space, that is, from the conditions of space and of its determination. And since these contain *a priori* in themselves the form of experience in general, they have objective reality; that is, they apply to possible things.

We shall now proceed to show the far-reaching utility and influence of this postulate of possibility. If I represent to myself a thing which is permanent, so that everything in it which changes belongs only to its state, I can never know from such a concept that a thing of this kind is possible. Or if I represent to myself something which is so constituted that if it is posited something else invariably and inevitably follows from it, this may certainly be so thought without contradiction; but this thought affords no means of judging whether this property (causality) is to be met with in any possible thing. Lastly, B 269 I can represent to myself diverse things (substances), which are so constituted that the state of the one carries with it some consequence in the state of the other, and this reciprocally; but I can never determine from these concepts, which contain a merely arbitrary synthesis, whether a relation of this kind can belong to any [possible] things. Only through the fact that these concepts express *a priori* the relations of perceptions in every experience, do we know their objective reality, that is, their transcendental truth, and this, indeed, independently of experience, though not independently of all relation to the form of an experience in general, and to the synthetic unity in which alone objects can be empirically known.

But if we should seek to frame quite new concepts of substances, forces, reciprocal actions, from the material which perception presents to us, without experience itself yielding the example of their connection, we should be occupying ourselves with mere fancies, of whose possibility there is no criterion since we have neither borrowed these concepts [directly] from experience, nor have taken experience as our instructress in their formation Such fictitious concepts, unlike the categories, can acquire the character of possibility not in *a priori* fashion, as conditions upon which all experience depends, but only *a posteriori* as being concepts which are given through experience itself. And, consequently, their possibility must either be known *a posteriori* and empirically, or it cannot be known at all. A substance which would be permanently present in space, but without filling it (like that mode of existence intermediate between matter and thinking being which some would seek to introduce), or a special ultimate mental power of *intuitively* anticipating the future (and not merely inferring it), or lastly a power of standing in community of thought with other men, however distant they may be—are concepts the possibility of which is altogether groundless, as they cannot be based on experience and its known laws; and without such confirmation they are arbitrary combinations of thoughts, which, although indeed free from contradiction, can make no claim to objective reality, and none, therefore, as to the possibility of an object such as we here profess to think. As regards reality, we obviously cannot think it *in concreto*, without calling experience to our aid. For reality is bound up with sensation, the matter of experience, not with that form of relation in regard to which we can, if we so choose, resort to a playful inventiveness.[1]

But I leave aside everything the possibility of which can

A 222

B 270

A 223

---

[1] [*in Erdichtungen spielen.*]

be derived only from its actuality in experience, and have here
in view only the possibility of things through *a priori* concepts;
B 271 and I maintain the thesis that their possibility can never be
established from such concepts taken in and by themselves,
but only when the concepts are viewed as formal and objective
conditions of experience in general.

It does, indeed, seem as if the possibility of a triangle could
be known from its concept in and by itself (the concept is certainly independent of experience), for we can, as a matter of
fact, give it an object completely *a priori*, that is, can construct
it. But since this is only the form of an object, it would remain
A 224 a mere product of imagination, and the possibility of its object
would still be doubtful. To determine its possibility, something
more is required, namely, that such a figure be thought under
no conditions save those upon which all objects of experience
rest. That space is a formal *a priori* condition of outer experiences, that the formative[1] synthesis through which we construct a triangle in imagination is precisely the same as that
which we exercise in the apprehension of an appearance, in
making for ourselves an empirical concept of it—these are the
considerations that alone enable us to connect the representation of the possibility of such a thing with the concept of it.
Similarly, since the concepts of continuous magnitudes, indeed
of magnitudes in general, are one and all synthetic, the possibility of such magnitudes is never clear from the concepts them-
B 272 selves, but only when they are viewed as formal conditions
of the determination of objects in experience in general. And
where, indeed, should we seek for objects corresponding to
these concepts if not in experience, through which alone objects are given to us? We can, indeed, prior to experience
itself, know and characterise the possibility of things, merely
by reference to the formal conditions under which in experience anything whatsoever is determined as object, and
therefore can do so completely *a priori*. But, even so, this is
possible only in relation to experience and within its limits.
A 225   The postulate bearing on the knowledge of things as
actual does not, indeed, demand immediate *perception* (and,
therefore, sensation of which we are conscious) of the object
whose existence is to be known. What we do, however,

---

[1] [*bildende.*]

require is the connection of the object with some actual perception, in accordance with the analogies of experience, which define[1] all real connection in an experience in general.[2]

In the *mere concept* of a thing no mark[3] of its existence is to be found. For though it may be so complete that nothing which is required for thinking the thing with all its inner determinations is lacking to it, yet existence has nothing to do with all this, but only with the question whether such a thing be so given us that the perception of it can, if need be, precede the concept. For that the concept precedes the perception signifies the concept's mere possibility; the perception which supplies the content to the concept is the sole mark of actuality. We can also, however, know the existence of the thing prior to its perception and, consequently, comparatively speaking, in an *a priori* manner, if only it be bound up with certain perceptions, in accordance with the principles of their empirical connection (the analogies). For the existence of the thing being thus bound up with our perceptions in a possible experience, we are able in the series of possible perceptions and under the guidance of the analogies to make the transition from our actual perception to the thing in question. Thus from the perception of the attracted iron filings we know of the existence of a magnetic matter pervading all bodies, although the constitution of our organs cuts us off from all immediate perception of this medium.[4] For in accordance with the laws of sensibility and the context of our perceptions, we should, were our senses more refined, come also in an experience[5] upon the immediate empirical intuition of it. The grossness of our senses does not in any way decide the form of possible experience in general. Our knowledge of the existence of things reaches, then, only so far as perception and its advance[6] according to empirical laws can extend. If we do not start from experience, or do not proceed in accordance with laws of the em-

B 273

A 226

B 274

---

[1] [*darlegen.*]
[2] [In the opening sentence of this paragraph I adopt a change in the order of the words, as suggested by Valentiner.]
[3] [*Charakter.*]   [4] [*dieses Stoffs.*]
[5] [If a comma be omitted from the text of A and B, we have what is perhaps the more natural reading: "the context of our perceptions in one experience, we should˙. . . come also upon . . ."]
[6] [Reading, with Wille, *Fortgang* for *Anhang.*]

pirical connection of appearances, our guessing or enquiring into the existence of anything will only be an idle pretence. [1] Idealism raises, however, what is a serious objection to these rules for proving existence mediately; and this is the proper place for its refutation.

*   *   *

Refutation of Idealism

Idealism—meaning thereby *material* idealism—is the theory which declares the existence of objects in space outside us either to be merely doubtful and indemonstrable or to be false and impossible. The former is the *problematic* idealism of Descartes, which holds that there is only one empirical assertion that is indubitably certain, namely, that 'I am'. The latter is the *dogmatic* idealism of Berkeley. He maintains that space, with all the things of which it is the inseparable condition, is something which is in itself impossible; and he therefore regards the things in space as merely imaginary entities.[2] Dogmatic idealism is unavoidable, if space be interpreted as a property that must belong to things in themselves. For in that case space, and everything to which it serves as condition, is a non-entity.[3] The ground on which this idealism rests has already been undermined by us in the Transcendental Aesthetic. Problematic idealism, which makes no such assertion, but merely pleads incapacity to prove, through immediate experience, any existence except our own, is, in so far as it allows of no decisive judgment until sufficient proof has been found, reasonable and in accordance with a thorough and philosophical mode of thought. The required proof must, therefore, show that we have *experience*, and not merely imagination of outer things; and this, it would seem, cannot be achieved save by proof that even our inner experience, which for Descartes is indubitable, is possible only on the assumption of outer experience.

B 275

---

[1] [This sentence, and the immediately following *Refutation of Idealism*, added in B.]
[2] [*Einbildungen.*]   [3] [*Unding.*]

Thesis

The mere, but empirically determined, consciousness of my own existence proves the existence of objects in space outside me.

Proof

I am conscious of my own existence as determined in time. All determination of time presupposes something *permanent* in perception. This permanent cannot, however, be something in me, since it is only through this permanent that my existence in time can itself be determined.[1] Thus perception of this permanent is possible only through a *thing* outside me and not through the mere *representation* of a thing outside me; and consequently the determination of my existence in time is possible only through the existence of actual things which I perceive outside me. B 276 Now consciousness [of my existence] in time is necessarily bound up with consciousness of the [condition of the] possibility of this time-determination; and it is therefore necessarily bound up with the existence of things outside me, as the condition of the time-determination. In other words, the consciousness of my existence is at the same time an immediate consciousness of the existence of other things outside me.

Note 1. It will be observed that in the foregoing proof the game played by idealism has been turned against itself, and with greater justice. Idealism assumed that the only immediate experience is inner experience, and that from it we can only *infer* outer things—and this, moreover, only in an untrustworthy manner, as in all cases where we are inferring from given effects to determinate causes. In this particular case, the cause of the representations, which we ascribe, perhaps falsely, to outer things, may lie in ourselves. But in the above proof it has been shown that outer experience is really

---

[1] [As stated by Kant in the Preface to B (above, p. 36 n.), this sentence should be altered as follows: "But this permanent cannot be an intuition in me. For all grounds of determination of my existence which are to be met with in me are representations; and as representations themselves require a permanent distinct from them, in relation to which their change, and so my existence in the time wherein they change, may be determined."]

B 277 immediate,[a] and that only by means of it is inner experience —not indeed the consciousness of my own existence, but the determination of it in time—possible. Certainly, the representation 'I am', which expresses the consciousness that can accompany all thought, immediately includes in itself the existence of a subject; but it does not so include any *knowledge* of that subject, and therefore also no empirical knowledge, that is, no experience of it. For this we require, in addition to the thought of something existing, also intuition, and in this case inner intuition, in respect of which, that is, of time, the subject must be determined. But in order so to determine it, outer objects are quite indispensable; and it therefore follows that inner experience is itself possible only mediately, and only through outer experience.

Note 2. With this thesis all employment of our cognitive faculty in experience, in the determination of time, entirely agrees. Not only are we unable to perceive[1] any determination of time save through change in outer relations (motion) relatively to the permanent in space (for instance, the motion of the sun relatively to objects on the earth), we

B 278 have nothing permanent on which, as intuition, we can base the concept of a substance, save only *matter*; and even this permanence is not obtained from outer experience, but is presupposed *a priori* as a necessary condition of determination of time, and therefore also as a determination of inner sense in respect of [the determination of] our own existence through the existence of outer things. The consciousness of myself in the representation 'I' is not an intuition, but a

---

[a] The *immediate* consciousness of the existence of outer things is, in the preceding thesis, not presupposed, but proved, be the possibility of this consciousness understood by us or not. The question as to its possibility would be this: whether we have an inner sense only, and no outer sense, but merely an outer imagination. It is clear, however, that in order even only to imagine something as B 277 outer, that is, to present it to sense in intuition, we must already have an outer sense, and must thereby immediately distinguish the mere receptivity of an outer intuition from the spontaneity which characterises every act of imagination. For should we merely be imagining an outer sense, the faculty of intuition, which is to be determined by the faculty of imagination, would itself be annulled.

[1] [Reading, with Grillo, *wahrnehmen* for *vornehmen*.]

merely *intellectual* representation of the spontaneity [1] of a thinking subject. This 'I' has not, therefore, the least predicate of intuition, which, as permanent, might serve as correlate for the determination of time in inner sense—in the manner in which, for instance, *impenetrability* serves in our *empirical* intuition of matter.

Note 3. From the fact that the existence of outer things is required for the possibility of a determinate consciousness of the self, it does not follow that every intuitive representation of outer things involves the existence of these things, for their representation can very well be the product merely of the imagination (as in dreams and delusions). Such representation is merely the reproduction of previous outer perceptions, which, as has been shown, are possible only through the reality of outer objects. All that we have here sought to prove is that inner experience in general is possible only through outer experience in general. Whether this or that B 279 supposed experience be not purely imaginary, must be ascertained from its special determinations, and through its congruence with the criteria of all real experience.[2]

*　　*　　*

Lastly, as regards the third postulate, it concerns material necessity in existence, and not merely formal and logical necessity in the connection of concepts. Since the existence of any object of the senses cannot be known completely *a priori*, but only comparatively *a priori*, relatively to some other previously given existence; and since, even so, we[3] can then A 227 arrive only at such an existence as must somewhere be contained in the context[4] of the experience, of which the given perception is a part, the necessity of existence can never be known from concepts, but always only from connection with that which is perceived, in accordance with universal laws of experience. Now there is no existence that can be known as necessary under the condition of other given appearances, save the existence of effects from given causes,

---

[1] [*Selbsttätigkeit.*] [2] [This concludes passage added in B.]
[3] [Reading, with Mellin, *man gleichwohl* for *gleichwohl.*]
[4] [*Zusammenhange.*]

in accordance with laws of causality. It is not, therefore, the existence of things (substances) that we can know to be necessary, but only the existence of their state; and this necessity
B 280 of the existence of their state we can know only from other states, which are given in perception, in accordance with empirical laws of causality. It therefore follows that the criterion of necessity lies solely in the law of possible experience, the law that everything which happens is determined *a priori* through its cause in the [field of] appearance. We thus know the necessity only of those *effects* in nature the causes of which are given to us, and the character[1] of necessity in existence extends no further than the field of possible experience, and even in this field is not applicable to the existence of things as substances, since substances can never be viewed as empirical effects—that is, as happening and coming to be. Necessity con-
A 228 cerns only the relations of appearances in conformity with the dynamical law of causality and the possibility grounded upon it of inferring *a priori* from a given existence (a cause) to another existence (the effect). That everything which happens is hypothetically necessary is a principle which subordinates alteration in the world to a law, that is, to a rule of necessary existence, without which there would be nothing that could be entitled nature. The proposition that nothing happens through blind chance (*in mundo non datur casus*) is therefore an *a priori* law of nature. So also is the proposition that no necessity in nature is blind, but always a conditioned and therefore intelligible necessity (*non datur fatum*). Both are laws through
B 281 which the play of alterations is rendered subject to a *nature of things* (that is, of things as appearances), or what amounts to the same thing, to the unity of understanding, in which[2] alone they can belong to *one* experience, that is, to the synthetic unity of appearances. Both belong to the class of dynamical principles. The first is really a consequence of the principle of causality, and so belongs to the analogies of experience. The second is a principle of modality; but this modality, while adding the concept of necessity to causal determination, itself stands under a rule of understanding. The principle of continuity forbids any leap in the series of appearances, that is, of alterations (*in mundo non datur saltus*);

[1] [*Merkmal.*]   [2] [Reading, with Erdmann, *welcher* for *welchem*.]

it also forbids, in respect of the sum of all empirical intuitions A 229
in space, any gaps or cleft between two appearances (*non
datur hiatus*); for so we may express the proposition, that
nothing which proves a vacuum, or which even admits it as a
part of empirical synthesis, can enter into experience. As regards
a void which may be conceived to lie beyond the field of possible
experience, that is, outside the world, such a question does not
come within the jurisdiction of the mere understanding—which
decides only upon questions that concern the use to be made
of given appearances for the obtaining of empirical knowledge. It is a problem for that ideal reason[1] which goes out
beyond the sphere of a possible experience and seeks to judge B 282
of that which surrounds and limits it; and is a problem which
will therefore have to be considered in the Transcendental
Dialectic. These four propositions (*in mundo non datur
hiatus, non datur saltus, non datur casus, non datur fatum*),
like all principles of transcendental origin, we can easily exhibit in their order, that is, in accordance with the order of
the categories, and so assign to each its proper place. But the
reader has now had sufficient practice to allow of his doing
this for himself, or of easily discovering the guiding principle
for so doing. They are all entirely at one in this, that they
allow of nothing in the empirical synthesis which may do
violence or detriment to the understanding and to the continuous connection of all appearances—that is, to the unity of A 230
the concepts of the understanding. For in the understanding
alone is possible the unity of experience, in which all perceptions must have their place.

   To enquire whether the field of possibility is larger than the
field which contains all actuality, and this latter, again, larger
than the sum of that which is necessary, is to raise somewhat
subtle questions which demand a synthetic solution and yet
come under the jurisdiction of reason alone. For they are
tantamount to the enquiry whether things as appearances one
and all belong to the sum and context[2] of a single experience,
of which every given perception is a part, a part which therefore cannot be connected with any other [series of] appearances,
or whether my perceptions can belong, in their general con- B 283
nection, to more than one possible experience. The under-

----

¹ [*für die idealische Vernunft.*]   ² [*Kontext.*]

standing, in accordance with the subjective and formal conditions of sensibility as well as of apperception, prescribes *a priori* to experience in general the rules which alone make experience possible. Other forms of intuition than space and time, other forms of understanding than the discursive forms of thought, or of knowledge through concepts, even if they should be possible, we cannot render in any way conceivable and comprehensible to ourselves; and even assuming that we could do so, they still would not belong to experience—the only kind of knowledge in which objects are given to us.

A 231   Whether other perceptions than those belonging to our whole possible experience, and therefore a quite different field of matter, may exist, the understanding is not in a position to decide. It can deal only with the synthesis of that which is given. Moreover, the poverty of the customary inferences through which we throw open a great realm of possibility, of which all that is actual (the objects of experience) is only a small part, is patently obvious. Everything actual is possible; from this proposition there naturally follows, in accordance with the logical rules of conversion, the merely particular proposition,

B 284   that some possible is actual; and this would seem to mean that much is possible which is not actual. It does indeed seem as if we were justified in extending the number of possible things beyond that of the actual, on the ground that something must be added to the possible to constitute the actual.[1] But this [alleged] process of adding to the possible I refuse to allow. For that which would have to be added to the possible, over and above the possible, would be impossible What can be added is only a relation to my understanding, namely, that in addition to agreement with the formal conditions of experience there should be connection with some perception. But whatever is connected with perception in accordance with empirical laws is actual, even although it is not immediately perceived. That yet another series of appearances in thoroughgoing connection with that which is given in perception, and consequently that more

A 232   than one all-embracing experience is possible, cannot be inferred from what is given; and still less can any such inference be drawn independently of anything being given—since

---

[1] [Reading, with Vaihinger, *jenem . . . dieses* for *jener . . . diese.*]

without material [1] nothing whatsoever can be thought. What is possible only under conditions which themselves are merely possible is not *in all respects* possible. But such [absolute] possibility is in question when it is asked whether the possibility of things extends further than experience can reach.

I have made mention of these questions only in order to omit nothing which is ordinarily reckoned among the concepts B 285 of understanding. But as a matter of fact absolute possibility, that which is in all respects valid, is no mere concept of understanding, and can never be employed empirically. It belongs exclusively to reason, which transcends all possible empirical employment of the understanding. We have therefore had to content ourselves with some merely critical remarks; the matter must otherwise be left in obscurity until we come to the proper occasion for its further treatment.

Before concluding this fourth section, and therewith the system of all principles of pure understanding, I must explain why I have entitled the principles of modality postulates. I interpret this expression not in the sense which some recent philosophical writers, wresting it from its proper mathematical A 233 significance, have given to it, namely, that to postulate should mean to treat a proposition as immediately certain, without justification or proof. For if, in dealing with synthetic propositions, we are to recognise them as possessing unconditioned validity, independently of deduction, on the evidence [merely] of their own claims, then no matter how evident they may be, all critique of understanding is given up. And since there is no lack of audacious pretensions, and these are supported by common belief (though that is no credential of their truth), the understanding lies open to every fancy, and is B 286 in no position to withhold approval of those assertions which, though illegitimate, yet press upon us, in the same confident tone, their claims to be accepted as actual axioms. Whenever, therefore, an *a priori* determination is synthetically added to the concept of a thing, it is indispensable that, if not a proof, at least a deduction of the legitimacy of such an assertion should be supplied.

The principles of modality are not, however, objectively synthetic. For the predicates of possibility, actuality, and

[1] [*Stoff*.]

necessity do not in the least enlarge the concept of which they are affirmed, adding something to the representation of the object. But since they are none the less synthetic, they are so

A 234 subjectively only, that is, they add to the concept of a thing (of something real),[1] of which otherwise they say nothing, the cognitive faculty from which it springs and in which it has its seat. Thus if it is in connection only with the formal conditions of experience, and so merely in the understanding, its object is called possible. If it stands in connection with perception, that is, with sensation as material[2] supplied by the senses, and through perception is determined by means of the understanding, the object is actual. If it is determined through the connection of per-

B 287 ceptions according to concepts, the object is entitled necessary. The principles of modality thus predicate of a concept nothing but the action of the faculty of knowledge through which it is generated. Now in mathematics a postulate means the practical proposition which contains nothing save the synthesis through which we first give ourselves an object and generate its concept—for instance, with a given line, to describe a circle on a plane from a given point. Such a proposition cannot be proved, since the procedure which it demands is exactly that through which we first generate the concept of such a figure. With exactly the same right we may postulate the principles of modality, since they do not increase our[3] concept of things,[a]

A 235 but only show the manner in which it is connected with the faculty of knowledge.

B 288   *General Note on the System of the Principles*[4]

That the possibility of a thing cannot be determined from the category alone, and that in order to exhibit the objective reality of the pure concept of understanding we must always

---

[a] Through the actuality of a thing I certainly posit more than the possibility of it, but not *in the thing*. For it can never contain more in its actuality than is contained in its complete possibility. But while possibility is merely a positing of the thing in relation to the understanding (in its empirical employment), actuality is at the same time a connection of it with perception.

---

[1] [In A (*realen*), in B (*Realen*).]   [2] [*Materie.*]
[3] [Reading, with Erdmann, *unsern* for *ihren.*]
[4] [This section, to end of chapter, added in B.]

have an intuition, is a very noteworthy fact. Take, for instance, the categories of relation. We cannot determine from mere concepts how (1) something can exist as subject only, and not as a mere determination of other things, that is, how a thing can be substance, or (2) how, because something is, something else must be, and how, therefore, a thing can be a cause, or (3) when several things exist, how because one of them is there, something follows in regard to the others and *vice versa*, and how in this way there can be a community of substances. This likewise applies to the other categories; for example, how a thing can be equal to a number of things taken together, that is, can be a quantity. So long as intuition is lacking, we do not know whether through the categories we are thinking an object, and whether indeed there can anywhere be an object suited to them. In all these ways, then, we obtain confirmation that the categories are not in themselves knowledge, but are merely *forms of thought* for the making of knowledge from given intuitions.

For the same reason it follows that no synthetic proposi-   B 289
tion can be made from mere categories. For instance, we are not in a position to say that in all existence there is substance, that is, something which can exist only as subject and not as mere predicate; or that everything is a quantum, etc. For if intuition be lacking, there is nothing which can enable us to go out beyond a given concept, and to connect another with it. No one, therefore, has ever yet succeeded in proving a synthetic proposition merely from pure concepts of the understanding—as, for instance, that everything which exists contingently has a cause. We can never get further than proving, that without this relation we are unable to comprehend the existence of the contingent, that is, are unable *a priori* through the understanding to know the existence of such a thing— from which it does not, however, follow that this is also a condition of the possibility of the things themselves. If the reader will go back to our proof of the principle of causality—that everything which happens, that is, every event, presupposes a cause—he will observe that we were able to prove it only of objects of possible experience; and even so, not from pure concepts, but only as a principle of the possibility of experience, and therefore of the knowledge of an object given in *empirical*

intuition. We cannot, indeed, deny that the proposition, that
B 290 everything contingent must have a cause, is patent to everyone from mere concepts. But the concept of the contingent
is then being apprehended as containing, not the category
of modality (as something the not-being of which can be
thought), but that of relation (as something which can exist
only as consequence[1] of something else); and it is then, of
course, an identical proposition—that which can exist only
as consequence has a cause. As a matter of fact, when we are
required to cite examples of contingent existence, we invariably have recourse to *alterations*, and not merely to the possibility of *entertaining the opposite in thought.*[a] Now alteration
B 291 is an event which, as such, is possible only through a cause, and
the not-being of which is therefore in itself possible. In other
words, we recognise contingency in and through the fact that
something can exist only as the effect of a cause; and if, therefore, a thing is assumed to be contingent, it is an analytic proposition to say that it has a cause.

But it is an even more noteworthy fact, that in order to
understand the possibility of things in conformity with the
categories, and so to demonstrate the *objective reality* of the
latter, we need, not merely intuitions, but intuitions that are in
all cases *outer intuitions.* When, for instance, we take the pure
concepts of *relation*, we find, firstly, that in order to obtain
something *permanent* in intuition corresponding to the concept of *substance*, and so to demonstrate the objective reality
of this concept, we require an intuition in space (of matter).

[a] We can easily think the non-existence of matter. From this
the ancients did not, however, infer its contingency. Even the
change from being to not-being of a given state of a thing, in which
all alteration consists, does not prove the contingency of this
state, on the ground of the reality of its opposite. For instance, that
a body should come to rest after having been in motion does not
prove the contingency of the motion as being the opposite of the
state of rest. For this opposite is *opposed* to the other only logically,
not *realiter*. To prove the contingency of its motion, we should have
to prove that *instead of* the motion at the preceding moment, it was
possible for the body to have been *then* at rest, not that it is *afterwards* at rest; for in the latter case the opposites are quite consistent
with each other.

[1] [*Folge.*]

For space alone is determined as permanent, while time, and therefore everything that is in inner sense, is in constant flux. Secondly, in order to exhibit *alteration* as the intuition corresponding to the concept of *causality*, we must take as our example motion, that is, alteration in space. Only in this way can we obtain the intuition of alterations, the possibility of which can never be comprehended through any pure understanding. For alteration is combination of contradictorily opposed determinations in the existence of one and the same thing. Now how it is[1] possible that from a given state of a thing an opposite state should follow, not only cannot be conceived by reason without an example, but is actually incomprehensible to reason without intuition. The intuition required is the intuition of the movement of a point in space. The presence of the point in different locations (as a sequence of opposite determinations) is what alone first yields to us an intuition of alteration. For in order that we may afterwards make inner alterations likewise thinkable, we must represent time (the form of inner sense) figuratively as a line, and the inner alteration through the drawing of this line (motion), and so in this manner by means of outer intuition make comprehensible the successive existence of ourselves in different states. The reason of this is that all alteration, if it is to be perceived as alteration, presupposes something permanent in intuition, and that in inner sense no permanent intuition is to be met with. Lastly, the possibility of the category of *community* cannot be comprehended through mere reason alone; and consequently its objective reality is only to be determined through intuition, and indeed through outer intuition in space. For how are we to think it to be possible, when several substances exist, that, from the existence of one, something (as effect) can follow in regard to the existence of the others, and *vice versa*; in other words, that because there is something in the one there must also in the others be something which is not to be understood solely from the existence of these others? For this is what is required in order that there be community; community is not conceivable as holding between things each of which, through its subsistence,[2] stands in complete isolation. Leibniz, in attributing to the substances of the

B 292

B 293

---

[1] [Reading, with Vorländer, *ist* for *sei.*]   [2] [*Subsistenz.*]

world, as thought through the understanding alone, a community, had therefore to resort to the mediating intervention of a Deity. For, as he justly recognised, a community of substances is utterly inconceivable as arising simply from their existence. We can, however, render the possibility of community—of substances as appearances—perfectly comprehensible, if we represent them to ourselves in space, that is, in outer intuition. For this already contains in itself *a priori* formal outer relations as conditions of the possibility of the real relations of action and reaction, and therefore of the possibility of community.

Similarly, it can easily be shown that the possibility of things as *quantities*, and therefore the objective reality of quantity, can be exhibited only in outer intuition, and that only through the mediation of outer intuition can it be applied also to inner sense. But, to avoid prolixity, I must leave the reader to supply his own examples of this.

These remarks are of great importance, not only in confirmation of our previous refutation of idealism, but even more, when we come to treat of *self-knowledge* by mere inner consciousness, that is, by determination of our nature without the aid of outer empirical intuitions—as showing us the limits of the possibility of this kind of knowledge.

The final outcome of this whole section is therefore this: all principles of the pure understanding are nothing more than principles *a priori* of the possibility of experience, and to experience alone do all *a priori* synthetic propositions relate — indeed, their possibility itself rests entirely on this relation.

TRANSCENDENTAL DOCTRINE OF JUDGMENT

(ANALYTIC OF PRINCIPLES)

CHAPTER III

THE GROUND OF THE DISTINCTION OF ALL OBJECTS IN GENERAL INTO PHENOMENA AND NOUMENA

WE have now not merely explored the territory of pure understanding, and carefully surveyed every part of it, but have also measured its extent, and assigned to everything in it its rightful place. This domain is an island, enclosed by nature itself within unalterable limits. It is the land of truth—enchanting name!—surrounded by a wide and stormy ocean, B 295 the native home of illusion, where many a fog bank and many a swiftly melting iceberg give the deceptive appearance of farther shores, deluding the adventurous seafarer ever anew A 236 with empty hopes, and engaging him in enterprises which he can never abandon and yet is unable to carry to completion. Before we venture on this sea, to explore it in all directions and to obtain assurance whether there be any ground for such hopes, it will be well to begin by casting a glance upon the map of the land which we are about to leave, and to enquire, first, whether we cannot in any case be satisfied with what it contains—are not, indeed, under compulsion to be satisfied, inasmuch as there may be no other territory upon which we can settle; and, secondly, by what title we possess even this domain, and can consider ourselves as secured against all opposing claims. Although we have already given a sufficient answer to these questions in the course of the Analytic, a summary statement of its solutions may nevertheless help to strengthen our conviction, by focussing the various considerations in their bearing on the questions now before us.

257

We have seen that everything which the understanding derives from itself is, though not borrowed from experience, at the disposal of the understanding solely for use in experi-

B 296 ence. The principles of pure understanding, whether constitutive *a priori*, like the mathematical principles, or merely regulative, like the dynamical, contain nothing but what

A 237 may be called the pure schema of possible experience. For experience obtains its unity only from the synthetic unity which the understanding originally and of itself confers upon the synthesis of imagination in its relation to apperception; and the appearances, as data for a possible knowledge, must already stand *a priori* in relation to, and in agreement with, that synthetic unity. But although these rules of understanding are not only true *a priori*, but are indeed the source of all truth (that is, of the agreement of our knowledge with objects), inasmuch as they contain in themselves the ground of the possibility of experience viewed as the sum of all knowledge wherein objects can be given to us, we are not satisfied with the exposition merely of that which is true, but likewise demand that account be taken of that which we desire to know. If, therefore, from this critical enquiry we learn nothing more than what, in the merely empirical employment of understanding, we should in any case have practised without any such subtle enquiry, it would seem as if the advantage derived from it by no means repays the labour expended. The reply may certainly be made that in the endeavour to extend our knowledge a meddlesome curiosity is far less injurious than the habit of always insisting,

B 297 before entering on any enquiries, upon antecedent proof of the utility of the enquiries—an absurd demand, since prior to completion of the enquiries we are not in a position to form the least conception of this utility, even if it were placed before our eyes. There is, however, one advantage which may be made comprehensible and of interest even to the most re-

A 238 fractory and reluctant learner, the advantage, that while the understanding, occupied merely with its empirical employment, and not reflecting upon the sources of its own knowledge, may indeed get along quite satisfactorily, there is yet one task to which it is not equal, that, namely, of determining the limits of its employment, and of knowing what it is that may lie within and what it is that lies without its own proper sphere. This demands just those deep enquiries which we have instituted. If the understanding in its empirical employment cannot distinguish whether certain questions lie within its horizon or not, it can never be assured of its claims or of its possessions, but must be prepared for many a humiliating disillusionment, whenever, as must unavoidably and constantly happen, it oversteps the limits of its own domain, and loses itself in opinions that are baseless and misleading.

If the assertion, that the understanding can employ its various principles and its various concepts solely in an empirical and never in a transcendental manner, is a proposition which can be known with certainty, it will yield important B 298 consequences. The transcendental employment of a concept in any principle is its application to things *in general and in themselves*; the empirical employment is its application *merely to appearances*; that is, to objects of a possible experience. That A 239 the latter application of concepts is alone feasible is evident from the following considerations. We demand in every concept, first, the logical form of a concept (of thought) in general, and secondly, the possibility of giving it an object to which it may be applied. In the absence of such object, it has no meaning and is completely lacking in content, though it may still contain the logical function which is required for making a concept out of any data that may be presented. Now the object cannot be given to a concept otherwise than in intuition; for though a pure intuition can indeed precede the object *a priori*, even this intuition can acquire its object, and therefore objective validity, only through the empirical intuition of which it is the mere form. Therefore all concepts, and with them all principles, even such as are possible *a priori*, relate to empirical intuitions, that is, to the data for a possible experience. Apart from this relation they have no objective validity, and in respect of their representations are a mere play of imagination or of understanding. Take, for instance, the concepts of mathematics, considering them first B 299 of all in their pure intuitions. Space has three dimensions; between two points there can be only one straight line, etc. Although all these principles, and the representation of the

object with which this science occupies itself, are generated
A 240 in the mind completely *a priori*, they would mean nothing,
were we not always able to present their meaning in appearances, that is, in empirical objects. We therefore demand
that a bare[1] concept be *made sensible*, that is, that an object
corresponding to it be presented in intuition. Otherwise the
concept would, as we say, be without *sense*, that is, without
meaning. The mathematician meets this demand by the construction of a figure, which, although produced *a priori*, is an
appearance present to the senses. In the same science the
concept of magnitude seeks its support and sensible meaning[2]
in number, and this in turn in the fingers, in the beads of the
abacus, or in strokes and points which can be placed before
the eyes. The concept itself is always *a priori* in origin, and
so likewise are the synthetic principles or formulas derived
from such concepts; but their employment and their relation
to their professed objects can in the end be sought nowhere
but in experience, of whose possibility they contain the formal
conditions.

B 300   That this is also the case with all categories and the principles derived from them, appears from the following consideration. We cannot define any one of them in any real[3]
fashion, that is, make the possibility of their object understandable,[4] without at once descending to the conditions of
sensibility, and so to the form of appearances—to which, as
A 241 their sole objects, they must consequently be limited. For if
this condition be removed, all meaning, that is, relation to the
object, falls away; and we cannot through any example make
comprehensible to ourselves what sort of a thing is to be meant
by such a concept.*

---

* [In A follows the passage, omitted in B:]
In the above statement of the table of categories, we relieved
ourselves of the task of defining each of them, as our purpose,
which concerned only their synthetic employment, did not
require such definition, and we are not called upon to incur
any responsibility through unnecessary undertakings from

[1] [*abgesonderten, i.e.* apart from all elements of sense.]
[2] [*Sinn.*]   [3] [*real* added in B.]
[4] ["that is, make . . . understandable" added in B.]

The concept of magnitude in general can never be explained except by saying that it is that determination of a thing whereby we are enabled to think how many times a unit is posited in it. But this how-many-times is based on successive repetition, and therefore on time and the synthesis of the homogeneous in time. Reality, in contradistinction to negation, can be explained only if we think time (as containing[1] all being) as either filled with being or as empty. If I leave out permanence (which is existence in all time), nothing remains in the concept of substance save only the logical representation of a subject—a representation which I endeavour to realise[2] by representing to myself something which can exist only as subject and never as {A 243
{B 301

which we can be relieved. It was no evasion but an important prudential maxim, not to embark upon the task of definition, attempting or professing to attain completeness and precision in the determination of a concept, so long as we can achieve our end with one or other of its properties, without requiring a complete enumeration of all those that constitute the complete concept. But we now perceive that the ground of this precaution lies still deeper. We realise that we are unable to define them even if we wished.[a] For if we remove all those conditions of sensibility which mark them out as concepts of   A 242 possible empirical employment, and view them as concepts of things in general and therefore of transcendental employment, all that we can then do with them is to regard the logical function in judgments [to which they give expression] as the condition of the possibility of the things themselves, without in the least being able to show how they can have application to an object, that is, how in pure understanding, apart from sensibility, they can have meaning and objective validity.

   [a] I here mean real definition—which does not merely substitute for the name of a thing other more intelligible words, but contains a clear property by which the defined *object* can always be known with certainty, and which makes the explained concept serviceable in application. Real explanation would be that which makes clear   A 242 not only the concept but also its *objective reality*. Mathematical explanations which present the object in intuition, in conformity with the concept, are of this latter kind.

   [1] [als den Inbegriff von.]   [2] [realisieren.]

predicate. But not only am I ignorant of any conditions under which this logical pre-eminence may belong to anything; I can neither put such a concept to any use, nor draw the least inference from it. For no object is thereby determined for its employment, and consequently we do not know whether it signifies anything whatsoever. If I omit from the concept of cause the time in which something follows upon something else in conformity with a rule, I should find in the pure category nothing further than that there is something from which we can conclude to the existence of something else. In that case not only would we be unable to distinguish cause and effect from one another, but since the power to draw such inferences requires conditions of which I know nothing, the concept would yield no indication how it applies to any object. The so-called principle, that everything accidental has a cause, presents itself indeed somewhat pompously, as self-sufficing in its own high dignity. But if I ask what is understood by accidental, and you reply, "That the not-being of which is possible," I would gladly know how you can determine this possibility of its not-being, if you do not represent a succession in the series of appearances and in it a being which follows upon not-being (or reversewise), that is, a change. For to say

A 244   that the not-being of a thing does not contradict itself, is a lame
B 302   appeal to a logical condition, which, though necessary to the concept, is very far from being sufficient for real possibility. I can remove in thought every existing substance without contradicting myself, but I cannot infer from this their objective contingency in existence, that is, that their[1] non-existence is possible. As regards the concept of community, it is easily seen that inasmuch as the pure categories of substance and causality admit of no explanation determinant of the object, neither is any such explanation possible of reciprocal causality in the relation of substances to one another (*commercium*). So long as the definition of possibility, existence, and necessity is sought solely in pure understanding, they cannot be explained save through an obvious tautology. For to substitute the logical possibility of the *concept* (namely, that the concept does not contradict itself) for the transcendental possibility of *things* (namely, that an object corresponds to

[1] [Reading, with Vaihinger, *ihres* for *seines*.]

the concept) can deceive and leave satisfied only the simple-minded.*ᵃ

---

* [In A follows the passage, omitted in B:]

There is something strange and even absurd in the assertion that there should be a concept which possesses a meaning and yet is not capable of any explanation. But the categories have this peculiar feature, that only in virtue of the general condition of sensibility can they possess a determinate meaning and relation to any object. Now when this condition has A 245 been omitted from the pure category, it can contain nothing but the logical function for bringing the manifold under a concept. By means of this function or form of the concept, thus taken by itself, we cannot in any way know and distinguish what object comes under it, since we have abstracted from the sensible condition through which alone objects can come under it. Consequently, the categories require, in addition to the pure concept of understanding, determinations of their application to sensibility in general (schemata¹). Apart from such application they are not concepts through which an object is known and distinguished from others, but only so many modes of thinking an object for possible intuitions, and of giving it meaning, under the requisite further conditions, in conformity with some function of the understanding, that is, *of defining it*. But they cannot themselves be defined. The logical functions of judgments in general, unity and plurality, assertion and denial, subject and predicate, cannot be defined without perpetrating a circle, since the definition must itself be a judgment, and so must already contain these functions. The pure categories are nothing but representations of things in general, so far as the manifold of their intuition must be thought through one or other of these logical functions. Magnitude is the determina-

ᵃ In a word, if all sensible intuition, the only kind of intuition which we possess, is removed, not one of these concepts can in any fashion *verify* itself, so as to show its *real* possibility. Only *logical* possibility then remains, that is, that the concept or thought is pos- B 303 sible. That, however, is not what we are discussing, but whether the concept relates to an object and so signifies something.²

¹ [Reading, with Valentiner, *schemata* for *schema*.]
² [Note added in B, presumably as a substitute for the passage omitted.]

B 303   From all this it undeniably follows that the pure concepts of understanding can *never* admit of *transcendental*[1] but *always* only of *empirical* employment, and that the principles of pure understanding can apply only to objects of the senses under the universal conditions of a possible experience, never to things in general without regard to the mode in which we are able to intuit them

Accordingly the Transcendental Analytic leads to this important conclusion, that the most the understanding can achieve *a priori* is to anticipate the form of a possible experience in general. And since that which is not appearance cannot be an object of experience, the understanding can never transcend those limits of sensibility within which alone objects

A 247   can be given to us. Its principles are merely rules for the exposition of appearances; and the proud name of an Ontology that presumptuously claims to supply, in systematic doctrinal form, synthetic *a priori* knowledge of things in general (for instance, the principle of causality) must, therefore, give place to the modest title of a mere Analytic of pure understanding

B 304   Thought is the act which relates given intuition to an object. If the mode[2] of this intuition is not in any way given, the object is merely transcendental, and the concept of understanding has only transcendental employment, namely, as the unity of the thought of a manifold in general. Thus no object is determined through a pure category in which abstraction is made of every condition of sensible intuition—the only kind of intuition possible to us. It then expresses only the

---

tion which can be thought only through a judgment which has
A 246   quantity (*judicium commune*); reality is that determination which can be thought only through an affirmative judgment; substance is that which, in relation to intuition, must be the last subject of all other determinations. But what sort of a thing it is that demands one of these functions rather than another, remains altogether undetermined. Thus the categories, apart from the condition of sensible intuition, of which they contain the synthesis, have no relation to any determinate object, cannot therefore define any object, and so do not in themselves have the validity of objective concepts.

[1] [Altered by Kant (*Nachträge*, cxxi) to *realen*.]   [2] [*Art*.]

thought of an object in general, according to different modes. Now the employment of a concept involves a function of judgment[1] whereby[2] an object is subsumed under the concept, and so involves at least the formal condition under which something can be given in intuition. If this condition of judgment (the schema) is lacking, all subsumption becomes impossible. For in that case nothing is given that could be subsumed under the concept. The merely transcendental employment of the categories is, therefore, really no employment at all,[3] and has no determinate object, not even one that is determinable in its mere form. It therefore follows that the pure category does not suffice for a synthetic *a priori* principle, that the principles of pure understanding are only of empirical, never of transcendental employment, and that outside the field of possible experience there can be no synthetic *a priori* principles.

It may be advisable, therefore, to express the situation as follows. The pure categories, apart from formal conditions of sensibility, have only transcendental meaning; nevertheless they may not be employed transcendentally, such employment being in itself impossible, inasmuch as all conditions of any employment in judgments[4] are lacking to them, namely, the formal conditions of the subsumption of any ostensible[5] object under these concepts. Since, then, as pure categories merely, they are not to be employed empirically, and cannot be employed transcendentally, they cannot, when separated from all sensibility, be employed in any manner whatsoever, that is, they cannot be applied to any ostensible object. They are the pure form of the employment of understanding in respect of objects in general, that is, of thought; but since they are merely its form, through them alone no object can be thought or determined.*

A 248

B 305

---

* [In A follows the passage, omitted in B:]

Appearances, so far as they are thought as objects according to the unity of the categories, are called *phaenomena*. But if I postulate things which are mere objects of understanding, and which, nevertheless, can be given as such to an intuition,

A 249

[1] [*Urteilskraft.*]   [2] [Reading, with Erdmann, *wodurch* for *worauf.*]
[3] [Kant (*Nachträge*, cxxvii) adds: "for the knowing of anything".]
[4] [*in Urteilen.*]   [5] [*angeblichen.*]

[1]But we are here subject to an illusion from which it is difficult to escape. The categories are not, as regards their origin, grounded in sensibility, like the *forms of intuition*, space and time; and they seem, therefore, to allow of an application extending beyond all objects of the senses. As a matter of fact they are nothing but *forms of thought*, which contain the merely logical faculty of uniting *a priori* in one consciousness the manifold given in intuition; and apart, therefore, from the only intuition that is possible to us, they have even less meaning than the pure sensible forms. Through these forms an object is at least given, whereas a mode of combining the manifold—a mode peculiar to our understanding—by itself, in the absence of that intuition wherein the manifold can alone be given, signifies nothing at all. At the same time, if we entitle certain objects, as appearances, sensible entities [2] (phenomena), then since we thus distinguish the mode in which we intuit them from the nature that

B 306

---

although not to one [3] that is sensible—given therefore [4] *coram intuitu intellectuali*—such things would be entitled *noumena* (*intelligibilia*).

Now we must bear in mind that the concept of appearances, as limited by the Transcendental Aesthetic, already of itself establishes [5] the objective reality of *noumena* and justifies the division of objects into *phaenomena* and *noumena*, and so of the world into a world of the senses and a world of the understanding (*mundus sensibilis et intelligibilis*), and indeed in such manner that the distinction does not refer merely to the logical form of our knowledge of one and the same thing, according as it is indistinct or distinct, but to the difference in the manner in which the two worlds can be first given to our knowledge, and in conformity with this difference, to the manner in which they are in themselves generically distinct from one another. For if the senses represent to us something merely *as it appears*, this something must also in itself be a

---

[1] [The four paragraphs, "But we are here . . . only in a *negative* sense" (p. 270, below), added in B.]
[2] [*Sinnenwesen*.]
[3] [Reading, with Vorländer, *einer* for *der*.]
[4] [Reading, with Vaihinger, *also* for *als*.]
[5] [*an die Hand gebe*.]

belongs to them in themselves, it is implied in this distinction that we place the latter, considered in their own nature, although we do not so intuit them, or that we place other possible things, which are not objects of our senses but are thought as objects merely through the understanding, in opposition to the former, and that in so doing we entitle them intelligible entities[1] (noumena). The question then arises, whether our pure concepts of understanding have meaning in respect of these latter, and so can be a way of knowing them.[2]

At the very outset, however, we come upon an ambiguity which may occasion serious misapprehension. The understanding, when it entitles an object in a [certain] relation mere phenomenon, at the same time forms, apart from that relation, a representation of an *object in itself*, and so comes to represent itself as also being able to form *concepts* of such objects. And since the understanding yields no concepts additional to the categories, it also supposes that the object in itself must at least be *thought* through these   B 307

---

thing, and an object of a non-sensible intuition, that is, of the understanding. In other words, a [kind of] knowledge must be possible, in which there is no sensibility, and which alone has reality that is absolutely objective. Through it objects will be represented *as they are*, whereas in the empirical employment of our understanding things will be known only *as they appear*.   A 250
If this be so, it would seem to follow that we cannot assert, what we have hitherto maintained, that the pure modes of knowledge yielded by our understanding are never anything more than principles of the exposition of appearance, and that even in their *a priori* application they relate only to the formal possibility of experience. On the contrary, we should have to recognise that in addition to the empirical employment of the categories, which is limited to sensible conditions, there is likewise a pure and yet objectively valid employment. For a field quite different from that of the senses would here lie open to us, a world which is thought as it were in the spirit[3] (or even perhaps intuited), and which would therefore be for the understanding a far nobler, not a less noble, object of contemplation.

[1] [*Verstandeswesen.*]   [2] [*eine Erkenntnisart derselben.*]   [3] [*im Geiste.*]

268 KANT'S CRITIQUE OF PURE REASON

pure concepts, and so is misled into treating the entirely *indeterminate* concept of an intelligible entity, namely, of a something in general outside our sensibility, as being a *determinate* concept of an entity that allows of being known in a certain [purely intelligible] manner by means of the understanding.

If by 'noumenon' we mean a thing so far as it is *not an object of our sensible intuition*, and so abstract from our mode of intuiting it, this is a noumenon in the *negative* sense of the term. But if we understand by it an *object* of a *non-sensible intuition*, we thereby presuppose a special mode of intuition, namely, the intellectual, which is not that which we possess, and of which we cannot comprehend even the possibility. This would be 'noumenon' in the *positive* sense of the term.

The doctrine of sensibility is likewise the doctrine of the noumenon in the negative sense, that is, of things which the understanding must think without this reference to our mode of intuition, therefore not merely as appearances but as things in themselves. At the same time the understanding is

---

All our representations are, it is true, referred by the understanding to some object; and since appearances are nothing but representations, the understanding refers them to a *something*, as the object of sensible intuition. But this something, thus conceived,[1] is only the transcendental object; and by that is meant a something = X, of which we know, and with the present constitution of our understanding can know, nothing whatsoever, but which,[2] as a correlate of the unity of apperception, can serve only for the unity of the manifold in sensible intuition. By means of this unity the understanding combines the manifold into the concept of an object. This transcendental object cannot be separated from the sensible data, for nothing

A 251 is then left through which it might be thought. Consequently it is not in itself an object of knowledge, but only the representation of appearances under the concept of an object in general —a concept which is determinable through the manifold of these appearances.

Just for this reason the categories represent no special object, given to the understanding alone, but only serve to deter-

[1] [*in so fern.*]   [2] [Reading, with Hartenstein, *welches* for *welcher.*]

well aware that in viewing things in this manner, as thus
apart from our mode of intuition, it cannot make any use of B 308
the categories. For the categories have meaning only in relation to the unity of intuition in space and time; and even this
unity they can determine, by means of general *a priori* connecting concepts, only because of the mere ideality of space
and time. In cases where this unity of time is not to be found,
and therefore in the case of the noumenon, all employment,
and indeed the whole meaning of the categories, entirely
vanishes; for we have then no means of determining whether
things in harmony with the categories are even possible. On
this point I need only refer the reader to what I have said in
the opening sentences of the *General Note* appended to the
preceding chapter.[1] The possibility of a thing can never be
proved merely from the fact that its concept is not self-contradictory, but only through its being supported by some
corresponding intuition. If, therefore, we should attempt to
apply the categories to objects which are not viewed as being
appearances, we should have to postulate an intuition other

---

mine the transcendental object, which is the concept of something in general, through that which is given in sensibility, in
order thereby to know appearances empirically under concepts
of objects.

The cause of our not being satisfied with the substrate of
sensibility, and of our therefore adding to the phenomena noumena which only the pure understanding can think, is simply
as follows. The sensibility (and its field, that of the appearances) is itself limited by the understanding in such fashion that
it does not have to do with things in themselves but only with
the mode in which, owing to our subjective constitution, they
appear. The Transcendental Aesthetic, in all its teaching, has
led to this conclusion; and the same conclusion also, of course,
follows from the concept of an appearance in general; namely,
that something which is not in itself appearance must correspond to it. For appearance can be nothing by itself, outside
our mode of representation. Unless, therefore, we are to move A 252
constantly in a circle, the word appearance must be recognised
as already indicating a relation to something, the immediate

[1] [Above, p. 252.]

than the sensible, and the object would thus be a noumenon in the *positive sense*. Since, however, such a type of intuition, intellectual intuition, forms no part whatsoever of our faculty of knowledge, it follows that the employment of the categories can never extend further than to the objects of experience. Doubtless, indeed, there are intelligible entities B 309 corresponding to the sensible entities; there may also be intelligible entities to which our sensible faculty of intuition has no relation whatsoever; but our concepts of understanding, being mere forms of thought for our sensible intuition, could not in the least apply to them. That, therefore, which we entitle 'noumenon' must be understood as being such only in a *negative* sense.

If I remove from empirical knowledge all thought (through categories), no knowledge of any object remains. For through mere intuition nothing at all is thought, and the fact that this affection of sensibility is in me does not [by itself] amount to a relation of such representation to any object. But if, on the A 254 other hand, I leave aside all intuition, the form of thought

---

representation of which is, indeed, sensible, but which, even apart from the constitution of our sensibility (upon which the form of our intuition is grounded), must be something in itself, that is, an object independent of sensibility.

There thus results the concept of a *noumenon*. It is not indeed in any way positive, and is not a determinate knowledge of anything, but signifies only the thought of something in general, in which I abstract from everything that belongs to the form of sensible intuition. But in order that a noumenon may signify a true object, distinguishable from all phenomena, it is not enough that I *free* my thought from all conditions of sensible intuition; I must likewise have ground for *assuming* another kind of intuition, different from the sensible, in which such an object may be given. For otherwise my thought, while indeed without contradictions, is none the less empty. We have not, indeed, been able to prove that sensible intuition is the only possible intuition, but only that it is so for us. But neither have we been able to prove that another kind of intuition is possible Consequently, although our thought can abstract from all[1]

[1] [Reading, with Hartenstein, *jeder* for *jener*.]

still remains—that is, the mode of determining an object for the manifold of a possible intuition. The categories accordingly extend further than sensible intuition, since they think objects in general, without regard to the special mode (the sensibility[1]) in which they may be given. But they do not thereby determine a greater sphere of objects. For we cannot assume that such objects can be given, without presupposing the possibility of another kind of intuition than the sensible; and we are by no means justified in so doing.

If the objective reality of a concept cannot be in any way B 310 known, while yet the concept contains no contradiction and also at the same time is connected with other modes of knowledge that involve given concepts which it serves to limit, I entitle that concept problematic. The concept of a *noumenon*—that is, of a thing which is not to be thought as object of the senses but as a thing in itself, solely through a pure understanding— is not in any way contradictory. For we cannot assert of sensibility that it is the sole possible kind of intuition. Further, the

sensibility, it is still an open question whether the notion of a noumenon be not a mere form of a concept, and whether, A 253 when this separation has been made, any object whatsoever is left.

The object to which I relate appearance in general is the transcendental object, that is, the completely indeterminate thought of *something* in general. This cannot be entitled the *noumenon*; for I know nothing of what it is in itself, and have no concept of it save as merely the object of a sensible intuition in general, and so as being one and the same for all appearances. I cannot think it through any category;[2] for a category is valid [only] for empirical intuition, as bringing it under a concept of object in general. A pure use of the category is indeed possible [logically], that is, without contradiction; but it has no objective validity, since the category is not then being applied to any intuition so as to impart to it the unity of an object. For the category is a mere function of thought, through which no object is given to me, and by which I merely think that which may be given in intuition.

---

¹ [Reading, with Erdmann, *die Sinnlichkeit* for *der Sinnlichkeit.*]
² [Reading, with Rosenkranz, *Kategorie* for *Kategorien.*]

concept of a noumenon is necessary, to prevent sensible intuition from being extended to things in themselves, and thus to limit the objective validity of sensible knowledge. The remaining A 255 things,[1] to which it does not apply, are entitled noumena, in order to show that this knowledge cannot extend its domain over everything which the understanding thinks. But none the less we are unable to comprehend how such noumena can be possible, and the domain that lies out beyond the sphere of appearances is for us empty. That is to say, we have an understanding which *problematically* extends further, but we have no intuition, indeed not even the concept of a possible intuition, through which objects outside the field of sensibility can be given, and through which the understanding can be employed *assertorically* beyond that field. The concept of a noumenon is thus a merely *limiting* B 311 *concept*, the function of which is to curb the pretensions of sensibility; and it is therefore only of negative employment At the same time it is no arbitrary invention; it is bound up with the limitation of sensibility, though it cannot affirm anything positive beyond the field of sensibility.

The division of objects into phenomena and noumena, and the world into a world of the senses and a world of the understanding, is therefore quite inadmissible in the positive sense,[2] although the distinction of concepts as sensible and intellectual is certainly legitimate. For no object can be determined for the latter concepts, and consequently they cannot be asserted to be objectively valid. If we abandon the senses, how shall we make A 256 it conceivable that our categories, which would be the sole remaining concepts for noumena, should still continue to signify something, since for their relation to any object more must be given than merely the unity of thought—namely, in addition, a possible intuition, to which they may be applied. None the less, if the concept of a noumenon be taken in a merely problematic sense, it is not only admissible, but as setting limits to sensibility is likewise indispensable. But in that case a noumenon is not for our understanding a special [kind of] object, namely, an *intelligible object*; the [sort of] understanding to which it might belong is itself a problem. For we cannot in

---

[1] [Reading, with Erdmann, *die übrigen* for *das übrige*.]
[2] [" in the positive sense " added in B.]

the least represent to ourselves the possibility of an understanding which should know its object, not discursively
through categories, but intuitively in a non-sensible intuition. B 312
What our understanding acquires through this concept of a
noumenon, is a negative extension; that is to say, understanding is not limited through sensibility; on the contrary,
it itself limits sensibility by applying the term noumena to
things in themselves (things not regarded as appearances).
But in so doing it at the same time sets limits to itself, recognising that it cannot know these noumena through any of the
categories, and that it must therefore think them only under
the title of an unknown something.

In the writings of modern philosophers I find the expressions *mundus sensibilis* and *intelligibilis*[a] used with a meaning altogether different from that of the ancients—a meaning A 257
which is easily understood, but which results merely in an
empty play upon words. According to this usage, some have
thought good to entitle the sum of appearances, in so far as
they are intuited, the world of the senses, and in so far as their
connection is thought in conformity with laws of understanding, the world of the understanding. Observational[1] astronomy, B 313
which teaches merely the observation of the starry heavens,
would give an account of the former; theoretical astronomy,
on the other hand, as taught according to the Copernican
system, or according to Newton's laws of gravitation, would
give an account of the second, namely, of an intelligible
world. But such a twisting of words is a merely sophistical
subterfuge; it seeks to avoid a troublesome question by
changing its meaning to suit our own convenience. Understanding and reason are, indeed, employed in dealing with
appearances; but the question to be answered is whether they
have also yet another employment, when the object is not a

---

[a] We must not, in place of the expression *mundus intelligibilis*,
use the expression ' an *intellectual* world ', as is commonly done
in German exposition. For only modes of knowledge are either
intellectual or sensuous.[2] What can only be an *object* of the one
or the other kind of intuition must be entitled (however harsh-
sounding) intelligible or sensible.[3]

[1] [Transposing, with Wille, *theoretische* and *kontemplative*.]
[2] [*intellektuell, oder sensitiv.*]   [3] [*intelligibel oder sensibel.*]

phenomenon (that is, is a noumenon); and it is in this latter sense that the object is taken, when it is thought as merely intelligible, that is to say, as being given to the understanding alone, and not to the senses. The question, therefore, is whether in addition to the empirical employment of the understanding —to its employment even in the Newtonian account of the structure of the universe—there is likewise possible a transcendental employment, which has to do with the noumenon as an object. This question we have answered in the negative.

A 258   When, therefore, we say that the senses represent objects *as they appear*, and the understanding objects *as they are*, the latter statement is to be taken, not in the transcendental, but in the merely empirical meaning of the terms, namely as meaning that the objects must be represented as objects of experience, that is, as appearances in thoroughgoing inter-

B 314   connection with one another, and not as they may be apart from their relation to possible experience (and consequently to any senses), as objects of the pure understanding. Such objects of pure understanding will always remain unknown to us; we can never even know whether such a transcendental or exceptional[1] knowledge is possible under any conditions—at least not if it is to be the same kind of knowledge as that which stands under our ordinary categories. *Understanding* and *sensibility*, with us, can determine objects *only when they are employed in conjunction*. When we separate them, we have intuitions without concepts, or concepts without intuitions—in both cases, representations which we are not in a position to apply to any determinate object.

If, after all these explanations, any one still hesitates to abandon the merely transcendental employment of the categories, let him attempt to obtain from them a synthetic proposition. An analytic proposition carries the understanding no further; for since it is concerned only with what is already thought in the concept, it leaves undecided whether this concept has in itself any relation to objects, or merely signifies

A 259   the unity of thought in general—complete abstraction being made from the mode in which an object may be given. The understanding [in its analytic employment] is concerned only to know what lies in the concept; it is indifferent as to the

---

[1] [Vaihinger reads *aussersinnliche* for *ausserordentliche*.]

object to which the concept may apply. The attempt must therefore be made with a synthetic and professedly tran- B 315 scendental principle, as, for instance, 'Everything that exists, exists as substance, or as a determination inherent in it', or 'Everything contingent exists as an effect of some other thing, namely, of its cause'. Now whence, I ask, can the understanding obtain these synthetic propositions, when the concepts are to be applied, not in their relation to possible experience, but to things in themselves (noumena)? Where is here that third something, which is always required for a synthetic proposition, in order that, by its mediation, the concepts which have no logical (analytic) affinity may be brought into connection with one another? The proposition can never be established, nay, more, even the possibility of any such pure assertion cannot be shown, without appealing to the empirical employment of the understanding, and thereby departing completely from the pure and non-sensible judgment. Thus the concept of pure and merely intelligible objects is completely lacking in all principles that might make possible its application. For we cannot think of any way in which such intelligible objects might be given. The problematic thought which leaves open a place for them serves only, like an empty space, for the limitation of empirical principles, without itself containing or A 260 revealing any other object of knowledge beyond the sphere of those principles

APPENDIX

THE AMPHIBOLY OF CONCEPTS OF REFLECTION[1]

ARISING FROM THE CONFUSION OF THE EMPIRICAL WITH THE TRANSCENDENTAL EMPLOYMENT OF UNDERSTANDING

Reflection[2] (*reflexio*) does not concern itself with objects themselves with a view to deriving concepts from them directly, but is that state of mind in which we first set ourselves to discover the subjective conditions under which [alone] we are able to arrive at concepts. It is the consciousness of the relation of given representations to our different sources of knowledge; and only by way of such consciousness can the relation of the sources of knowledge to one another be rightly determined. Prior to all further treatment of our representations,[3] this question must first be asked: In which of our cognitive faculties are our representations connected together? Is it the understanding, or is it the senses, by[4] which they are combined or compared? Many a judgment is accepted owing to custom or is grounded in inclination; but since no reflection precedes it, or at least none follows critically upon it, it is taken as having originated in the understanding. An *examination* (*i.e.* the direction of our attention to the grounds of the truth of a judgment) is not indeed required in every case; for if the judgment is immediately certain (for instance, the judgment that between two points there can only be one straight line), there can be no better evidence of its truth than the judgment itself. All judgments, however, and indeed all comparisons, require *reflection*, *i.e.* distinction of the cognitive faculty to which the given concepts belong. The act by which I confront

---

[1] [*der Reflexionsbegriffe.*]   [2] [*Überlegung.*]
[3] [Reading, with Erdmann, *Vorstellungen* for *Vorstellung.*]
[4] [Reading, with Erdmann, *von* for *vor.*]

the comparison of representations with the cognitive faculty to which it belongs, and by means of which I distinguish whether it is as belonging to the pure understanding or to sensible intuition that they are to be compared with each other, I call *transcendental reflection*. Now the relations[1] in which concepts in a state of mind[2] can stand to one another are those of *identity* and *difference*, of *agreement* and *opposition*, of the *inner* and the *outer*, and finally of the *determinable* and the *determination* (matter and form). The right determining of the relation depends on the answer to the question, in which faculty of knowledge they belong together *subjectively*—in the sensibility or in the understanding. For the difference between the faculties makes a great difference to the mode in which we have to think the relations.

Before constructing any objective judgment we compare A 262 the concepts to find[3] in them *identity* (of many representations under one concept) with a view to *universal* judgments, *difference* with a view to *particular* judgments, *agreement* B 318 with a view to *affirmative* judgments, *opposition* with a view to *negative* judgments, etc. For this reason we ought, it seems, to call the above-mentioned concepts, concepts of comparison (*conceptus comparationis*). If, however, the question is not about the logical form, but about the content of the concepts, *i.e.* whether things are themselves identical or different, in agreement or in opposition, etc., then since the things can have a twofold relation to our faculty of knowledge, namely, to sensibility and to understanding, it is the place to which they belong in this regard that determines the mode in which they belong to one another. For this reason the interrelations of given representations can be determined only through transcendental reflection, that is, through [consciousness of] their relation to one or other of the two kinds of knowledge. Whether things are identical or different, in agreement or opposition, etc., cannot be established at once from the concepts themselves by mere comparison (*comparatio*), but solely by means of transcendental consideration (*reflexio*), through distinction of the cognitive faculty to which they belong. We may therefore say

---

[1] [Reading, with Hartenstein, *Die Verhältnisse . . . sind* for *Das Verhältnis . . . sind.*] [2] [*in einem Gemütszustande.*]
[3] [Adding, with Erdmann, *zu treffen.*]

that *logical reflection* is a mere act of comparison; for since
we take no account whatsoever of the faculty of knowledge to
which the given representations belong, the representations
B 319   must be treated as being, so far as their place in the mind is
concerned, all of the same order. *Transcendental reflection*, on
the other hand, since it bears on the objects themselves, contains the ground of the possibility of the objective comparison
of representations with each other, and is therefore altogether
A 263   different from the former type of reflection.[1] Indeed they do
not even belong to the same faculty of knowledge. This transcendental consideration is a duty from which nobody who
wishes to make any *a priori* judgments about things can claim
exemption. We shall now take it in hand, and in so doing shall
obtain no little light for the determining of the real business
of the understanding.

1. *Identity* and *Difference*.—If an object is presented to us
on several occasions but always with the same inner determinations (*qualitas et quantitas*), then if it be taken as object of
pure understanding, it is always one and the same, only one
thing (*numerica identitas*), not many. But if it is appearance,
we are not concerned to compare concepts; even if there is
no difference whatever as regards the concepts, difference of
spatial position at one and the same time is still an adequate
ground for the *numerical difference* of the object, that is, of the
object of the senses. Thus in the case of two drops of water
we can abstract altogether from all internal difference (of
A 264   quality and quantity), and the mere fact that they have been
intuited simultaneously in different spatial positions is suffi-
B 320   cient justification for holding them to be numerically different.
Leibniz took the appearances for things-in-themselves, and so
for intelligibilia, *i.e.* objects of the pure understanding (although, on account of the confused character of our representations of them, he still gave them the name of phenomena),
and on that assumption his principle of the identity of indiscernibles (*principium identitatis indiscernibilium*) certainly
could not be disputed. But since they are objects of sensibility,
in relation to which the employment of the understanding is
not pure but only empirical, plurality and numerical difference
are already given us by space itself, the condition of outer

---

[1] [Reading, with Vaihinger, *ersteren* for *letzteren*.]

appearances. For one part of space, although completely similar and equal to another part, is still outside the other, and for this very reason is a different part, which when added to it constitutes with it a greater space. The same must be true of all things which exist simultaneously in the different spatial positions, however similar and equal they may otherwise be.

2. *Agreement* and *Opposition.*—If reality is represented only by the pure understanding (*realitas noumenon*), no opposition can be conceived between the realities, *i.e.* no relation of such a kind that, when combined in the same subject, they A 265 cancel each other's consequences and take a form like 3 – 3 = 0. On the other hand, the real in appearance (*realitas phaeno-menon*) may certainly allow of opposition. When such realities B 321 are combined in the same subject, one may wholly or partially destroy the consequences of another, as in the case of two moving forces in the same straight line, in so far as they either attract or impel a point in opposite directions, or again in the case of a pleasure counterbalancing pain.

3. The *Inner* and the *Outer.*—In an object of the pure understanding that only is inward which has no relation whatsoever (so far as its existence is concerned) to anything different from itself. It is quite otherwise with a *substantia phaenomenon* in space; its inner determinations are nothing but relations, and it itself is entirely made up of mere relations. We are acquainted with substance in space only through forces which are active in this and that space, either bringing other objects to it (attraction), or preventing them penetrating into it (repulsion and impenetrability). We are not acquainted with any other properties constituting the concept of the substance which appears in space and which we call matter. As object of pure understanding, on the other hand, every substance must have inner determinations and powers which pertain to its inner reality. But what inner accidents can I entertain in thought, save only those which my inner sense presents to me? They A 266 must be something which is either itself a *thinking*[1] or analogous to thinking. For this reason Leibniz, regarding substances as noumena, took away from them, by the manner in B 322 which he conceived them, whatever might signify outer relation, including also, therefore, *composition*, and so made

[1] [*ein* Denken.]

them all, even the constituents of matter, simple subjects with powers of representation—in a word, MONADS.

4. *Matter* and *Form*.—These two concepts underlie all other reflection, so inseparably are they bound up with all employment of the understanding. The one [matter] signifies the determinable in general, the other [form] its determination—both in the transcendental sense, abstraction being made from all differences in that which is given and from the mode in which it is determined Logicians formerly gave the name 'matter' to the universal, and the name 'form' to the specific difference. In any judgment we can call the given concepts logical matter (*i.e.* matter for the judgment), and their relation (by means of the copula) the form of the judgment. In every being the constituent elements of it (*essentialia*) are the matter, the mode in which they are combined in one thing the essential form. Also as regards things in general unlimited reality was viewed as the matter of all possibility, and its limitation (negation) as being the form by which one thing is distinguished from others according to transcendental concepts. The understanding, in order that it may be in a position to determine anything in definite fashion, demands that something be first given, at least in concept. Consequently in the concept of the pure understanding matter is prior to form; and for this reason Leibniz first assumed things (monads), and within them a power of representation, in order afterwards to found on this their outer relation and the community of their states (*i.e.* of the representations). Space and time —the former through the relation of substances, the latter through the connection of their determinations among themselves—were thus, on this view, possible as grounds and consequents. This, in fact, is how it would necessarily be, if the pure understanding could be directed immediately to objects, and if space and time were determinations of things-in-themselves. But if they are only sensible intuitions, in which we determine all objects merely as appearances, then the form of intuition (as a subjective property of sensibility) is prior to all matter (sensations); space and time come before all appearances and before all data of experience, and are indeed what make the latter at all possible. The intellectualist philosopher could not endure to think of the form as preceding

A 267

B 323

the things themselves and determining their possibility—a perfectly just criticism on the assumption that we intuit things as they really are, although in confused representation. But A 268 since sensible intuition is a quite specific subjective condition, which lies *a priori* at the foundation of all perception, as its B 324 original form, it follows that the form is given by itself, and that so far is the matter (or the things themselves which appear[1]) from serving as the foundation (as we should have to judge if we followed mere concepts) that on the contrary its own possibility presupposes a formal intuition (time and space) as antecedently given.

NOTE TO THE AMPHIBOLY OF CONCEPTS OF REFLECTION

Let me call the place which we assign to a concept, either in sensibility or in pure understanding, its *transcendental location*. Thus the decision as to the place which belongs to every concept according to difference in the use to which it is put, and the directions for determining this place for all concepts according to rules, is a *transcendental topic*. This doctrine, in distinguishing the cognitive faculty to which in each case the concepts properly belong, will provide a sure safeguard against the surreptitious employment of pure understanding and the delusions which arise therefrom. We may call every concept, every heading, under which many items of knowledge fall, a *logical location*. On this is based the *logical topic* of Aristotle, of which teachers and orators could make use in order under given headings of thought to find what {A 269 / B 325} would best suit the matter in hand, and then, with some appearance of thoroughness, to argue or be eloquent about it.

The transcendental topic, on the other hand, contains no more than the above-mentioned four headings of all comparison and distinction. They are distinguished from categories by the fact that they do not present the object according to what constitutes its concept (quantity, reality), but only serve to describe in all its manifoldness the comparison of the representations which is prior to the concept of things. But this comparison requires in the first place a reflection, that is, a determination of the location to which the repre-

[1] [Reading, with 4th edition, *erscheinen* for *erschienen*.]

sentations of the things that are being compared belong, namely, whether they are thought by the pure understanding or given in appearance by sensibility.

Concepts can be compared logically without our troubling to which faculty their objects belong, that is, as to whether their objects are noumena for the understanding, or are phenomena for the sensibility. But if we wish to advance to the objects with these concepts, we must first resort to transcendental reflection, in order to determine for which cognitive faculty they are to be objects, whether for pure understanding or for sensibility. In the absence of such reflection, the use of these concepts is very unsafe, giving birth to alleged synthetic principles, which the critical reason cannot recognise, and which are based on nothing better than a transcendental amphiboly, that is, a confounding of an object of pure understanding with appearance.

A 270
B 326

Having no such transcendental topic, and being therefore deceived by the amphiboly of the concepts of reflection, the celebrated Leibniz erected an *intellectual system of the world*, or rather believed that he could obtain knowledge of the inner nature of things by comparing all objects merely with the understanding and with the separated,[1] formal concepts of its thought. Our table of concepts of reflection gives us the unexpected advantage of putting before our eyes the distinctive features of his system in all its parts, and at the same time the chief ground of this peculiar way of thinking, which indeed rested on nothing but a misunderstanding. He compared all things with each other by means of concepts alone, and naturally found no other differences save those only through which the understanding distinguishes its pure concepts from one another. The conditions of sensible intuition, which carry with them their own differences, he did not regard as original, sensibility being for him only a confused mode of representation, and not a separate source of representations. Appearance was, on his view, the representation of the *thing in itself*. Such representation is indeed, as he recognised, different in logical form from knowledge through the understanding, since, owing to its usual lack of analysis, it introduces a certain admixture of accompanying representations

A 271
B 327

---

[1] [*abgesonderten*]

into the concept of the thing, an admixture which the understanding knows how to separate from it. In a word, Leibniz *intellectualised* appearances, just as Locke, according to his system of *noogony* (if I may be allowed the use of such expressions), *sensualised* all concepts of the understanding, *i.e.* interpreted them as nothing more than empirical or abstracted concepts of reflection. Instead of seeking in understanding and sensibility two sources of representations which, while quite different, can supply objectively valid judgments of things only in *conjunction* with each other, each of these great men holds to one only of the two, viewing it as in immediate relation to things in themselves. The other faculty is then regarded as serving only to confuse or to order the representations which this selected faculty yields.

Leibniz therefore compared the objects of the senses with each other merely in regard to understanding, taking them as things in general. *First*, he compared them in so far as they are to be judged by understanding to be identical or to be different. And since he had before him only their concepts and not their position in intuition (wherein alone the objects can be given), and left entirely out of account the transcendental place of these concepts (whether the object is to be reckoned among appearances or things in themselves), it inevitably followed that he should extend his principle of $\left\{\begin{smallmatrix} \text{A } 272 \\ \text{B } 328 \end{smallmatrix}\right.$ the identity of indiscernibles, which is valid only of concepts of things in general, to cover also the objects of the senses (*mundus phaenomenon*), and that he should believe that in so doing he had advanced our knowledge of nature in no small degree. Certainly, if I know a drop of water in all its internal determinations as a thing in itself, and if the whole concept of any one drop is identical with that of every other, I cannot allow that any drop is different from any other. But if the drop is an appearance in space, it has its location not only in understanding (under concepts) but in sensible outer intuition (in space), and the physical locations are there quite indifferent to the inner determinations of the things. A location *b* can contain a thing which is completely similar and equal to another in a location *a*, just as easily as if the things were inwardly ever so different. Difference of locations, without any further conditions, makes the plurality and distinction of objects, as appearances, not only possible but also necessary. Consequently, the above so-called law is no law of nature. It is only an analytic rule for[1] the comparison of things through mere concepts.

Secondly, the principle that realities (as pure assertions) never logically conflict with each other is an entirely true proposition as regards the relation of concepts, but has not the least meaning in regard either to nature or to anything in itself. For real conflict certainly does take place; there are cases where $A - B = 0$, that is, where two realities combined in one subject cancel one another's effects. This is brought before our eyes incessantly by all the hindering and counteracting processes in nature, which, as depending on forces, must be called *realitates phaenomena.* General mechanics can indeed give the empirical condition of this conflict in an *a priori* rule, since it takes account of the opposition in the direction of forces, a condition totally ignored by the transcendental concept of reality. Although Herr von Leibniz did not indeed announce the above proposition with all the pomp of a new principle, he yet made use of it for new assertions, and his successors expressly incorporated it into their Leibnizian-Wolffian system. Thus, according to this principle all evils are merely consequences of the limitations of created beings, that is, negations, since negations alone conflict with reality. (This is indeed the case as regards the mere concept of a thing in general, but not as regards things as appearances.) Similarly his disciples consider it not only possible, but even natural, to combine all reality in one being, without fear of any conflict. For the only conflict which they recognise is that of contradiction, whereby the concept of a thing is itself removed. They do not admit the conflict of reciprocal injury, in which each of two real grounds destroys the effect of the other—a conflict which we can represent to ourselves only in terms of conditions presented to us in sensibility.

Thirdly, Leibniz's monadology has no basis whatsoever save his mode of representing the distinction of inner and outer merely in relation to the understanding. Substances in general must have some *internal* nature, which is therefore free from all outer relations, and consequently also from com-

A 273
B 329

B 330
A 274

---

[1] [Reading, with the 4th edition, *der* for *oder.*]

position. The simple is therefore the basis of that which is inner in things-in-themselves. But that which is inner in the state of a substance cannot consist in place, shape, contact, or motion (these determinations being all outer relations), and we can therefore assign to substances no inner state save that through which we ourselves inwardly determine our sense, namely, the *state of the representations*. This, therefore, completed the conception of the monads, which, though they have to serve as the basic material of the whole universe, have no other active power save only that which consists in representations, the efficacy of which is confined, strictly speaking, to themselves.

For this very reason his principle of the possible reciprocal *community of substances* had to be a *pre-established harmony*, {B 331 / A 275} and could not be a physical influence. For since everything is merely inward, *i.e.* concerned with its own representations, the state of the representations of one substance could not stand in any effective connection whatever with that of another. There had to be some third cause, determining all substances whatsoever, and so making their states correspond to each other, not indeed by an occasional special intervention in each particular case (*systema assistentiae*), but by the unity of the idea of a cause valid for all substances, and in which they must one and all obtain their existence and permanence, and consequently also their reciprocal correspondence, according to universal laws.

Fourthly, Leibniz's famous *doctrine of time and space*, in which he intellectualised these forms of sensibility, owed its origin entirely to this same fallacy[1] of transcendental reflection. If I attempt, by the mere understanding, to represent to myself outer relations of things, this can only be done by means of a concept of their reciprocal action; and if I seek to connect two states of one and the same thing, this can only be in the order of grounds and consequences. Accordingly, Leibniz conceived space as a certain order in the community of substances, and time as the dynamical sequence of their states. That which space and time seem to possess as proper to themselves, in independence of things, he ascribed to the *confusion* {B 332 / A 276} in their concepts, which has led us to regard what is a mere

[1] [*Täuschung.*]

form of dynamical relations as being a special intuition, self-subsistent and antecedent to the things themselves. Thus space and time were for him the intelligible form of the connection of things (substances and their states) in themselves; and the things were intelligible substances (*substantiae noumena*). And since he allowed sensibility no mode of intuition peculiar to itself but sought for all representation of objects, even the empirical, in the understanding, and left to the senses nothing but the despicable task of confusing and distorting the representations of the former, he had no option save to treat the [intellectualised] concepts as being likewise valid of appearances.

But even if we could by pure understanding say anything synthetically in regard to *things-in-themselves* (which, however, is impossible), it still could not be applied to appearances, which do not represent things-in-themselves. In dealing with appearances I shall always be obliged to compare my concepts, in transcendental reflection, solely under the conditions of sensibility; and accordingly space and time will not be determinations of things-in-themselves but of appearances. A 277 | What the things-in-themselves may be I do not know, nor do B 333 | I need to know, since a thing can never come before me except in appearance.

The remaining concepts of reflection have to be dealt with in the same manner. Matter is *substantia phaenomenon*. That which inwardly belongs to it I seek in all parts of the space which it occupies, and in all effects which it exercises, though admittedly these can only be appearances of outer sense. I have therefore nothing that is absolutely, but only what is comparatively inward and is itself again composed of outer relations. The absolutely inward [nature] of matter, as it would have to be conceived by pure understanding, is nothing but a phantom;[1] for matter is not among the objects of pure understanding, and the transcendental object which may be the ground of this appearance that we call matter is a mere something of which we should not understand what it is, even if someone were in a position to tell us. For we can understand only that which brings with it, in intuition, something corresponding to our words. If by the complaints—*that we have no*

[1] [*Grille.*]

insight whatsoever into the inner [nature] of things—it be meant that we cannot conceive by pure understanding what the things which appear to us may be in themselves, they are entirely illegitimate and unreasonable. For what is demanded is that we should be able to know things, and therefore to intuit them, without senses, and therefore that we should have a faculty of knowledge altogether different from the human, and this not only in degree but as regards intuition likewise in kind—in other words, that we should be not men but beings[1] of whom we are unable to say whether they are even possible, much less how they are constituted. Through observation and analysis of appearances we penetrate to nature's inner recesses, and no one can say how far this knowledge may in time extend. But with all this knowledge, and even if the whole of nature were revealed to us, we should still never be able to answer those transcendental questions which go beyond nature. The reason of this is that it is not given to us to observe our own mind with any other intuition than that of inner sense; and that it is yet precisely in the mind that the secret of the source of our sensibility is located. The relation of sensibility to an object and what the transcendental ground of this [objective] unity may be, are matters undoubtedly so deeply concealed that we, who after all know even ourselves only through inner sense and therefore as appearance, can never be justified in treating sensibility as being a suitable instrument of investigation for discovering anything save always still other appearances—eager as we yet are to explore their non-sensible cause.

{ A 278
{ B 334

What makes this critique of conclusions based merely on acts of reflection so exceedingly useful is that it renders manifest the nullity of all conclusions about objects which are compared with each other solely in the understanding, and at the same time confirms our principal contention, namely, that although appearances are not included as things-in-themselves among the objects of pure understanding, they are yet the only objects in regard to which our knowledge can possess objective reality, that is, in respect of which there is an intuition corresponding to the concepts.

{ A 279
{ B 335

If we reflect in a merely logical fashion, we are only com-

[1] [*Wesen.*]

paring our concepts with each other in the understanding, to
find whether both have the same content, whether they are
contradictory or not, whether something is contained within
the concept or is an addition from outside, which of the two
is given and which should serve only as a mode of thinking
what is given. But if I apply these concepts to an object in
general (in the transcendental sense), without determining
whether it be an object of sensible or of intellectual intuition,
limitations are at once revealed in the very notion of this
object which forbid[1] any non-empirical employment of the
concepts, and by this very fact prove that the representation
of an object as a thing in general is not only *insufficient*, but,
when taken without sensible determination, and independently of any empirical condition, *self-contradictory*. The conclusion is that we must either abstract from any and every
object (as in logic), or, if we admit an object, must think it
under the conditions of sensible intuition. For the intelligible
would require a quite peculiar intuition which we do not
B 336   possess, and in the absence of this would be *for us* nothing at
A 280   all; and, on the other hand, it is also evident that appearances
could not be objects in themselves. If I think to myself merely
things in general, the difference in their outer relations cannot
constitute a difference in the things themselves; on the contrary, it presupposes this difference. And if there is no inward
difference between the concept of the one and the concept of the
other, I am only positing one and the same thing in different
relations. Further, the addition of one sheer[2] affirmation
(reality) to another increases the positive in them; nothing is
withdrawn or inhibited; accordingly the real in things cannot
be in conflict with itself—and so on.

*   *   *

As we have shown, the concepts of reflection, owing to a
certain misinterpretation, have exercised so great an influence
upon the employment of the understanding that they have
misled even one of the most acute of all philosophers into a
supposititious system of intellectual knowledge, which under-

---

[1] [Reading, with Vaihinger, *nicht empirischen . . . verwehren* for *empirischen
. . . verkehren.*]
[2] [*blossen.*]

takes to determine its objects without any assistance from the senses. For this reason the exposition of the cause of what is deceptive—occasioning these false principles—in the amphiboly of these concepts, is of great utility as a reliable method of determining and securing the limits of the understanding.

It is indeed true that whatever universally agrees with or contradicts a concept also agrees with or contradicts every particular which is contained under it (*dictum de omni et nullo*); but it would be absurd to alter this logical principle so as to read:—what is not contained in a universal concept is also not included in the particular concepts which stand under it. For these are particular concepts just because they include in themselves more than is thought in the universal. Nevertheless it is upon this latter principle that the whole intellectual system of Leibniz is based; and with this principle it therefore falls, together with all the ambiguities (in the employment of the understanding) that have thence arisen. B 337 A 281

The principle of the identity of indiscernibles is really based on the presupposition, that if a certain distinction is not found in the concept of a thing in general, it is also not to be found in the things themselves, and consequently that all things which are not distinguishable from one another in their concepts (in quality or quantity) are completely identical (*numero eadem*). Because in the mere concept of a thing in general we abstract from the many necessary conditions of its[1] intuition, the conditions from which we have abstracted are, with strange presumption, treated as not being there at all, and nothing is allowed to the thing beyond what is contained in its concept. B 338

The concept of a cubic foot of space, wherever and however often I think it, is in itself throughout one and the same. But two cubic feet are nevertheless distinguished in space by the mere difference of their locations (*numero diversa*); these locations are conditions of the intuition wherein the object of this concept is given; they do not, however, belong to the concept but entirely to sensibility.[2] Similarly there is no conflict in the concept of a thing unless a negative statement is combined with an affirmative; merely affirmative concepts cannot, when combined, produce any cancellation. But in the sensible A 282

---

[1] [Reading, with Erdmann, *seiner* for *einer*.]
[2] [*zur ganzen Sinnlichkeit*.]

intuition, wherein reality (*e.g.* motion) is given, there are conditions (opposite directions), which have been omitted in the concept of motion in general, that make possible a conflict (though not indeed a logical one), namely, as producing from what is entirely positive a zero (= o). We are not, therefore, in a position to say that since conflict is not to be met with in the concepts of reality, all reality is in[1] agreement with itself.[a]

B 339⎫
A 283⎭

According to mere concepts the inner is the substratum of all relational[2] or outer determinations. If, therefore, I abstract from all conditions of intuition and confine myself to the concept of a thing in general, I can abstract from all outer relation, and there must still be left a concept of something which signifies no relation, but inner determinations only. From this it seems to follow that in whatever is a thing (substance) there is something which is absolutely inward and precedes all outer determinations, inasmuch as it is what first makes them possible; and consequently, that this substratum, as no longer containing in itself any outer relations, is *simple*. (Corporeal things are never anything save relations only, at least of their parts external to each other.) And since we know of no determinations which are absolutely inner except those [given] through our inner sense, this substratum is not only simple; it is likewise (in analogy with our inner sense) determined through *representations*; in other words, all things are really

B 340 *monads*, simple beings endowed with representations. These contentions would be entirely justified, if beyond the con-
A 284 cept of a thing in general there were no further conditions under which alone objects of outer intuition can be given us —those from which the pure concept has [as a matter of fact]

---

[a] If we here wished to resort to the usual subterfuge, maintaining as regards *realitates noumena* that they at least do not act in opposition to each other, it would be incumbent on us to produce an ex-
B 339 ample of such pure and non-sensuous reality, that it may be discerned whether such a concept represents something or nothing. But no example can be obtained otherwise than from experience, which never yields more than phenomena. This proposition has therefore no further meaning than that a concept which only includes affirmation includes no negation—a proposition which we have never doubted.

---

[1] [Reading, with Hartenstein, *in Einstimmung* for *Einstimmung*.]
[2] [Reading, with Hartenstein, *Verhältnis-* for *Verhältnis*.]

made abstraction. For under these further conditions, as we find, an abiding appearance in space (impenetrable extension) can contain only relations and nothing at all that is absolutely inward, and yet be the primary substratum of all outer perception. Through mere concepts I cannot, indeed, think what is outer without thinking something that is inner;[1] and this for the sufficient reason that concepts of relation presuppose things which are absolutely [*i.e.* independently] given, and without these are impossible. But something is contained in intuition which is not to be met with in the mere concept of a thing; and this yields the substratum, which could never be known through mere concepts, namely, a[2] space which with all that it contains consists solely of relations, formal or, it may be, also real. Because, without an absolutely inner element, a thing can never be represented *by mere concepts*, I may not therefore claim that there is *not* also in the things themselves which are subsumed under these concepts, and *in their intuition*, something external that has no basis in anything wholly inward. Once we have abstracted from all conditions of intuition, there is, I admit, nothing left in the mere concept but the inner in B 341
general and its interrelations, through which alone the external is possible. But this necessity, which is founded solely on abstraction, does not arise in the case of things as given in intuition with determinations that express mere relations, with- A 285
out having anything inward as their basis; for such are not things in themselves but merely appearances. All that we know in matter is merely relations (what we call the inner determinations of it are inward only in a comparative sense), but among these relations some are self-subsistent and permanent, and through these we are given a determinate object. The fact that, if I abstract from these relations, there is nothing more left for me to think does not rule out the concept of a thing as appearance, nor indeed the concept of an object *in abstracto*. What it does remove is all possibility of an object determinable through mere concepts, that is, of a noumenon. It is certainly startling to hear that a thing is to be taken as consisting wholly of relations. Such a thing is, however, mere appearance, and cannot be thought through pure categories;

---

[1] [Reading, with the 4th edition, *Inneres* for *Innerem*.]
[2] [Reading, with Mellin, *einen* for *ein*.]

what it itself consists in is the mere relation of something in general to the senses. Similarly, if we begin with mere concepts, we cannot think the relations of things *in abstracto* in any other manner than by regarding one thing as the cause of determinations in another, for that is how our understanding conceives of relations. But since we are in that case disregarding all intuition, we have ruled ourselves out from any kind of recognition of the special mode in which the different elements of the manifold determine each other's positions, that is, of the form of sensibility (space), which yet is presupposed in all empirical causality.

If by merely intelligible objects we mean those things which are thought[1] through pure categories, without any schema of sensibility, such objects are impossible. For the condition of the objective employment of all our concepts of understanding is merely the mode of our sensible intuition, by which objects are given us; if we abstract from these objects, the concepts have no relation to any object. Even if we were willing to assume a kind of intuition other than this our sensible kind, the functions of our thought would still be without meaning in respect to it. If, however, we have in mind only objects of a non-sensible intuition, in respect of which our categories are admittedly not valid, and of which therefore we can never have any knowledge whatsoever (neither intuition nor concept), noumena in this purely negative sense must indeed be admitted. For this is no more than saying that our kind of intuition does not extend to all things, but only to objects of our senses, that consequently its objective validity is limited, and that a place therefore remains open for some other kind of intuition, and so for things as its objects. But in that case the concept of a noumenon is problematic, that is, it is the representation of a thing of which we can neither say that it is possible nor that it is impossible; for we are acquainted with no kind of intuition but our own sensible kind and no kind of concepts but the categories, and neither of these is appropriate to a non-sensible object. We cannot, therefore, positively extend the sphere of the objects of our thought beyond the conditions of our sensibility, and assume besides appearances objects of pure thought, that is,

---

[1] [Altered by Kant (*Nachträge*, cl) to: "are known by us".]

noumena, since such objects have no assignable positive meaning. For in regard to the categories we must admit that they are not of themselves adequate to the knowledge of things in themselves, and that without the data of sensibility they would be merely subjective forms of the unity of understanding, having no object. Thought is in itself, indeed, no product of the senses, and in so far is also not limited by them; but it does not therefore at once follow that it has a pure employment of its own, unaided by sensibility, since it is then without an object. We cannot call the noumenon such an *object*; signifying, as it does, the problematic concept of an object for a quite different intuition and a quite different B 344 understanding from ours, it is itself a problem. The concept of the noumenon is, therefore, not the concept of an object, but is a problem unavoidably bound up with the limitation of our sensibility—the problem, namely, as to whether there may not be objects entirely disengaged from any such kind of intuition. This is a question which can only be answered A 288 in an indeterminate manner, by saying that as sensible intuition does not extend to all things without distinction, a place remains open for other and different objects; and consequently that these latter must not be absolutely denied, though—since we are without a determinate concept of them (inasmuch as no category can serve that purpose)—neither can they be asserted as objects for our understanding.

Understanding accordingly limits sensibility, but does not thereby extend its own sphere. In the process of warning the latter that it must not presume to claim applicability to things-in-themselves but only to appearances, it does indeed think for itself an object in itself, but only as transcendental object, which is the cause of appearance and therefore not itself appearance, and which can be thought neither as quantity nor as reality nor as substance, etc. (because these concepts always require sensible forms in which they determine an object). We are completely ignorant whether it is to be met with in us or outside us, whether it would be at once removed with the cessation of sensibility, or whether in the absence of B 345 sensibility it would still remain. If we are pleased to name this object noumenon for the reason that its representation is not sensible, we are free to do so. But since we can apply

to it none[1] of the concepts of our understanding, the representation remains for us empty, and is of no service except
A 289 to mark the limits of our sensible knowledge and to leave open a space which we can fill neither through possible experience nor through pure understanding.

The critique of this pure understanding, accordingly, does not permit us to create a new field of objects beyond those which may be presented to it as appearances, and so to stray into intelligible worlds; nay, it does not allow of our entertaining even the concept of them. The error, which quite obviously is the cause of this mistaken venture, and which indeed excuses though it does not justify it, lies in employing the understanding, contrary to its vocation, transcendentally, and in making objects, that is, possible intuitions, conform to concepts, not concepts to possible intuitions, on which alone their objective validity rests. This error, in turn, is due to the fact that apperception, and with it thought, precedes all possible determinate ordering of representations. Consequently what we do is to think something in general; and while on the one
B 346 hand we determine it in sensible fashion, on the other hand we distinguish from this mode of intuiting it the universal object represented *in abstracto*. What we are then left with is a mode of determining the object by thought alone—a merely logical form without content, but which yet seems to us to be a mode in which the object exists in itself (*noumenon*) without regard to intuition, which is limited to our senses.

* * *

A 290 Before we leave the Transcendental Analytic we must add some remarks which, although in themselves not of special importance, might nevertheless be regarded as requisite for the completeness of the system. The supreme concept with which it is customary to begin a transcendental philosophy is the division into the possible and the impossible. But since all division presupposes a concept to be divided, a still higher one is required, and this is the concept of an object in general, taken problematically, without its having been decided whether it is something or nothing. As the categories are the only concepts which refer to objects in general, the

[1] [Reading, with Erdmann, *keinen* for *keine*.]

distinguishing of an object, whether it is something or
nothing, will proceed according to the order and under the
guidance of the categories.

  1. To the concepts of all, many, and one there is opposed   B 347
the concept which cancels everything, that is, *none.* Thus the
object of a concept to which no assignable intuition whatsoever corresponds is = nothing. That is, it is a concept without
an object (*ens rationis*), like noumena, which cannot be
reckoned among the possibilities, although they must not for
that reason be declared to be also impossible; or like certain
new fundamental forces, which though entertained in thought   A 291
without self-contradiction are yet also in our thinking unsupported by any example from experience, and are therefore
not to be counted as possible.

  2. Reality is *something*; negation is *nothing*, namely, a
concept of the absence of an object, such as shadow, cold
(*nihil privativum*).

  3. The mere form of intuition, without substance, is in
itself no object, but the merely formal condition of an object
(as appearance), as pure space and pure time (*ens imaginarium*). These are indeed something, as forms of intuition,
but are not themselves objects which are intuited.

  4. The object of a concept which contradicts itself is   B 348
nothing, because the concept is nothing, is the impossible,
e.g. a two-sided rectilinear figure (*nihil negativum*).   ◂

  The table of this division of the concept of *nothing* would
therefore have to be drawn up as follows. (The corresponding
division of *something* follows directly from it):

Nothing,   A 292
as

I
Empty concept without object,
ens rationis.

2   3
Empty object of a concept,   Empty intuition without object,
nihil privativum.   *ens imaginarium.*

4
Empty object without concept,
nihil negativum.

We see that the *ens rationis*[1] (1) is distinguished from the *nihil negativum*[2] (4), in that the former is not to be counted among possibilities because it is mere fiction (although not self-contradictory), whereas the latter is opposed to possibility in that the concept cancels itself. Both, however, are empty concepts. On the other hand, the *nihil privativum* (2) and the *ens imaginarium* (3) are empty *data* for concepts. If light were not given to the senses we could not represent darkness, and if extended beings were not perceived we could not represent space. Negation and the mere form of intuition, in the absence of a something real, are not objects.

B 349

---

[1] [*Gedankending.*]   [2] [*Undinge.*]

SECOND DIVISION

TRANSCENDENTAL DIALECTIC

INTRODUCTION

I

TRANSCENDENTAL ILLUSION

WE have already entitled dialectic in general a *logic of illusion*.[1] This does not mean a doctrine of *probability*; for probability is truth, known however on insufficient grounds, and the knowledge of which, though thus imperfect, is not on that account deceptive; and such doctrine, accordingly, is not to be separated from the analytic part of logic. Still less justification have we for regarding *appearance* and *illusion* as being identi-   B 350
cal. For truth or illusion is not in the object, in so far as it is intuited, but in the judgment about it, in so far as it is thought It is therefore correct to say that the senses do not err—not because they always judge rightly but because they do not judge at all. Truth and error, therefore, and consequently also illusion as leading to error, are only to be found in the judgment, *i.e.* only in the relation of the object to our understanding. In any knowledge which completely accords with the laws of understanding there is no error. In a representation of the   A 294
senses—as containing no judgment whatsoever—there is also no error. No natural force can of itself deviate from its own laws. Thus neither the understanding by itself (uninfluenced by another cause), nor the senses by themselves, would fall into error. The former would not, since, if it acts only according to its own laws, the effect (the judgment) must necessarily be in conformity with these laws; conformity with the laws

[1] [*Schein.*]

297

of the understanding is the formal element in all truth. In the senses there is no judgment whatsoever, neither a true nor a false judgment. Now since we have no source of knowledge besides these two, it follows that error is brought about solely by the unobserved influence of sensibility on the understanding, through which it happens that the subjective grounds of the judgment enter into union with the objective grounds and make these latter deviate from their true function,[a]—just as a body in motion would always of itself continue in a straight line in the same direction, but if influenced by another force acting in another direction starts off into curvilinear motion. In order to distinguish the specific action of understanding from the force which is intermixed with it, it is necessary to regard the erroneous judgment as the diagonal between two forces—forces which determine the judgment in different directions that enclose, as it were, an angle—and to resolve this composite action into the simple actions of the understanding and of the sensibility. In the case of pure *a priori* judgments this is a task which falls to be discharged by transcendental reflection, through which, as we have already shown, every representation is assigned its place in the corresponding faculty of knowledge, and by which the influence of the one upon the other is therefore likewise distinguished.

We are not here concerned with empirical (*e.g.* optical) illusion, which occurs in the empirical employment of rules of understanding that are otherwise correct, and through which the faculty of judgment is misled by the influence of imagination; we are concerned only with *transcendental illusion*, which exerts its influence on principles that are in no wise intended for use in experience, in which case we should at least have had a criterion of their correctness. In defiance of all the warnings of criticism, it carries us altogether beyond the empirical employment of categories and puts us off with a merely deceptive extension of *pure understanding*. We shall entitle the principles whose application is confined entirely within the limits of possible

B 351   [a] Sensibility, when subordinated to understanding, as the object upon which the latter exercises its function, is the source of real modes of knowledge. But the same sensibility, in so far as it influences the operation of understanding, and determines it to make judgments, is the ground of error.

experience, *immanent*; and those, on the other hand, which A 296
profess to pass beyond these limits, *transcendent*. In the case of
these latter, I am not referring to the *transcendental* employment or misemployment of the categories, which is merely an
error of the faculty of judgment when it is not duly curbed by
criticism, and therefore does not pay sufficient attention to the
bounds of the territory within which alone free play is allowed
to pure understanding. I mean actual principles which incite
us to tear down all those boundary-fences and to seize possession of an entirely new domain which recognises no limits of
demarcation. Thus *transcendental* and *transcendent* are not
interchangeable terms. The principles of pure understanding,
which we have set out above, allow only of empirical and not
of transcendental employment, that is, employment extend- B 353
ing beyond the limits of experience. A principle, on the other
hand, which takes away these limits, or even commands us
actually to transgress them, is called *transcendent*. If our
criticism can succeed in disclosing the illusion in these alleged
principles, then those principles which are of merely empirical
employment may be called, in opposition to the others, *immanent* principles of pure understanding.

Logical illusion, which consists in the mere imitation
of the form of reason (the illusion of formal fallacies), arises
entirely from lack of attention to the logical rule. As soon
as attention is brought to bear on the case that is before us, A 297
the illusion completely disappears. Transcendental illusion,
on the other hand, does not cease even after it has been detected and its invalidity clearly revealed by transcendental
criticism (*e.g.* the illusion in the proposition: the world must
have a beginning in time). The cause of this is that there are
fundamental rules and maxims for the employment of our
reason (subjectively regarded as a faculty of human knowledge), and that these have all the appearance of being objective principles. We therefore take the subjective necessity
of a connection of our concepts, which is to the advantage of
the understanding, for an objective necessity in the determination of things in themselves. This is an *illusion* which
can no more be prevented than we can prevent the sea B 354
appearing higher at the horizon than at the shore, since we see
it through higher light rays; or to cite a still better example,

than the astronomer can prevent the moon from appearing larger at its rising, although he is not deceived by this illusion.

The transcendental dialectic will therefore content itself with exposing the illusion of transcendent judgments, and at the same time taking precautions that we be not deceived by it. That the illusion should, like logical illusion, actually disappear and cease to be an illusion, is something which transcendental dialectic can never be in a position to achieve. For here we have to do with a *natural* and inevitable *illusion*, which rests on subjective principles, and foists them upon us as objective; whereas logical dialectic in its exposure of deceptive inferences has to do merely with an error in the following out of principles, or with an illusion artificially created in imitation of such inferences. There exists, then, a natural and unavoidable dialectic of pure reason—not one in which a bungler might entangle himself through lack of knowledge, or one which some sophist has artificially invented to confuse thinking people, but one inseparable from human reason, and which, even after its deceptiveness has been exposed, will not cease to play tricks with reason and continually entrap it into momentary aberrations ever and again calling for correction.

A 298

B 355

II

PURE REASON AS THE SEAT OF TRANSCENDENTAL ILLUSION

A

Reason in general

All our knowledge starts with the senses, proceeds from thence to understanding, and ends with reason, beyond which there is no higher faculty to be found in us for elaborating the matter of intuition and bringing it under the highest unity of thought. Now that I have to give an explanation of this highest faculty of knowledge, I find myself in some difficulty. Reason, like understanding, can be employed in a merely formal, that is, logical manner, wherein it abstracts from all content of knowledge. But it is also capable of a real use, since it contains within itself the source of certain concepts and principles,

A 299

which it does not borrow either from the senses or from the understanding. The former faculty has long since been defined by logicians as the faculty of making mediate inferences (in distinction from immediate inferences, *consequentiis immediatis*); but the nature of the other faculty, which itself gives birth to concepts, is not to be understood from this definition. Now since we are here presented with a division of reason into a logical and a transcendental faculty, we are constrained to seek for a B 356 higher concept of this source of knowledge which includes both concepts as subordinate to itself. Following the analogy of concepts of understanding, we may expect that the logical concept will provide the key to the transcendental, and that the table of the functions of the former will at once give us the genealogical tree of the concepts of reason.

In the first part of our transcendental logic we treated the understanding as being the faculty of rules; reason we shall here distinguish from understanding by entitling it the *faculty of principles.*

The term 'principle' is ambiguous, and commonly sig-   A 300 nifies any knowledge which can be used as a principle, although in itself, and as regards its proper origin, it is no principle. Every universal proposition, even one derived from experience, through induction, can serve as major premiss in a syllogism; but it is not therefore itself a principle. The mathematical axioms (*e.g.* that there can only be one straight line between two points) are instances of universal *a priori* knowledge, and are therefore rightly called principles, relatively to the cases which can be subsumed under them. But I cannot therefore say that I apprehend this property of straight lines in general and in itself, from principles; I apprehend it   B 357 only in pure intuition.

Knowledge from principles is, therefore, that knowledge alone in which I apprehend the particular in the universal through concepts. Thus every syllogism is a mode of deducing knowledge from a principle. For the major premiss always gives a concept through which everything that is subsumed under the concept as under a condition is known from the concept according to a principle. Now since any universal knowledge can serve as major premiss in a syllogism, and since the understanding presents us with universal *a priori* propositions

of this kind, they can also be called principles in respect of
their possible employment.

A 301   But if we consider them in themselves in relation to their
origin, these fundamental propositions of pure understanding
are anything rather than knowledge based on concepts. For
they would not even be possible *a priori*, if we were not supported by pure intuition (in mathematics), or by conditions of
a possible experience in general. That everything that happens
has a cause cannot be inferred merely from the concept of
happening in general; on the contrary, it is this fundamental
proposition which shows how in regard to that which happens
we are in a position to obtain in experience any concept whatsoever that is really determinate.

The understanding can, then, never supply any synthetic
modes of knowledge derived from concepts; and it is such
B 358 modes of knowledge that are properly, without qualification,[1]
to be entitled 'principles'. All universal propositions, however,
may be spoken of as 'principles' in a comparative sense.

It has long been wished—and sometime perhaps (who
knows when!) may be fulfilled—that instead of the endless
multiplicity of civil laws we should be able to fall back on their
general principles. For it is in these alone that we can hope to
find the secret of what we are wont to call the simplifying of
legislation. In this domain, however, the laws are only limitations imposed upon our freedom in order that such freedom
may completely harmonise with itself; hence they are directed
to something which is entirely our own work, and of which we
ourselves, through these concepts, can be the cause. But that
A 302   objects in themselves, the very nature of things, should stand
under principles, and should be determined according to mere
concepts, is a demand which, if not impossible, is at least quite
contrary to common sense.[2] But however that may be (it is
a question which we still have to discuss), it is now at least
evident that knowledge derived from principles which are
genuinely such is something quite different from knowledge
obtained merely through the understanding. The latter may,
indeed, also take the form of a principle and thus be prior to
some other knowledge, but in itself, in so far as it is syn-

[1] [*schlechthin.*]
[2] [*sehr Widersinnisches.*]

thetic, it does not depend on thought alone, nor contain in itself a universal obtained from concepts.

Understanding may be regarded as a faculty which secures   B 359
the unity of appearances by means of rules, and reason as being the faculty which secures the unity of the rules of understanding under principles. Accordingly, reason never applies itself directly to experience or to any object, but to understanding, in order to give to the manifold knowledge of the latter an *a priori* unity by means of concepts, a unity which may be called the unity of reason, and which is quite different in kind from any unity that can be accomplished by the understanding.

This is the universal concept of the faculty of reason in so far as it has been possible to make it clear in the total absence of examples. These will be given in the course of our argument.

B   A 303

The Logical Employment of Reason

A distinction is commonly made between what is immediately known and what is merely inferred. That in a figure which is bounded by three straight lines there are three angles, is known immediately; but that the sum of these angles is equal to two right angles, is merely inferred. Since we have constantly to make use of inference, and so end by becoming completely accustomed to it, we no longer take notice of this distinction, and frequently, as in the so-called deceptions of the senses, treat as being immediately perceived what has really only been inferred. In every process of reasoning there is a fundamental proposi-   B 360
tion, and[1] another, namely the conclusion, which is drawn from it, and[1] finally, the inference (logical sequence[2]) by which the truth of the latter is inseparably connected with the truth of the former. If the inferred judgment is already so contained in the earlier judgment that it may be derived from it without the mediation of a third representation, the inference is called immediate (*consequentia immediata*)—I should prefer to entitle it inference of the understanding. But if besides the knowledge contained in the primary proposition still another judg-

---

[1] [*und* added in 2nd edition.]
[2] [*Konsequens.*]

ment is needed to yield the conclusion, it is to be entitled an inference of the reason.[1] In the proposition: "All men are mortal", there are already contained the propositions: "some men are mortal", "some mortal beings are men", "nothing A 304 that is not mortal is a man"; and these are therefore immediate conclusions from it. On the other hand, the proposition: "All learned beings are mortal", is not contained in the fundamental judgment (for the concept of learned beings does not occur in it at all), and it can only be inferred from it by means of a mediating judgment.

In every syllogism I first think a *rule* (the major premiss) through the *understanding*. Secondly, I *subsume* something known under the condition of the rule by means of *judgment*[2] (the minor premiss). Finally, what is thereby known I *deter-* B 361 *mine* through the predicate of the rule, and so *a priori* through *reason* (the conclusion). The relation, therefore, which the major premiss, as the rule, represents between what is known and its condition is the ground of the different kinds of syllogism. Consequently, syllogisms, like judgments, are of three kinds, according to the different ways in which, in the understanding, they express the relation of what is known[3]; they are either *categorical*, *hypothetical*, or *disjunctive*.

If, as generally happens, the judgment that forms the conclusion is set as a problem—to see whether it does not follow from judgments already given, and through which a quite different object is thought—I look in the understanding for the assertion of this conclusion, to discover whether it is not there found to stand under certain conditions according to a uni- A 305 versal rule. If I find such a condition, and if the object of the conclusion can be subsumed under the given condition, then the conclusion is deduced from the rule, *which is also valid for other objects of knowledge*. From this we see that in inference reason endeavours to reduce the varied and manifold knowledge obtained through the understanding to the smallest number of principles (universal conditions) and thereby to achieve in it the highest possible unity.

---

[1] [*Vernunftschluss*, here distinguished from *Verstandesschluss*, is Kant's usual term for 'syllogism', and is so translated in other passages as, *e.g.*, in the next paragraph.]

[2] [*Urteilskraft*.]   [3] [*des Erkenntnisses.*]

C

The Pure Employment of Reason

Can we isolate reason, and is it, so regarded, an independent source of concepts and judgments which spring from it alone, and by means of which it relates to objects; or is it a merely subordinate faculty, for imposing on given modes of knowledge a certain form, called logical—a faculty through which what is known by means of the understanding is determined in its interrelations, lower rules being brought under higher (namely, those the condition of which includes in its own sphere the condition of the lower), as far as this can be done through [processes of] comparison? This is the question with which we are now provisionally occupying ourselves. As a matter of fact, multiplicity of rules and unity of principles is a demand of reason, for the purpose of bringing the understanding into thoroughgoing accordance with itself, just as the understanding brings the manifold of intuition under concepts A 306 and thereby connects the manifold.[1] But such a principle does not prescribe any law for objects, and does not contain any general ground of the possibility of knowing or of determining objects as such; it is merely a subjective law for the orderly management of the possessions of our understanding, that by comparison of its concepts it may reduce them to the smallest possible number; it does not justify us in demanding from the objects such uniformity as will minister to the convenience B 363 and extension of our understanding; and we may not, therefore, ascribe to the maxim any objective validity. In a word, the question is, does reason in itself, that is, does pure reason, contain *a priori* synthetic principles and rules, and in what may these principles consist?

The formal and logical procedure of reason in syllogisms gives us sufficient guidance as to the ground on which the transcendental principle of pure reason in its synthetic knowledge will rest.

In the first place, reason in the syllogism does not concern itself with intuitions, with a view to bringing them under rules (as the understanding does with its categories), but with con-

---

[1] [Reading, with Erdmann, *jenes* for *jene*.]

cepts and judgments. Accordingly, even if pure reason does concern itself with objects, it has no immediate relation to these and the intuition of them, but only to the understanding and its judgments—which deal at first hand with the senses and their intuition for the purpose of determining their object. The unity of reason is therefore not the unity of a possible experience, but is essentially different from such unity, which is that of understanding. That everything which happens has a cause, is not a principle known and prescribed by reason. That principle makes the unity of experience possible, and borrows nothing from reason, which, apart from this relation to possible experience, could never, from mere concepts, have imposed any such synthetic unity.

Secondly, reason, in its logical employment, seeks to discover the universal condition of its judgment (the conclusion), and the syllogism is itself nothing but a judgment made by means of the subsumption of its condition under a universal rule (the major premiss). Now since this rule is itself subject to the same requirement of reason, and the condition of the condition must therefore be sought (by means of a prosyllogism) whenever practicable, obviously the principle peculiar to reason in general, in its logical employment, is:—to find for the conditioned knowledge obtained through the understanding the unconditioned whereby its unity is brought to completion.

But this logical maxim can only become a principle of *pure reason* through our assuming that if the conditioned is given, the whole series of conditions, subordinated to one another—a series which is therefore itself unconditioned— is likewise given, that is, is contained in the object and its connection.

Such a principle of pure reason is obviously *synthetic*; the conditioned is analytically related to some condition but not to the unconditioned. From the principle there must also follow various synthetic propositions, of which pure understanding—inasmuch as it has to deal only with objects of a possible experience, the knowledge and synthesis of which is always conditioned—knows nothing. The unconditioned, if its actuality be granted, is[1] especially to be considered in respect of all the determinations which distinguish it from whatever

---

[1] [Reading, with 4th edition, *wird* for *kann*.]

is conditioned, and thereby must yield material for many synthetic *a priori* propositions.

The principles[1] arising from this supreme principle[2] of pure reason will, however, be *transcendent* in relation to all appearances, *i.e.* there can never be any adequate empirical employment of the principle. It will therefore be entirely different from all principles of understanding, the employment of which is wholly *immanent*, inasmuch as they have as their theme[3] only the possibility of experience. Take the principle, that the series of conditions (whether in the synthesis of appearances, or even in the thinking of things in general) extends to the unconditioned. Does it, or does it not, have objective applicability? What are its implications as regards the empirical employment of understanding? Or is there A 309 no such objectively valid principle of reason, but only a logical precept, to advance towards completeness by an ascent to ever higher conditions and so to give to our knowledge the greatest possible unity of reason? Can it be that this requirement of reason has been wrongly treated in being viewed as a transcendental principle of pure reason, and that B 366 we have been overhasty in postulating such an unbounded completeness of the series of conditions in the objects themselves? In that case, what other misunderstandings and delusions may have crept into the syllogisms, whose major premiss (perhaps rather an assumption than a postulate) is derived from pure reason, and which proceed from experience upwards to its conditions? To answer these questions will be our task in the Transcendental Dialectic, which we shall now endeavour to develop from its deeply concealed sources in human reason. We shall divide the Dialectic into two books, the first on the *transcendent concepts* of pure reason, the second on its transcendent and *dialectical inferences*.

[1] [*Grundsätze.*]   [2] [*Prinzip.*]   [3] [*zu ihrem Thema.*]

THE TRANSCENDENTAL DIALECTIC

Book I

THE CONCEPTS OF PURE REASON

WHATEVER we may have to decide as to the possibility of the concepts derived from pure reason, it is at least true that they are not to be obtained by mere reflection but only by inference. Concepts of understanding are also thought *a* B 367 *priori* antecedently to experience and for the sake of experience, but they contain nothing more than the unity of reflection upon appearances, in so far as these appearances must necessarily belong to a possible empirical consciousness. Through them alone is knowledge and the determination of an object possible. They first provide the material required for making inferences, and they are not preceded by any *a priori* concepts of objects from which they could be inferred. On the other hand, their objective reality is founded solely on the fact that, since they constitute the intellectual form of all experience, it must always be possible to show their application in experience.

The title 'concept of reason' already gives a preliminary indication that we are dealing with something which does not allow of being confined within experience, since it concerns a knowledge of which any empirical knowledge (perhaps A 311 even the whole of possible experience or of its empirical synthesis) is only a part. No actual experience has ever been completely adequate to it, yet to it every actual experience belongs. Concepts of reason enable us to *conceive*, concepts of understanding to *understand*—([as employed in reference to] perceptions). If the concepts of reason contain the unconditioned, they are concerned with something to which all experience is subor-

dinate, but which is never itself an object of experience—
something to which reason leads in its inferences from experience, and in accordance with which it estimates and gauges
the degree of its empirical employment, but which is never
itself a member of the empirical synthesis. If, none the less,   B 368
these concepts possess objective validity, they may be called
conceptus ratiocinati (rightly inferred concepts); if, however,
they have no such validity, they have surreptitiously obtained
recognition through having at least an illusory appearance
of being inferences, and may be called *conceptus ratiocinantes*
(pseudo-rational concepts). But since this can be established
only in the chapter on the dialectical inferences of pure reason,
we are not yet in a position to deal with it. Meantime, just as
we have entitled the pure concepts of understanding categories, so we shall give a new name to the concepts of pure
reason, calling them transcendental ideas. This title we shall
now explain and justify

FIRST BOOK OF THE TRANSCENDENTAL   A 312
DIALECTIC

Section 1

THE IDEAS IN GENERAL

Despite the great wealth of our languages, the thinker often
finds himself at a loss for the expression which exactly fits his
concept, and for want of which he is unable to be really intelligible to others or even to himself. To coin new words is to ad-   B 369
vance a claim to legislation in language that seldom succeeds;
and before we have recourse to this desperate expedient it is
advisable to look about in a dead and learned language, to see
whether the concept and its appropriate expression are not
already there provided. Even if the old-time usage of a term
should have become somewhat uncertain through the carelessness of those who introduced it, it is always better to hold fast
to the meaning which distinctively belongs to it (even though
it remain doubtful whether it was originally used in precisely
this sense) than to defeat our purpose by making ourselves
unintelligible.

For this reason, if there be only a single word the established meaning of which exactly agrees with a certain concept,
A 313 then, since it is of great importance that this concept be distinguished from related concepts, it is advisable to economise in the use of the word and not to employ it, merely for the sake of variety, as a synonym for some other expression, but carefully to keep to its own proper meaning. Otherwise it may easily happen that the expression ceasing to engage the attention in one specific sense, and being lost in the multitude of other words of very different meaning, the thought also is lost which it alone could have preserved.

B 370   Plato made use of the expression '*idea*' in such a way as quite evidently to have meant by it something which not only can never be borrowed from the senses but far surpasses even the concepts of understanding (with which Aristotle occupied himself), inasmuch as in experience nothing is ever to be met with that is coincident with it.[1] For Plato ideas are archetypes of the things themselves, and not, in the manner of the categories, merely keys to possible experiences. In his view they have issued from highest reason, and from that source have come to be shared in by human reason, which, however, is now no longer in its original state, but is constrained laboriously to recall, by a process of reminiscence (which is named philosophy), the old ideas, now very much obscured. I shall not engage here in any literary enquiry into the meaning which
A 314 this illustrious philosopher attached to the expression. I need only remark that it is by no means unusual, upon comparing the thoughts which an author has expressed in regard to his subject, whether in ordinary conversation or in writing, to find that we understand him better than he has understood himself. As he has not sufficiently determined his concept, he has sometimes spoken, or even thought, in opposition to his own intention.

Plato very well realised that our faculty of knowledge feels a much higher need than merely to spell out appearances ac-
B 371 cording to a synthetic unity, in order to be able to read them as experience. He knew that our reason naturally exalts itself to modes of knowledge which so far transcend the bounds of experience that no given empirical object can ever coincide[2]

---

[1] [*damit Kongruierendes.*]   [2] [*kongruieren.*]

with them, but which must none the less be recognised as having their own reality, and which are by no means mere fictions of the brain.

Plato found the chief instances of his ideas in the field of the practical,[a] that is, in what rests upon freedom, which in its turn rests upon modes of knowledge that are a peculiar product A 315 of reason. Whoever would derive the concepts of virtue from experience and make (as many have actually done) what at best can only serve as an example in an imperfect kind of exposition, into a pattern from which to derive knowledge, would make of virtue something which changes according to time and circumstance, an ambiguous monstrosity not admitting of the formation of any rule. On the contrary, as we are well aware, if anyone is held up as a pattern of virtue, the true B 372 original with which we compare the alleged pattern and by which alone we judge of its value is to be found only in our minds. This original is the idea of virtue, in respect of which the possible objects of experience may serve as examples (proofs that what the concept of reason commands is in a certain degree practicable), but not as archetype. That no one of us will ever act in a way which is adequate to what is contained in the pure idea of virtue is far from proving this thought to be in any respect chimerical. For it is only by means of this idea that any judgment as to moral worth or its opposite is possible; and it therefore serves as an indispensable foundation for every approach to moral perfection—however the obstacles in human nature, to the degree of which there are no assignable limits, may keep us far removed from its complete achievement.

The *Republic* of Plato has become proverbial as a striking A 316 example of a supposedly visionary perfection, such as can exist

---

[a] He also, indeed, extended his concept so as to cover speculative knowledge, provided only the latter was pure and given completely *a priori*. He even extended it to mathematics, although the object of that science is to be found nowhere except in *possible* experience. In this I cannot follow him, any more than in his mystical deduction of these ideas, or in the extravagances whereby he, so to speak, hypostatised them—although, as must be allowed, the exalted language, which he employed in this sphere, is quite capable of a milder interpretation that accords with the nature of things.

only in the brain of the idle thinker; and Brucker[1] has ridiculed the philosopher for asserting that a prince can rule well only in so far as he participates in the ideas. We should, however, be better advised to follow up this thought, and, where the great philosopher leaves us without help, to place it, through fresh efforts, in a proper light, rather than to set it aside as use-

B 373   less on the very sorry and harmful pretext of impracticability. A constitution allowing *the greatest possible human freedom* in accordance with laws by which *the freedom of each is made to be consistent with that of all others*—I do not speak of the greatest happiness, for this will follow of itself—is at any rate a necessary idea, which must be taken as fundamental not only in first projecting a constitution but in all its laws. For at the start we are required to abstract from the actually existing hindrances, which, it may be, do not arise unavoidably out of human nature, but rather are due to a quite remediable cause, the neglect of the pure ideas in the making of the laws. Nothing, indeed, can be more injurious, or more unworthy of a philosopher, than the vulgar appeal to so-called adverse experience. Such experience would never have existed at all, if

A 317   at the proper time those institutions had been established in accordance with ideas, and if ideas had not been displaced by crude conceptions which, just because they have been derived from experience, have nullified all good intentions. The more legislation and government are brought into harmony with the above idea, the rarer would punishments become, and it is therefore quite rational to maintain, as Plato does, that in a perfect state no punishments whatsoever would be required. This perfect state may never, indeed, come into being; none the less

B 374   this does not affect the rightfulness of the idea, which, in order to bring the legal organisation of mankind ever nearer to its greatest possible perfection, advances this maximum as an archetype. For what the highest degree may be at which mankind may have to come to a stand, and how great a gulf may still have to be left between the idea and its realisation, are questions which no one can, or ought to, answer. For the issue depends on freedom; and it is in the power of freedom to pass beyond any and every specified limit.

---

[1] [Johann Jakob Brucker (1696–1770). The reference is probably to vol. i. pp. 726-7 of his *Historia Critica Philosophica* (pub. 1742–4).]

But it is not only where human reason exhibits genuine causality, and where ideas are operative causes (of actions and their objects), namely, in the moral sphere, but also in regard to nature itself, that Plato rightly discerns clear proofs of an origin from ideas. A plant, an animal, the orderly arrangement of the cosmos—presumably therefore the entire natural world —clearly show that they are possible only according to ideas, and that though no single creature in the conditions of its individual existence coincides with the idea of what is most perfect in its kind—just as little as does any human being with the idea of humanity, which he yet carries in his soul as the archetype of his actions—these ideas are none the less completely determined in the Supreme Understanding, each as an individual and each as unchangeable, and are the original causes of things. But only the totality of things, in their interconnection as constituting the universe, is com- pletely adequate to the idea. If we set aside the exaggerations in Plato's methods of expression, the philosopher's spiritual flight from the ectypal mode of reflecting upon[1] the physical world-order to the architectonic ordering of it according to ends, that is, according to ideas, is an enterprise which calls for respect and imitation. It is, however, in regard to the principles of morality, legislation, and religion, where the experience, in this case of the good, is itself made possible only by the ideas—incomplete as their empirical expression must always remain—that Plato's teaching exhibits its quite peculiar merits. When it fails to obtain recognition, this is due to its having been judged in accordance with precisely those empirical rules, the invalidity of which, regarded as principles, it has itself demonstrated. For whereas, so far as nature is concerned, experience supplies the rules and is the source of truth, in respect of the moral laws it is, alas, the mother of illusion! Nothing is more reprehensible than to derive the laws prescribing what *ought to be done* from what *is done*, or to impose upon them the limits by which the latter is circumscribed.

But though the following out of these considerations is what gives to philosophy its peculiar dignity, we must meantime occupy ourselves with a less resplendent, but still meri-

A 318

B 375

A 319

[1] [*von der copeilichen Betrachtung.*]

torious task, namely, to level the ground, and to render it
B 376 sufficiently secure for moral edifices of these majestic dimensions. For this ground has been honeycombed by subterranean
workings which reason, in its confident but fruitless search
for hidden treasures, has carried out in all directions, and
which threaten the security of the superstructures. Our present
duty is to obtain insight into the transcendental employment
of pure reason, its principles and ideas, that we may be in a
position to determine and estimate its influence and true value.
Yet, before closing these introductory remarks, I beseech
those who have the interests of philosophy at heart (which is
more than is the case with most people) that, if they find
themselves convinced by these and the following considerations, they be careful to preserve the expression 'idea' in
its original meaning, that it may not become one of those
expressions which are commonly used to indicate any and
every species of representation, in a happy-go-lucky confusion, to the consequent detriment of science. There is no lack
of terms suitable for each kind of representation, that we
A 320 should thus needlessly encroach upon the province of any one
of them. Their serial arrangement[1] is as follows. The genus
is *representation*[2] in general (*repraesentatio*). Subordinate to
it stands representation with consciousness (*perceptio*). A
perception[3] which relates solely to the subject as the modification of its state is *sensation*[4] (*sensatio*), an objective perception
B 377 is *knowledge*[5] (*cognitio*). This is either *intuition*[6] or *concept*[7]
(*intuitus vel conceptus*). The former relates immediately to the
object and is single, the latter refers to it mediately by means
of a feature which several things may have in common. The
concept is either an *empirical* or a *pure concept*. The pure concept, in so far as it has its origin in the understanding alone
(not in the pure image of sensibility), is called a *notion*.[8] A
concept formed from notions and transcending the possibility
of experience is an *idea*[9] or concept of reason. Anyone who
has familiarised himself with these distinctions must find it
intolerable to hear the representation of the colour, red, called
an idea. It ought not even to be called a concept of understanding, a notion.

---

[1] [*Stufenleiter.*]   [2] [*Vorstellung.*]   [3] [*Perception.*]   [4] [*Empfindung.*]
[5] [*Erkenntnis.*]   [6] [*Anschauung.*]   [7] [*Begriff.*]   [8] [*Notio.*]   [9] [*Idee.*]

FIRST BOOK OF THE TRANSCENDENTAL
DIALECTIC

Section 2

THE TRANSCENDENTAL IDEAS

The Transcendental Analytic has shown us how the mere
logical form of our knowledge may in itself contain original
pure *a priori* concepts, which represent objects prior to all
experience, or, speaking more correctly, indicate the synthetic
unity which alone makes possible an empirical knowledge of   B 378
objects. The form of judgments (converted into a concept of
the synthesis of intuitions) yielded categories which direct all
employment of understanding in experience. Similarly, we
may presume that the form of syllogisms,[1] when applied to
the synthetic unity of intuitions under the direction of the
categories, will contain the origin of special *a priori* concepts,
which we may call pure concepts of reason, or *transcendental
ideas*, and which will determine according to principles how
understanding is to be employed in dealing with experience
in its totality.[2]

The function of reason in its inferences consists[3] in the
universality of knowledge [which it yields] according to concepts, the syllogism being itself a judgment which is determined *a priori* in the whole extent of its conditions. The pro-   A 322
position, 'Caius is mortal', I could indeed derive from experience by means of the understanding alone. But I am in pursuit
of a concept (in this case, the concept 'man') that contains the
condition under which the predicate (general term for what
is asserted) of this judgment is given; and after I have subsumed the predicate under this condition taken in its whole
extension ('All men are mortal'), I proceed, in accordance
therewith, to determine the knowledge of my object ('Caius
is mortal').

Accordingly, in the conclusion of a syllogism we restrict a

---

[1] [The reader will bear in mind that the German term here translated
'syllogism' is *Vernunftschluss.*]
[2] [*im Ganzen der gesamten Erfahrung*].
[3] [Reading, with Adickes, *besteht* for *bestand.*]

B 379   predicate to a certain object, after having first thought it in the major premiss in its whole extension under a given condition. This complete quantity of the extension in relation to such a condition is called *universality* (*universalitas*). In the synthesis of intuitions we have corresponding to this the *allness* (*universitas*) or *totality* of the conditions. The transcendental concept of reason is, therefore, none other than the concept of the *totality* of the *conditions* for any given conditioned. Now since it is the *unconditioned* alone which makes possible the totality of conditions, and, conversely, the totality of conditions is always itself unconditioned, a pure concept of reason can in general be explained by the concept of the unconditioned, conceived as containing a ground of the synthesis of the conditioned.

A 323   The number of pure concepts of reason will be equal to the number of kinds of relation which the understanding represents to itself by means of the categories. We have therefore to seek for an *unconditioned*, first, of the *categorical* synthesis in a *subject*; secondly, of the *hypothetical* synthesis of the members of a *series*; thirdly, of the *disjunctive* synthesis of the parts in a *system*.

There is thus precisely the same number of kinds of syllogism, each of which advances through prosyllogisms to the unconditioned: first, to the subject which is never itself a pre-
B 380   dicate; secondly, to the presupposition which itself presupposes nothing further; thirdly, to such an aggregate of the members of the division of a concept as requires nothing further to complete the division. The pure concepts of reason —of totality in the synthesis of conditions—are thus at least necessary as setting us the task of extending the unity of understanding, where possible, up to the unconditioned, and are grounded in the nature of human reason. These transcendental concepts may, however, be without any suitable corresponding employment *in concreto*, and may therefore have no other utility than that of so directing the understanding that, while it is extended to the uttermost, it is also at the same time brought into complete consistency with itself.

A 324   But while we are here speaking of the totality of conditions and of the unconditioned, as being equivalent titles for all concepts of reason, we again come upon an expression with which we cannot dispense, and which yet, owing to an ambiguity that attaches to it through long-standing misuse, we also cannot with safety employ. The word *'absolute'* is one of the few words which in their original meaning were adapted to a concept that no other word in the same language exactly suits. Consequently its loss, or what amounts to the same thing, looseness in its employment, must carry with it B 381 the loss of the concept itself. And since, in this case, the concept is one to which reason devotes much of its attention, it cannot be relinquished without greatly harming all transcendental philosophy. The word *'absolute'* is now often used merely to indicate that something is true of a thing considered *in itself*, and therefore of its *inward* nature. In this sense the *absolutely possible* would mean that which in itself (*interne*) is possible—which is, in fact, the *least* that can be said of an object. On the other hand, the word is also sometimes used to indicate that something is valid in all respects, without limitation, *e.g.* absolute despotism, and in this sense the *absolutely possible* would mean what is *in every relation* (in all respects)[1] *possible*—which is the *most* that can be said of the possibility A 325 of a thing. Now frequently we find these two meanings combined. For example, what is internally impossible is impossible in any relation, and therefore absolutely impossible. But in most cases the two meanings are infinitely far apart, and I can in no wise conclude that because something is in itself possible, it is therefore also possible in every relation, and so absolutely possible. Indeed, as I shall subsequently show, *absolute* necessity is by no means always dependent on inner necessity, and must not, therefore, be treated as synonymous with it. If the opposite of something is internally impossible, this opposite B 382 is, of course, impossible in all respects, and the thing itself is therefore absolutely necessary. But I cannot reverse the reasoning so as to conclude that if something is absolutely necessary its opposite is *internally* impossible, *i.e.* that the *absolute* necessity of things is an *inner* necessity. For this inner necessity is in certain cases a quite empty expression to which we cannot attach any concept whatsoever, whereas the concept of the necessity of a thing in all relations (to everything possible) involves certain quite special determinations.

---

[1] [With Erdmann, bracketing *in aller Absicht*.]

Since the loss of a concept that is of great importance for speculative science can never be a matter of indifference to the philosopher, I trust that the fixing and careful preservation of the expression, on which the concept depends, will likewise be not indifferent to him.

A 326   It is, then, in this wider sense that I shall use the word '*absolute*', opposing it to what is valid only comparatively, that is, in some particular respect. For while the latter is restricted by conditions, the former is valid without restriction.

Now the transcendental concept of reason is directed always solely towards absolute totality in the synthesis of conditions, and never terminates save in what is absolutely, that is, in all relations, unconditioned. For pure reason leaves every-

B 383   thing to the understanding—the understanding [alone] applying immediately to the objects of intuition, or rather to their synthesis in the imagination. Reason concerns itself exclusively with absolute totality in the employment of the concepts of the understanding, and endeavours to carry the synthetic unity, which is thought in the category, up to the completely unconditioned. We may call this unity of appearances the *unity of reason*, and that expressed by the category the *unity of understanding*. Reason accordingly occupies itself solely with the employment of understanding, not indeed in so far as the latter contains the ground of possible experience (for the concept of the absolute totality of conditions is not applicable in any experience, since no experience is unconditioned), but solely in order to prescribe to the understanding its direction towards a certain unity of which it has itself no concept, and in such manner as to unite all the acts of the understanding,

A 327   in respect of every object, into an *absolute* whole. The objective employment of the pure concepts of reason is, therefore, always *transcendent*, while that of the pure concepts of understanding must, in accordance with their nature, and inasmuch as their application is solely to possible experience, be always *immanent*.

I understand by idea a necessary concept of reason to which no corresponding[1] object can be given in sense-experience.[2] Thus the pure concepts of reason, now under con-

B 384   sideration, are *transcendental ideas*. They are concepts of pure

---

[1] [*kongruierender.*]   [2] [*in den Sinnen.*]

reason, in that they view all knowledge gained in experience as being determined through an absolute totality of conditions. They are not arbitrarily invented; they are imposed by the very nature of reason itself, and therefore stand in necessary relation to the whole employment of understanding. Finally, they are transcendent and overstep the limits of all experience; no object adequate to the transcendental idea can ever be found within experience. If I speak of an idea, then as regards its object, viewed as an object of pure understanding, I am saying a *great deal*, but as regards its relation to the subject, that is, in respect of its actuality under empirical conditions, I am for the same reason saying *very little*, in that, as being the concept of a maximum, it can never be correspondingly given *in concreto*. Since in the merely speculative employment of reason the latter [namely, to determine the actuality of the A 328 idea under empirical conditions] is indeed our whole purpose, and since the approximation to a concept, which yet is never actually reached, puts us in no better position than if the concept were entirely abortive, we say of such a concept—it is *only* an idea. The absolute whole of all appearances—we might thus say—*is only an idea*; since we can never represent it in image, it remains a *problem* to which there is no solution. But since, on the other hand, in the practical employment of understanding, our sole concern is with the carrying out of rules, the idea B 385 of practical reason can always be given actually *in concreto*, although only in part; it is, indeed, the indispensable condition of all practical employment of reason. The practice of it is always limited and defective, but is not confined within determinable boundaries, and is therefore always under the influence of the concept of an absolute completeness. The practical idea is, therefore, always in the highest degree fruitful, and in its relation to our actual activities is indispensably necessary. Reason is here, indeed, exercising causality, as actually bringing about that which its concept contains; and of such wisdom we cannot, therefore, say disparagingly *it is only an idea*. On the contrary, just because it is the idea of the necessary unity of all possible ends, it must as an original, and at least restrictive condition, serve as standard in all that bears on the practical.

Although we must say of the transcendental concepts of A 329 reason that *they are only ideas*, this is not by any means to be taken as signifying that they are superfluous and void. For even if they cannot determine any object, they may yet, in a fundamental and unobserved fashion, be of service to the understanding as a canon for its extended and consistent employment. The understanding does not thereby obtain more knowledge of any object than it would have by means of its own concepts, but for the acquiring of such knowledge it receives better and more extensive guidance. Further—what B 386 we need here no more than mention—concepts of reason may perhaps make possible a transition from the concepts of nature to the practical concepts, and in that way may give support to the moral ideas themselves, bringing them into connection with the speculative knowledge of reason. As to all this, we must await explanation in the sequel.

In accordance with our plan we leave aside the practical ideas, and consider reason only in its speculative, or rather, restricting ourselves still further, only in its transcendental employment. Here we must follow the path that we have taken in the deduction of the categories; we must consider the logical form of knowledge through reason, to see whether perhaps reason may not thereby be likewise a source of concepts which enable us to regard objects in themselves as determined synthetically *a priori*, in relation to one or other of the functions of reason.

A 330   Reason, considered as the faculty of a certain logical form of knowledge, is the faculty of inferring, *i.e.* judging mediately (by the subsumption of the condition of a possible judgment under the condition of a given judgment). The given judgment is the universal rule (major premiss). The subsumption of the condition of another possible judgment under the condition of the rule is the minor premiss. The actual judgment which applies the assertion of the rule to[1] the *subsumed* B 387 *case* is the conclusion. The rule states something universally, subject to a certain condition. The condition of the rule is found to be fulfilled in an actual case. What has been asserted to be universally valid under that condition is therefore to be regarded as valid also in the actual case, which involves that condition. It is very evident, therefore, that reason arrives at

---

[1] [Reading, with 4th edition, *zu* for *in*.]

knowledge by means of acts of the understanding which constitute a series of conditions. Thus if I arrive at the proposition that all bodies are alterable, only by beginning with the more remote knowledge (in which the concept of body does not occur, but which nevertheless contains the condition of that concept), namely, that everything composite is alterable; if I then proceed from this to a proposition which is less remote and stands under the condition of the last-named proposition, namely, that bodies are composite; and if from this I finally pass to a third proposition, which connects the more remote knowledge (alterable) with the knowledge actually before me, and so conclude that bodies are alterable—by this procedure I have arrived at knowledge (a conclusion) by means of a series of conditions (the premises). Now every series the exponent of which is given (in categorical or hypothetical judgment) can be continued; consequently this same activity of reason leads to *ratiocinatio polysyllogistica*, which[1] is a series of inferences that can be prolonged indefinitely on the side either of the conditions (*per prosyllogismos*) or of the conditioned (*per episyllogismos*). A 331

B 388

But we soon become aware that the chain or series of prosyllogisms, that is, of inferred knowledge on the side of the grounds or conditions of a given knowledge, in other words, of the *ascending* series of syllogisms, must stand in a different relation to the faculty of reason from that of the *descending* series, that is, of the advance of reason in the direction of the conditioned, by means of episyllogisms. For since in the former case the knowledge (*conclusio*) is given only as conditioned, we cannot arrive at it by means of reason otherwise than on the assumption that all the members of the series on the side of the conditions are given (totality in the series of the premises); only on this assumption is the judgment before us possible *a priori*: whereas on the side of the conditioned, in respect of consequences, we only think a series *in process of becoming*, not one already presupposed or given *in its completeness*, and therefore an advance that is merely potential. If, therefore, knowledge be viewed as conditioned, reason is constrained to regard the series of conditions in the ascending line as completed and as given in their totality. But if the same knowledge A 332

1 [Reading, with Erdmann, *welche* for *welches*.]

B 389 is viewed as a condition of yet other knowledge, and this knowledge as constituting a series of consequences in a descending line, reason can be quite indifferent as to how far this advance extends *a parte posteriori*, and whether a totality of the series is possible at all. For it does not need such a series in order to be able to draw its conclusion, this being already sufficiently determined and secured by its grounds *a parte priori*. The series of premisses on the side of the conditions may have a *first* member, as its highest condition, or it may have no such member, in which case it is without limits *a parte priori*. But however this may be, and even admitting that we can never succeed in comprehending a totality of conditions,[1] the series must none the less contain such a totality, and the entire series must be unconditionally true if the conditioned, which is regarded as a consequence resulting from it, is to be counted as true. This is a requirement of reason, which announces its knowledge as being determined *a priori* and as necessary, either in itself, in which case it needs no grounds, or, if it be derivative, as a member of a series of grounds, which itself, as a series, is unconditionally true.

A 333
B 390

FIRST BOOK OF THE TRANSCENDENTAL DIALECTIC

Section 3

SYSTEM OF THE TRANSCENDENTAL IDEAS

We are not at present concerned with logical dialectic, which abstracts from all the content of knowledge and confines itself to exposing the fallacies concealed in the form of syllogisms, but with a transcendental dialectic which has to contain, completely *a priori*, the origin of certain modes of knowledge derived from pure reason as well as of certain inferred concepts, the object of which can never be given empirically and which therefore lie entirely outside [the sphere of] the faculty of pure understanding. From the natural relation which the transcendental employment of our knowledge, alike in inferences and in judgments, must bear to its logical

[1] [Reading, with Erdmann, *Bedingungen* for *Bedingung*.]

employment, we have gathered that there can be only three kinds of dialectical inference, corresponding to the three kinds of inference through which reason can arrive at knowledge by means of principles, and that in all of these its business is to ascend from the conditioned synthesis, to which understanding always remains restricted, to the unconditioned, which understanding can never reach.

The relations which are to be universally found in all our representations are (1) relation to the subject; (2) relation to objects, either as appearances or as objects of thought in general. If we combine the subdivision with the main division, all relation of representations, of which we can form either a concept or an idea, is then threefold: (1) the relation to the subject; (2) the relation to the manifold of the object in the [field of] appearance; (3) the relation to all things in general. {B 391 A 334

Now all pure concepts in general are concerned with the synthetic unity of representations, but [those of them which are] concepts of pure reason (transcendental ideas) are concerned with the unconditioned synthetic unity of all conditions in general. All transcendental ideas can therefore be arranged in three classes, the *first* containing the absolute (unconditioned) *unity* of the *thinking subject*, the *second* the absolute *unity of the series of conditions of appearance*, the *third* the absolute *unity of the condition of all objects of thought in general*.[1]

The thinking subject is the object[2] of *psychology*, the sumtotal of all appearances (the world) is the object of *cosmology*, and the thing[3] which contains the highest condition of the possibility of all that can be thought (the being of all beings) the object of *theology*. Pure reason thus furnishes the idea for a transcendental doctrine of the soul (*psychologia rationalis*), for a transcendental science of the world (*cosmologia rationalis*), and, finally, for a transcendental knowledge of God (*theologia transzendentalis*). The understanding is not in a position to yield even the mere project of any one of these sciences, not even though it be supported by the highest logical employment of reason, that is, by all the conceivable inferences through which we seek to advance from one of its objects (appearance) to all others, up to the most remote B 392 A 335

---

[1] [Following Erdmann, in italicising *überhaupt*.]
[2] [*der Gegenstand.*]   [3] [*das Ding.*]

members of the empirical synthesis; each of these sciences is
an altogether pure and genuine product, or problem, of pure
reason.

In what precise modes the pure concepts of reason come
under these three headings of all transcendental ideas will be
fully explained in the next chapter. They follow the guiding-
thread of the categories. For pure reason never relates directly
to objects, but to the concepts which understanding frames
in regard to objects. Similarly it is only by the process of
completing our argument that it can be shown how reason,
simply by the synthetic employment of that very function of
which it makes use in categorical syllogisms, is necessarily
brought to the concept of the absolute unity of the *thinking
subject*, how the logical procedure used in hypothetical syllogisms leads to the idea[1] of the completely unconditioned *in a
series* of given conditions, and finally how the mere form of
the disjunctive syllogism must necessarily involve the highest
concept of reason, that of a *being of all beings*—a thought
which, at first sight, seems utterly paradoxical.

B 393
A 336

No *objective deduction*, such as we have been able to give
of the categories, is, strictly speaking, possible in the case of
these transcendental ideas. Just because they are only ideas
they have, in fact, no relation to any object that could be given
as coinciding with them. We can, indeed, undertake a subjective derivation[2] of them from the nature of our reason; and
this has been provided in the present chapter.

As is easily seen, what pure reason alone has in view is
the absolute totality of the synthesis *on the side of the conditions* (whether of inherence, of dependence, or of concurrence); it is not concerned with absolute completeness *on the
side of the conditioned*. For the former alone is required in
order to presuppose the whole series of the conditions, and
to present it *a priori* to the understanding. Once we are given
a complete (and unconditioned) condition, no concept of
reason is required for the continuation of the series; for every
step in the forward direction from the condition to the *conditioned* is carried through by the understanding itself. The

B 394

---

[1] [Reading, with Erdmann, *Vernunftschlüssen die Idee vom* for *Ideen die
vom.*]

[2] [Reading, with Mellin, *Ableitung* for *Anleitung.*]

transcendental ideas thus serve only for *ascending*, in the series of conditions, to the unconditioned, that is, to principles. As regards the *descending* to the conditioned, reason does, A 337 indeed, make a very extensive logical employment of the laws of understanding, but no kind of transcendental employment; and if we form an idea of the absolute totality of such a synthesis (of the *progressus*), as, for instance, of the whole series of all *future* alterations in the world, this is a creation of the mind (*ens rationis*) which is only arbitrarily thought, and not a necessary presupposition of reason. For the possibility of the conditioned presupposes the totality of its conditions, but not of its consequences. Such a concept is not, therefore, one of the transcendental ideas; and it is with these alone that we have here to deal.

Finally, we also discern that a certain connection and unity is evident among the transcendental ideas themselves, and that by means of them pure reason combines all its modes of knowledge into a system. The advance from the knowledge of oneself (the soul) to the knowledge of the world, and by means of this to the original being, is so natural that it seems to resemble the logical advance of reason from premises B 395 to conclusion.[a] Whether this is due to a concealed relationship of the same kind as subsists between the logical and the transcendental procedure, is one of the questions that await answer

[a] [Note added in 2nd edition.] Metaphysics has as the proper object of its enquiries three ideas only: *God, freedom,* and *immortality* —so related that the second concept, when combined with the first, should lead to the third as a necessary conclusion. Any other matters with which this science may deal serve merely as a means of arriving at these ideas and of establishing their reality. It does not need the ideas for the purposes of natural science, but in order to pass beyond nature. Insight into them would render *theology* and *morals*, and, through the union of these two, likewise *religion*, and therewith the highest ends of our existence, entirely and exclusively dependent on the faculty of speculative reason. In a systematic representation of the ideas, the order cited, the *synthetic*, would be the most suitable; but in the investigation which must necessarily precede it the *analytic*, or reverse order, is better adapted to the purpose of completing our great project, as enabling us to start from what is immediately given us in experience—advancing from the doctrine of the *soul*, to the doctrine of the *world*, and thence to the knowledge of *God*.

A 338   in the course of these enquiries. Indeed, we have already,
        in a preliminary manner, obtained an answer to the question,
B 396   since in treating of the transcendental concepts of reason,
        which, in philosophical theory, are commonly confused with
        others, and not properly distinguished even from concepts of
        understanding, we have been able to rescue them from their
        ambiguous position, to determine their origin, and at the
        same time, in so doing, to fix their precise number (to which
        we can never add), presenting them in a systematic connec-
        tion, and so marking out and enclosing a special field for pure
        reason.

THE TRANSCENDENTAL DIALECTIC

BOOK II

THE DIALECTICAL INFERENCES OF PURE REASON

ALTHOUGH a purely transcendental idea is, in accordance with the original laws of reason, a quite necessary product of reason, its object, it may yet be said, is something of which we have no concept. For in respect of an object which is adequate to the demands of reason, it is not, in fact, possible that we should ever be able to form a concept of the under- A 339 standing, that is, a concept that allows of being exhibited and intuited in a possible experience. But we should be better advised and less likely to be misunderstood if we said that B 397 although we cannot have any knowledge of the object which corresponds to an idea, we yet have a problematic concept of it.

The transcendental (subjective) reality of the pure concepts of reason depends on our having been led to such ideas by a necessary syllogism.[1] There will therefore be syllogisms which contain no empirical premisses, and by means of which we conclude from something which we know to something else of which we have no concept, and to which, owing to an inevitable illusion, we yet ascribe objective reality. These conclusions are, then, rather to be called *pseudo-rational*[2] than rational, although in view of their origin they may well lay claim to the latter title, since they are not fictitious and have not arisen fortuitously, but have sprung from the very nature of reason. They are sophistications not of men but of pure reason itself. Even the wisest of men cannot free himself from them. After long effort he perhaps succeeds in guarding himself against

---

[1] [*Vernunftschluss.*]   [2] [*vernünftelnde.*]

actual error; but he will never be able to free himself from the
illusion, which unceasingly mocks and torments him.

There are, then, only three kinds of dialectical syllogisms
—just so many as there are ideas in which their conclusions
result. In the *first* kind of syllogism I conclude from the
transcendental concept of the subject, which contains nothing
manifold, the absolute unity of this subject itself, of which,
however, even in so doing, I possess no concept whatsoever.
This dialectical inference I shall entitle the transcendental
paralogism. The *second* kind of pseudo-rational inference is
directed to the transcendental concept of the absolute totality
of the series of conditions for any given appearance. From the
fact that my concept of the unconditioned synthetic unity of the
series, as thought in a certain way, is always self-contradictory,
I conclude that there is really a unity of the opposite kind,
although of it also I have no concept. The position of reason in
these dialectical inferences I shall entitle the *antinomy* of pure
reason. Finally, in the *third* kind of pseudo-rational inference,
from the totality of the conditions under which objects in
general, in so far as they can be given me, have to be thought,
I conclude to the absolute synthetic unity of all conditions of
the possibility of things in general, *i.e.* from things which I do
not know through the merely transcendental concept of them
I infer an *ens entium*, which I know even less through any
transcendental[1] concept, and of the unconditioned necessity
of which I can form no concept whatsoever. This dialectical
syllogism I shall entitle the *ideal* of pure reason.

A 341
B 399

SECOND BOOK OF THE TRANSCENDENTAL DIALECTIC

CHAPTER I

THE PARALOGISMS OF PURE REASON

A logical paralogism is a syllogism which is fallacious in
form, be its content what it may. A transcendental paralogism
is one in which there is a transcendental ground, constraining
us to draw a formally invalid conclusion. Such a fallacy is

---

[1] [Reading, with the 4th edition, *transcendental* for *transcendent*.]

therefore grounded in the nature of human reason, and gives rise to an illusion which cannot be avoided, although it may, indeed, be rendered harmless.

We now come to a concept which was not included in the general list of transcendental concepts but which must yet be counted as belonging to that list, without, however, in the least altering it or declaring it defective. This is the concept or, if the term be preferred, the judgment, 'I think'. As is easily seen, this is the vehicle of all concepts, and therefore also of transcendental concepts, and so is always included in the conceiving of these latter, and is itself transcendental. But it can have no special designation, because it serves only to introduce all our thought, as belonging to consciousness. Meanwhile, however free it be of empirical admixture (impressions of the senses), it yet enables us to distinguish, through the nature of our faculty of representation, two kinds of objects. 'I', as thinking, am an object of inner sense, and am called 'soul'. That which is an object of the outer senses is called 'body'. Accordingly the expression 'I', as a thinking being, signifies the object of that psychology which may be entitled the 'rational doctrine of the soul', inasmuch as I am not here seeking to learn in regard to the soul anything more than can be inferred, independently of all experience (which determines me more specifically and *in concreto*), from this concept 'I', so far as it is present in all thought.

The *rational* doctrine of the soul is really an undertaking of this kind; for if in this science the least empirical element of my thought, or any special perception of my inner state, were intermingled with the grounds of knowledge, it would no longer be a rational but an *empirical* doctrine of the soul. Thus we have here what professes to be a science built upon the single proposition 'I *think*'. Whether this claim be well or ill grounded, we may, very fittingly, in accordance with the nature of a transcendental philosophy, proceed to investigate. The reader must not object that this proposition, which expresses the perception of the self, contains an inner experience, and that the rational doctrine of the soul founded upon it is never pure and is therefore to that extent based upon an empirical principle. For this inner perception is nothing more than the mere apperception '*I think*', by which even tran-

B 400

A 342

B 401

A 343

scendental concepts are made possible; what we assert in them is 'I think substance, cause', etc. For inner experience in general and its possibility, or perception in general and its relation to other perception, in which no special distinction or empirical determination is given, is not to be regarded as empirical knowledge but as knowledge of the empirical in general, and has to be reckoned with the investigation of the possibility of any and every experience, which is certainly a transcendental enquiry. The least object of perception (for example, even pleasure or displeasure[1]), if added[2] to the universal representation of self-consciousness, would at once transform rational psychology into empirical psychology.

'*I think*' is, therefore, the sole text of rational psychology, and from it the whole of its teaching has to be developed. Obviously, if this thought is to be related to an object (myself), it can contain none but transcendental predicates of that object, since the least empirical predicate would destroy the rational purity of the science and its independence of all experience.

A 344 }
B 402 }

All that is here required is that we follow the guidance of the categories, with this difference only, that since our starting-point is a given thing, 'I' as thinking being, we begin with the category of substance, whereby a thing in itself is represented, and so proceed backwards through the series, without, however, otherwise changing the order adopted in the table of the categories. The topic of the rational doctrine of the soul, from which everything else that it contains must be derived, is accordingly as follows:

I

The soul is *substance*.[3]

2	3
As regards its quality it is *simple*.	As regards the different times in which it exists, it is numerically identical, that is, *unity* (not plurality).

[1] [*Unlust.*]
[2] [Reading, with Erdmann, *welches* for *welche*.]
[3] [In his private copy of the *Critique* [Nachträge, No. CLXI] Kant has changed this to: The soul exists as substance.]

4

It is in relation to *possible* objects in space.[a]

All the concepts of pure psychology arise from these ele- $\begin{Bmatrix} \text{A } 345 \\ \text{B } 403 \end{Bmatrix}$ ments, simply by way of combination, without admission of any other principle. This substance, merely as object of inner sense, gives the concept of *immateriality*; as simple substance, that of *incorruptibility*; its identity, as intellectual substance, *personality*; all these three together, *spirituality*; while the relation to objects in space gives *commercium* with bodies, and so leads us to represent the thinking substance as the principle of life in matter, that is, as soul *(anima)*, and as the ground of *animality*. This last, in turn, as limited by spirituality, gives the concept of *immortality*.

In connection with these concepts we have four paralogisms of a transcendental psychology—which is wrongly regarded as a science of pure reason—concerning the nature of our thinking being. We can assign no other basis for this teaching than the B 404 simple, and in itself completely empty, representation '*I*'; and we A 346 cannot even say that this is a concept, but only that it is a bare consciousness which accompanies all concepts. Through this I or he or it (the thing) which thinks, nothing further is represented than a transcendental subject of the thoughts = X. It is known only through the thoughts which are its predicates, and of it, apart from them, we cannot have any concept whatsoever, but can only revolve in a perpetual circle, since any judgment upon it has always already made use of its representation. And the reason why this inconvenience is inseparably bound up with it, is that consciousness in itself is not a representation distinguishing a particular object, but a form

---

[a] The reader who has difficulty in guessing the psychological meaning of these expressions taken in their transcendental abstractness, and in discovering why the last-mentioned attribute of the soul belongs to the category of *existence*, will find the terms sufficiently B 403 explained and justified in the sequel. Further, I have to apologise for the Latin expressions which, contrary to good taste, have usurped the place of their German equivalents, both in this section and in the work as a whole. My excuse is that I have preferred to lose somewhat in elegance of language rather than to increase, in however minor a degree, the reader's difficulties.

of representation in general, that is, of representation in so far as it is to be entitled knowledge; for it is only of knowledge that I can say that I am thereby thinking something.

It must, on first thoughts, seem strange that the condition under which alone I think, and which is therefore merely a property of myself as subject, should likewise be valid for everything that thinks, and that on a seemingly empirical proposition we can presume to base an apodeictic and universal judgment, namely, that that which thinks must, in all cases, be constituted as the voice of self-consciousness declares it to be constituted in my own self. The reason is this: we must assign to things, necessarily and *a priori*, all the properties that constitute the conditions under which alone we think them. Now I cannot have any representation whatsoever of a thinking being, through any outer experience, but only through self-consciousness. Objects of this kind are, therefore, nothing more than the transference of this consciousness of mine to other things, which in this way alone can be represented as thinking beings. The proposition, 'I think', is, however, here taken only problematically, not in so far as it may contain perception of an existent (the Cartesian *cogito, ergo sum*), but in respect of its mere possibility, in order to see what properties applicable to its subject (be that subject actually existent or not) may follow from so simple a proposition.

If our knowledge of thinking beings in general, by means of pure reason, were based on more than the *cogito*, if we likewise made use of observations concerning the play of our thoughts and the natural laws of the thinking self to be derived from these thoughts, there would arise an empirical psychology, which would be a kind of *physiology* of inner sense, capable perhaps of explaining the appearances of inner sense, but never of revealing such properties as do not in any way belong to possible experience (*e.g.* the properties of the simple), nor of yielding any *apodeictic* knowledge regarding the nature of thinking beings in general. It would not, therefore, be a *rational* psychology.

Since the proposition 'I think' (taken problematically) contains the form of each and every judgment of the understanding and accompanies all categories as their vehicle, it is evident that the inferences from it admit only of a transcendental

B 405

A 347

B 406

A 348

employment of the understanding. And since this employment excludes any admixture of experience, we cannot, after what has been shown above, entertain any favourable anticipations in regard to its methods of procedure. We therefore propose to follow it, with a critical eye, through all the predicaments of pure psychology.

[*The Paralogisms of Pure Reason: as in 1st edition.*][1]

FIRST PARALOGISM: OF SUBSTANTIALITY

That, the representation of which is the *absolute subject* of our judgments and cannot therefore be employed as determination of another thing, is *substance.*

I, as a thinking being, am the *absolute subject* of all my possible judgments, and this representation of myself cannot be employed as predicate of any other thing.

Therefore I, as thinking being (soul), am *substance.*

Critique of the First Paralogism of Pure Psychology

In the analytical part of the Transcendental Logic we have shown that pure categories, and among them that of substance, have in themselves no objective meaning, save in so far as they rest upon an intuition, and are applied to the manifold A 349 of this intuition, as functions of synthetic unity. In the absence of this manifold, they are merely functions of a judgment, without content. I can say of any and every thing that it is substance, in the sense that I distinguish it from mere predicates and determinations of things. Now in all our thought the 'I' is the subject, in which thoughts inhere only as determinations; and this 'I' cannot be employed as the determination of another thing. Everyone must, therefore, necessarily regard himself as substance, and thought as [consisting] only [in] accidents of his being, determinations of his state.

But what use am I to make of this concept of a substance? That I, as a thinking being, *persist* for myself, and do not in any natural manner either *arise* or *perish*, can by no means be

---

[1] ["The Paralogisms of Pure Reason," as here given up to p. 367, were omitted in B. As restated in B, they are given below, pp. 368 to 383.]

deduced from it. Yet there is no other use to which I can put the concept of the substantiality of my thinking subject, and apart from such use I could very well dispense with it.

So far from being able to deduce these properties merely from the pure category of substance, we must, on the contrary, take our start from the permanence of an object given in experience as permanent. For only to such an object can the concept of *substance* be applied in a manner that is empirically serviceable. In the above proposition, however, we have not taken as our basis any experience; the inference is merely A 350 from the concept of the relation which all thought has to the 'I' as the common subject in which it inheres. Nor should we, in resting it upon experience, be able, by any sure observation, to demonstrate such permanence. The 'I' is indeed in all thoughts, but there is not in this representation the least trace of intuition, distinguishing the 'I' from other objects of intuition. Thus we can indeed perceive that this representation is invariably present in all thought, but not that it is an abiding and continuing intuition, wherein the thoughts, as being transitory, give place to one another.

It follows, therefore, that the first syllogism of transcendental psychology, when it puts forward the constant logical subject of thought as being knowledge of the real subject in which the thought inheres, is palming off upon us what is a mere pretence of new insight. We do not have, and cannot have, any knowledge whatsoever of any such subject. Consciousness is, indeed, that which alone makes all representations to be thoughts, and in it, therefore, as the transcendental subject, all our perceptions must be found; but beyond this logical meaning of the 'I', we have no knowledge of the subject in itself, which as substratum underlies this 'I', as it does all thoughts. The proposition, '*The soul is substance*', may, however, quite well be allowed to stand, if only it be recognised that this concept [of the soul as substance] does not carry us[1] a single step further, and so cannot yield us any of the A 351 usual deductions of the pseudo-rational doctrine of the soul, as, for instance, the everlasting duration of the human soul in all changes and even in death—if, that is to say, we recognise that this concept signifies a substance only in idea, not in reality.

---

[1] [Reading, with Hartenstein, *uns* for *unser*.]

SECOND PARALOGISM: OF SIMPLICITY

That, the action of which can never be regarded as the concurrence of several things acting, is *simple*.

Now the soul, or the thinking 'I', is such a being. Therefore, etc.

Critique of the Second Paralogism of Transcendental Psychology

This is the Achilles of all dialectical inferences in the pure doctrine of the soul. It is no mere sophistical play, contrived by a dogmatist in order to impart to his assertions a superficial plausibility, but an inference which appears to withstand even the keenest scrutiny and the most scrupulously exact investigation. It is as follows.

Every *composite* substance is an aggregate of several substances, and the action of a composite, or whatever inheres in it as thus composite, is an aggregate of several actions or accidents, distributed among the plurality of the substances. Now an effect which arises from the concurrence of many acting A 352 substances is indeed possible, namely, when this effect is external only (as, for instance, the motion of a body is the combined motion of all its parts). But with thoughts, as internal accidents belonging to a thinking being, it is different. For suppose it be the composite that thinks: then every part of it would be a part of the thought, and only all of them taken together would contain the whole thought. But this cannot consistently be maintained. For representations (for instance, the single words of a verse), distributed among different beings, never make up a whole thought (a verse), and it is therefore impossible that a thought should inhere in what is essentially composite. It is therefore possible only in a *single* substance, which, not being an aggregate of many, is absolutely simple.[a]

The so-called *nervus probandi* of this argument lies in the proposition, that if a multiplicity of representations are to form a single representation, they must be contained in the

[a] This proof can very easily be given the customary syllogistic correctness of form. But for my purpose it is sufficient to have made clear, though in popular fashion, the bare ground of proof.

absolute unity of the thinking subject. No one, however, can prove this proposition from *concepts*. For how should he set A 353 about the task of achieving this? The proposition, 'A thought can only be the effect of the absolute unity of the thinking being', cannot be treated as analytic. For the unity of the thought, which consists of many representations, is collective, and as far as mere concepts can show, may relate just as well to the collective unity of different substances acting together (as the motion of a body is the composite motion of all its parts) as to the absolute unity of the subject. Consequently, the necessity of presupposing, in the case of a composite thought, a simple substance, cannot be demonstrated in accordance with the principle of identity. Nor will anyone venture to assert that the proposition allows of being known synthetically and completely *a priori* from mere concepts—not, at least, if he understands the ground of the possibility of *a priori* synthetic propositions, as above explained.

It is likewise impossible to derive this necessary unity of the subject, as a condition of the possibility of every thought, from experience. For experience yields us no knowledge of necessity, apart even from the fact that the concept of absolute unity is quite outside its province. Whence then are we to derive this proposition upon which the whole psychological syllogism depends?

It is obvious that, if I wish to represent to myself a thinking being, I must put myself in his place, and thus substitute, as it were, my own subject for the object I am seeking to A 354 consider (which does not occur in any other kind of investigation), and that we demand the absolute unity of the subject of a thought, only because otherwise we could not say, '*I* think' (the manifold in one representation). For although the whole of the thought could be divided and distributed among many subjects, the subjective '*I*' can never be thus divided and distributed, and it is this 'I' that we presuppose in all thinking.

Here again, as in the former paralogism, the formal proposition of apperception, 'I think', remains the sole ground to which rational psychology can appeal when it thus ventures upon an extension of its knowledge. This proposition, however, is not itself an experience, but the form of apperception, which belongs to and precedes every experience; and as such it must always be taken only in relation to some possible knowledge, as a *merely subjective condition* of that knowledge. We have no right to transform it into a condition of the possibility of a knowledge of objects, that is, into a *concept* of thinking being in general. For we are not in a position to represent such being to ourselves save by putting ourselves, with the formula of our consciousness, in the place of every other intelligent being.

Nor is the simplicity of myself (as soul) really *inferred* from the proposition, 'I think'; it[1] is already involved in every thought. The proposition, '*I am simple*', must be regarded as an immediate expression of apperception, just as what is A 355 referred to as the Cartesian inference, *cogito, ergo sum*, is really a tautology, since the *cogito (sum cogitans)* asserts my existence immediately. '*I am simple*' means nothing more than that this representation, 'I', does not contain in itself the least manifoldness and that it is absolute (although merely logical) unity.

Thus the renowned psychological proof is founded merely on the indivisible unity of a representation, which governs only the verb in its relation to a person. It is obvious that in attaching 'I' to our thoughts[2] we designate the subject of inherence only transcendentally, without noting in it any quality whatsoever—in fact, without knowing anything of it either by direct acquaintance or otherwise.[3] It means a something in general (transcendental subject), the representation of which must, no doubt, be simple, if only for the reason that there is nothing determinate in it. Nothing, indeed, can be represented that is simpler than that which is represented through the concept of a mere something. But the simplicity of the representation of a subject is not *eo ipso* knowledge of the simplicity of the subject itself, for we abstract altogether from its properties when we designate it solely by the entirely empty expression 'I', an expression which I can apply to every thinking subject.

This much, then, is certain, that through the 'I', I always A 356

---

[1] [Reading, with Erdmann, *die* for *der*.]
[2] [Reading, with Erdmann, *den* for *dem*.]
[3] [*etwas von ihm zu kennen, oder zu wissen.*]

entertain the thought of an absolute, but logical, unity of the subject (simplicity). It does not, however, follow that I thereby know the actual simplicity of my subject. The proposition, 'I am substance', signifies, as we have found, nothing but the pure category, of which I can make no use (empirically) *in concreto*; and I may therefore legitimately say: 'I am a simple substance', that is, a substance the representation of which never contains a synthesis of the manifold. But this concept, as also the proposition, tells us nothing whatsoever in regard to myself as an object of experience, since the concept of substance is itself used only as a function of synthesis, without any underlying intuition, and therefore without an object. It concerns only the condition of our knowledge; it does not apply to any assignable object. We will test the supposed usefulness of the proposition by an experiment.

Everyone must admit that the assertion of the simple nature of the soul is of value only in so far as I can thereby distinguish this subject from all matter, and so can exempt it from the dissolution to which matter is always liable. This is indeed, strictly speaking, the only use for which the above proposition is intended, and is therefore generally expressed A 357 as 'The soul is not corporeal'. If, then, I can show that, although we allow full objective validity—the validity appropriate to a judgment of pure reason derived solely from pure categories—to this cardinal proposition of the rational doctrine of the soul (that is, that everything which thinks is a simple substance), we still cannot make the least use of this proposition in regard to the question of its dissimilarity from or relation to matter, this will be the same as if I had relegated this supposed psychological insight to the field of mere ideas, without any real objective use.

In the Transcendental Aesthetic we have proved, beyond all question, that bodies are mere appearances of our outer sense and not things in themselves. We are therefore justified in saying that our thinking subject is not corporeal; in other words, that, inasmuch as it is represented by us as object of inner sense, it cannot, in so far as it thinks, be an object of outer sense, that is, an appearance in space. This is equivalent to saying that thinking beings, *as such*, can never be found by us among outer appearances, and that their thoughts, consciousness, desires, etc., cannot be outwardly intuited. All these belong to inner sense. This argument does, in fact, seem to be so natural and so popular that even the commonest understanding appears to have always relied upon it, and thus already, from the earliest times, to have regarded souls as quite different entities from their bodies.   A 358

But although extension, impenetrability, cohesion, and motion—in short, everything which outer senses can give us —neither are[1] nor contain thoughts, feeling, desire, or resolution, these never being objects of outer intuition, nevertheless the something which underlies the outer appearances and which so affects our sense that it obtains the representations of space, matter, shape, etc., may yet, when viewed as noumenon (or better, as transcendental object), be at the same time the subject of our thoughts. That the mode in which our outer sense is thereby affected gives us no intuition of representations, will, etc., but only of space and its determinations, proves nothing to the contrary. For this something is not extended, nor is it impenetrable or composite, since all these predicates concern only sensibility and its intuition, in so far as we are affected by certain (to us otherwise unknown) objects. By such statements we are not, however, enabled to know what kind of an object it is, but only to recognise that if it be considered in itself, and therefore apart from any relation to the outer senses, these predicates of outer appearances cannot be assigned to it. On the other hand, the predicates of inner sense, representations and thought, are not inconsistent with its nature. Accordingly, even granting the human soul to be simple in nature, such simplicity by no means suffices to distinguish it from matter, in respect of the substratum of the latter—if, that is to say, we consider matter, as indeed we ought to, as mere appearance.   A 359

If matter were a thing in itself, it would, as a composite being, be entirely different from the soul, as a simple being. But matter is mere outer appearance, the substratum of which cannot be known through any predicate that we can assign to it. I can therefore very well admit the possibility that it is in itself simple, although owing to the manner in which it affects our senses it produces in us the intuition of the extended and so of

---

[1] [Reading, with Erdmann, *sind* for *sein*.]

the composite. I may further assume that the substance which in relation to our outer sense possesses extension is in itself the possessor of thoughts, and that these thoughts can by means of its own inner sense be consciously represented. In this way, what in one relation is entitled corporeal would in another relation be at the same time a thinking being, whose thoughts we cannot intuit, though we can indeed intuit their signs in the [field of] appearance. Accordingly, the thesis that only souls (as particular kinds of substances) think, would have to be given up; and we should have to fall back on the common expression that men think, that is, that the very same being which, as outer appearance, is extended, is (in itself) internally a subject, and is not composite, but is simple and thinks.

A 360

But, without committing ourselves in regard to such hypotheses, we can make this general remark. If I understand by soul a thinking being in itself, the question whether or not it is the same in kind as matter—matter not being a thing in itself, but merely a species of representations in us—is by its very terms illegitimate. For it is obvious that a thing in itself is of a different nature from the determinations which constitute only its state.

If, on the other hand, we compare the thinking 'I' not with matter but with the intelligible[1] that lies at the basis of the outer appearance which we call matter, we have no knowledge whatsoever of the intelligible, and therefore are in no position to say that the soul is in any inward respect different from it.

The simple consciousness is not, therefore, knowledge of the simple nature of the self as subject, such as might enable us to distinguish it from matter, as from a composite being.

If, therefore, in the only case[2] in which this concept can be of service, namely, in the comparison of myself with objects of outer experience, it does not suffice for determining what is specific and distinctive in the nature of the self, then though we may still profess to know that the thinking 'I', the soul (a name for the transcendental object of inner sense), is simple, such a way of speaking has no sort of application to real objects, and therefore cannot in the least extend our knowledge.

A 361

---

[1] [mit dem Intelligibilen.]
[2] [Following Erdmann, in omitting ihn.]

Thus the whole of rational psychology is involved in the collapse of its main support. Here as little as elsewhere can we hope to extend our knowledge through mere concepts—still less by means of the merely subjective form of all our concepts, consciousness—in the absence of any relation to possible experience. For [as we have thus found], even the fundamental concept of a *simple nature* is such that it can never be met with in any experience, and such, therefore, that there is no way of attaining to it, as an objectively valid concept.

THIRD PARALOGISM: OF PERSONALITY

That which is conscious of the numerical identity of itself at different times is in so far a *person*
Now the soul is conscious, etc.
Therefore it is a person.

Critique of the Third Paralogism of Transcendental Psychology

If I want to know through experience, the numerical identity of an external object, I shall pay heed to that permanent A 362 element in the appearance to which as subject everything else is related as determination, and note its identity throughout the time in which the determinations change. Now I am an object of inner sense, and all time is merely the form of inner sense. Consequently, I refer each and all of my successive determinations to the numerically identical self, and do so throughout time, that is, in the form of the inner intuition of myself. This being so, the personality of the soul has to be regarded not as inferred but as a completely identical proposition of self-consciousness in time; and this, indeed, is why[1] it is valid *a priori*. For it really says nothing more than that in the whole time in which I am conscious of myself, I am conscious of this time as belonging to the unity of myself; and it comes to the same whether I say that this whole time is in me, as individual unity, or that I am to be found as numerically identical in all this time.

In my own consciousness, therefore, identity of person is unfailingly met with. But if I view myself from the standpoint of another person (as object of his outer intuition), it is this

[1] [*die Ursache, weswegen.*]

outer observer who first represents *me in time*, for in the apperception *time* is represented, strictly speaking, only *in me*. Although he admits, therefore, the 'I', which accompanies, and indeed with complete identity, all representations at all times in *my* consciousness, he will draw no inference from this to the objective permanence of myself. For just as the time in which the observer sets me is not the time of my own but of his sensibility, so the identity which is necessarily bound up with my consciousness is not therefore bound up with his, that is, with the consciousness which contains the outer intuition of my subject.

A 363

The identity of the consciousness of myself at different times is therefore only a formal condition of my thoughts and their coherence, and in no way proves the numerical identity of my subject. Despite the logical identity of the 'I', such a change may have occurred in it as does not allow of the retention of its identity, and yet we may ascribe to it the same-sounding[1] 'I', which in every different state, even in one involving change of the [thinking] subject, might still retain the thought of the preceding subject and so hand it over to the subsequent subject.[a]

A 364

Although the dictum of certain ancient schools, that everything in the world is *in a flux* and nothing is *permanent* and abiding, cannot be reconciled with the admission of substances, it is not refuted by the unity of self-consciousness.

[a] An elastic ball which impinges on another similar ball in a straight line communicates to the latter its whole motion, and therefore its whole state (that is, if we take account only of the positions in space). If, then, in analogy with such bodies, we postulate substances such that the one communicates to the other representations together with the consciousness of them, we can conceive a whole series of substances of which the first transmits its state together with its consciousness to the second, the second its own state with that of the preceding substance to the third, and this in turn the states of all the preceding substances together with its own consciousness and with their consciousness to another. The last substance would then be conscious of all the states of the previously changed substances, as being its own states, because they would have been transferred to it together with the consciousness of them. And yet it would not have been one and the same person in all these states.

A 364

[1] [*gleichlautende.*]

For we are unable from our own consciousness to determine whether, as souls, we are permanent or not. Since we reckon as belonging to our identical self only that of which we are conscious, we must necessarily judge that we are one and the same throughout the whole time of which we are conscious. We cannot, however, claim that this judgment would be valid from the standpoint of an outside observer. For since the only permanent appearance which we encounter in the soul is the representation 'I' that accompanies and connects them all, we are unable to prove that this 'I', a mere thought, may not be in the same state of flux as the other thoughts which, by means of it, are linked up with one another.

It is indeed strange that personality, and its presupposi- A 365 tion, permanence, and therefore the substantiality of the soul, should have to be proved *at this stage and not earlier.* For could we have presupposed these latter [permanence and substantiality], there would follow, not indeed the continuance of consciousness, yet at least the possibility of a continuing consciousness in an abiding subject, and that is already sufficient for personality. For personality does not itself at once cease because its activity is for a time interrupted. This permanence, however, is in no way given prior to that numerical identity of our self which we infer from identical apperception, but on the contrary is inferred first from the numerical identity. (If the argument proceeded aright, the concept of substance, which is applicable only empirically, would first be brought in after such proof of numerical identity.) Now, since this identity of person [presupposing, as it does, numerical identity] in nowise follows from the identity of the 'I' in the consciousness of all the time in which I know myself, we could not, earlier in the argument, have founded upon it the substantiality of the soul.

Meanwhile we may still retain the concept of personality —just as we have retained the concept of substance and of the simple—in so far as it is merely transcendental, that is, concerns[1] the unity of the subject, otherwise unknown to us, in the determinations of which there is a thoroughgoing connection through apperception. Taken in this way, the concept is necessary for practical employment and is sufficient for

[1] [Reading, with Adickes, *d.i. Einheit des Subjektes betrifft.*]

A 366   such use; but we can never parade it as an extension of our
self-knowledge through pure reason, and as exhibiting to us
from the mere concept of the identical self an unbroken continuance of the subject. For this concept revolves perpetually
in a circle, and does not help us in respect to any question
which aims at synthetic knowledge. What matter may be as a
thing in itself (transcendental object) is completely unknown
to us, though, owing to its being represented as something external, its permanence as appearance can indeed be observed.
But if I want to observe the mere 'I' in the change of all representations, I have no other *correlatum* to use in my comparisons
except again myself, with the universal conditions of my consciousness. Consequently, I can give none but tautological
answers to all questions, in that I substitute my concept and
its unity for the properties which belong to myself as object,
and so take for granted that which the questioner has desired
to know.

FOURTH PARALOGISM: OF IDEALITY

(IN REGARD TO OUTER RELATION)

That, the existence of which can only be inferred as a cause
of given perceptions, has a merely doubtful existence.

A 367   Now all outer appearances are of such a nature that their
existence is not immediately perceived, and that we can only
infer them as the cause of given perceptions.

Therefore the existence of all objects of the outer senses is
doubtful. This uncertainty I entitle the ideality of outer appearances, and the doctrine of this ideality is called *idealism*, as
distinguished from the counter-assertion of a possible certainty
in regard to objects of outer sense, which is called *dualism*.

Critique of the Fourth Paralogism of Transcendental Psychology

Let us first examine the premisses. We are justified, [it is
argued], in maintaining that only what is in ourselves can be
perceived immediately, and that my own existence is the sole
object of a mere perception. The existence, therefore, of an
actual object outside me (if this word 'me' be taken in the

intellectual [not in the empirical] sense) is never given directly in perception. Perception is a modification of inner sense, and the existence of the outer object can be added to it only in thought, as being its outer cause, and accordingly as being inferred. For the same reason, Descartes was justified in limiting all perception, in the narrowest sense of that term, to the proposition, 'I, as a thinking being, exist.' Obviously, since A 368 what is without is not in me, I cannot encounter it in my apperception, nor therefore in any perception, which, properly regarded, is merely the determination of apperception.

I am not, therefore, in a position to *perceive* external things, but can only infer their existence from my inner perception, taking the inner perception as the effect of which something external is the proximate cause. Now the inference from a given effect to a determinate cause is always uncertain, since the effect may be due to more than one cause. Accordingly, as regards the relation of the perception to its cause, it always remains doubtful whether the cause be internal or external; whether, that is to say, all the so-called outer perceptions are not a mere play of our inner sense, or whether they stand in relation to actual external objects as their cause. At all events, the existence of the latter is only inferred, and is open to all the dangers of inference, whereas the object of inner sense (I myself with all my representations) is immediately perceived, and its existence does not allow of being doubted.

The term '*idealist*' is not, therefore, to be understood as applying to those who deny the existence of external objects of the senses, but only to those who do not admit that their existence is known through immediate perception, and who therefore conclude that we can never, by way of any possible A 369 experience, be completely certain as to their reality.

Before exhibiting our paralogism in all its deceptive illusoriness, I have first to remark that we must necessarily distinguish two types of idealism, the transcendental and the empirical. By *transcendental idealism* I mean the doctrine that appearances are to be regarded as being, one and all, representations only, not things in themselves, and that time and space are therefore only sensible forms of our intuition, not determinations given as existing by themselves, nor conditions of objects viewed as things in themselves. To this idealism there is opposed a *transcendental realism* which regards time and space as something given in themselves, independently of our sensibility. The transcendental realist thus interprets outer appearances (their reality being taken as granted) as things-in-themselves, which exist independently of us and of our sensibility, and which are therefore outside us—the phrase 'outside us' being interpreted in conformity with pure concepts of understanding. It is, in fact, this transcendental realist who afterwards plays the part of empirical idealist. After wrongly supposing that objects of the senses, if they are to be external, must have an existence by themselves, and independently of the senses, he finds that, judged from this point of view, all our sensuous representations are inadequate to establish their reality.

A 370   The transcendental idealist, on the other hand, may be an empirical realist or, as he is called, a *dualist*; that is, he may admit the existence of matter without going outside his mere self-consciousness, or assuming anything more than the certainty of his representations, that is, the *cogito, ergo sum*. For he considers this matter and even its inner possibility to be appearance merely; and appearance, if separated from our sensibility, is nothing. Matter is with him, therefore, only a species of representations (intuition), which are called external, not as standing in relation to objects *in themselves external*, but because they relate perceptions to the space in which all things are external to one another, while yet the space itself is in us.

From the start, we have declared ourselves in favour of this transcendental idealism; and our doctrine thus removes all difficulty in the way of accepting the existence of matter on the unaided testimony of our mere self-consciousness, or of declaring it to be thereby proved in the same manner as the existence of myself as a thinking being is proved. There can be no question that I am conscious of my representations; these representations and I myself, who have the representations, therefore exist. External objects (bodies), however, are mere appearances, and are therefore nothing but a species of my representations, the objects of which are something only through these representations. Apart from them they are
A 371   nothing. Thus external things exist as well as I myself, and

both, indeed, upon the immediate witness of my self-consciousness. The only difference is that the representation of myself, as the thinking subject, belongs to inner sense only, while the representations which mark extended beings belong also to outer sense. In order to arrive at the reality of outer objects I have just as little need to resort to inference as I have in regard to the reality of the object of my inner sense, that is, in regard to the reality of my thoughts. For in both cases alike the objects are nothing but representations, the immediate perception (consciousness) of which is at the same time a sufficient proof of their reality.

The transcendental idealist is, therefore, an empirical realist, and allows to matter, as appearance, a reality which does not permit of being inferred, but is immediately perceived. Transcendental realism, on the other hand, inevitably falls into difficulties, and finds itself obliged to give way to empirical idealism, in that it regards the objects of outer sense as something distinct from the senses themselves, treating mere appearances as self-subsistent beings, existing outside us. On such a view as this, however clearly we may be conscious[1] of our representation of these things, it is still far from certain that, if the representation exists, there exists also the object corresponding to it. In our system, on the other hand, these external things, namely matter, are in all their configurations and alterations nothing but mere appearances, that is, representations in us, of the reality of which we are immediately conscious. A 372

Since, so far as I know, all psychologists who adopt empirical idealism are transcendental realists, they have certainly proceeded quite consistently in ascribing great importance to empirical idealism, as one of the problems in regard to which the human mind is quite at a loss how to proceed. For if we regard outer appearances as representations produced in us by their objects, and if these objects be things existing in themselves outside us, it is indeed impossible to see how we can come to know the existence of the objects otherwise than by inference from the effect to the cause; and this being so, it must always remain doubtful whether the cause in question be in us or outside us. We can indeed admit that something, which

---

[1] [*bei unserem besten Bewusstsein.*]

may be (in the transcendental sense) outside us, is the cause of our outer intuitions, but this is not the object of which we are thinking in the representations of matter and of corporeal things; for these are merely appearances, that is, mere kinds of representation, which are never to be met with save in us, and the reality of which depends on immediate consciousness, just as does the consciousness of my own thoughts. The transcendental object is equally unknown in respect to inner and to

A 373 outer intuition. But it is not of this that we are here speaking, but of the empirical object, which is called an *external* object if it is represented *in space*, and an *inner* object if it is represented only *in its time-relations*. Neither space nor time, however, is to be found save *in us*.

The expression '*outside us*' is thus unavoidably ambiguous in meaning, sometimes signifying what *as thing in itself* exists apart from us, and sometimes what belongs solely to outer *appearance*. In order, therefore, to make this concept, in the latter sense—the sense in which the psychological question as to the reality of our outer intuition has to be understood—quite unambiguous, we shall distinguish *empirically external* objects from those which may be said to be external in the transcendental sense, by explicitly entitling the former '*things which are to be found in space*'

Space and time are indeed *a priori* representations, which dwell in us as forms of our sensible intuition, before any real object, determining our sense through sensation, has enabled us to represent the object under those sensible relations. But the material or real element, the something which is to be intuited in space, necessarily presupposes perception. Perception exhibits the reality of something in space; and in the absence of perception no power of imagination can invent and

A 374 produce that something. It is sensation, therefore, that indicates a reality in space or[1] in time, according as it is related to the one or to the other mode of sensible intuition. (Once sensation is given—if referred to an object in general, though not as determining that object, it is entitled perception—thanks to its manifoldness we can picture in imagination many objects which have no empirical place in space or time outside the imagination.)[2]

---

[1] [Reading, with Erdmann, *oder* for *und*.]
[2] [Brackets not in text.]

This admits of no doubt; whether we take pleasure and pain, or the sensations of the outer senses, colours, heat, etc., perception is that whereby the material required to enable us to think objects of sensible intuition must first be given. This perception, therefore (to consider, for the moment, only outer intuitions), represents something real in space. For, in the first place, while space is the representation of a mere possibility of coexistence, perception is the representation of a reality. Secondly, this reality is represented in outer sense, that is, in space. Thirdly, space is itself nothing but mere representation, and therefore nothing in it can count as real save only what is represented in it;*a* and conversely, what is given in it, that is, represented through perception, is also real in it. For if it A 375 were not real, that is, immediately given through empirical intuition, it could not be pictured in imagination, since what is real in intuitions cannot be invented *a priori*.

All outer perception, therefore, yields immediate proof of something real[1] in space, or rather is the real itself. In this sense empirical realism is beyond question; that is, there corresponds to our outer intuitions something real in space. Space itself, with all its appearances, as representations, is, indeed, only in me, but nevertheless the real, that is, the material of all objects of outer intuition, is actually given in this space, independently of all imaginative invention. Also, it is impossible that in *this space* anything *outside us* (in the transcendental sense) should be given, space itself being nothing outside our sensibility. Even the most rigid idealist cannot, therefore, require a proof that the object outside us (taking 'outside' in the strict [transcendental] sense) corresponds to A 376 our perception. For if there be any such object, it could not be

---

a We must give full credence to this paradoxical but correct proposition, that there is nothing in space save what is represented in it. For space is itself nothing but representation, and whatever is in it must therefore be contained in the representation. Nothing whatso- A 375 ever is in space, save in so far as it is actually represented in it. It is a proposition which must indeed sound strange, that a thing can exist only in the representation of it, but in this case the objection falls, inasmuch as the things with which we are here concerned are not things in themselves, but appearances only, that is, representations.

[1] [*wirkliches*. In this section, as elsewhere, Kant uses *Wirklichkeit* and *Realität* as synonymous terms.]

represented and intuited as outside us, because such representation and intuition presuppose space, and reality in space, being the reality of a mere representation, is nothing other than perception itself. The real of outer appearances is therefore real in perception only, and can be real in no other way.

From perceptions knowledge of objects can be generated, either by mere play of imagination or by way of experience; and in the process there may, no doubt, arise illusory representations to which the objects do not correspond, the deception being attributable sometimes to a delusion of imagination (in dreams) and sometimes to an error of judgment (in so-called sense-deception). To avoid such deceptive illusion, we have to proceed according to the rule: *Whatever is connected with a perception according to empirical laws, is actual.* But such deception, as well as the provision against it, affects idealism quite as much as dualism, inasmuch as we are concerned only with the form of experience. Empirical idealism, and its mistaken questionings as to the objective reality of our outer perceptions, is already sufficiently refuted, when it has been shown that outer perception yields immediate proof of something actual in space, and that this space, although in itself only a mere form of representations, has objective reality in relation to all outer appearances, which also are nothing else than mere representations; and when it has likewise been shown that in the absence of perception even imagining and dreaming are not possible, and that our outer senses, as regards the data from which experience can arise, have therefore their actual corresponding objects in space.

The *dogmatic idealist* would be one who *denies* the existence of matter, the *sceptical idealist* one who *doubts* its existence, because holding it to be incapable of proof.[1] The former must base his view on supposed contradictions in the possibility of there being such a thing as matter at all—a view with which we have not yet been called upon to deal. The following section on dialectical inferences, which represents reason as in strife with itself in regard to the concepts which it makes for itself of the possibility of what[2] belongs to the

A 377

---

[1] [Reading, with Erdmann, *es . . . es* for *sie . . . sie.*]

[2] [Reading, with Hartenstein and Kehrbach, *die sie sich . . . dessen macht* for *die sich . . . dessen.*]

connection of experience, will remove this difficulty. The sceptical idealist, however, who merely challenges the ground of our assertion and denounces as insufficiently justified our conviction of the existence of matter, which we thought to base on immediate perception, is a benefactor of human reason in so far as he compels us, even in the smallest advances of ordinary experience, to keep on the watch, lest we consider as a well-earned possession what we perhaps obtain only illegitimately. We are now in a position to appreciate the value of these idealist objections. Unless we mean to contradict ourselves in our commonest assertions, they drive us by main force to view all our perceptions, whether we call them inner or outer, as a consciousness only of what is dependent on our sensibility. They also compel us to view the outer objects of these perceptions not as things in themselves, but only as representations, of which, as of every other representation, we can become immediately conscious, and which are entitled outer because they depend on what we call 'outer sense', whose intuition is space. Space itself, however, is nothing but an inner mode of representation in which certain perceptions are connected with one another. A 378

If we treat outer objects as things in themselves, it is quite impossible to understand how we could arrive at a knowledge of their reality outside us, since we have to rely merely on the representation which is in us. For we cannot be sentient [of what is] outside ourselves, but only [of what is] in us, and the whole of our self-consciousness therefore yields nothing save merely our own determinations. Sceptical idealism thus constrains us to have recourse to the only refuge still open, namely, the ideality of all appearances, a doctrine which has already been established in the Transcendental Aesthetic independently of these consequences, which we could not at that stage foresee. If then we ask, whether it follows that in the doctrine of the soul dualism alone is tenable, we must answer: 'Yes, certainly; but dualism only in the empirical sense'. That is to say, in the connection of experience matter, as substance in the [field of] appearance, is really given to outer sense, just as the thinking 'I', also as substance in the [field of] appearance, is given to inner sense. Further, appearances in both fields[1] A 379

1 [beiderseits.]

must be connected with each other according to the rules which this category introduces into that connection of our outer as well as of our inner perceptions whereby they constitute one experience. If, however, as commonly happens, we seek to extend the concept of dualism, and take it in the transcendental sense, neither it nor the two counter-alternatives—*pneumatism* on the one hand, *materialism* on the other—would have any sort of basis, since we should then have misapplied our concepts, taking the difference in the mode of representing objects, which, as regards what they are in themselves, still remain unknown to us, as a difference in the things themselves. Though the 'I', as represented through inner sense in time, and objects in space outside me, are specifically quite distinct appearances, they are not for that reason thought as being different things. Neither the *transcendental object* which underlies outer appearances nor that which underlies inner intuition, is in itself either matter or a thinking being, but a ground (to us unknown) of the appearances which supply to us the empirical concept of the former as well as of the latter mode of existence.

If then, as this critical argument obviously compels us to do, we hold fast to the rule above established, and do not push our questions beyond the limits within which possible experience can present us with its object, we shall never dream of seeking to inform ourselves about the objects of our senses as they are in themselves, that is, out of all relation to the senses. But if the psychologist takes appearances for things in themselves, and as existing in and by themselves, then whether he be a materialist who admits into his system nothing but matter alone, or a spiritualist who admits only thinking beings (that is, beings with the form of our inner sense), or a dualist who accepts both, he will always, owing to this misunderstanding, be entangled in pseudo-rational speculations as to how that which is not a thing in itself, but only the appearance of a thing in general, can exist by itself.

A 381

Consideration of Pure Psychology as a whole, in view of these Paralogisms

If we compare the *doctrine of the soul* as the physiology of inner sense, with the *doctrine of the body* as a physiology of the object of the outer senses, we find that while in both much can be learnt empirically, there is yet this notable difference In the latter science much that is *a priori* can be synthetically known from the mere concept of an extended impenetrable being, but in the former nothing whatsoever that is *a priori* can be known synthetically from the concept of a thinking being. The cause is this. Although both are appearances, the appearance to outer sense has something fixed or abiding which supplies a substratum as the basis of its transitory determinations and therefore a synthetic concept, namely, that of space and of an appearance in space; whereas time, which is the sole form of our inner intuition, has nothing abiding, and therefore yields knowledge only of the change of determinations, not of any object that can be thereby determined. For in what we entitle 'soul', everything is in continual flux and there is nothing abiding except (if we must so express ourselves) the 'I', which is simple solely because its representation has no content, and therefore no manifold, and for this reason seems to represent, or (to use a more correct   A 382 term) denote, a simple object. In order that it should be possible, by pure reason, to obtain knowledge of the nature of a thinking being in general, this 'I' would have to be an intuition which, in being presupposed in all thought (prior to all experience), might as intuition yield *a priori* synthetic propositions. This 'I' is, however, as little an intuition as it is a concept of any object; it is the mere form of consciousness, which can accompany the two kinds of representation and which is in a position to elevate them to the rank of knowledge only in so far as something else is given in intuition which provides material for a representation of an object. Thus the whole of rational psychology, as a science surpassing all powers of human reason, proves abortive, and nothing is left for us but to study our soul under the guidance of experience, and to confine ourselves to those questions which do not go beyond the limits within which a content can be provided for them by possible inner experience.

But although rational psychology cannot be used to extend knowledge, and when so employed is entirely made up of paralogisms, still we cannot deny it a considerable negative value, if it is taken as nothing more than a critical treatment of our dialectical inferences, those that arise from the common and natural reason of men.

A 383   Why do we have resort to a doctrine of the soul founded exclusively on pure principles of reason? Beyond all doubt, chiefly in order to secure our thinking self against the danger of materialism. This is achieved by means of the pure concept[1] of our thinking self which we have just given. For by this teaching so completely are we freed from the fear that on the removal of matter all thought, and even the very existence of thinking beings, would be destroyed, that on the contrary it is clearly shown, that if I remove the thinking subject the whole corporeal world must at once vanish: it is nothing save an appearance in the sensibility of our subject and a mode of its representations

I admit that this does not give me any further knowledge of the properties of this thinking self, nor does it enable me to determine its permanence or even that it exists independently of what we may conjecture to be the transcendental substratum of outer appearances; for the latter is just as unknown to me as is the thinking self. But it is nevertheless possible that I may find cause, on other than merely speculative grounds, to hope for an independent and continuing existence of my thinking nature, throughout all possible change of my state. In that case much will already have been gained if, while freely confessing my own ignorance, I am yet in a position to repel the dogmatic assaults of a speculative op-
A 384   ponent, and to show him that he can never know more of the nature of the self[2] in denying the possibility of my expectations than I can know in clinging to them.

Three other dialectical questions, constituting the real goal of rational psychology, are grounded on this transcendental illusion in our psychological concepts, and cannot be decided except by means of the above enquiries: namely (1) of the possibility of the communion[3] of the soul with an organised body, *i.e.* concerning animality and the state of the soul in the life of man; (2) of the beginning of this communion, that is, of the soul in and before birth; (3) of the end of this communion, that is, of the soul in and after death (the question of immortality).

---

[1] [*Vernunftbegriff.*]   [2] [*meines Subjekts.*]   [3] [*Gemeinschaft.*]

Now I maintain that all the difficulties commonly found in these questions, and by means of which, as dogmatic objections, men seek to gain credit for a deeper insight into the nature of things than any to which the ordinary understanding can properly lay claim, rest on a mere delusion by which they hypostatise what exists merely in thought, and take it as a real object existing, in the same character, outside the thinking subject. In other words, they regard extension, which is nothing but appearance, as a property of outer things that subsists A 385 even apart from our sensibility, and hold that motion is due to these things and really occurs in and by itself, apart from our senses. For matter, the communion of which with the soul arouses so much questioning, is nothing but a mere form, or a particular way of representing an unknown object by means of that intuition which is called outer sense. There may well be something outside us to which this appearance, which we call matter, corresponds; in its character of appearance it is not, however, outside us, but is only a thought in us, although this thought, through the above-mentioned outer sense, represents it as existing outside us. Matter, therefore, does not mean a kind of substance quite distinct and heterogeneous from the object of inner sense (the soul), but only the distinctive nature of those appearances of objects—in themselves unknown to us—the representations of which we call outer as compared with those which we count as belonging to inner sense, although like all other thoughts these outer representations belong only to the thinking subject. They have, indeed, this deceptive property that, representing objects in space, they detach themselves as it were from the soul and appear to hover outside it. Yet the very space in which they are intuited is nothing but a representation, and no counterpart of the same quality is to be found outside the soul. Consequently, the question is no longer of the communion of the A 386 soul with other known substances of a different kind outside us, but only of the connection of the representations of inner sense with the modifications of our outer sensibility—as to how these can be so connected with each other according to settled laws that they exhibit the unity of a coherent experience.

As long as we take inner and outer appearances together as mere representations in experience, we find nothing absurd and strange in the association[1] of the two kinds of senses. But as soon as we hypostatise outer appearances and come to regard them not as representations but *as things existing by themselves outside us, with the same quality as that with which they exist in us,* and as bringing to bear on our thinking subject the activities which they exhibit as appearances in relation to each other, then the efficient causes outside us assume a character which is irreconcilable with their effects in us. For the cause relates only to outer sense, the effect to inner sense—senses which, although combined in one subject, are extremely unlike each other. In outer sense we find no other outer effects save changes of place, and no forces except mere tendencies which issue in spatial relations as their effects. Within us, on the other hand, the effects are thoughts, among which is not to be found any relation of place, motion, shape, or other spatial determination, and we altogether lose the thread of the causes in the effects to which they are supposed to have given rise in inner sense. We ought, however, to bear in mind that bodies are not objects in themselves which are present to us, but a mere appearance of we know not what unknown object; that motion is not the effect of this unknown cause, but only the appearance of its influence on our senses Neither bodies nor motions are anything outside us; both alike are mere representations in us; and it is not, therefore, the motion of matter that produces representations in us; the motion itself is representation only, as also is the matter which makes itself known in this way. Thus in the end the whole difficulty which we have made for ourselves comes to this, how and why the representations of our sensibility are so interconnected that those which we entitle outer intuitions can be represented according to empirical laws as objects outside us—a question which is not in any way bound up with the supposed difficulty of explaining the origin of our representations from quite heterogeneous efficient causes outside us. That difficulty has arisen from our taking the appearances of an unknown cause as being the cause itself outside us, a view which can result in nothing but confusion. In the case of judgments in which a misapprehension has taken deep root through long custom, it is impossible at once to give to their correction that clarity

A 387

A 388

[1] [*Gemeinschaft.*]

which can be achieved in other cases where no such inevitable illusion confuses the concept. Our freeing of reason from sophistical theories can hardly, therefore, at this stage have the clearness which is necessary for its complete success. The following comments will, I think, be helpful as contributing towards this ultimate clarity.

All *objections* can be divided into *dogmatic, critical*, and *sceptical*. A dogmatic objection is directed against a *proposition*, a critical objection against the *proof* of a proposition. The former requires an insight into the nature of the object such that we can maintain the opposite of what the proposition has alleged in regard to this object. It is therefore itself dogmatic, claiming acquaintance with the constitution of the object fuller than that of the counter-assertion. A critical objection, since it leaves the validity or invalidity of the proposition unchallenged, and assails only the proof, does not presuppose fuller acquaintance with the object or oblige us to claim superior knowledge of its nature; it shows only that the assertion is unsupported, not that it is wrong. A sceptical objection sets assertion and counter-assertion in mutual opposition to each other as having equal weight, treating each in turn as dogma and the other as the objection thereto. And the conflict, as the being thus seemingly dogmatic on both the oppos- A 389 ing sides, is taken as showing that all judgment in regard to the object is completely null and void. Thus dogmatic and sceptical objections alike lay claim to such insight into their object as is required to assert or to deny something in regard to it. A critical objection, on the other hand, confines itself to pointing out that in the making of the assertion something has been presupposed that is void and merely fictitious; and it thus overthrows the theory by removing its alleged foundation without claiming to establish anything that bears directly upon the constitution of the object.

So long as we hold to the ordinary concepts of our reason with regard to the communion in which our thinking subject stands with the things outside us, we are dogmatic, looking upon them as real objects existing independently of us, in accordance with a certain transcendental dualism which does not assign these outer appearances to the subject as representations, but sets them, just as they are given us in sensible intuition, as objects outside us, completely separating them from the thinking subject. This subreption is the basis of all theories in regard to the communion between soul and body. The objective reality thus assigned to appearances is never brought into question. On the contrary, it is taken for granted; the theorising is merely as to the mode in which it has to be explained and understood. There A 390 are three usual systems devised on these lines, and they are indeed the only possible systems: that of *physical influence*, that of predetermined *harmony*, and that of *supernatural intervention*.

The two last methods of explaining the communion between the soul and matter are based on objections to the first view, which is that of common sense. It is argued, namely, that what appears as matter cannot by its immediate influence be the cause of representations, these being effects which are quite different in kind from matter. Now those who take this line cannot attach to what they understand by 'object of outer senses' the concept of a matter which is nothing but appearance, and so itself a mere representation produced by some sort of outer objects. For in that case they would be saying that the representations of outer objects (appearances) cannot be outer causes of the representations in our mind; and this would be a quite meaningless objection, since no one could dream of holding that what he has once come to recognise as mere representation, is an outer cause. On our principles they can establish their theory only by showing that that which is the true (transcendental) object of our outer senses cannot be the cause of those representations (appearances) which we A 391 comprehend under the title 'matter'. No one, however, can have the right to claim that he knows anything in regard to the transcendental cause of our representations of the outer senses; and their assertion is therefore entirely groundless. If, on the other hand, those who profess to improve upon the doctrine of physical influence keep to the ordinary outlook of transcendental dualism, and suppose matter, as such, to be a thing-in-itself (not the mere appearance of an unknown thing), they will direct their objection to showing that such an outer object, which in itself exhibits no causality save that of movements, can never be the efficient cause of representations, but that a

third entity must intervene to establish, if not reciprocal interaction, at least correspondence and harmony between the two.
But in arguing in this way, they begin their refutation by admitting into their dualism the πρῶτον ψεῦδος of [a doctrine of]
physical influence, and consequently their objection is not so
much a disproof of natural influence as of their own dualistic
presupposition. For the difficulties in regard to the connection
of our thinking nature with matter have their origin, one and
all, in the illicitly assumed dualistic view, that matter as such
is not appearance, that is, a mere representation of the mind
to which an unknown object corresponds, but is the object in
itself as it exists outside us independently of all sensibility.

As against the commonly accepted doctrine of physical in- A 392
fluence, an objection of the dogmatic type is not, therefore,
practicable. For if the opponent of the doctrine accepts the
view that matter and its motion are mere appearances and so
themselves mere representations, his difficulty is then simply
this, that it is impossible that the unknown object of our sensibility should be the cause of the representations in us. He cannot, however, have the least justification for any such contention, since no one is in a position to decide what an unknown
object may or may not be able to do. And this transcendental
idealism, as we have just proved, he cannot but concede. His
only way of escape would be frankly to hypostatise representations, and to set them outside himself as real things .

The doctrine of physical influence, in its ordinary form,
is, however, subject to a well-founded *critical* objection. The
alleged communion between two kinds of substances, the
thinking and the extended, rests on a crude dualism, and
treats the extended substances, which are really nothing
but mere representations of the thinking subject, as existing
by themselves. This mistaken interpretation of physical influence can thus be effectively disposed of: we have shown
that the proof of it is void and illicit.

The much-discussed question of the communion between
the thinking and the extended, if we leave aside all that is A 393
merely fictitious, comes then simply to this: *how in a thinking
subject outer intuition*, namely, that of space, with its filling-
in of shape and motion, *is possible*. And this is a question
which no man can possibly answer. This gap in our knowledge

can never be filled; all that can be done is to indicate it through the ascription of outer appearances to that transcendental object which is the cause of this species of representations, but of which we can have no knowledge whatsoever and of which we shall never acquire any concept. In all problems which may arise in the field of experience we treat these appearances as objects in themselves, without troubling ourselves about the primary ground of their possibility (as appearances). But to advance beyond these limits the concept of a transcendental object would be indispensably required.

The settlement of all disputes or objections which concern the state of the thinking nature prior to this communion (prior to life), or after the cessation of such communion (in death), rests upon these considerations regarding the communion between thinking beings and extended beings. The opinion that the thinking subject has been capable of thought prior to any communion with bodies would now appear as an assertion that, prior to the beginning of the species of sensibility in virtue of which something appears to us in space, those transcendental objects, which in our present state appear as bodies, could have been intuited in an entirely different manner. The opinion that the soul after the cessation of all communion with the corporeal world could still continue to think, would be formulated as the view that, if that species of sensibility, in virtue of which transcendental objects, at present quite unknown to us, appear as a material world, should cease, all intuition of the transcendental objects would not for that reason be removed, and it would still be quite possible that those same unknown objects should continue to be known by the thinking subject, though no longer, indeed, in the quality of bodies

Now on speculative principles no one can give the least ground for any such assertion. Even the possibility of what is asserted cannot be established; it can only be assumed. But it is equally impossible for anyone to bring any valid dogmatic objection against it. For whoever he may be, he knows just as little as I or anybody else of the absolute inner cause of outer corporeal appearances. Since he cannot, therefore, offer any justification for claiming to know on what the outer appearances in our present state (that of life) really rest, neither can he know that the condition of all outer intuition, or the thinking subject itself, will cease with this state A 395 (in death).

Thus all controversy in regard to the nature of the thinking being and its connection with the corporeal world is merely a result of filling the gap where knowledge is wholly lacking to us with paralogisms of reason, treating our thoughts as things and hypostatising them. Hence originates an imaginary science, imaginary both in the case of him who affirms and of him who denies, since all parties either suppose some knowledge of objects of which no human being has any concept, or treat their own representations as objects, and so revolve in a perpetual circle of ambiguities and contradictions. Nothing but the sobriety of a critique, at once strict and just, can free us from this dogmatic delusion, which through the lure of an imagined felicity keeps so many in bondage to theories and systems. Such a critique confines all our speculative claims rigidly to the field of possible experience; and it does this not by shallow scoffing at ever-repeated failures or pious sighs over the limits of our reason, but by an effective determining of these limits in accordance with established principles, inscribing its *nihil ulterius* on those Pillars of Hercules which nature herself has erected in order that the voyage of our reason may be extended no further than the continuous coastline of experience A 396 itself reaches—a coast we cannot leave without venturing upon a shoreless ocean which, after alluring us with ever-deceptive prospects, compels us in the end to abandon as hopeless all this vexatious and tedious endeavour.

*   *   *

We still owe the reader a clear general exposition of the transcendental and yet natural illusion in the paralogisms of pure reason, and also a justification of the systematic ordering of them which runs parallel with the table of the categories. We could not have attempted to do so at the beginning of this section without running the risk of becoming obscure or of clumsily anticipating the course of our argument. We shall now try to fulfil this obligation.

All *illusion* may be said to consist in treating the *subjective* condition of thinking as being knowledge of the *object*. Further in the Introduction to the Transcendental Dialectic we have

shown that pure reason concerns itself solely with the totality
of the synthesis of the conditions, for a given conditioned. Now
since the dialectical illusion of pure reason cannot be an empirical illusion, such as occurs in certain specific instances of
empirical knowledge, it will relate to what is universal in the
conditions of thinking, and there will therefore be only three
A 397 cases of the dialectical employment of pure reason.

    1. The synthesis of the conditions of a thought in general.
    2. The synthesis of the conditions of empirical thinking.
    3. The synthesis of the conditions of pure thinking.

In all these three cases pure reason occupies itself only
with the absolute totality of this synthesis, that is, with that
condition which is itself unconditioned. On this division is
founded the threefold transcendental illusion which gives
occasion for the three main sections of the Dialectic, and for
the three pretended sciences of pure reason—transcendental
psychology, cosmology, and theology. Here we are concerned
only with the first.

Since, in thinking in general, we abstract from all relation
of the thought to any object (whether of the senses or of the
pure understanding), the synthesis of the conditions of a
thought in general (No. 1) is not objective at all, but merely a
synthesis of the thought with the subject,[1] which is mistaken
for a synthetic representation of an object.

It follows from this that the dialectical inference to the
condition[2] of all thought in general, which is itself unconditioned, does not commit a material[3] error (for it abstracts
A 398 from all content or objects), but is defective in form alone, and
must therefore be called a paralogism.

Further, since the one condition which accompanies all
thought is the 'I' in the universal proposition 'I think',
reason has to deal with this condition in so far as it is itself
unconditioned. It is only the formal condition, namely, the
logical unity of every thought, in which I abstract from all
objects; but nevertheless it is represented as an object which I
think, namely, I myself and its unconditioned unity.

If anyone propounds to me the question, 'What is the con-

---

    [1] [*blos eine Synthesis des Gedankens mit dem Subjekt.*]
    [2] [Reading *Bedingung* for *Bedingungen.*]   [3] [*im Inhalte.*]

stitution[1] of a thing which thinks?', I have no *a priori* knowledge wherewith to reply. For the answer has to be synthetic—an analytic answer will perhaps explain what is meant by thought, but beyond this cannot yield any knowledge of that upon which this thought depends for its possibility. For a synthetic solution, however, intuition is always required; and owing to the highly general character of the problem, intuition has been left entirely out of account. Similarly no one can answer in all its generality the question, 'What must a thing be, to be movable?' For the question contains no trace of the answer, viz. impenetrable extension (matter). But although I have no general answer to the former question, it still seems as if I could reply in the special case of the proposition which expresses self-consciousness—'I think'. For this 'I' is the primary A 399 subject, that is, substance; it is simple, etc. But these would then have to be propositions derived from experience, and in the absence of a universal rule which expresses the conditions of the possibility of thought in general and *a priori*, they could[2] not contain any such non-empirical predicates. Suspicion is thus thrown on the view, which at first seemed to me so plausible, that we can form judgments about the nature of a thinking being, and can do so from concepts alone. But the error in this way of thinking has not yet been detected.

Further investigation into the origin of the attributes which I ascribe to myself as a thinking being in general can, however, show in what the error consists. These attributes are nothing but pure categories, by which I do not think a determinate object but only the unity of the representations—in order to determine an object for them. In the absence of an underlying intuition the category cannot by itself yield a concept of an object; for by intuition alone is the object given, which thereupon is thought in accordance with the category. If I am to declare a thing to be a substance in the [field of] appearance, predicates of its intuition must first be given me, and I must be able to distinguish in these the permanent from the transitory and the substratum (the thing itself) from what is merely inherent in it. If I call a A 400 thing in the [field of] appearance *simple*, I mean by this that the intuition of it, although a part of the appearance, is not

---

[1] [*Beschaffenheit.*]
[2] [Reading, with Wille, *könnten* for *könnte.*]

itself capable of being divided into parts, etc. But if I know
something as simple in concept only and not in the [field of]
appearance, I have really no knowledge whatsoever of the
object, but only of the concept which I make for myself of a
something in general that does not allow of being intuited. I
say that I think something as completely simple, only because
I have really nothing more to say of it than merely that it is
something.

Now the bare apperception, 'I', is in concept substance, in
concept simple, etc.; and in this sense all those psychological
doctrines are unquestionably true. Yet this does not give us
that knowledge of the soul for which we are seeking. For since
none of these predicates are valid of intuition, they cannot
have any consequences which are applicable to objects of
experience, and are therefore entirely void. The concept of
substance does not teach me that the soul endures by itself,
nor that it is a part of outer intuitions which cannot itself be
divided into parts, and cannot therefore arise or perish by any
natural alterations. These are properties which would make
the soul known to me in the context of experience and might
A 401 reveal something concerning its origin and future state. But
if I say, in terms of the[1] mere category, 'The soul is a simple
substance', it is obvious that since the bare concept of substance (supplied by the understanding) contains nothing beyond the requirement that a thing be represented as being
subject in itself, and not in turn predicate of anything else,
nothing follows from this as regards the permanence of the
'I', and the attribute 'simple' certainly does not aid in adding
this permanence. Thus, from this source, we learn nothing
whatsoever as to what may happen to the soul in the changes
of the natural world. If we could be assured that the soul is a
simple part of matter, we could use this knowledge, with the
further assistance of what experience teaches in this regard, to
deduce the permanence, and, as involved in its simple nature,
the indestructibility of the soul. But of all this, the concept
of the 'I', in the psychological principle 'I think', tells us
nothing.

That the being which thinks in us is under the impression
that it knows itself through pure categories, and precisely

---

[1] [Reading, with Rosenkranz, *die blosse* for *blosse.*]

through those categories which in each type of category[1] express absolute unity, is due to the following reason. Apperception is itself the ground of the possibility of the categories, which on their part represent nothing but the synthesis of the manifold of intuition, in so far as the manifold has unity in apperception. Self-consciousness in general is therefore the representation of that which is the condition of all unity, and itself is unconditioned. We can thus say of the thinking 'I' (the soul) which regards itself as substance, as simple, as   A 402 numerically identical at all times, and as the correlate of all existence, from which all other existence must be inferred, that it does *not* know *itself through the categories*, but knows the categories, and through them all objects, in the absolute unity of apperception, and so *through itself*. Now it is, indeed, very evident that I cannot know as an object that which I must presuppose in order to know any object, and that the determining self (the thought) is distinguished from the self that is to be determined (the thinking subject) in the same way as knowledge is distinguished from its object. Nevertheless there is nothing more natural and more misleading than the illusion which leads us to regard the unity in the synthesis of thoughts as a perceived unity in the subject of these thoughts. We might call it the subreption of the hypostatised consciousness (*apperceptionis*[2] *substantiatae*).

If we desire to give a logical title to the paralogism contained in the dialectical syllogisms of the rational doctrine of the soul, then in view of the fact that their premisses are correct, we may call it a *sophisma figurae dictionis*.[3] Whereas the major premiss, in dealing with the condition, makes a merely transcendental use of the category, the minor premiss and the conclusion, in dealing with the soul which has been subsumed under this condition, use the same category empirically. Thus, for instance, in the paralogism of substantiality,[4] the con-   A 403 cept of substance is a pure intellectual concept, which in the absence of the conditions of sensible intuition admits only of transcendental use, that is, admits of no use whatsoever. But in the minor premiss the very same concept is applied to the object

---

[1] [*unter jedem Titel derselben.*]
[2] [Reading, with Hartenstein, *apperceptionis* for *apperceptiones.*]
[3] [*i.e.* of ambiguous middle.]
[4] [Reading, with Adickes, *Substanzialität* for *Simplizität.*]

of all inner experience without our having first ascertained and established the condition of such employment *in concreto*, namely, the permanence of this object. We are thus making an empirical, but in this case inadmissible, employment of the category.[1]

Finally, in order to show the systematic interconnection of all these dialectical assertions of a pseudo-rational doctrine of the soul in an order determined by pure reason, and so to show that we have them in their completeness, we may note that apperception has been carried through all the classes of the categories but only in reference to those concepts of understanding which in each class form the basis of the unity of the others in a possible perception, namely, subsistence, reality, unity (not plurality), and existence. Reason here represents all of these as conditions, which are themselves unconditioned, of the possibility of a thinking being. Thus the soul knows in itself—

A 404   (1) *the unconditioned unity of relation, i.e.* that it itself is not inherent [in something else] but *self-subsistent.*

  (2) *the unconditioned unity of quality,* that is, that it is not a real whole but *simple.*[a]

  (3) *the unconditioned unity in the plurality in time, i.e.* that it is not numerically different at different times but *one* and *the very same subject.*

  (4) *the unconditioned unity of existence in space, i.e.* that it is not the consciousness of many things outside it, but the consciousness *of the existence of itself* only, and of other things merely as its *representations.*

A 405   Reason is the faculty of principles. The assertions of pure psychology do not contain empirical predicates of the soul but those predicates, if there be any such, which are meant to determine the object in itself independently of experience, and so by mere reason. They ought, therefore, to be founded on principles and universal concepts bearing on the nature of

---

[a] How the simple here again corresponds to the category of reality I am not yet in a position to explain. This will be shown in the next chapter on the occasion of this same concept being put by reason to yet another use.

[1] [For a more consistent account of the nature of paralogism cf. B 410-411.]

thinking beings in general. But instead we find that the single representation, 'I am', governs them all. This representation just because it expresses the pure formula of all my experience in general[1] announces itself as a universal proposition valid for all thinking beings; and since it is at the same time in all respects unitary, it carries with it the illusion of an absolute unity of the conditions of thought in general, and so extends itself further than possible experience can reach.

[1] [*unbestimmt.*]

THE PARALOGISMS OF PURE REASON[1]

[AS RESTATED IN SECOND EDITION]

SINCE[2] the proposition 'I think' (taken problematically) contains the form of each and every judgment of understanding and accompanies all categories as their vehicle, it is evident that the inferences from it admit only of a transcendental employment of the understanding. And since this employment excludes any admixture of experience, we cannot, after what has been shown above, entertain any favourable anticipations in regard to its methods of procedure. We therefore propose to follow it, with a critical eye, through all the predicaments of pure psychology. But for the sake of brevity the examination had best proceed in an unbroken continuity.

The following general remark may, at the outset, aid us in our scrutiny of this kind of argument. I do not know an object merely in that I think, but only in so far as I determine a given intuition with respect to the unity of consciousness in which all thought consists. Consequently, I do not know myself through being conscious of myself as thinking, but only when I am conscious of the[3] intuition of myself as determined with respect to the function of thought. *Modi* of self-consciousness in B 407 thought are not by themselves concepts of objects (categories), but are mere functions which do not give thought an object to be known, and accordingly do not give even myself as object. The object is not the consciousness of the *determining* self, but only that[4] of the *determinable* self, that is, of my inner intuition (in so far as its manifold can be combined in accordance with the universal condition of the unity of apperception in thought).

[1] [What follows, up to p. 383, is Kant's restatement of the Paralogisms, in B.]
[2] [In sequence to p. 332, above.]   [3] [Reading, with Grillo, *der* for *die*.]
[4] [Reading, with Hartenstein, *das* for *die*.]

(1) In all judgments I am the *determining* subject of that relation which constitutes the judgment. That the 'I', the 'I' that thinks, can be regarded always as *subject*, and as something which does not belong to thought as a mere predicate, must be granted. It is an apodeictic and indeed *identical* proposition; but it does not mean that I, as *object*, am for myself a *self-subsistent* being or *substance*. The latter statement goes very far beyond the former, and demands for its proof data which are not to be met with in thought, and perhaps (in so far as I have regard to the thinking self merely as such) are more than I shall ever find in it.

(2) That the 'I' of apperception, and therefore the 'I' in every act of thought, is *one*,[1] and cannot be resolved into a plurality of subjects, and consequently signifies a logically simple subject, is something already contained in the very concept of thought, and is therefore an analytic proposition. But this does not mean that the thinking 'I' is a simple *sub-*   B 408 *stance*. That proposition would be synthetic. The concept of substance always relates to intuitions which cannot in me be other than sensible, and which therefore lie entirely outside the field of the understanding and its thought. But it is of this thought that we are speaking when we say that the 'I' in thought is simple. It would, indeed, be surprising if what in other cases requires so much labour to determine—namely, what, of all that is presented in intuition, is substance, and further, whether this substance can be simple (*e.g.* in the parts of matter)—should be thus given me directly, as if by revelation, in the poorest of all representations.

(3) The proposition, that in all the manifold of which I am conscious I am identical with myself, is likewise implied in the concepts themselves, and is therefore an analytic proposition. But this identity of the subject, of which I can be conscious in all my[2] representations, does not concern any intuition of the subject, whereby it is given as object, and cannot therefore signify the identity of the person, if by that is understood the consciousness of the identity of one's own substance, as a thinking being, in all change of its states. No mere analysis of the proposition 'I think' will suffice to prove such a proposi-

---

[1] [*ein Singular.*]
[2] [Reading, with Erdmann, *meinen* for *seinen*.]

B 409   tion; for that we should require various synthetic judgments, based upon given intuition.

(4) That I distinguish my own existence as that of a thinking being, from other things outside me—among them my body—is likewise an analytic proposition; for *other* things are such as I think to be *distinct* from myself. But I do not thereby learn whether this consciousness of myself would be even possible apart from things outside me through which representations are given to me, and whether, therefore, I could exist merely as thinking being (*i.e.* without existing in human form).

The analysis, then, of the consciousness of myself in thought in general, yields nothing whatsoever towards the knowledge of myself as object. The logical exposition of thought in general has been mistaken for a metaphysical determination of the object.

Indeed, it would be a great stumbling-block, or rather would be the one unanswerable objection, to our whole critique, if there were a possibility of proving *a priori* that all thinking beings are in themselves simple substances, and that consequently (as follows from this same mode of proof) personality is inseparable from them, and that they are conscious of their existence as separate and distinct from all matter. For by such procedure we should have taken a step beyond the world of sense, and have entered into the field of noumena;

B 410   and no one could then deny our right of advancing yet further in this domain, indeed of settling in it, and, should our star prove auspicious, of establishing claims to permanent possession. The proposition, 'Every thinking being is, as such, a simple substance', is a synthetic *a priori* proposition; it is synthetic in that it goes beyond the concept from which it starts, and adds to the thought in general [*i.e.* to the concept of a thinking being] the mode of [its] existence: it is *a priori*, in that it adds to the concept a predicate (that of simplicity) which cannot be given in any experience. It would then follow that *a priori* synthetic propositions are possible and admissible, not only, as we have asserted, in relation to objects of possible experience, and indeed as principles of the possibility of this experience, but that they are applicable to things in general and to things in themselves—a result that would make an end of our whole critique, and would constrain us to acquiesce in the old-time procedure. Upon closer consideration we find, however, that there is no such serious danger. The whole procedure of rational psychology is determined by a paralogism, which is exhibited in the following syllogism:

That which cannot be thought otherwise than as subject does not exist otherwise than as subject, and is therefore substance.

A thinking being, considered merely as such, cannot be thought otherwise than as subject. B 411

Therefore it exists also only as subject, that is, as substance.

In the major premiss we speak of a being that can be thought in general, in every relation, and therefore also as it may be given in intuition. But in the minor premiss we speak of it only in so far as it regards itself, as subject, simply in relation to thought and the unity of consciousness, and not as likewise in relation to the intuition through which it[1] is given as object to thought. Thus the conclusion is arrived at fallaciously, *per sophisma figurae dictionis.*[a]

That we are entirely right in resolving this famous argu- B 412 ment into a paralogism will be clearly seen, if we call to mind what has been said in the General Note to the Systematic Representation of the Principles and in the Section on Noumena. For it has there been proved that the concept of a thing

---

[a] 'Thought' is taken in the two premisses in totally different senses: in the major premiss, as relating to an object in general and therefore to an object as it may be given in intuition; in the minor premiss, only as it consists in relation to self-consciousness. In this latter sense, no object whatsoever is being thought; all that is being represented is simply the relation to self as subject (as the form of thought). In the former premiss we are speaking of *things* which cannot be thought otherwise than as subjects; but in the latter premiss we speak not of *things* but of *thought* (abstraction being B 412 made from all objects) in which the 'I' always serves as the subject of consciousness. The conclusion cannot, therefore, be, 'I cannot exist otherwise than as subject', but merely, 'In thinking my existence, I cannot employ myself, save as subject of the judgment [therein involved]'. This is an identical proposition, and casts no light whatsoever upon the mode of my existence.

[1] [Reading, with Vorländer, *es* for *sie.*]

which can exist by itself as subject and never as mere predicate, carries with it no objective reality; in other words, that we cannot know whether there is any object to which the concept is applicable—as to the possibility of such a mode of existence we have no means of deciding—and that the concept[1] therefore yields no knowledge whatsoever. If by the term 'substance' be meant an object which can be given, and if it is to yield knowledge, it must be made to rest on a permanent intuition, as being that through which alone the object of our concept can be given, and as being, therefore, the indispensable condition B 413 of the objective reality of the concept. Now in inner intuition there is nothing permanent, for the 'I' is merely the consciousness of my thought. So long, therefore, as we do not go beyond mere thinking, we are without the necessary condition for applying the concept of substance, that is, of a self-subsistent subject, to the self as a thinking being. And with the objective reality of the concept of substance, the allied concept of simplicity likewise vanishes; it is transformed into a merely logical qualitative unity of self-consciousness in thought in general, which has to be present whether the subject be composite or not.

REFUTATION OF MENDELSSOHN'S[2] PROOF OF THE PERMANENCE OF THE SOUL

This acute philosopher soon noticed that the usual argument by which it is sought to prove that the soul—if it be admitted to be a simple being—cannot cease to be through *dissolution*, is insufficient for its purpose, that of proving the necessary continuance of the soul, since it may be supposed to pass out of existence through simply *vanishing*. In his *Phaedo* he endeavoured to prove that the soul cannot be subject to such a process of vanishing, which would be a true annihilation, by showing that a simple being cannot cease to exist. His argument is that since the soul cannot be diminished, and so gradually lose something of its exist-B 414 ence, being by degrees changed into nothing (for since it has no parts, it has no multiplicity in itself), there would be

---

[1] [Reading, with Erdmann, *er* for *es*.]
[2] [Moses Mendelssohn (1729-86): *Phädon* (1767) (*Gesammelte Schriften*, 1843, ii. p. 151 ff.).]

no time between a moment in which it is and another in which it is not—which is impossible. He failed, however, to observe that even if we admit the simple nature of the soul, namely, that it contains no manifold of constituents external to one another, and therefore no extensive quantity, we yet cannot deny to it, any more than to any other existence, intensive quantity, that is, a degree of reality in respect of all its faculties, nay, in respect of all that constitutes its existence, and that this degree of reality may diminish through all the infinitely many smaller degrees. In this manner the supposed substance—the thing, the permanence of which has not yet been proved—may be changed into nothing, not indeed by dissolution, but by gradual loss (*remissio*) of its powers, and so, if I may be permitted the use of the term, by elanguescence. For consciousness itself has always a degree, which always allows of diminution,[a] and the same must also hold of the faculty of being conscious of the self, and likewise of all the other faculties. Thus the permanence of the soul, regarded merely as object of inner sense, remains undemonstrated, and indeed indemonstrable. Its permanence during life is, of course, evident *per se*,[1] since the thinking being (as man) is itself likewise an object of the outer senses. But this is very far from satisfying the rational psychologist who undertakes to prove from mere concepts its absolute permanence beyond this life.[b]

B 415

[a] Clearness is not, as the logicians assert, the consciousness of a representation. A certain degree of consciousness, though it be insufficient for recollection, must be met with even in many obscure representations, since in the absence of all consciousness we should make no distinction between different combinations of obscure representations, which yet we are able to do in respect of the characters of many concepts, such as those of right or equity, or as when the musician in improvising strikes several keys at once. But a representation is clear, when the consciousness suffices for the *consciousness of the distinction* of this representation from others. If it suffices for distinguishing, but not for consciousness of the distinction, the representation must still be entitled obscure. There are therefore infinitely many degrees of consciousness, down to its complete vanishing.

B 415

[b] Some philosophers, in making out a case for a new possibility, consider that they have done enough if they can defy others to show

1 [*für sich klar ist.*]

B 416   If we take the above propositions in *synthetic* connection, as valid for all thinking beings, as indeed they must be taken in the system of rational psychology, and proceed from the category of relation, with the proposition, 'All think-
B 417   ing beings are, as such, substances', backwards through the series of the propositions, until the circle is completed, we

---

any contradiction in their assumptions. This is the procedure [1] of all
B 416   those who profess to comprehend the possibility of thought—of which they have an example only in the empirical intuitions of our human life—even after this life has ceased. But those who resort to such a method of argument can be quite nonplussed by the citation of other possibilities which are not a whit more adventurous. Such is the possibility of the division of a *simple substance* into several substances, and conversely the fusing together (coalition) of several into one simple substance. For although divisibility presupposes a composite, it does not necessarily require a composite of substances, but only of degrees (of the manifold powers) of one and the same substance. Now just as we can think all powers and faculties of the soul, even that of consciousness, as diminished by one half, but in such a way that the substance still remains, so also, without contradiction, we can represent this extinguished half as being preserved, not in the soul, but outside it; and we can likewise hold that since everything which is real in it, and which therefore has a degree—in other words, its entire existence, from which nothing is lacking—has been halved, another separate substance would then come into existence outside it. For the multiplicity which has been divided existed before, not indeed as a multiplicity of substances, but as the multiplicity of every reality proper to the substance, that is, of the quantum of existence in it; and the unity of substance was therefore only a mode of existence, which in virtue of this division has been trans-
B 417   formed into a plurality of subsistence. Similarly, several simple substances might be fused into one, without anything being lost except only the plurality of subsistence, inasmuch as the one substance would contain the degree of reality of all the former substances together. We might perhaps also represent the simple substances which yield us the appearance [which we entitle] matter as producing—not indeed by a mechanical or chemical influence upon one another, but by an influence unknown to us, of which the former influence would be merely the appearance—the souls of children, that is, as producing them through such *dynamical* division of the parent souls, considered as *intensive quantities*, and those parent souls as making good their loss through coalition with new material of the same kind.

---

[1] [Reading, with Mellin, *tun* for *sind*.]

come at last to the *existence*[1] of these thinking beings. Now in this system of rational psychology these beings are taken not only as being conscious of their existence independently of outer things, but as also being able, in and by themselves, to determine that existence in respect of the permanence which   B 418 is a necessary characteristic of substance. This rationalist system is thus unavoidably committed to *idealism*, or at least to problematic idealism. For if the existence of outer things is not in any way required for determination of one's own existence in time, the assumption of their existence is a quite gratuitous assumption, of which no proof can ever be given.

If, on the other hand, we should proceed *analytically*, starting from the proposition 'I think', as a proposition that already in itself includes an existence as given, and therefore modality, and analysing it in order to ascertain its content, and so to discover whether and how this 'I' determines its existence in space or time solely through that content,[2] then the propositions of the rational doctrine of the soul would not begin with the concept of a thinking being in general, but with a reality, and we should infer from the manner in which this reality is thought, after everything empirical in it has been removed, what it is that belongs to a thinking being in general.   B 419 This is shown in the following table:

I am far from allowing any serviceableness or validity to such fancies; and as the principles of our Analytic have sufficiently demonstrated, no other than an empirical employment of the categories (including that of substance) is possible. But if the rationalist is bold enough, out of the mere faculty of thought, without any permanent intuition whereby an object might be given, to construct a self-subsistent being, and this merely on the ground that the unity of apperception in thought does not allow of its being explained [as arising] out of the composite, instead of admitting, as he ought to do, that he is unable to explain   B 418 the possibility of a thinking nature,[3] why should not the *materialist*, though he can as little appeal to experience in support of his [conjectured] possibilities, be justified in being equally daring, and in using his principle to establish the opposite conclusion, while still preserving the formal unity upon which his opponent has relied.

---

[1] [Cf. above, p. 330. As there noted, Kant, in his private copy of the *Critique*, has changed 'The soul is substance' to 'The soul exists as substance'.]
[2] [*bloss dadurch.*]   [3] [*einer denkenden Natur.*]

1. *I think,*

2. *as subject,*   3. *as simple subject,*

4. *as identical subject
in every state of my thought.*

In the second proposition it has not been determined whether I can exist and be thought as subject only, and not also as a predicate of another being, and accordingly the concept of a subject is here taken in a merely logical sense, and it remains undetermined whether or not we are to understand by it a substance. Similarly, the third proposition establishes nothing in regard to the constitution or subsistence of the subject; none the less in this proposition the absolute unity of apperception, the simple 'I' in the representation to which all combination or separation that constitutes thought relates, has its own importance. For apperception is something real, and its simplicity is already given in the mere fact of its possibility. Now in space there is nothing real which can be simple; points, which are the only simple things in space, are merely limits, not themselves anything that can as parts serve to constitute B 420 space. From this follows the impossibility of any explanation in *materialist* terms of the constitution of the self as a merely thinking subject. But since my existence is taken in the first proposition as given—for it does not say that every thinking being exists, which would be to assert its absolute necessity and therefore to say too much, but only, '*I exist thinking*'—the proposition is empirical, and can determine my existence only in relation to my representations in time. But since for this purpose I again require something permanent, which, so far as I think myself, is in no way given to me in inner intuition, it is quite impossible, by means of this simple self-consciousness, to determine the manner in which I exist, whether it be as substance or as accident. Thus, if materialism is disqualified from explaining my existence, spiritualism is equally incapable of doing so; and the conclusion is that in no way whatsoever can we know anything of the constitution of the soul, so far as the possibility of its separate existence is concerned.

How, indeed, should it be possible, by means of the unity

of consciousness—which we only know because we cannot but make use of it, as indispensable for the possibility of experience—to pass out beyond experience (our existence in this life), and even to extend our knowledge to the nature of all thinking beings in general, through the empirical, but in B 421 respect of every sort of intuition the quite indeterminate proposition, 'I think'?

Rational psychology exists not as *doctrine*, furnishing an addition to our knowledge of the self, but only as *discipline*. It sets impassable limits to speculative reason in this field, and thus keeps us, on the one hand, from throwing ourselves into the arms of a soulless materialism, or, on the other hand, from losing ourselves in a spiritualism which must be quite unfounded so long as we remain in this present life. But though it furnishes no positive doctrine, it reminds us that we should regard this refusal of reason to give satisfying response to our inquisitive probings into what is beyond the limits of this present life as reason's hint to divert our self-knowledge from fruitless and extravagant speculation to fruitful practical employment. Though in such practical employment it is directed always to objects of experience only, it derives its principles from a higher source, and determines us to regulate our actions as if our destiny reached infinitely far beyond experience, and therefore far beyond this present life.

From all this it is evident that rational psychology owes its origin simply to misunderstanding. The unity of consciousness, which underlies the categories, is here mistaken for an intuition of the subject as object, and the category of substance is then applied to it. But this unity is only unity in B 422 *thought*, by which alone no object is given, and to which, therefore, the category of substance, which always presupposes a given *intuition*, cannot be applied. Consequently, this subject cannot be known. The subject of the categories cannot by thinking the categories acquire a concept of itself as an object of the categories. For in order to think them, its pure self-consciousness, which is what was to be explained, must itself be presupposed. Similarly, the subject, in which the representation of time has its original ground, cannot thereby determine its own existence in time. And if this latter is impossible, the former, as a determination of the self (as a thinking being in general) by means of the categories, is equally so.[a]

B 423   Thus the expectation of obtaining knowledge which while extending beyond the limits of possible experience is likewise to further the highest interests of humanity, is found, so far as speculative philosophy professes to satisfy it, to

B 424   be grounded in deception, and to destroy itself in the attempt at fulfilment. Yet the severity of our criticism has rendered reason a not unimportant service in proving the impossibility of dogmatically determining, in regard to an object of experience, anything that lies beyond the limits of experience. For in so doing it has secured reason against all possible assertions of the opposite. That cannot be achieved save in one or other

---

[a] The 'I think' is, as already stated, an empirical proposition, and contains within itself the proposition 'I exist'. But I cannot say 'Everything which thinks, exists'. For in that case the property of thought would render all beings which possess it necessary beings. My existence cannot, therefore, be regarded as an inference from the proposition 'I think', as Descartes sought to contend—for it would then have to be preceded by the major premiss 'Everything which thinks, exists'—but is identical with it. The 'I think' expresses an indeterminate empirical intuition, *i.e.* perception (and

B 423   thus shows that sensation, which as such belongs to sensibility, lies at the basis of this existential proposition) But the 'I think' precedes the experience which is required to determine the object of perception through the category in respect of time; and the existence here [referred to] is not a category. The category as such does not apply to an indeterminately given object but only to one of which we have a concept and about which we seek to know whether it does or does not exist outside the concept. An indeterminate perception here signifies only something real that is given, given indeed to thought in general, and so not as appearance, nor as thing in itself (*noumenon*), but as something which actually[1] exists, and which in the proposition, 'I think', is denoted[2] as such. For it must be observed, that when I have called the proposition, 'I think', an empirical proposition, I do not mean to say thereby, that the 'I' in this proposition is an empirical representation. On the contrary, it is purely intellectual, because belonging to thought in general. Without some empirical representation to supply the material for thought, the *actus*, 'I think', would not, indeed, take place; but the empirical is only the condition of the application, or of the employment, of the pure intellectual faculty.

[1] [*in der Tat.*]   [2] [*bezeichnet.*]

of two ways. Either we have to prove our proposition apodeictically; or, if we do not succeed in this, we have to seek out the sources of this inability, which, if they are traceable to the necessary limits of our reason, must constrain all opponents to submit to this same law of renunciation in respect of all claims to dogmatic assertion.

Yet nothing is thereby lost as regards the right, nay, the necessity, of postulating a future life in accordance with the principles of the practical employment of reason, which is closely bound up with its speculative employment. For the merely speculative proof has never been able to exercise any influence upon the common reason of men. It so stands upon the point of a hair, that even the schools preserve it from falling only so long as they keep it unceasingly spinning round like a top; even in their own eyes it yields no abiding foundation upon which anything could be built. The proofs which are serviceable for the world at large all preserve their entire value B 425 undiminished, and indeed, upon the surrender of these dogmatic pretensions, gain in clearness and in natural force. For reason is then located in its own peculiar sphere, namely, the order of ends, which is also at the same time an order of nature; and since it is in itself not only a theoretical but also a practical faculty, and as such is not bound down to natural conditions, it is justified in extending the order of ends, and therewith our own existence, beyond the limits of experience and of life. If we judged according to *analogy with the nature* of living beings in this world, in dealing with which reason must necessarily accept the principle that no organ, no faculty, no impulse, indeed nothing whatsoever is either superfluous or disproportioned to its use, and that therefore nothing is purposeless, but everything exactly conformed to its destiny in life—if we judged by such an analogy we should have to regard man, who alone can contain in himself the final end of all this order, as the only creature that is excepted from it. Man's natural endowments—not merely his talents and the impulses to enjoy them, but above all else the moral law within him—go so far beyond all the utility and advantage which he may derive from them in this present life, that he learns thereby to prize the mere consciousness of a righteous will as being, apart from all advantageous consequences, apart even from the B 426 shadowy reward of posthumous fame, supreme over all other values; and so feels an inner call to fit himself, by his conduct in this world, and by the sacrifice of many of its advantages, for citizenship in a better world upon which he lays hold in idea. This powerful and incontrovertible proof is reinforced by our ever-increasing knowledge of purposiveness in all that we see around us, and by contemplation of the immensity of creation, and therefore also by the consciousness of a certain illimitableness in the possible extension of our knowledge, and of a striving commensurate therewith. All this still remains to us; but we must renounce the hope of comprehending, from the merely theoretical knowledge of ourselves, the necessary continuance of our existence.

CONCLUSION, IN REGARD TO THE SOLUTION OF THE PSYCHOLOGICAL PARALOGISM

The dialectical illusion in rational psychology arises from the confusion of an idea of reason—the idea of a pure intelligence—with the completely undetermined concept of a thinking being in general. I think myself on behalf of a possible experience, at the same time abstracting from all actual experience; and I conclude therefrom that I can be conscious of my existence even apart from experience and its empirical conditions. In so doing I am confusing the possible *abstraction* from my empirically determined existence with the supposed consciousness of a possible *separate* existence of my thinking self, and I thus come to believe that I have *knowledge* that what is substantial in me is the transcendental subject. But all that I really have in thought is simply the unity of consciousness, on which, as the mere form of knowledge, all determination is based.

B 427

The task of explaining the communion of the soul with the body does not properly belong to the psychology with which we are here dealing. For this psychology proposes to prove the personality of the soul even apart from this communion (that is, after death), and is therefore *transcendent* in the proper sense of that term. It does, indeed, occupy itself with an object of experience, but only in that aspect in which[1]

---

[1] [*nur sofern.*]

it ceases to be an object of experience. Our teaching, on the other hand, does supply a sufficient answer to this question. The difficulty peculiar to the problem consists, as is generally recognised, in the assumed heterogeneity of the object of inner sense (the soul) and the objects of the outer senses, the formal condition of their intuition being, in the case of the former, time only, and in the case of the latter, also space. But if we consider that the two kinds of objects thus differ from each other, not inwardly but only in so far as one *appears* outwardly to the other, and that what, as thing in itself, underlies the appearance of B 428 matter, perhaps after all may not be so heterogeneous in character, this difficulty vanishes, the only question that remains being how in general a communion of substances is possible. This, however, is a question which lies outside the field of psychology, and which the reader, after what has been said in the Analytic regarding fundamental powers and faculties, will not hesitate to regard as likewise lying outside the field of all human knowledge

General Note on the Transition from Rational Psychology to Cosmology

The proposition, 'I think' or 'I exist thinking', is an empirical proposition. Such a proposition, however, is conditioned by empirical intuition, and is therefore also conditioned by the object [that is, the self] which is thought [in its aspect] as appearance. It would consequently seem that on our theory the soul, even in thought, is completely transformed into appearance, and that in this way our consciousness itself, as being a mere illusion,[1] must refer in fact to nothing.

Thought, taken by itself, is merely the logical function, and therefore the pure spontaneity of the combination of the manifold of a merely possible intuition, and does not exhibit the subject of consciousness as appearance; and this for the B 429 sufficient reason that thought takes no account whatsoever of the mode of intuition, whether it be sensible or intellectual. I thereby represent myself to myself neither as I am nor as I appear to myself. I think myself only as I do any object in general from whose mode of intuition I abstract. If I here re-

[1] [*Schein.*]

present myself as *subject* of thoughts or as *ground* of thought, these modes of representation do not signify the categories of substance or of cause. For the categories are those functions of thought (of judgment) as already applied to our sensible intuition, such intuition being required if I seek to *know* myself. If, on the other hand, I would be conscious of myself simply as thinking, then since I am not considering how my own self[1] may be given in intuition, the self may be mere appearance to me, the 'I' that thinks, but is no mere appearance in so far as I think; in the consciousness of myself in mere thought I am the *being itself*, although nothing in myself is thereby given for thought.

The proposition, 'I think', in so far as it amounts to the assertion, '*I exist thinking*', is no mere logical function, but determines the subject (which is then at the same time object) in respect of existence, and cannot take place without inner sense, the intuition of which presents the object not as thing in itself but merely as appearance. There is here, therefore, not simply spontaneity of thought, but also receptivity of intuition, that is, the thought of myself applied to the empirical intuition of myself.[2] Now it is to this intuition that the thinking self would have to look for the conditions of the employment of its logical functions as categories of substance, cause, etc., if it is not merely to distinguish itself as object in itself, through the 'I', but is also to determine the mode of its existence, that is, to know itself as noumenon. This, however, is impossible, since the inner empirical intuition is sensible and yields only data of appearance, which furnish nothing to the object of *pure consciousness* for the knowledge of its separate existence, but can serve only for the obtaining of experience.

Should it be granted that we may in due course discover, not in experience but in certain laws of the pure employment of reason—laws which are not merely logical rules, but which while holding *a priori* also concern our existence—ground for regarding ourselves as *legislating* completely *a priori* in regard to our own *existence*, and as determining this existence, there would thereby be revealed a spontaneity through which our reality would be determinable, independently of the conditions of empirical intuition. And we should also become

B 430

---

[1] [*mein eigenes Selbst.*]   [2] [*ebendesselben Subjekts.*]

aware that in the consciousness of our existence there is contained a something *a priori*, which can serve to determine our existence—the complete determination of which is possible B 431 only in sensible terms—as being related, in respect of a certain inner faculty, to a non-sensible intelligible world.

But this would not be of the least service in furthering the attempts of rational psychology. In this marvellous faculty, which the consciousness of the moral law first reveals to me, I should indeed have, for the determination of my existence, a principle which is purely intellectual. But through what predicates would that determination have to be made? They could be no other than those which must be given to me in sensible intuition; and thus I should find myself, as regards rational psychology, in precisely the same position as before, namely, still in need of sensible intuitions to confer meaning on my concepts of understanding (substance, cause, etc.), through which alone I can have knowledge of myself; and these intuitions can never aid me in advancing beyond the field of experience. Nevertheless, in respect of the practical employment, which is always directed to objects of experience, I should be justified in applying these concepts, in conformity with their analogical meaning when employed theoretically, to freedom and the subject that is possessed of freedom. In so doing, however, I should understand by these concepts the merely logical functions of subject and predicate, of ground and consequence, in accordance with which the acts or effects are so determined conformably to those [moral] laws, that B 432 they always allow of being explained, together with the laws of nature, in accordance with the categories of substance and cause, although they have their source in an entirely different principle. These observations are designed merely to prevent a misunderstanding to which the doctrine of our self-intuition, as appearance, is particularly liable. We shall have occasion to make further application of them in the sequel.

THE TRANSCENDENTAL DIALECTIC

BOOK II

CHAPTER II

THE ANTINOMY OF PURE REASON

WE have shown in the introduction to this part of our work that all transcendental illusion of pure reason rests on dialectical inferences whose schema is supplied by logic in the A 406 three formal species of syllogisms—just as the categories find their logical schema in the four functions of all judgments. The first type of these pseudo-rational inferences deals with the unconditioned unity of the subjective conditions of all representations in general (of the subject or soul), in correspondence with the *categorical* syllogisms, the major premiss of which is a principle asserting the relation of a predicate to a subject. B 433 The second type of dialectical argument follows the analogy of the *hypothetical* syllogisms. It has as its content the unconditioned unity of the objective conditions in the [field of] appearance. In similar fashion, the third type, which will be dealt with in the next chapter, has as its theme the unconditioned unity of the objective conditions of the possibility of objects in general.

But there is one point that calls for special notice. Transcendental paralogism produced a purely one-sided illusion in regard to the idea of the subject of our thought. No illusion which will even in the slightest degree support the opposing assertion is caused by the concepts of reason. Consequently, although transcendental paralogism, in spite of a favouring illusion, cannot disclaim the radical defect through which in the fiery ordeal of critical investigation it dwindles into mere semblance, such advantage as it offers is altogether on the side of pneumatism.

A completely different situation arises when reason is applied to the *objective* synthesis of appearances. For in this A 407 domain, however it may endeavour to establish its principle of unconditioned unity, and though it indeed does so with great though illusory appearance of success, it soon falls into such contradictions that it is constrained, in this cosmological field, to desist from any such pretensions.

We have here presented to us a new phenomenon of human reason—an entirely natural antithetic, in which there is no need of making subtle enquiries or of laying snares for the unwary, but into which reason of itself quite unavoidably falls. B 434 It certainly guards reason from the slumber of *fictitious* conviction such as is generated by a purely one-sided illusion, but at the same time subjects it to the temptation either of abandoning itself to a sceptical despair, or of assuming an obstinate attitude, dogmatically committing itself to certain assertions, and refusing to grant a fair hearing to the arguments for the counter-position. Either attitude is the death of sound philosophy, although the former might perhaps be entitled the *euthanasia* of pure reason.

Before considering the various forms of opposition and dissension to which this conflict or antinomy of the laws of pure reason gives rise, we may offer a few remarks in explanation and justification of the method which we propose to employ in the treatment of this subject. I entitle all transcendental ideas, in so far as they refer to absolute totality in the synthesis of appearances, *cosmical concepts*, partly be- A 408 cause this unconditioned totality also underlies the concept —itself only an idea—of the world-whole; partly because they concern only the synthesis of appearances, therefore only empirical synthesis When, on the contrary, the absolute totality is that of the synthesis of the conditions of all possible things in general, it gives rise to an *ideal* of B 435 pure reason which, though it may indeed stand in a certain relation to the cosmical concept, is quite distinct from it. Accordingly, just as the paralogisms of pure reason formed the basis of a dialectical psychology, so the antinomy of pure reason will exhibit to us the transcendental principles of a pretended pure rational cosmology. But it will not do so in order to show this science to be valid and to adopt it. As the title, conflict of reason, suffices to show, this pretended science can be exhibited only in its bedazzling but false illusoriness, as an idea which can never be reconciled with appearances.

THE ANTINOMY OF PURE REASON

Section 1

SYSTEM OF COSMOLOGICAL IDEAS

In proceeding to enumerate these ideas with systematic precision according to a principle, we must bear in mind two points. In the first place we must recognise that pure and transcendental concepts can issue only from the understanding. Reason does not really generate any concept. The most it can do is to *free* a concept of *understanding* from the unavoidable limitations of possible experience, and so to endeavour to extend it beyond the limits of the empirical, though still, indeed, in terms of its relation to the empirical. This is achieved in the following manner. For a given conditioned, reason demands on the side of the conditions—to which as the conditions of synthetic unity the understanding subjects all appearances—absolute totality, and in so doing converts the category into a transcendental idea. For only by carrying the empirical synthesis as far as the unconditioned is it enabled to render it absolutely complete; and the unconditioned is never to be met with in experience, but only in the idea. Reason makes this demand in accordance with the principle that if *the conditioned is given, the entire sum of conditions, and consequently the absolutely unconditioned* (through which alone the conditioned has been possible) *is also given*. The transcendental ideas are thus, in the *first* place, simply categories extended to the unconditioned, and can be reduced to a table arranged according to the [fourfold] headings of the latter. In the *second* place, not all categories are fitted for such employment, but only those in which the synthesis constitutes a *series* of conditions subordinated to, not co-ordinated with,

A 409

B 436

one another, and generative of a [given] conditioned. Absolute totality is demanded by reason only in so far as the ascending series of conditions relates to a given conditioned. A 410 It is not demanded in regard to the descending line of consequences, nor in reference to the aggregate of co-ordinated conditions of these consequences. For in the case of the given B 437 conditioned, conditions are presupposed, and are considered as given together with it. On the other hand, since consequences do not make their conditions possible, but rather presuppose them, we are not called upon, when we advance to consequences or descend from a given condition to the conditioned, to consider whether the series does or does not cease; the question as to the totality of the series is not in any way a presupposition of reason

Thus we necessarily think time as having completely elapsed up to the given moment, and as being itself given in this completed form. This holds true, even though such completely elapsed time is not determinable by us. But since the future is not the condition of our attaining to the present, it is a matter of entire indifference, in our comprehension of the latter, how we may think of future time, whether as coming to an end or as flowing on to infinity. We have, as it were, the series *m, n, o*, in which *n* is given as conditioned by *m*, and at the same time as being the condition of *o*. The series ascends from the conditioned *n* to *m* (*l, k, i*, etc.), and also descends from the condition *n* to the conditioned *o* (*p, q, r*, etc.). Now I must presuppose the first series in order to be able to view *n* as given. According to reason, with its demand for totality of conditions, *n* is possible only by means of that series. Its A 411 possibility does not, however, rest upon the subsequent series, *o, p, q, r*. This latter series may not therefore be regarded as B 438 given, but only as allowing of being given (*dabilis*).

I propose to name the synthesis of a series which begins, on the side of the conditions, from the condition which stands nearest to the given appearance and so passes to the more remote conditions, the *regressive* synthesis; and that which advances, on the side of the conditioned, from the first consequence to the more distant, the *progressive*. The first proceeds *in antecedentia*, the second *in consequentia*. The cosmological ideas deal, therefore, with the totality of the regressive synthesis proceeding *in antecedentia*, not *in consequentia*. The problem of pure reason suggested by the progressive form of totality is gratuitous and unnecessary, since the raising of it is not required for the complete comprehension of what is given in appearance. For that we require to consider only the grounds, not the consequences.

In arranging the table of ideas in accordance with the table of categories, we first take the two original *quanta* of all our intuition, *time* and *space*. Time is in itself a series, and indeed the formal condition of all series. In it, in regard to a given present, the antecedents can be *a priori* distinguished as conditions (the past) from the consequents (the future). The

A 412 transcendental idea of the absolute totality of the series of con-
B 439 ditions of any given conditioned therefore refers only to all *past* time; and in conformity with the idea of reason past time, as condition of the given moment, is necessarily thought as being given in its entirety. Now in space, taken in and by itself, there is no distinction between progress and regress. For as its parts are co-existent, it is an *aggregate, not a series*. The present moment can be regarded only as conditioned by past time, never as conditioning it, because this moment comes into existence only through past time, or rather through the passing of the preceding time. But as the parts of space are co-ordinated with, not subordinated to, one another, one part is not the condition of the possibility of another; and unlike time, space does not in itself constitute a series. Nevertheless the synthesis of the manifold parts of space, by means of which we apprehend space, is successive, taking place in time and containing a series. And since in this series of the aggregated spaces (as for instance of the feet in a rood) of the given space, those which are thought in extension of the given space are always *the condition of the limits* of the given space, the *measuring* of a space is also to be regarded as a synthesis of a series of the conditions of a given conditioned, only with this difference that the side of

A 413 the conditions is not in itself distinct from that of the condi-
B 440 tioned, and that in space *regressus* and *progressus* would therefore seem to be one and the same. Inasmuch as one part of space is not given through the others but only limited by them, we must consider each space, in so far as it is limited, as being also conditioned, in that it presupposes another space as the

condition of its limits, and so on. In respect of limitation the advance in space is thus also a regress, and the transcendental idea of the absolute totality of the synthesis in the series of conditions likewise applies to space. I can as legitimately enquire regarding the absolute totality of appearance in space as of that in past time. Whether an answer to this question is ever possible, is a point which will be decided later.

Secondly, reality in space, *i.e. matter*, is a conditioned. Its internal conditions are its parts, and the parts of these parts its remote conditions. There thus occurs a regressive synthesis, the absolute totality of which is demanded by reason. This can be obtained only by a completed division in virtue of which the reality of matter vanishes either into nothing or into what is no longer matter—namely, the simple. Here also, then, we have a series of conditions, and an advance to the unconditioned.

Thirdly, as regards the categories of real relation between appearances, that of substance with its accidents is not adapted to being a transcendental idea. That is to say, in it reason finds no ground for proceeding regressively to conditions. Accidents, in so far as they inhere in one and the same substance, are co-ordinated with each other, and do not constitute a series. Even in their relation to substance they are not really subordinated to it, but are the mode of existence of the substance itself. What in this category may still, however, seem to be an idea of transcendental reason, is the concept of the[1] *substantial*. But since this means no more than the concept of object in general, which subsists in so far as we think in it merely the transcendental subject apart from all predicates, whereas we are here dealing with the unconditioned only as it may exist in the series of appearances, it is evident that the substantial cannot be a member of that series. This is also true of substances in community. They are mere aggregates, and contain nothing on which to base a series.[2] For we cannot say of them, as we can of spaces, whose limits are never determined in and by themselves but only through some other space, that they are subordinated to each other as conditions of the possibility of one another. There thus remains only the category of *causality*. It presents a series of causes of a given

B 441
A 414

---

[1] [Reading, with Erdmann, *vom* for *von*.]
[2] [*keinen Exponenten einer Reihe haben*.]

390 KANT'S CRITIQUE OF PURE REASON

B 442   effect such that we can proceed to ascend from the latter as the conditioned to the former as conditions, and so to answer the question of reason.

A 415   Fourthly, the concepts of the possible, the actual, and the necessary do not lead to any series, save in so far as the *accidental* in existence must always be regarded as conditioned, and as pointing in conformity with the rule of the understanding to a condition under which it is necessary, and this latter in turn to a higher condition, until reason finally attains unconditioned necessity only in the totality of the series.

When we thus select out those categories which necessarily lead to a series in the synthesis of the manifold, we find that there are but four cosmological ideas, corresponding to the four titles of the categories:

B 443   **1.**

Absolute completeness
of the *Composition*
of the given whole of all appearances.

2.

Absolute completeness
in the *Division*
of a given whole in the [field of] appearance.

3.

Absolute completeness
in the *Origination*
of an appearance.

4.

Absolute completeness
as regards *Dependence* of *Existence*
of the alterable in the [field of] appearance.

A 416   There are several points which here call for notice. In the first place, the idea of absolute totality concerns only the exposition of *appearances*, and does not therefore refer to the pure concept, such as the understanding may form, of a totality of *things in general*. Appearances are here regarded as given; what reason demands is the absolute completeness of the conditions of their possibility, in so far as these conditions constitute a series. What reason prescribes is therefore an absolutely (that is to say, in every respect) complete synthesis, whereby the appearance may be exhibited[1] in accordance with the laws of understanding.

---

[1] [*exponiert.*]

Secondly, what reason is really seeking in this serial, regressively continued, synthesis of conditions, is solely the un-   B 444
conditioned. What it aims at is, as it were, such a completeness
in the series of premisses as will dispense with the need of presupposing other premisses. This *unconditioned* is always contained in the *absolute totality of the series* as represented in
imagination.[1] But this absolutely complete synthesis is again
only an idea; for we cannot know, at least at the start of this
enquiry, whether such a synthesis is possible in the case of appearance. If we represent everything exclusively through pure
concepts of understanding, and apart from conditions of sensible intuition, we can indeed at once assert that for a given conditioned, the whole series of conditions subordinated to each
other is likewise given. The former is given only through the
latter. When, however, it is with appearances that we are dealing, we find a special limitation due to the manner in which
conditions are given, namely, through the successive synthesis   A 417
of the manifold of intuition—a synthesis which has to be
made complete through the regress. Whether this completeness is sensibly possible is a further problem; the idea of it
lies in reason, independently alike of the possibility or of the
impossibility of our connecting with it any adequate empirical
concepts. Since, then, the *unconditioned* is necessarily contained in the absolute totality of the regressive synthesis of
the manifold in the [field of] appearance—the synthesis being
executed in accordance with those categories which represent
appearance as a series of conditions to a given conditioned—
reason here adopts the method of starting from the idea of   B 445
totality, though what it really has in view is the *unconditioned*,
whether of the entire series or of a part of it. Meantime, also,
it leaves undecided whether and how this totality is attainable.

This unconditioned may be conceived in either of two
ways. It may be viewed as consisting of the entire series in
which all the members without exception are conditioned and
only the totality of them is absolutely unconditioned. This
regress is to be entitled infinite. Or alternatively, the absolutely
unconditioned is only a part of the series—a part to which the
other members are subordinated, and which does not itself stand

---

[1] [*Einbildung*.]

392 KANT'S CRITIQUE OF PURE REASON

under any other condition.*a* On the first view, the series *a parte*
A 418 *priori* is without limits or beginning, *i.e.* is infinite, and at the
same time is given in its entirety. But the regress in it is never
completed, and can only be called potentially infinite. On the
B 446 second view, there is a first member of the series which in
respect of past time is entitled, *the beginning of the world*, in
respect of space, *the limit of the world*, in respect of the parts
of a given limited whole, the *simple*, in respect of causes,
absolute *self-activity* (freedom), in respect of the existence of
alterable things, absolute *natural necessity*.

We have two expressions, *world* and *nature*, which sometimes coincide. The former signifies the mathematical sum-
total of all appearances and the totality of their synthesis, alike
in the great and in the small, that is, in the advance alike through
composition and through division. This same world is entitled
A 419 nature*b* when it is viewed as a dynamical whole. We are not
then concerned with the aggregation in space and time, with
B 447 a view to determining it as a magnitude, but with the unity in
the *existence* of appearances. In this case the condition of that
which happens is entitled the cause. Its unconditioned causality in the [field of] appearance is called *freedom*, and its
conditioned causality is called *natural* cause[1] in the narrower
[adjectival] sense. The conditioned in existence in general is
termed contingent and the unconditioned necessary. The un-

a The absolute totality of the series of conditions to a given conditioned is always unconditioned, since outside it there are no further
conditions in respect of which it could be conditioned. But this
absolute totality of such a series is only an idea, or rather a problematic concept, the possibility of which has to be investigated, especially in regard to the manner in which the unconditioned (the transcendental idea really at issue) is involved therein.

B 446 *b* Nature, taken adjectivally (*formaliter*), signifies the connection of the determinations of a thing according to an inner principle
of causality. By nature, on the other hand, taken substantively
(*materialiter*), is meant the sum of appearances in so far as they
stand, in virtue of an inner principle of causality, in thoroughgoing interconnection. In the first sense we speak of the nature of
fluid matter, of fire, etc. The word is then employed in an adjectival
manner. When, on the other hand, we speak of the things of nature,
we have in mind a self-subsisting whole.

[1] [*Natur-ursache.*]

conditioned necessity of *appearances* may be entitled natural necessity.

The ideas with which we are now dealing I have above entitled cosmological ideas, partly because by the term 'world' we mean the sum of all *appearances*, and it is exclusively to the unconditioned in the *appearances* that our ideas are directed, partly also because the term 'world', in the transcendental sense, signifies the absolute *totality* of all existing things, and we direct our attention solely to the *completeness* of the synthesis, even though that is only attainable in the A 420 regress to its conditions. Thus despite the objection that these ideas are one and all transcendent, and that although they do not in kind surpass the object, namely, appearances, but are concerned exclusively with the world of sense, not with noumena, they yet carry the synthesis to a degree which transcends all possible experience, I none the less still hold that they may quite appropriately be entitled *cosmical concepts.*[1] In respect of the distinction between the mathematically and the B 448 dynamically unconditioned at which the regress aims, I might, however, call the first two concepts cosmical in the narrower sense, as referring to the world of the great and the small, and the other two *transcendent concepts of nature.*[2] This distinction has no special immediate value; its significance will appear later.

THE ANTINOMY OF PURE REASON

Section 2

ANTITHETIC OF PURE REASON

If thetic be the name for any body of dogmatic doctrines, antithetic may be taken as meaning, not dogmatic assertions of the opposite, but the conflict of the doctrines of seemingly dogmatic knowledge (*thesis cum antithesi*) in which no one assertion can establish superiority over another. The antithetic does A 421 not, therefore, deal with one-sided assertions. It treats only of the conflict of the doctrines of reason with one another and the causes of this conflict. The transcendental antithetic is an enquiry into the antinomy of pure reason, its causes and out-

[1] [*Weltbegriffe.*]   [2] [*Naturbegriffe.*]

come. If in employing the principles of understanding we do
B 449 not merely apply our reason to objects of experience, but
venture to extend these principles beyond the limits of experience, there arise *pseudo-rational* doctrines which can neither
hope for confirmation in experience nor fear refutation by it.
Each of them is not only in itself free from contradiction, but
finds conditions of its necessity in the very nature of reason—
only that, unfortunately, the assertion of the opposite has, on
its side, grounds that are just as valid and necessary.

The questions which naturally arise in connection with
such a dialectic of pure reason are the following: (1) In what
propositions is pure reason unavoidably subject to an antinomy? (2) On what causes does this antinomy depend? (3)
Whether and in what way, despite this contradiction, does
there still remain open to reason a path to certainty?

A dialectical doctrine of pure reason must therefore be
distinguished from all sophistical propositions in two respects.
A 422 It must not refer to an arbitrary question such as may be raised
for some special purpose, but to one which human reason
must necessarily encounter in its progress. And secondly, both
it and its opposite must involve no mere artificial illusion such
as at once vanishes upon detection, but a natural and un-
B 450 avoidable illusion, which even after it has ceased to beguile
still continues to delude though not to deceive us, and which
though thus capable of being rendered harmless can never be
eradicated.

Such dialectical doctrine relates not to the unity of understanding in empirical concepts, but to the unity of reason in
mere ideas. Since this unity of reason involves a synthesis according to rules, it must conform to the understanding; and
yet as demanding absolute unity of synthesis it must at the
same time harmonise with reason. But the conditions of this
unity are such that when it is adequate to reason it is too great
for the understanding; and when suited to the understanding,
too small for reason. There thus arises a conflict which cannot
be avoided, do what we will.

These pseudo-rational assertions thus disclose a dialectical
battlefield in which the side permitted to open the attack is
A 423 invariably victorious, and the side constrained to act on the
defensive is always defeated. Accordingly, vigorous fighters, no

matter whether they support a good or a bad cause, if only they contrive to secure the right to make the last attack, and are not required to withstand a new onslaught from their opponents, may always count upon carrying off the laurels. We can easily understand that while this arena should time and again be contested, and that numerous triumphs should be gained by both sides, the last decisive victory always leaves the B 451 champion of the good cause master of the field, simply because his rival is forbidden to resume the combat. As impartial umpires, we must leave aside the question whether it is for the good or the bad cause that the contestants are fighting. They must be left to decide the issue for themselves. After they have rather exhausted than injured one another, they will perhaps themselves perceive the futility of their quarrel, and part good friends.

This method of watching, or rather provoking, a conflict of assertions, not for the purpose of deciding in favour of one or other side, but of investigating whether the object of controversy is not perhaps a deceptive appearance which each vainly strives to grasp, and in regard to which, even if there were no opposition to be overcome, neither can arrive at any A 424 result,—this procedure, I say, may be entitled the *sceptical method*. It is altogether different from *scepticism*—a principle of technical and scientific ignorance, which undermines the foundations of all knowledge, and strives in all possible ways to destroy its reliability and steadfastness. For the sceptical method aims at certainty. It seeks to discover the point of B 452 misunderstanding in the case of disputes which are sincerely and competently conducted by both sides, just as from the embarrassment of judges in cases of litigation wise legislators contrive to obtain instruction regarding the defects and ambiguities of their laws. The antinomy which discloses itself in the application of laws is for our limited wisdom the best criterion of the legislation[1] that has given rise to them. Reason, which does not in abstract speculation easily become aware of its errors, is hereby awakened to consciousness of the factors[2] [that have to be reckoned with] in the determination of its principles

[1] [*der Nomothetik.*]
[2] [*Momente.*]

But it is only for transcendental philosophy that this sceptical method is essential. Though in all other fields of enquiry it can, perhaps, be dispensed with, it is not so in this field. In mathematics its employment would, indeed, be absurd; for in mathematics no false assertions can be concealed and rendered invisible, inasmuch as the proofs must always proceed under the guidance of pure intuition and by means of a synthesis that is always evident. In experimental philosophy the delay caused by doubt may indeed be useful; no misunderstanding is, however, possible which cannot easily be removed; and the final means of deciding the dispute, whether found early or late, must in the end be supplied by experience. Moral philosophy can also present its principles, together with their practical consequences, one and all *in concreto*, in what are at least possible experiences; and the misunderstanding due to abstraction is thereby avoided. But it is quite otherwise with transcendental assertions which lay claim to insight into what is beyond the field of all possible experiences. Their abstract synthesis can never be given in any *a priori* intuition, and they are so constituted that what is erroneous in them can never be detected by means of any experience. Transcendental reason consequently admits of no other test than the endeavour to harmonise its various assertions. But for the successful application of this test the conflict into which they fall with one another must first be left to develop free and untrammelled. This we shall now set about arranging.[a]

A 426 }
B 454 }   THE ANTINOMY OF PURE REASON   { A 427
                                              { B 455

FIRST CONFLICT OF THE TRANSCENDENTAL IDEAS

Thesis	*Antithesis*
The world has a beginning in time, and is also limited as regards space.	The world has no beginning, and no limits in space; it is infinite as regards both time and space.

[a] The antinomies follow one another in the order of the transcendental ideas above enumerated [p. 390].

Proof

If we assume that the world has no beginning in time, then up to every given moment an ete·nity has elapsed, and there has passed away in the world an infinite series of successive states of things. Now the infinity of a series consists in the fact that it can never be completed through successive synthesis. It thus follows that it is impossible for an infinite world-series to have passed away, and that a beginning of the world is therefore a necessary condition of the world's existence. This was the first point that called for proof.

As regards the second point, let us again assume the opposite, namely, that the world is an infinite given whole of co-existing things. Now the magnitude of a quantum which is not given in intuition[a] as within certain limits, can be thought only through the synthesis of its parts, and the totality of such a quantum only through a synthesis that is brought to completion through repeated addition of

A 428
B 456

Proof

For let us assume that it has a beginning. Since the beginning is an existence which is preceded by a time in which the thing is not, there must have been a preceding time in which the world was not, *i.e.* an empty time. Now no coming to be of a thing is possible in an empty time, because no part of such a time possesses, as compared with any other, a distinguishing condition of existence rather than of non-existence; and this applies whether the thing is supposed to arise of itself or through some other cause. In the world many series of things can, indeed, begin; but the world itself cannot have a beginning, and is therefore infinite in respect of past time.

As regards the second point, let us start by assuming the opposite, namely, that the world in space is finite and limited, and consequently exists in an empty space which is unlimited. Things will therefore not only be

---

[a] An indeterminate quantum can be intuited as a whole when it is such that though enclosed within limits we do not require to con- B 654 struct its totality through measurement, that is, through the successive synthesis of its parts. For the limits, in cutting off anything further, themselves determine its completeness.

unit to unit.^a In order, therefore, to think, as a whole, the world which fills all spaces, the successive synthesis of the parts of an infinite world must be viewed as completed, that is, an infinite time must be viewed as having elapsed in the enumeration of all co-existing things. This, however, is impossible. An infinite aggregate of actual things cannot therefore be viewed as a given whole, nor consequently as simultaneously given. The world is, therefore, as regards extension in space, not infinite, but is enclosed within limits. This was the second point in dispute.

related *in space* but also related *to space*. Now since the world is an absolute whole beyond which there is no object of intuition, and therefore no correlate with which the world stands in relation, the relation of the world to empty space would be a relation of it to no *object*. But such a relation, and consequently the limitation of the world by empty space, is nothing. The world cannot, therefore, be limited in space; that is, it is infinite in respect of extension.^b

{ A 429
{ B 457

---

^a The concept of totality is in this case simply the representation of the completed synthesis of its parts; for, since we cannot obtain the concept from the intuition of the whole—that being in this case impossible—we can apprehend it only through the synthesis of the parts viewed as carried, at least in idea, to the completion of the infinite.

B 457   ^b Space is merely the form of outer intuition (formal intuition). It is not a real object which can be outwardly intuited. Space, as prior to all things which determine (occupy or limit) it, or rather which give an empirical intuition in accordance with its form, is, under the name of absolute space, nothing but the mere possibility of outer appearances in so far as they either exist in themselves or can be added to given appearances. Empirical intuition is not, therefore, a composite of appearances and space (of perception and empty intuition). The one is not the correlate of the other in a synthesis; they are connected in one and the same empirical intuition as matter and form of the intuition. If we attempt to set one of these two factors outside the other, space outside all appearances, there arise all sorts of empty determinations of outer intuition, which yet are not possible perceptions. For example, a determination of the relation of the motion (or rest) of the world to infinite empty space

I. *On the Thesis*

In stating these conflicting arguments I have not sought to elaborate sophisms. That is to say, I have not resorted to the method of the special pleader who attempts to take advantage of an opponent's carelessness—freely allowing the appeal to a misunderstood law, in order that he may be in a position to establish his own unrighteous claims by the refutation of that law. Each of the above proofs arises naturally out of the matter in dispute, and no advantage has been taken of the openings afforded by erroneous conclusions arrived at by dogmatists in either party.

I might have made a pretence of establishing the thesis in the usual manner of the dogmatists, by starting from a defective concept of the infinitude of a given magnitude. I might have argued that a magnitude is infinite if a greater than itself, as determined by the multiplicity of given units which it

II. *On the Antithesis*

The proof of the infinitude of the given world-series and of the world-whole, rests upon the fact that, on the contrary assumption, an empty time and an empty space, must constitute the limit of the world. I am aware that attempts have been made to evade this conclusion by arguing that a limit of the world in time and space is quite possible without our having to make the impossible assumption of an absolute time prior to the beginning of the world, or of an absolute space extending beyond the real world. With the latter part of this doctrine, as held by the philosophers of the Leibnizian school, I am entirely satisfied. Space is merely the form of outer intuition; it is not a real object which can be outwardly intuited; it is not a correlate of the appearances, but the form of the appearances themselves. And since space is thus no object but only the form of possible objects, it cannot be

is a determination which can never be perceived, and is therefore the predicate of a mere thought-entity.

contains, is not possible. Now no multiplicity is the greatest, since one or more units can always be added to it. Consequently an infinite given magnitude, and therefore an infinite world (infinite as regards the elapsed series or as regards extension) is impossible; it must be limited in both respects. Such is the line that my proof might have followed. But the above concept is not adequate to what we mean by an infinite whole. It does not represent *how great* it is, and consequently is not the concept of a *maximum*. Through it we think only its relation to any assignable unit in respect to which it is greater than all number. According as the unit chosen is greater or smaller, the infinite would be greater or smaller. Infinitude, however, as it consists solely in the relation to the given unit, would always remain the same. The absolute magnitude of the whole would not, therefore, be known in this way; indeed, the above

A 432
B 460

regarded as something absolute in itself that determines the existence of things. Things, as appearances, determine space, that is, of all its possible predicates of magnitude and relation they determine this or that particular one to belong to the real. Space, on the other hand, viewed as a self-subsistent something, is nothing real in itself; and cannot, therefore, determine the magnitude or shape of real things. Space, it further follows, whether full or empty,[a] may be limited by appearances, but appearances cannot be limited *by an empty space* outside them. This is likewise true of time. But while all this may be granted, it yet cannot be denied that these two non-entities,[1] empty space outside the world and empty time prior to it, have to be assumed if we are to assume a limit to the world in space and in time.

A 43
B 46

The method of argument which professes to enable us to avoid the above consequence (that of having to

---

[a] It will be evident that what we here desire to say is that *empty space*, so far as it is *limited by appearances*, that is, empty space *within the world*, is at least not contradictory of transcendental principles and may therefore, so far as they are concerned, be admitted. This does not, however, amount to an assertion of its possibility.

B 461

[1] [*Undinge.*]

concept does not really deal with it.

The true transcendental concept of infinitude is this, that the successive synthesis of units required for the enumeration of a quantum can never be completed.ᵃ Hence it follows with complete certainty that an eternity of actual successive states leading up to a given (the present) moment cannot have elapsed, and that the world must therefore have a beginning.

In the second part of the thesis the difficulty involved in a series that is infinite and yet has elapsed does not arise, since the manifold of a world which is infinite in respect of extension is given as *co-existing*. But if we are to think the totality of such a multiplicity, and yet cannot appeal to limits that of themselves constitute it a totality in intuition, we have to account for a concept which in this case cannot proceed from the whole to the determinate multiplicity of the parts, but which must demonstrate the possibility of a whole by means of the successive synthesis of the parts. Now since this syn-

assume that if the world has limits in time and space, the infinite void must determine the magnitude in which actual things are to exist) consists in surreptitiously substituting for the sensible world some intelligible world of which we know nothing; for the first beginning (an existence preceded by a time of non-existence) an existence in general which presupposes no other condition whatsoever; and for the limits of extension boundaries of the world-whole—thus getting rid of time and space. But we are here treating only of the *mundus phaenomenon* and its magnitude, and cannot therefore abstract from the aforesaid conditions of sensibility without destroying the very being of that world. If the sensible world is limited, it must necessarily lie in the infinite void. If that void, and consequently space in general as *a priori* condition of the possibility of appearances, be set aside, the entire sensible world vanishes. This world is all that is given us in our problem. The *mundus intelligibilis* is nothing but the general concept of a

---

ᵃ This quantum therefore contains a quantity (of given units) which is greater than any number—which is the mathematical concept of the infinite.

thesis must constitute a never to be completed series, I cannot think a totality either prior to the synthesis or by means of the synthesis. For the concept of totality is in this case itself the representation of a completed synthesis of the parts. And since this completion is impossible, so likewise is the concept of it.

world in general, in which abstraction is made from all conditions of its intuition, and in reference to which, therefore, no synthetic proposition, either affirmative or negative, can possibly be asserted.

A 434 }
B 462 }   THE ANTINOMY OF PURE REASON   { A 435
{ B 463

SECOND CONFLICT OF THE TRANSCENDENTAL IDEAS

Thesis

Every composite substance in the world is made up of simple parts, and nothing anywhere exists save the simple or what is composed of the simple.

Antithesis

No composite thing in the world is made up of simple parts, and there nowhere exists in the world anything simple.

Proof

Let us assume that composite substances are not made up of simple parts. If all composition be then removed in thought, no composite part, and (since we admit no simple parts) also no simple part, that is to say, nothing at all, will remain, and accordingly no substance will be given. Either, therefore, it is impossible to remove in thought all composition, or after its removal there must remain something which

Proof

Assume that a composite thing (as substance) is made up of simple parts. Since all external relation, and therefore all composition of substances, is possible only in space, a space must be made up of as many parts as are contained in the composite which occupies it. Space, however, is not made up of simple parts, but of spaces. Every part of the composite must therefore occupy a space. But the absolutely first parts exists without composition, that is, the simple. In the former case the composite would not be made up of substances; composition, as applied to substances, is only an accidental relation in independence of which they must still persist as self-subsistent beings. Since this contradicts our supposition, there remains only the original supposition, that a composite of substances in the world is made up of simple parts.

It follows, as an immediate consequence, that the things in the world are all, without exception, simple beings; that composition is merely an external state of these beings; and that although we can never so isolate these elementary substances as to take them out of this state of composition, reason must think them as the primary subjects of all composition, and therefore, as simple beings, prior to all composition.

of every composite are simple. The simple therefore occupies a space. Now since everything real, which occupies a space, contains in itself a manifold of constituents external to one another, and is therefore composite; and since a real composite is not made up of accidents (for accidents could not exist outside one another, in the absence of substance) but of substances, it follows that the simple would be a composite of substances — which is self-contradictory.

The second proposition of the antithesis, that nowhere in the world does there exist anything simple, is intended {A 437 / B 465} to mean only this, that the existence of the absolutely simple cannot be established by any experience or perception, either outer or inner; and that the absolutely simple is therefore a mere idea, the objective reality of which can never be shown in any possible experience, and which, as being without an object, has no application in the explanation[1] of the appearances. For if we assumed that in experience an object might be found for this transcendental idea, the empirical intuition of such an object

{436 / 464}

---

[1] [*Exposition.*]

would have to be known as one that contains no manifold [factors] external to one another and combined into unity. But since from the non-consciousness of such a manifold we cannot conclude to its complete impossibility in every kind of intuition of an object; and since without such proof absolute simplicity can never be established, it follows that such simplicity cannot be inferred from any perception whatsoever. An absolutely simple object can never be given in any possible experience. And since by the world of sense we must mean the sum of all possible experiences, it follows that nothing simple is to be found anywhere in it.

This second proposition of the antithesis has a much wider application than the first. Whereas the first proposition banishes the simple only from the intuition of the composite, the second excludes it from the whole of nature. Accordingly it has not been possible to prove this second proposition by reference to the concept of a given object of outer intuition (of the composite), but only by reference to its relation to a possible experience in general.

OBSERVATION ON THE SECOND ANTINOMY

I. *On the Thesis*

When I speak of a whole as necessarily made up of simple parts, I am referring only to a substantial whole that is composite in the strict sense of the term 'composite', that is, to that accidental unity of the manifold which, given as *separate* (at least in thought), is brought into a mutual connection, and thereby constitutes a unity. Space should properly be called not *compositum* but *totum*, since its parts are possible only in the whole, not the whole through the parts. It might, indeed, be called a *compositum ideale*, but not *reale*. This, however, is a mere subtlety. Since space is not a composite made up of substances (nor even of real accidents), if I remove all compositeness from it, nothing remains, not even the point. For a point is possible only as the limit of a space, and so of a composite. Space and time do not, therefore, consist of simple parts. What belongs only to the state of a substance, even though it has a magnitude, *e.g.* alteration, does not consist of the simple;

II. *On the Antithesis*

Against the doctrine of the infinite divisibility of matter, the proof of which is purely mathematical, objections have been raised by the monadists. These objections, however, at once lay the monadists open to suspicion. For however evident mathematical proofs may be, they decline to recognise that the proofs are based upon insight into the constitution of space, in so far as space is in actual fact the formal condition of the possibility of all matter. They regard them merely as inferences from abstract but arbitrary concepts, and so as not being applicable to real things. How can it be possible to invent a different kind of intuition from that given in the original intuition of space, and how can the *a priori* determinations of space fail to be directly applicable to what is only possible in so far as it fills this space! Were we to give heed to them, then beside the mathematical point, which, while simple, is not a part but only the limit of a space, we should have to conceive physical points as being likewise

that is to say, a certain degree of alteration does not come about through the accretion of many simple alterations. Our inference from the composite to the simple applies only to self-subsisting things. Accidents of the state [of a thing] are not self-subsisting. Thus the proof of the necessity of the simple, as the constitutive parts of the substantially composite, can easily be upset (and therewith the thesis as a whole), if it be extended too far and in the absence of a limiting qualification be made to apply to everything composite—as has frequently happened.

Moreover I am here speaking only of the simple in so far as it is necessarily given in the composite—the latter being resolvable into the simple, as its constituent parts. The word *monas*, in the strict sense in which it is employed by Leibniz, should refer only to the simple which is *immediately* given as simple substance (*e.g.* in self-consciousness), and not to an element of the composite. This latter is better entitled *atomus*.[1] As I am seeking to prove the [existence of] simple substances only as elements in the composite, I

simple, and yet as having the distinguishing characteristic of being able, as parts of space, to fill space through their mere aggregation. Without repeating the many familiar and conclusive refutations of this absurdity—it being quite futile to attempt to reason away by sophistical manipulation of purely discursive concepts the evident demonstrated truth of mathematics—I make only one observation, that when philosophy here plays tricks with {A 44 B 46} mathematics, it does so because it forgets that in this discussion we are concerned only with *appearances* and their condition. Here it is not sufficient to find for the pure concept of the composite formed by the understanding the concept of the simple; what has to be found is an intuition of the simple for the intuition of the composite (matter). But by the laws of sensibility, and therefore in objects of the senses, this is quite impossible. Though it may be true that when a whole, made up of substances, is thought by the pure understanding alone, we must, prior to all composition of it, have the simple, this does not hold of the

A 442
B 470

---

[1] [*den Atomus*. This use of the term as a masculine is peculiar to Kant.]

might entitle the thesis[1] of the second antinomy, transcendental *atomistic*. But as this word has long been appropriated to signify a particular mode of explaining bodily appearances (*moleculae*), and therefore presupposes empirical concepts, the thesis may more suitably be entitled the dialectical principle of *monadology*.

totum substantiale phaenomenon which, as empirical intuition in space, carries with it the necessary characteristic that no part of it is simple, because no part of space is simple. The monadists have, indeed, been sufficiently acute to seek escape from this difficulty by refusing to treat space as a condition of the possibility of the objects of outer intuition (bodies), and by taking instead these and the dynamical relation of substances as the condition of the possibility of space. But we have a concept of bodies only as appearances; and as such they necessarily presuppose space as the condition of the possibility of all outer appearance. This evasion of the issue is therefore futile, and has already been sufficiently disposed of in the Transcendental Aesthetic. The argument of the monadists would indeed be valid if bodies were things in themselves.

The second dialectical assertion has this peculiarity, that over against it stands a dogmatic assertion which is the only one of all the pseudo-rational assertions that undertakes to afford manifest evidence, in an empirical

{ A 443
{ B 471

---

[1] [Reading, with Mellin and Valentiner, *These* for *Antithese*.]

object, of the reality of that which we have been ascribing only to transcendental ideas, namely, the absolute simplicity of substance—I refer to the assertion that the object of inner sense, the ' I ' which there thinks, is an absolutely simple substance. Without entering upon this question (it has been fully considered above), I need only remark, that if (as happens in the quite bare representation, ' I ') anything is thought as object only, without the addition of any synthetic determination of its intuition, nothing manifold and no compositeness can be perceived in such a representation. Besides, since the predicates through which I think this object are merely intuitions of inner sense, nothing can there be found which shows a manifold [of elements] external to one another, and therefore real compositeness. Self-consciousness is of such a nature that since the subject which thinks is at the same time its own object, it cannot divide itself, though it can divide the determinations which inhere in it ; for in regard to itself every object is absolute unity. Nevertheless, when this subject is viewed *outwardly*, as an object of intuition, it must exhibit [some sort of] compositeness in its appearance; and it must always be viewed in this way if we wish to know whether or not there be in it a manifold [of elements] *external* to one another.

THIRD CONFLICT OF THE TRANSCENDENTAL IDEAS

Thesis	*Antithesis*

Thesis

Causality in accordance with laws of nature is not the only causality from which the appearances of the world can one and all be derived. To explain these appearances it is necessary to assume that there is also another causality, that of freedom.

Antithesis

There is no freedom; everything in the world takes place solely in accordance with laws of nature.

Proof

Let us assume that there is no other causality than that in accordance with laws of nature. This being so, everything which *takes place* presupposes a preceding state upon which it inevitably follows according to a rule. But the preceding state must itself be something which has taken place (having come to be in a time in which it previously was not); for if it

Proof

Assume that there is freedom in the transcendental sense, as a special kind of causality in accordance with which the events in the world can have come about, namely, a power of absolutely beginning a state, and therefore also of absolutely beginning a series of consequences of that state; it then follows that not only will a series have its absolute beginning

had always existed, its consequence also would have always existed, and would not have only just arisen. The causality of the cause through which something takes place is itself, therefore, something that has *taken place*, which again presupposes, in accordance with the law of nature, a preceding state and its causality, and this in similar manner a still earlier state, and so on. If, therefore, everything takes place solely in accordance with laws of nature, there will always be only a relative[1] and never a first beginning, and consequently no completeness of the series on the side of the causes that arise the one from the other. But the law of nature is just this, that nothing takes place without a cause *sufficiently* determined *a priori*. The proposition that no causality is possible save in accordance with laws of nature, when taken in unlimited universality, is therefore self-contradictory; and this cannot, therefore, be regarded as the sole kind of causality.

We must, then, assume a causality through which something takes place, the cause of which is not itself deter-

A 446
B 474

in this spontaneity, but that the very determination of this spontaneity to originate the series, that is to say, the causality itself, will have an absolute beginning; there will be no antecedent through which this act, in taking place, is determined in accordance with fixed laws. But every beginning of action presupposes a state of the not yet acting cause; and a *dynamical* beginning of the action, if it is also a first beginning, presupposes a state which has no *causal* connection with the preceding state of the cause, that is to say, in nowise follows from it. Transcendental freedom thus stands opposed to the law of causality; and the kind of connection which it assumes as holding between the successive states of the active causes renders all unity of experience impossible. It is not to be met with in any experience, and is therefore an empty thought-entity.

In nature alone, therefore, [not in freedom], must we seek for the connection and order of cosmical events. Freedom (independence) from the laws of nature is no doubt a liberation from compulsion, but also from the guidance

A 4
B 4

[1] [*subalternen.*]

mined, in accordance with necessary laws, by another cause antecedent to it, that is to say, an *absolute spontaneity* of the cause, whereby a series of appearances, which proceeds in accordance with laws of nature, begins *of itself*. This is transcendental freedom, without which, even in the [ordinary] course of nature, the series of appearances on the side of the causes can never be complete of all rules. For it is not permissible to say that the *laws* of freedom enter into the causality exhibited in the course of nature, and so take the place of natural laws. If freedom were determined in accordance with laws, it would not be freedom; it would simply be nature under another name. Nature and transcendental freedom differ as do conformity to law and lawlessness. Nature does indeed impose upon the understanding the exacting task of always seeking the origin of events ever higher in the series of causes, their causality being always conditioned. But in compensation it holds out the promise of thoroughgoing unity of experience in accordance with laws. The illusion of freedom, on the other hand, offers a point of rest to the enquiring understanding in the chain of causes, conducting it to an unconditioned causality which begins to act of itself. This causality is, however, blind, and abrogates those rules through which alone a completely coherent experience is possible.

A 448 ⎫   OBSERVATION ON THE THIRD ANTINOMY   ⎧ A 449
B 476 ⎭   ⎩ B 477

I. *On the Thesis*

The transcendental idea of freedom does not by any means constitute the whole content of the psychological concept of that name, which is mainly empirical. The transcendental idea stands only for the absolute spontaneity of an action, as the proper ground of its imputability. This, however, is, for philosophy, the real stumbling-block; for there are insurmountable difficulties in the way of admitting any such type of unconditioned causality. What has always so greatly embarrassed speculative reason in dealing with the question of the freedom of the will, is its strictly transcendental aspect. The problem, properly viewed, is solely this: whether we must admit a power of *spontaneously* beginning a series of successive things or states. How such a power is possible is not a question which requires to be answered in this case, any more than in regard to causality in accordance with the laws of nature. For, [as we have found], we have to remain satisfied with the

II. *On the Antithesis*

The defender of an omnipotent nature (transcendental *physiocracy*), in maintaining his position against the pseudo-rational arguments offered in support of the counter-doctrine of freedom, would argue as follows. *If you do not, as regards time, admit anything as being mathematically first in the world, there is no necessity, as regards causality, for seeking something that is dynamically first.* What authority have you for inventing an absolutely first state of the world, and therefore an absolute beginning of the ever-flowing series of appearances, and so of procuring a resting-place for your imagination by setting bounds to limitless nature? Since the substances in the world have always existed—at least the unity of experience renders necessary such a supposition—there is no difficulty in assuming that change of their states, that is, a series of their alterations, has likewise always existed, and therefore that a first beginning, whether mathematical or dynamical, is not to be

a priori knowledge that this latter type of causality must be presupposed; we are not in the least able to comprehend how it can be possible that through one existence the existence of another is determined, and for this reason must be guided by experience alone. The necessity of a first beginning, due to freedom, of a series of appearances we have demonstrated only in so far as it is required to make an origin of the world conceivable; for all the later following states can be taken as resulting according to purely natural laws. But since the power of spontaneously beginning a series in time is thereby proved (though not understood), it is now also permissible for us to admit within the course of the world different series as capable in their causality of beginning of themselves, and so to attribute to their substances a power of acting from freedom. And we must not allow ourselves to be prevented from drawing this conclusion by a misapprehension, namely that, as a series occurring in the world can have only a relatively first beginning, being always preceded in the world by some other state of things, no

450
478

looked for. The possibility of such an infinite derivation, without a first member to which all the rest is merely a sequel, cannot indeed, in respect of its possibility, be rendered comprehensible. But if for this reason you refuse to recognise this enigma in nature, you will find yourself compelled to reject many fundamental synthetic properties and forces, which as little admit of comprehension. The possibility even of alteration itself would have to be denied. For were you not assured by experience that alteration actually occurs, you would never be able to excogitate *a priori* the possibility of such a ceaseless sequence of being and not-being.

A 451
B 479

Even if a transcendental power of freedom be allowed, as supplying a beginning of happenings in the world, this power would in any case have to be outside the world (though any such assumption that over and above the sum of all possible intuitions there exists an object which cannot be given in any possible perception, is still a very bold one). But to ascribe to substances in the world itself such a power, can never be permissible; for, should this

absolute first beginning of a series is possible during the course of the world. For the absolutely first beginning of which we are here speaking is not a beginning in time, but in causality. If, for instance, I at this moment arise from my chair, in complete freedom, without being necessarily determined thereto by the influence of natural causes, a new series, with all its natural consequences *in infinitum*, has its absolute beginning in this event, although as regards time this event is only the continuation of a preceding series. For this resolution and act of mine do not form part of the succession of purely natural effects, and are not a mere continuation of them. In respect of its happening, natural causes exercise over it no determining influence whatsoever. It does indeed follow upon them, but without arising out of them; and accordingly, in respect of causality though not of time, must be entitled an absolutely first beginning of a series of appearances.

This requirement of reason, that we appeal in the series of natural causes to a first beginning, due to freedom, is amply confirmed when we observe that all the philo-

be done, that connection of appearances determining one another with necessity according to universal laws, which we entitle nature, and with it the criterion of empirical truth, whereby experience is distinguished from dreaming, would almost entirely disappear. Side by side with such a lawless faculty of freedom, nature [as an ordered system] is hardly thinkable; the influences of the former would so unceasingly alter the laws of the latter that the appearances which in their natural course are regular and uniform would be reduced to disorder and incoherence.

sophers of antiquity, with the sole exception of the Epicurean School, felt themselves obliged, when explaining cosmical movements, to assume a *prime mover*, that is, a freely acting cause, which first and of itself began this series of states. They made no attempt to render a first beginning conceivable through nature's own resources.

FOURTH CONFLICT OF THE TRANSCENDENTAL IDEAS

Thesis

There belongs to the world, either as its part or as its cause, a being that is absolutely necessary.

Antithesis

An absolutely necessary being nowhere exists in the world, nor does it exist outside the world as its cause.

Proof

The sensible world, as the sum-total of all appearances, contains a series of alterations. For without such a series even the representation of serial time, as a condition of the possibility of the sensible world, would not be given us.[a] But every alteration stands under its condition, which precedes it in time and renders

Proof

If we assume that the world itself is necessary, or that a necessary being exists in it, there are then two alternatives. Either there is a beginning in the series of alterations which is absolutely necessary, and therefore without a cause, or the series itself is without any beginning, and although contingent and

[a] Time, as the formal condition of the possibility of changes, is indeed objectively prior to them; subjectively, however, in actual consciousness, the representation of time, like every other, is given only in connection with perceptions.

it necessary. Now every conditioned that is given presupposes, in respect of its existence, a complete series of conditions up to the unconditioned, which alone is absolutely necessary. Alteration thus existing as a consequence of the absolutely necessary, the existence of something absolutely necessary must be granted. But this necessary existence itself belongs to the sensible world. For if it existed outside that world, the series of alterations in the world would derive its beginning from a necessary cause A 454⎫ which would not itself belong B 482⎭ to the sensible world. This, however, is impossible. For since the beginning of a series in time can be determined only by that which precedes it in time, the highest condition of the beginning of a series of changes must exist in the time when the series as yet was not (for a beginning is an existence preceded by a time in which the thing that begins did not yet exist). Accordingly the causality of the necessary cause of

conditioned in all its parts, none the less, as a whole, is absolutely necessary and unconditioned. The former alternative, however, conflicts with the dynamical law of the determination of all appearances in time; and the latter alternative contradicts itself, since the existence of a series [1] cannot be necessary if no single member [2] of it is necessary.

If, on the other hand, we assume that an absolutely necessary cause of the world exists outside the world, then this cause, as the highest member in the series of the ⎧A 45 causes of changes in the ⎩B 48 world, must begin the existence of the latter and their series.[a] Now this cause must itself begin to act, and its causality would therefore be in time, and so would belong to the sum of appearances, that is, to the world. It follows that it itself, the cause, would not be outside the world—which contradicts our hypothesis. Therefore neither in the world, nor outside the world (though in causal con-

---

[a] The word 'begin' is taken in two senses; first as *active*, signifying that as cause it begins (*infit*) a series of states which is its effect; secondly as *passive*, signifying the causality which begins to operate (*fit*) in the cause itself. I reason here from the former to the latter meaning.

[1] [*Menge.*]   [2] [*Teil.*]

alterations, and therefore the cause itself, must belong to time and so to appearance— time being possible only as the form of appearance. Such causality cannot, therefore, be thought apart from that sum of all appearances which constitutes the world of sense. Something absolutely necessary is therefore contained in the world itself, whether this something be the whole series of alterations in the world or a part of the series.

nection with it), does there exist any absolutely necessary being.

A 456⎫   ⎧A 457
B 484⎭ OBSERVATION ON THE FOURTH ANTINOMY ⎨B 485

I. *On the Thesis*

In proving the existence of a necessary being I ought not, in this connection, to employ any but the *cosmological* argument, that, namely, which ascends from the conditioned in the [field of] appearance to the unconditioned in concept, this latter being regarded as the necessary condition of the absolute totality of the series. To seek proof of this from the mere idea of a supreme being belongs to another principle of reason, and will have to be treated separately.

The pure cosmological proof, in demonstrating the existence of a necessary being,

II. *On the Antithesis*

The difficulties in the way of asserting the existence of an absolutely necessary highest cause, which we suppose ourselves to meet as we ascend in the series of appearances, cannot be such as arise in connection with mere concepts of the necessary existence of a thing in general. The difficulties are not, therefore, ontological, but must concern the causal connection of a series of appearances for which a condition has to be assumed that is itself unconditioned, and so must be cosmological, and relate to empirical laws. It must be shown that regress in the

has to leave unsettled whether this being is the world itself or a thing[1] distinct from it. To establish the latter view, we should require principles which are no longer cosmological and do not continue in the series of appearances. For we should have to employ concepts of contingent beings in general (viewed as objects of the understanding alone) and a principle which will enable us to connect these, by means of mere concepts, with a necessary being. But all this belongs to a *transcendent* philosophy; and that we are not yet in a position to discuss.

If we begin our proof cosmologically, resting it upon the series of appearances and the regress therein according to empirical laws of causality, we must not afterwards suddenly deviate from this mode of argument, passing over to something that is not a member of the series. Anything taken as condition must be viewed precisely in the same manner in which we viewed the relation of the conditioned to its condition in the series which is supposed to carry us by continuous advance to the supreme condition. If, then, this relation is

A 458}
B 486}

series of causes (in the sensible world) can never terminate in an empirically unconditioned condition, and that the cosmological argument from the contingency of states of the world, as evidenced by their alterations, does not support the assumption of a first and absolutely originative cause of the series.

A strange situation is disclosed in this antinomy. From the same ground on which, in the thesis, the existence of an original being was inferred, its non-existence is inferred in the antithesis, and this with equal stringency. We were first assured that *a necessary being exists* because the whole of past time comprehends the series of all conditions and therefore also the unconditioned (that is, the necessary); we are now assured that *there is no necessary being*, and precisely for the reason that the whole of past time comprehends the series of all conditions (which therefore are one and all themselves conditioned). The explanation is this. The former argument takes account only of *the absolute totality* of the series of conditions determining each other in time,

{A 459
{B 487

---

[1] [*ein Ding.*]

sensible and falls within the province of the possible empirical employment of understanding, the highest condition or cause can bring the regress to a close only in accordance with the laws of sensibility, and therefore only in so far as it itself belongs to the temporal series. The necessary being must therefore be regarded as the highest member of the cosmical series. Nevertheless certain thinkers have allowed themselves the liberty of making such a *saltus* (μετάβασις εἰς ἄλλο γένος). From the alterations in the world they have inferred their empirical contingency, that is, their dependence on empirically determining causes, and so have obtained an ascending series of empirical conditions. And so far they were entirely in the right. But since they could not find in such a series any first beginning, or any highest member, they passed suddenly from the empirical concept of contingency, and laid hold upon the pure category, which then gave rise to a strictly intelligible series the completeness of which rested on the existence of an absolutely necessary cause. Since this cause

and so reaches what is unconditioned and necessary. The latter argument, on the other hand, takes into consideration the *contingency* of everything which is determined in the temporal series (everything being preceded by a time in which the condition must itself again be determined as conditioned), and from this point of view everything unconditioned and all absolute necessity completely vanish. Nevertheless, the method of argument in both cases is entirely in conformity even with ordinary human reason, which frequently falls into conflict with itself through considering its object from two different points of view. M. de Mairan[1] regarded the controversy between two famous astronomers, which arose from a similar difficulty in regard to choice of standpoint, as a sufficiently remarkable phenomenon to justify his writing a special treatise upon it. The one had argued that the *moon revolves on its own axis*, because it always turns the same side towards the earth. The other drew the opposite conclusion that *the moon does not revolve on its own axis*, because it always

{A 461
{B 489

---

[1] [J. J. D. de Mairan (1678–1771).]

was not bound down to any sensible conditions, it was freed from the temporal condition which would require that its causality should itself have a beginning. But such procedure is entirely illegitimate, as may be gathered from what follows.

In the strict meaning of the category, the contingent is so named because its contradictory opposite is possible. Now we cannot argue from empirical contingency to intelligible contingency. When anything is altered, the opposite of its state is actual at another time, and is therefore possible. This present state is not, however, the contradictory opposite of the preceding state. To obtain such a contradictory opposite we require to conceive, that in the same time in which the preceding state was, its opposite could have existed in its place, and this can never be inferred from [the fact of] the alteration. A body which was in motion (= A) comes to rest (= non-A). Now from the fact that a state opposite to the state A follows upon the state A, we cannot argue that the contradictory opposite of A is possible, and that A is therefore contingent. To prove such a

A 460
B 488

turns the same side towards the earth. Both inferences were correct, according to the point of view which each chose in observing the moon's motion

conclusion, it would have to be shown that in place of the motion, and at the time at which it occurred, there could have been rest. All that we know is that rest was real in the time that followed upon the motion, and was therefore likewise possible. Motion at one time and rest at another time are not related as contradictory opposites. Accordingly the succession of opposite determinations, that is, alteration, in no way establishes contingency of the type represented in the concepts of pure understanding; and cannot therefore carry us to the existence of a necessary being, similarly conceived in purely intelligible terms. Alteration proves only empirical contingency; that is, that the new state, in the absence of a cause which belongs to the preceding time, could never of itself have taken place. Such is the condition prescribed by the law of causality. This cause, even if it be viewed as absolutely necessary, must be such as can be thus met with in time, and must belong to the series of appearances.

THE ANTINOMY OF PURE REASON

Section 3

THE INTEREST OF REASON IN THESE CONFLICTS

We have now completely before us the dialectic play of cosmological ideas. The ideas are such that an object congruent with them can never be given in any possible experience, and that even in thought reason is unable to bring them into harmony with the universal laws of nature. Yet they are not arbitrarily conceived. Reason, in the continuous advance of empirical synthesis, is necessarily led up to them whenever it endeavours to free from all conditions and apprehend in its unconditioned totality that which according to the rules of experience can never be determined save as conditioned. These pseudo-rational assertions are so many attempts to solve four natural and unavoidable problems of reason. There are just so many, neither more nor fewer, owing to the fact that there are just four series of synthetic presuppositions which impose *a priori* limitations on the empirical synthesis.

The proud pretensions of reason, when it strives to extend its domain beyond all limits of experience, we have represented only in dry formulas that contain merely the ground of their
legal claims. As befits a transcendental philosophy, they have been divested of all empirical features, although only in connection therewith can their full splendour be displayed. But in this empirical application, and in the progressive extension of the employment of reason, philosophy, beginning with the field of our experiences and steadily soaring to these lofty ideas, displays a dignity and worth such that, could it but make good its pretensions, it would leave all other human science far behind. For it promises a secure foundation for our highest expectations in respect of those ultimate ends towards which all the endeavours of reason must ultimately converge. Whether the world has a beginning [in time] and any limit to its extension in space; whether there is anywhere, and perhaps in my thinking self, an indivisible and indestructible unity, or nothing but what is divisible and transitory; whether I am free in my actions or, like other beings, am led by the hand of

nature and of fate; whether finally there is a supreme cause
of the world, or whether the things of nature and their order
must as the ultimate object terminate thought—an object that
even in our speculations can never be transcended: these are
questions for the solution of which the mathematician would
gladly exchange the whole of his science. For mathematics
can yield no satisfaction in regard to those highest ends that $\begin{cases} \text{A 464} \\ \text{B 492} \end{cases}$
most closely concern humanity. And yet the very dignity of
mathematics (that pride of human reason) rests upon this,
that it guides reason to knowledge of nature in its order and
regularity—alike in what is great in it and in what is small—
and in the extraordinary unity of its moving forces, thus
rising to a degree of insight far beyond what any philosophy
based on ordinary experience would lead us to expect; and
so gives occasion and encouragement to an employment of
reason that is extended beyond all experience, and at the same
time supplies it with the most excellent materials for support-
ing its investigations—so far as the character of these permits
—by appropriate intuitions.

  Unfortunately for speculation, though fortunately perhaps
for the practical interests of humanity, reason, in the midst of
its highest expectations, finds itself so compromised by the
conflict of opposing arguments, that neither its honour nor
its security allows it to withdraw and treat the quarrel with
indifference as a mere mock fight; and still less is it in a position to command peace, being itself directly interested in the
matters in dispute. Accordingly, nothing remains for reason
save to consider whether the origin of this conflict, whereby
it is divided against itself, may not have arisen from a mere
misunderstanding. In such an enquiry both parties, perchance, $\begin{cases} \text{A 465} \\ \text{B 493} \end{cases}$
may have to sacrifice proud claims; but a lasting and peaceful
reign[1] of reason over understanding and the senses would
thereby be inaugurated.

  For the present we shall defer this thorough enquiry, in
order first of all to consider upon which side we should prefer
to fight, should we be compelled to make choice between
the opposing parties. The raising of this question, how we
should proceed if we consulted only our interest and not
the logical criterion of truth, will decide nothing in regard to

――――――――
  ¹ [Regiment.]

the contested rights of the two parties, but has this advantage, that it enables us to comprehend why the participants in this quarrel, though not influenced by any superior insight into the matter under dispute, have preferred to fight on one side rather than on the other. It will also cast light on a number of incidental points, for instance, the passionate zeal of the one party and the calm assurance of the other; and will explain why the world hails the one with eager approval, and is implacably prejudiced against the other.

Comparison of the principles which form the starting-points of the two parties is what enables us, as we shall find, to determine the standpoint from which alone this preliminary enquiry can be carried out with the required thoroughness. In the assertions of the antithesis we observe a perfect uniformity in manner of thinking and complete unity of maxims, namely a principle of pure *empiricism*, applied not only in explanation of the appearances within the world, but also in the solution of the transcendental ideas of the world itself, in its totality. The assertions of the thesis, on the other hand, presuppose, in addition to the empirical mode of explanation employed within the series of appearances, intelligible beginnings[1]; and to this extent its maxim is complex.[2] But as its essential and distinguishing characteristic is the presupposition of intelligible beginnings, I shall entitle it the *dogmatism* of pure reason.

In the determination of the cosmological ideas, we find on the side of *dogmatism*, that is, of the thesis:

First, a certain *practical interest* in which every well-disposed man, if he has understanding of what truly concerns him, heartily shares. That the world has a beginning, that my thinking self is of simple and therefore indestructible nature, that it is free in its voluntary actions and raised above the compulsion of nature, and finally that all order in the things constituting the world is due to a primordial being,[3] from which everything derives its unity and purposive connection—these are so many foundation stones of morals and religion. The antithesis robs us of all these supports, or at least appears to do so.

Secondly, reason has a *speculative interest* on the side of

A 466
B 494

---

[1] [*intellektuelle Anfänge.*]   [2] [*nicht einfach.*]   [3] [*Urwesen.*]

the thesis. When the transcendental ideas are postulated and
employed in the manner prescribed by the thesis, the entire {A 467 / B 495}
chain of conditions and the derivation of the conditioned can
be grasped completely *a priori*. For we then start from the
unconditioned. This is not done by the antithesis, which for
this reason is at a very serious disadvantage. To the question
as to the conditions of its synthesis it can give no answer which
does not lead to the endless renewal of the same enquiry.
According to the antithesis, every given beginning compels us
to advance to one still higher; every part leads to a still smaller
part; every event is preceded by another event as its cause; and
the conditions of existence in general rest always again upon
other conditions, without ever obtaining unconditioned footing and support in any self-subsistent thing, viewed as primordial being.

Thirdly, the thesis has also the advantage of *popularity*;
and this certainly forms no small part of its claim to favour.
The common understanding finds not the least difficulty in the
idea of the unconditioned beginning of all synthesis. Being
more accustomed to descend to consequences than to ascend
to grounds, it does not puzzle over the possibility of the absolutely first; on the contrary, it finds comfort in such concepts,
and at the same time a fixed point to which the thread by
which it guides its movements can be attached. In the restless
ascent from the conditioned to the condition, always with one
foot in the air, there can be no satisfaction.

In the determination of the cosmological ideas, we find on {A 468 / B 496}
the side of *empiricism*, that is, of the *antithesis*: first, no such
practical interest (due to pure principles of reason) as is provided for the thesis by morals and religion. On the contrary,
pure empiricism appears to deprive them of all power and influence. If there is no primordial being distinct from the world,
if the world is without beginning and therefore without an
Author, if our will is not free, if the soul is divisible and
perishable like matter, *moral* ideas and principles lose all
validity, and share in the fate of the *transcendental* ideas
which served as their theoretical support.

But secondly, in compensation, empiricism yields advantages to the speculative[1] interest of reason, which are very

[1] ['Speculative' means for Kant theoretical, in distinction from the 'practical'.]

attractive and far surpass those which dogmatic teaching bearing on the ideas of reason can offer. According to the principle of empiricism the understanding is always on its own proper ground, namely, the field of genuinely possible experiences, investigating their laws, and by means of these laws affording indefinite extension to the sure and comprehensible knowledge which it supplies. Here every object, both in itself and in its relations, can and ought to be represented in intuition, or at least in concepts for which the corresponding images can be clearly and distinctly provided in given similar intuitions. There is no necessity to leave the chain of the natural order and to resort to ideas, the objects of which are not known, because, as mere thought-entities, they can never be given. Indeed, the understanding is not permitted to leave its proper business, and under the pretence of having brought it to completion to pass over into the sphere of idealising reason and of transcendent concepts—a sphere in which it is no longer necessary for it to observe and investigate in accordance with the laws of nature, but only to *think* and to *invent*,[1] in the assurance that it cannot be refuted by the facts of nature, not being bound by the evidence which they yield, but presuming to pass them by or even to subordinate them to a higher authority, namely, that of pure reason.

A 469 / B 497

The empiricist will never allow, therefore, that any epoch of nature is to be taken as the absolutely first, or that any limit of his insight into the extent of nature is to be regarded as the widest possible. Nor does he permit any transition from the objects of nature—which he can analyse through observation and mathematics, and synthetically determine in intuition (the extended)—to those which neither sense nor imagination can ever represent *in concreto* (the simple). Nor will he admit the legitimacy of assuming in nature itself any power that operates independently of the laws of nature (freedom), and so of encroaching upon the business of the understanding, which is that of investigating, according to necessary rules, the origin of appearances. And, lastly, he will not grant that a cause ought ever to be sought outside nature, in an original being. We know nothing but nature, since it alone can present objects to us and instruct us in regard to their laws.

A 470 / B 498

[1] [*dichten.*]

If the empirical philosopher had no other purpose in pro-pounding his antithesis than to subdue the rashness and pre-sumption of those who so far misconstrue the true vocation of reason as to boast of insight and knowledge just where true in-sight and knowledge cease, and to represent as furthering spec-ulative interests that which is valid only in relation to practical interests (in order, as may suit their convenience, to break the thread of physical enquiries, and then under the pretence of ex-tending knowledge to fasten it to transcendental ideas, through which we really know only that we know nothing); if, I say, the empiricist were satisfied with this, his principle would be a maxim urging moderation in our pretensions, modesty in our assertions, and yet at the same time the greatest possible extension of our understanding, through the teacher fittingly assigned to us, namely, through experience. If such were our procedure, we should not be cut off from employing intel-lectual *presuppositions* and *faith* on behalf of our practical interest; only they could never be permitted to assume the title and dignity of science and rational insight. *Knowledge,* which as such is speculative, can have no other object than that supplied by experience; if we transcend the limits thus imposed, the synthesis which seeks, independently of experi-ence, new species of knowledge, lacks that substratum of intuition upon which alone it can be exercised.

{A 471
{B 499

But when empiricism itself, as frequently happens, be-comes dogmatic in its attitude towards ideas, and confidently denies whatever lies beyond the sphere of its intuitive know-ledge, it betrays the same lack of modesty; and this is all the more reprehensible owing to the irreparable injury which is thereby caused to the practical interests of reason.

The contrast between the teaching of Epicurus[a] and that of Plato is of this nature.

[a] It is, however, open to question whether Epicurus ever pro-pounded these principles as objective assertions. If perhaps they were for him nothing more than maxims for the speculative employ-ment of reason, then he showed in this regard a more genuine philo-sophical spirit than any other of the philosophers of antiquity. That, in explaining the appearances, we must proceed as if the field of our enquiry were not circumscribed by any limit or beginning of the world; that we must assume the material composing the world to be such as it must be if we are to learn about it from experience;

428   KANT'S CRITIQUE OF PURE REASON

A 472 }
B 500 }   Each of the two types of philosophy says more than it
knows. Epicurus encourages and furthers knowledge, though
to the prejudice of the practical; Plato supplies excellent
practical principles, but permits reason to indulge in ideal
explanations of natural appearances, in regard to which a
speculative knowledge is alone possible to us—to the neglect
of physical investigation.

Finally, as regards the third factor which has to be considered in a preliminary choice between the two conflicting
parties, it is extremely surprising that empiricism should be so
universally unpopular. The common understanding, it might
be supposed, would eagerly adopt a programme which promises to satisfy it through exclusively empirical knowledge
and the rational connections there revealed—in preference to
the transcendental dogmatism which compels it to rise to
concepts far outstripping the insight and rational faculties
A 473 }
B 501 } of the most practised thinkers. But this is precisely what commends such dogmatism to the common understanding. For it
then finds itself in a position in which the most learned can
claim no advantage over it. If it understands little or nothing
about these matters, no one can boast of understanding much
more; and though in regard to them it cannot express itself in
so scholastically correct a manner as those with special training, nevertheless there is no end to the plausible arguments
which it can propound, wandering as it does amidst mere ideas,
about which no one knows anything, and in regard to which
it is therefore free to be as eloquent as it pleases; whereas

---

that we must postulate no other mode of the production of events
than one which will enable them to be [regarded as] determined
through unalterable laws of nature; and finally that no use must be
A 472 }
B 500 } made of any cause distinct from the world—all these principles still
[retain their value]. They are very sound principles (though seldom
observed) for extending the scope of speculative philosophy, while
at the same time [enabling us] to discover the principles of morality
without depending for this discovery upon alien [*i.e.* non-moral,
theoretical] sources; and it does not follow in the least that those
who require us, so long as we are occupied with mere speculation,
to *ignore* these dogmatic propositions [that there is a limit and
beginning to the world, a Divine Cause, etc.], can justly be accused
of wishing to *deny* them.

when matters that involve the investigation of nature are in
question, it has to stand silent and to admit its ignorance. Thus
indolence and vanity combine in sturdy support of these principles. Besides, although the philosopher finds it extremely
hard to accept a principle for which he can give no justification, still more to employ concepts the objective reality of which
he is unable to establish, nothing is more usual in the case of
the common understanding. It insists upon having something
from which it can make a confident start. The difficulty of even
conceiving this presupposed starting-point does not disquiet
it. Since it is unaware what conceiving really means, it never
occurs to it to reflect upon the assumption; it accepts as known
whatever is familiar to it through frequent use. For the
common understanding, indeed, all speculative interests pale
before the practical; and it imagines that it comprehends and   B 502
knows what its fears or hopes incite it to assume or to believe.   A 474
Thus *empiricism* is entirely devoid of the popularity of transcendentally idealising reason[1]; and however prejudicial such
empiricism[2] may be to the highest practical principles, there
is no need to fear that it will ever pass the limits of the Schools,
and acquire any considerable influence in the general life or
any real favour among the multitude.

Human reason is by nature architectonic. That is to say, it
regards all our knowledge as belonging to a possible system,
and therefore allows only such principles as do not at any rate
make it impossible for any knowledge that we may attain to
combine into a system with other knowledge. But the propositions of the antithesis are of such a kind that they render the
completion of the edifice of knowledge quite impossible. They
maintain that there is always to be found beyond every state
of the world a more ancient state, in every part yet other parts
similarly divisible, prior to every event still another event
which itself again is likewise generated, and that in existence
in general everything is conditioned, an unconditioned and
first existence being nowhere discernible. Since, therefore,
the antithesis thus refuses to admit as first or as a beginning
anything that could serve as a foundation for building, a

---

[1] [Reading, with Erdmann, *aller Popularität der transcendental-idealisierenden Vernunft* for *der transcendental-idealisierenden aller Popularität.*]

[2] [Reading, with Mellin, *er . . . er* for *sie . . . sie.*]

complete edifice of knowledge is, on such assumptions, alto-

gether impossible. Thus the architectonic interest of reason—
the demand not for empirical but for pure *a priori* unity of
reason—forms a natural recommendation for the assertions
of the thesis.

If men could free themselves from all such interests, and
consider the assertions of reason irrespective of their consequences, solely in view of the intrinsic force of their grounds,
and were the only way of escape from their perplexities to
give adhesion to one or other of the opposing parties, their
state would be one of continuous vacillation. To-day it would
be their conviction that the human will is *free*; to-morrow,
dwelling in reflection upon the indissoluble chain of nature,
they would hold that freedom is nothing but self-deception,
that everything is simply *nature*. If, however, they were
summoned to action, this play of the merely speculative
reason would, like a dream, at once cease, and they would
choose their principles exclusively in accordance with practical interests. Since, however, it is fitting that a reflective and
enquiring being should devote a certain amount of time to
the examination of his own reason, entirely divesting himself
of all partiality and openly submitting his observations to the
judgment of others, no one can be blamed for, much less pro-

hibited from, presenting for trial the two opposing parties,
leaving them, terrorised by no threats, to defend themselves as
best they can, before a jury of like standing with themselves,
that is, before a jury of fallible men.

THE ANTINOMY OF PURE REASON

Section 4

THE ABSOLUTE NECESSITY OF A SOLUTION OF THE
TRANSCENDENTAL PROBLEMS OF PURE REASON

To profess to solve all problems and to answer all questions
would be impudent boasting, and would argue such extravagant self-conceit as at once to forfeit all confidence. Nevertheless there are sciences the very nature of which requires that
every question arising within their domain should be com-

pletely answerable in terms of what is known, inasmuch as the
answer must issue from the same sources from which the
question proceeds. In these sciences it is not permissible to
plead unavoidable ignorance; the solution can be demanded.
We must be able, in every possible case, in accordance with a
rule, to know what is *right* and what is *wrong*, since this concerns our obligation, and we have no obligation to that which
we cannot know. In the explanation of natural appearances, $\begin{cases} A\ 477 \\ B\ 505 \end{cases}$
on the other hand, much must remain uncertain and many
questions insoluble, because what we know of nature is by no
means sufficient, in all cases, to account for what has to be explained. The question, therefore, is whether in transcendental
philosophy there is any question relating to an object presented to pure reason which is unanswerable by this reason,
and whether we may rightly excuse ourselves from giving a
decisive answer. In thus excusing ourselves, we should have
to show that any knowledge which we can acquire still leaves
us in complete uncertainty as to what should be ascribed to
the object, and that while we do indeed have a concept sufficient to raise a question, we are entirely lacking in materials
or power to answer the same.

Now I maintain that transcendental philosophy is unique
in the whole field of speculative knowledge, in that no question which concerns an object given to pure reason can be
insoluble for this same human reason, and that no excuse of
an unavoidable ignorance, or of the problem's unfathomable
depth, can release us from the obligation to answer it thoroughly and completely. That very concept which puts us in a
position to ask the question must also qualify us to answer it,
since, as in the case of right and wrong, the object is not to be
met with outside the concept.

In transcendental philosophy, however, the only questions $\begin{cases} A\ 478 \\ B\ 506 \end{cases}$
to which we have the right to demand a sufficient answer
bearing on the constitution of the object, and from answering
which the philosopher is nót permitted to excuse himself on
the plea of their impenetrable obscurity, are the cosmological.
These questions [bearing on the constitution of the object]
must refer exclusively to cosmological ideas. For the object
must be given empirically, the question being only as to its
conformity to an idea. If, on the other hand, the object is

transcendental, and therefore itself unknown; if, for instance, the question be whether that something, the appearance of which (in ourselves) is thought (soul), is in itself a simple being, whether there is an absolutely necessary cause of all things, and so forth, what we have then to do is in each case to seek an object for our idea; and we may well confess that this object is unknown to us, though not therefore impossible.^a The cosmological ideas alone have the peculiarity that they can presuppose their object, and the empirical synthesis required for its concept, as being given. The question which arises out of these ideas refers only to the advance in this synthesis, that is, whether it should be carried so far as to contain absolute totality—such totality, since it cannot be given in any experience, being no longer empirical. Since we are here dealing solely with a thing as object of a possible experience, not as a thing in itself, the answer to the transcendent cosmological question cannot lie anywhere save in the idea. We are not asking what is the constitution of any object in itself, nor as regards possible experience are we enquiring what can be given *in concreto* in any experience. Our sole question is as to what lies in the idea, to which the empirical synthesis can do no more than merely approximate; the question must therefore be capable of being solved entirely from the idea. Since the idea is a mere creature of reason, reason cannot disclaim its responsibility and saddle it upon the unknown object.

A 479
B 507

^a Although to the question, what is the constitution of a transcendental object, no answer can be given stating *what it is*, we can yet reply that the *question* itself is *nothing*, because there is no given object [corresponding] to it. Accordingly all questions dealt with in the transcendental doctrine of the soul are answerable in this latter manner, and have indeed been so answered; its questions refer to the transcendental subject of all inner appearances, which is not itself appearance and consequently not *given* as object, and in which none of the categories (and it is to them that the question is really directed) meet with the conditions required for their application. We have here a case where the common saying holds, that no answer is itself an answer. A question as to the constitution of that something which cannot be thought through any determinate predicate—inasmuch as it is completely outside the sphere of those objects which can be given to us—is entirely null and void.

A 479
B 507

It is not so extraordinary as at first seems the case, that a $\left\{\begin{array}{l}\text{A } 480 \\ \text{B } 508\end{array}\right.$
science should be in a position to demand and expect none but
assured answers to all the questions within its domain (*quae-
stiones domesticae*), although up to the present they have perhaps not been found. In addition to transcendental philosophy,
there are two pure rational sciences, one purely speculative,
the other with a practical content, namely, pure mathematics
and pure ethics. Has it ever been suggested that, because of
our necessary ignorance of the conditions, it must remain uncertain what exact relation, in rational or irrational numbers,
a diameter bears to a circle? Since no adequate solution in
terms of rational numbers is possible, and no solution in terms
of irrational numbers has yet been discovered, it was concluded that at least the impossibility of a solution can be
known with certainty, and of this impossibility Lambert[1] has
given the required proof. In the universal principles of morals
nothing can be uncertain, because the principles are either
altogether void and meaningless, or must be derived from
the concepts of our reason. In natural science, on the other
hand, there is endless conjecture, and certainty is not to be
counted upon. For the natural appearances are objects which
are given to us independently of our concepts, and the key to
them lies not in us and our pure thinking, but outside us; and
therefore in many cases, since the key is not to be found, an $\left\{\begin{array}{l}\text{A } 481 \\ \text{B } 509\end{array}\right.$
assured solution is not to be expected. I am not, of course, here
referring to those questions of the Transcendental Analytic
which concern the deduction of our pure knowledge; we are
at present treating only of the certainty of judgments with
respect to their objects and not with respect to the source of
our concepts themselves.

The obligation of an at least critical solution of the questions which reason thus propounds to itself, we cannot, therefore, escape by complaints of the narrow limits of our reason,
and by confessing, under the pretext of a humility based on self-
knowledge, that it is beyond the power of our reason to determine whether the world exists from eternity or has a beginning; whether cosmical space is filled with beings to infinitude,

---

[1] [J. H. Lambert (1728–77). The proof that π is incommensurable, Lambert
communicated, in a memoir on transcendental magnitudes, to the Berlin Academy
in 1768.]

or is enclosed within certain limits; whether anything in the world is simple, or everything such as to be infinitely divisible; whether there is generation and production through freedom, or whether everything depends on the chain of events in the natural order; and finally whether there exists any being completely unconditioned and necessary in itself, or whether everything is conditioned in its existence and therefore dependent on external things and itself contingent. All these questions refer to an object which can be found nowhere save in our thoughts, namely, to the absolutely unconditioned totality of the synthesis of appearances. If from our own concepts we are unable to assert and determine anything certain, we must not throw the blame upon the object as concealing itself from us. Since such an object is nowhere to be met with outside our idea, it is not possible for it to be given. The cause of failure we must seek in our idea itself. For so long as we obstinately persist in assuming that there is an actual object corresponding to the idea, the problem, as thus viewed, allows of no solution. A clear exposition of the dialectic which lies within our concept itself would soon yield us complete certainty how we ought to judge in reference to such a question

A 482 \
B 510 /

The pretext that we are unable to obtain certainty in regard to these problems can be at once met with the following question which certainly calls for a clear answer: Whence come those ideas, the solution of which involves us in such difficulty? Is it, perchance, appearances that demand explanation, and do we, in accordance with these ideas, have to seek only the principles or rules of their exposition? Even if we suppose the whole of nature to be spread out before us, and that of all that is presented to our intuition nothing is concealed from our senses and consciousness, yet still through no experience could the object of our ideas be known by us *in concreto*. For that purpose, in addition to this exhaustive intuition, we should require what is not possible through any empirical knowledge, namely, a completed synthesis and the consciousness of its absolute totality. Accordingly our question does not require to be raised in the explanation of any given appearance, and is therefore not a question which can be regarded as imposed on us by the object itself. The object can never come before us, since it cannot be given through any possible experience. In all

A 483 \
B 511 /

possible perceptions we always remain involved in *conditions*, whether in space or in time, and come upon nothing unconditioned requiring us to determine whether this unconditioned is to be located in an absolute beginning of synthesis, or in an absolute totality of a series that has no beginning. In its empirical meaning, the term 'whole' is always only comparative. The absolute whole of quantity (the universe), the whole of division, of derivation, of the condition of existence in general, with all questions as to whether it is brought about through finite synthesis or through a synthesis requiring infinite extension, have nothing to do with any possible experience. We should not, for instance, in any wise be able to explain the appearances of a body better, or even differently, in assuming that it consisted either of simple or of inexhaustibly composite parts; for neither a simple appearance nor an infinite composition can ever come before us. Appearances demand explanation only so far as the conditions of their explanation are given in perception; but all that may ever be given in this B 512 way, when taken together in an *absolute whole*, is not[1] itself A 484 a perception. Yet it is just the explanation of this very whole that is demanded in the transcendental problems of reason.

Thus the solution of these problems can never be found in experience, and this is precisely the reason why we should not say that it is uncertain what should be ascribed to the object [of our idea]. For as our object is only in our brain, and cannot be given outside it, we have only to take care to be at one with ourselves, and to avoid that amphiboly which transforms our idea into a supposed representation of an object that is empirically given and therefore to be known according to the laws of experience. The dogmatic solution is therefore not only uncertain, but impossible. The critical solution, which allows of complete certainty, does not consider the question objectively, but in relation to the foundation of the knowledge upon which the question is based.

---

[1] [Reading, with Mellin, *keine* for *eine*.]

THE ANTINOMY OF PURE REASON

Section 5

Sceptical Representation of the Cosmological Questions in the Four Transcendental Ideas

We should of ourselves desist from the demand that our questions be answered dogmatically, if from the start we understood that whatever the dogmatic answer might turn out to be it would only increase our ignorance, and cast us from one inconceivability into another, from one obscurity into another still greater, and perhaps even into contradictions. If our question is directed simply to a yes or no, we are well advised to leave aside the supposed grounds of the answer, and first consider what we should gain according as the answer is in the affirmative or in the negative. Should we then find that in both cases the outcome is mere nonsense,[1] there will be good reason for instituting a critical examination of our question, to determine whether the question does not itself rest on a groundless presupposition, in that it plays with an idea the falsity of which can be more easily detected through study of its application and consequences than in its own separate representation.
This is the great utility of the sceptical mode of dealing with the questions which pure reason puts to pure reason. By its means we can deliver ourselves, at but a small cost, from a great body of sterile dogmatism, and set in its place a sober critique, which as a true cathartic will effectively guard us against such groundless beliefs and the supposed polymathy to which they lead.

If therefore, in dealing with a cosmological idea, I were able to appreciate beforehand that whatever view may be taken of the unconditioned in the successive synthesis of appearances, it must either be *too large* or *too small* for any *concept of the understanding*, I should be in a position to understand that since the cosmological idea has no bearing save upon an object of experience which has to be in conformity with a possible concept of the understanding, it must be

---

[1] [Kant here plays on the double meaning of *sinnleeres*, "empty of sense" and "nonsense".]

entirely empty and without meaning; for its object, view it as we may, cannot be made to agree with it. This is in fact the case with all cosmical concepts; and this is why reason, so long as it holds to them, is involved in an unavoidable antinomy. For suppose:—

First, that *the world has no beginning*: it is then *too large* for our concept, which, consisting as it does in a successive regress, can never reach the whole eternity that has elapsed. Or suppose that *the world has a beginning*, it will then, in the necessary empirical regress, be *too small* for the concept of $\begin{cases} \text{A } 487 \\ \text{B } 515 \end{cases}$ the understanding. For since the beginning still presupposes a time which precedes it, it is still not unconditioned; and the law of the empirical employment of the understanding therefore obliges us to look for a higher temporal condition; and the world [as limited in time] is therefore obviously too *small* for this law.

This is also true of the twofold answer to the question regarding the magnitude of the world in space. If it is *infinite* and unlimited, it is too *large* for any possible empirical concept. If it is *finite* and limited, we have a right to ask what determines these limits. Empty space is no self-subsistent correlate of things, and cannot be a condition at which we could stop; still less can it be an empirical condition, forming part of a possible experience. (For how can there be any experience of the absolutely void?) And yet to obtain absolute totality in the *empirical* synthesis it is always necessary that the unconditioned be an empirical concept. Consequently, a *limited* world is too *small* for our concept.

Secondly, if every appearance in space (matter) consists of infinitely many parts, the regress in the division will always be *too large* for our concept; while if the *division* of space is to *stop* at any member of the division (the simple), the regress will be *too small* for the idea of the unconditioned. For this member always still allows of a regress to further parts con- $\begin{cases} \text{A } 488 \\ \text{B } 516 \end{cases}$ tained in it.

Thirdly, if we suppose that nothing happens in the world save in accordance with the laws of *nature*, the causality of the cause will always itself be something that happens, making necessary a regress to a still higher cause, and thus a continuation of the series of conditions *a parte priori* without end.

Nature, as working always through efficient causes, is thus too *large* for any of the concepts which we can employ in the synthesis of cosmical events.

If, in certain cases, we admit the occurrence of self-caused events, that is, generation through *freedom*, then by an unavoidable law of nature the question 'why' still pursues us, constraining us, in accordance with the law of causality [which governs] experience,[1] to pass beyond such events; and we thus find that such totality of connection is too *small* for our necessary empirical concept.

Fourthly, if we admit *an absolutely necessary being* (whether it be the world itself, or something in the world, or the cause of the world), we set it in a time *infinitely* remote from any given point of time, because otherwise it would be dependent upon another being antecedent to it. But such an existence is then too large for our empirical concept, and is unapproachable through any regress, however far this be carried.

A 489⎫
B 517⎭ If, again, we hold that everything belonging to the world (whether as conditioned or as condition) is *contingent*, any and every given existence is too *small* for our concept. For we are constrained always still to look about for some other existence upon which it is dependent.

We have said that in all these cases the cosmical idea is either too large or too small for the empirical regress, and therefore for any possible concept of the understanding. We have thus been maintaining that the fault lies with the idea, in being too large or too small for that to which it is directed, namely, possible experience. Why have we not expressed ourselves in the opposite manner, saying that in the former case the empirical concept is always too small for the idea, and in the latter too large, and that the blame therefore attaches to the empirical regress? The reason is this. Possible experience is that which can alone give reality to our concepts; in its absence a concept is a mere idea, without truth, that is, without relation to any object. The possible empirical concept is therefore the standard by which we must judge whether the idea is a mere idea and thought-entity, or whether it finds its object in the world. For we can say of anything that it is too large

¹ [*der Erfahrung*.]

or too small relatively to something else, only if the former is required for the sake of the latter, and has to be adapted to it. Among the puzzles propounded in the ancient dialectical Schools was the question, whether, if a ball cannot pass through a hole, we should say that the ball is too large or the hole too small. In such a case it is a matter of indifference how we choose to express ourselves, for we do not know which exists for the sake of the other. In the case, however, of a man and his coat, we do not say that a man is too tall for his coat, but that the coat is too short for the man.

{A 490
{B 518

We have thus been led to what is at least a well-grounded suspicion that the cosmological ideas, and with them all the mutually conflicting pseudo-rational assertions, may perhaps rest on an empty and merely fictitious concept of the manner in which the object of these ideas is given to us; and this suspicion may set us on the right path for laying bare the illusion which has so long led us astray.

THE ANTINOMY OF PURE REASON

Section 6

TRANSCENDENTAL IDEALISM AS THE KEY TO THE
SOLUTION OF THE COSMOLOGICAL DIALECTIC

We have sufficiently proved in the Transcendental Aesthetic that everything intuited in space or time, and therefore all objects of any experience possible to us, are nothing but appearances, that is, mere representations, which, in the manner in which they are represented, as extended beings, or as series of alterations, have no independent existence outside our thoughts. This doctrine I entitle *transcendental idealism*.[a] The realist in the transcendental meaning of this term, treats these modifications of our sensibility as self-subsistent things, that is, treats *mere representations* as things in themselves.

{A 491
{B 519

It would be unjust to ascribe to us that long-decried

[a] I have also, elsewhere, sometimes entitled it *formal* idealism, to distinguish it from *material* idealism, that is, from the usual type of idealism which doubts or denies the existence of outer things themselves. [Note added in B.]

empirical idealism, which, while it admits the genuine reality
of space, denies the existence of the extended beings in it, or
at least considers their existence doubtful, and so does not
in this regard allow of any properly demonstrable distinction
between truth and dreams. As to the appearances of inner
sense in time, empirical idealism finds no difficulty in regarding them as real things; indeed it even asserts that this inner
experience is the sufficient as well as the only proof of the
actual existence of its object (in itself, with[1] all this time-
determination).

B 520   Our transcendental idealism, on the contrary, admits the
reality of the objects of outer intuition, as intuited in space, and
of all changes in time, as represented by inner sense. For since
space is a form of that intuition which we entitle outer, and
A 492   since without objects in space there would be no empirical representation whatsoever, we can and must regard the extended
beings in it as real; and the same is true of time. But this space
and this time, and with them all appearances, are not in themselves *things*; they are nothing but representations, and cannot
exist outside our mind. Even the inner and sensible intuition
of our mind (as object of consciousness) which is represented
as being determined by the succession of different states in
time, is not the self proper, as it exists in itself—that is, is not
the transcendental subject—but only an appearance that has
been given to the sensibility of this, to us unknown, being.
This inner appearance cannot be admitted to exist in any such
manner in and by itself; for it is conditioned by time, and time
cannot be a determination of a thing in itself. The empirical
truth of appearances in space and time is, however, sufficiently
B 521   secured; it is adequately distinguished from dreams, if both
dreams and genuine appearances cohere truly and completely
in one experience, in accordance with empirical laws.

The objects of experience, then, are *never* given *in themselves*, but only in experience, and have no existence outside it.
A 493   That there may be inhabitants in the moon, although no one
has ever perceived them, must certainly be admitted. This,
however, only means that in the possible advance of experience we may encounter them. For everything is real which
stands in connection with a perception in accordance with the

---

[1] [Reading, with Erdmann, *selbst, mit*.]

laws of empirical advance. They are therefore real if they
stand in an empirical connection with my actual consciousness,
although they are not for that reason real in themselves, that
is, outside this advance of experience.

Nothing is really given us save perception and the empirical advance from this to other possible perceptions. For the
appearances, as mere representations, are in themselves real
only in perception, which perception is in fact nothing but the
reality of an empirical representation, that is, appearance. To
call an appearance a real thing prior to our perceiving it, either
means that in the advance of experience we must meet with
such a perception, or it means nothing at all. For if we were
speaking of a thing in itself, we could indeed say that it exists
in itself apart from relation to our senses and possible experience. But we are here speaking only of an appearance in space   B 522
and time, which[1] are not determinations of things in themselves but only of our sensibility. Accordingly, that which is in
space and time is an appearance; it is not anything in itself   A 494
but consists merely of representations, which, if not given in
us—that is to say, in perception—are nowhere to be met with.

The faculty of sensible intuition is strictly only a receptivity, a capacity of being affected in a certain manner with
representations,[2] the relation of which to one another is a pure
intuition of space and of time (mere forms of our sensibility),
and which, in so far as they are connected in this manner in
space and time, and are determinable according to laws of the
unity of experience, are entitled *objects*. The non-sensible cause
of these representations is completely unknown to us, and cannot
therefore be intuited by us as object. For such an object would
have to be represented as neither in space nor in time (these
being merely conditions of sensible representation), and apart
from such conditions we cannot think any intuition. We may,
however, entitle the purely intelligible cause of appearances in
general the transcendental object, but merely in order to have
something corresponding to sensibility viewed as a receptivity.
To this transcendental object we can ascribe the whole extent
and connection of our possible perceptions, and can say that it   B 523
is given in itself prior to all experience. But the appearances,

---

[1] [Reading, with Vorländer, *die beide* for *die beides*.]
[2] [*mit Vorstellungen affiziert zu werden*.]

while conforming to it, are not given in themselves, but only in this experience, being mere representations, which as percep-

A 495 tions can mark out[1] a real object only in so far as the perception connects with all others according to the rules of the unity of experience. Thus we can say that the real things of past time are given in the transcendental object of experience; but they are objects for me and real in past time only in so far as I repre-sent to myself (either by the light of history or by the guiding-clues of causes and effects) that a regressive series of possible perceptions in accordance with empirical laws, in a word, that the course of the world, conducts us to a past time-series as con-dition of the present time—a series which, however, can be re-presented as actual not in itself but only in the connection of a possible experience. Accordingly, all events which have taken place in the immense periods that have preceded my own ex-istence mean really nothing but the possibility of extending the chain of experience from the present perception back to the conditions which determine this perception in respect of time.

If, therefore, I represent to myself all existing objects of the senses in all time and in all places, I do not set them in space and time [as being there] prior to experience. This

B 524 representation is nothing but the thought of a possible ex-perience in its absolute completeness. Since the objects are nothing but mere representations, only in such a possible

A 496 experience are they given. To say that they exist prior to all my experience is only to assert that they are to be met with if, starting from perception, I advance to that part of experience to which they belong. The cause of the empirical conditions of this advance (that which determines what mem-bers I shall meet with, or how far I can meet with any such in my regress) is transcendental, and is therefore necessarily unknown to me. We are not, however, concerned with this transcendental cause, but only with the rule of the advance in the experience in which objects, that is to say, appearances, are given to me. Moreover, in outcome it is a matter of in-difference whether I say that in the empirical advance in space I can meet with stars a hundred times farther removed than the outermost now perceptible to me, or whether I say that they are perhaps to be met with in cosmical space even

---

[1] [bedeuten.]

though no human being has ever perceived or ever will perceive them. For even supposing they were given as things in themselves, without relation to possible experience, it still remains true that they are nothing to me, and therefore are not objects, save in so far as they are contained in the series of the empirical regress. Only in another sort of relation, when these appearances would be used for the cosmological idea of an absolute whole, and when, therefore, we are dealing with a B 525 question which oversteps the limits of possible experience, does distinction of the mode in which we view the reality of those objects of the senses become of importance, as serving A 497 to guard us against a deceptive error which is bound to arise if we misinterpret our empirical concepts.

THE ANTINOMY OF PURE REASON

Section 7

CRITICAL SOLUTION OF THE COSMOLOGICAL CONFLICT OF REASON WITH ITSELF

The whole antinomy of pure reason rests upon the dialectical argument: If the conditioned is given, the entire series of all its conditions is likewise given; objects of the senses are given as conditioned; therefore, etc. Through this syllogism, the major premiss of which appears so natural and evident, as many cosmological ideas are introduced as there are differences in the conditions (in the synthesis of appearances) that constitute a series. The ideas postulate absolute totality of these series; and thereby they set reason in unavoidable conflict with itself. We shall be in a better position to detect what is deceptive in this pseudo-rational argument, if we first B 526 correct and define some of the concepts employed in it.

In the first place, it is evident beyond all possibility of doubt, that if the conditioned is given, a regress in the series of A 498 all its conditions is *set* us *as a task*.[1] For it is involved in the very concept of the conditioned that something is referred to a condition, and if this condition is again itself conditioned, to a more remote condition, and so through all the members of the

---

[1] [*aufgegeben.*]

series. The above proposition is thus analytic, and has nothing to fear from a transcendental criticism. It is a logical postulate of reason, that through the understanding we follow up and extend as far as possible that connection of a concept with its conditions which directly results from the concept itself.

Further, if the conditioned as well as its condition are things in themselves, then upon the former being given, the regress to the latter is not only *set as a task*, but therewith already really *given*. And since this holds of all members of the series, the complete series of the conditions, and therefore the unconditioned, is given therewith, or rather is presupposed in view of the fact that the conditioned, which is only possible through the complete series, is given. The synthesis of the conditioned with its condition is here a synthesis of the mere understanding, which represents things *as they are*, without

B 527 considering whether and how we can obtain knowledge of them. If, however, what we are dealing with are appearances —as mere representations appearances cannot be given save

A 499 in so far as I attain knowledge of them, or rather attain them in themselves, for they are nothing but empirical modes of knowledge—I cannot say, in the same sense of the terms, that if the conditioned is given, all its conditions (as appearances) are likewise given, and therefore cannot in any way infer the absolute totality of the series of its conditions. The *appearances* are in their apprehension themselves nothing but an empirical synthesis in space and time, and are given only in *this synthesis*. It does not, therefore, follow, that if the conditioned, in the [field of] appearance, is given, the synthesis which constitutes its empirical condition is given therewith and is presupposed. This synthesis first occurs in the regress, and never exists without it. What we can say is that a *regress* to the conditions, that is, a continued empirical synthesis, on the side of the conditions, is enjoined or *set as a task*, and that *in this regress* there can be no lack of given conditions.

These considerations make it clear that the major premiss of the cosmological inference takes the conditioned in the transcendental sense of a pure category, while the minor premiss takes it in the empirical sense of a concept of the understanding applied to mere appearances. The argument thus

B 528 commits that dialectical fallacy which is entitled *sophisma*

figurae dictionis. This fallacy is not, however, an artificial A 500
one; a quite natural illusion of our common reason leads
us, when anything is given as conditioned, thus to assume in
the major premiss, as it were *without thought or question*, its
conditions and their series. This assumption is indeed simply
the logical requirement that we should have adequate premisses for any given conclusion. Also, there is no reference to a
time-order in the connection of the conditioned with its condition; they are presupposed as given *together* with it. Further,
it is no less natural, in the minor premiss, to regard appearances both as things in themselves and as objects given to the
pure understanding, than to proceed as we have done in the
major, in which we have [similarly] abstracted from all those
conditions of intuition under which alone objects can be given.
Yet in so doing we have overlooked an important distinction
between the concepts. The synthesis of the conditioned with
its conditions (and the whole series of the latter) does not in
the major premiss carry with it any limitation through time
or any concept of succession. The empirical synthesis, on the
other hand, that is, the series of the conditions in appearance,
as subsumed in the minor premiss, is necessarily successive,
the members of the series being given only as following upon
one another in time; and I have therefore, in this case, no right
to assume the absolute *totality* of the synthesis and of the
series thereby represented. In the major premiss all the mem- B 529
bers of the series are given in themselves, without any condition of time, but in this minor premiss they are possible only
through the successive regress, which is given only in the A 501
process in which it is actually carried out.

When this error has thus been shown to be involved in the
argument upon which both parties alike base their cosmological assertions, both might justly be dismissed, as being
unable to offer any sufficient title in support of their claims.
But the quarrel is not thereby ended—as if one or both of the
parties had been proved to be wrong in the actual doctrines
they assert, that is, in the conclusions of their arguments. For
although they have failed to support their contentions by valid
grounds of proof, nothing seems to be clearer than that since
one of them asserts that the world has a beginning and the
other that it has no beginning and is from eternity, one of the

two must be in the right. But even if this be so, none the less, since the arguments on both sides are equally clear, it is impossible to decide between them. The parties may be commanded to keep the peace before the tribunal of reason; but the controversy none the less continues. There can therefore be no way of settling it once for all and to the satisfaction of both sides, save by their becoming convinced that the very fact of their being able so admirably to refute one another is evidence that they are really quarrelling about nothing, and that a certain transcendental illusion has mocked them with a reality where none is to be found. This is the path which we shall now proceed to follow in the settlement of a dispute that defies all attempts to come to a decision.

B 530
A 502

*   *   *

Zeno of Elea, a subtle dialectician, was severely reprimanded by Plato as a mischievous Sophist who, to show his skill, would set out to prove a proposition through convincing arguments and then immediately overthrow them by other arguments equally strong. Zeno maintained, for example, that God (probably conceived by him as simply the world) is neither finite nor infinite, neither in motion nor at rest, neither similar nor dissimilar to any other thing. To the critics of his procedure he appeared to have the absurd intention of denying both of two mutually contradictory propositions. But this accusation does not seem to me to be justified. The first of his propositions I shall consider presently more in detail. As regards the others, if by the word 'God' he meant the universe, he would certainly have to say that it is neither abidingly present in its place, that is, at rest, nor that it changes its place, that is, is in motion; because all places are in the universe, and the universe is not, therefore, itself in any place. Again, if the universe comprehends in itself everything that exists, it cannot be either similar or dissimilar to any other thing, because there is no *other* thing, nothing outside it, with which it could be compared. If two opposed judgments presuppose an inadmissible condition, then in spite of their opposition, which does not amount to a contradiction strictly so-called, both fall to the ground, inasmuch as the condition, under which alone either of them can be maintained, itself falls.

B 531
A 503

If it be said that all bodies have either a good smell or a smell that is not good, a third case is possible, namely, that a body has no smell at all; and both the conflicting propositions may therefore be false. If, however, I say: all bodies are either good-smelling or not good-smelling (*vel suaveolens vel non suaveolens*), the two judgments are directly contradictory to one another, and the former only is false, its contradictory opposite, namely, that some bodies are not good-smelling, comprehending those bodies also which have no smell at all. Since, in the previous opposition (*per disparata*), smell, the contingent condition of the concept of the body,[1] was not removed by the opposed judgment, but remained attached to it, the two judgments were not related as *contradictory* opposites.

If, therefore, we say that the world is either infinite in extension or is not infinite (*non est infinitus*), and if the former proposition is false, its contradictory opposite, that the world is not infinite, must be true. And I should thus deny the existence of an infinite world, without affirming in its place a finite world. But if we had said that the world is either infinite or finite { A 504 / B 532 } (non-infinite), both statements might be false. For in that case we should be regarding the world in itself as determined in its magnitude, and in the opposed judgment we do not merely remove the infinitude, and with it perhaps the entire separate existence of the world, but attach a determination to the world, regarded as a thing actually existing in itself. This assertion may, however, likewise be false; the world may not be given as a thing in itself, nor as being in its magnitude either infinite or finite. I beg permission to entitle this kind of opposition *dialectical*, and that of contradictories *analytical*. Thus of two dialectically opposed judgments both may be false; for the one is not a mere contradictory of the other, but says something more than is required for a simple contradiction.

If we regard the two propositions, that the world is infinite in magnitude and that it is finite in magnitude, as contradictory opposites, we are assuming that the world, the complete series of appearances, is a thing in itself that remains even if I suspend the infinite or the finite regress in the series of its appearances. If, however, I reject this assumption, or

---

[1] [Reading, with Hartenstein, *des Körpers* for *der Körper*.]

rather this accompanying transcendental illusion, and deny
that the world is a thing in itself, the contradictory opposition
of the two assertions is converted into a merely dialectical
opposition. Since the world does not exist in itself, independently of the regressive series of my representations, it exists
in itself neither as an *infinite* whole nor as a *finite* whole. It
exists only in the empirical regress of the series of appearances, and is not to be met with as something in itself. If, then,
this series is always conditioned, and therefore can never be
given as complete, the world is not an unconditioned whole,
and does not exist as such a whole, either of infinite or of
finite magnitude.

What we have here said of the first cosmological idea,
that is, of the absolute totality of magnitude in the [field
of] appearance, applies also to all the others. The series of
conditions is only to be met with in the regressive synthesis
itself, not in the [field of] appearance viewed as a thing given
in and by itself, prior to all regress. We must therefore say that
the number of parts in a given appearance is in itself neither
finite nor infinite. For an appearance is not something existing
in itself, and its parts are first given in and through the regress
of the decomposing synthesis,[1] a regress which is never given
in absolute completeness, either as finite or as infinite. This
also holds of the series of subordinated causes, and of the
series that proceeds from the conditioned to unconditioned
necessary existence. These series can never be regarded as
being in themselves in their totality either finite or infinite.
Being series of subordinated *representations*, they exist only
in the dynamical regress, and prior to this regress can have no
existence in themselves as self-subsistent series of things.

Thus the antinomy of pure reason in its cosmological ideas
vanishes when it is shown that it is merely dialectical, and
that it is a conflict due to an illusion which arises from our
applying to appearances that exist only in our representations,
and therefore, so far as they form a series, not otherwise than
in a successive regress, that idea of absolute totality which
holds only as a condition of things in themselves. From this
antinomy we can, however, obtain, not indeed a dogmatic, but
a critical and doctrinal advantage. It affords indirect proof of

---

[1] [*der dekomponierenden Synthesis.*]

the transcendental ideality of appearances—a proof which ought to convince any who may not be satisfied by the direct proof given in the Transcendental Aesthetic. This proof would consist in the following dilemma. If the world is a whole existing in itself, it is either finite or infinite. But both alternatives are false (as shown in the proofs of the antithesis and thesis respectively). It is therefore also false that the world (the sum of all appearances) is a whole existing in itself. From this {B 535 A 507 it then follows that appearances in general are nothing outside our representations—which is just what is meant by their transcendental ideality.

This remark is of some importance. It enables us to see that the proofs given in the fourfold antinomy are not merely baseless deceptions. On the supposition that appearances, and the sensible world which comprehends them all, are things in themselves, these proofs are indeed well-grounded. The conflict which results from the propositions thus obtained shows, however, that there is a fallacy in this assumption, and so leads us to the discovery of the true constitution of things, as objects of the senses. While the transcendental dialectic does not by any means favour scepticism, it certainly does favour the sceptical method, which can point to such dialectic as an example of its great services. For when the arguments of reason are allowed to oppose one another in unrestricted freedom, something advantageous, and likely to aid in the correction of our judgments, will always accrue, though it may not be what we set out to find.

THE ANTINOMY OF PURE REASON   {A 508 B 536

Section 8

THE REGULATIVE PRINCIPLE OF PURE REASON IN ITS APPLICATION TO THE COSMOLOGICAL IDEAS

Since no maximum of the series of conditions in a sensible world, regarded as a thing in itself, is *given* through the cosmological principle of totality, but can only be *set as a task* that calls for regress in the series of conditions, the principle of pure reason has to be amended in these terms; and it then preserves its validity, not indeed as the *axiom* that we think the totality as actually in the object, but as a *problem* for the understanding, and therefore for the subject, leading it to undertake and to carry on, in accordance with the completeness prescribed by the idea, the regress in the series of conditions of any given conditioned. For in our sensibility, that is, in space and time, every condition to which we can attain in the exposition of given appearances is again conditioned. For they are not objects in themselves—were they such, the absolutely unconditioned might be found in them—but simply empirical representations which must always find in intuition the condition that determines them in space and time. The principle of reason is thus properly only a *rule*, pre-

A 509
B 537

scribing a regress in the series of the conditions of given appearances, and forbidding it to bring the regress to a close by treating anything at which it may arrive as absolutely unconditioned. It is not a principle of the possibility of experience and of empirical knowledge of objects of the senses, and therefore not a principle of the understanding; for every experience, in conformity with the given [forms of] intuition, is enclosed within limits. Nor is it a *constitutive* principle of reason, enabling us to extend our concept of the sensible world beyond all possible experience. It is rather a principle of the greatest possible continuation and extension of experience, allowing no empirical limit to hold as absolute. Thus it is a principle of reason which serves as a *rule*, postulating what we ought to do in the regress, but *not anticipating* what is present[1] *in the object as it is in itself, prior to all regress*. Accordingly I entitle it a *regulative* principle of reason, to distinguish it from the principle of the absolute totality of the series of conditions, viewed as actually present in the object (that is, in the appearances),[2] which would be a constitutive cosmological principle. I have tried to show by this distinction that there is no such constitutive principle, and so to prevent what otherwise, through a transcendental subreption, inevitably takes place, namely, the ascribing of objective reality to an idea that serves merely as a rule.

In order properly to determine the meaning of this rule of

[1] [*gegeben.*]
[2] [*als im Objekte (den Erscheinungen) an sich selbst gegeben.*]

pure reason, we must observe, first, that it cannot tell us *what* $\left\{\begin{array}{l}\text{A } 510 \\ \text{B } 538\end{array}\right.$
the object is, but only *how the empirical regress is to be carried
out* so as to arrive at the complete concept of the object. If it
attempted the former task, it would be a constitutive principle,
such as pure reason can never supply. It cannot be regarded
as maintaining that the series of conditions for a given conditioned is in itself either finite or infinite. That would be to
treat a mere idea of absolute totality, which is only produced
in the idea, as equivalent to thinking an object that cannot be
given in any experience. For in terms of it we should be ascribing to a series of appearances an objective reality which
is independent of empirical synthesis. This idea of reason can
therefore do no more than prescribe a rule to the regressive
synthesis in the series of conditions; and in accordance with
this rule the synthesis must proceed from the conditioned,
through all subordinate conditions, up to the unconditioned.
Yet it can never reach this goal, for the absolutely unconditioned is not to be met with in experience.

We must therefore first of all determine what we are to
mean by the synthesis of a series, in cases in which the synthesis is never complete. In this connection two expressions
are commonly employed, which are intended to mark a distinction, though without correctly assigning the ground of the
distinction. Mathematicians speak solely of a *progressus in
infinitum*. Philosophers, whose task it is to examine concepts, $\left\{\begin{array}{l}\text{A } 511 \\ \text{B } 539\end{array}\right.$
refuse to accept this expression as legitimate, substituting for
it the phrase *progressus in indefinitum*. We need not stop to
examine the reasons for such a distinction, or to enlarge upon
its useful or useless employment. We need only determine
these concepts with such accuracy as is required for our particular purposes.

Of a straight line we may rightly say that it can be produced to infinity. In this case the distinction between an infinite and an indeterminately great advance (*progressus in indefinitum*) would be mere subtlety. When we say, 'Draw a line',
it sounds indeed more correct to add *in indefinitum* than *in
infinitum*. Whereas the latter means that you *must* not cease
producing it—which is not what is intended—the former means
only, produce it as far as you *please*; and if we are referring
only to what it is in our *power* to do, this expression is quite

correct, for we can always make the line longer, without end. So is it in all cases in which we speak only of the *progress*, that is, of the *advance* from the condition to the conditioned: this possible advance proceeds, without end, in the series of appearances. From a given pair of parents the descending line of generation may proceed without end, and we can quite

A 512
B 540
well regard the line as actually so continuing in the world. For in this case reason never requires an absolute totality of the series, since it does not presuppose that totality as a condition and as given (*datum*), but only as something conditioned, that allows of being given (*dabile*), and is added to without end.

Quite otherwise is it with the problem: how far the regress extends, when it ascends in a series from something given as conditioned to its conditions. Can we say that the regress is *in infinitum*, or only that it is indeterminately far extended (*in indefinitum*)? Can we, for instance, ascend from the men now living, through the series of their ancestors, *in infinitum*; or can we only say that, so far as we have gone back, we have never met with an empirical ground for regarding the series as limited at any point, and that we are therefore justified and at the same time obliged, in the case of every ancestor, to search further for progenitors, though not indeed to presuppose them?

We answer: when the whole is given in empirical intuition, the regress in the series of its inner conditions proceeds *in infinitum*; but when a member only of the series is given, starting from which the regress has to proceed to absolute totality, the regress is only of indeterminate character (*in*

B 541
A 513
indefinitum). Accordingly, the division of a body, that is, of a portion of matter given between certain limits, must be said to proceed *in infinitum*. For this matter is given as a whole, and therefore with all its possible parts, in empirical intuition. Since the condition of this whole is its part, and the condition of this part is the part of the part, and so on, and since in this regress of decomposition an unconditioned (indivisible) member of this series of conditions is never met with, not only is there never any empirical ground for stopping in the division, but the further members of any continued division are themselves empirically given prior to the continuation of the division The division, that is to say, goes on *in infinitum*. On

the other hand, since the series of ancestors of any given man is not given in its absolute totality in any possible experience, the regress proceeds from every member in the series of generations to a higher member, and no empirical limit is encountered which exhibits a member as absolutely unconditioned. And since the members, which might supply the condition, are not contained in an empirical intuition of the whole, prior to the regress, this regress does not proceed *in infinitum*, by division of the given, but only indefinitely far, searching for further members additional to those that are given, and which are themselves again always given as conditioned.

In neither case, whether the regress be *in infinitum* or *in* {A 514 / B 542} *indefinitum*, may the series of conditions be regarded as being given as infinite in the object. The series are not things in themselves, but only appearances, which, as conditions of one another, are given only in the regress itself. The question, therefore, is no longer how great this series of conditions may be in itself, whether it be finite or infinite, for it is nothing in itself; but how we are to carry out the empirical regress, and how far we should continue it. Here we find an important distinction in regard to the rule governing such procedure. When the whole is empirically given, it is *possible* to proceed back in the series of its inner conditions *in infinitum*. When the whole is not given, but has first to be given through empirical regress, we can only say that the *search* for still higher conditions of the series is *possible in infinitum*. In the former case we could say: there are always more members, empirically given, than I can reach through the regress of decomposition; in the latter case, however, the position is this: we can always proceed still further in the regress, because no member is empirically given as absolutely unconditioned; and since a higher member is therefore always possible, the enquiry regarding it is necessary. In the one case we necessarily *find* further members of the series; in the other case, since no experience is absolutely limited, the {A 515 / B 543} necessity is that we *enquire* for them. For either we have no perception which sets an absolute limit to the empirical regress, in which case we must not regard the regress as completed, or we have a perception limiting our series, in which case the perception cannot be part of the series traversed (for that which *limits* must be distinct from that which *is* thereby *limited*), and we must therefore continue our regress to this condition also, and the regress is thus again resumed.

These observations will be set in their proper light by their application in the following section.

THE ANTINOMY OF PURE REASON

Section 9

THE EMPIRICAL EMPLOYMENT OF THE REGULATIVE PRINCIPLE OF REASON, IN RESPECT OF ALL COSMOLOGICAL IDEAS

We have already, on several occasions, shown that no transcendental employment can be made of the pure concepts either of the understanding or of reason; that the [assertion of] absolute totality of the series of conditions in the sensible world rests on a transcendental employment of reason in which reason demands this unconditioned completeness from what it assumes to be a thing in itself; and that since the sensible world contains no such completeness, we are never justified in enquiring, as regards the absolute magnitude of the series in the sensible world, whether it be limited or *in itself* unlimited, but only how far we ought to go in the empirical regress, when we trace experience back to its conditions, obeying the rule of reason, and therefore resting content with no answer to its questions save that which is in conformity with the object.

A 516
B 544

What therefore alone remains to us is the validity of the principle of reason as a rule for the *continuation* and magnitude of a possible experience; its invalidity as a constitutive principle of appearances [viewed as things] in themselves has been sufficiently demonstrated. If we can keep these conclusions steadily in view, the self-conflict of reason will be entirely at an end. For not only will this critical solution destroy the illusion which set reason at variance with itself, but will replace it by teaching which, in correcting the misinterpretation that has been the sole source of the conflict, brings reason into agreement with itself. A principle which otherwise would be *dialectical* will thus be converted into a *doctrinal* principle. In fact, if this principle can be upheld as determining, in accordance with its subjective significance, and yet also in conformity with the objects of experience, the greatest possible empirical use of understanding, the outcome will be much the same as if it were—what is impossible from pure reason—an axiom which $\begin{cases} A\ 517 \\ B\ 545 \end{cases}$ determined *a priori* the objects in themselves. For only in proportion as the principle is effective in directing the widest possible *empirical* employment of the understanding, can it exercise, in respect of the objects of experience, any influence in extending and correcting our knowledge.

I

Solution of the Cosmological Idea of the Totality of the Composition of the Appearances of a Cosmic Whole

Here, as in the other cosmological questions, the regulative principle of reason is grounded on the proposition that in the empirical regress we can have *no experience of an absolute limit*, that is, no experience of any condition as being one that *empirically* is absolutely unconditioned. The reason is this: such an experience would have to contain a limitation of appearances by nothing, or by the void, and in the continued regress we should have to be able to encounter this limitation in a perception—which is impossible.

This proposition, which virtually states that the only conditions which we can reach in the empirical regress are conditions which must themselves again be regarded as empirically conditioned, contains the rule *in terminis*, that however $\begin{cases} A\ 518 \\ B\ 546 \end{cases}$ far we may have advanced in the ascending series, we must always enquire for a still higher member of the series, which may or may not become known to us through experience.

For the solution, therefore, of the first cosmological problem we have only to decide whether in the regress to the unconditioned magnitude of the universe, in time and space, this never limited ascent can be called a regress to infinity, or only an indeterminately continued regress (*in indefinitum*).

The quite general representation of the series of all past states of the world, as well as of all the things which coexist in cosmic space, is itself merely a possible empirical regress which I think to myself, though in an indeterminate manner. Only in this way can the concept of such a series of conditions for a given perception arise at all.[a] Now we have the cosmic

A 519}
B 547}

whole only in concept, never, as a whole, in intuition. We cannot, therefore, argue from the magnitude of the cosmic whole to the magnitude of the regress, determining the latter in accordance with the former; on the contrary, only by reference to the magnitude of the empirical regress am I in a position to make for myself a concept of the magnitude of the world. But of this empirical regress the most that we can ever know is that from every given member of the series of conditions we have always still to advance empirically to a higher and more remote member. The magnitude of the whole of appearances is not thereby determined in any absolute manner; and we cannot therefore say that this regress proceeds to infinity. In doing so we should be anticipating members which the regress has not yet reached, representing their number as so great that no empirical synthesis could attain thereto, and so should be determining the magnitude of the world (although only negatively) prior to the regress— which is impossible. Since the world is not given me, in its totality, through any intuition, neither is its magnitude given me prior to the regress. We cannot, therefore, say anything at all in regard to the magnitude of the world, not even that there is in it a regress *in infinitum*. All that we can do is to seek for the concept of its magnitude according to the rule which determines the empirical regress in it. This rule says no more than that, however far we may have attained in the series of empirical conditions, we should never assume an absolute

A 520}
B 548}

limit, but should subordinate every appearance, as conditioned, to another as its condition, and that we must advance to this condition. This is the *regressus in indefinitum*, which, as it determines no magnitude in the object, is clearly enough distinguishable from the *regressus in infinitum*.

[a] This cosmic series can, therefore, be neither greater nor smaller than the possible empirical regress upon which alone its concept rests. And since this regress can yield neither a determinate infinite nor a determinate finite (that is, anything absolutely limited), it is evident that the magnitude of the world can be taken neither as finite nor as infinite. The regress, through which it is represented, allows of neither alternative.

I cannot say, therefore, that the world is *infinite* in space or as regards past time. Any such concept of magnitude, as being that of a given infinitude, is empirically impossible, and therefore, in reference to the world as an object of the senses, also absolutely impossible. Nor can I say that the regress from a given perception to all that limits it in a series, whether in space or in past time, proceeds to *infinity*; that would be to presuppose that the world has infinite magnitude. I also cannot say that the regress is *finite*; an absolute limit is likewise empirically impossible. Thus I can say nothing regarding the whole object of experience, the world of sense; I must limit my assertions to the rule which determines how experience, in conformity with its object, is to be obtained and further extended.

Thus the first and negative answer to the cosmological problem regarding the magnitude of the world is that the world has no first beginning in time and no outermost limit in space.

For if we suppose the opposite, the world would be limited on the one hand by empty time and on the other by empty {A 521 / B 549} space. Since, however, as appearance, it cannot in itself be limited in either manner—appearance not being a thing in itself—these limits of the world would have to be given in a possible experience, that is to say, we should require to have a perception of limitation by absolutely empty time or space. But such an experience, as completely empty of content, is impossible. Consequently, an absolute limit of the world is impossible empirically, and therefore also absolutely.[a]

The affirmative answer likewise directly follows, namely, that the regress in the series of appearances, as a determination of the magnitude of the world, proceeds *in indefinitum*.

---

[a] It may be noted that this proof is presented in a very different manner from the dogmatic proof of the antithesis of the first antinomy. In that argument we regarded the sensible world, in accordance with the common and dogmatic view, as a thing given in itself, in its totality, prior to any regress; and we asserted that unless it occupies all time and all places, it cannot have any determinate position whatsoever in them. The conclusion also was therefore different from that given above; for in the dogmatic proof we inferred the actual infinity of the world.

This is equivalent to saying that, although the sensible world has no absolute magnitude, the empirical regress (through which alone it can be given on the side of its conditions) has its own rule, namely, that it must always advance from every member of the series, as conditioned, to one still more remote; doing so by means either of our own experience, or of the guiding-thread of history, or of the chain of effects and causes. And as the rule further demands, our sole and constant aim must be the extension of the possible empirical employment of the understanding, this being the only proper task of reason in the application of its principles.

A 522
B 550

This rule does not prescribe a determinate empirical regress that must proceed without end in some one kind of appearance, *e.g.* that in proceeding from a living person through a series of progenitors we must never expect to meet with a first pair, or that in the series of cosmic bodies we must never admit an outermost sun. All that the rule requires is that the advance from appearances be to appearances; for even if these latter yield no actual perception (as is the case when for our consciousness they are too weak in degree to become experience), as appearances they none the less still belong to a possible experience.

All beginning is in time and all limits of the extended are in space. But space and time belong only to the world of sense. Accordingly, while appearances *in the world* are conditionally limited, *the world itself* is neither conditionally nor unconditionally limited.

Similarly, since the world can never be given as *complete*, and since even the series of conditions for that which is given as conditioned cannot, as a cosmic series, be given as *complete*, the concept of the magnitude of the world is given only through the regress and not in a collective intuition prior to it. But the regress consists only in the *determining* of the magnitude, and does not give any *determinate* concept. It does not, therefore, yield any concept of a magnitude which, in relation to a certain [unit-] measure, can be described as infinite. In other words, the regress does not proceed to the infinite, as if the infinite could be given, but only indeterminately far, in order [by means of the regress] to give that empirical magnitude which first becomes actual in and through this very regress.

A 523
B 551

II

*Solution of the Cosmological Idea of the Totality of
Division of a Whole given in Intuition*

If we divide a whole which is given in intuition, we proceed from something conditioned to the conditions of its possibility. The division of the parts (*subdivisio* or *decompositio*) is a regress in the series of these conditions. The absolute totality of this series would be given only if the regress could reach *simple* parts. But if all the parts in a continuously progressing decomposition are themselves again divisible, the division, that is, the regress from the conditioned to its conditions, proceeds *in infinitum*. For the conditions (the parts) are themselves contained in the conditioned, and since this is given complete in an intuition that is enclosed between {A 524 B 552} limits, the parts are one and all given together with the conditioned. The regress may not, therefore, be entitled merely a regress *in indefinitum*. This was permissible in regard to the first cosmological idea, since it required an advance from the conditioned to its conditions, which, as outside it, were not given through and along with it, but were first added to it in the empirical regress. We are not, however, entitled to say of a whole which is divisible to infinity, that *it is made up of infinitely many parts*. For although all parts are contained in the intuition of the whole, *the whole division* is not so contained, but consists only in the continuous decomposition, that is, in the regress itself, whereby the series first becomes actual. Since this regress is infinite, all the members or parts at which it arrives are contained in the given whole, viewed as an *aggregate*. But the whole *series of the division* is not so contained, for it is a successive infinite and never *whole*, and cannot, therefore, exhibit an infinite multiplicity, or any combination of an infinite multiplicity in a whole.

This general statement is obviously applicable to space. Every space intuited as within limits is such a whole, the parts of which, as obtained by decomposition, are always themselves spaces. Every limited space is therefore infinitely divisible.

From this a second application of the statement quite {A 525 B 553} naturally follows, namely, to an outer appearance enclosed

within limits, that is, to body. Its divisibility is grounded in
the divisibility of space, which constitutes the possibility of the
body as an extended whole. Body is therefore infinitely divisible, without consisting, however, of infinitely many parts.

It may seem, indeed, that a body, since it has to be represented in space as *substance*, will, as regards the law of the
divisibility of space, differ from space. We may certainly grant
that decomposition can never remove all compositeness from
space; for that would mean that space, in which there is
nothing self-subsistent, had ceased to be space, which is impossible. On the other hand, the assertion that if all compositeness
of matter be thought away nothing at all will remain, does not
appear to be compatible with the concept of a substance which
is meant to be the subject of all compositeness, and which
must persist in the elements of the composite, even although
the connection in space, whereby they constitute a body, be
removed. But while this is true of a thing in itself, as thought
through a pure concept of the understanding, it does not hold
of that which we entitle substance in the [field of] *appearance*.
For this latter is not an absolute subject, but only an abiding
image[1] of sensibility; it is nothing at all save as an intuition,
in which unconditionedness is never to be met with.

A 526⎱
B 554⎰

But although this rule of progress *in infinitum* undoubtedly
applies to the subdivision of an appearance, viewed as a mere
filling of space, it cannot be made to apply to a whole in which
already, as given, the parts are so definitely distinguished off
from one another that they constitute a *quantum discretum*.
We cannot assume that every part of an organised whole is
itself again so organised that, in the analysis of the parts to
infinity, still other organised parts[2] are always to be met with;
in a word, that the whole is organised to infinity. This is not a
thinkable hypothesis. It is true, indeed, that the parts of matter,
[as found] in their decomposition *in infinitum*, may be organised. The infinitude of the division of a given appearance in
space is grounded solely on the fact that, through this infinitude, only the divisibility (in itself, as regards the number of its
parts, absolutely indeterminate) is given—the parts themselves
being given and determined only through the subdivision. In
a word, the whole is not in itself already divided. The number

[1] [*beharrliches Bild.*]   [2] [*Kunstteile.*]

of parts, therefore, which a division may determine in a whole,
will depend upon how far we care to advance in the regress of
the division. On the other hand, in the case of an organic body {A 527
conceived as organised *in infinitum* the whole is represented {B 555
as already divided into parts, and as yielding to us, prior to all
regress, a determinate and yet infinite number of parts. This,
however, is self-contradictory. This infinite involution is regarded as an infinite (that is, never to be completed) series,
and yet at the same time as completed in a [discrete] complex.[1] Infinite divisibility belongs to appearance only in so
far as it is a *quantum continuum*; it is inseparable from the
occupation of space, which is indeed its ground. To view anything as being a *quantum discretum*, is to take the number of
units in it as being determined, and therefore as being in every
case equal to some number. How far organisation can go in an
organised body, only experience can show; and although, so
far as our experience has gone, we may not have arrived with
certainty at any inorganic part, the *possibility* of experiencing
such parts must at least be recognised. When, however, we
have in mind the transcendental division of an appearance
in general, the question how far it may extend does not await
an answer from experience; it is decided by a principle of
reason which prescribes that, in the decomposition of the extended, the empirical regress, in conformity with the nature of
this appearance, be never regarded as absolutely completed.

Concluding Note on the Solution of the Mathematical-trans- {A 528
cendental Ideas, and Preliminary Observation on the Solution of {B 556
the Dynamical-transcendental Ideas.

   In representing the antinomy of pure reason, through all
the transcendental ideas, in tabular form, and in showing that
the ground of this conflict and the only means of removing it
is by declaring both the opposed assertions to be false, we have
represented the conditions as, in all cases, standing to the conditioned in relations of space and time. This is the assumption
ordinarily made by the common understanding, and to it the
conflict is exclusively due. On this view all the dialectical
representations of totality, in the series of conditions for a
given conditioned, are throughout of the same character. The

_____
[1] [*Zusammennehmung.*]

condition is always a member of a series along with the conditioned, and so is *homogeneous* with it. In such a series
the regress was never thought as completed, or if it had to be
so thought, a member, in itself conditioned, must have been
falsely supposed to be a first member, and therefore to be
unconditioned; the object, that is, the conditioned, might not
always be considered merely according to its magnitude, but at
least the series of its conditions was so regarded. Thus arose the
difficulty—a difficulty which could not be disposed of by any
compromise but solely by cutting the knot—that reason made
the series either too long or too short for the understanding, so
that the understanding could never be equal to the prescribed
idea.

But in all this we have been overlooking an essential distinction that obtains among the objects, that is, among those
concepts of understanding which reason endeavours to raise
to ideas. According to the table of categories given above, two
of these concepts imply a *mathematical*, the other two a
dynamical synthesis of appearances. Hitherto it has not been
necessary to take account of this distinction; for just as in the
general representation of all transcendental ideas we have
been conforming to conditions within the [field of] appearance,
so in the two mathematical-transcendental ideas the only
object we have had in mind is object as appearance. But now
that we are proceeding to consider how far *dynamical* concepts of the understanding are adequate to the idea of reason,
the distinction becomes of importance, and opens up to us an
entirely new view of the suit in which reason is implicated.
This suit, in our previous trial of it, has been *dismissed* as
resting, on both sides, on false presuppositions. But since in
the dynamical antinomy a presupposition compatible with the
pretensions of reason may perhaps be found, and since the
judge may perhaps make good what is lacking in the pleas
which both sides have been guilty of misstating, the suit may
be settled to the satisfaction of both parties, a procedure impossible in the case of the mathematical antinomies.

If we consider solely the *extension*[1] of the series of conditions, and whether the series are adequate to the idea, or the
idea too large or too small for the series, the series are indeed in

A 529
B 557

A 530
B 558

---

[1] [*Erstreckung.*]

these respects all homogeneous. But the concept of the under-standing, which underlies these ideas, may contain either a synthesis solely of the *homogeneous* (which is presupposed alike in the composition and in the division of every magni-tude), or a synthesis of the *heterogeneous*. For the hetero-geneous can be admitted as at least possible in the case of dynamical synthesis, alike in causal connection and in the connection of the necessary with the contingent.

Hence in the mathematical connection of the series of appearances no other than a *sensible* condition is admissible, that is to say, none that is not itself a part of the series. On the other hand, in the dynamical series of sensible conditions, a heterogeneous condition, not itself a part of the series, but *purely intelligible*, and as such outside the series, can be allowed. In this way reason obtains satisfaction and the {A 531 {B 559 unconditioned is set prior to the appearances, while yet the invariably conditioned character of the appearances is not obscured, nor their series cut short, in violation of the principles prescribed by the understanding.

Inasmuch as the dynamical ideas allow of a condition of appearances outside the series of the appearances, that is, a condition which is not itself appearance, we arrive at a con-clusion altogether different from any that was possible in the case of the mathematical antinomy.[1] In it we were obliged to denounce both the opposed dialectical assertions as false. In the dynamical series, on the other hand, the completely conditioned, which is inseparable from the series considered as appearances, is bound up with a condition which, while indeed empirically unconditioned, is also *non-sensible*. We are thus able to obtain satisfaction for *understanding* on the one hand and for *reason* on the other.[a] The dialectical

---

[a] Understanding does not admit *among appearances* any condi-tion which can itself be empirically unconditioned. But if for some conditioned in the [field of] appearance we can conceive an *intellig-ible* condition, not belonging to the series of appearances as one of its members, and can do so without in the least interrupting the series of empirical conditions, such a condition may be accepted as *empirically unconditioned*, without prejudice to the continuity of the empirical regress.

[1] [Reading, with Hartenstein, *der mathematischen Antinomie* for *der Anti-nomie*.]

arguments, which in one or other way sought unconditioned totality in mere appearances, fall to the ground, and the propositions of reason, when thus given this more correct interpretation, may *both* alike be *true*. This can never be the case with those cosmological ideas which refer only to a mathematically unconditioned unity; for in them no condition of the series of appearances can be found that is not itself appearance, and as appearance one of the members of the series.

III

Solution of the Cosmological Idea[1] *of Totality in the Derivation of Cosmical Events from their Causes*

When we are dealing with what happens there are only two kinds of causality conceivable by us; the causality is either according to *nature* or arises from *freedom*. The former is the connection in the sensible world of one state with a preceding state on which it follows according to a rule. Since the causality of appearances rests on conditions of time, and the preceding state, if it had always existed, could not have produced an effect which first comes into being in time, it follows that the causality of the cause of that which happens or comes into being must itself also have *come into being*, and that in accordance with the principle of the understanding it must in its turn itself require a cause.

By freedom, on the other hand, in its cosmological meaning, I understand the power of beginning a state *spontaneously*.[2] Such causality will not, therefore, itself stand under another cause determining it in time, as required by the law of nature. Freedom, in this sense, is a pure transcendental idea, which, in the first place, contains nothing borrowed from experience, and which, secondly, refers to an object that cannot be determined or given in any experience. That everything which happens has a cause is a universal law, conditioning the very possibility of all experience. Hence the causality of the cause, which *itself happens* or comes to be, must itself in turn have a cause; and thus the entire field of experience, however far it may extend, is transformed into a sum-total of the merely natural. But since in this way no absolute totality of

---

[1] [Reading, with Erdmann, *Idee* for *Ideen*.]　　　[2] [*von selbst*.]

conditions determining causal relation can be obtained, reason creates for itself the idea of a spontaneity which can begin to act of itself, without requiring to be determined to action by an antecedent cause in accordance with the law of causality.

It should especially be noted that the practical concept of freedom is based on this *transcendental* idea, and that in the latter lies the real source of the difficulty by which the question of the possibility of freedom has always been beset. Freedom in the practical sense is the will's[1] independence of $\left\{ \begin{smallmatrix} A & 534 \\ B & 562 \end{smallmatrix} \right.$ coercion through sensuous impulses. For a will is sensuous, in so far as it is *pathologically affected*, *i.e.* by sensuous motives;[2] it is *animal* (*arbitrium brutum*), if it can be pathologically *necessitated*. The human will is certainly an *arbitrium sensitivum*, not, however, *brutum* but *liberum*. For sensibility does not necessitate its action. There is in man a power of self-determination, independently of any coercion through sensuous impulses.

Obviously, if all causality in the sensible world were mere nature, every event would be determined by another in time, in accordance with necessary laws. Appearances, in determining the will, would have in the actions of the will their natural effects, and would render the actions necessary. The denial of transcendental freedom must, therefore, involve the elimination of all practical freedom. For practical freedom presupposes that although something has not happened, it *ought* to have happened, and that its cause, [as found] in the [field of] appearance, is not, therefore, so determining that it excludes a causality of our will—a causality which, independently of those natural causes, and even contrary to their force and influence, can produce something that is determined in the time-order in accordance with empirical laws, and which can therefore begin a series of events *entirely of itself*.

Here then, as always happens when reason, in venturing $\left\{ \begin{smallmatrix} A & 535 \\ B & 563 \end{smallmatrix} \right.$ beyond the limits of possible experience, comes into conflict with itself, the problem is not really *physiological* but *transcendental*. The question as to the possibility of freedom does indeed concern psychology; since it rests on dialectical arguments of pure reason, its treatment and solution belong exclusively to transcendental philosophy. Before attempting

---

[1] [*Willkür.*]   [2] [*Bewegursachen.*]

this solution, a task which transcendental philosophy cannot decline, I must define somewhat more accurately the procedure of transcendental philosophy in dealing with the problem.

If appearances were things in themselves, and space and time forms of the existence of things in themselves, the conditions would always be members of the same series as the conditioned; and thus, in the present case, as in the other transcendental ideas, the antinomy would arise, that the series must be too large or too small for the understanding. But the dynamical concepts of reason, with which we have to deal in this and the following section, possess this peculiarity that they are not concerned with an object considered as a magnitude, but only with its existence. Accordingly we can abstract from the magnitude of the series of conditions, and consider only the dynami-

A 536
B 564

cal relation of the condition to the conditioned. The difficulty which then meets us, in dealing with the question regarding nature and freedom, is whether freedom is possible at all, and if it be possible, whether it can exist along with the universality of the natural law of causality. Is it a truly disjunctive proposition to say that every effect in the world must arise *either* from nature *or* from freedom; or must we not rather say that in one and the same event, in different relations, both can be found? That all events in the sensible world stand in thoroughgoing connection in accordance with unchangeable laws of nature is an established principle of the Transcendental Analytic, and allows of no exception. The question, therefore, can only be whether freedom is completely excluded by this inviolable rule, or whether an effect, notwithstanding its being thus determined in accordance with nature, may not at the same time be grounded in freedom. The common but fallacious presupposition of the *absolute reality* of appearances here manifests its injurious influence, to the confounding of reason. For if appearances are things in themselves, freedom cannot be upheld. Nature will then be the complete and sufficient determining cause of every event. The condition of the event will be such as can be found only in the series of appearances; both it and its effect will be necessary in accordance with the law of

A 537
B 565

nature. If, on the other hand, appearances are not taken for more than they actually are; if they are viewed not as things in themselves, but merely as representations, connected according to empirical laws, they must themselves have grounds which are not appearances. The effects of such an intelligible cause appear, and accordingly can be determined through other appearances, but its causality is not so determined. While the effects are to be found in the series of empirical conditions, the intelligible cause, together with its causality, is outside the series. Thus the effect may be regarded as free in respect of its intelligible cause, and at the same time in respect of appearances as resulting from them according to the necessity of nature. This distinction, when stated in this quite general and abstract manner, is bound to appear extremely subtle and obscure, but will become clear in the course of its application. My purpose has only been to point out that since the thoroughgoing connection of all appearances, in a context of nature, is an inexorable law, the inevitable consequence of obstinately insisting upon the reality of appearances is to destroy all freedom. Those who thus follow the common view have never been able to reconcile nature and freedom.

Possibility of Causality through Freedom, in Harmony with the $\begin{cases} \text{A } 538 \\ \text{B } 566 \end{cases}$ *Universal Law of Natural Necessity.*

Whatever in an object of the senses is not itself appearance, I entitle *intelligible*. If, therefore, that which in the sensible world must be regarded as appearance has in itself a faculty which is not an object of sensible intuition, but through which it can be the cause of appearances, the *causality* of this being can be regarded from two points of view. Regarded as the causality of a thing in itself, it is *intelligible* in its *action*; regarded as the causality of an appearance in the world of sense, it is *sensible* in its *effects*. We should therefore have to form both an empirical and an intellectual concept of the causality of the faculty of such a subject, and to regard both as referring to one and the same effect. This twofold manner of conceiving the faculty possessed by an object of the senses does not contradict any of the concepts which we have to form of appearances and of a possible experience. For since they are not things in themselves, they must rest upon a transcendental object which determines them as mere representations; and consequently there is nothing to prevent us from ascribing to this transcendental $\begin{cases} \text{A } 539 \\ \text{B } 567 \end{cases}$

object, besides the quality in terms of which[1] it appears, a *causality* which is not appearance, although its *effect* is to be met with in appearance. Every efficient cause must have a *character*,[2] that is, a law of its causality, without which it would not be a cause. On the above supposition, we should, therefore, in a subject belonging to the sensible world have, first, an *empirical character*, whereby its actions, as appearances, stand in thoroughgoing connection with other appearances in accordance with unvarying laws of nature. And since these actions can be derived from the other appearances, they constitute together with them a single series in the order of nature. Secondly, we should also have to allow the subject an *intelligible character*, by which it is indeed the cause of those same actions [in their quality] as appearances, but which does not itself stand under any conditions of sensibility, and is not itself appearance. We can entitle the former the character of the thing in the [field of] appearance, and the latter its character as thing in itself.

Now this acting subject would not, in its intelligible character, stand under any conditions of time; time is only a condition of appearances, not of things in themselves. In this subject no *action* would *begin* or *cease*, and it would not, there-

A 540⎫
B 568⎭ fore, have to conform to the law of the determination of all that is alterable in time, namely, that everything *which happens* must have its cause in the *appearances* which precede it. In a word, its causality, so far as it is intelligible,[3] would not have a place in the series of those empirical conditions through which the event is rendered necessary in the world of sense. This intelligible character can never, indeed, be immediately known, for nothing can be perceived except in so far as it appears. It would have to be *thought* in accordance with the empirical character—just as we are constrained to think a transcendental object as underlying appearances, though we know nothing of what it is in itself.

In its empirical character, therefore, this subject, as appearance, would have to conform to all the laws of causal determination. To this extent it could be nothing more than a part of the world of sense, and its effects, like all other

---

[1] [*dadurch.*]   [2] [*Charakter.*]
[3] [*intellektuell.* In all other cases Kant employs the less misleading term *intelligibel.*]

appearances, must be the inevitable outcome of nature. In proportion as outer appearances are found to influence it, and in proportion as its empirical character, that is, the law of its causality, becomes known through experience, all its actions must admit of explanation in accordance with the laws of nature. In other words, all that is required for their complete and necessary determination must be found in a possible experience.

In its intelligible character (though we can only have a general concept of that character) this same subject must be { A 541 / B 569 } considered to be free from all influence of sensibility and from all determination through appearances. Inasmuch as it is *noumenon*, nothing *happens* in it; there can be no change requiring dynamical determination in time, and therefore no causal dependence upon appearances. And consequently, since natural necessity is to be met with only in the sensible world, this active being must in its actions be independent of, and free from all such necessity. No action begins *in* this active being itself; but we may yet quite correctly say that the active being *of itself* begins its effects in the sensible world. In so doing, we should not be asserting that the effects in the sensible world can begin of themselves; they are always predetermined through antecedent empirical conditions, though solely through their empirical character (which is no more than the appearance of the intelligible), and so are only possible as a continuation of the series of natural causes. In this way freedom and nature, in the full sense of these terms, can exist together, without any conflict, in the same actions, according as the actions are referred to their intelligible or to their sensible cause.

Explanation of the Cosmological Idea of Freedom in its con- { A 542 / B 570 } *nection with Universal Natural Necessity.*

I have thought it advisable to give this outline sketch of the solution of our transcendental problem, so that we may be the better enabled to survey the course which reason has to adopt in arriving at the solution. I shall now proceed to set forth the various factors involved in this solution, and to consider each in detail.

That everything which happens has a cause, is a law of nature. Since the causality of this cause, that is, the *action* of

the cause, is antecedent in time to the effect which has *ensued* upon it, it cannot itself have always existed, but must have *happened*, and *among the appearances* must have a cause by which it in turn is determined. Consequently, all events are empirically determined in an order of nature. Only in virtue of this law can appearances constitute a *nature* and become objects of experience. This law is a law of the understanding, from which no departure can be permitted, and from which no appearance may be exempted. To allow such exemption would be to set an appearance outside all possible experience,
A 543 ⎱
B 571 ⎰ to distinguish it from all objects of possible experience, and so to make of it a mere thought-entity, a phantom of the brain.

This would seem to imply the existence of a chain of causes which in the regress to their conditions allows of no *absolute totality*. But that need not trouble us. The point has already been dealt with in the general discussion of the antinomy into which reason falls when in the series of appearances it proceeds to the unconditioned. Were we to yield to the illusion of transcendental realism, neither nature nor freedom would remain. The only question here is this:—Admitting that in the whole series of events there is nothing but natural necessity, is it yet possible to regard one and the same event as being in one aspect merely an effect of nature and in another aspect an effect due to freedom; or is there between these two kinds of causality a direct contradiction?

Among the causes in the [field of] appearance there certainly cannot be anything which could begin a series absolutely and of itself. Every action, [viewed] as appearance, in so far as it gives rise to an event, is itself an event or happening, and presupposes another state wherein its cause is to be found. Thus everything which happens is merely a continuation of the series, and nothing that begins of itself is a possible mem-
A 544 ⎱
B 572 ⎰ ber of the series. The actions of natural causes in the time-sequence are thus themselves effects; they presuppose causes antecedent to them in the temporal series. An *original* act, such as can by itself bring about what did not exist before, is not to be looked for in the causally connected appearances.

Now granting that effects are appearances and that their cause is likewise appearance, is it necessary that the causality of their cause should be exclusively empirical? May it not rather be, that while for every effect in the [field of] appearance a connection with its cause in accordance with the laws of empirical causality is indeed required, this empirical causality, without the least violation of its connection with natural causes, is itself an effect of a causality that is not empirical but intelligible? This latter causality would be the action of a cause which, in respect of appearances, is original, and therefore, as pertaining to this faculty, not appearance but intelligible; although it must otherwise, in so far as it is a link in the chain of nature, be regarded as entirely belonging to the world of sense.

The principle of the causal connection of appearances is required in order that we may be able to look for and to determine the natural conditions of natural events, that is to say, their causes in the [field of] appearance. If this principle be admitted, and be not weakened through any exception, the requirements of the understanding, which in its empirical employment sees in all happenings nothing but nature, and is $\left\{ \begin{matrix} A & 545 \\ B & 573 \end{matrix} \right.$ justified in so doing, are completely satisfied; and physical explanations may proceed on their own lines without interference. These requirements are not in any way infringed, if we assume, even though the assumption should be a mere fiction, that some among the natural causes have a faculty which is intelligible only, inasmuch as its determination to action never rests upon empirical conditions, but solely on grounds of understanding. We must, of course, at the same time be able to assume that the *action* of these causes *in the [field of] appearance* is in conformity with all the laws of empirical causality. In this way the acting subject, as *causa phaenomenon*, would be bound up with nature through the indissoluble dependence of all its actions, and only as we ascend from the empirical object to the transcendental should we find that this subject, together with all its causality in the [field of] appearance, has in its *noumenon*[1] certain conditions which must be regarded as purely intelligible. For if in determining in what ways appearances can serve as causes we follow the rules of nature, we need not concern ourselves what kind of ground for these appearances and their connection may have to be thought as existing in the transcendental subject, which is empirically

---

[1] [Reading, with Hartenstein, *noumenon* for *phaenomenon*.]

unknown to us. This intelligible ground does not have to be considered in empirical enquiries; it concerns only thought

in the pure understanding; and although the effects of this thought and action of the pure understanding are to be met with in the appearances, these appearances must none the less be capable of complete causal explanation in terms of other appearances in accordance with natural laws. We have to take their strictly empirical character as the supreme ground of explanation, leaving entirely out of account their intelligible character (that is, the transcendental cause of their empirical character) as being completely unknown, save in so far as the empirical serves for its sensible sign.

Let us apply this to experience. Man is one of the appearances of the sensible world, and in so far one of the natural causes the causality of which must stand under empirical laws. Like all other things in nature, he must have an empirical character. This character we come to know through the powers and faculties which he reveals in his actions.[1] In lifeless, or merely animal, nature we find no ground for thinking that any faculty is conditioned otherwise than in a merely sensible manner. Man, however, who knows all the rest of nature solely through the senses, knows himself also through pure[2] apperception; and this, indeed, in acts and inner determinations which he cannot regard as impressions of the senses. He is thus to himself, on the one hand phenomenon, and on the other hand, in respect of certain faculties the

action of which cannot be ascribed to the receptivity of sensibility, a purely[3] intelligible object. We entitle these faculties understanding and reason. The latter, in particular, we distinguish in a quite peculiar and especial way from all empirically conditioned powers. For it views its objects exclusively[3] in the light of ideas, and in accordance with them determines the understanding, which then proceeds to make an empirical use of its own similarly pure concepts.

That our reason has causality, or that we at least represent it to ourselves as having causality, is evident from the *imperatives* which in all matters of conduct we impose as rules upon our active powers. '*Ought*' expresses a kind of necessity and of connection with grounds which is found nowhere else in the

---

[1] [*Wirkungen.*]   [2] [*blosse.*]   [3] [*bloss.*]

whole of nature. The understanding can know in nature only what is, what has been, or what will be. We cannot say that anything in nature *ought to be* other than what in all these time-relations it actually is. When we have the course of nature alone in view, '*ought*' has no meaning whatsoever. It is just as absurd to ask what ought to happen in the natural world as to ask what properties a circle ought to have. All that we are justified in asking is: what happens in nature? what are the properties of the circle?

This '*ought*' expresses a possible action the ground of which cannot be anything but a mere concept; whereas in the case of a merely natural action the ground must always be an appearance. The action to which the '*ought*' applies must indeed be possible under natural conditions. These conditions, however, do not play any part in determining the will itself, but only in determining the effect and its consequences in the [field of] appearance. No matter how many natural grounds or how many sensuous impulses may impel me to *will*, they can never give rise to the '*ought*', but only to a willing which, while very far from being necessary, is always conditioned; and the '*ought*' pronounced by reason confronts such willing with a limit and an end—nay more, forbids or authorises it. Whether what is willed be an object of mere sensibility (the pleasant) or of pure reason (the good), reason will not give way to any ground which is empirically given. Reason does not here follow the order of things as they present themselves in appearance, but frames for itself with perfect spontaneity an order of its own according to ideas, to which it adapts the empirical conditions, and according to which it declares actions to be necessary, even although they have never taken place, and perhaps never will take place. And at the same time reason also presupposes that it can have causality in regard to all these actions, since otherwise no empirical effects could be expected from its ideas. {A 548 / B 576

Now, in view of these considerations, let us take our stand, and regard it as at least possible for reason to have causality with respect to appearances. Reason though it be, it must none the less exhibit an empirical character. For every cause presupposes a rule according to which certain appearances follow as effects; and every rule requires uniformity in the effects. This uniformity is, indeed, that upon which the {A 549 / B 577 concept of cause (as a faculty) is based, and so far as it must be exhibited by mere appearances may be named the empirical character of the cause. This character is permanent, but its effects, according to variation in the concomitant and in part limiting conditions, appear in changeable forms.

Thus the will of every man has an empirical character, which is nothing but a certain causality of his reason, so far as that causality exhibits, in its effects in the [field of] appearance, a rule from which we may gather what, in their kind and degrees, are the actions of reason and the grounds thereof, and so may form an estimate concerning the subjective principles of his will. Since this empirical character must itself be discovered from the appearances which are its effect and from the rule to which experience shows them to conform, it follows that all the actions of men in the [field of] appearance are determined in conformity with the order of nature, by their empirical character and by the other causes which co-operate with that character; and if we could exhaustively investigate all the appearances of men's wills, there would not be found a single human action which we could not predict with certainty, and recognise as proceeding necessarily from its antecedent conditions. So far, then, as regards this empirical character there is no freedom; and yet it is only in the light of this character that man can be studied—if, that is to say, we are simply *observing*, and in the manner of anthropology seeking to institute a physiological investigation into the motive causes of his actions.

But when we consider these actions in their relation to reason—I do not mean speculative reason, by which we endeavour *to explain* their coming into being, but reason in so far as it is itself the cause *producing* them—if, that is to say, we compare them with [the standards of] reason in its *practical* bearing, we find a rule and order altogether different from the order of nature. For it may be that all that *has happened* in the course of nature, and in accordance with its empirical grounds must inevitably have happened, *ought not to have happened*. Sometimes, however, we find, or at least believe that we find, that the ideas of reason have in actual fact proved their causality in respect of the actions of men, as appearances; and that these actions have taken place, not because they were

A 550
B 578

determined by empirical causes, but because they were determined by grounds of reason.

Granted, then, that reason may be asserted to have causality in respect of appearance, its action can still be said to be free, even although its empirical character (as a mode of sense[1]) is completely and necessarily determined in all its detail. This empirical character is itself determined in the intelligible character (as a mode of thought[2]). The latter, however, we do not know; we can only indicate its nature by means of appearances; and these really yield an immediate knowledge only of the mode of sense, the empirical character.[a] The action, in so far as it can be ascribed to a mode of thought as its cause, does not *follow* therefrom in accordance with empirical laws; that is to say, it is not *preceded* by the conditions of pure reason, but only by their effects in the [field of] appearance of inner sense. Pure reason, as a purely intelligible faculty, is not subject to the form of time, nor consequently to the conditions of succession in time. The causality of reason in its intelligible character does not, in producing an effect, *arise* or begin to be at a certain time. For in that case it would itself be subject to the natural law of appearances, in accordance with which causal series are determined in time; and its causality would then be nature, not freedom. Thus all that we are justified in saying is that, if reason can have causality in respect of appearances, it is a faculty *through* which the sensible condition of an empirical series of effects first begins. For the condition which lies in reason is not sensible, and therefore does not itself begin to be. And thus what we failed to find in any empirical series is disclosed as being possible, namely, that the condition of a successive series of events may itself be empirically unconditioned. For

$\left\{ \begin{matrix} A\ 551 \\ B\ 579 \end{matrix} \right.$

$\left\{ \begin{matrix} A\ 552 \\ B\ 580 \end{matrix} \right.$

---

[a] The real morality of actions, their merit or guilt, even that of our own conduct, thus remains entirely hidden from us. Our imputations can refer only to the empirical character. How much of this character is ascribable to the pure effect of freedom, how much to mere nature, that is, to faults of temperament for which there is no responsibility, or to its happy constitution (*merito fortunae*), can never be determined; and upon it therefore no perfectly just judgments can be passed.

[1] [*Sinnesart.*]   [2] [*Denkungsart.*]

here the condition is *outside* the series of appearances (in the intelligible), and therefore is not subject to any sensible condition, and to no time-determination through an antecedent cause.

The same cause does, indeed, in another relation, belong to the series of appearances. Man is himself an appearance. His will has an empirical character, which is the empirical cause of all his actions. There is no condition determining man in accordance with this character which is not contained in the series of natural effects, or which is not subject to their law—the law according to which there can be no empirically unconditioned causality of that which happens in time. Therefore no given action (since it can be perceived only as appearance) can begin absolutely of itself. But of pure reason we cannot say that the state wherein the will is determined is preceded and itself determined by some other state. For since reason is not itself an appearance, and is not subject to any conditions of sensibility, it follows that even as regards its causality there is in it no time-sequence, and that the dynamical law of nature, which determines succession in time in accordance with rules, is not applicable to it.

A 553
B 581

Reason is the abiding condition of all those actions of the will under [the guise of] which man appears. Before ever they have happened, they are one and all predetermined in the empirical character. In respect of the intelligible character, of which the empirical character is the sensible schema, there can be no *before* and *after*; every action, irrespective of its relation in time to other appearances, is the immediate effect of the intelligible character of pure reason. Reason therefore acts freely; it is not dynamically determined in the chain of natural causes through either outer or inner grounds antecedent in time. This freedom ought not, therefore, to be conceived only negatively as independence of empirical conditions. The faculty of reason, so regarded, would cease to be a cause of appearances. It must also be described in positive terms, as the power of originating a series of events. In reason itself nothing begins; as unconditioned condition of every voluntary act, it admits of no conditions antecedent to itself in time. Its effect has, indeed, a beginning in the series of appearances, but never in this series an absolutely first beginning.

A 554
B 582

In order to illustrate this regulative principle of reason by an example of its empirical employment—not, however, to confirm it, for it is useless to endeavour to prove transcendental propositions by examples—let us take a voluntary action, for example, a malicious lie by which a certain confusion has been caused in society. First of all, we endeavour to discover the motives to which it has been due, and then, secondly, in the light of these, we proceed to determine how far the action and its consequences can be imputed to the offender. As regards the first question, we trace the empirical character of the action to its sources, finding these in defective education, bad company, in part also in the viciousness of a natural disposition insensitive to shame, in levity and thoughtlessness, not neglecting to take into account also the occasional causes that may have intervened. We proceed in this enquiry just as we should in ascertaining for a given natural effect the series of its determining causes. But although we believe that the action is thus determined, we none the less blame the agent, not indeed on account {A 555 / B 583} of his unhappy disposition, nor on account of the circumstances that have influenced him, nor even on account of his previous way of life; for we presuppose that we can leave out of consideration what this way of life may have been, that we can regard the past series of conditions as not having occurred and the act as being completely unconditioned by any preceding state, just as if the agent in and by himself began in this action an entirely new series of consequences. Our blame is based on a law of reason whereby we regard reason as a cause that irrespective of all the above-mentioned empirical conditions could have determined, and ought to have determined, the agent to act otherwise. This causality of reason we do not regard as only a co-operating agency, but as complete in itself, even when the sensuous impulses do not favour but are directly opposed to it; the action is ascribed to the agent's intelligible character; in the moment when he utters the lie, the guilt is entirely his. Reason, irrespective of all empirical conditions of the act, is completely free, and the lie is entirely due to its default.

Such imputation clearly shows that we consider reason to be unaffected by these sensible influences, and not liable to alteration. Its appearances—the modes in which it manifests

A 556⎱
B 584⎰ itself in its effects—do alter; but in itself [so we consider] there is no preceding state determining the state that follows. That is to say, it does not belong to the series of sensible conditions which render appearances necessary in accordance with laws of nature. Reason is present in all the actions of men at all times and under all circumstances, and is always the same; but it is not itself in time, and does not fall into any new state in which it was not before. In respect to new states, it is *determining*, not *determinable*. We may not, therefore, ask why reason has not determined *itself* differently, but only why it has not through its causality determined the *appearances* differently. But to this question no answer is possible. For a different intelligible character would have given a different empirical character. When we say that in spite of his whole previous course of life the agent could have refrained from lying, this only means that the act is under the immediate power of reason, and that reason in its causality is not subject to any conditions of appearance or of time. Although difference of time makes a fundamental difference to appearances in their relations to one another—for appearances are not things in themselves and therefore not causes in themselves—it can make no difference to the relation in which the action stands to reason.

A 557⎱
B 585⎰ Thus in our judgments in regard to the causality of free actions, we can get as far as the intelligible cause, but not beyond it. We can know that it is free, that is, that it is deter‐ mined independently of sensibility, and that in this way it may be the sensibly unconditioned condition of appearances. But to explain why in the given circumstances the intelligible char‐ acter should give just these appearances and this empirical character transcends all the powers of our reason, indeed all its rights of questioning, just as if we were to ask why the trans‐ cendental object of our outer sensible intuition gives intuition in *space* only and not some other mode of intuition. But the problem which we have to solve does not require us to raise any such questions. Our problem was this only: whether freedom and natural necessity can exist without conflict in one and the same action; and this we have sufficiently answered. We have shown that since freedom may stand in relation to a quite different kind of conditions from those of natural necessity, the law of the latter does not affect the former, and that both

may exist, independently of one another and without inter-
fering with each other

*   *   *

The reader should be careful to observe that in what has
been said our intention has not been to establish the *reality*
of freedom as one of the faculties which contain the cause of {A 558 B 586}
the appearances of our sensible world. For that enquiry, as it
does not deal with concepts alone, would not have been transcendental. And further, it could not have been successful,
since we can never infer from experience anything which cannot be thought in accordance with the laws of experience. It
has not even been our intention to prove the *possibility* of
freedom. For in this also we should not have succeeded, since
we cannot from mere concepts *a priori* know the possibility
of any real ground and its causality. Freedom is here being
treated only as a transcendental idea whereby reason is led to
think that it can begin the series of conditions in the [field of]
appearance by means of the sensibly unconditioned, and so
becomes involved in an antinomy with those very laws which
it itself prescribes to the empirical employment of the understanding. What we have alone been able to show, and what we
have alone been concerned to show, is that this antinomy rests
on a sheer illusion, and that causality through freedom is at
least *not incompatible with* nature.

IV

Solution of the Cosmological Idea of the Totality of the De- {A 559 B 587}
  pendence of Appearances as regards their Existence in
  general

In the preceding subsection we have considered the changes
of the sensible world in so far as they form a dynamical
series, each member being subordinate to another as effect to
cause. We shall now employ this series of states merely to
guide us in our search for an existence that may serve as
the supreme condition of all that is alterable, that is, in
our search for *necessary being*. We are concerned here, not
with unconditioned causality, but with the unconditioned
existence of substance itself. The series which we have in

view is, therefore, really a series of concepts, not a series of intuitions in which one intuition is the condition of the other.

But it is evident that since everything in the sum-total of appearances is alterable, and therefore conditioned in its existence, there cannot be in the whole series of dependent existence any unconditioned member the existence of which can be regarded as absolutely necessary. Hence, if appearances were things in themselves, and if, as would then follow, the condition and the conditioned always belonged to one and the same series of intuitions, by no possibility could a necessary being exist as the condition of the existence of appearances in the world of sense.

A 560
B 588

The dynamical regress is distinguished in an important respect from the mathematical. Since the mathematical regress is concerned only with the combining of parts to form a whole or the division of a whole into parts, the conditions of this series must always be regarded as parts of the series, and therefore as homogeneous and as appearances. In the dynamical regress, on the other hand, we are concerned, not with the possibility of an unconditioned whole of given parts, or with an unconditioned part for a given whole, but with the derivation of a state from its cause, or of the contingent existence of substance itself from necessary existence.[1] In this latter regress, it is not, therefore, necessary that the condition should form part of an empirical series along with the conditioned.

A way of escape from this apparent antinomy thus lies open to us. Both of the conflicting propositions may be true, if taken in different connections. All things in the world of sense may be contingent, and so have only an empirically conditioned existence, while yet there may be a non-empirical condition of the whole series; that is, there may exist an unconditionally necessary being. This necessary being, as the intelligible condition of the series, would not belong to it as a member, not even as the highest member of it, nor would it render any member of the series empirically unconditioned. The whole sensible world, so far as regards the empirically conditioned existence of all its various members, would be left unaffected. This way of conceiving how an unconditioned

A 561
B 589

[1] [Reading *dem* for *der*.]

being may serve as the ground of appearance differs from that which we followed in the preceding subsection, in dealing with the empirically unconditioned causality of freedom. For there the thing itself was as cause (*substantia phaenomenon*) conceived to belong to the series of conditions, and only its *causality* was thought as intelligible. Here, on the other hand, the necessary being must be thought as entirely outside the series of the sensible world (as *ens extramundanum*), and as purely intelligible. In no other way can it be secured against the law which renders all appearances contingent and dependent.

The *regulative principle of reason*, so far as it bears upon our present problem, is therefore this, that everything in the sensible world has an empirically conditioned existence, and that in no one of its qualities can it be unconditionally necessary; that for every member in the series of conditions we must expect, and as far as possible seek, an empirical condition in some possible experience; and that nothing justifies us in deriving an existence from a condition outside the empirical series or even in regarding it in its place within the series as absolutely independent and self-sufficient. At the same time this principle does not in any way debar us from recognising that the whole series may rest upon some intelligible being {A 562 / B 590} that is free from all empirical conditions and itself contains the ground of the possibility of all appearances.

In these remarks we have no intention of proving the unconditionally necessary existence of such a being, or even of establishing the possibility of a purely intelligible condition of the existence of appearances in the sensible world. Just as, on the one hand, we limit reason, lest in leaving the guiding-thread of the empirical conditions it should go straying into the *transcendent*, adopting grounds of explanation that are incapable of any representation *in concreto*, so, on the other hand, we limit the law of the purely empirical employment of the understanding, lest it should presume to decide as to the possibility of things in general, and should declare the intelligible to be *impossible*, merely on the ground that it is not of any use in explaining appearances. Thus all that we have shown is that the thoroughgoing contingency of all natural things, and of all their empirical conditions, is quite consistent with the optional assumption of a necessary, though purely intelligible, condition; and that as there is no real contradiction between the two assertions, *both may be true*. Such an absolutely necessary being, as conceived by the understanding,[1] may be in itself impossible, but this can in no wise be inferred from the universal contingency and dependence of everything belonging to the sensible world, nor from the principle which interdicts us from stopping at any one of its contingent members and from appealing to a cause outside the world. Reason proceeds by one path in its empirical use, and by yet another path in its transcendental use.

A 563
B 591

The sensible world contains nothing but appearances, and these are mere representations which are always sensibly conditioned; in this field things in themselves are never objects to us. It is not therefore surprising that in dealing with a member of the empirical series, no matter what member it may be, we are never justified in making a leap out beyond the context[2] of sensibility. To do so is to treat the appearances as if they were things in themselves which exist apart from their transcendental ground, and which can remain standing while we seek an outside cause of their existence. This certainly would ultimately be the case with contingent *things*, but not with mere *representations* of things, the contingency of which is itself merely phenomenon, and can lead to no other regress than that which determines the phenomena, that is, solely to the empirical regress. On the other hand, to think an *intelligible* ground of the appearances, that is, of the sensible world, and to think it as free from the contingency of appearances, does not conflict either with the unlimited empirical regress in the series of appearances nor with their thoroughgoing contingency. That, indeed, is all that we had to do in order to remove the apparent antinomy; and it can be done in this way only. If for everything conditioned in its existence the condition is always sensible, and therefore belongs to the series, it must itself in turn be conditioned, as we have shown in the antithesis of the fourth antinomy. Either, therefore, reason through its demand for the unconditioned must remain in conflict with itself, or this unconditioned must be posited outside the series, in the intelligible. Its necessity will not then

A 564
B 592

----

¹ [*Verstandeswesen.*]   ² [*ausser dem Zusammenhange.*]

require, or allow of, any empirical condition; so far as appearances are concerned, it will be unconditionally necessary.

The empirical employment of reason, in reference to the conditions of existence in the sensible world, is not affected by the admission of a purely intelligible being; it proceeds, in accordance with the principle of thoroughgoing contingency, from empirical conditions to higher conditions which are always again empirical. But it is no less true, when what we have in view is the pure employment of reason, in reference to ends,[1] that this regulative principle does not exclude the assumption of an intelligible cause which is *not* in the series. For the intelligible cause then signifies only the purely transcendental and to us unknown ground of the possibility of the sensible series in general. Its existence as independent of all sensible conditions and as in respect of these conditions unconditionally necessary, is not inconsistent with the unlimited contingency of appearances, that is to say, with the never-ending regress in the series of empirical conditions.

$\begin{cases} A\ 565 \\ B\ 593 \end{cases}$

Concluding Note on the whole Antinomy of Pure Reason.

So long as reason, in its concepts, has in view simply the totality of conditions in the sensible world, and is considering what satisfaction in this regard it can obtain for them, our ideas are at once transcendental and *cosmological.* Immediately, however, the unconditioned (and it is with this that we are really concerned) is posited in that which lies entirely outside the sensible world, and therefore outside all possible experience, the ideas become *transcendent.* They then no longer serve only for the completion of the empirical employment of reason —an[2] idea [of completeness] which must always be pursued, though it can never be completely achieved. On the contrary, they detach themselves completely from experience, and make for themselves objects for which experience supplies no material, and whose objective reality is not based on completion of the empirical series but on pure *a priori* concepts. Such transcendent ideas have a purely intelligible object; and this object may indeed be admitted as a transcendental object, but only if we likewise admit that, for the rest, we have no know-

---

[1] [*Zwecke.*]
[2] [Reading, with Erdmann, *die* for *der.*]

ledge in regard to it, and that it cannot be thought as a determinate thing in terms of distinctive inner predicates. As it is independent of all empirical concepts, we are cut off from any

A 566
B 594

reasons that could establish the possibility of such an object, and have not the least justification for assuming it. It is a mere thought-entity. Nevertheless the cosmological idea which has given rise to the fourth antinomy impels us to take this step. For the existence of appearances, which is never self-grounded but always conditioned, requires us to look around for something different from all appearances, that is, for an intelligible object in which this contingency may terminate. But once we have allowed ourselves to assume a self-subsistent reality entirely outside the field of sensibility, appearances can only be viewed[1] as contingent modes whereby beings that are themselves intelligences represent intelligible objects. Consequently, the only resource remaining to us is the use of analogy, by which we employ the concepts of experience in order to form some sort of concept of intelligible things—things of which as they are in themselves we have yet not the least knowledge. Since the contingent is not to be known save through experience, and we are here concerned with things which are not to be in any way objects of experience, we must derive the knowledge of them from that which is in itself necessary, that is, from pure concepts of things in general. Thus the

A 567
B 595

very first step which we take beyond the world of sense obliges us, in seeking for such new knowledge, to begin with an enquiry into absolutely necessary being, and to derive from the concepts of it the concepts of all things in so far as they are purely intelligible. This we propose to do in the next chapter.

[1] [Reading, with Hartenstein, *anzusehen sind* for *anzusehen.*]

TRANSCENDENTAL DIALECTIC

BOOK II

CHAPTER III

THE IDEAL OF PURE REASON

Section 1

THE IDEAL IN GENERAL

WE have seen above that no objects can be represented through pure *concepts of understanding*, apart from the conditions of sensibility. For the conditions of the objective reality of the concepts are then absent, and nothing is to be found in them save the mere form of thought. If, however, they are applied to appearances, they can be exhibited *in concreto*, because in the appearances they obtain the appropriate material for concepts of experience—a concept of experience being nothing but a concept of understanding *in concreto*. But *ideas* are even further removed from objective reality than are categories, for no appearance can be found in which they can be represented *in concreto*. They contain a certain completeness to which no possible empirical know- $\begin{cases} \text{A } 568 \\ \text{B } 596 \end{cases}$ ledge ever attains. In them reason aims only at a systematic unity, to which it seeks to approximate the unity that is empirically possible, without ever completely reaching it.

But what I entitle the *ideal* seems to be further removed from objective reality even than the idea. By the ideal I understand the idea, not merely *in concreto*, but *in individuo*, that is, as an individual[1] thing, determinable or even determined by the idea alone.

Humanity [as an idea] in its complete perfection contains not only all the essential qualities which belong to human nature and constitute our concept of it—and these so extended

---

[1] [*einzelnes.*]

485

as to be in that complete conformity with their ends which would be our idea of perfect humanity—but also everything which, in addition to this concept, is required for the complete determination of the idea. For of all contradictory predicates one only [of each pair] can apply to the idea of the perfect man. What to us is an ideal was in Plato's view an *idea of the divine understanding*, an individual[1] object of its pure intuition, the most perfect of every kind of possible being, and the archetype[2] of all copies in the [field of] appearance.

A 569
B 597

Without soaring so high, we are yet bound to confess that human reason contains not only ideas, but ideals also, which although they do not have, like the Platonic ideas, creative power, yet have *practical* power (as regulative principles), and form the basis of the possible perfection of certain *actions*. Moral concepts, as resting on something empirical (pleasure or displeasure), are not completely pure concepts of reason. None the less, in respect of the principle whereby reason sets bounds to a freedom which is in itself without law, these concepts (when we attend merely to their form) may well serve as examples of pure concepts of reason. Virtue, and therewith human wisdom in its complete purity, are ideas. The wise man (of the Stoics) is, however, an ideal, that is, a man existing in thought only, but in complete conformity with the idea of wisdom. As the idea gives the *rule*, so the ideal in such a case serves as the *archetype* for the complete determination of the copy; and we have no other standard for our actions than the conduct of this divine man within us, with which we compare and judge ourselves, and so reform ourselves, although we can never attain to the perfection thereby prescribed. Although we cannot concede to these ideals objective reality (existence), they are not therefore to be regarded as figments of the brain; they supply reason with a standard which is indispensable to it, providing it, as they do, with a

A 570
B 598

concept of that which is entirely complete in its kind, and thereby enabling it to estimate and to measure the degree and the defects of the incomplete. But to attempt to realise the ideal in an example, that is, in the [field of] appearance, as, for instance, to depict the [character of the perfectly] wise man in a romance, is impracticable. There is indeed something absurd,

---

[1] [*einzelnes.*]   [2] [*Urgrund.*]

and far from edifying, in such an attempt, inasmuch as the
natural limitations, which are constantly doing violence to the
completeness of the idea, make the illusion that is aimed at
altogether impossible, and so cast suspicion on the good itself
—the good that has its source in the idea—by giving it the air
of being a mere fiction.

Such is the nature of the ideal of reason, which must
always rest on determinate concepts and serve as a rule and
archetype, alike in our actions and in our critical judgments.
The products of the imagination are of an entirely different
nature; no one can explain or give an intelligible concept of
them; each is a kind of *monogram*, a mere set of particular
qualities, determined by no assignable rule, and forming
rather a blurred sketch drawn from diverse experiences than a
determinate image—a representation such as painters and
physiognomists profess to carry in their heads, and which they
treat as being an incommunicable shadowy image[1] of their
creations or even of their critical judgments. Such representations may be entitled, though improperly, ideals of
sensibility, inasmuch as they are viewed as being models
(not indeed realisable) of possible empirical intuitions, and yet $\left\{ \begin{array}{l} \text{A } 571 \\ \text{B } 599 \end{array} \right.$
furnish no rules that allow of being explained and examined.

Reason, in its ideal, aims, on the contrary, at complete
determination in accordance with *a priori* rules. Accordingly
it thinks for itself an object which it regards as being completely determinable in accordance with principles. The
conditions that are required for such determination are not,
however, to be found in experience, and the concept itself is
therefore transcendent.

CHAPTER III

Section 2

THE TRANSCENDENTAL IDEAL

(*Prototypon Transcendentale*)

Every concept is, in respect of what is not contained in it,
undetermined, and is subject to the principle of *determin-*

[1] [*Schattenbild.*]

ability According to this principle, of *every two* contradictorily opposed predicates only one can belong to a concept.
This principle is based on the law of contradiction, and is
therefore a purely logical principle. As such, it abstracts from
the entire content of knowledge and is concerned solely with
its logical form.

But every *thing*, as regards its possibility, is likewise subject to the principle of *complete* determination, according to
which if *all the possible* predicates of *things* be taken together
with their contradictory opposites, then one of each pair of
contradictory opposites must belong to it. This principle[1] does
not rest merely on the law of contradiction; for, besides considering each thing in its relation to the two contradictory
predicates, it also considers it in its relation to *the sum-total
of all possibilities*, that is, to the sum-total of all predicates of
things. Presupposing this sum as being an *a priori* condition,
it proceeds to represent everything as deriving its own possibility from the share which it possesses in this sum of all
possibilities.[a] The principle of complete determination concerns, therefore, the content, and not merely the logical form.
It is the principle of the synthesis of all predicates which are
intended to constitute the complete concept of a thing, and not
simply a principle of analytic representation in reference merely
to one of two contradictory predicates. It contains a transcendental presupposition, namely, that of the material *for all
possibility*, which in turn is regarded as containing *a priori*
the data *for the particular possibility* of each and every thing.

The proposition, *everything which exists is completely determined*, does not mean only that one of every pair of *given*
contradictory predicates, but that one of every [pair of] *possible*

A 572 }
B 600 }

A 573 }
B 601 }

[a] In accordance with this principle, each and every thing is therefore related to a common correlate, the sum of all possibilities. If this
correlate (that is, the material for all possible predicates) should be
found in the idea of some one thing, it would prove an affinity of all
possible things, through the identity of the ground of their complete
determination. Whereas the *determinability* of every *concept* is subordinate to the *universality* (*universalitas*) of the principle of excluded middle, the *determination* of a *thing* is subordinate to the
totality (*universitas*) or sum of all possible predicates.

[1] [Reading, with Erdmann, *Dieser . . . er . . . er . . . er* for *Dieses . . . es
. . . es . . . es.*]

predicates, must always belong to it. In terms of this proposition the predicates are not merely compared with one another logically, but the thing itself is compared, in transcendental fashion, with the sum of all possible predicates. What the proposition therefore asserts is this: that to know a thing completely, we must know every possible [predicate], and must determine it thereby, either affirmatively or negatively. The complete determination is thus a concept, which, in its totality, can never be exhibited *in concreto*. It is based upon an idea, which has its seat solely in the faculty of reason—the faculty which prescribes to the understanding the rule of its complete employment.

Although this idea of the *sum-total of all possibility*, in so far as it serves as the condition of the complete determination of each and every thing, is itself undetermined in respect of the predicates which may constitute it, and is thought by us as being nothing more than the sum-total of all possible predicates, we yet find, on closer scrutiny, that this idea, as a primordial concept, excludes a number of predicates which as derivative are already given through other predicates or which { A 574 / B 602 } are incompatible with others; and that it does, indeed, define itself as a concept that is completely determinate *a priori*. It thus becomes the concept of an individual[1] object which is completely determined through the mere idea, and must therefore be entitled an *ideal* of pure reason.

When we consider all possible predicates, not merely logically, but transcendentally, that is, with reference to such content as can be thought *a priori* as belonging to them, we find that through some of them we represent a being, through others a mere not-being. Logical negation, which is indicated simply through the word *not*, does not properly refer to a concept, but only to its relation to another concept in a judgment, and is therefore quite insufficient to determine a concept in respect of its content. The expression *non-mortal* does not enable us to declare that we are thereby representing in the object a mere not-being; the expression leaves all content unaffected. A transcendental negation, on the other hand, signifies not-being in itself, and is opposed to transcendental affirmation, which is a something the very concept of which

---

[1] [*einzelnen.*]

in itself expresses a being. Transcendental affirmation is therefore entitled reality,[1] because through it alone, and so far only

A 575
B 603

as it reaches, are objects something (things), whereas its opposite, negation, signifies a mere want, and, so far as it alone is thought, represents the abrogation of all thinghood.[2]

Now no one can think a negation determinately, save by basing it upon the opposed affirmation. Those born blind cannot have the least notion of darkness, since they have none of light. The savage knows nothing of poverty, since he has no acquaintance with wealth. The ignorant have no concept of their ignorance, because they have none of knowledge, etc.[a] All concepts of negations are thus derivative; it is the realities which contain the data, and, so to speak, the material or transcendental content, for the possibility and complete determination of all things.

If, therefore, reason employs in the complete determination of things a transcendental substrate that contains, as it were, the whole store of material from which all possible predicates of things must be taken, this substrate cannot be

A 576
B 604

anything else than the idea of an *omnitudo realitatis*.[3] All true negations are nothing but limitations—a title which would be inapplicable, were they not thus based upon the unlimited, that is, upon "the All."[4]

But the concept of what thus possesses all reality is just the concept of a *thing in itself* as completely determined; and since in all possible [pairs of] contradictory predicates one predicate, namely, that which belongs to being absolutely, is to be found in its determination, the concept of an *ens realissimum* is the concept of an individual[5] being. It is therefore a transcendental *ideal* which serves as basis for the complete deter-

[a] The observations and calculations of astronomers have taught us much that is wonderful; but the most important lesson that they have taught us has been by revealing the abyss of our *ignorance*, which otherwise we could never have conceived to be so great. Reflection upon the ignorance thus disclosed must produce a great change in our estimate of the purposes for which our reason should be employed. [In both A and B this note is attached, presumably by inadvertence, to the preceding sentence.]

[1] [*Realität (Sachheit)*.]　　　[2] [*die Aufhebung alles Dinges*.]
[3] [*von einem All der Realität* (omnitudo realitatis).]
[4] [*das All*.]　　　[5] [*einzelnen*.]

mination that necessarily belongs to all that exists. This ideal
is the supreme and complete material condition of the possibility of all that exists—the condition to which all thought of
objects, so far as their content is concerned, has to be traced
back. It is also the only true[1] ideal of which human reason is
capable. For only in this one case is a concept of a thing—a concept which is in itself universal—completely determined in and
through itself, and known as the representation of an individual.[2]

The logical determination of a concept by reason is based
upon a disjunctive syllogism, in which the major premiss
contains a logical division (the division of the sphere of a
universal concept), the minor premiss limiting this sphere to
a certain part, and the conclusion determining the concept by ${A\ 577 \atop B\ 605}$
means of this part. The universal concept of a reality in general
cannot be divided *a priori*, because without experience we do
not know any determinate kinds of reality which would be contained under that genus. The transcendental major premiss
which is presupposed in the complete determination of all
things is therefore no other than the representation of the sum
of all reality; it is not merely a concept which, as regards its
transcendental content, comprehends all predicates *under
itself*; it also contains them *within itself*; and the complete
determination of any and every thing rests on the limitation of
this *total* reality,[3] inasmuch as part of it is ascribed to the thing,
and the rest is excluded—a procedure which is in agreement
with the 'either—or' of the disjunctive major premiss and with
the determination of the object, in the minor premiss, through
one of the members of the division. Accordingly, reason, in employing the transcendental ideal as that by reference to which
it determines all possible things, is proceeding in a manner
analogous with its procedure in disjunctive syllogisms—this,
indeed, is the principle upon which I have based the systematic division of all transcendental ideas, as parallel with, and
corresponding to, the three kinds of syllogism.

It is obvious that reason, in achieving its purpose, that,
namely, of representing the necessary complete determination
of things, does not presuppose the existence of a being that ${A\ 578 \atop B\ 606}$
corresponds to this ideal, but only the idea of such a being, and
this only for the purpose of deriving from an unconditioned

---
[1] [*eigentliche.*]   [2] [*Individuum.*]   [3] [*dieses All der Realität.*]

R 2

totality of complete determination the conditioned totality, that is, the totality of the limited. The ideal is, therefore, the archetype[1] (*prototypon*) of all things, which one and all, as imperfect copies (*ectypa*), derive from it the material of their possibility, and while approximating to it in varying degrees, yet always fall very far short of actually attaining it.

All possibility of things (that is, of the synthesis of the manifold, in respect of its content) must therefore be regarded as derivative, with only one exception, namely, the possibility of that which includes in itself all reality. This latter possibility must be regarded as original. For all negations (which are the only predicates through which anything can be distinguished from the *ens realissimum*) are merely limitations of a greater, and ultimately of the highest, reality; and they therefore presuppose this reality, and are, as regards their content, derived from it. All manifoldness of things is only a correspondingly varied mode of limiting the concept of the highest reality which forms their common substratum, just as all figures are only possible as so many different modes of limiting infinite space. The object of the ideal of reason, an object which is present to us only in and through reason, is therefore entitled the *primordial being* (*ens originarium*). As it has nothing above it, it is also entitled the *highest being* (*ens summum*); and as everything that is con-

A 579
B 607 } ditioned is subject to it, the *being of all beings* (*ens entium*). These terms are not, however, to be taken as signifying the objective relation of an actual object to other things, but of an *idea to concepts*. We are left entirely without knowledge as to the existence of a being of such outstanding pre-eminence.

We cannot say that a primordial being consists of a number of derivative beings, for since the latter presuppose the former they cannot themselves constitute it. The idea of the primordial being must therefore be thought as simple.

Consequently, the derivation of all other possibility from this primordial being cannot, strictly speaking, be regarded as a *limitation* of its supreme reality, and, as it were, a *division* of it. For in that case the primordial being would be treated as a mere aggregate of derivative beings; and this, as we have just shown, is impossible, although in our first rough statements we have used such language. On the contrary, the supreme

[1] [*Urbild.*]

reality must condition the possibility of all things as their *ground*, not as their *sum*; and the manifoldness of things must therefore rest, not on the limitation of the primordial being itself, but on all that follows from it, including therein all our sensibility, and all reality in the [field of] appearance —existences of a kind which cannot, as ingredients, belong to the idea of the supreme being.

If, in following up this idea of ours, we proceed to hypos- $\left\{\begin{smallmatrix}A & 580 \\ B & 608\end{smallmatrix}\right.$ tatise it, we shall be able to determine the primordial being through the mere concept of the highest reality, as a being that is one, simple, all-sufficient, eternal, etc. In short, we shall be able to determine it, in its unconditioned completeness, through all predicaments. The concept of such a being is the concept of *God*, taken in the transcendental sense; and the ideal of pure reason, as above defined, is thus the object of a transcendental *theology*.

In any such use of the transcendental idea we should, however, be overstepping the limits of its purpose and validity. For reason, in employing it as a basis for the complete determination of things, has used it only as the *concept* of all reality, without requiring that all this reality be objectively given and be itself a thing. Such a thing is a mere fiction in which we combine and realise the manifold of our idea in an ideal, as an individual[1] being. But we have no right to do this, nor even to assume the possibility of such an hypothesis. Nor do any of the consequences which flow from such an ideal have any bearing upon the complete determination of things, or exercise in that regard the least influence; and it is solely as aiding in their determination that the idea has been shown to be necessary.

But merely to describe the procedure of our reason and its $\left\{\begin{smallmatrix}A & 581 \\ B & 609\end{smallmatrix}\right.$ dialectic does not suffice; we must also endeavour to discover the sources of this dialectic, that we may be able to explain, as a phenomenon of the understanding, the illusion to which it has given rise. For the ideal, of which we are speaking, is based on a natural, not on a merely arbitrary idea. The question to be raised is therefore this: how does it happen that reason regards all possibility of things as derived from one single fundamental possibility, namely, that of the highest

[1] [*besonderen.*]

reality, and thereupon presupposes this to be contained in an individual[1] primordial being?

The answer is obvious from the discussions in the Transcendental Analytic. The possibility of the objects of the senses is a relation of these objects to our thought, in which something (namely, the empirical form) can be thought *a priori*, while that which constitutes the matter, reality in the [field of] appearance (that which corresponds to sensation), must be given, since otherwise it could not even be thought, nor its possibility represented. Now an object of the senses can be completely determined only when it is compared with all the predicates that are possible in the [field of] appearance, and by means of them [2] is represented either affirmatively or negatively. But since that which constitutes the thing itself, namely, the real in the [field of] appearance, must be given—otherwise the thing could not be conceived at all—and since that wherein the real of all appearances is given is experience, considered as single and all-embracing, the material for the possibility of all objects of the senses must be presupposed as given in one whole; [3] and it is upon the limitation of this whole that all possibility of empirical objects, their distinction from each other and their complete determination, can alone be based. No other objects, besides those of the senses, can, as a matter of fact, be given to us, and nowhere save in the context of a possible experience; and consequently nothing is an object *for us*, unless it presupposes the sum [4] of all empirical reality as the condition of its possibility. Now owing to a natural illusion we regard this principle, which applies only to those things which are given as objects of our senses, as being a principle which must be valid of things in general. Accordingly, omitting this limitation, we treat the empirical principle of our concepts of the possibility of things, viewed as appearances, as being a transcendental principle of the possibility of things in general.

If we thereupon proceed to hypostatise this idea of the sum of all reality, that is because we substitute dialectically for the *distributive* unity of the empirical employment of the understanding, the *collective* unity of experience as a whole;

A 582
B 610

---

[1] [*besonderen*.]   [2] [Reading, with Hartenstein, *dieselben* for *dieselbe*.]
[3] [*in einem Inbegriffe*.]   [4] [*Inbegriff*.]

and then thinking this whole [realm] of appearance as one
single thing that contains all empirical reality in itself; and
then again, in turn, by means of the above-mentioned tran- {A 583
                                                             {B 611
scendental subreption, substituting for it the concept of a thing
which stands at the source of the possibility of all things, and
supplies the real conditions for their complete determination.[a]

CHAPTER III

Section 3

THE ARGUMENTS OF SPECULATIVE REASON IN PROOF
OF THE EXISTENCE OF A SUPREME BEING

Notwithstanding this pressing need of reason to presuppose something that may afford the understanding a sufficient
foundation for the complete determination of its concepts, it
is yet much too easily conscious of the ideal and merely fictitious character of such a presupposition to allow itself, on
this ground alone, to be persuaded that a mere creature of its {A 584
                                                                {B 612
own thought is a real being—were it not that it is impelled from
another direction to seek a resting-place in the regress from
the conditioned, which is given, to the unconditioned. This
unconditioned is not, indeed, given as being in itself real, nor
as having a reality that follows from its mere concept; it is,
however, what alone can complete the series of conditions
when we proceed to trace these conditions to their grounds.
This is the course which our human reason, by its very nature,
leads all of us, even the least reflective, to adopt, though not
everyone continues to pursue it. It begins not with concepts,
but with common experience, and thus bases itself on some-

[a] This ideal of the *ens realissimum*, although it is indeed a mere
representation, is first *realised*, that is, made into an object, then
hypostatised, and finally, by the natural progress of reason towards
the completion of unity, is, as we shall presently show, *personified*.
For the regulative unity of experience is not based on the appearances themselves (on sensibility alone), but on the connection of the
manifold through the *understanding* (in an apperception); and consequently the unity of the supreme reality and the complete determinability (possibility) of all things seems to lie in a supreme
understanding, and therefore in an *intelligence*.

thing actually existing. But if this ground does not rest upon the immovable rock of the absolutely necessary, it yields beneath our feet. And this latter support is itself in turn without support, if there be any empty space beyond and under it, and if it does not itself so fill all things as to leave no room for any further question—unless, that is to say, it be infinite in its reality.

If we admit something as existing, no matter what this something may be, we must also admit that there is something which exists *necessarily*. For the contingent exists only under the condition of some other contingent existence as its cause, and from this again we must infer yet another cause, until we are brought to a cause which is not contingent, and which is therefore unconditionally necessary. This is the argument upon which reason bases its advance to the primordial being.

A 585
B 613

Now reason looks around for a concept that squares with so supreme a mode of existence as that of unconditioned necessity—not for the purpose of inferring *a priori* from the concept the existence of that for which it stands (for if that were what it claimed to do, it ought to limit its enquiries to mere concepts, and would not then require a given existence as its basis), but solely in order to find among its various concepts that concept which is in no respect incompatible with absolute necessity. For that there must be something that exists with absolute necessity, is regarded as having been established by the first step in the argument. If, then, in removing everything which is not compatible with this necessity, only one existence remains, this existence must be the absolutely necessary being, whether or not its necessity be comprehensible, that is to say, deducible from its concept alone.

Now that which in its concept contains a therefore for every wherefore, that which is in no respect defective, that which is in every way sufficient as a condition, seems to be precisely the being to which absolute necessity can fittingly be ascribed. For while it contains the conditions of all that is possible, it itself does not require and indeed does not allow of any condition, and therefore satisfies, at least in this one feature, the concept of unconditioned necessity. In this respect all other concepts must fall short of it; for since they are deficient and in need of completion, they cannot have as

A 586
B 614

their characteristic this independence of all further conditions. We are not indeed justified in arguing that what does not contain the highest and in all respects complete condition is therefore itself conditioned in its existence. But we are justified in saying that it does not possess that one feature through which alone reason is in a position, by means of an *a priori* concept, to know, in regard to any being, that it is unconditioned.

The concept of an *ens realissimum* is therefore, of all concepts of possible things, that which best squares with the concept of an unconditionally necessary being; and though it may not be completely adequate to it, we have no choice in the matter, but find ourselves constrained to hold to it. For we cannot afford to dispense with the existence of a necessary being; and once its existence is granted, we cannot, in the whole field of possibility, find anything that can make a better grounded claim [than the *ens realissimum*] to such pre-eminence in the mode of its existence.

Such, then, is the natural procedure of human reason. It begins by persuading itself of the existence of *some* necessary being. This being it apprehends as having an existence that is unconditioned. It then looks around for the concept of that which is independent of any condition, and finds it in that which is itself the sufficient condition of all else, that is, in that which contains all reality. But that which is all-containing and without limits is absolute unity, and involves the concept of a single being that is likewise the supreme being. Accordingly, we conclude that the supreme being, as primordial ground of all things, must exist by absolute necessity. {A 587 B 615}

If what we have in view is the *coming to a decision*—if, that is to say, the existence of some sort of necessary being is taken as granted, and if it be agreed further that we must come to a decision as to what it is—then the foregoing way of thinking must be allowed to have a certain cogency. For in that case no better choice can be made, or rather we have no choice at all, but find ourselves compelled to decide in favour of the absolute unity of complete reality, as the ultimate source of possibility. If, however, we are not required to come to any decision, and prefer to leave the issue open until the weight of the evidence is such as to compel assent; if, in other words, what we have to do is merely to *estimate* how much we really

know in the matter, and how much we merely flatter ourselves
that we know, then the foregoing argument is far from appearing in so advantageous a light, and special favour is
required to compensate for the defectiveness of its claims.

For if we take the issue as being that which is here stated,
namely, *first*, that from any given existence (it may be, merely
my own existence) we can correctly infer the existence of an
unconditionally necessary being; *secondly*, that we must regard
a being which contains all reality, and therefore every condition, as being absolutely unconditioned, and that in this concept of an *ens realissimum* we have therefore found the concept
of a thing to which we can also ascribe absolute necessity—
granting all this, it by no means follows that the concept of a
limited being which does not have the highest reality is for that
reason incompatible with absolute necessity. For although
I do not find in its concept that unconditioned which is involved in the concept of the totality of conditions, we are not
justified in concluding that its existence must for this reason
be conditioned; just as I cannot say, in the case of a hypothetical syllogism, that where a certain condition (in the case
under discussion, the condition of completeness in accordance
with [pure] concepts) does not hold, the conditioned also does
not hold. On the contrary, we are entirely free to hold that
any limited beings whatsoever, notwithstanding their being
limited, may also be unconditionally necessary, although we
cannot infer their necessity from the universal concepts which
we have of them. Thus the argument has failed to give us the
least concept of the properties of a necessary being, and indeed
is utterly ineffective.

But this argument continues to have a certain importance
and to be endowed with an authority of which we cannot,
simply on the ground of this objective insufficiency, at once
proceed to divest it. For granting that there are in the idea of
reason obligations which are completely valid, but which in
their application to ourselves would be lacking in all reality—
that is, obligations to which there would be no motives—save
on the assumption that there exists a supreme being to give
effect and confirmation to the practical laws, in such a situation we should be under an obligation to follow those concepts
which, though they may not be objectively sufficient, are yet,

A 588}
B 616}

A 589}
B 617}

according to the standard of our reason, preponderant, and in comparison with which we know of nothing that is better and more convincing. The duty of deciding would thus, by a practical addition, incline the balance so delicately preserved by the indecisiveness of speculation. Reason would indeed stand condemned in its own judgment—and there is none more circumspect—if, when impelled by such urgent motives, it should fail, however incomplete its insight, to conform its judgment to those pleas which are at least of greater weight than any others known to us.

Though this argument, as resting on the inner insufficiency of the contingent, is in actual fact transcendental, it is yet so simple and natural that, immediately it is propounded, it commends itself to the commonest understanding. We see things alter, come into being, and pass away; and these, or at least their state, must therefore have a cause. But the same question can be raised in regard to every cause that can be $\begin{cases} \text{A 590} \\ \text{B 618} \end{cases}$ given in experience. Where, therefore, can we more suitably locate the *ultimate* causality than where there also exists the *highest* causality, that is, in that being which contains primordially in itself the sufficient ground of every[1] possible effect, and the concept of which we can also very easily entertain by means of the one attribute of an all-embracing perfection. This supreme cause we then proceed to regard as absolutely necessary, inasmuch as we find it absolutely necessary that we should ascend to it, and find no ground for passing beyond it. And thus, in all peoples, there shine amidst the most benighted polytheism some gleams of monotheism, to which they have been led, not by reflection and profound speculation, but simply by the natural bent of the common understanding, as step by step it has come to apprehend its own requirements.

There are only three possible ways of proving the existence of God by means of speculative reason.

All the paths leading to this goal begin either from determinate experience and the specific constitution of the world of sense as thereby known, and ascend from it, in accordance with laws of causality, to the supreme cause outside the

[1] [Reading, with Erdmann, *jeder* for *der*.]

world; or they start from experience which is purely indeterminate, that is, from experience of existence in general; or finally they abstract from all experience, and argue completely *a priori*, from mere concepts, to the existence of a supreme cause. The first proof is the *physico-theological*, the second the *cosmological*, the third the *ontological*. There are, and there can be, no others.

A 591
B 619

I propose to show that reason is as little able to make progress on the one path, the empirical, as on the other path, the transcendental, and that it stretches its wings in vain in thus attempting to soar above the world of sense by the mere power of speculation. As regards the order in which these arguments should be dealt with, it will be exactly the reverse of that which reason takes in the progress of its own development, and therefore of that which we have ourselves followed in the above account. For it will be shown that, although experience is what first gives occasion to this enquiry, it is the *transcendental concept* which in all such endeavours marks out the goal that reason has set itself to attain, and which is indeed its sole guide in its efforts to achieve that goal. I shall therefore begin with the examination of the transcendental proof, and afterwards enquire what effect the addition of the empirical factor can have in enhancing the force of the argument

A 592
B 620

CHAPTER III

Section 4

THE IMPOSSIBILITY OF AN ONTOLOGICAL PROOF OF THE EXISTENCE OF GOD

It is evident, from what has been said, that the concept of an absolutely necessary being is a concept of pure reason, that is, a mere idea the objective reality of which is very far from being proved by the fact that reason requires it. For the idea instructs us only in regard to a certain unattainable completeness, and so serves rather to limit the understanding than to extend it to new objects. But we are here faced by what is indeed strange and perplexing, namely, that while the inference from a given existence in general to some absolutely necessary being seems to be both imperative and legitimate, all those conditions under which alone the understanding can form a concept of such a necessity are so many obstacles in the way of our doing so.

In all ages men have spoken of an *absolutely necessary* being, and in so doing have endeavoured, not so much to understand whether and how a thing of this kind allows even of being thought, but rather to prove its existence. There is, of course, no difficulty in giving a verbal definition of the concept, namely, that it is something the non-existence of which is impossible. But this yields no insight into the conditions $\{ \begin{smallmatrix} A\ 593 \\ B\ 621 \end{smallmatrix}$ which make it necessary[1] to regard the non-existence of a thing as absolutely unthinkable. It is precisely these conditions that we desire to know, in order that we may determine whether or not, in resorting to this concept, we are thinking anything at all. The expedient of removing all those conditions which the understanding indispensably requires in order to regard something as necessary, simply through the introduction of the word *unconditioned*, is very far from sufficing to show whether I am still thinking anything in the concept of the unconditionally necessary, or perhaps rather nothing at all.

Nay more, this concept, at first ventured upon blindly, and now become so completely familiar, has been supposed to have its meaning exhibited in a number of examples; and on this account all further enquiry into its intelligibility has seemed to be quite needless. Thus the fact that every geometrical proposition, as, for instance, that a triangle has three angles, is absolutely necessary, has been taken as justifying us in speaking of an object which lies entirely outside the sphere of our understanding as if we understood perfectly what it is that we intend to convey by the concept of that object.

All the alleged examples are, without exception, taken from *judgments*, not from *things* and their existence. But the unconditioned necessity of judgments is not the same as an absolute necessity of things. The absolute necessity of the judgment is only a conditioned necessity of the thing, or of the predicate in the judgment. The above proposition does not $\{ \begin{smallmatrix} A\ 594 \\ B\ 622 \end{smallmatrix}$

[1] [Reading, with Noiré, *notwendig* for *unmöglich*.]

declare that three angles are absolutely necessary, but that, under the condition that there is a triangle (that is, that a triangle is given), three angles will necessarily be found in it. So great, indeed, is the deluding influence exercised by this logical necessity that, by the simple device of forming an *a priori* concept of a thing in such a manner as to include existence within the scope of its meaning, we have supposed ourselves to have justified the conclusion that because existence necessarily belongs to the object of this concept—always under the condition that we posit the thing as given (as existing)—we are also of necessity, in accordance with the law of identity, required to posit the existence of its object, and that this being is therefore itself absolutely necessary—and this, to repeat, for the reason that the existence of this being has already been thought in a concept which is assumed arbitrarily and on condition that we posit its object.

If, in an identical proposition, I reject the predicate while retaining the subject, contradiction results; and I therefore say that the former belongs necessarily to the latter. But if we reject subject and predicate alike, there is no contradiction; for nothing is then left that can be contradicted. To posit a triangle, and yet to reject its three angles, is self-contradictory; but there is no contradiction in rejecting the triangle together with its three angles. The same holds true of the concept of an absolutely necessary being. If its existence is rejected, we reject the thing itself with all its predicates; and no question of contradiction can then arise. There is nothing outside it that would then be contradicted, since the necessity of the thing is not supposed to be derived from anything external; nor is there anything internal that would be contradicted, since in rejecting the thing itself we have at the same time rejected all its internal properties. 'God is omnipotent' is a necessary judgment. The omnipotence cannot be rejected if we posit a Deity, that is, an infinite being; for the two concepts are identical. But if we say, 'There is no God', neither the omnipotence nor any other of its predicates is given; they are one and all rejected together with the subject, and there is therefore not the least contradiction in such a judgment.

We have thus seen that if the predicate of a judgment is rejected together with the subject, no internal contradiction can result, and that this holds no matter what the predicate may be. The only way of evading this conclusion is to argue that there are subjects which cannot be removed, and must always remain. That, however, would only be another way of saying that there are absolutely necessary subjects; and that is the very assumption which I have called in question, and the possibility of which the above argument professes to establish. For I cannot form the least concept of a thing which, should it be rejected with all its predicates, leaves behind a contra- $\left\{ \begin{matrix} A\ 596 \\ B\ 624 \end{matrix} \right.$ diction; and in the absence of contradiction I have, through pure *a priori* concepts alone, no criterion of impossibility.

Notwithstanding all these general considerations, in which every one must concur, we may be challenged with a case which is brought forward as proof that in actual fact the contrary holds, namely, that there is one concept, and indeed only one, in reference to which the not-being or rejection of its object is in itself contradictory, namely, the concept of the *ens realissimum*. It is declared that it possesses all reality, and that we are justified in assuming that such a being is possible (the fact that a concept does not contradict itself by no means proves the possibility of its object: but the contrary assertion I am for the moment willing to allow).[a] Now [the argument proceeds] 'all reality' includes existence; existence is therefore contained in the concept of a thing that is possible. If, then, this thing is rejected, the internal possibility of the thing is $\left\{ \begin{matrix} A\ 597 \\ B\ 625 \end{matrix} \right.$ rejected—which is self-contradictory.

My answer is as follows. There is already a contradiction in introducing the concept of existence—no matter under what title it may be disguised—into the concept of a thing which we profess to be thinking solely in reference to its possibility. If that be allowed as legitimate, a seeming victory has been

[a] A concept is always possible if it is not self-contradictory. This is the logical criterion of possibility, and by it the object of the concept is distinguishable from the *nihil negativum*. But it may none the less be an empty concept, unless the objective reality of the synthesis through which the concept is generated has been specifically proved; and such proof, as we have shown above, rests on principles of possible experience, and not on the principle of analysis (the law of contradiction). This is a warning against arguing directly from the logical possibility of concepts to the real possibility of things.

won; but in actual fact nothing at all is said: the assertion is a mere tautology. We must ask: Is the proposition that *this or that thing* (which, whatever it may be, is allowed as possible) *exists*, an analytic or a synthetic proposition? If it is analytic, the assertion of the existence of the thing adds nothing to the thought of the thing; but in that case either the thought, which is in us, is the thing itself, or we have presupposed an existence as belonging to the realm of the possible, and have then, on that pretext, inferred its existence from its internal possibility—which is nothing but a miserable tautology. The word 'reality', which in the concept of the thing sounds other than the word 'existence' in the concept of the predicate, is of no avail in meeting this objection. For if all positing (no matter what it may be that is posited) is entitled reality, the thing with all its predicates is already posited in the concept of the subject, and is assumed as actual; and in the predicate this is merely repeated. But if, on the other hand, we admit, as every reasonable person must, that all existential propositions are synthetic, how can we profess to maintain that the predicate of existence cannot be rejected without contradiction? This is a feature which is found only in analytic propositions, and is indeed precisely what constitutes their analytic character.

A 598 }
B 626 }

I should have hoped to put an end to these idle and fruitless disputations in a direct manner, by an accurate determination of the concept of existence, had I not found that the illusion which is caused by the confusion of a logical with a real predicate (that is, with a predicate which determines a thing) is almost beyond correction. Anything we please can be made to serve as a logical predicate; the subject can even be predicated of itself; for logic abstracts from all content. But a *determining* predicate is a predicate which is added to the concept of the subject and enlarges it. Consequently, it must not be already contained in the concept.

'*Being*' is obviously not a real predicate; that is, it is not a concept of something which could[1] be added to the concept of a thing. It is merely the positing of a thing, or of certain determinations, as existing in themselves. Logically, it is merely the copula of a judgment. The proposition, 'God is omnipotent',

---

[1] [Reading, with Erdmann, *könnte* for *könne*.]

contains two concepts, each of which has its object—God and omnipotence. The small word 'is' adds no new predicate, but only serves to posit the predicate *in its relation* to the subject. If, $\left\{\begin{smallmatrix}\text{A } 599 \\ \text{B } 627\end{smallmatrix}\right.$ now, we take the subject (God) with all its predicates (among which is omnipotence), and say 'God is', or 'There is a God', we attach no new predicate to the concept of God, but only posit the subject in itself with all its predicates, and indeed posit it as being an *object* that stands in relation to my *concept*. The content of both must be one and the same; nothing can have been added to the concept, which expresses merely what is possible, by my thinking its object (through the expression 'it is') as given absolutely. Otherwise stated, the real contains no more than the merely possible. A hundred real thalers do not contain the least coin more than a hundred possible thalers. For as the latter signify the concept, and the former the object and the positing of the object, should the former contain more than the latter, my concept would not, in that case, express the whole object, and would not therefore be an adequate concept of it. My financial position is, however, affected very differently by a hundred real thalers than it is by the mere concept of them (that is, of their possibility). For the object, as it actually exists, is not analytically contained in my concept, but is added to my concept (which is a determination of my state) synthetically; and yet the conceived hundred thalers are not themselves in the least increased through thus acquiring existence outside my concept.

By whatever and by however many predicates we may $\left\{\begin{smallmatrix}\text{A } 600 \\ \text{B } 628\end{smallmatrix}\right.$ think a thing—even if we completely determine it—we do not make the least addition to the thing when we further declare that this thing *is*. Otherwise, it would not be exactly the same thing that exists, but something more than we had thought in the concept; and we could not, therefore, say that the exact object of my concept exists. If we think in a thing every feature of reality except one,[1] the missing reality is not added by my saying that this defective thing exists. On the contrary, it exists with the same defect with which I have thought it, since otherwise what exists would be something different from what I thought. When, therefore, I think a being as the supreme reality, without any defect, the question still remains whether

---

[1] [*alle Realität ausser einer.*]

it exists or not. For though, in my concept, nothing may be lacking of the possible real content of a thing in general, something is still lacking in its relation to my whole state of thought, namely, [in so far as I am unable to assert] that knowledge of this object is also possible *a posteriori*. And here we find the source of our present difficulty. Were we dealing with an object of the senses, we could not confound the existence of the thing with the mere concept of it. For through the concept the object is thought only as conforming to the *universal conditions* of possible empirical knowledge in general, whereas through its existence it is thought as belonging to the context of experience as a whole. In being thus connected with the *content* of experience as a whole, the concept of the object is not, however, in the least enlarged; all that has happened is that our thought has thereby obtained an additional possible perception. It is not, therefore, surprising that, if we attempt to think existence through the pure category alone, we cannot specify a single mark distinguishing it from mere possibility.

A 601
B 629

Whatever, therefore, and however much, our concept of an object may contain, we must go outside it, if we are to ascribe existence to the object. In the case of objects of the senses, this takes place through their connection with some one of our perceptions, in accordance with empirical laws. But in dealing with objects of pure thought, we have no means whatsoever of knowing their existence, since it would have to be known in a completely *a priori* manner. Our consciousness of all existence (whether immediately through perception, or mediately through inferences which connect something with perception) belongs exclusively to the unity of experience; any [alleged] existence outside this field, while not indeed such as we can declare to be absolutely impossible, is of the nature of an assumption which we can never be in a position to justify.

The concept of a supreme being is in many respects a very useful idea; but just because it is a mere idea, it is altogether incapable, by itself alone, of enlarging our knowledge in regard to what exists. It is not even competent to enlighten us as to the *possibility* of any existence beyond that which is known in and through experience.[1] The analytic criterion of

A 602
B 630

[1] [*in Ansehung der Möglichkeit eines Mehreren.*]

possibility, as consisting in the principle that bare positives (realities) give rise to no contradiction, cannot be denied to it. But since the realities are not given to us in their specific characters; since even if they were, we should still[1] not be in a position to pass judgment; since the criterion of the possibility of synthetic knowledge is never to be looked for save in experience, to which the object of an idea cannot belong,[2] the connection of all real properties in a thing is a synthesis, the possibility of which we are unable to determine *a priori*. And thus the celebrated Leibniz is far from having succeeded in what he plumed himself on achieving—the comprehension *a priori* of the possibility of this sublime ideal being.

The attempt to establish the existence of a supreme being by means of the famous ontological argument of Descartes is therefore merely so much labour and effort lost; we can no more extend our stock of [theoretical] insight by mere ideas, than a merchant can better his position by adding a few noughts to his cash account.

CHAPTER III   {A 603
B 631

Section 5

THE IMPOSSIBILITY OF A COSMOLOGICAL PROOF OF
THE EXISTENCE OF GOD

To attempt to extract from a purely arbitrary idea the existence of an object corresponding to it is a quite unnatural procedure and a mere innovation of scholastic subtlety. Such an attempt would never have been made if there had not been antecedently, on the part of our reason, the need to assume as a basis of existence in general something necessary (in which our regress may terminate); and if, since this necessity must be unconditioned and certain *a priori*, reason had not, in consequence, been forced to seek a concept which would satisfy, if possible, such a demand, and enable us to know an existence in a completely *a priori* manner. Such a concept was supposed to have been found in the idea of an *ens realissimum*; and that

---

[1] [Reading, with B, *da aber* for *weil aber*.]
[2] [Reading, with Wille, *stattfände* for *stattfinde*.]

idea was therefore used only for the more definite knowledge of that necessary being, of the necessary existence of which we were already convinced, or persuaded, on other grounds. This natural procedure of reason was, however, concealed from view, and instead of ending with this concept, the attempt was made to begin with it, and so to deduce from it that

A 604
B 632

necessity of existence which it was only fitted to supplement. Thus arose the unfortunate ontological proof, which yields satisfaction neither to the natural and healthy understanding nor to the more academic demands of strict proof.

The *cosmological proof*, which we are now about to examine, retains the connection of absolute necessity with the highest reality, but instead of reasoning, like the former proof, from the highest reality to necessity of existence, it reasons from the previously given unconditioned necessity of some being to the unlimited reality of that being. It thus enters upon a course of reasoning which, whether rational or only pseudo-rational, is at any rate natural, and the most convincing not only for common sense but even for speculative understanding. It also sketches the first outline of all the proofs in natural theology, an outline which has always been and always will be followed, however much embellished and disguised by superfluous additions. This proof, termed by Leibniz the proof *a contingentia mundi*, we shall now proceed to expound and examine.

It runs thus: If anything exists, an absolutely necessary being must also exist. Now I, at least, exist. Therefore an absolutely necessary being exists. The minor premiss contains

A 605
B 633

an experience, the major premiss the inference from there being any experience at all to the existence of the necessary.[a] The proof therefore really begins with experience, and is not wholly *a priori* or ontological. For this reason, and because the object of all possible experience is called the world, it is entitled the *cosmological* proof. Since, in dealing with the objects

---

[a] This inference is too well known to require detailed statement. It depends on the supposedly transcendental law of natural causality: that everything contingent has a cause, which, if itself contingent, must likewise have a cause, till the series of subordinate causes ends with an absolutely necessary cause, without which it would have no completeness.

of experience, the proof abstracts from all special properties through which this world may differ from any other possible world, the title also serves to distinguish it from the physico-theological proof, which is based upon observations of the particular properties of the world disclosed to us by our senses.

The proof then proceeds as follows: The necessary being can be determined in one way only, that is, by one out of each possible pair of opposed predicates. It must therefore be *completely* determined through its own concept. Now there is only one possible concept which determines a thing completely *a priori*, namely, the concept of the *ens realissimum*. The concept of the *ens realissimum* is therefore the only concept $\left\{\begin{smallmatrix} \text{A 606} \\ \text{B 634} \end{smallmatrix}\right.$ through which a necessary being can be thought. In other words, a supreme being necessarily exists.

In this cosmological argument there are combined so many pseudo-rational principles that speculative reason seems in this case to have brought to bear all the resources of its dialectical skill to produce the greatest possible transcendental illusion. The testing of the argument may meantime be postponed while we detail in order the various devices whereby an old argument is disguised as a new one, and by which appeal is made to the agreement of two witnesses, the one with credentials of pure reason and the other with those of experience. In reality the only witness is that which speaks in the name of pure reason; in the endeavour to pass as a second witness it merely changes its dress and voice. In order to lay a secure foundation for itself, this proof takes its stand on experience, and thereby makes profession of being distinct from the ontological proof, which puts its entire trust in pure *a priori* concepts. But the cosmological proof uses this experience only for a single step in the argument, namely, to conclude the existence of a necessary being. What properties this being may have, the empirical premiss cannot tell us. Reason therefore abandons experience altogether, and endeavours to discover from mere concepts what properties an absolutely $\left\{\begin{smallmatrix} \text{A 607} \\ \text{B 635} \end{smallmatrix}\right.$ necessary being must have, that is, which among all possible things contains in itself the conditions (*requisita*) essential to absolute necessity. Now these, it is supposed, are nowhere to be found save in the concept of an *ens realissimum*; and the conclusion is therefore drawn, that the *ens realissimum* is the absolutely necessary being. But it is evident that we are here presupposing that the concept of the highest reality is completely adequate to the concept of absolute necessity of existence; that is, that the latter can be inferred from the former. Now this is the proposition maintained by the ontological proof; it is here being assumed in the cosmological proof, and indeed made the basis of the proof; and yet it is an assumption with which this latter proof has professed to dispense. For absolute necessity is an existence determined from mere concepts. If I say, the concept of the *ens realissimum* is a concept, and indeed the only concept, which is appropriate and adequate to necessary existence, I must also admit that necessary existence can be inferred from this concept. Thus the so-called cosmological proof really owes any cogency which it may have to the ontological proof from mere concepts. The appeal to experience is quite superfluous; experience may perhaps lead us to the concept of absolute necessity, but is unable to demonstrate this necessity as belonging to any determinate thing. For immediately we endeavour to do so, we must abandon all experience and search among pure concepts to discover whether any one of them contains the conditions of the possibility of an absolutely necessary being. If in this way we can determine the possibility of a necessary being, we likewise establish its existence. For what we are then saying is this: that of all possible beings there is one which carries with it absolute necessity, that is, that this being exists with absolute necessity.

Fallacious and misleading arguments are most easily detected if set out in correct syllogistic form. This we now proceed to do in the instance under discussion.

If the proposition, that every absolutely necessary being is likewise the most real of all beings, is correct (and this is the *nervus probandi* of the cosmological proof), it must, like all affirmative judgments, be convertible, at least *per accidens*. It therefore follows that some *entia realissima* are likewise absolutely necessary beings. But one *ens realissimum* is in no respect different from another, and what is true of *some* under this concept is true also of *all*. In this case, therefore, I can convert the proposition *simpliciter*, not only *per accidens*, and say that every *ens realissimum* is a necessary being. But

A 608
B 636

since this proposition is determined from its[1] *a priori* concepts alone, the mere concept of the *ens realissimum* must carry with it the absolute necessity of that being; and this is precisely what the ontological proof has asserted and what the cosmological proof has refused to admit, although the conclusions {A 609 / B 637} of the latter are indeed covertly based on it.

Thus the second path upon which speculative reason enters in its attempt to prove the existence of a supreme being is not only as deceptive as the first, but has this additional defect, that it is guilty of an *ignoratio elenchi*. It professes to lead us by a new path, but after a short circuit brings us back to the very path which we had deserted at its bidding.

I have stated that in this cosmological argument there lies hidden a whole nest of dialectical assumptions, which the transcendental critique can easily detect and destroy. These deceptive principles I shall merely enumerate, leaving to the reader, who by this time will be sufficiently expert in these matters, the task of investigating them further, and of refuting them.

We find, for instance, (1) the transcendental principle whereby from the contingent we infer a cause. This principle is applicable only in the sensible world; outside that world it has no meaning whatsoever. For the mere intellectual concept of the contingent cannot give rise to any synthetic proposition, such as that of causality. The principle of causality has no meaning and no criterion for its application save only in the sensible world. But in the cosmological proof it is precisely in order to enable us to advance beyond the sensible world that it is employed. (2) The inference to a first cause, from the im- {A 610 / B 638} possibility of an infinite series of causes, given one after the other, in the sensible world. The principles of the employment of reason do not justify this conclusion even within the world of experience, still less beyond this world in a realm into which this series can never be extended. (3) The unjustified self-satisfaction of reason in respect of the completion of this series. The removal of all the conditions without which no concept of necessity is possible is taken by reason to be a completion of the concept of the series, on the ground that we can then conceive nothing further. (4) The confusion between the

---

[1] [Erdmann would read *reinen* in place of *seinen*.]

logical possibility of a concept of all reality united into one (without inner contradiction) and the transcendental possibility of such a reality. In the case of the latter there is needed a principle to establish the practicability of such a synthesis, a principle which itself, however, can apply only to the field of possible experiences—etc.

The procedure of the cosmological proof is artfully designed to enable us to escape having to prove the existence of a necessary being *a priori* through mere concepts. Such proof would require to be carried out in the ontological manner, and that is an enterprise for which we feel ourselves to be altogether incompetent. Accordingly, we take as the starting-point of our inference an actual existence (an experience in general), and advance, in such manner as we can, to some absolutely necessary condition of this existence. We have then no need to show the possibility of this condition. For if it has been proved to exist, the question as to its possibility is entirely superfluous. If now we want to determine more fully the nature of this necessary being, we do not endeavour to do so in the manner that would be really adequate, namely, by discovering from its concept the necessity of its existence. For could we do that, we should be in no need of an empirical starting-point. No, all we seek is the negative condition (*conditio sine qua non*), without which a being would not be absolutely necessary. And in all other kinds of reasoning from a given consequence to its ground this would be legitimate; but in the present case it unfortunately happens that the condition which is needed for absolute necessity is only to be found in one single being. This being must therefore contain in its concept all that is required for absolute necessity, and consequently it enables me to infer this absolute necessity *a priori*. I must therefore be able also to reverse the inference, and to say: Anything to which this concept (of supreme reality) applies is absolutely necessary. If I cannot make this inference (as I must concede, if I am to avoid admitting the ontological proof), I have come to grief in the new way that I have been following, and am back again at my starting-point. The concept of the supreme being satisfies all questions *a priori* which can be raised regarding the inner determinations of a thing, and is therefore an ideal that is quite unique, in that the concept, while universal, also at the same time designates an

A 611 ⎫
B 639 ⎭

A 612 ⎫
B 640 ⎭

individual as being among the things that are possible. But it does not give satisfaction concerning the question of its own existence—though this is the real purpose of our enquiries—and if anyone admitted the existence of a necessary being but wanted to know which among all [existing] things is to be identified with that being, we could not answer: "This, not that, is the necessary being."

We may indeed be allowed to *postulate* the existence of an all-sufficient being, as the cause of all possible effects, with a view to lightening the task of reason in its search for the unity of the grounds of explanation. But in presuming so far as to say that such a being *necessarily exists*, we are no longer giving modest expression to an admissible hypothesis, but are confidently laying claim to apodeictic certainty. For the knowledge of what we profess to know as absolutely necessary must itself carry with it absolute necessity.

The whole problem of the transcendental ideal amounts to this: either, given absolute necessity, to find a concept which possesses it, or, given the concept of something, to find that something to be absolutely necessary. If either task be possible, so must the other; for reason recognises that only as absolutely necessary which follows of necessity from its concept. But both tasks are quite beyond our utmost efforts to *satisfy* our understanding in this matter; and equally unavailing are all attempts to induce it to acquiesce in its incapacity. $\left\{ \begin{array}{l} \text{A 613} \\ \text{B 641} \end{array} \right.$

Unconditioned necessity, which we so indispensably require as the last bearer of all things, is for human reason the veritable abyss. Eternity itself, in all its terrible sublimity, as depicted by a Haller,[1] is far from making the same overwhelming impression on the mind; for it only *measures* the duration of things, it does not *support* them. We cannot put aside, and yet also cannot endure the thought, that a being, which we represent to ourselves as supreme amongst all possible beings, should, as it were, say to itself: 'I am from eternity to eternity, and outside me there is nothing save what is through my will, *but whence then am I?*' All support here fails us; and the *greatest* perfection, no less than the *least* perfection, is unsubstantial and baseless for the merely speculative reason, which

---

[1] [Albrecht von Haller (1708-1777), a writer on medical and kindred subjects, author of *Die Alpen* and other poems.]

makes not the least effort to retain either the one or the other, and feels indeed no loss in allowing them to vanish entirely.

Many forces in nature, which manifest their existence through certain effects, remain for us inscrutable; for we cannot track them sufficiently far by observation. Also, the transcendental object lying at the basis of appearances (and with it the reason why our sensibility is subject to certain supreme conditions rather than to others) is and remains for us inscrutable. The thing itself[1] is indeed given, but we can have no insight into its nature. But it is quite otherwise with an ideal of pure reason; it can never be said to be inscrutable. For since it is not required to give any credentials of its reality save only the need on the part of reason to complete all synthetic unity by means of it; and since, therefore, it is in no wise given as thinkable *object*, it cannot be inscrutable in the manner in which an object is. On the contrary it[2] must, as a mere idea, find its place and its solution in the nature of reason, and must therefore allow of investigation. For it is of the very essence of reason that we should be able to give an account of all our concepts, opinions, and assertions, either upon objective or, in the case of mere illusion, upon subjective grounds.

A 614
B 642

DISCOVERY AND EXPLANATION
of the Dialectical Illusion in all Transcendental Proofs of the Existence of a Necessary Being

Both the above proofs were transcendental, that is, were attempted independently of empirical principles. For although the cosmological proof presupposes an experience in general, it is not based on any particular property of this experience but on pure principles of reason, as applied to an existence given through empirical consciousness in general. Further, it soon abandons this guidance and relies on pure concepts alone. What, then, in these transcendental proofs is the cause of the dialectical but natural illusion which connects the concepts of necessity and supreme reality, and which realises and hypostatises what can be an idea only? Why are we constrained to assume that some one among existing things is in itself

A 615
B 643

---

[1] [*die Sache selbst.*]   [2] [Reading, with Hartenstein, *es* for *er.*]

necessary, and yet at the same time to shrink back from the existence of such a being as from an abyss? And how are we to secure that reason may come to an agreement with itself in this matter, and that from the wavering condition of a diffident approval, ever again withdrawn, it may arrive at settled insight?

There is something very strange in the fact, that once we assume something to exist we cannot avoid inferring that something exists necessarily. The cosmological argument rests on this quite natural (although not therefore certain) inference. On the other hand, if I take the concept of anything, no matter what, I find that the existence of this thing can never be represented by me as absolutely necessary, and that, whatever it may be that exists, nothing prevents me from thinking its non-existence. Thus while I may indeed be obliged to assume something necessary as a condition of the existent in general, I cannot think any particular thing as in itself necessary. In other words, I can never *complete* the regress to the ${\begin{smallmatrix} A\ 616 \\ B\ 644 \end{smallmatrix}}$ conditions of existence save by assuming a necessary being, and yet am never in a position to *begin* with such a being.

If I am constrained to think something necessary as a condition of existing things, but am unable to think any particular thing as in itself necessary, it inevitably follows that necessity and contingency do not concern the things themselves; otherwise there would be a contradiction. Consequently, neither of these two principles can be objective. They may, however, be regarded as subjective principles of reason. The one calls upon us to seek something necessary as a condition of all that is given as existent, that is, to stop nowhere until we have arrived at an explanation which is complete *a priori*; the other forbids us ever to hope for this completion, that is, forbids us to treat anything empirical as unconditioned and to exempt ourselves thereby from the toil of its further derivation. Viewed in this manner, the two principles, as merely heuristic and *regulative*, and as concerning only the formal interest of reason, can very well stand side by side. The one prescribes that we are to philosophise about nature as if there were a necessary first ground for all that belongs to existence—solely, however, for the purpose of bringing systematic unity into our knowledge, by always pursuing such

an idea, as an imagined ultimate ground. The other warns us
A 617} not to regard any determination whatsoever of existing things
B 645} as such an ultimate ground, that is, as absolutely necessary,
but to keep the way always open for further derivation, and
so to treat each and every determination as always conditioned by something else. But if everything which is perceived
in things must necessarily be treated by us as conditioned,
nothing that allows of being empirically given can be regarded as absolutely necessary.

Since, therefore, the absolutely necessary is only intended
to serve as a principle for obtaining the greatest possible
unity among appearances, as being their ultimate ground;
and since—inasmuch as the second rule commands us always to regard all empirical causes of unity as themselves
derived—we can never reach this unity within the world, it
follows that we must regard the absolutely necessary as being
outside the world.

While the philosophers of antiquity regard all form in
nature as contingent, they follow the judgment of the common
man in their view of matter as original and necessary. But if,
instead of regarding matter relatively, as *substratum* of appearances, they had considered it *in itself*, and as regards its
existence, the idea of absolute necessity would at once have
disappeared. For there is nothing which absolutely binds
reason to accept such an existence; on the contrary it can always annihilate it in thought, without contradiction; absolute
necessity is a necessity that is to be found in thought alone.
A 618} This belief must therefore have been due to a certain regu-
B 646} lative principle. In fact extension and impenetrability (which
between them make up the concept of matter) constitute the
supreme empirical principle[1] of the unity of appearances;
and this principle, so far as it is empirically unconditioned,
has the character of a regulative principle. Nevertheless,
since every determination of the matter which constitutes what
is real in appearances, including impenetrability, is an effect
(action) which must have its cause and which is therefore
always derivative in character, matter is not compatible with
the idea of a necessary being as a principle of all derived unity.
(For its real properties, being derivative, are one and all only

[1] [*Prinzipium.* Kant's more usual term is *Prinzip.*]

conditionally necessary, and so allow of being removed—
wherewith the whole existence of matter would be removed.)
If this were not the case, we should have reached the ultimate ground of unity by empirical means—which is forbidden by the second regulative principle. It therefore follows
that matter, and in general whatever belongs to the world,
is not compatible with the idea of a necessary original being,
even when the latter is regarded simply as a principle of the
greatest empirical unity. That being or principle must be set
outside the world, leaving us free to derive the appearances
of the world and their existence from other appearances, with
unfailing confidence, just as if there were no necessary being,
while yet we are also free to strive unceasingly towards the
completeness of that derivation, just as if such a being were ⎰A 619
presupposed as an ultimate ground.   ⎱B 647

As follows from these considerations, the ideal of the
supreme being is nothing but a *regulative principle* of reason,
which directs us to look upon all connection in the world *as if*
it originated from an all-sufficient necessary cause. We can
base upon the ideal the rule of a systematic and, in accordance with universal laws, necessary unity in the explanation
of that connection; but the ideal is not an assertion of an
existence necessary in itself. At the same time we cannot avoid
the transcendental subreption, by which this formal principle
is represented as constitutive, and by which this unity is hypostatised. We proceed here just as we do in the case of space.
Space is only a principle[1] of sensibility, but since it is the
primary source and condition of all shapes, which are only so
many limitations of itself, it is taken as something absolutely
necessary, existing in its own right, and as an object given *a
priori* in itself. In the same way, since the systematic unity of
nature cannot be prescribed as a principle for the empirical
employment of our reason, except in so far as we presuppose
the idea of an *ens realissimum* as the supreme cause, it is
quite natural that this latter idea should be represented as an
actual object, which, in its character of supreme condition, is
also necessary—thus changing a *regulative* into a *constitutive* ⎰A 620
principle. That such a substitution has been made becomes   ⎱B 648
evident, when we consider this supreme being, which relatively

[1] [*Prinzipium.*]

to the world is absolutely (unconditionally) necessary, as a thing in and by itself. For we are then unable to conceive what can be meant by its necessity. The concept of necessity is only to be found in our reason, as a formal condition of thought; it does not allow of being hypostatised as a material condition of existence.

CHAPTER III

Section 6

THE IMPOSSIBILITY OF THE PHYSICO-THEOLOGICAL PROOF

If, then, neither the concept of things in general nor the experience of any *existence in general* can supply what is required, it remains only to try whether a *determinate experience*, the experience of the things of the present world, and the constitution and order of these, does not provide the basis of a proof which may help us to attain to an assured conviction of a supreme being. Such proof we propose to entitle the *physico-theological*. Should this attempt also fail, it must follow that no satisfactory proof of the existence of a being corresponding to our transcendental idea can be possible by pure speculative reason.

A 621 }
B 649 }   In view of what has already been said, it is evident that we can count upon a quite easy and conclusive answer to this enquiry. For how can any experience ever be adequate to an idea? The peculiar nature of the latter consists just in the fact that no experience can ever be equal to it. The transcendental idea of a necessary and all-sufficient original being is so overwhelmingly great, so high above everything empirical, the latter being always conditioned, that it leaves us at a loss, partly because we can never find in experience material sufficient to satisfy such a concept, and partly because it is always in the sphere of the conditioned that we carry out our search, seeking there ever vainly for the unconditioned—no law of any empirical synthesis giving us an example of any such unconditioned or providing the least guidance in its pursuit.

If the supreme being should itself stand in this chain of

conditions, it would be a member of the series, and like the lower members which it precedes, would call for further enquiry as to the still higher ground from which it follows. If, on the other hand, we propose to separate it from the chain, and to conceive it as a purely intelligible being, existing apart from the series of natural causes, by what bridge can reason contrive to pass over to it? For all laws governing the transition from effects to causes, all synthesis and extension of our knowledge, refer to nothing but possible experience, and therefore solely to objects of the sensible world, and apart from them can have $\begin{cases} \text{A 622} \\ \text{B 650} \end{cases}$ no meaning whatsoever.

This world presents to us so immeasurable a stage of variety, order, purposiveness, and beauty, as displayed alike in its infinite extent and in the unlimited divisibility of its parts, that even with such knowledge as our weak understanding can acquire of it, we are brought face to face with so many marvels immeasurably great, that all speech loses its force, all numbers their power to measure, our thoughts themselves all definiteness, and that our judgment of the whole resolves itself into an amazement which is speechless, and only the more eloquent on that account. Everywhere we see a chain of effects and causes, of ends and means, a regularity in origination and dissolution. Nothing has of itself come into the condition in which we find it to exist, but always points to something else as its cause, while this in turn commits us to repetition of the same enquiry. The whole universe must thus sink into the abyss of nothingness, unless, over and above this infinite chain of contingencies, we assume something to support it— something which is original and independently self-subsistent, and which as the cause of the origin of the universe secures also at the same time its continuance. What magnitude are we to ascribe to this supreme cause—admitting that it is supreme in respect of all things in the world? We are not acquainted with the whole content of the world, still less do we know $\begin{cases} \text{A 623} \\ \text{B 651} \end{cases}$ how to estimate its magnitude by comparison with all that is possible. But since we cannot, as regards causality, dispense with an ultimate and supreme being,[1] what is there to prevent us ascribing to it a degree of perfection that sets it *above everything else that is possible?* This we can easily do—though

---

[1] [*ein äusserstes und oberstes Wesen.*]

only through the slender outline of an abstract concept—by representing this being to ourselves as combining in itself all possible perfection, as in a single substance. This concept is in conformity with the demand of our reason for parsimony of principles; it is free from self-contradiction, and is never decisively contradicted by any experience; and it is likewise of such a character that it contributes to the extension of the employment of reason within experience, through the guidance which it yields in the discovery of order and purposiveness.

This proof always deserves to be mentioned with respect. It is the oldest, the clearest, and the most accordant with the common reason of mankind. It enlivens the study of nature, just as it itself derives its existence and gains ever new vigour from that source. It suggests ends and purposes, where our observation would not have detected them by itself, and extends our knowledge of nature by means of the guiding-concept of a special unity, the principle of which is outside nature. This knowledge again reacts on its cause, namely, upon the idea which has led to it, and so strengthens the belief in a supreme Author [of nature] that the belief acquires the force of an irresistible conviction.

A 624
B 652

It would therefore not only be uncomforting but utterly vain to attempt to diminish in any way the authority of this argument. Reason, constantly upheld by this ever-increasing evidence, which, though empirical, is yet so powerful, cannot be so depressed through doubts suggested by subtle and abstruse speculation, that it is not at once aroused from the indecision of all melancholy reflection, as from a dream, by one glance at the wonders of nature and the majesty of the universe—ascending from height to height up to the all-highest, from the conditioned to its conditions, up to the supreme and unconditioned Author [of all conditioned being].

But although we have nothing to bring against the rationality and utility of this procedure, but have rather to commend and to further it, we still cannot approve the claims, which this mode of argument would fain advance, to apodeictic certainty and to an assent founded on no special favour or support from other quarters. It cannot hurt the good cause, if the dogmatic

language of the overweening sophist be toned down to the $\left\{\begin{smallmatrix} \text{A } 625 \\ \text{B } 653 \end{smallmatrix}\right.$
more moderate and humble requirements of a belief adequate
to quieten our doubts, though not to command unconditional
submission. I therefore maintain that the physico-theological
proof can never by itself establish the existence of a supreme
being, but must always fall back upon the ontological argument to make good its deficiency. It only serves as an introduction to the ontological argument; and the latter therefore
contains (in so far as a speculative proof is possible at all) *the
one possible ground of proof* with which human reason can
never dispense.[1]

The chief points of the physico-theological proof are as
follows: (1) In the world we everywhere find clear signs of an
order in accordance with a determinate purpose, carried out
with great wisdom; and this in a universe which is indescrib-
ably varied in content and unlimited in extent. (2) This purposive order is quite alien to the things of the world, and only
belongs to them contingently; that is to say, the diverse things
could not of themselves have co-operated, by so great a combination of diverse means, to the fulfilment of determinate
final purposes, had they not been chosen and designed for
these purposes by an ordering rational principle in conformity
with underlying ideas. (3) There exists, therefore, a sublime
and wise cause (or more than one), which must be the cause
of the world not merely as a blindly working all-powerful
nature, by *fecundity*, but as intelligence, through *freedom*.
(4) The unity of this cause may be inferred from the unity of
the reciprocal relations existing between the parts of the world,
as members of an artfully arranged structure—inferred with $\left\{\begin{smallmatrix} \text{A } 626 \\ \text{B } 654 \end{smallmatrix}\right.$
certainty in so far as our observation suffices for its verification,
and beyond these limits with probability, in accordance with
the principles of analogy.

We need not here criticise natural reason too strictly in
regard to its conclusion from the analogy between certain
natural products and what our human art produces when we
do violence to nature, and constrain it to proceed not according
to its own ends but in conformity with ours—appealing to the
similarity of these particular natural products with houses,
ships, watches. Nor need we here question its conclusion that

---

[1] [*vorbeigehen.*]

522   KANT'S CRITIQUE OF PURE REASON

there lies at the basis of nature a causality similar to that responsible for artificial products, namely, an understanding and a will; and that the inner possibility of a self-acting[1] nature (which is what makes all art, and even, it may be, reason itself, possible) is therefore derived from another, though superhuman, art—a mode of reasoning which could not perhaps withstand a searching transcendental criticism. But at any rate we must admit that, if we are to specify a cause at all, we cannot here proceed more securely than by analogy with those purposive productions of which alone the cause and mode of action are fully known to us. Reason could never be justified in abandoning the causality which it knows for grounds of explanation which are obscure, of which it does not have any knowledge, and which are incapable of proof.

On this method of argument, the purposiveness and harmonious adaptation of so much in nature can suffice to prove the contingency of the form merely, not of the matter, that is, not of the substance in the world. To prove the latter we should have to demonstrate that the things in the world would not of themselves be capable of such order and harmony, in accordance with universal laws, if they were not *in their substance* the product of supreme wisdom. But to prove this we should require quite other grounds of proof than those which are derived from the analogy with human art. The utmost, therefore, that the argument can prove is an *architect* of the world who is always very much hampered by the adaptability of the material in which he works, not a *creator* of the world to whose idea everything is subject. This, however, is altogether inadequate to the lofty purpose which we have before our eyes, namely, the proof of an all-sufficient primordial being. To prove the contingency of matter itself, we should have to resort to a transcendental argument, and this is precisely what we have here set out to avoid.

The inference, therefore, is that the order and purposiveness everywhere observable throughout the world may be regarded as a completely contingent arrangement, and that we may argue to the existence of a cause *proportioned* to it. But the concept of this cause must enable us to know some-

A 627
B 655

---

[1] [*freiwirkenden*.]

thing quite *determinate* about it, and can therefore be no other than the concept of a being who possesses all might, wisdom, etc., in a word, all the perfection which is proper to an all-sufficient being. For the predicates—'very great', 'astounding', 'immeasurable' in power and excellence—give no determinate concept at all, and do not really tell us what the thing is in itself. They are only relative representations of the magnitude of the object, which the observer, in contemplating the world, compares with himself and with his capacity of comprehension, and which are equally terms of eulogy whether we be magnifying the object or be depreciating the observing subject in relation to that object. Where we are concerned with the magnitude (of the perfection) of a thing, there is no determinate concept except that which comprehends all possible perfection; and in that concept only the allness (*omnitudo*) of the reality is completely determined. {A 628 B 656

Now no one, I trust, will be so bold as to profess that he comprehends the relation of the magnitude of the world as he has observed it (alike as regards both extent and content) to omnipotence, of the world order to supreme wisdom, of the world unity to the absolute unity of its Author, etc. Physico-theology is therefore unable to give any determinate concept of the supreme cause of the world, and cannot therefore serve as the foundation of a theology which is itself in turn to form the basis of religion.

To advance to absolute totality by the empirical road is utterly impossible. None the less this is what is attempted in the physico-theological proof. What, then, are the means which have been adopted to bridge this wide abyss? {A 629 B 657

The physico-theological argument can indeed lead us to the point of admiring the greatness, wisdom, power, etc., of the Author of the world, but can take us no further. Accordingly, we then abandon the argument from empirical grounds of proof, and fall back upon the contingency which, in the first steps of the argument, we had inferred from the order and purposiveness of the world. With this contingency as our sole premiss, we then advance, by means of transcendental concepts alone, to the existence of an absolutely necessary being, and [as a final step] from the concept of the absolute necessity of the first cause to the completely determinate or determinable concept of that necessary being, namely, to the concept of an all-embracing reality. Thus the physico-theological proof, failing in its undertaking, has in face of this difficulty suddenly fallen back upon the cosmological proof; and since the latter is only a disguised ontological proof, it has really achieved its purpose by pure reason alone—although at the start it disclaimed all kinship with pure reason and professed to establish its conclusions on convincing evidence derived from experience.

Those who propound the physico-theological argument have therefore no ground for being so contemptuous in their attitude to the transcendental mode of proof, posing as clear-sighted students of nature, and complacently looking down upon that proof as the artificial product of obscure speculative refinements. For were they willing to scrutinise their own procedure, they would find that, after advancing some considerable way on the solid ground of nature and experience, and finding themselves just as far distant as ever from the object which discloses itself to their reason, they suddenly leave this ground, and pass over into the realm of mere possibilities, where they hope upon the wings of ideas to draw near to the object—the object that has refused itself to all their *empirical* enquiries. For after this tremendous leap, when they have, as they think, found firm ground, they extend their concept—the *determinate* concept, into the possession of which they have now come, they know not how—over the whole sphere of creation. And the ideal, [which this reasoning thus involves, and] which is entirely a product of pure reason, they then elucidate by reference to experience, though inadequately enough, and in a manner far below the dignity of its object; and throughout they persist in refusing to admit that they have arrived at this knowledge or hypothesis by a road quite other than that of experience.

Thus the physico-theological proof of the existence of an original or supreme being rests upon the cosmological proof, and the cosmological upon the ontological. And since, besides these three, there is no other path open to speculative reason, the ontological proof from pure concepts of reason is the only possible one, if indeed any proof of a proposition so far exalted above all empirical employment of the understanding is possible at all.

A 630
B 658

CHAPTER III $\left\{\begin{array}{l}\text{A } 631 \\ \text{B } 659\end{array}\right.$

Section 7

CRITIQUE OF ALL THEOLOGY BASED UPON SPECULATIVE
PRINCIPLES OF REASON

If I understand by theology knowledge of the original
being, it is based either solely upon reason (*theologia rationalis*) or upon revelation (*revelata*). The former thinks its object
either through pure reason, solely by means of transcendental
concepts (*ens originarium, realissimum, ens entium*), in which
case it is entitled *transcendental* theology, or through a concept borrowed from nature (from the nature of our soul)—a
concept of the original being as a supreme intelligence—and
it would then have to be called *natural* theology. Those who
accept only a transcendental theology are called *deists*; those
who also admit a natural theology are called *theists*. The
former grant that we can know the existence of an original
being solely through reason, but maintain that our concept
of it is transcendental only, namely, the concept of a being
which possesses all reality, but which we are unable to determine in any more specific fashion. The latter assert that
reason is capable of determining its object more precisely
through analogy with nature, namely, as a being which,
through understanding and freedom, contains in itself the
ultimate ground of everything else. Thus the deist represents this being merely as a *cause of the world* (whether by $\left\{\begin{array}{l}\text{A } 632 \\ \text{B } 660\end{array}\right.$
the necessity of its nature or through freedom, remains undecided), the theist as the *Author of the world*.

Transcendental theology, again, either proposes to deduce
the existence of the original being from an experience in
general (without determining in any more specific fashion the
nature of the world to which the experience belongs), and is
then entitled *cosmo-theology*; or it believes that it can know the
existence of such a being through mere concepts, without the
help of any experience whatsoever, and is then entitled *onto-theology*.

Natural theology infers the properties and the existence of an Author of the world from the constitution, the order and unity, exhibited in the world—a world in which we have to recognise two kinds of causality with their rules, namely, nature and freedom. From this world natural theology ascends to a supreme intelligence, as the principle either of all natural or of all moral order and perfection. In the former case it is entitled *physico-theology*, in the latter *moral theology*.[a]

Since we are wont to understand by the concept of God not merely an eternal nature that works blindly, as the root-source of all things, but a supreme being who through understanding and freedom is the Author of all things; and since it is in this sense only that the concept interests us, we could, strictly speaking, deny to the *deist* any belief in God, allowing him only the assertion of an original being or supreme cause. However, since no one ought to be accused of denying what he only does not venture to assert, it is less harsh and more just to say that the *deist* believes in a *God*, the *theist* in a *living God* (*summa intelligentia*). We shall now proceed to enquire what are the possible sources of all these endeavours of reason.

For the purposes of this enquiry, theoretical knowledge may be defined as knowledge of what *is*, practical knowledge as the representation of what *ought to be*. On this definition, the theoretical employment of reason is that by which I know *a priori* (as necessary) that something is, and the practical that by which it is known *a priori* what ought to happen. Now if it is indubitably certain that something is or that something ought to happen, but this certainty is at the same time only conditional, then a certain determinate condition of it can be absolutely necessary, or can be an optional and contingent presupposition. In the former case the condition is postulated (*per thesin*); in the latter case it is assumed (*per hypothesin*). Now since there are practical laws which are absolutely necessary, that is, the moral laws, it must follow that if these necessarily presuppose the existence of any being as the condition of

A 633
B 661
A 634
B 662

---

[a] Not theological ethics: for this contains moral laws, which *presuppose* the existence of a supreme ruler of the world. Moral theology, on the other hand, is a conviction of the existence of a supreme being—a conviction which bases itself on moral laws.[1]

[1] [*welche sich auf sittliche Gesetze gründet* substituted in B for *welche auf sittliche Gesetze gegründet ist.*]

the possibility of their *obligatory* power, this existence must be *postulated*; and this for the sufficient reason that the conditioned, from which the inference is drawn to this determinate condition, is itself known *a priori* to be absolutely necessary. At some future time we shall show that the moral laws do not merely presuppose the existence of a supreme being, but also, as themselves in a different connection absolutely necessary, justify us in postulating it, though, indeed, only from a practical point of view. For the present, however, we are leaving this mode of argument aside.

Where we are dealing merely with what is (not with what ought to be), the conditioned, which is given to us in experience, is always thought as being likewise contingent. That which conditions it is not, therefore, known as absolutely necessary, but serves only as something relatively necessary or rather as *needful*; in itself and *a priori* it is an arbitrary presupposition, assumed by us in our attempt to know the conditioned by means of reason. If, therefore, in the field of theoretical knowledge, the absolute necessity of a thing were to be known, this could only be from *a priori* concepts, and never by positing it as a cause relative to an existence given in experience.

Theoretical knowledge is *speculative* if it concerns an object, or those concepts of an object, which cannot be reached in any experience. It is so named to distinguish it from *the* {A 635 / B 663} *knowledge of nature*, which concerns only those objects or predicates of objects which can be given in a possible experience.

The principle by which, from that which happens (the empirically contingent) [viewed] as [an] effect, we infer a cause, is a principle of the knowledge of nature, but not of speculative knowedge. For, if we abstract from what it is as a principle that contains the condition of all possible experience, and leaving aside all that is empirical attempt to assert it of the contingent in general, there remains not the least justification for any synthetic proposition such as might show us how to pass from that which is before us to something quite different (called its cause). In this merely speculative employment any meaning whose objective reality admits of being made intelligible *in concreto*, is taken away not only from the concept of the contingent but from the concept of a cause.

If we infer from the existence of *things* in the world the existence of their cause, we are employing reason, not in the knowledge of nature, but in *speculation*. For the former type of knowledge treats as empirically contingent, and refers to a cause, not the things themselves (substances), but only that which *happens*, that is, their *states*. That substance (matter) is itself contingent in its existence would have to be known in a

A 636 ⎫
B 664 ⎭ purely speculative manner. Again, even if we were speaking only of the form of the world, the way in which things are connected and change, and sought to infer from this a cause entirely distinct from the world, this would again be a judgment of purely speculative reason, since the object which we are inferring is not an object of a possible experience. So employed, the principle of causality, which is only valid within the field of experience, and outside this field has no application, nay, is indeed meaningless, would be altogether diverted from its proper use

Now I maintain that all attempts to employ reason in theology in any merely speculative manner are altogether fruitless and by their very nature null and void, and that the principles of its employment in the study of nature do not lead to any theology whatsoever. Consequently, the only theology of reason which is possible is that which is based upon moral laws or seeks guidance from them. All synthetic principles of reason allow only of an immanent employment; and in order to have knowledge of a supreme being we should have to put them to a transcendent use, for which our understanding is in no way fitted. If the empirically valid law of causality is to lead to the original being, the latter must belong to the chain of objects of experience, and in that case it would, like all appearances, be

A 637 ⎫
B 665 ⎭ itself again conditioned. But even if the leap beyond the limits of experience, by means of the dynamical law of the relation of effects to their causes, be regarded as permissible, what sort of a concept could we obtain by this procedure? It is far from providing the concept of a supreme being, since experience never gives us the greatest of all possible effects, such as would be required to provide the evidence for a cause of that kind. Should we seek to make good this lack of determination in our concept, by means of a mere idea of [a being that possesses] the highest perfection and original necessity, this may indeed be granted

as a favour; it cannot be demanded as a right on the strength of an incontrovertible proof. The physico-theological proof, as combining speculation and intuition, might therefore perhaps give additional weight to other proofs (if such there be); but taken alone, it serves only to prepare the understanding for theological knowledge, and to give it a natural leaning in this direction, not to complete the work in and by itself.

All this clearly points to the conclusion that transcendental questions allow only of transcendental answers, that is, answers exclusively based on concepts that are *a priori*, without the least empirical admixture. But the question under consideration is obviously synthetic, calling for an extension of our knowledge beyond all limits of experience, namely, to the existence of a being that is to correspond to a mere idea of ours, an idea that cannot be paralleled in any experience. $\begin{cases} \text{A 638} \\ \text{B 666} \end{cases}$ Now as we have already proved, synthetic *a priori* knowledge is possible only in so far as it expresses the formal conditions of a possible experience; and all principles are therefore only of immanent validity, that is, they are applicable only to objects of empirical knowledge, to appearances. Thus all attempts to construct a theology through purely speculative reason, by means of a transcendental procedure, are without result.

But even if anyone prefers to call in question all those proofs which have been given in the Analytic, rather than allow himself to be robbed of his conviction of the conclusiveness of the arguments upon which he has so long relied, he still cannot refuse to meet my demand that he should at least give a satisfactory account how, and by what kind of inner illumination, he believes himself capable of soaring so far above all possible experience, on the wings of mere ideas. New proofs, or attempts to improve upon the old ones, I would ask to be spared. There is not indeed, in this field, much room for choice, since all merely speculative proofs in the end bring us always back to one and the same proof, namely, the ontological; and I have therefore no real ground to fear the fertile ingenuity of the dogmatic champions of supersensible[1] reason. I shall not, however, decline the challenge $\begin{cases} \text{A 639} \\ \text{B 667} \end{cases}$ to discover the fallacy in any attempt of this kind, and so to nullify its claims; and this I can indeed do without

---

[1] [*sinnenfreien.*]

considering myself a particularly combative person. But by such means I should never succeed in eradicating the hope of better fortune in those who have once become accustomed to dogmatic modes of persuasion; and I therefore confine myself to the moderate demand, that they give, in terms which are universal and which are based on the nature of the human understanding and of all our other sources of knowledge, a satisfactory answer to this one question: how we can so much as make a beginning in the proposed task of extending our knowledge entirely *a priori*, and of carrying it into a realm where no experience is possible to us, and in which there is therefore no means of establishing the objective reality of any concept that we have ourselves invented. In whatever manner the understanding may have arrived at a concept, the existence of its object is never, by any process of analysis, discoverable within it; for the knowledge of the *existence* of the object consists precisely in the fact that the object is posited in itself, *beyond the [mere] thought of it*.[1] Through concepts alone, it is quite impossible to advance to the discovery of new objects and supernatural[2] beings; and it is useless to appeal to experience, which in all cases yields only appearances.

But although reason, in its merely speculative employment, is very far from being equal to so great an undertaking, namely, to demonstrate the existence of a supreme being,

A 640
B 668
it is yet of very great utility in *correcting* any knowledge of this being which may be derived from other sources, in making it consistent with itself and with every point of view from which intelligible objects may be regarded,[3] and in freeing it from everything incompatible with the concept of an original being and from all admixture of empirical limitations

Transcendental theology is still, therefore, in spite of all its disabilities, of great importance in its negative employment, and serves as a permanent censor of our reason, in so far as the latter deals merely with pure ideas which, as such, allow of no criterion that is not transcendental. For if, in some other relation, perhaps on practical grounds, the *presupposition* of a supreme and all-sufficient being, as highest intelli-

---

[1] [*ausser dem Gedanken.*]   [2] [*überschwenglicher.*]
[3] [*mit sich selbst und jeder intelligibilen Absicht.*]

gence, established its validity beyond all question, it would be of the greatest importance accurately to determine this concept on its transcendental side, as the concept of a necessary and supremely real being, to free it from whatever, as belonging to mere appearance (anthropomorphism in its wider sense), is out of keeping with the supreme reality, and at the same time to dispose of all counter-assertions, whether *atheistic*, *deistic*, or *anthropomorphic*. Such critical treatment is, indeed, far from being difficult, inasmuch as the same grounds which have enabled us to demonstrate the inability of human reason to maintain the existence of such a being must {A 641 / B 669} also suffice to prove the invalidity of all counter-assertions. For from what source could we, through a purely speculative employment of reason, derive the knowledge that there is no supreme being as ultimate ground of all things, or that it has none of the attributes which, arguing from their consequences, we represent to ourselves as analogical with the dynamical realities of a thinking being, or (as the anthropomorphists contend) that it must be subject to all the limitations which sensibility inevitably imposes on those intelligences which are known to us through experience.

Thus, while for the merely speculative employment of reason the supreme being remains a mere *ideal*, it is yet *an ideal without a flaw*, a concept which completes and crowns the whole of human knowledge. Its objective reality cannot indeed be proved, but also cannot be disproved, by merely speculative reason. If, then, there should be a moral theology that can make good this deficiency, transcendental theology, which before was problematic only, will prove itself indispensable in determining the concept of this supreme being and in constantly testing reason, which is so often deceived by sensibility, and which is frequently out of harmony with its own ideas. Necessity, infinity, unity, existence outside the world (and not as world-soul), eternity as free from conditions of time, omnipresence as free from conditions of space, omni- {A 642 / B 670} potence, etc. are purely transcendental predicates, and for this reason the purified concepts of them, which every theology finds so indispensable, are only to be obtained from transcendental theology.

APPENDIX TO THE TRANSCENDENTAL DIALECTIC

THE REGULATIVE EMPLOYMENT OF THE IDEAS OF PURE REASON

The outcome of all dialectical attempts of pure reason does not merely confirm what we have already proved in the Transcendental Analytic, namely, that all those conclusions of ours which profess to lead us beyond the field of possible experience are deceptive and without foundation; it likewise teaches us this further lesson, that human reason has a natural tendency to transgress these limits, and that transcendental ideas are just as natural to it as the categories are to understanding—though with this difference, that while the categories lead to truth, that is, to the conformity of our concepts with the object, the ideas produce what, though a mere illusion, is none the less irresistible, and the harmful influence of which we can barely succeed in neutralising even by means of the severest criticism.

Everything that has its basis in the nature of our powers must be appropriate to, and consistent with, their right employment—if only we can guard against a certain misunderstanding and so can discover the proper direction of these powers. We are entitled, therefore, to suppose that transcendental ideas have their own good, proper, and therefore *immanent* use, although, when their meaning is misunderstood, and they are taken for concepts of real things, they become transcendent in their application and for that very reason can be delusive. For it is not the idea in itself, but its use only, that can be either transcendent or immanent (that is, either range beyond all possible experience or find employment within its limits), according as it is applied to an object which is supposed to correspond to it, or is directed solely to the use of understanding in general, in respect of those objects that fall to be dealt with by the understanding. All errors of subreption are to be ascribed to a defect of judgment,[1] never to understanding or to reason.

Reason is never in immediate relation to an object, but

A 643 }
B 671 }

[1] [*Urteilskraft.*]

only to the understanding; and it is only through the understanding that it has its own [specific] empirical employment.
It does not, therefore, *create* concepts (of objects) but only
orders them, and gives them that unity which they can have
only if they be employed in their widest possible application,
that is, with a view to obtaining totality in the various series.
The understanding does not concern itself with this totality,
but only with that connection through which, in accordance
with *concepts*, such *series* of conditions *come into being*.
Reason has, therefore, as its sole object, the understanding $\left\{\begin{matrix}\text{A 644}\\\text{B 672}\end{matrix}\right.$
and its effective application. Just as the understanding unifies
the manifold in the object by means of concepts, so reason
unifies the manifold of concepts by means of ideas, positing
a certain collective unity as the goal of the activities of the
understanding, which otherwise are concerned solely with
distributive unity.

I accordingly maintain that transcendental ideas never
allow of any constitutive employment. When regarded in
that mistaken manner, and therefore as supplying concepts
of certain objects, they are but pseudo-rational, merely dialectical concepts. On the other hand, they have an excellent,
and indeed indispensably necessary, regulative employment,
namely, that of directing the understanding towards a certain
goal upon which the routes marked out by all its rules converge, as upon their point of intersection. This point is indeed
a mere idea, a *focus imaginarius*, from which, since it lies
quite outside the bounds of possible experience, the concepts
of the understanding do not in reality proceed; none the less
it serves to give to these concepts the greatest [possible] unity
combined with the greatest [possible] extension. Hence arises
the illusion that the lines have their source in[1] a real object
lying outside the field of empirically possible knowledge—just
as objects reflected in a mirror are seen as behind it. Never-
theless this illusion (which need not, however, be allowed $\left\{\begin{matrix}\text{A 645}\\\text{B 673}\end{matrix}\right.$
to deceive us) is indispensably necessary if we are to direct
the understanding beyond every given experience (as part of
the sum of possible experience), and thereby to secure its
greatest possible extension, just as, in the case of mirror-
vision, the illusion involved is indispensably necessary if,

---

[1] [Reading, with Mellin, *geflossen* for *ausgeschlossen*.]

besides the objects which lie before our eyes, we are also to see those which lie at a distance behind our back.

If we consider in its whole range the knowledge obtained for us by the understanding, we find that what is peculiarly distinctive of reason in its attitude to this body of knowledge, is that it prescribes and seeks to achieve its *systematisation*, that is, to exhibit the connection of its parts in conformity with a single principle. This unity of reason always presupposes an idea, namely, that of the form of a whole of knowledge—a whole which is prior to the determinate knowledge of the parts and which contains the conditions that determine *a priori* for every part its position and relation to the other parts. This idea accordingly postulates a complete unity in the knowledge obtained by the understanding, by which this knowledge is to be not a mere contingent aggregate, but a system connected according to necessary laws. We may not say that this idea is a concept of the object, but only of the thoroughgoing unity of such concepts, in so far as that unity serves as a rule for the understanding. These concepts of reason are not derived from nature; on the contrary, we interrogate nature in accordance with these ideas, and consider our knowledge as defective so long as it is not adequate to them. By general admission, *pure earth, pure water, pure air*, etc., are not to be found. We require, however, the concepts of them (though, in so far as their complete purity is concerned, they have their origin solely in reason) in order properly to determine the share which each of these natural causes has in producing appearances. Thus in order to explain the chemical interactions of bodies in accordance with the idea of a mechanism, every kind of matter is reduced to earths (*qua* mere weight), to salts and inflammable substances (*qua* force), and to water and air as vehicles (machines, as it were, by which the first two produce their effects). The modes of expression usually employed are, indeed, somewhat different; but the influence of reason on the classifications of the natural scientist is still easily detected.

A 646
B 674

If reason is a faculty of deducing the particular from the universal, and if the universal is already *certain in itself* and given, only *judgment*[1] is required to execute the process of

---

[1] [*Urteilskraft.*]

subsumption, and the particular is thereby determined in a necessary manner. This I shall entitle the apodeictic use of reason. If, however, the universal is admitted as *problematic* only, and is a mere idea, the particular is certain, but the universality of the rule of which it is a consequence is still a problem. Several particular instances, which are one and all certain, are scrutinised in view of the rule, to see whether they follow from it. If it then appears that all particular instances which can be cited follow from the rule, { A 647 / B 675 } we argue to its universality, and from this again to all particular instances, even to those which are not themselves given. This I shall entitle the hypothetical employment of reason.

The hypothetical employment of reason, based upon ideas viewed as problematic concepts, is not, properly speaking, *constitutive*, that is, it is not of such a character that, judging in all strictness, we can regard it as proving the truth of the universal rule which we have adopted as hypothesis. For how are we to know all the possible consequences which, as actually following from the adopted principle, *prove* its universality? The hypothetical employment of reason is regulative only; its sole aim is, so far as may be possible, to bring unity into the body of our detailed knowledge, and thereby to *approximate* the rule to universality.

The hypothetical employment of reason has, therefore, as its aim the systematic unity of the knowledge of understanding, and this unity is the *criterion of the truth* of its rules. The systematic unity (as a mere idea) is, however, only a *projected* unity, to be regarded not as given in itself, but as a problem only. This unity aids us in discovering a principle for the understanding in its manifold [1] and special modes of employment, directing its attention to cases which are not given, and thus rendering it more coherent.[2]

But the only conclusion which we are justified in drawing { A 648 / B 676 } from these considerations is that the systematic unity of the manifold knowledge of understanding, as prescribed by reason, is a *logical* principle. Its function is to assist the understanding by means of ideas, in those cases in which the understanding cannot by itself establish rules, and at the same time to give

---

[1] [Reading, with Valentiner, *mannigfaltigen* for *Mannigfaltigen*.]
[2] [*zusammenhängend*.]

to the numerous and diverse rules of the understanding unity or system under a single principle, and thus to secure coherence in every possible way. But to say that the constitution of the objects or the nature of the understanding which knows them as such, is in itself determined to systematic unity, and that we can in a certain measure postulate this unity *a priori*, without reference to any such special interest of reason, and that we are therefore in a position to maintain that knowledge of the understanding in all its possible modes (including empirical knowledge) has the unity required by reason, and stands under common principles from which all its various modes can, in spite of their diversity, be deduced —that would be to assert a *transcendental* principle of reason, and would make the systematic unity necessary, not only subjectively and logically, as method, but objectively also.

We may illustrate this by an instance of the employment of reason. Among the various kinds of unity which conform to the concepts of the understanding, is that of the causality of a substance, which is called power.[1] The various appearances of one and the same substance show at first sight so great a diversity, that at the start we have to assume just as many different powers as there are different effects. For instance, in the human mind we have sensation, consciousness, imagination, memory, wit, power of discrimination, pleasure, desire, etc. Now there is a logical maxim which requires that we should reduce, so far as may be possible, this seeming diversity, by comparing these with one another and detecting their hidden identity. We have to enquire whether imagination combined with consciousness may not be the same thing as memory, wit, power of discrimination, and perhaps even identical with understanding and reason. Though logic is not capable of deciding whether a *fundamental power* actually exists, the idea of such a power is the problem involved in a systematic representation of the multiplicity of powers. The logical principle of reason calls upon us to bring about such unity as completely as possible; and the more the appearances of this and that power are found to be identical with one another, the more probable it becomes that they are simply different manifestations of one and the same power,

A 649⎱
B 677⎰

---

[1] [*Kraft.*]

which may be entitled, relatively to the more specific powers, the *fundamental power*. The same is done with the other powers.

The relatively fundamental powers must in turn be compared with one another, with a view to discovering their harmony, and so to bring them nearer to a single radical, that is, absolutely fundamental, power. But this unity of reason is purely hypothetical. We do not assert that such a power must necessarily be met with, but that we must seek it in the interests of reason, that is, of establishing certain principles for the manifold rules which experience may supply to us. $\begin{cases} \text{A } 650 \\ \text{B } 678 \end{cases}$ We must endeavour, wherever possible, to bring in this way systematic unity into our knowledge.

On passing, however, to the transcendental employment of understanding, we find that this idea of a fundamental power is not treated merely as a problem for the hypothetical use of reason, but claims to have objective reality, as postulating the systematic unity of the various powers of a substance, and as giving expression to an apodeictic principle of reason. For without having made any attempt to show the harmony of these various powers, nay, even after all attempts to do so have failed, we yet presuppose that such a unity does actually exist, and this not only, as in the case cited, on account of the unity of the substance, but also in those cases in which, as with matter in general, we encounter powers which, though to a certain extent homogeneous, are likewise diverse. In all such cases reason presupposes the systematic unity of the various powers, on the ground that special natural laws fall under more general laws, and that parsimony in principles is not only an economical requirement of reason, but is one of nature's own laws.

It is, indeed, difficult to understand how there can be a logical principle by which reason prescribes the unity of rules, unless we also presuppose a transcendental principle whereby such a systematic unity is *a priori* assumed to be necessarily inherent in the objects. For with what right can reason, in its $\begin{cases} \text{A } 651 \\ \text{B } 679 \end{cases}$ logical employment, call upon us to treat the multiplicity of powers exhibited in nature as simply a disguised unity, and to derive this unity, so far as may be possible, from a fundamental power—how can reason do this, if it be free to admit as likewise possible that all powers may be heterogeneous, and that such systematic unity of derivation may not be in conformity with nature? Reason would then run counter to its own vocation, proposing as its aim an idea quite inconsistent with the constitution of nature. Nor can we say that reason, while proceeding in accordance with its own principles, has arrived at knowledge of this unity through observation of the accidental constitution of nature. The law of reason which requires us to seek for this unity, is a necessary law, since without it we should have no reason at all, and without reason no coherent employment of the understanding, and in the absence of this no sufficient criterion of empirical truth. In order, therefore, to secure an empirical criterion we have no option save to presuppose the systematic unity of nature as objectively valid and necessary.

Although philosophers have not always acknowledged this transcendental principle, even to themselves, or indeed been conscious of employing it, we none the less find it covertly implied, in remarkable fashion, in the principles upon which they proceed. That the manifold respects in which individual things differ do not exclude identity of species, that the various species A 652⎱ must be regarded merely as different determinations of a few B 680⎰ genera, and these, in turn, of still higher genera, and so on; in short, that we must seek for a certain systematic unity of all possible empirical concepts, in so far as they can be deduced from higher and more general concepts—this is a logical principle, a rule of the Schools, without which there could be no employment of reason. For we can conclude from the universal to the particular, only in so far as universal properties are ascribed to things as being the foundation upon which the particular properties rest.

That such unity is to be found in nature, is presupposed by philosophers in the well-known scholastic maxim, that rudiments[1] or principles must not be unnecessarily multiplied (*entia praeter necessitatem non esse multiplicanda*). This maxim declares that things by their very nature supply material for the unity of reason, and that the seemingly infinite variety need not hinder us from assuming that behind this variety there is a unity of fundamental properties—properties from which the

[1] [*Anfänge.*]

diversity can be derived through repeated determination. This unity, although it is a mere idea, has been at all times so eagerly sought, that there has been need to moderate the desire for it, not to encourage it. A great advance was made when chemists succeeded in reducing all salts to two main genera, acids and alkalies; and they endeavour to show that even this difference is merely a variety, or diverse manifestation, of one and the {A 653 / B 681} same fundamental material. Chemists have sought, step by step, to reduce the different kinds of earths (the material of stones and even of metals) to three, and at last to two; but, not content with this, they are unable to banish the thought that behind these varieties there is but one genus, nay, that there may even be a common principle for the earths and the salts. It might be supposed that this is merely an economical contrivance whereby reason seeks to save itself all possible trouble, a hypothetical attempt, which, if it succeeds, will, through the unity thus attained, impart probability to the presumed principle of explanation. But such a selfish purpose can very easily be distinguished from the idea. For in conformity with the idea everyone presupposes that this unity of reason accords with nature itself, and that reason—although indeed unable to determine the limits of this unity—does not here beg but command.

If among the appearances which present themselves to us, there were so great a variety—I do not say in form, for in that respect the appearances might resemble one another; but in content, that is, in the manifoldness of the existing entities—that even the acutest human understanding could never by comparison of them detect the slightest similarity (a possibility which is quite conceivable), the logical law of genera would have no sort of standing; we should not even have the concept of a genus, or indeed any other universal concept; and {A 654 / B 682} the understanding itself, which has to do solely with such concepts, would be non-existent. If, therefore, the logical principle of genera is to be applied to nature (by which I here understand those objects only which are given to us), it presupposes a transcendental principle. And in accordance with this latter principle, homogeneity is necessarily presupposed in the manifold of possible experience (although we are not in a position to determine in *a priori* fashion its degree); for in the absence

of homogeneity, no empirical concepts, and therefore no experience, would be possible.

The logical principle of genera, which postulates identity,
is balanced by another principle, namely, that of *species*,
which calls for manifoldness and diversity in things, notwithstanding their agreement as coming under the same genus,
and which prescribes to the understanding that it attend to the
diversity no less than to the identity. This principle (of discrimi-
native observation, that is, of the faculty of distinction) sets
a limit to possible indiscretion in the former principle (of the
faculty of wit [1]); and reason thus exhibits a twofold, self-con-
flicting interest, on the one hand interest in *extent* (universality) in respect of genera, and on the other hand in *content* (de-
terminateness) in respect of the multiplicity of the species. In
the one case the understanding thinks more *under* its concepts,
in the other more *in* them. This twofold interest manifests itself also among students of nature in the diversity of their ways
of thinking. Those who are more especially speculative are,
we may almost say, hostile to heterogeneity, and are always on
the watch for the unity of the genus; those, on the other hand,
who are more especially empirical, are constantly endeavouring to differentiate nature in such manifold fashion as almost
to extinguish the hope of ever being able to determine its appearances in accordance with universal principles.

A 655
B 683

This latter mode of thought is evidently based upon a logical principle which aims at the systematic completeness of all
knowledge—prescribing that, in beginning with the genus, we
descend to the manifold which may be contained thereunder,
in such fashion as to secure extension for the system, just as in
the alternative procedure, that of ascending to the genus, we
endeavour to secure the unity of the system. For if we limit
our attention to the sphere of the concept which marks out a
genus, we can no more determine how far it is possible to proceed in the [logical] division of it, than we can judge merely
from the space which a body occupies how far it is possible to
proceed in the [physical] division of its parts. Consequently,

---

[1] [In his *Anthropologie*, i. § 42, Kant defines wit (*ingenium*) as the faculty by
which we determine the universal appropriate to the particular, in contrast to the
faculty of judgment, by which we determine the particular that accords with the
universal.]

every genus requires diversity of species, and these in turn diversity of subspecies; and since no one of these subspecies is ever itself without a sphere (extent as *conceptus communis*), reason, in being carried to completion, demands that no species be regarded as being in itself the lowest. For since the species is always a concept, containing only what is common to different things, it is not completely determined. It cannot, therefore, be directly related to an individual, and other concepts, that is, subspecies, must always be contained under it. This law of specification can be formulated as being the principle: *entium varietates non temere esse minuendas.*

$\begin{cases} \text{A } 656 \\ \text{B } 684 \end{cases}$

But it is easily seen that this logical law would be without meaning and application if it did not rest upon a *transcendental* law of specification, which does not indeed demand an actual *infinity* of differences in the things which can be objects to us —the logical principle, as affirming only the *indeterminateness* of the logical sphere in respect of possible division, gives no occasion for any such assertion—but which none the less imposes upon the understanding the obligation of seeking under every discoverable species for subspecies, and under every difference for yet smaller differences. For if there were no *lower* concepts, there could not be *higher* concepts. Now the understanding can have knowledge only through concepts, and therefore, however far it carries the process of division, never through mere intuition, but always again through *lower* concepts. The knowledge of appearances in their complete determination, which is possible only through the understanding, demands an endless progress in the specification of our concepts, and an advance to yet other remaining differences, from which we have made abstraction in the concept of the species, and still more so in that of the genus.

This law of specification cannot be derived from experience, which can never open to our view any such extensive prospects. Empirical specification soon comes to a stop in the distinction of the manifold, if it be not guided by the antecedent transcendental law of specification, which, as a principle of reason, leads us to seek always for further differences, and to suspect their existence even when the senses are unable to disclose them. That absorbent earths are of different kinds (chalk and muriatic earths), is a discovery that was possible

$\begin{cases} \text{A } 657 \\ \text{B } 685 \end{cases}$

only under the guidance of an antecedent rule of reason—reason proceeding on the assumption that nature is so richly diversified that we may presume the presence of such differences, and therefore prescribing to the understanding the task of searching for them. Indeed it is only on the assumption of differences in nature, just as it is also only under the condition that its objects exhibit homogeneity, that we can have any faculty of understanding whatsoever. For the diversity of that which is comprehended under a concept is precisely what gives occasion for the employment of the concept and the exercise of the understanding.

Reason thus prepares the field for the understanding: (1) through a principle of the *homogeneity* of the manifold under higher genera; (2) through a principle of the *variety* of the homogeneous under lower species; and (3) in order to complete the systematic unity, a further law, that of the *affinity* of all concepts—a law which prescribes that we proceed from each
A 658⎫
B 686⎭ species to every other by gradual increase of the diversity. These we may entitle the principles of *homogeneity*, *specification*, and *continuity* of forms. The last named arises from union of the other two, inasmuch as only through the processes of ascending to the higher genera and of descending to the lower species do we obtain the idea of systematic connection in its completeness.   For all the manifold differences are then related to one another, inasmuch as they one and all spring from one highest genus, through all degrees of a more and more widely extended determination.

The systematic unity, prescribed by the three logical principles, can be illustrated in the following manner.   Every concept may be regarded as a point which, as the station for an observer, has its own horizon, that is, a variety of things which can be represented, and, as it were, surveyed from that standpoint. This horizon must be capable of containing an infinite number of points, each of which has its own narrower horizon; that is, every species contains subspecies, according to the principle of specification, and the logical horizon consists exclusively of smaller horizons (subspecies), never of points which possess no extent (individuals). But for different horizons, that is, genera, each of which is determined by its own concept, there can be a common horizon, in reference to which, as from a common centre, they can all be surveyed; and from this higher genus we can proceed until we arrive at the $\left\{\begin{smallmatrix} \text{A } 659 \\ \text{B } 687 \end{smallmatrix}\right.$ highest of all genera, and so at the universal and true horizon, which is determined from the standpoint of the highest concept, and which comprehends under itself all manifoldness—genera, species, and subspecies.

We are carried to this highest standpoint by the law of homogeneity, and to all lower standpoints, and their greatest possible variety, by the law of specification. And since there is thus no void in the whole sphere of all possible concepts, and since nothing can be met with outside this sphere, there arises from the presupposition of this universal horizon and of its complete division, the principle: *non datur vacuum formarum*, that is, that there are not different, original, first genera, which are isolated from one another, separated, as it were, by an empty intervening space; but that all the manifold genera are simply divisions of one single highest and universal genus. From this principle there follows, as its immediate consequence: *datur continuum formarum*, that is, that all differences of species border upon one another, admitting of no transition from one to another *per saltum*, but only through all the smaller degrees of difference that mediate between them. In short, there are no species or subspecies which (in the view of reason) are the nearest possible to each other; still other intermediate species are always possible, the difference of which from each of the former is always smaller than the $\left\{\begin{smallmatrix} \text{A } 660 \\ \text{B } 688 \end{smallmatrix}\right.$ difference between these.

The first law thus keeps us from resting satisfied with an excessive number of different original genera, and bids us pay due regard to homogeneity; the second, in turn, imposes a check upon this tendency towards unity, and insists that before we proceed to apply a universal concept to individuals we distinguish subspecies within it. The third law combines these two laws by prescribing [1] that even amidst the utmost manifoldness we observe homogeneity in the gradual transition from one species to another, and thus recognise a relationship of the different branches, as all springing from the same stem.

This logical law of the *continuum specierum* (*formarum logicarum*) presupposes, however, a transcendental law (*lex*

---

[1] [Reading, with Hartenstein, *es* for *sie*.]

continui in natura), without which the former law would only lead the understanding astray, causing it[1] to follow a path which is perhaps quite contrary to that prescribed by nature itself. This law must therefore rest upon pure transcendental, not on empirical, grounds. For if it rested on empirical grounds, it would come later than the systems, whereas in actual fact it has itself given rise to all that is systematic in our knowledge of nature. The formulation of these laws is not due to any secret design of making an experiment, by putting them forward as merely tentative suggestions. Such anticipations, when confirmed, yield strong evidence in support of the view that the hypothetically conceived unity is well-grounded; and such evidence has therefore in this respect a certain utility. But it is evident that the laws contemplate the parsimony of fundamental causes, the manifoldness of effects, and the consequent affinity of the parts of nature as being in themselves in accordance both with reason and with nature. Hence these principles carry their recommendation directly in themselves, and not merely as methodological devices.

A 661
B 689

But it is easily seen that this continuity of forms is a mere idea, to which no congruent object can be discovered in experience. For in the first place, the species in nature are actually divided, and must therefore constitute a *quantum discretum*. Were the advance in the tracing of their affinity continuous, there would be a true infinity of intermediate members between any two given species, which is impossible. And further, in the second place, we could not make any determinate empirical use of this law, since it instructs us only in quite general terms that we are to seek for grades of affinity, and yields no criterion whatsoever as to how far, and in what manner, we are to prosecute the search for them.

A 662
B 690

If we place these principles of systematic unity in the order appropriate to their empirical employment, they will stand thus: *manifoldness, affinity, unity*, each being taken, as an idea,[2] in the highest degree of its completeness. Reason presupposes the knowledge which is obtained by the understanding and which stands in immediate relation to experience, and

---

[1] [Reading, with Erdmann, *er* for *sie*.]
[2] [Reading, with Erdmann, *Idee* for *Ideen*.]

seeks for the unity of this knowledge in accordance with ideas
which go far beyond all possible experience. The affinity of
the manifold (as, notwithstanding its diversity, coming under
a principle of unity) refers indeed to things, but still more to
their properties and powers. Thus, for instance, if at first our imperfect experience leads us to regard the orbits of the planets
as circular, and if we subsequently detect deviations therefrom,
we trace the deviations to that which can change the circle,
in accordance with a fixed law, through all the infinite intermediate degrees, into one of these divergent orbits. That is to
say, we assume that the movements of the planets which are
not circular will more or less approximate to the properties of a
circle; and thus we come upon the idea of an ellipse. Since the
comets do not, so far as observation reaches, return in any such
courses, their paths exhibit still greater deviations. What we
then do is to suppose that they proceed in a parabolic course,
which is akin to the ellipse, and which in all our observations $\begin{cases} \text{A } 663 \\ \text{B } 691 \end{cases}$
is indistinguishable from an ellipse that has its major axis in-
definitely extended. Thus, under the guidance of these principles, we discover a unity in the generic forms of the orbits,
and thereby a unity in the cause of all the laws of planetary
motion, namely, gravitation. And we then extend our con-
quests still further, endeavouring to explain by the same principle all variations and seeming departures from these rules;
finally, we even go on to make additions such as experience
can never confirm, namely, to conceive, in accordance with
the rules of affinity, hyperbolic paths of comets, in the course
of which these bodies entirely leave our solar system, and
passing from sun to sun, unite the most distant parts of the
universe—a universe which, though for us unlimited, is
throughout held together by one and the same moving force.

The remarkable feature of these principles, and what in
them alone concerns us, is that they seem to be transcendental,
and that although they contain mere ideas for the guidance of
the empirical employment of reason—ideas which reason
follows only as it were asymptotically, *i.e.* ever more closely
without ever reaching them—they yet possess, as synthetic
a priori propositions, objective but indeterminate validity, and
serve as rules for possible experience. They can also be employed with great advantage in the elaboration of experience,

as heuristic principles. A transcendental deduction of them
cannot, however, be effected; in the case of ideas, as we have
shown above, such a deduction is never possible.

A 664
B 692

In the Transcendental Analytic we have distinguished the
dynamical principles of the understanding, as merely regulative principles of *intuition*, from the *mathematical*, which, as
regards intuition, are constitutive. None the less these dynamical laws are constitutive in respect of *experience*, since they
render the *concepts*, without which there can be no experience, possible *a priori*. But principles of pure reason can
never be constitutive in respect of empirical *concepts*; for since
no schema of sensibility corresponding to them can ever be
given, they can never have an object *in concreto*. If, then, we
disallow such empirical employment of them, as constitutive
principles, how are we to secure for them a regulative employment, and therewith some sort of objective validity, and
what can we mean by such regulative employment?

The understanding is an object for reason, just as sensibility is for the understanding. It is the business of reason to
render the unity of all possible empirical acts of the understanding systematic; just as it is of the understanding to connect the manifold of the appearances by means of concepts,
and to bring it under empirical laws. But the acts of the understanding are, without the schemata of sensibility, *undetermined*; just as the *unity of reason* is in itself *undetermined*, as
regards the conditions under which, and the extent to which,
the understanding ought to combine its concepts in systematic
fashion. But although we are unable to find in *intuition* a
schema for the complete systematic unity of all concepts of the
understanding, an *analogon* of such a schema must necessarily
allow of being given. This analogon is the idea of the *maximum* in the division and unification of the knowledge of the
understanding under one principle. For what is greatest and
absolutely complete can be determinately thought, all restricting conditions, which give rise to an indeterminate
manifoldness, being left aside. Thus the idea of reason is
an analogon of a schema of sensibility; but with this difference, that the application of the concepts of the understanding
to the schema of reason does not yield knowledge of the object
itself (as is the case in the application of categories to their

A 665
B 693

sensible schemata), but only a rule or principle for the systematic unity of all employment of the understanding. Now since every principle which prescribes *a priori* to the understanding thoroughgoing unity in its employment, also holds, although only indirectly, of the object of experience, the principles of pure reason must also have objective reality in respect of that object, not, however, in order to *determine* anything in it,[1] but only in order to indicate the procedure whereby the empirical and determinate employment of the understanding can be brought into complete harmony with itself. This is achieved by bringing its employment, so far as may be possible, into connection with the principle of thoroughgoing unity, and by determining its procedure in the light of this principle.

B 694
A 666

I entitle all subjective principles which are derived, not from the constitution of an object but from the interest of reason in respect of a certain possible perfection of the knowledge of the object, *maxims* of reason. There are therefore maxims of speculative reason, which rest entirely on its speculative interest, although they may seem to be objective principles.

When merely regulative principles are treated as constitutive, and are therefore employed as objective principles, they may come into conflict with one another. But when they are treated merely as *maxims*, there is no real conflict, but merely those differences in the interest of reason that give rise to differing modes of thought. In actual fact, reason has only one single interest, and the conflict of its maxims is only a difference in, and a mutual limitation of, the methods whereby this interest endeavours to obtain satisfaction.

Thus one thinker may be more particularly interested in *manifoldness* (in accordance with the principle of specification), another thinker in *unity* (in accordance with the principle of aggregation).[2] Each believes that his judgment has been arrived at through insight into the object, whereas it really rests entirely on the greater or lesser attachment to one of the two principles. And since neither of these principles is based on objective grounds, but solely on the interest of reason, the

A 667
B 695

---

[1] [Reading, with Wille, *ihm* for *ihnen*.]
[2] [*Aggregation*.]

title 'principles' is not strictly applicable; they may more fittingly be entitled 'maxims'. When we observe intelligent people disputing in regard to the characteristic properties of men, animals, or plants—even of bodies in the mineral realm—some assuming, for instance, that there are certain special hereditary characteristics in each nation, certain well-defined inherited differences in families, races, etc., whereas others are bent upon maintaining that in all such cases nature has made precisely the same provision for all, and that it is solely to external accidental conditions that the differences are due, we have only to consider what sort of an object it is about which they are making these assertions, to realise that it lies too deeply hidden to allow of their speaking from insight into its nature. The dispute is due simply to the twofold interest of reason, the one party setting its heart upon, or at least adopting, the one interest, and the other party the other. The differences between the maxims of manifoldness and of unity in nature thus easily allow of reconciliation. So long, however, as the maxims are taken as yielding objective insight, and until a way has been discovered of adjusting their conflicting claims, and of satisfying reason in that regard, they will not only give rise to disputes but will be a positive hindrance, and cause long delays in the discovery of truth.

A 668 ⎱
B 696 ⎰

Similar observations are relevant in regard to the assertion or denial of the widely discussed law of the *continuous gradation* of created beings, which was propounded by Leibniz,[1] and admirably supported by Bonnet.[2] It is simply the following out of that principle of affinity which rests on the interest of reason. For observation and insight into the constitution of nature could never justify us in the objective assertion of the law. The steps of this ladder, as they are presented to us in experience, stand much too far apart; and what may seem to us small differences are usually in nature itself such wide gaps, that from any such observations we can come to no decision in regard to nature's ultimate design—especially if we bear in mind that in so great a multiplicity of things there can never be much difficulty in finding similarities and approximations. On the other hand, the method of looking for order in nature

---

[1] [Leibniz: *Nouveaux Essais*, Liv. iii. ch. 6.]

[2] [Charles Bonnet (1726-93): *Betrachtungen über die Natur*, pp. 29-85.]

in accordance with such a principle, and the maxim which prescribes that we regard such order—leaving, however, undetermined where and how far—as grounded in nature as such, is certainly a legitimate and excellent regulative principle of reason. In this regulative capacity it goes far beyond what experience or observation can verify; and though not itself determining anything, yet serves to mark out the path towards systematic unity.

THE FINAL PURPOSE OF THE NATURAL DIALECTIC OF HUMAN REASON

{A 669
{B 697

The ideas of pure reason can never be dialectical in themselves; any deceptive illusion to which they give occasion must be due solely to their misemployment. For they arise from the very nature of our reason; and it is impossible that this highest tribunal of all the rights and claims of speculation should itself be the source of deceptions and illusions. Presumably, therefore, the ideas have their own good and appropriate vocation as determined by the natural disposition of our reason. The mob of sophists, however, raise against reason the usual cry of absurdities and contradictions, and though unable to penetrate to its innermost designs, they none the less inveigh against its prescriptions. Yet it is to the beneficent influences exercised by reason that they owe the possibility of their own self-assertiveness, and indeed that very culture[1] which enables them to blame and to condemn what reason requires of them.

We cannot employ an *a priori* concept with any certainty without having first given a transcendental deduction of it. The ideas of pure reason do not, indeed, admit of the kind of deduction that is possible in the case of the categories. But if they are to have the least objective validity, no matter how indeterminate that validity may be, and are not to be mere empty thought-entities[2] (*entia rationis ratiocinantis*), a deduction of them must be possible, however greatly (as we admit) it may differ from that which we have been able to give of the categories. This will complete the critical work of pure reason, and is what we now propose to undertake.

{A 670
{B 698

[1] [*Kultur.*]   [2] [*Gedankendinge.*]

There is a great difference between something being given
to my reason as an *object absolutely*, or merely as an *object in
the idea*. In the former case our concepts are employed to determine the object; in the latter case there is in fact only a schema
for which no object, not even a hypothetical one, is directly
given, and which only enables us to represent to ourselves
other objects in an indirect manner, namely in their systematic
unity, by means of their relation to this idea. Thus I say that
the concept of a highest intelligence is a mere idea, that is
to say, its objective reality is not to be taken as consisting in
its referring directly to an object (for in that sense we should
not be able to justify its objective validity). It is only a schema
constructed in accordance with the conditions of the greatest
possible unity of reason—the schema of the concept of a thing
in general, which serves only to secure the greatest possible systematic unity in the empirical employment of our reason. We
then, as it were, derive the object of experience from the supposed object of this idea, viewed as the ground or cause of the
object of experience. We declare, for instance, that the things
of the world must be viewed *as if* they received their existence
from a highest intelligence. The idea is thus really only a heuristic, not an ostensive concept. It does not show us how an
object is constituted, but how, under its guidance, we should
seek to determine the constitution and connection of the objects
of experience. If, then, it can be shown that the three transcendental ideas (the psychological, the cosmological, and the theological), although they do not directly relate to, or determine,
any object corresponding to them, none the less, as[1] rules of the
empirical employment of reason, lead us to systematic unity,
under the presupposition of such an *object in the idea*; and
that they thus contribute to the extension of empirical knowledge, without ever being in a position to run counter to it,
we may conclude that it is a necessary maxim of reason to
proceed always in accordance with such ideas. This, indeed,
is the transcendental deduction of all ideas of speculative
reason, not as *constitutive* principles for the extension of our
knowledge to more objects than experience can give, but as
regulative principles of the systematic unity of the manifold
of empirical knowledge in general, whereby this empirical

A 671
B 699

---

[1] [Reading, with Grillo, *als* for *alle*.]

knowledge is more adequately secured within its own limits and more effectively improved than would be possible, in the absence of such ideas, through the employment merely of the principles of the understanding.

I shall endeavour to make this clearer. In conformity with $\begin{cases} \text{A } 672 \\ \text{B } 700 \end{cases}$ these ideas as principles we shall, *first*, in psychology, under the guidance of inner experience, connect all the appearances, all the actions and receptivity of our mind, *as if* the mind were a simple substance which persists with personal identity (in this life at least), while its states, to which those of the body belong only as outer conditions, are in continual change. *Secondly*, in cosmology, we must follow up the conditions of both inner and outer natural appearances, in an enquiry which is to be regarded as never allowing of completion, just *as if* the series of appearances were in itself endless, without any first or supreme member. We need not, in so doing, deny that, outside all appearances, there are purely intelligible grounds of the appearances; but as we have no knowledge of these whatsoever, we must never attempt to make use of them in our explanations of nature. *Thirdly*, and finally, in the domain of theology, we must view everything that can belong to the context of possible experience *as if* this experience formed an absolute but at the same time completely dependent and *sensibly* conditioned unity, and yet also at the same time *as if* the sum of all appearances (the sensible world itself) had a single, highest and all-sufficient ground beyond itself, namely, a self-subsistent, original, creative reason. For it is in the light of this idea of a creative reason that we so guide the empirical $\begin{cases} \text{A } 673 \\ \text{B } 701 \end{cases}$ employment of *our* reason as to secure its greatest possible extension—that is, by viewing all objects *as if* they drew their origin from such an archetype. In other words, we ought not to derive the inner appearances of the soul from a simple thinking substance but from one another, in accordance with the idea of a simple being; we ought not to derive the order and systematic unity of the world from a supreme intelligence, but to obtain from the idea of a supremely wise cause the rule according to which reason in connecting empirical causes and effects in the world may be employed to best advantage, and in such manner as to secure satisfaction of its own demands.

Now there is nothing whatsoever to hinder us from *as-*

suming these ideas to be also objective, that is, from hypostatising them—except in the case of the cosmological ideas,
where reason, in so proceeding, falls into antinomy. The
psychological and theological ideas contain no antinomy,
and involve no contradiction. How, then, can anyone dispute
their [possible] objective reality? He who denies their possibility must do so with just as little knowledge [of this possi-
bility] as we can have in affirming it. It is not, however, a
sufficient ground for assuming anything, that there is no
positive hindrance to our so doing; we are not justified in
introducing thought-entities[1] which transcend all our concepts, though without contradicting them, as being real and
determinate objects, merely on the authority of a speculative
reason that is bent upon completing the tasks which it has
set itself. They ought not to be assumed as existing in
themselves, but only as having the reality of a schema—the
schema of the regulative principle of the systematic unity of
all knowledge of nature. They should be regarded only as
analoga of real things, not as in themselves real things. We
remove from the object of the idea the conditions which limit
the concept provided by our understanding, but which also
alone make it possible for us to have a determinate concept of anything. What we then think is a something of
which, as it is in itself, we have no concept whatsoever, but
which we none the less represent to ourselves as standing to
the sum of appearances in a relation analogous to that in
which appearances stand to one another.

A 674
B 702

If, in this manner, we assume such ideal beings, we do not
really extend our knowledge beyond the objects of possible
experience; we extend only the empirical unity of such experience, by means of the systematic unity for which the schema
is provided by the idea—an idea which has therefore no claim
to be a constitutive, but only a regulative principle. For
to allow that we posit a thing, a something, a real being,
corresponding to the idea, is not to say that we profess
to extend our knowledge of things by means of transcendental[2] concepts. For this being is posited only in the idea and
not in itself; and therefore only as expressing the systematic

---

[1] [*Gedankenwesen.*]
[2] [Reading, with the 4th edition, *transcendentalen* for *transcendenten.*]

unity which is to serve as a rule for the empirical employ- $\begin{cases} A\ 675 \\ B\ 703 \end{cases}$
ment of reason. It decides nothing in regard to the ground of
this unity or as to what may be the inner character of the being
on which as cause the unity depends.

Thus the transcendental, and the only determinate, concept which the purely speculative reason gives us of God is, in
the strictest sense, *deistic*; that is, reason does not determine
the objective validity of such a concept, but yields only the
idea of something which is the ground of the highest and
necessary unity of all empirical reality. This something we
cannot think otherwise than on the analogy of a real substance that, in conformity with laws of reason, is the cause
of all things. This, indeed, is how we must think it, in
so far as we venture to think it as a special object, and do
not rather remain satisfied with the mere idea of the regulative principle of reason, leaving aside the completion of
all conditions of thought as being too surpassingly great
for the human understanding. The latter procedure is, however, inconsistent with the pursuit of that complete systematic unity in our knowledge to which reason at least sets
no limits.

This, then, is how matters stand: if we assume a divine
being, we have indeed no concept whatsoever either of the
inner possibility of its supreme perfection or of the necessity
of its existence; but, on the other hand, we are in a position $\begin{cases} A\ 676 \\ B\ 704 \end{cases}$
to give a satisfactory answer to all those questions which
relate to the contingent, and to afford reason the most complete satisfaction in respect to that highest unity after which
it is seeking in its empirical employment. The fact, however,
that we are unable to satisfy reason in respect to the assumption itself, shows that it is the speculative interest of reason,
not any insight, which justifies it in thus starting from a point
that lies so far above its sphere; and in endeavouring, by this
device, to survey its objects as constituting a complete whole.

We here come upon a distinction bearing on the procedure
of thought in dealing with one and the same assumption, a
distinction which is somewhat subtle, but of great importance
in transcendental philosophy. I may have sufficient ground to
assume something, in a relative sense (*suppositio relativa*), and
yet have no right to assume it absolutely (*suppositio absoluta*).

This distinction has to be reckoned with in the case of a merely regulative principle. We recognise the necessity of the principle, but have no knowledge of the source of its necessity; and in assuming that it has a supreme ground, we do so solely in order to think its universality more determinately. Thus, for instance, when I think as existing a being that corresponds to a mere idea, indeed to a transcendental idea, I have no right to assume any such thing as in itself exist-

A 677
B 705

ing, since no concepts through which I am able to think any object as determined suffice for such a purpose—the conditions which are required for the objective validity of my concepts being excluded by the idea itself. The concepts of reality, substance, causality, even that of necessity in existence, apart from their use in making possible the empirical knowledge of an object, have no meaning whatsoever, such as might serve to determine any object. They can be employed, therefore, to explain the possibility of things in the world of sense, but not to explain the possibility of the *universe itself*. Such a ground of explanation would have to be outside the world, and could not therefore be an object of a possible experience. None the less, though I cannot assume such an inconceivable being [as existing] in itself, I may yet assume it as the object of a mere idea, relatively to the world of sense. For if the greatest possible empirical employment of my reason rests upon an idea (that of systematically complete unity, which I shall presently be defining more precisely), an idea which, although it can never itself be adequately exhibited in experience, is yet indispensably necessary in order that we may approximate to the highest possible degree of empirical unity, I shall not only be entitled, but shall also be constrained, to realise this idea, that is, to posit for it a real object. But I may posit it only as a something which I do not at all know in itself, and to which, as a ground of that systematic unity, I

A 678
B 706

ascribe, in relation to this unity, such properties as are analogous to the concepts employed by the understanding in the empirical sphere. Accordingly, in analogy with realities in the world, that is, with substances, with causality and with necessity, I think a being which possesses all this in the highest perfection; and since this idea depends merely on my reason, I can think this being as *self-subsistent reason,* which through ideas of the greatest harmony and unity is the cause of the universe. I thus omit all conditions which might limit the idea, solely in order, under countenance of such an original ground, to make possible systematic unity of the manifold in the universe, and thereby the greatest possible empirical employment of reason. This I do by representing all connections *as if* they were the ordinances of a supreme reason, of which our reason is but a faint copy. I then proceed to think this supreme being exclusively through concepts which, properly, are applicable only in the world of sense. But since I make none but a relative use of the transcendental assumption, namely, as giving the substratum of the greatest possible unity of experience, I am quite in order in thinking a being which I distinguish from the world of sense, through properties which belong solely to that world. For I do not seek, nor am I justified in seeking, to know this object of my idea according to what it may be in itself. There are no concepts available for any such purpose; even the concepts of {A 679 / B 707} reality, substance, causality, nay, even that of necessity in existence, lose all meaning, and are empty titles for [possible] concepts, themselves entirely without content, when we thus venture with them outside the field of the senses. I think to myself merely the relation of a being, in itself completely unknown to me, to the greatest possible systematic unity of the universe, solely for the purpose of using it as a schema of the regulative principle of the greatest possible empirical employment of my reason.

If it be the transcendental object of our idea that we have in view, it is obvious that we cannot thus, in terms of the concepts of reality, substance, causality, etc., presuppose its reality *in itself*, since these concepts have not the least application to anything that is entirely distinct from the world of sense. The supposition which reason makes of a supreme being, as the highest cause, is, therefore relative only; it is devised solely for the sake of systematic unity in the world of sense, and is a mere something in idea, of which, as it may be *in itself*, we have no concept This explains why, in relation to what is given to the senses as existing, we require the idea of a primordial being *necessary in itself*, and yet can never form the slightest concept of it or of its absolute necessity.

We are now in a position to have a clear view of the outcome of the whole Transcendental Dialectic, and accurately to define the final purpose of the ideas of pure reason, which become dialectical only through heedlessness and misapprehension. Pure reason is in fact occupied with nothing but itself. It can have no other vocation. For what is given to it does not consist in objects that have to be brought to the unity of the empirical concept, but in those modes of knowledge supplied by the understanding that require to be brought to the unity of the concept of reason—that is, to unity of connection in conformity with a principle. The unity of reason is the unity of system; and this systematic unity does not serve objectively as a principle that extends the application of reason to objects, but subjectively as a maxim that extends its application to all possible empirical knowledge of objects. Nevertheless, since the systematic connection which reason can give to the empirical employment of the understanding not only furthers its extension, but also guarantees its correctness, the principle of such systematic unity is so far also objective, but in an indeterminate manner (*principium vagum*). It is not a constitutive principle that enables us to determine anything in respect of its direct object, but only a merely regulative principle and maxim, to further and strengthen *in infinitum* (indeterminately) the empirical employment of reason—never in any way proceeding counter to the laws of its empirical employment, and yet at the same time opening out new paths which are not within the cognisance of the understanding.

But reason cannot think this systematic unity otherwise than by giving to the idea of this unity an object; and since experience can never give an example of complete systematic unity, the object which we have to assign to the idea is not such as experience can ever supply. This object, as thus entertained by reason (*ens rationis ratiocinatae*), is a mere idea; it is not assumed as a something that is real absolutely and *in itself*, but is postulated only problematically (since we cannot reach it through any of the concepts of the understanding) in order that we may view all connection of the things of the world of sense *as if* they had their ground in such a being. In thus proceeding, our sole purpose is to secure that systematic unity which is indispensable to reason, and which while furthering in every way the empirical knowledge obtainable by the understanding can never interfere to hinder or obstruct it.

We misapprehend the meaning of this idea if we regard it as the assertion or even as the assumption of a real thing, to which we may proceed to ascribe the ground of the systematic order of the world. On the contrary, what this ground which eludes our concepts may be in its own inherent constitution is left entirely undetermined; the idea is posited only as being the point of view from which alone that unity, which is so essential to reason and so beneficial to the understanding, can be further extended. In short, this transcendental {A 682 / B 710} thing is only the schema of the regulative principle by which reason, so far as lies in its power, extends systematic unity over the whole field of experience.

The first object of such an idea is the 'I' itself, viewed simply as thinking nature or soul. If I am to investigate the properties with which a thinking being is in itself endowed, I must interrogate experience. For I cannot even apply any one of the categories to this object, except in so far as the schema of the category is given in sensible intuition. But I never thereby attain to a systematic unity of all appearances of inner sense. Instead, then, of the empirical concept (of that which the soul actually is), which cannot carry us far, reason takes the concept of the empirical unity of all thought; and by thinking this unity as unconditioned and original, it forms from it a concept of reason, that is, the idea of a simple substance, which, unchangeable in itself (personally identical), stands in association with other real things outside it; in a word, the idea of a simple self-subsisting intelligence. Yet in so doing it has nothing in view save principles of systematic unity in the explanation of the {A 683 / B 711} appearances of the soul. It is endeavouring to represent all determinations as existing in a single subject, all powers, so far as possible, as derived from a single fundamental power, all change as belonging to the states of one and the same permanent being, and all *appearances* in space as completely different from the actions of *thought*. The simplicity and other properties of substance are intended to be only the schema of this regulative principle, and are not presupposed as being the actual ground of the properties of the soul. For these may rest on altogether different grounds, of which we can know nothing. The soul in itself could not be known through these assumed predicates, not even if we regarded them as absolutely valid in respect of it. For they constitute a mere idea which cannot be represented *in concreto*. Nothing but advantage can result from the psychological idea thus conceived, if only we take heed that it is not viewed as more than a mere idea, and that it is therefore taken as valid only relatively to the systematic employment of reason in determining the appearances of our soul. For no empirical laws of bodily appearances, which are of a totally different kind, will then intervene in the explanation of what belongs exclusively to *inner sense*. No windy hypotheses of generation, extinction, and palingenesis of souls will be permitted. The consideration of this object of inner sense will thus be kept completely pure and will not be confused by the introduction of heterogeneous properties. Also, reason's investigations will be directed to reducing the grounds of explanation in this field, so far as may be possible, to a single principle. All this will be best attained through such a schema, viewed *as if* it were a real being; indeed it is attainable in no other way. The psychological idea can signify nothing but the schema of a regulative concept. For were I to enquire whether *the soul in itself* is of spiritual nature, the question would have no meaning. In employing such a concept I not only abstract from corporeal nature, but from nature in general, that is, from all predicates of any possible experience, and therefore from all conditions requisite for thinking an object for such a concept; yet only as related to an object can the concept be said to have a meaning.

A 684
B 712

The second regulative idea of merely speculative reason is the concept of the world in general. For nature is properly the only given object in regard to which reason requires regulative principles. This nature is twofold, either thinking or corporeal. To think the latter, so far as regards its inner possibility, that is, to determine the application of the categories to it, we need no idea, that is, no representation which transcends experience. Nor, indeed, is any idea possible in this connection, since in dealing with corporeal nature we are guided solely by sensible intuition. The case is different from that of the fundamental psychological concept ('I'), which contains *a priori* a certain form of thought, namely, the unity of thought. There therefore remains for pure reason nothing but nature in general, and the completeness of the conditions in nature in accordance with some principle. The absolute totality of the series of these conditions, in the derivation of their members, is an idea which can never be completely realised in the empirical employment of reason, but which yet serves as a rule that prescribes how we ought to proceed in dealing with such series, namely, that in explaining appearances, whether in their regressive or in their ascending order, we ought to treat the series *as if* it were in itself infinite, that is, *as if* it proceeded *in indefinitum*. When, on the other hand, reason is itself regarded as the determining cause, as in [the sphere of] freedom, that is to say, in the case of practical principles, we have to proceed as if we had before us an object, not of the senses, but of the pure understanding. In this practical sphere the conditions are no longer in the series of appearances; they can be posited outside the series, and the series of states can therefore be regarded *as if* it had an absolute beginning, through an intelligible cause. All this shows that the cosmological ideas are nothing but simply regulative principles, and are very far from positing, in the manner of constitutive principles, an actual totality of such series. The fuller treatment of this subject will be found in the chapter on the antinomy of pure reason.

{A 685
{B 713

The third idea of pure reason, which contains a merely relative supposition of a being that is the sole and sufficient cause of all cosmological series, is the idea of *God*. We have not the slightest ground to assume in an absolute manner (to suppose in itself) the object of this idea; for what can enable us to believe in or assert a being of the highest perfection and one absolutely necessary by its very nature, merely on the basis of its concept, or if we did how could we justify our procedure? It is only by way of its relation to the world that we can attempt to establish the necessity of this supposition; and it then becomes evident that the idea of such a being, like all speculative ideas, seeks only to formulate the command of reason, that all connection in the world be viewed in accordance with the principles of a systematic unity—*as if* all such connection had its source in one single all-embracing being, as the supreme and

{A 686
{B 714

all-sufficient cause. It is thus evident that reason has here no other purpose than to prescribe its own formal rule for the extension of its empirical employment, and not any extension *beyond all limits of empirical employment*. Consequently it is evident that this idea does not, in any concealed fashion, involve any principle that claims, in its application to possible experience, to be constitutive in character.

This highest formal unity, which rests solely on concepts of reason, is the *purposive*[1] unity of things. The *speculative* interest of reason makes it necessary to regard all order in the world as if it had originated in the purpose[2] of a supreme reason. Such a principle opens out to our reason, as applied in the field of experience, altogether new views as to how the things of the world may be connected according to teleological[3] laws, and so enables it to arrive at their greatest systematic unity. The assumption of a supreme intelligence, as the one and only cause of the universe, though in the idea alone, can therefore always benefit reason and can never injure it. Thus if, in studying the shape of the earth (which is round, but somewhat flattened),[a] of the mountains, seas, etc., we assume it to be the outcome of wise purposes on the part of an Author of the world, we are enabled to make in this way a number of discoveries. And provided we restrict ourselves to a merely regulative use of this principle, even error cannot do us any serious harm. For the worst that can happen would be that where we expected a teleological connection (*nexus finalis*), we find only a mechanical or physical connection (*nexus effectivus*). In such a case, we merely fail to find the additional unity; we do not destroy the unity upon which reason insists in its empirical

A 687
B 715

A 688
B 716

[a] The advantage arising from the spherical shape of the earth is well known. But few are aware that its spheroidal flattening alone prevents the continental elevations, or even the smaller hills, thrown up perhaps by earthquakes, from continuously, and indeed quite appreciably in a comparatively short time, altering the position of the axis of the earth. The protuberance of the earth at the equator forms so vast a mountain that the impetus of all the other mountains can never produce any observable effect in changing the position of the earth's axis. And yet, wise as this arrangement is, we feel no scruples in explaining it from the equilibrium of the formerly fluid mass of the earth.

[1] [*zweckmässige*.]   [2] [*Absicht*.]   [3] [*teleologischen*.]

employment. But even a disappointment of this sort cannot affect the teleological law itself, in its general bearing. For although an anatomist can be convicted of error when he assigns to some member of an animal body an end[1] which it can be clearly shown not to subserve, it is yet quite impossible to *prove* in any given case that an arrangement of nature, be it what it may, subserves no end whatsoever. Accordingly, medical physiology extends its very limited empirical knowledge of the ends served by the articulation of an organic body, by resorting to a principle for which pure reason has alone been responsible; and it carries this principle so far as to assume confidently, and with general approval, that everything in an animal has its use, and subserves some good purpose. If this assumption be treated as constitutive it goes much further than observation has thus far been able to justify; and we must therefore conclude that it is nothing more than a regulative principle of reason, to aid us in securing the highest possible systematic unity, by means of the idea of the purposive causality of the supreme cause of the world—*as if* this being, as supreme intelligence, acting in accordance with a supremely wise purpose, were the cause of all things.

If, however, we overlook this restriction of the idea to a merely regulative use, reason is led away into mistaken paths. {A 689 B 717} For it then leaves the ground of experience, which alone can contain the signs that mark out its proper course, and ventures out beyond it to the incomprehensible and unsearchable, rising to dizzy heights where it finds itself entirely cut off from all possible action in conformity with experience.

The first error which arises from our using the idea of a supreme being in a manner contrary to the nature of an idea, that is, constitutively, and not regulatively only, is the error of *ignava ratio*.[a] We may so entitle every principle which makes

[a] This was the title given by the ancient dialecticians to a sophistical argument, which ran thus: If it is your fate to recover from this illness, you will recover, whether you employ a physician or not. Cicero states that this mode of argument has been so named, because, if we conformed to it, reason would be left without any use in life. On the same ground I apply the name also to the sophistical argument of pure reason.

[1] [*Zweck.*]

us regard our investigation into nature, on any subject, as
A 690
B 718 absolutely complete, disposing reason to cease from further
enquiry, as if it had entirely succeeded in the task which it had
set itself. Thus the psychological idea, when it is employed as
a constitutive principle to explain the appearances of our soul,
and thereby to extend our knowledge of the self beyond the
limits of experience (its state after death), does indeed simplify
the task of reason; but it interferes with, and entirely ruins,
our use of reason in dealing with nature under the guidance
of our experiences. The dogmatic spiritualist explains the
abiding and unchanging unity of a person throughout all
change of state, by the unity of the thinking substance, of
which, as he believes, he has immediate perception in the 'I';
or he explains the interest which we take in what can happen
only after our death, by means of our consciousness of the immaterial nature of the thinking subject; and so forth. He thus
dispenses with all empirical investigation of the cause of these
inner appearances, so far as that cause is to be found in physical grounds of explanation; and to his own great convenience,
though at the sacrifice of all real insight, he professes, in reliance upon the assumed authority of a transcendent reason, to
have the right to ignore those sources of knowledge which are
immanent in experience. These detrimental consequences are
even more obvious in the dogmatic treatment of our idea of a
supreme intelligence, and in the theological system of nature
A 691
B 719 (physico-theology) which is falsely based upon it. For in
this field of enquiry, if instead of looking for causes in the
universal laws of material mechanism, we appeal directly to
the unsearchable decree of supreme wisdom, all those ends
which are exhibited in nature, together with the many ends
which are only ascribed by us to nature, make our investigation of the causes a very easy task, and so enable us to
regard the labour of reason as completed, when, as a matter
of fact, we have merely dispensed with its employment—an
employment which is wholly dependent for guidance upon the
order of nature and the series of its alterations, in accordance
with the universal laws which they are found to exhibit.[1] This
error can be avoided, if we consider from the teleological point
of view not merely certain parts of nature, such as the distribu-

[1] [nach ihren inneren und allgemeinen Gesetzen.]

tion of land, its structure, the constitution and location of the mountains, or only the organisation of the vegetable and animal kingdoms, but make this systematic unity of nature completely *universal*, in relation to the idea of a supreme intelligence. For we then treat nature as resting upon a purposiveness, in accordance with universal laws, from which no special arrangement is exempt, however difficult it may be to establish this in any given case. We then have a regulative principle of the systematic unity of teleological connection— a connection which we do not, however, predetermine. What we may presume to do is to follow out the physico-mechanical {A 692 / B 720} connection in accordance with universal laws, in the hope of discovering what the teleological connection actually is. In this way alone can the principle of purposive unity aid always in extending the employment of reason in reference to experience, without being in any instance prejudicial to it.

The second error arising from the misapprehension of the above principle of systematic unity is that of *perversa ratio* (ὕστερον πρότερον). The idea of systematic unity should be used only as a regulative principle to guide us in seeking for such unity in the connection of things, according to universal laws of nature; and we ought, therefore, to believe that we have approximated to completeness in the employment of the principle only in proportion as we are in a position to verify such unity in empirical fashion—a completeness which is never, of course, attainable. Instead of this the reverse procedure is adopted. The reality of a principle of purposive unity is not only presupposed but hypostatised; and since the concept of a supreme intelligence is in itself completely beyond our powers of comprehension, we proceed to determine it in an anthropomorphic manner, and so to impose ends upon nature, forcibly and dictatorially, instead of pursuing the more reasonable course of searching for them by the path of physical investigation. And thus teleology, which is intended to aid us merely in completing the unity of nature in accordance with universal laws, not only tends to abrogate such unity, but also prevents reason from carrying out its own {A 693 / B 721} professed purpose, that of proving from nature, in conformity with these laws,[1] the existence of a supreme intelligent cause.

---

[1] [Reading, with Wille, *nach diesen* for *nach diesem*.]

For if the most complete purposiveness cannot be presupposed a priori *in* nature, that is, *as belonging to its essence*, how can we be required to search for it, and through all its gradations to approximate to the supreme perfection of an Author of all things, a perfection that, as absolutely necessary, must be knowable *a priori*? The regulative principle prescribes that systematic unity as a *unity in nature*, which is not known merely empirically but is presupposed *a priori* (although in an indeterminate manner), be presupposed absolutely, and consequently as following from the essence of things. If, however, I begin with a supreme purposive being as the ground of all things, the unity of nature is really surrendered, as being quite foreign and accidental to the nature of things, and as not capable of being known from its own universal laws. There then arises a vicious circle; we are assuming just that very point which is mainly in dispute.

To take the regulative principle of the systematic unity of nature as being a constitutive principle, and to hypostatise, and presuppose as a cause, that which serves, merely in idea, as the ground of the consistent employment of reason, is simply to confound reason. The investigation of nature takes its own independent course, keeping to the chain of natural causes in conformity with their universal laws. It does indeed, in so doing, proceed in accordance with the idea of an Author of the universe, but not in order to deduce therefrom the purposiveness for which it is ever on the watch, but in order to obtain knowledge of the existence of such an Author from this purposiveness. And by seeking this purposiveness in the essence of the things of nature, and so far as may be possible in the essence of things in general, it seeks to know the existence of this supreme being as absolutely necessary. Whether this latter enterprise succeed or not, the idea remains always true in itself, and justified in its use, provided it be restricted to the conditions of a merely regulative principle.

Complete purposive unity constitutes what is, in the absolute sense, perfection. If we do not find this unity in the essence of the things which go to constitute the entire object of experience, that is, of all our objectively valid knowledge, and therefore do not find it in the universal and necessary laws of nature, how can we profess to infer directly from this unity the idea of a supreme and absolutely necessary perfection of an original being, as the source of all causality? The greatest possible systematic unity, and consequently also purposive unity, is the training school for the use of reason, and is indeed the very foundation of the possibility of its greatest possible employment. The idea of such unity is, therefore, inseparably bound $\left\{\begin{smallmatrix} A\ 695 \\ B\ 723 \end{smallmatrix}\right.$ up with the very nature of our reason. This same idea is on that account legislative for us; and it is therefore very natural that we should assume a corresponding legislative reason (*intellectus archetypus*), from which, as the object of our reason, all systematic unity of nature is to be derived.

In discussing the antinomy of pure reason we have stated that the questions propounded by pure reason must in every case admit of an answer, and that in their regard it is not permissible to plead the limits of our knowledge (a plea which in many questions that concern nature is as unavoidable as it is relevant). For we are not here asking questions in regard to the nature of things, but only such questions as arise from the very nature of reason, and which concern solely its own inner constitution. We are now in a position to confirm this assertion—which at first sight may have appeared rash—so far as regards the two questions in which pure reason is most of all interested; and thus finally to complete our discussion of the dialectic of pure reason.

If, in connection with a transcendental theology,[a] we ask, *first*, whether there is anything distinct from the world, which $\left\{\begin{smallmatrix} A\ 696 \\ B\ 724 \end{smallmatrix}\right.$ contains the ground of the order of the world and of its connection in accordance with universal laws, the answer is that there *undoubtedly* is. For the world is a sum of appearances; and there must therefore be some transcendental ground of the appearances, that is, a ground which is thinkable only by the pure understanding. If, *secondly*, the question be, whether this being is substance, of the greatest reality, necessary, etc.,

---

[a] After what I have already said regarding the psychological idea and its proper vocation, as a principle for the merely regulative $\left\{\begin{smallmatrix} A\ 696 \\ B\ 724 \end{smallmatrix}\right.$ employment of reason, I need not dwell at any length upon the transcendental illusion by which the systematic unity of all the manifoldness of inner sense is hypostatised. The procedure is very similar to that which is under discussion in our criticism of the theological ideal.

we reply that *this question is entirely without meaning*. For all categories through which we can attempt to form a concept of such an object allow only of empirical employment, and have no meaning whatsoever when not applied to objects of possible experience, that is, to the world of sense. Outside this field they are merely titles of concepts, which we may admit, but through which [in and by themselves] we can understand nothing. If, *thirdly*, the question be, whether we may not at least think this being, which is distinct from the world, in *analogy* with the objects of experience, the answer is: certainly, but only as object in *idea* and not in reality, namely, only as being a substratum, to us unknown, of the systematic unity, order, and purposiveness of the arrangement of the world—an idea which reason is constrained to form as the regulative principle of its investigation of nature. Nay, more, we may freely, without laying ourselves open to censure, admit into this idea certain anthropomorphisms which are helpful to the principle in its regulative capacity. For it is always an idea only, which does not relate directly to a being distinct from the world, but to the regulative principle of the systematic unity of the world, and only by means of a schema of this unity, namely, through the schema of a supreme intelligence which, in originating the world, acts in accordance with wise purposes. What this primordial ground of the unity of the world may be in itself, we should not profess to have thereby decided, but only how we should use it, or rather its idea, in relation to the systematic employment of reason in respect of the things of the world.

But the question may still be pressed: Can we, on such grounds, assume a wise and omnipotent Author of the world? *Undoubtedly* we may; and we not only may, but *must*, do so. But do we then extend our knowledge beyond the field of possible experience? *By no means*. All that we have done is merely to presuppose a something, a merely transcendental object, of which, as it is in itself, we have no concept whatsoever. It is only in relation to the systematic and purposive ordering of the world, which, if we are to study nature, we are constrained to presuppose, that we have thought this unknown being *by analogy* with an intelligence (an empirical concept); that is, have endowed it, in respect of the ends and perfection

A 697
B 725

A 698
B 726

which are to be grounded upon it, with just those properties which, in conformity with the conditions of our reason, can be regarded as containing the ground of such systematic unity. This idea is thus valid only in respect of the *employment* of our reason *in reference to the world*. If we ascribed to it a validity that is absolute and objective, we should be forgetting that what we are thinking is a being in idea only; and in thus taking our start from a ground which is not determinable through observation of the world, we should no longer be in a position to apply the principle in a manner suited to the empirical employment of reason.

But, it will still be asked, can I make any such use of the concept and of the presupposition of a supreme being in the rational consideration of the world? Yes, it is precisely for this purpose that reason has resorted to this idea. But may I then proceed to regard seemingly purposive arrangements as purposes,[1] and so derive them from the divine will, though, $\begin{cases} \text{A } 699 \\ \text{B } 727 \end{cases}$ of course, mediately through certain special natural means, themselves established in furtherance of that divine will? Yes, we can indeed do so; but only on condition that we regard it as a matter of indifference whether it be asserted that divine wisdom has disposed all things in accordance with its supreme ends, or that the idea of supreme wisdom is a regulative principle in the investigation of nature and a principle of its systematic and purposive unity, in accordance with universal laws, even in those cases in which we are unable to detect that unity. In other words, it must be a matter of complete indifference to us, when we perceive such unity, whether we say that God in his wisdom has willed it to be so, or that nature has wisely arranged it thus. For what has justified us in adopting the idea of a supreme intelligence as a schema of the regulative principle is precisely this greatest possible systematic and purposive unity—a unity which our reason has required as a regulative principle that must underlie all investigation of nature. The more, therefore, we discover purposiveness in the world, the more fully is the legitimacy of our idea confirmed. But since the sole aim of that principle was to guide us in seeking a necessary unity of nature, and that in the greatest possible degree, while we do indeed,

[1] [*zweckähnliche Anordnungen als Absichten.*]

in so far as we attain that unity, owe it to the idea of a supreme

A 700\
B 728 being, we cannot, without contradicting ourselves, ignore the universal laws of nature—with a view to discovering which the idea was alone adopted—and look upon this purposiveness of nature as contingent and hyperphysical in its origin. For we were not justified in assuming above nature a being with those qualities, but only in adopting the idea of such a being in order to view the appearances[1] as systematically connected with one another in accordance with the principle of a causal determination.

For the same reasons, in thinking the cause of the world, we are justified in representing it in our idea not only in terms of a certain subtle anthropomorphism (without which we could not think anything whatsoever in regard to it), namely, as a being that has understanding, feelings of pleasure and displeasure, and desires and volitions corresponding to these, but also in ascribing to it a perfection which, as infinite, far transcends any perfection that our empirical knowledge of the order of the world can justify us in attributing to it. For the regulative law of systematic unity prescribes that we should study nature *as if* systematic and purposive unity, combined with the greatest possible manifoldness, were everywhere to be met with, *in infinitum*. For although we may succeed in discovering but little of this perfection of the world, it is nevertheless required by the legislation of our reason that we must

A 701\
B 729 always search for and surmise it; and it must always be beneficial, and can never be harmful, to direct our investigations into nature in accordance with this principle. But it is evident that in this way of representing the principle as involving the idea of a supreme Author, I do not base the principle upon the existence and upon the knowledge of such a being, but upon its idea only, and that I do not really derive anything from this being, but only from the idea of it—that is, from the nature of the things of the world, in accordance with such an idea. A certain, unformulated consciousness of the true use of this concept of reason seems indeed to have inspired the modest and reasonable language of the philosophers of all times, since they speak of the wisdom and providence of nature and of divine wisdom, just as if nature and divine wisdom were

---

[1] [Reading, with Hartenstein, *die* for *der*.]

equivalent expressions—indeed, so long as they are dealing solely with speculative reason, giving preference to the former mode of expression, on the ground that it enables us to avoid making profession of more than we are justified in asserting, and that it likewise directs reason to its own proper field, namely, nature.

Thus pure reason, which at first seemed to promise nothing less than the extension of knowledge beyond all limits of experience, contains, if properly understood, nothing but regulative principles, which, while indeed prescribing greater unity than the empirical employment of understanding can achieve, yet still, by the very fact that they place the goal of its endeavours at so great a distance, carry its agreement with {A 702 / B 730} itself, by means of systematic unity, to the highest possible degree. But if, on the other hand, they be misunderstood, and be treated as constitutive principles of transcendent knowledge, they give rise, by a dazzling and deceptive illusion, to persuasion and a merely fictitious knowledge, and therewith to contradictions and eternal disputes.

*　　*　　*

Thus all human knowledge begins with intuitions, proceeds from thence to concepts, and ends with ideas. Although in respect of all three elements it possesses *a priori* sources of knowledge, which on first consideration seem to scorn the limits of all experience, a thoroughgoing critique convinces us that reason, in its speculative employment, can never with these elements transcend the field of possible experience, and that the proper vocation of this supreme faculty of knowledge is to use all methods, and the principles of these methods, solely for the purpose of penetrating to the innermost secrets of nature, in accordance with every possible principle of unity —that of ends being the most important—but never to soar beyond its limits, outside which there is *for us* nothing but empty space. The critical examination, as carried out in the Transcendental Analytic, of all propositions which may seem {A 703 / B 731} to extend our knowledge beyond actual experience, has doubtless sufficed to convince us that they can never lead to anything more than a possible experience. Were it not that we are suspicious of abstract and general doctrines, however clear, and were it not that specious and alluring prospects tempt us to escape from the compulsion which these doctrines impose, we might have been able to spare ourselves the laborious interrogation of all those dialectical witnesses that a transcendent reason brings forward in support of its pretensions. For we should from the start have known with complete certainty that all such pretensions, while perhaps honestly meant, must be absolutely groundless, inasmuch as they relate to a kind of knowledge to which man can never attain. But there is no end to such discussions, unless we can penetrate to the true cause of the illusion by which even the wisest are deceived. Moreover, the resolution of all our transcendent knowledge into its elements (as a study of our inner nature) is in itself of no slight value, and to the philosopher is indeed a matter of duty. Accordingly, fruitless as are all these endeavours of speculative reason, we have none the less found it necessary to follow them up to their primary sources. And since the dialectical illusion does not merely deceive us in our judgments, but also, because of the interest which we take in these judgments, has a certain natural attraction which it will always continue to possess, we have thought it advisable, with a view to the prevention of such errors in the future, to draw up in full detail what we may describe as being the records of this lawsuit, and to deposit them in the archives of human reason.

B 732
A 704

II

TRANSCENDENTAL DOCTRINE OF METHOD $\{\begin{smallmatrix} \text{A } 705 \\ \text{B } 733 \end{smallmatrix}$

TRANSCENDENTAL DOCTRINE OF METHOD

IF we look upon the sum of all knowledge of pure speculative $\begin{cases} \text{A 707} \\ \text{B 735} \end{cases}$ reason as an edifice for which we have at least the idea within ourselves, it can be said that in the Transcendental Doctrine of Elements we have made an estimate of the materials, and have determined for what sort of edifice and for what height and strength of building they suffice. We have found, indeed, that although we had contemplated building a tower which should reach to the heavens, the supply of materials suffices only for a dwelling-house, just sufficiently commodious for our business on the level of experience, and just sufficiently high to allow of our overlooking it. The bold undertaking that we had designed is thus bound to fail through lack of material —not to mention the babel of tongues, which inevitably gives rise to disputes among the workers in regard to the plan to be followed, and which must end by scattering them over all the world, leaving each to erect a separate building for himself, according to his own design. At present, however, we are concerned not so much with the materials as with the plan; and inasmuch as we have been warned not to venture at random upon a blind project which may be altogether beyond our capacities, and yet cannot well abstain from building a secure home for ourselves, we must plan our building in conformity with the material which is given to us, and which is also at the same time appropriate to our needs.

I understand, therefore, by Transcendental Doctrine of Method the determination of the formal conditions of a com- $\begin{cases} \text{A 708} \\ \text{B 736} \end{cases}$ plete system of pure reason. In this connection, we shall have to treat of a *discipline*, a *canon*, an *architectonic*, and finally a *history* of pure reason, and to provide (in its transcendental reference) what, in relation to the use of the understanding in general, the Schools have attempted, though very unsatisfactorily, under the title of a *practical logic*. For since universal logic is not confined to any particular kind of knowledge made possible by the understanding (for instance, not to its pure knowledge) and is also not confined to certain objects, it cannot, save by borrowing knowledge from other sciences, do more than present the titles of *possible methods* and the technical terms which are used for purposes of systematisation in all kinds of sciences; and this serves only to acquaint the novice in advance with names the meaning and use of which he will not learn till later.

TRANSCENDENTAL DOCTRINE OF METHOD

CHAPTER I

THE DISCIPLINE OF PURE REASON

Owing to the general desire for knowledge, negative judgments, that is, those which are such not merely as regards their form but also as regards their content, are not held in any very high esteem. They are regarded rather as the jealous enemies A 709 of our unceasing endeavour to extend our knowledge, and it B 737 almost requires an apology to win for them even tolerance, not to say favour and high repute.

As far as *logical* form is concerned, we can make negative any proposition we like; but in respect to the content of our knowledge in general, which is either extended or limited by a judgment, the task peculiar to negative judgments is that of *rejecting error*. Accordingly, negative propositions intended to reject false knowledge, where yet no error is possible, are indeed true but empty, that is, are not suited to their purpose, and just for this reason are often quite absurd, like the proposition of the Schoolman, that Alexander could not have conquered any countries without an army.

But where the limits of our possible knowledge are very narrow, where the temptation to judge is great, where the illusion that besets us is very deceptive and the harm that results from the error is considerable, there the *negative* instruction, which serves solely to guard us from errors, has even more importance than many a piece of positive information by which our knowledge is increased. The compulsion, by which the constant tendency to disobey certain rules is restrained and finally extirpated, we entitle *discipline*. It is distinguished from *culture*, which is intended solely to give a certain kind of skill, and not to cancel any habitual mode of action already present. Towards the development of a talent, which has al- {A 710 B 738} ready in itself[1] an impulse to manifest itself, discipline will therefore contribute in a negative,[a] culture and doctrine in a positive, fashion.

That temperament and our various talents (such as imagination and wit) which incline to allow themselves a free and unlimited activity are in many respects in need of a discipline, everyone will readily admit. But that reason, whose proper duty it is to prescribe a discipline for all other endeavours, should itself stand in need of such discipline may indeed seem strange; and it has, in fact, hitherto escaped this humiliation, only because, in view of its stately guise and established standing, nobody could lightly come to suspect it of idly substituting fancies for concepts, and words for things.

There is no need of a critique of reason in its empirical em- {A 711 B 739} ployment, because in this field its principles are always subject to the test of experience. Nor is it needed in mathematics, where the concepts of reason must be forthwith exhibited *in concreto* in pure intuition, so that everything unfounded and arbitrary in them is at once exposed. But where neither empirical nor pure intuition keeps reason to a visible track, when, that is to say, reason is being considered in its transcendental employment, in accordance with mere concepts, it stands so greatly in need of a discipline, to restrain its tendency towards extension beyond the narrow limits of possible experience and to guard it against extravagance and error, that the whole

---

[a] I am well aware that in the terminology of the Schools the title *discipline* is commonly used as synonymous with instruction. However, there are so many other cases where discipline in the sense of *training by constraint* is carefully distinguished from instruction in the sense of *teaching*, and the very nature of things itself makes it so imperative that we should preserve the only expressions suitable for this distinction, that it is desirable that the former term should never be used in any but the negative sense.

[1] [Reading, with Erdmann, *von sich* for *vor sich*.]

philosophy of pure reason has no other than this strictly negative utility. Particular errors can be got rid of by *censure*, and their causes by *criticism*. But where, as in the case of pure reason, we come upon a whole system of illusions and fallacies, intimately bound together and united under common principles, a quite special negative legislation seems to be required, erecting a system of precautions and self-examination under the title of a *discipline*, founded on the nature of reason and the objects of its pure employment—a system in face of which no pseudo-rational illusion will be able to stand, but will at once betray itself, no matter what claims it may advance for exceptional treatment.

A 712 }
B 740 } But it is well to note that in this second main division of the transcendental Critique the discipline of pure reason is not directed to the content but only to the method of knowledge through pure reason. The former has already been considered in the Doctrine of Elements. But there is so much similarity in the mode of employing reason, whatever be the object to which it is applied, while yet, at the same time, its transcendental employment is so essentially different from every other, that without the admonitory negative teaching of a discipline, specially devised for the purpose, we cannot hope to avoid the errors which inevitably arise from pursuing in improper fashion methods which are indeed suitable to reason in other fields, only not in this transcendental sphere.

CHAPTER I

Section I

THE DISCIPLINE OF PURE REASON IN ITS DOGMATIC
EMPLOYMENT

Mathematics presents the most splendid example of the successful extension of pure reason, without the help of experience. Examples are contagious, especially as they quite naturally flatter a faculty which has been successful in one field, [leading it] to expect the same good fortune in other fields. Thus pure
A 713 }
B 741 } reason hopes to be able to extend its domain as successfully and securely in its transcendental as in its mathematical em-

ployment, especially when it resorts to the same method as
has been of such obvious utility in mathematics. It is therefore
highly important for us to know whether the method of attaining apodeictic certainty which is called *mathematical* is identical with the method by which we endeavour to obtain the
same certainty in philosophy, and which in that field would
have to be called *dogmatic*.

Philosophical knowledge is the *knowledge gained by reason
from concepts*; mathematical knowledge is the knowledge
gained by reason from the *construction* of concepts. To *construct* a concept means to exhibit *a priori* the intuition which
corresponds to the concept. For the construction of a concept
we therefore need a *non-empirical* intuition. The latter must,
as intuition, be a *single* object, and yet none the less, as the
construction of a concept (a universal representation), it must
in its representation express universal validity for all possible
intuitions which fall under the same concept. Thus I construct
a triangle by representing the object which corresponds to this
concept either by imagination alone, in pure intuition, or in
accordance therewith also on paper, in empirical intuition—in
both cases completely *a priori*, without having borrowed the
pattern from any experience. The single figure which we draw
is empirical, and yet it serves to express the concept, without {A 714
B 742
impairing its universality. For in this empirical intuition we
consider only the act whereby we construct the concept, and
abstract from the many determinations (for instance, the magnitude of the sides and of the angles), which are quite indifferent, as not altering the concept 'triangle'.

Thus philosophical knowledge considers the particular
only in the universal, mathematical knowledge the universal
in the particular, or even in the single instance, though still
always *a priori* and by means of reason. Accordingly, just as
this single object is determined by certain universal conditions
of construction, so the object of the concept, to which the single
object corresponds merely as its schema, must likewise be
thought as universally determined.

The essential difference between these two kinds of knowledge through reason consists therefore in this formal difference, and does not depend on difference of their material or
objects. Those who propose to distinguish philosophy from

mathematics by saying that the former has as its object *quality* only and the latter *quantity* only, have mistaken the effect for the cause. The form of mathematical knowledge is the cause why it is limited exclusively to quantities. For it is the concept of quantities only that allows of being constructed, that is, ex- hibited *a priori* in intuition; whereas qualities cannot be pre- sented in any intuition that is not empirical. Consequently reason can obtain a knowledge of qualities only through con- cepts. No one can obtain an intuition corresponding to the con- cept of reality otherwise than from experience; we can never come into possession of it *a priori* out of our own resources, and prior to the empirical consciousness of reality. The shape of a cone we can form for ourselves in intuition, unassisted by any experience, according to its concept alone, but the colour of this cone must be previously given in some experience or other. I cannot represent in intuition the concept of a cause in general except in an example supplied by experience; and similarly with other concepts. Philosophy, as well as mathe- matics, does indeed treat of quantities, for instance, of totality, infinity, etc. Mathematics also concerns itself with qualities, for instance, the difference between lines and surfaces, as spaces of different quality, and with the continuity of extension as one of its qualities. But although in such cases they have a common object, the mode in which reason handles that object is wholly different in philosophy and in mathematics. Philo- sophy confines itself to universal concepts; mathematics can achieve nothing by concepts alone but hastens at once to intui- tion, in which it considers the concept *in concreto*, though not empirically, but only in an intuition which it presents *a priori*, that is, which it has constructed, and in which whatever follows from the universal conditions of the construction must be uni- versally valid of the object of the concept thus constructed.

Suppose a philosopher be given the concept of a triangle and he be left to find out, in his own way, what relation the sum of its angles bears to a right angle. He has nothing but the concept of a figure enclosed by three straight lines, and possessing three angles. However long he meditates on this concept, he will never produce anything new. He can analyse and clarify the concept of a straight line or of an angle or of the number three, but he can never arrive at any properties not already contained in these concepts. Now let the geometrician take up these questions. He at once begins by constructing a triangle. Since he knows that the sum of two right angles is exactly equal to the sum of all the adjacent angles which can be constructed from a single point on a straight line, he prolongs one side of his triangle and obtains two adjacent angles, which together are equal to two right angles. He then divides the external angle by drawing a line parallel to the opposite side of the triangle, and observes that he has thus obtained an external adjacent angle which is equal to an internal angle—and so on. In this fashion, through a chain of inferences guided throughout by intuition, he arrives at a fully evident and universally valid solution of the problem. {A 717 B 745}

But mathematics does not only construct magnitudes (*quanta*) as in geometry; it also constructs magnitude as such (*quantitas*), as in algebra In this it abstracts completely from the properties of the object that is to be thought in terms of such a concept of magnitude. It then chooses a certain notation for all constructions of magnitude as such (numbers),[1] that is, for addition, subtraction, extraction of roots, etc. Once it has adopted a notation for the general concept of magnitudes so far as their different relations are concerned, it exhibits in intuition, in accordance with certain universal rules, all the various operations through which the magnitudes are produced and modified. When, for instance, one magnitude is to be divided by another, their symbols are placed together, in accordance with the sign for division, and similarly in the other processes; and thus in algebra by means of a symbolic construction, just as in geometry by means of an ostensive construction (the geometrical construction of the objects themselves), we succeed in arriving at results which discursive knowledge could never have reached by means of mere concepts.

Now what can be the reason of this radical difference in the fortunes of the philosopher and the mathematician, both of whom practise the art of reason, the one making his way by means of concepts, the other by means of intuitions which he exhibits *a priori* in accordance with concepts? The cause is {A 718 B 746} evident from what has been said above, in our exposition of the

---

[1] [Reading, with Hartenstein and Erdmann (*Zahlen*), *als . . . Wurzeln usw.* for (*Zahlen, als . . . Subtraktion usw*).]

fundamental transcendental doctrines. We are not here concerned with analytic propositions, which can be produced by mere analysis of concepts (in this the philosopher would certainly have the advantage over his rival), but with synthetic propositions, and indeed with just those synthetic propositions that can be known *a priori*. For I must not restrict my attention to what I am actually thinking in my concept of a triangle (this is nothing more than the mere definition); I must pass beyond it to properties which are not contained in this concept, but yet belong to it. Now this is impossible unless I determine my object in accordance with the conditions either of empirical or of pure intuition. The former would only give us an empirical proposition (based on the measurement of the angles), which would not have universality, still less necessity; and so would not at all serve our purpose. The second method of procedure is the mathematical one, and in this case is the method of geometrical construction, by means of which I combine in a pure intuition (just as I do in empirical intuition) the manifold which belongs to the schema of a triangle in general, and therefore to its concept. It is by this method that universal synthetic propositions must be constructed.

It would therefore be quite futile for me to philosophise upon the triangle, that is, to think about it discursively. I should not be able to advance a single step beyond the mere definition, which was what I had to begin with. There is indeed a transcendental synthesis [framed] from concepts alone, a synthesis with which the philosopher is alone competent to deal; but it relates only to a thing in general, as defining the conditions under which the perception of it can belong to possible experience. But in mathematical problems there is no question of this, nor indeed of existence at all, but only of the properties of the objects in themselves, [that is to say], solely in so far as these properties are connected with the concept of the objects.

In the above example we have endeavoured only to make clear the great difference which exists between the discursive employment of reason in accordance with concepts and its intuitive employment by means of the construction of concepts. This naturally leads on to the question, what can be the cause which necessitates such a twofold employment of reason, and how we are to recognise whether it is the first or the second method that is being employed.

All our knowledge relates, finally, to possible intuitions, for it is through them alone that an object is given. Now an *a priori* concept, that is, a concept which is not empirical, either already includes in itself a pure intuition (and if so, it can be constructed), or it includes nothing but the synthesis of possible intuitions which are not given *a priori*. In this latter case we can indeed make use of it in forming synthetic *a priori* judgments, but only discursively in accordance with concepts, never intuitively through the construction of the concept.

{A 720
B 748

The only intuition that is given *a priori* is that of the mere form of appearances, space and time. A concept of space and time, as quanta, can be exhibited *a priori* in intuition, that is, constructed, either in respect of the quality (figure) of the quanta, or through number in their quantity only (the mere synthesis of the homogeneous manifold). But the matter of appearances, by which *things* are given us in space and time, can only be represented in perception, and therefore *a posteriori*. The only concept which represents *a priori* this empirical content of appearances is the concept of a *thing* in general, and the *a priori* synthetic knowledge of this thing in general can give us nothing more than the mere rule of the synthesis of that which perception may give *a posteriori*. It can never yield an *a priori* intuition of the real object, since this must necessarily be empirical.

Synthetic propositions in regard to *things* in general, the intuition of which does not admit of being given *a priori*, are transcendental. Transcendental propositions can never be given through construction of concepts, but only in accordance with concepts that are *a priori*. They contain nothing but the rule according to which we are to seek empirically for a certain synthetic unity of that which is incapable of intuitive representation *a priori* (that is, of perceptions). But these synthetic principles cannot exhibit *a priori* any one of their concepts in a specific instance; they can only do this *a posteriori*, by means of experience, which itself is possible only in conformity with these principles

{A 721
B 749

If we are to judge synthetically in regard to a concept, we must go beyond this concept and appeal to the intuition in which it is given. For should we confine ourselves to what is contained in the concept, the judgment would be merely analytic, serving only as an explanation of the thought, in terms of what is actually contained in it. But I can pass from the concept to the corresponding pure or empirical intuition, in order to consider it in that intuition *in concreto*, and so to know, either *a priori* or *a posteriori*, what are the properties of the object of the concept. The *a priori* method gives us our rational and mathematical knowledge through the construction of the concept, the *a posteriori* method our merely empirical (mechanical) knowledge, which is incapable of yielding necessary and apodeictic propositions. Thus I might analyse my empirical concept of gold without gaining anything more than merely an enumeration of everything that I actually think in using the word, thus improving the logical character of my knowledge but not in any way adding to it. But I take the material body, familiarly known by this name, and obtain perceptions by means of it; and these perceptions yield various propositions which are synthetic but empirical. When the concept is mathematical, as in the concept of a triangle, I am in a position to construct the concept, that is, to give it *a priori* in intuition, and in this way to obtain knowledge which is at once synthetic and rational. But if what is given me is the *transcendental* concept of a reality, substance, force, etc., it indicates neither an empirical nor a pure intuition, but only the synthesis of empirical intuitions, which, as being empirical, cannot be given *a priori*. And since the synthesis is thus unable to advance *a priori*, beyond the concept, to the corresponding intuition, the concept cannot yield any determining synthetic proposition, but only a principle of the synthesis [a] of possible

A 722
B 750

[a] With the concept of cause I do really go beyond the empirical concept of an event (something happening), yet I do not pass to the intuition which exhibits the concept of cause *in concreto*, but to the time-conditions in general, which in experience may be found to be in accord with this concept. I therefore proceed merely in accordance with concepts; I cannot proceed by means of the construction of concepts, since the concept is a rule of the synthesis of perceptions, and the latter are not pure intuitions, and so do not permit of being *given a priori*.

empirical intuitions. A transcendental proposition is therefore synthetic knowledge through reason, in accordance with mere concepts; and it is discursive, in that while it is what alone makes possible any synthetic unity of empirical knowledge, it yet gives us no intuition *a priori*.

There is thus a twofold employment of reason; and while $\begin{cases} \text{A } 723 \\ \text{B } 751 \end{cases}$ the two modes of employment resemble each other in the universality and *a priori* origin of their knowledge, in outcome they are very different. The reason is that in the [field of] appearance, in terms of which[1] all objects are given us, there are two elements, the form of intuition (space and time), which can be known and determined completely *a priori*, and the matter (the physical element) or content—the latter signifying something which is met with in space and time and which therefore contains an existent[2] corresponding to sensation. In respect to this material element, which can never be given in any determinate fashion otherwise than empirically, we can have nothing *a priori* except indeterminate concepts of the synthesis of possible sensations, in so far as they belong, in a possible experience, to the unity of apperception. As regards the formal element, we can determine our concepts in *a priori* intuition, inasmuch as we create for ourselves, in space and time, through a homogeneous synthesis, the objects themselves —these objects being viewed simply as *quanta*. The former method is called the employment of reason in accordance with concepts; in so employing it[3] we can do nothing more than bring appearances under concepts, according to their actual content. The concepts cannot be made determinate in this manner,[4] save only empirically, that is, *a posteriori* (although always in accordance with these concepts as rules of an empirical synthesis). The other method is the employment of reason through the construction of concepts; and since the concepts here re- $\begin{cases} \text{A } 724 \\ \text{B } 752 \end{cases}$ late to an *a priori* intuition, they are for this very reason themselves *a priori* and can be given in a quite determinate fashion in pure intuition, without the help of any empirical data. The consideration of everything which exists in space or time, in regard to the questions, whether and how far it is a quantum

---

[1] [*als wodurch.*]
[2] [*Dasein.*]
[3] [Reading, with Erdmann, *in dem* for *indem.*]
[4] [Reading, with Erdmann, *dadurch* for *darauf.*]

or not, whether we are to ascribe to it positive being or the absence of such, how far this something occupying space or time is a primary substratum or a mere determination [of substance], whether there be a relation of its existence to some other existence, as cause or effect, and finally in respect of its existence whether it is isolated or is in reciprocal relation to and dependence upon others—these questions, as also the question of the possibility of this existence, its actuality and necessity, or the opposites of these, one and all belong altogether to knowledge obtained by reason from concepts, such knowledge being termed *philosophical*. But the determination of an intuition *a priori* in space (figure), the division of time (duration), or even just the knowledge of the universal element in the synthesis of one and the same thing in time and space, and the magnitude of an intuition that is thereby generated (number),—all this is the work of reason through construction of concepts, and is called *mathematical*.

The great success which attends reason in its mathematical employment quite naturally gives rise to the expectation that it, or at any rate its method, will have the same success in other fields as in that of quantity. For this method has the advantage of being able to realise all its concepts in intuitions, which it can provide *a priori*, and by which it becomes, so to speak, master of nature; whereas pure philosophy is all at sea when it seeks through *a priori* discursive concepts to obtain insight in regard to the natural world, being unable to intuit *a priori* (and thereby to confirm) their reality. Nor does there seem to be, on the part of the experts in mathematics, any lack of self-confidence as to this procedure—or on the part of the vulgar of great expectations from their skill—should they apply themselves to carry out their project. For, since they have hardly ever attempted to philosophise in regard to their mathematics (a hard task!), the specific difference between the two employments of reason has never so much as occurred to them. Current, empirical rules, which they borrow from ordinary consciousness, they treat as being axiomatic. In the question as to the source of the concepts of space and time they are not in the least interested, although it is precisely with these concepts (as the only original quanta) that they are themselves occupied. Similarly, they think it unnecessary to investigate

A 725
B 753

the origin of the pure concepts of understanding and in so doing to determine the extent of their validity; they care only to make use of them. In all this they are entirely in the right, provided only they do not overstep the proper limits, that is, the limits of the natural world. But, unconsciously, they pass from the field of sensibility to the precarious ground of pure and even transcendental concepts, a ground (*instabilis tellus, innabilis unda*) that permits them neither to stand nor to swim, and where their hasty tracks are soon obliterated. In mathematics, on the other hand, their passage gives rise to a broad highway, which the latest posterity may still tread with confidence.

$\left\{ \begin{matrix} A\ 726 \\ B\ 754 \end{matrix} \right.$

We have made it our duty to determine, with exactitude and certainty, the limits of pure reason in its transcendental employment. But the pursuit of such transcendental knowledge has this peculiarity, that in spite of the plainest and most urgent warnings men still allow themselves to be deluded by false hopes, and therefore to postpone the total abandonment of all proposed attempts to advance beyond the bounds of experience into the enticing regions of the intellectual world. It therefore becomes necessary to cut away the last anchor of these fantastic hopes, that is, to show that the pursuit of the mathematical method cannot be of the least advantage in this kind of knowledge (unless it be in exhibiting more plainly the limitations of the method); and that mathematics[1] and philosophy, although in natural science they do, indeed, go hand in hand, are none the less so completely different, that the procedure of the one can never be imitated by the other.

The exactness of mathematics rests upon definitions, axioms and demonstrations. I shall content myself with showing that none of these, in the sense in which they are understood by the mathematician, can be achieved or imitated by the philosopher. I shall show that in philosophy the geometrician can by his method build only so many houses of cards, just as in mathematics the employment of a philosophical method results only in mere talk. Indeed it is precisely in knowing its limits that philosophy consists; and even the mathematician, unless his talent is of such a specialised character that it naturally confines itself to its proper field, cannot afford to ignore the warnings of philosophy, or to behave as if he were superior to them.

$\left\{ \begin{matrix} A\ 727 \\ B\ 755 \end{matrix} \right.$

[1] [*Messkunst.*]

1. *Definitions.*—To *define*, as the word itself indicates, really only means to present the complete, original concept of a thing within the limits of its concept.[a] If this be our standard, an *empirical* concept cannot be defined at all, but only *made explicit.* For since we find in it only a few characteristics of a certain species of sensible object, it is never certain that we are not using the word, in denoting one and the same object, sometimes so as to stand for more, and sometimes so as to

A 728
B 756 } stand for fewer characteristics. Thus in the concept of *gold* one man may think, in addition to its weight, colour, malleability, also its property of resisting rust, while another will perhaps know nothing of this quality. We make use of certain characteristics only so long as they are adequate for the purpose of making distinctions; new observations remove some properties and add others; and thus the limits of the concept are never assured. And indeed what useful purpose could be served by defining an empirical concept, such, for instance, as that of water? When we speak of water and its properties, we do not stop short at what is thought in the word, water, but proceed to experiments. The word, with the few characteristics which we attach to it, is more properly to be regarded as merely a designation than as a concept of the thing; the so-called definition is nothing more than a determining of the word. In the second place, it is also true that no concept given *a priori*, such as substance, cause, right, equity, etc., can, strictly speaking, be defined. For I can never be certain that the clear representation of a given concept, which as given may still be confused, has been completely effected, unless I know that it is adequate to its object. But since the concept of it may, as given, include many obscure representations, which we overlook in our analysis, although we are constantly making use of them in our application of the concept, the completeness of the analysis of my concept is always in doubt, and a multiplicity

---

[a] *Completeness* means clearness and sufficiency of characteristics; by *limits* is meant the precision shown in there not being more of these characteristics than belong to the complete concept; by *original* is meant that this determination of these limits is not derived from anything else, and therefore does not require any proof; for if it did, that would disqualify the supposed explanation from standing at the head of all the judgments regarding its object.

THE DISCIPLINE OF PURE REASON   587

of suitable examples suffices only to make the completeness *probable*, never to make it *apodeictically* certain.   ⌈A 729
⌊B 757 Instead of the term, definition, I prefer to use the term, *exposition*, as being a more guarded term, which the critic can accept as being up to a certain point valid, though still entertaining doubts as to the completeness of the analysis. Since, then, neither empirical concepts nor concepts given *a priori* allow of definition, the only remaining kind of concepts, upon which this mental operation[1] can be tried, are arbitrarily invented concepts. A concept which I have invented I can always define; for since it is not given to me either by the nature of understanding or by experience, but is such as I have myself deliberately made it to be, I must know what I have intended to think in using it. I cannot, however, say that I have thereby defined a true object.[2] For if the concept depends on empirical conditions, as *e.g.* the concept of a ship's clock, this arbitrary concept of mine does not assure me of the existence or of the possibility of its object. I do not even know from it whether it has an object at all, and my explanation may better be described as a declaration of my project than as a definition of an object. There remain, therefore, no concepts which allow of definition, except only those which contain an arbitrary synthesis that admits of *a priori* construction. Consequently, mathematics is the only science that has definitions. For the object which it thinks it exhibits *a priori* in intuition, and this object certainly cannot contain either more or less than the concept, since it is through the definition[3] that   ⌈A 730
⌊B 758 the concept of the object is given—and given originally, that is, without its being necessary to derive the definition[3] from any other source. The German language has for the [Latin] terms *exposition, explication, declaration,* and *definition* only one word, *Erklärung,*[4] and we need not, therefore, be so stringent in our requirements as altogether to refuse to philosophical explanations[5] the honourable title, definition. We shall confine ourselves simply to remarking that while philosophical definitions are never more than expositions of given concepts, mathematical definitions are constructions of con-

---

[1] [*dieses Kunststück.*]   [2] [*einen wahren Gegenstand.*]
[3] [*Erklärung.*]
[4] [This term Kant usually employs in the sense of explanation; but, as above indicated, it is used in the preceding sentence in the sense of definition.]
[5] [*Erklärungen.*]

cepts, originally framed by the mind itself; and that while the former can be obtained only by analysis (the completeness of which is never apodeictically certain), the latter are produced synthetically. Whereas, therefore, mathematical definitions *make* their concepts, in philosophical definitions concepts are only *explained*. From this it follows:

(*a*) That in philosophy we must not imitate mathematics by beginning with definitions, unless it be by way simply of experiment. For since the definitions are analyses of given concepts, they presuppose the prior presence of the concepts, although in a confused state; and the incomplete exposition must precede the complete. Consequently, we can infer a good deal from a few characteristics, derived from an incomplete analysis, without having yet reached the complete exposition, that is, the definition. In short, the definition in all its precision and clarity ought, in philosophy, to come rather at the end than at the beginning of our enquiries.[a] In mathematics, on the other hand, we have no concept whatsoever prior to the definition, through which the concept itself is first given. For this reason mathematical science must always begin, and it can always begin, with the definition.

(*b*) That mathematical definitions can never be in error. For since the concept is first given through the definition, it includes nothing except precisely what the definition intends should be understood by it. But although nothing incorrect can be introduced into its content, there may sometimes, though rarely, be a defect in the form in which it is clothed, namely as regards precision. Thus the common explanation of the circle that it is a *curved* line every point in which is equidistant

A 731
B 759

---

[a] Philosophy is full of faulty definitions, especially of definitions which, while indeed containing some of the elements required, are yet not complete. If we could make no use of a concept till we had defined it, all philosophy would be in a pitiable plight. But since a good and safe use can still be made of the elements obtained by analysis so far as they go, defective definitions, that is, propositions which are properly not definitions, but are yet true, and are therefore approximations to definitions, can be employed with great advantage. In mathematics definition belongs *ad esse*, in philosophy *ad melius esse*. It is desirable to attain an adequate definition, but often very difficult. The jurists are still without a definition of their concept of right.

from one and the same point (the centre), has the defect that $\left\{\begin{matrix} \text{A 732} \\ \text{B 760} \end{matrix}\right.$
the determination, curved, is introduced unnecessarily. For
there must be a particular theorem, deduced from the definition and easily capable of proof, namely, that if all points
in a line are equidistant from one and the same point, the line
is curved (no part of it straight). Analytic definitions, on the
other hand, may err in many ways, either through introducing
characteristics which do not really belong to the concept, or by
lacking that completeness which is the essential feature of a
definition. The latter defect is due to the fact that we can never
be quite certain of the completeness of the analysis. For these
reasons the mathematical method of definition does not admit
of imitation in philosophy.

2. *Axioms.*—These, in so far as they are immediately
certain, are synthetic *a priori* principles. Now one concept
cannot be combined with another synthetically and also at the
same time immediately, since, to be able to pass beyond either
concept, a third something is required to mediate our knowledge. Accordingly, since philosophy is simply what reason
knows by means of concepts, no principle deserving the name
of an axiom is to be found in it. Mathematics, on the other
hand, can have axioms, since by means of the construction of
concepts in the intuition of the object it can combine the predicates of the object both *a priori* and immediately, as, for
instance, in the proposition that three points always lie in a $\left\{\begin{matrix} \text{A 733} \\ \text{B 761} \end{matrix}\right.$
plane. But a synthetic principle derived from concepts alone
can never be immediately certain, for instance, the proposition
that everything which happens has a cause. Here I must look
round for a third something, namely, the condition of time-
determination in an experience; I cannot obtain knowledge of
such a principle directly and immediately from the concepts
alone. Discursive principles are therefore quite different from
intuitive principles, that is, from axioms; and always require
a deduction. Axioms, on the other hand, require no such deduction, and for the same reason are evident—a claim which
the philosophical principles can never advance, however great
their certainty. Consequently, the synthetic propositions of pure,
transcendental reason are, one and all, infinitely removed from
being as evident—which is yet so often arrogantly claimed
on their behalf—as the proposition that *twice two make four.*

In the Analytic I have indeed introduced some axioms of intuition into the table of the principles of pure understanding;
but the principle[1] there applied is not itself an axiom, but
serves only to specify the principle[2] of the possibility of axioms
in general, and is itself no more than a principle[1] derived from
concepts. For the possibility of mathematics must itself be
demonstrated in transcendental philosophy. Philosophy has
therefore no axioms, and may never prescribe its *a priori*
principles in any such absolute manner, but must resign itself
to establishing its authority in their regard by a thorough
deduction.

A 734
B 762

3. *Demonstrations.*—An apodeictic proof can be called a
demonstration, only in so far as it is intuitive. Experience
teaches us what is, but does not teach us that it could not
be other than what it is. Consequently, no empirical grounds
of proof can ever amount to apodeictic proof. Even from *a
priori* concepts, as employed in discursive knowledge, there
can never arise intuitive certainty, that is, [demonstrative]
evidence, however apodeictically certain the judgment may
otherwise be. Mathematics alone, therefore, contains demonstrations, since it derives its knowledge not from concepts
but from the construction of them, that is, from intuition,
which can be given *a priori* in accordance with the concepts.
Even the method of algebra with its equations, from which
the correct answer, together with its proof, is deduced by reduction, is not indeed geometrical in nature, but is still con-
structive in a way characteristic of the science.[3] The concepts
attached to the symbols, especially concerning the relations
of magnitudes, are presented in intuition; and this method,
in addition to its heuristic advantages, secures all inferences
against error by setting each one before our eyes. While
philosophical knowledge must do without this advantage,
inasmuch as it has always to consider the universal *in
abstracto* (by means of concepts), mathematics can consider
the universal *in concreto* (in the single intuition) and yet at the
same time through pure *a priori* representation, whereby all
errors are at once made evident. I should therefore prefer to

A 735
B 763

---

[1] [*Grundsatz.*]   [2] [*Prinzipium.*]
[3] [*charakteristische Konstruktion.* The meaning in which Kant uses this phrase
is doubtful. It might also be translated 'construction by means of symbols'.]

call the first kind *acroamatic* (discursive) *proofs*, since they may be conducted by the agency of words alone (the object in thought), rather than *demonstrations* which, as the term itself indicates, proceed in and through the intuition of the object.

From all this it follows that it is not in keeping with the nature of philosophy, especially in the field of pure reason, to take pride in a dogmatic procedure, and to deck itself out with the title and insignia of mathematics, to whose ranks it does not belong, though it has every ground to hope for a sisterly union with it. Such pretensions are idle claims which can never be satisfied, and indeed must divert philosophy from its true purpose, namely, to expose the illusions of a reason that forgets its limits, and by sufficiently clarifying our concepts to recall it from its presumptuous speculative pursuits to modest but thorough self-knowledge. Reason must not, therefore, in its transcendental endeavours, hasten forward with sanguine expectations, as though the path which it has traversed led directly to the goal, and as though the accepted premisses could be so securely relied upon that there can be no need of constantly returning to them and of considering whether we may not perhaps, in the course of the inferences, discover defects which have been overlooked in the principles, and which render it necessary either to determine these principles more {A 736 B 764} fully or to change them entirely.

I divide all apodeictic propositions, whether demonstrable or immediately certain, into *dogmata* and *mathemata*. A synthetic proposition directly derived from concepts is a *dogma*; a synthetic proposition, when directly obtained through the construction of concepts, is a *mathema*. Analytic judgments really teach us nothing more about the object than what the concept which we have of it already contains; they do not extend our knowledge beyond the concept of the object, but only clarify the concept. They cannot therefore rightly be called dogmas (a word which might perhaps be translated *doctrines*).[1] Of the two kinds of synthetic *a priori* propositions only those belonging to philosophical knowledge can, according to the ordinary usage of words, be entitled dogmas; the propositions of arithmetic or geometry would hardly be so

[1] [*Lehrsprüche.*]

named. The customary use of words thus confirms our interpretation of the term, namely, that only judgments derived
from concepts can be called dogmatic, not those based on the
construction of concepts.

Now in the whole domain of pure reason, in its merely
speculative employment, there is not to be found a single
synthetic judgment directly derived from concepts. For, as we
have shown, ideas cannot form the basis of any objectively
valid synthetic judgment. Through concepts of understanding
pure reason does, indeed, establish secure principles, not however directly from concepts alone, but always only indirectly
through relation of these concepts to something altogether contingent, namely, *possible experience*. When such experience
(that is, something as object of possible experiences) is presupposed, these principles are indeed apodeictically certain;
but in themselves, directly, they can never be known *a priori*.
Thus no one can acquire insight into the proposition that
everything which happens has its cause, merely from the concepts involved. It is not, therefore, a dogma, although from
another point of view, namely, from that of the sole field of
its possible employment, that is, experience, it can be proved
with complete apodeictic certainty. But though it needs proof,
it should be entitled a *principle*, not a *theorem*, because it has
the peculiar character that it makes possible the very experience which is its own ground of proof, and that in this experience it must always itself be presupposed.

Now if in the speculative employment of pure reason there
are no dogmas, to serve as its special subject-matter,[1] all
dogmatic methods, whether borrowed from the mathematician
or specially invented, are as such inappropriate. For they only
serve to conceal defects and errors, and to mislead philosophy,
whose true purpose is to present every step of reason in the
clearest light. Nevertheless its method can always be *systematic*. For our reason is itself, subjectively, a system, though in
its pure employment, by means of mere concepts, it is no more
than a system whereby our investigations can be conducted
in accordance with principles of unity, the material being provided by *experience* alone. We cannot here discuss the method
peculiar to transcendental philosophy; we are at present con-

A 737
B 765

A 738
B 766

---

[1] [*auch dem Inhalte nach.*]

cerned only with a critical estimate of what may be expected from our faculties—whether we are in a position to build at all; and to what height, with the material at our disposal (the pure *a priori* concepts), we may hope to carry the edifice.

Reason must in all its undertakings subject itself to criticism; should it limit freedom of criticism by any prohibitions, it must harm itself, drawing upon itself a damaging suspicion. Nothing is so important through its usefulness, nothing so sacred, that it may be exempted from this searching examination, which knows no respect for persons. Reason depends on this freedom for its very existence. For reason has no dictatorial authority; its verdict is always simply the agreement of free citizens, of whom each one must be permitted {A 739 / B 767} to express, without let or hindrance, his objections or even his veto.

But while reason can never refuse to submit to criticism, it does not always have cause to fear it. In its dogmatic (non-mathematical) employment it is not, indeed, so thoroughly conscious of such exact observation of its own supreme laws, as not to feel constrained to present itself with diffidence, nay, with entire renunciation of all assumed dogmatic authority, to the critical scrutiny of a *higher* judicial reason.

The situation is, however, quite otherwise, when reason has to deal not with the verdict of a judge, but with the claims of a fellow-citizen, and against these has only to act in self-defence. For since these are intended to be just as dogmatic in denial as its own are in affirmation, it is able to justify itself κατ' ἄνθρωπον, in a manner which ensures it against all interference, and provides it with a title to secure possession that need fear no outside claims, although κατ' ἀλήθειαν the title cannot itself be conclusively proved.

By the polemical employment of pure reason I mean the

defence of its propositions as against the dogmatic counter-propositions through which they are denied. Here the contention is not that its own assertions may not, perhaps, be false,

A 740
B 768

but only that no one can assert the opposite with apodeictic certainty, or even, indeed, with a greater degree of likelihood. We do not here hold our possessions upon sufferance; for although our title to them may not be satisfactory, it is yet quite certain that no one can ever be in a position to prove the illegality of the title.

It is grievous, indeed, and disheartening, that there should be any such thing as an antithetic of pure reason, and that reason, which is the highest tribunal for all conflicts, should thus be at variance with itself. We had to deal, in a previous chapter, with such an antithetic; but it turned out to be only an apparent conflict, resting upon a misunderstanding. In accordance with the common prejudice, it took appearances as being things in themselves, and then required an absolute completeness of their synthesis in the one mode or in the[1] other (this being equally impossible in either way)—a demand which is not at all permissible in respect of appearances. There was, therefore, no real *self-contradiction of reason* in the propounding of the two propositions, that the series of appearances *given in themselves* has an absolutely first beginning, and that this series is absolutely and *in itself* without any beginning. For the two propositions are quite consistent with each other, inasmuch as *appearances*, in respect of their existence (as appearances), are *in themselves* nothing at all, that is, [so regarded] are something self-contradictory; for the assumption [that they do thus exist in themselves] must naturally lead to self-contradictory inferences.

A 741
B 769

But there are other cases in which we cannot allege any such misunderstanding, and in which we cannot, therefore, dispose of the conflict of reason in the above manner—when, for instance, it is asserted, on the one hand, theistically, that there is a supreme being, and on the other hand, atheistically, that there is no supreme being; or as in psychology, that everything which thinks is endowed with absolute and abiding unity and is therefore distinct from all transitory material unity, and, in opposition thereto, that the soul is not immaterial unity

---

[1] [Reading, with Vorländer, *die andere* for *andere*.]

and cannot be exempt from transitoriness. For since in these cases the understanding has to deal only with *things in themselves* and not with appearances, the object of such questions is free from any foreign element that is in contradiction with its nature. There would indeed be a real conflict, if pure reason had anything to say on the negative side which amounted to a positive ground for its negative contentions. For so far as concerns criticism of the grounds of proof offered by those who make dogmatic affirmations, the criticism[1] can be freely admitted, without our having on that account to give up these affirmations, which have at least the interest of reason in their favour—an interest to which the opposite party cannot appeal.

I do not at all share the opinion which certain excellent and thoughtful men (such as Sulzer[2]), in face of the weakness of the arguments hitherto employed, have so often been led to express, that we may hope sometime to discover conclusive demonstrations of the two cardinal propositions of our reason—that there is a God, and that there is a future life. On the contrary, I am certain that this will never happen. For {A 742 / B 770} whence will reason obtain ground for such synthetic assertions, which do not relate to objects of experience and their inner possibility. But it is also apodeictically certain that there will never be anyone who will be able to assert the *opposite* with the least show [of proof], much less, dogmatically. For since he could prove this only through pure reason, he must undertake to prove that a supreme being, and the thinking subject in us [viewed] as pure intelligence, are *impossible*. But whence will he obtain the modes of knowledge which could justify him in thus judging synthetically in regard to things that lie beyond all possible experience. We may therefore be so[3] completely assured that no one will ever prove the opposite, that there is no need for us to concern ourselves with formal arguments. We are always in a position to accept these propositions —propositions which are so very closely bound up with the speculative interest of our reason in its empirical employment, and which, moreover, are the sole means of reconciling the

---

[1] [Reading, with Wille, *ihr* for *ihm*.]
[2] [J. G. Sulzer (1720–1779).]
[3] [Reading, with Erdmann, *so ganz* for *ganz*.]

speculative with the practical interest. As against our opponent, who must not be considered here as a critic only, we are equipped with our *non liquet*, which cannot fail to disconcert him. At the same time we do not mind his turning this argument upon ourselves, since we always have in reserve the subjective maxim of reason, which is necessarily lacking to our opponent, and under its protection can look upon all his vain attacks with a tranquil indifference.

A 743}
B 771}

There is thus no real antithetic of pure reason. For the arena for such an antithetic would have to be located in the domain of pure theology and psychology; and in that domain no combatant can be adequately equipped, or have weapons that we need fear. Ridicule and[1] boasting form his whole armoury, and these can be laughed at, as mere child's play. This is a comforting consideration, and affords reason fresh courage; for upon what could it rely, if, while it alone is called upon to remove all errors, it should yet be at variance with itself, and without hope of peace and quiet possession.

Everything which nature has itself instituted is good for some purpose. Even poisons have their use. They serve to counteract other poisons generated in our bodily humours, and must have a place in every complete pharmacopoeia. The objections against the persuasions and complacency of our purely speculative reason arise from the very nature of reason itself, and must therefore have their own good use and purpose, which ought not to be disdained. Why has Providence placed many things which are closely bound up with our highest in-

A 744}
B 772}

terests so far beyond our reach that we are only permitted to apprehend them in a manner lacking in clearness and subject to doubt—in such fashion that our enquiring gaze is more excited than satisfied? We may, indeed, be in doubt whether it serves any useful purpose, and whether it is not perhaps even harmful, to venture upon bold utterances in regard to such uncertain matters. But there can be no manner of doubt that it is always best to grant reason complete liberty, both of enquiry and of criticism, so that it may not be hindered in attending to its own proper interests. These interests are no less furthered by the limitation than by the extension of its speculations, and will always suffer when outside influences

[1] [Reading, with 5th edition, *und* for *oder*.]

intervene to divert it from its proper path, and to constrain it by what is irrelevant to its own proper ends.

Allow, therefore, your opponent to speak in the name of reason, and combat him only with weapons of reason. For the rest, have no anxiety as to the outcome in its bearing upon our practical interests, since in a merely speculative dispute they are never in any way affected. The conflict serves only to disclose a certain antinomy of reason which, inasmuch as it is due to the very nature of reason, must receive a hearing and be scrutinised. Reason is benefited by the consideration of its object from both sides, and its judgment is corrected in being thus limited. What is here in dispute is not the practical interests of reason but the mode of their presentation.[1] For although we have to surrender the language of *knowledge*, $\begin{cases} \text{A 745} \\ \text{B 773} \end{cases}$ we still have sufficient ground to employ, in the presence of the most exacting reason, the quite legitimate language of a firm *faith*.

If we should ask the dispassionate David Hume, [by temperament] so peculiarly fitted for balanced judgment, what led him to undermine, through far-fetched subtleties so elaborately thought out,[2] the conviction which is so comforting and beneficial for mankind, that their reason has sufficient insight for the assertion and for the determinate conception of a supreme being, he would answer: 'Solely in order to advance reason in its self-knowledge, and because of a certain indignation at the violence that is done to reason by those who, while boasting of its powers, yet hinder it from candid admission of the weaknesses which have become obvious to it through its own self-examination'. If, on the other hand, we should ask Priestley,[3] who was wholly devoted to the *empirical* employment of reason and out of sympathy with all transcendent speculation, what motives had induced him— himself a pious and zealous teacher of religion—to pull down two such pillars of all religion as the freedom and immortality of the soul (the hope of a future life is for him only the expectation of the miracle of resurrection), he would not be able to give

---

[1] [*nicht die* Sache, *sondern der* Ton.]
[2] [The reference is to Hume's *Dialogues concerning Natural Religion* (1779).]
[3] [Joseph Priestley (1733–1804): *Disquisitions relating to Matter and Spirit* (1777); *The Doctrine of Philosophical Necessity* (1777).]

any other answer than that he was concerned for the interest of reason, which must suffer when we seek to exempt certain objects from the laws of material nature, the only laws which we can know and determine with exactitude. It would be unjust to decry the latter (who knew how to combine his paradoxical teaching with the interests of religion), and so to give pain to a well-intentioned man, simply because he is unable to find his bearings, having strayed outside the field of natural science. And the same favour must be accorded to the no less well disposed and in his moral character quite blameless Hume, when he insists upon the relevance, in this field, of his subtly thought-out speculations. For, as he rightly held, their object lies entirely outside the limits of natural science, in the domain of pure ideas.

What, then, is to be done, especially in view of the danger which would thus seem to threaten the best interests of mankind?[1] Nothing is more natural, nothing is more reasonable, than the decision which we are hereby called upon to make. Leave such thinkers free to take their own line. If they exhibit talent, if they initiate new and profound enquiries, in a word, if they show reason, reason always stands to gain. If we resort to other means than those of untrammelled reason, if we raise the cry of high treason, and act as if we were summoning the vulgar to extinguish a conflagration—the vulgar who have no understanding of such subtle enquiries—we make ourselves ridiculous. For the question at issue is not as to what, in these enquiries, is beneficial or detrimental to the best interests of mankind, but only how far reason can advance by means of speculation that abstracts from all interests, and whether such speculation can count for anything, or must not rather be given up in exchange for the practical. Instead, therefore, of rushing into the fight, sword in hand, we should rather play the part of the peaceable onlooker, from the safe seat of the critic. The struggle is indeed toilsome to the combatants, but for us can be entertaining; and its outcome—certain to be quite bloodless—must be of advantage as contributing to our theoretical insight. For it is indeed absurd to look to reason for enlightenment, and yet to prescribe beforehand which side she must necessarily favour. Besides, reason is already of itself so confined and held

A 746
B 774

A 747
B 775

---

[1] [dem gemeinen Besten.]

within limits by reason, that we have no need to call out the guard, with a view to bringing the civil power to bear upon that party whose alarming superiority may seem to us to be dangerous. In this dialectic no victory is gained that need give us cause for anxiety.

Reason does indeed stand in sore need of such dialectical debate; and it is greatly to be wished that the debate had been instituted sooner and with unqualified public approval. For in that case criticism would sooner have reached a ripe maturity, and all these disputes would of necessity at once have come to an end, the opposing parties having learned to recognise the illusions and prejudices which have set them at variance.

There is in human nature a certain disingenuousness, which, like everything that comes from nature, must finally $\left\{ {A\ 748 \atop B\ 776} \right.$ contribute to good ends, namely, a disposition to conceal our real sentiments, and to make show of certain assumed sentiments which are regarded as good and creditable. This tendency to conceal ourselves and to assume the appearance of what contributes to our advantage, has, undoubtedly, not only *civilised* us, but gradually, in a certain measure, *moralised* us. For so long as we were not in a position to see through the outward show of respectability, honesty, and modesty, we found in the seemingly genuine examples of goodness with which we were surrounded a school for self-improvement. But this disposition to represent ourselves as better than we are, and to give expression to sentiments which we do not share, serves as a merely *provisional* arrangement, to lead us from the state of savage rudeness, and to allow of our assuming at least the *outward bearing*[1] of what we know to be good. But later, when true principles have been developed, and have become part of our way of thought, this duplicity must be more and more earnestly combated; otherwise it corrupts the heart, and checks the growth of good sentiments with the rank weeds of fair appearances.

I am sorry to observe the same disingenuousness, misrepresentation, and hypocrisy even in the utterances of speculative thought, where there are far fewer hindrances to our making, as is fitting, frank and unreserved admission of our thoughts, and no advantage whatsoever in acting otherwise. $\left\{ {A\ 749 \atop B\ 777} \right.$

[1] [*die Manier.*]

For what can be more prejudicial to the interests of knowledge than to communicate even our very thoughts in a falsified form, to conceal doubts which we feel in regard to our own assertions, or to give an appearance of conclusiveness to grounds of proofs which we ourselves recognise to be insufficient. So long as mere personal vanity is what breeds these secret devices—and this is generally the case with those speculative judgments which concern no special interest and do not easily allow of apodeictic certainty—it is counteracted, *in the process of enlisting general acceptance*, by the vanity of others; and thus in the end the result is the same as would have been obtained, though much sooner, by entirely sincere and honest procedure. When the common people are of opinion that those who indulge in subtle questionings aim at nothing less than to shake the very foundations of public welfare, it may, indeed, seem not only prudent but permissible, and indeed even commendable, to further the good cause through sophistical arguments rather than allow its supposed antagonists the advantage of having made us lower our tone to that of a merely practical conviction, and of having compelled us to admit our lack of speculative and apodeictic certainty. I cannot, however, but think that nothing is so entirely incompatible with the purpose of maintaining a good cause as deceit, hypocrisy, and fraud. Surely the least that can be demanded is that in a matter of pure speculation, when weighing the considerations cited by reason, we should proceed in an entirely sincere manner. If we could confidently count even upon this little, the conflict of speculative reason regarding the important questions of God, the immortality of the soul, and freedom, would long ago have been decided, or would very soon be brought to a conclusion. Thus it often happens that purity of purpose is in inverse ratio to the goodness of the cause, and that candour and honesty are perhaps more likely to be found among its assailants than among its defenders.

A 750
B 778

I shall therefore assume that I have readers who do not wish to see a righteous cause defended in an unrighteous manner; and that they will consequently take it as agreed, that, according to our principles of criticism, and having regard not to what commonly happens, but to what ought to happen, there can, properly speaking, be no polemic of pure reason.

For how can two persons carry on a dispute about a thing the reality of which neither of them can present in actual or even in possible experience—a dispute in which they brood over the mere idea of the thing, in order to extract from it something *more than the idea*, namely, the reality of the object itself? What means have they of ending the dispute, since neither of them can make his thesis genuinely comprehensible and certain, but only attack and refute that of his opponent? For this is the fate of all assertions of pure reason: that since they transcend the conditions of all possible experience, outside which the authentication of truth is in no wise possible, while at the same time they have to make use of the laws of the understanding—laws which are adapted only for empirical employment, but without which no step can be taken in synthetic thought—neither side can avoid exposing its weakness, and each can therefore take advantage of the weakness of the other.

{A 751
{B 779

The critique of pure reason can be regarded as the true tribunal for all disputes of pure reason; for it is not involved in these disputes—disputes which are immediately concerned with objects—but is directed to the determining and estimating of the rights of reason in general, in accordance with the principles of their first institution.

In the absence of this critique reason is, as it were, in the state of nature, and can establish and secure its assertions and claims only through *war*. The critique, on the other hand, arriving at all its decisions in the light of fundamental principles of its own institution, the authority of which no one can question, secures to us the peace of a legal order, in which our disputes have to be conducted solely by the recognised methods of *legal action*. In the former state, the disputes are ended by a victory to which both sides lay claim, and which is generally followed by a merely temporary armistice, arranged by some mediating authority; in the latter, by a *judicial sentence* which, as it strikes at the very root of the conflicts, effectively secures an eternal peace. The endless disputes of a merely dogmatic reason thus finally constrain us to seek relief in some critique of reason itself, and in a legislation based upon such criticism. As Hobbes maintains, the state of nature is a state of injustice and violence, and we have no option save to abandon it and submit ourselves to the constraint of law, which

{A 752
{B 780

limits our freedom solely in order that it may be consistent with the freedom of others and with the common good of all.

This freedom will carry with it the right to submit openly for discussion the thoughts and doubts with which we find ourselves unable to deal, and to do so without being decried as troublesome and dangerous citizens. This is one of the original rights of human reason, which recognises no other judge than that universal human reason in which everyone has his say. And since all improvement of which our state is capable must be obtained from this source, such a right is sacred and must not be curtailed. Indeed we are very ill-advised in decrying as dangerous any bold assertions against, or audacious attacks upon, the view which already has on its side the approval of the largest and best portion of the community; in so doing we are ascribing to them an importance which they are not entitled to claim. Whenever I hear that a writer of real ability has demonstrated away the freedom of the human will, the hope of a future life, and the existence of God, I am eager to read the book, for I expect him by his talents to increase my insight into these matters. Already, before having opened it, I am perfectly certain that he has not justified any one of his specific claims; not because I believe that I am in possession of conclusive proofs of these important propositions, but because the transcendental critique, which has disclosed to me all the resources of our pure reason, has completely convinced me that, as reason is incompetent to arrive at affirmative assertions in this field, it is equally unable, indeed even less able, to establish any negative conclusion in regard to these questions. For from what source will the freethinker derive his professed knowledge[1] that there is, for example, no supreme being? This proposition is outside the field of possible experience, and therefore beyond the limits of all human insight. The reply of the *dogmatic* defender of the good cause I should not read at all. I know beforehand that he will attack the sophistical arguments of his opponent simply in order to gain acceptance for his own; and I also know that a quite familiar line of false argument does not yield so much material for new observations as one that is novel and ingeniously elaborated.

A 753
B 781

---

[1] [Reading, with Wille, *der Freigeist seine angebliche Kenntnis* for *der angebliche Freigeist seine Kenntnis*.]

The opponent of religion is indeed, in his own way, no less dogmatic, but he affords me a welcome opportunity of apply- {A 754 B 782} ing and, in this or that respect, amending the principles of my Critique, while at the same time I need be in no fear of these principles being in the least degree endangered.

But must not the young, at least, when entrusted to our academical teaching, be warned against such writings, and preserved from a premature knowedge of such dangerous propositions, until their faculty of judgment is mature, or rather until the doctrine which we seek to instil into them has taken such firm root, that they are able effectively to withstand all persuasion to contrary views, from whatever quarter it may come?

If we are to insist on holding to dogmatic procedure in matters of pure reason, and on disposing of our opponents in strictly polemical fashion, that is, by ourselves taking sides in the controversy, and therefore equipping ourselves with proofs in support of the opposite assertions, certainly this procedure would *for the time being* be the most expedient; but *in the long run* nothing would be more foolish and ineffective than to keep youthful reason thus for a period under tutelage. This will indeed guard the young temporarily against perversion. But when, later, either curiosity or the fashion of the age brings such writings under their notice, will their youthful conviction then stand the test? Whoever, in withstanding the attacks of his opponent, has at his disposal only dogmatic weapons, and is unable to develop the dialectic which lies concealed in his own breast no less than in that of his an- {A 755 B 783} tagonist, [is in a dangerous position]. He sees sophistical arguments, which have the attraction of novelty, set in opposition to sophistical arguments which no longer have that attraction, but, on the contrary, tend to arouse the suspicion that advantage has been taken of his youthful credulity. And accordingly he comes to believe that there can be no better way of showing that he has outgrown childish discipline than by casting aside these well-meant warnings; and accustomed as he is to dogmatism, he drinks deep draughts of the poison, which destroys his principles by a counter-dogmatism.

In academic teaching we ought to pursue the course exactly opposite to that which is here recommended, provided always that the teaching is based on thorough instruction in the criticism of pure reason. For in order to bring the principles of this criticism into operation as soon as possible, and to show their sufficiency even when dialectical illusion is at its height, it is absolutely necessary that the attacks which seem so terrible to the dogmatist should be made to exercise their full force upon the pupil's reason, which though still weak has been enlightened through criticism, and that the pupil should thus be allowed the opportunity of testing for himself, one by one, by reference to the critical principles, how groundless are the assertions of those who have launched these attacks. As it is by no means difficult for him to resolve these arguments into thin air, he early begins to feel his own capacity to secure himself against such injurious deceptions, which must finally lose for him all their illusory power. Those same blows which destroy the structures of the enemy must indeed be equally destructive to any speculative structure which he may perchance himself wish to erect. This does not, however, in the least disturb him, since he has no need of any such shelter, being still in possession of good expectations in the practical sphere, where he may confidently hope to find firmer ground upon which to erect his own rational and beneficial system.

A 756
B 784

There is, therefore, properly speaking, no polemic in the field of pure reason. Both parties beat the air, and wrestle with their own shadows, since they go beyond the limits of nature, where there is nothing that they can seize and hold with their dogmatic grasp. Fight as they may, the shadows which they cleave asunder grow together again forthwith, like the heroes in Valhalla, to disport themselves anew in the bloodless contests.

But neither can we admit that there is any sceptical employment of pure reason, such as might be entitled the principle of *neutrality* in all its disputes. To set reason at variance with itself, to supply it with weapons on both sides, and then to look on, quietly and scoffingly, at the fierce struggle, is not, from the dogmatic point of view, a seemly spectacle, but appears to suggest a mischievous and malevolent disposition. If, however, we consider the invincible obstinacy and the boastfulness of those who argue dogmatically, and who refuse to allow their claims to be moderated by any criticism, there

A 757
B 785

is really no other available course of action than to set against the boasting of the one side the no less justified boasting of the other, in the hope that the resistance thus offered to reason may at least serve to disconcert it, to awaken some doubts as to its pretensions, and to make it willing to give a hearing to criticism. But to allow ourselves simply to acquiesce in these doubts, and thereupon to set out to commend the conviction and admission of our ignorance not merely as a remedy against the complacency of the dogmatists, but likewise as the right method of putting an end to the conflict of reason with itself, is a futile procedure, and can never suffice to overcome the restlessness of reason. At best it is merely a means of awakening it from its sweet dogmatic dreams, and of inducing it to enter upon a more careful examination of its own position. Since, however, the sceptical method of escaping from the troublesome affairs of reason appears to be, as it were, a short cut by which we can arrive at a permanent peace in philosophy, or [if it be not that], is at least the road favoured by those who would feign make show of having a philosophical justification for their contemptuous dislike of all enquiries of this kind, I consider it necessary to exhibit this way of thinking in its true light.

The Impossibility of a Sceptical Satisfaction of Pure Reason in its Internal Conflicts

{A 758
{B 786

The consciousness of my ignorance (unless at the same time this ignorance is recognised as being necessary), instead of ending my enquiries, ought rather to be itself the reason for entering upon them. All ignorance is either ignorance of things or ignorance of the function and limits of knowledge. If ignorance is only [1] accidental, it must incite me, in the former regard to a *dogmatic* enquiry concerning things (objects), in the latter regard to a *critical* enquiry concerning the limits of my possible knowledge. But that my ignorance is absolutely necessary, and that I am therefore absolved from all further enquiry, cannot be established empirically, from *observation*, but only through an *examination*, critically conducted, of the primary sources of our knowledge. The determination of the limits of our reason cannot, therefore, be made save on *a priori*

---

[1] [Reading, with Erdmann, *nur* for *nun*.]

grounds; on the other hand, that limitation of it which consists merely in an indeterminate knowledge of an ignorance never to be completely removed, can be recognised *a posteriori* by reference to that which, notwithstanding all we know, still remains to be known. The former knowledge of our ignorance, which is possible only through criticism of reason itself, is *science*; the latter is nothing but *perception*, and we cannot say how far the inferences from perception may extend. If I represent the earth as it appears to my senses, as a flat surface, with a circular horizon,[1] I cannot know how far it extends. But experience teaches me that wherever I may go, I always see a space around me in which[2] I could proceed further; and thus I know the limits of my actual knowledge of the earth at any given time, but not the limits of all possible geography. But if I have got so far as to know that the earth is a sphere and that its surface is spherical, I am able even from a small part of it, for instance, from the magnitude of a degree, to know determinately, in accordance with principles *a priori*, the diameter, and through it the total superficial area of the earth; and although I am ignorant of the objects which this surface may contain, I yet have knowledge in respect of its circuit, magnitude, and limits.

A 759 / B 787

The sum of all the possible objects of our knowledge appears to us to be a plane, with an apparent horizon—namely, that which in its sweep comprehends it all, and which has been entitled by us the idea of unconditioned totality. To reach this concept empirically is impossible, and all attempts to determine it *a priori* in accordance with an assured principle have proved vain. None the less all the questions raised by our pure reason are as to what may be outside the horizon,[3] or, it may be, on its boundary line.

A 760 / B 788

The celebrated David Hume was one of those geographers of human reason who have imagined that they have sufficiently disposed of all such questions by setting them outside the horizon of human reason—a horizon which yet he was not able to determine. Hume dwelt in particular upon the principle of causality, and quite rightly observed that its truth, and even the objective validity of the concept of efficient cause in

[1] [*als einen Teller*.]   [2] [Reading, with Erdmann, *darin* for *dahin*.]
[3] [Reading, with Erdmann, *dem Horizont* for *diesem Horizonte*.]

general, is based on no insight, that is, on no *a priori* knowledge, and that its authority cannot therefore be ascribed to
its necessity, but merely to its general utility in the course of
experience, and to a certain subjective necessity which it
thereby acquires, and which he entitles custom. From the
incapacity of our reason to make use of this principle in any
manner that transcends experience, he inferred the nullity of
all pretensions of reason to advance beyond the empirical.

A procedure of this kind—subjecting the facts[1] of reason
to examination, and if necessary to blame—may be entitled
the *censorship* of reason. This censorship must certainly lead
to *doubt* regarding all transcendent employment of principles.
But this is only the second step, and does not by any means ⟨ A 761
complete the work of enquiry. The first step in matters of pure ⟨ B 789
reason, marking its infancy, is *dogmatic*. The second step is
sceptical; and indicates that experience has rendered our judgment wiser and more circumspect. But a third step, such as
can be taken only by fully matured judgment, based on assured principles of proved universality, is now necessary,
namely, to subject to examination, not the facts of reason, but
reason itself, in the whole extent of its powers, and as regards
its aptitude for pure *a priori* modes of knowledge. This is not
the censorship but the *criticism* of reason, whereby not its
present *bounds*[2] but its determinate [and necessary] *limits*,[3]
not its ignorance on this or that point but its ignorance in
regard to all possible questions of a certain kind, are demonstrated from principles, and not merely arrived at by way of
conjecture. Scepticism is thus a resting-place for human
reason, where it can reflect upon its dogmatic wanderings and
make survey of the region in which it finds itself, so that for
the future it may be able to choose its path with more certainty.
But it is no dwelling-place for permanent settlement. Such can
be obtained only through perfect certainty in our knowledge,
alike of the objects themselves and of the limits within which ⟨ A 762
all our knowledge of objects is enclosed. ⟨ B 790

Our reason is not like a plane indefinitely far extended,
the limits of which we know in a general way only; but must
rather be compared to a sphere, the radius of which can be
determined from the curvature of the arc of its surface—that

---

[1] [*die Fakta.*]   [2] [*Schränken.*]   [3] [*Grenzen.*]

is to say, from the nature of synthetic *a priori* propositions
—and whereby we can likewise specify with certainty its
volume and its limits. Outside this sphere (the field of experience) there is nothing that can be an object for reason; nay, the
very questions in regard to such supposed objects relate only
to subjective principles of a complete determination of those
relations which can come under the concepts of the understanding and which can be found within the empirical sphere

We are actually in possession of *a priori* synthetic modes
of knowledge,[1] as is shown by the principles of understanding
which anticipate experience. If anyone is quite unable to
comprehend the possibility of these principles, he may at first
be inclined to doubt whether they actually dwell in us *a
priori*; but he cannot on this account declare that they are
beyond the powers of the understanding, and so represent all
the steps which reason takes under their guidance as being null
and void. All that he can say is that if we could have insight into
their origin and authenticity, we should be able to determine
the scope and limits of our reason, but that until we can have
such insight any assertions as to the limits of reason are made
at random. And on this ground a general doubt regarding all
dogmatic philosophy, proceeding as such philosophy does without criticism of reason itself, is entirely justified; but we cannot
therefore altogether deny to reason the right to take such forward steps, once we have prepared and secured the way for
them by a more thorough preparation of the ground. For all
the concepts, nay, all the questions, which pure reason presents
to us, have their source not in experience, but exclusively in
reason itself, and must therefore allow of solution and of being
determined in regard to their validity or invalidity. We have no
right to ignore these problems, as if their solution really de-
pended on the nature of things, and as if we might therefore,
on the plea of our incapacity, decline to occupy ourselves with
their further investigation; for since reason is the sole begetter
of these ideas, it is under obligation to give an account of their
validity or of their illusory, dialectical nature.

All sceptical polemic should properly be directed only
against the dogmatist, who, without any misgivings as to his
fundamental objective principles, that is, without criticism,

A 763
B 791

[1] [Reading, with Erdmann, *Erkenntnisse* for *Erkenntnis*.]

proceeds complacently upon his adopted path; it should be designed simply to put him out of countenance and thus to bring him to self-knowledge. In itself, however, this polemic is of no avail whatsoever in enabling us to decide what it is that we can and what it is that we cannot know. All unsuccessful dogmatic attempts of reason are facts,[1] and it is always of {A 764 / B 792} advantage to submit them to the censorship of the sceptic. But this can decide nothing regarding those expectations of reason which lead it to hope for better success in its future attempts, and to build claims on this foundation; and consequently no mere censorship can put an end to the dispute regarding the rights of human reason.

Hume is perhaps the most ingenious of all the sceptics, and beyond all question is without rival in respect of the influence which the sceptical procedure can exercise in awakening reason to a thorough self-examination. It will therefore well repay us to make clear to ourselves, so far as may be relevant to our purpose, the course of the reasoning, and the errors, of so acute and estimable a man—a course of reasoning which at the start was certainly on the track of truth.

Hume was perhaps aware, although he never followed the matter out, that in judgments of a certain kind we pass beyond our concept of the object. I have entitled this kind of judgments *synthetic*. There is no difficulty as to how, by means of experience, I can pass beyond the concept which I previously have. Experience is in itself a synthesis of perceptions, whereby the concept which I have obtained by means of a perception is increased through the addition of other perceptions. But we suppose ourselves to be able to pass *a priori* beyond our concept, and so to extend our knowledge. This we {A 765 / B 793} attempt to do either through the pure understanding, in respect of that which is at least capable of being an *object of experience*, or through pure reason, in respect of such properties of things, or indeed even of the existence of such things, as can never be met with in experience. Our sceptical philosopher did not distinguish these two kinds of judgments, as he yet ought to have done, but straightway proceeded to treat this self-increment of concepts, and, as we may say, this spontaneous generation on the part of our understanding and of our reason,

[1] [*Fakta.*]

without impregnation by experience, as being impossible. He therefore regarded all the supposed *a priori* principles of these faculties as fictitious, and concluded that they are nothing but a custom-bred habit arising from experience and its laws, and are consequently merely empirical, that is, rules that are in themselves contingent, and to which we ascribe a supposititious necessity and universality. In support of his assertion of this startling thesis, he cited the universally recognised principle of the relation between cause and effect. For since no faculty of understanding can carry us from the concept of a thing to the existence of something else that is thereby universally and necessarily given, he believed that he was therefore in a position to conclude that in the absence of experience we have nothing that can increase our concept and justify us in propounding a judgment which thus enlarges

A 766 }
B 794 }

itself *a priori*. That sunlight should melt wax and yet also harden clay, no understanding, he pointed out, can discover from the concepts which we previously possessed of these things, much less infer them according to a law. Only experience is able to teach us such a law. But, as we have discovered in the Transcendental Logic, although we can never pass *immediately* beyond the content of the concept which is given us, we are nevertheless able, in relation to a third thing, namely, *possible* experience, to know the law of its connection with other things, and to do so in an *a priori* manner. If, therefore, wax, which was formerly hard, melts, I can know *a priori* that *something* must have preceded, ([that something being] for instance [in this case] the heat of the sun), upon which the melting has followed according to a fixed law, although *a priori*, independently of experience, I could not determine, *in any specific manner*, either the cause from the effect, or the effect from the cause. Hume was therefore in error in inferring from the contingency of our determination *in accordance with the law* the contingency of the *law* itself. The passing beyond the concept of a thing to possible experience (which takes place *a priori* and constitutes the objective reality of the concept) he confounded with the synthesis of the objects of actual experience, which is always empirical. He thus confounds a principle of affinity, which has its seat in the understanding and affirms necessary connection, with a rule of association, which exists only in the imitative faculty of im- {A 767 / B 795} agination, and which can exhibit only contingent, not objective, connections.

The sceptical errors of this otherwise singularly acute thinker arose chiefly from a defect which he shares in common with all dogmatists, namely, that he did not make a systematic review of all the various kinds of *a priori* synthesis ascribable to the understanding. For he would then have found, to mention only one of many possible examples, that *the principle of permanence* is a principle of this character, and that, like the principle of causality, it anticipates experience. He would thus have been able to prescribe determinate limits to the activities whereby the understanding and pure reason extend themselves *a priori*. Instead of so doing, he merely *restricts* the understanding, without defining its *limits*, and while creating a general mistrust fails to supply any determinate knowledge of the ignorance which for us is unavoidable. For while subjecting to censorship certain principles of the understanding, he makes no attempt to assess the understanding itself, in respect of all its powers, by the assay-balance of criticism; while rightly denying to the understanding what it cannot really supply, he goes on to deny it all power of extending itself *a priori*, and this in spite of his never having tested it as a whole. Thus the fate that waits upon all scepticism likewise befalls Hume, namely, that his own sceptical teaching comes to be doubted, as being based only on facts which are contingent, not on principles {A 768 / B 796} which can constrain to a necessary renunciation of all right to dogmatic assertions.

Further, he draws no distinction between the well-grounded claims of the understanding and the dialectical pretensions of reason, though it is indeed chiefly against the latter that his attacks are directed. Accordingly that peculiarly characteristic ardour with which reason insists upon giving free rein to itself, has not in the least been disturbed but only temporarily impeded. It does not feel that it has been shut out from the field in which it is wont to disport itself; and so, in spite of its being thwarted in this and that direction, it cannot be made entirely to desist from these ventures. On the contrary, the attacks lead only to counter-preparations, and make us the more obstinate in insisting upon our own views. But a complete review of all the powers of reason—and the conviction thereby obtained of the certainty of its claims to a modest territory, as also of the vanity of higher pretensions— puts an end to the conflict, and induces it to rest satisfied with a limited but undisputed patrimony.

To the uncritical dogmatist, who has not surveyed the sphere of his understanding, and therefore has not determined, in accordance with principles, the limits of his possible knowledge, these sceptical attacks are not only dangerous but even destructive. For he does not know beforehand how far his powers extend, and indeed believes that their limits can be determined by the simple method of trial and failure. In consequence of this, if on being attacked there is a single one of his assertions that he is unable to justify, or which involves illusion for which he also cannot account in terms of any principles, suspicion falls on all his contentions, however plausible they may appear.

A 769
B 797

The sceptic is thus the taskmaster who constrains the dogmatic reasoner to develop a sound critique of the understanding and reason. When we have advanced thus far, we need fear no further challenge, since we have learned to distinguish our real possessions from that which lies entirely outside them; and as we make no claims in regard to this latter domain, we cannot become involved in any dispute in respect to it. While, therefore, the sceptical procedure cannot of itself yield any *satisfying* answer to the questions of reason, none the less it *prepares the way* by arousing reason to circumspection, and by indicating the radical measures which are adequate to secure it in its legitimate possessions.

CHAPTER I

Section 3

THE DISCIPLINE OF PURE REASON IN REGARD TO HYPOTHESES

Since criticism of our reason has at last taught us that we cannot by means of its pure and speculative employment arrive at any knowledge whatsoever, may it not seem that a proportionately wider field is opened for *hypotheses?* For are we not at liberty, where we cannot make assertions, at least to invent theories and to have opinions?[1]

If the imagination is not simply to be *visionary*,[2] but is to be *inventive*[3] under the strict surveillance of reason, there must {A 770 / B 798} always previously be something that is completely certain, and not invented[4] or merely a matter of opinion, namely, the *possibility* of the object itself. Once that is established, it is then permissible to have recourse to opinion in regard to its actuality; but this opinion, if it is not to be groundless, must be brought into connection with what is actually given and so far certain, as serving to account for what is thus given. Then, and only then, can the supposition be entitled an *hypothesis.*

As we cannot form the least conception *a priori* of the possibility of dynamical connection, and as the categories[5] of the pure understanding do not suffice for devising any such conception, but only for apprehending it when met with in experience, we cannot, in accordance with these categories, creatively imagine[6] any object in terms of any new quality that does not allow of being given in experience; and we cannot, therefore, make use of such an object in any legitimate hypothesis; otherwise we should be resting reason on empty figments of the brain,[7] and not on concepts of things. Thus it is not permissible to invent any new original powers, as, for instance, an understanding capable of intuiting its objects without the aid of senses; or a force of attraction without any contact; or a new kind of substance existing in space and yet not impenetrable. Nor is it legitimate to postulate a form of communion of substances which is different from any revealed in experience, a presence that is not spatial, {A 771 / B 799} a duration that is not temporal. In a word, our reason can employ as conditions of the possibility of things only the conditions of possible experience; it can never proceed to form concepts of things quite independently of these conditions. Such concepts, though not self-contradictory, would be without an object.

---

[1] [*zu dichten und zu meinen.*]   [2] [*schwärmen.*]
[3] [*dichten soll.*]   [4] [*erdichtet.*]
[5] [Reading, with Vorländer, *Kategorien . . . dienen* for *Kategorie . . . dient.*]
[6] [*ursprünglich aussinnen.*]   [7] [*leere Hirngespinste.*]

The concepts of reason are, as we have said, mere ideas, and have no object that can be met with in any experience. None the less they do not on this account signify objects that having been invented are thereupon assumed to be possible. They are thought only problematically, in order that upon them (as heuristic fictions), we may base regulative principles of the systematic employment of the understanding in the field of experience. Save in this connection they are merely thought-entities,[1] the possibility of which is not demonstrable, and which therefore do not allow of being employed, in the character of hypotheses, in explanation of the actual appearances. It is quite permissible to *think* the soul as simple, in order, in conformity with this *idea*, to employ as the principle of our interpretation of its inner appearances a complete and necessary unity of all its faculties; and this in spite of the fact that this unity is such as can never be apprehended *in concreto*. But to *assume* the soul as a simple substance (a transcendent concept), would be [to propound] a proposition which is not only indemonstrable—as is the case with many physical hypotheses—but is hazarded in a quite blind and arbitrary fashion. For the simple can never be met with in any experience whatsoever; and if by substance be here meant the permanent object of sensible intuition, the possibility of a *simple appearance* is quite incomprehensible Reason does not afford any sufficient ground for assuming, [even] as a matter of opinion, merely intelligible beings, or merely intelligible properties of things belonging to the sensible world, although (as we have no concepts of their possibility or impossibility) we also cannot lay claim to any insight that justifies us in dogmatically denying them.

A 772 | B 800 |

In the explanation of given appearances, no things or grounds of explanation can be adduced other than those which have been found to stand in connection with given appearances in accordance with the already known laws of the appearances. A *transcendental hypothesis*, in which a mere idea of reason is used in explanation of natural existences,[2] would really be no explanation; so to proceed would be to explain something, which in terms of known empirical principles we do not understand sufficiently, by something which

---

[1] [*Gedankendinge.*]   [2] [*Naturdinge.*]

we do not understand at all. Moreover, the principle of such an hypothesis would at most serve only for the satisfaction of reason, not for the furtherance of the employment of the understanding in respect of objects. Order and purposiveness in nature must themselves be explained from natural grounds and according to natural laws; and the wildest hypotheses, if $\begin{Bmatrix} A\ 773 \\ B\ 801 \end{Bmatrix}$ only they are physical, are here more tolerable than a hyperphysical hypothesis, such as the appeal to a divine Author, assumed simply in order that we may have an explanation. That would be a principle of *ignava ratio*; for we should be passing over all causes the objective reality of which, at least as regards their possibility, can be ascertained in the course of experience, in order to rest in a mere idea—an idea that is very comforting to reason. As regards the absolute totality of the ground of explanation of the series of these causes, such totality need suggest no difficulty in respect of natural existences;[1] since these existences are nothing but appearances, we need never look to them for any kind of completeness[2] in the synthesis of the series of conditions.

It can never be permissible, in the speculative employment of reason, to resort to transcendental hypotheses, and to presume that we can make good the lack of physical grounds of explanation by appealing to the hyperphysical. The objection to such procedure is twofold: partly, that reason, so far from being in the least advanced thereby, is cut off from all progress in its own employment; partly, that this license would in the end deprive reason of all the fruits that spring from the cultivation of its own proper domain, namely, that of experience. For whenever the explanation of natural existences is found to be difficult, there is always at hand a transcendental ground of explanation which relieves us from further investigation, $\begin{Bmatrix} A\ 774 \\ B\ 802 \end{Bmatrix}$ and our enquiry is brought to an end not through insight, but by the aid of a principle which while utterly incomprehensible has from the start been so constructed as necessarily to contain the concept of what is absolutely primordial.

The second requirement for the admissibility of an hypothesis is its adequacy in accounting *a priori* for those consequences which are [*de facto*] given. If for this purpose we have to call in auxiliary hypotheses, they give rise to the sus-

---

[1] [*Weltobjekte.*]   [2] [*etwas Vollendetes.*]

picion that they are mere fictions; for each of them requires the same justification as is necessary in the case of the fundamental hypothesis, and they are not, therefore, in a position to bear reliable testimony. If we assume an absolutely perfect cause, we need not be at a loss in explaining the purposiveness, order, and vastness which are displayed in the world; but in view of what, judged at least by our concepts, are the obvious deviations and evils, other new hypotheses are required in order to uphold the original hypothesis in face of the objections which these suggest. If the simple self-sufficiency of the human soul has been employed to account for its appearances, it is controverted by certain difficulties, due to those phenomena which are similar to the changes that take place in matter (growth and decay), and we have therefore to seek the aid of new hypotheses, which are not indeed without plausibility, but which yet have no credentials save what is conferred upon them by that opinion—the fundamental hypothesis—which they have themselves been called in to support.

A 775 }
B 803 }

If the instances here cited as examples of the assertions made by reason—the incorporeal unity of the soul and the existence of a supreme being—are propounded not as hypotheses, but as dogmas proved *a priori*, I am not at present concerned with them, save to remark that in that case care must be taken that the proof has the apodeictic certainty of a demonstration. For to set out to show no more than that the reality of such ideas is *probable* is as absurd as to think of proving a proposition of geometry merely as a probability. Reason, when employed apart from all experience, can know propositions entirely *a priori*, and as necessary, or it can know nothing at all. Its judgments, therefore, are never opinions; either it must abstain from all judgment, or must affirm with apodeictic certainty. Opinions and probable judgments as to what belongs to things can be propounded only in explanation of what is actually given, or as consequences that follow in accordance with empirical laws from what underlies the actually given. They are therefore concerned only with the series of the objects of experience. Outside this field, to form *opinions* is merely to play with thoughts. For we should then have to presuppose yet another opinion—the opinion that we may perhaps arrive at the truth by a road that is uncertain.

But although, in dealing with the merely speculative ques- { A 776
B 804 tions of pure reason, hypotheses are not available for the purposes of basing propositions upon them, they are yet entirely permissible for the purposes of defending propositions; that is to say, they may not be employed in any dogmatic, but only in polemical fashion. By the defence of propositions I do not mean the addition of fresh grounds for their assertion, but merely the nullifying of the sophistical arguments by which our opponent professes to invalidate this assertion. Now all synthetic propositions of pure reason have this peculiarity, that while in asserting the reality of this or that idea we can never have knowledge sufficient to give certainty to our proposition, our opponent is just as little able to assert the opposite. This equality of fortune [in the ventures] of human reason does not, in speculative modes of knowledge, favour either of the two parties, and it is consequently the fitting battle-ground for their never-ending feuds. But as will be shown, reason has, in respect of its *practical employment*, the right to postulate what in the field of mere speculation it can have no kind of right to assume without sufficient proof. For while all such assumptions do violence to [the principle of] completeness of speculation, that is a principle with which the practical interest is not at all concerned. In the practical sphere reason has rights of possession, of which it does not require to offer proof, and of which, in fact, it could not supply proof. The burden of proof { A 777
B 805 accordingly rests upon the opponent. But since the latter knows just as little of the object under question, in trying to prove its non-existence, as does the former in maintaining its reality, it is evident that the former, who is asserting something as a practically necessary supposition, is at an advantage (*melior est conditio possidentis*). For he is at liberty to employ, as it were in self-defence, on behalf of his own good cause, the very same weapons that his opponent employs against that cause, that is, hypotheses. These are not intended to strengthen the proof of his position, but only to show that the opposing party has much too little understanding of the matter in dispute to allow of his flattering himself that he has the advantage in respect of speculative insight.

Hypotheses are therefore, in the domain of pure reason, permissible only as weapons of war, and only for the purpose

of defending a right, not in order to establish it. But the opposing party we must always look for in ourselves. For speculative reason in its transcendental employment is *in itself*
dialectical; the objections which we have to fear lie in ourselves. We must seek them out, just as we would do in the
case of claims that, while old, have never become superannu-
ated, in order that by annulling them we may establish a
permanent peace. External quiescence is merely specious.
The root of these disturbances, which lies deep in the nature
A 778
B 806 } of human reason, must be removed. But how can we do so,
unless we give it freedom, nay, nourishment, to send out
shoots so that it may discover itself to our eyes, and that it
may then be entirely destroyed? We must, therefore, bethink
ourselves of objections which have never yet occurred to any
opponent, and indeed lend him our weapons, and grant him
the most favourable position which he could possibly desire.
We have nothing to fear in all this, but much to hope for;
namely, that we may gain for ourselves a possession which
can never again be contested.

Thus for our complete equipment we require among other
things the hypotheses of pure reason. For although they are
but leaden weapons, since they are not steeled by any law of experience, they are yet as effective as those which our opponents
can employ against us. If, therefore, having assumed (in some
non-speculative connection) the nature of the soul to be immaterial and not subject to any corporeal change, we are met
by the difficulty that nevertheless experience seems to prove
that the exaltation and the derangement of our mental powers
are alike in being merely diverse modifications of our organs,
we can weaken the force of this proof by postulating that our
body may be nothing more than a fundamental appearance
which in this our present state (in this life) serves as a condition
of our whole faculty of sensibility, and therewith of all our
thought, and that separation from the body may therefore
be regarded as the end of this sensible employment of our
faculty of knowledge and the beginning of its intellectual
A 779
B 807 } employment. Thus regarded, the body would not be the cause
of thought, but merely a restrictive condition of it, and therefore, while indeed furthering the sensible and animal life, it
would because of this very fact have to be considered a hind-

rance to the pure and spiritual life. The dependence of the animal and sensible upon the bodily constitution would then in nowise prove the dependence of our entire life upon the state of our organs. We might go yet further, and discover quite new objections, which either have never been suggested or have never been sufficiently developed.

Generation, in man as in non-rational creatures, is dependent upon opportunity, often indeed upon sufficiency of food, upon the moods and caprices of rulers, nay, even upon vice. And this makes it very difficult to suppose that a creature whose life has its first beginning in circumstances so trivial and so entirely dependent upon our own choice, should have an existence that extends to all eternity. As regards the continuance (here on earth) of the species as a whole, this difficulty is negligible, since accident in the individual case is still subject to a general law, but as regards each individual it certainly seems highly questionable to expect so potent an effect from causes so insignificant. But to meet these objections we can propound a transcendental hypothesis, namely, that all life is, strictly speaking, intelligible only, is not subject to changes of time, and neither begins in birth nor ends $\begin{cases} \text{A } 780 \\ \text{B } 808 \end{cases}$ in death; that[1] this life is an appearance only, that is, a sensible representation of the purely spiritual life, and that the whole sensible world is a mere picture[2] which in our present mode of knowledge hovers before us, and like a dream has in itself no objective reality; that if we could intuit ourselves and things *as they are*, we should see ourselves in a world of spiritual beings,[3] our sole and true community with which has not begun through birth and will not cease through bodily death—both birth and death being mere appearances.

Now of all this we have not the least knowledge. We plead it only in hypothetical fashion, to meet the attack; we are not actually asserting it. For it is not even an idea of reason, but is a concept *devised* merely for the purposes of self-defence. None the less we are here proceeding in entire conformity with reason. Our opponent falsely represents the absence of empirical conditions as itself amounting to proof of the total

---

[1] [Reading, with Valentiner, *werde; dass* for *werde. Dass.*]
[2] [*ein blosses Bild.*]   [3] [*geistiger Naturen.*]

impossibility of our belief, and is therefore proceeding on the assumption that he has exhausted all the possibilities. What we are doing is merely to show that it is just as little possible for him to comprehend the whole field of possible things through mere laws of experience as it is for us to reach, outside experience, any conclusions justifiable for our reason. Anyone who employs such hypothetical means of defence against the rash and presumptuous negations of his opponent must not be considered to intend the adoption of these opinions as his own; he abandons them, as soon as he has disposed of the dogmatic pretensions of his opponent. For though a merely negative attitude to the assertions of others may seem very modest and moderate, to proceed to represent the objections to an assertion as proofs of the counter-assertion is to make claims no less presumptuous and visionary than if the positive position and its affirmations had been adopted.

It is evident, therefore, that in the speculative employment of reason hypotheses, regarded as opinions, have no validity in themselves, but only relatively to the transcendent pretensions of the opposite party. For to make principles of possible experience conditions of the possibility of things in general is just as transcendent a procedure as to assert the objective reality of [transcendent] concepts, the objects of which cannot be found anywhere save outside the limits of all possible experience. What pure reason judges *assertorically*, must (like everything that reason knows) be necessary; otherwise nothing at all is asserted Accordingly, pure reason does not, in point of fact, contain any opinions whatsoever. The hypotheses, above referred to, are merely *problematic* judgments, which at least cannot be refuted, although they do not indeed allow of any proof. They are therefore nothing but [1] private opinions. Nevertheless, we cannot properly dispense with them as weapons against the misgivings which are apt to occur; they are necessary even to secure our inner tranquillity. We must preserve to them this character, carefully guarding against the assumption of their independent authority or absolute validity, since otherwise they would drown reason in fictions and delusions.

A 781
B 809

A 782
B 810

---

[1] [Reading, with Hartenstein, *reine* for *keine*.]

Chapter I

Section 4

THE DISCIPLINE OF PURE REASON IN REGARD TO ITS PROOFS

What distinguishes the proofs of transcendental synthetic propositions from all other proofs which yield an *a priori* synthetic knowledge is that, in the case of the former, reason may not apply itself, by means of its concepts, directly to the object, but must first establish the objective validity of the concepts and the possibility of their *a priori* synthesis. This rule is not made necessary merely by considerations of prudence, but is essential to the very possibility of the proofs themselves. If I am to pass *a priori* beyond the concept of an object, I can do so only with the help of some special guidance, supplied from outside this concept. In mathematics it is *a priori* intuition which guides my synthesis; and thereby all our conclusions can be drawn immediately from pure intuition. $\begin{Bmatrix} A\ 783 \\ B\ 811 \end{Bmatrix}$ In transcendental knowledge, so long as we are concerned only with concepts of the understanding, our guide is the possibility of experience. Such proof does not show that the given concept (for instance, of that which happens) leads *directly* to another concept (that of a cause); for such a transition would be a *saltus* which could not be justified. The proof proceeds by showing that experience itself, and therefore the object of experience, would be impossible without a connection of this kind. Accordingly, the proof must also at the same time show the possibility of arriving synthetically and *a priori* at some knowledge of things which was not contained in the concepts of them. Unless this requirement be met, the proofs, like streams which break their banks, run wildly at random, whithersoever the current of hidden association may chance to lead them. The semblance of conviction which rests upon subjective causes of association, and which is regarded as insight into a natural affinity, cannot balance the misgivings to which so hazardous a course must rightly give rise. On this account, all attempts to prove the principle of sufficient reason have, by the universal admission of those concerned, been fruitless; and prior to our own transcendental criticism it was considered better, since that principle could not be surrendered, boldly to appeal to the common sense of mankind—an expedient which always

A 784⎫
B 812⎭

is a sign that the cause of reason is in desperate straits—rather than to attempt new dogmatic proofs.

But if the proposition to be proved is an assertion of pure reason, and if I am therefore proposing to pass beyond my empirical concepts by means of mere ideas, justification of such a step in synthesis (supposing it to be possible) is all the more necessary as a precondition of any attempt to prove the proposition itself. However plausible the alleged proof of the simple nature of our thinking substance, derived from the unity of apperception, may be, it is faced by the unavoidable difficulty, that since the [notion of] absolute simplicity is not a concept which can be immediately related to a perception, but, as an idea, would have to be inferred, there can be no understanding how the bare consciousness (which is, or at least can be, contained *in all thought*), though it is indeed so far a simple representation, should conduct us to the consciousness and the knowledge of *a thing in which* thought alone can be contained. If I represent to myself the power of a[1] body in motion, it is so far for me absolute unity, and my representation of it is simple; and I can therefore express this representation by the motion of a point—for the volume of the body is not here a relevant consideration, and can be thought, without diminution of the moving power, as small as we please, and therefore even

A 785⎫
B 813⎭

as existing in a point. But I may not therefore conclude that if nothing be given to me but the moving power of a body, the body can be thought as simple substance—merely because its representation abstracts from the magnitude of its volume and is consequently simple. The simple arrived at by abstraction is entirely different from the simple as an object; though the 'I', taken in abstraction, can contain *in itself* no manifold, in its other meaning, as signifying the soul itself, it can be a highly complex concept, as containing *under itself*, and as denoting, what is very composite.[2] I thus detect in these arguments a paralogism But in order to be armed against this

---

[1] [Reading, with Hartenstein, *eines* for *meines*.]
[2] [*sehr vieles*.]

paralogism (for without some forewarning we should not entertain any suspicion in regard to the proof), it is indispensably necessary to have constantly at hand a criterion of the possibility of those synthetic propositions which are intended to prove more than experience yields. This criterion consists in the requirement that proof should not proceed directly to the desired predicate but only by means of a principle that will demonstrate the possibility of extending our given concept in an *a priori* manner to ideas, and of realising the latter. If this precaution be always observed, if before attempting any proof, we discreetly take thought as to how, and with what ground for hope, we may expect such an extension through pure reason, and whence, in such a case, this insight, which is not developed from concepts, and also cannot be anticipated in reference to any possible experience, is yet to be derived, we can by so doing spare ourselves much difficult and yet fruitless labour, not expecting from reason what obviously exceeds its power—or rather, since reason, when obsessed by passionate desire for the speculative enlargement of its domain, is not easily to be restrained, by subjecting it to the discipline of self-control. {A 786 / B 814}

The first rule is, therefore, not to attempt any transcendental proofs until we have considered, with a view to obtaining justification for them, from what source we propose to derive the principles on which the proofs are to be based, and with what right we may expect success in our inferences. If they are principles of the understanding (for instance, that of causality), it is useless to attempt, by means of them, to attain to ideas of pure reason; such principles are valid only for objects of possible experience. If they are principles of pure reason, it is again labour lost. Reason has indeed principles of its own; but regarded as objective principles, they are one and all dialectical, and can have no validity save as regulative principles for its employment in experience, with a view to making experience systematically coherent. But if such professed proofs are propounded, we must meet their deceptive power of persuasion with the *non liquet* of our matured judgment; and although we may not be able to detect the illusion involved, we are yet entirely within our rights in demanding a deduction of the principles employed in them; {A 787 / B 815} and if these principles have their source in reason alone, the demand is one which can never be met. And there is thus no need for us to concern ourselves with the particular nature and with the refutation of each and every groundless illusion; at the tribunal of a critical reason, which insists upon laws, this entire dialectic, so inexhaustible in its artifices, can be disposed of in bulk.

The second peculiarity of transcendental proofs is that only *one* proof can be found for each transcendental proposition. If I am inferring not from concepts but from the intuition which corresponds to a concept, be it a pure intuition as in mathematics, or an empirical intuition as in natural science, the intuition which serves as the basis of the inference supplies me with manifold material for synthetic propositions, material which I can connect in more than one way, so that, as it is permissible for me to start from more than one point, I can arrive at the same proposition by different paths.

In the case of transcendental propositions, however, we start always from *one* concept only, and assert the synthetic condition of the possibility of the object in accordance with this concept. Since outside this concept there is nothing further through which the object could be determined, there can therefore be only one ground of proof. The proof can contain nothing more than the determination of an object in general in accordance with this one single concept. In the Transcendental Analytic, for instance, we derived the principle that everything which happens has a cause, from the condition under which alone a concept of happening in general is objectively possible—namely, by showing that the determination of an event in time, and therefore the event as belonging to experience, would be impossible save as standing under such a dynamical rule. This is the sole possible ground of proof; for the event, in being represented, has objective validity, that is, truth, only in so far as an object is determined for the concept by means of the law of causality. Other proofs of this principle have, indeed, been attempted, for instance, from the contingency [of that which happens]. But on examining this argument, we can discover no mark of contingency save only the *happening*, that is, the existence of the object preceded by its non-existence, and thus are brought back to the same

A 788
B 816

ground of proof as before. Similarly, if the proposition, that everything which thinks is simple, is to be proved, we leave out of account the manifold of thought, and hold only to the concept of the 'I', which is simple and to which all thought is related. The same is true of the transcendental proof of the existence of God; it is based solely on the coincidence[1] of the concepts of the most real being and of necessary being, and is not to be looked for anywhere else.

{ A 789
{ B 817

This caution reduces the criticism of the assertions of reason to very small compass. When reason is conducting its business through concepts only, there is but one possible proof, if, that is to say, there be any possible proof at all. If, therefore, we observe the dogmatist coming forward with ten proofs, we can be quite sure that he really has none. For had he one that yielded—as must always be required in matters of pure reason—apodeictic proof, what need would he have of the others? His purpose can only be that of the parliamentary advocate, who intends his various arguments for different groups, in order to take advantage of the weakness of those before whom he is pleading—hearers who, without entering deeply into the matter, desire to be soon quit of it, and therefore seize upon whatever may first happen to attract their attention, and decide accordingly.

The third rule peculiar to pure reason, in so far as it is to be subjected to a discipline in respect of transcendental proofs, is that its proofs must never be *apagogical*, but always *ostensive*. The direct or ostensive proof, in every kind of knowledge, is that which combines with the conviction of its truth insight into the sources of its truth; the apagogical proof, on the other hand, while it can indeed yield certainty, cannot enable us to comprehend truth in its connection with the grounds of its possibility. The latter is therefore to be regarded rather as a last resort than as a mode of procedure which satisfies all the requirements of reason. In respect of convincing power, it has, however, this advantage over the direct proofs, that contradiction always carries with it more clearness of representation than the best connection, and so approximates to the intuitional certainty of a demonstration.

{ A 790
{ B 818

The real reason why apagogical proofs are employed in

[1] [*Reziprokabilität.*]

various sciences would seem to be this. When the grounds from which this or that knowledge has to be derived are too numerous or too deeply concealed, we try whether we may not arrive at the knowledge in question through its consequences. Now this *modus ponens*, that is, the inference to the truth of an assertion from the truth of its consequences, is only permissible when all its possible consequences are [known to be] true; for in that case there is only one possible ground for this being so, and that ground must also be true. But this procedure is impracticable; to discover all possible consequences of any given proposition exceeds our powers. None the less this mode of reasoning is resorted to, although indeed with a certain special modification, when we endeavour to prove something merely as an hypothesis. The modification made is that we admit the conclusion as holding according to analogy, namely, on the ground that if all the many consequences examined by us agree with an assumed ground, all other possible consequences will also agree with it. But from the

A 791 }
B 819 }

nature of the argument, it is obvious that an hypothesis can never, on such evidence, be transformed into demonstrated truth. The *modus tollens* of reasoning, which proceeds from consequences to their grounds, is not only a quite rigorous but also an extremely easy mode of proof. For if even a single false consequence can be drawn from a proposition, the proposition is itself false. Instead, then, as in an ostensive proof, of reviewing the whole series of grounds that can lead us to the truth of a proposition, by means of a complete insight into its possibility, we require only to show that a single one of the consequences resulting from its opposite is false, in order to prove that this opposite is itself false, and that the proposition which we had to prove is therefore true.

The apagogic method of proof is, however, permissible only in those sciences where it is impossible mistakenly to *substitute* what is subjective in our representations for what is objective, that is, for the knowledge of that which is in the object. Where such substitution tends to occur, it must often happen that the opposite of a given proposition contradicts only the subjective conditions of thought, and not the object, or that the two propositions contradict each other only under a subjective condition which is falsely treated as being objective; the condition being false, both can be false, without it being possible to infer from the falsity of the one to the truth of the other.

In mathematics this subreption is impossible; and it is ⎰A 792
there, therefore, that apagogical proofs have their true place. ⎱B 820
In natural science, where all our knowledge is based upon empirical intuitions, the subreption can generally be guarded against through repeated comparison of observations; but in this field this mode of proof is for the most part of little importance. The transcendental enterprises of pure reason, however, are one and all carried on within the domain proper to dialectical illusion, that is, within the domain of the subjective, which in its premisses presents itself to reason, nay, forces itself upon reason, as being objective. In this field, therefore, it can never be permissible, so far as synthetic propositions are concerned, to justify assertions by disproving their opposite. For either this refutation is nothing but the mere representation of the conflict of the opposite opinion with the subjective conditions under which alone anything can be conceived by our reason, which does not in the least contribute to the disproof of the thing itself—just as, for instance, we must recognise that while the unconditioned necessity of the existence of a being is altogether inconceivable to us, and that every speculative proof of a necessary supreme being is therefore rightly to be opposed on *subjective* grounds, we have yet no right to deny the possibility of such a primordial being *in itself*—or else both parties, those who adopt the affirmative no less than those who adopt the negative position, have been deceived by transcendental illusion, and base their assertions upon an impossible concept of the object. In that case we can apply the rule: *non entis nulla sunt predicata*; that ⎰A 793
is, all that is asserted of the object, whether affirmatively or ⎱B 821
negatively, is erroneous, and consequently we cannot arrive apagogically at knowledge of the truth through refutation of the opposite. If, for instance, it be assumed that the sensible world is given *in itself* in its totality, it is *false* that it must be *either* infinite in space *or* finite and limited. Both contentions are false. For appearances (as mere representations) which yet are to be given *in themselves* (as objects) are something impossible; and though the infinitude of this imaginary whole would

indeed be unconditioned, it would contradict (since everything
in appearances is conditioned) the unconditioned determination of magnitude, [that is, of totality], which is presupposed
in the concept.

The apagogic method of proof is the real deluding influence by which those who reason dogmatically have always held
their admirers. It may be compared to a champion who seeks
to uphold the honour and incontestable rights of his adopted
party by offering battle to all who would question them. Such
boasting proves nothing, however, in regard to the merits of the
issue but only in regard to the respective strength of the combatants, and this indeed only in respect of those who take the
offensive. The spectators, observing that each party is alter-
nately conqueror and conquered, are often led to have sceptical doubts in regard to the very object of the dispute. They
are not, however, justified in adopting such an attitude; it is
sufficient to declare to the combatants: *non defensoribus istis
tempus eget.* Everyone must defend his position directly, by a
legitimate proof that carries with it a transcendental deduction
of the grounds upon which it is itself made to rest. Only when
this has been done, are we in a position to decide how far its
claims allow of rational justification. If an opponent relies on
subjective grounds, it is an easy matter to refute him. The
dogmatist cannot, however, profit by this advantage. His own
judgments are, as a rule, no less dependent upon subjective
influences; and he can himself in turn be similarly cornered by
his opponent. But if both parties proceed by the direct method,
either they will soon discover the difficulty, nay, the impossibility, of showing ground for their assertions, and will be left
with no resort save to appeal to some form of prescriptive
authority; *or* our criticism will easily discover the illusion to
which their dogmatic procedure is due, compelling pure
reason to relinquish its exaggerated pretensions in the realm
of speculation, and to withdraw within the limits of its proper
territory—that of practical principles.

A 794
B 822

CHAPTER II

THE CANON OF PURE REASON

IT is humiliating to human reason that it achieves nothing in its pure employment, and indeed stands in need of a discipline to check its extravagances, and to guard it against the deceptions which arise therefrom. But, on the other hand, reason is reassured and gains self-confidence, on finding that it itself can and must apply this discipline, and that it is not called upon to submit to any outside censorship; and, moreover, that the limits which it is compelled to set to its speculative employment likewise limit the pseudo-rational pretensions of all its opponents, and that it can secure against all attacks whatever may remain over from its former exaggerated claims. The greatest and perhaps the sole use of all philosophy of pure reason is therefore only negative; since it serves not as an organon for the extension but as a discipline for the limitation of pure reason, and, instead of discovering truth, has only the modest merit of guarding against error.

There must, however, be some source of positive modes of knowledge which belong to the domain of pure reason, and which, it may be, give occasion to error solely owing to misunderstanding, while yet in actual fact they form the goal to- $\left\{\begin{smallmatrix} A\ 796 \\ B\ 824 \end{smallmatrix}\right.$ wards which reason is directing its efforts. How else can we account for our inextinguishable desire to find firm footing somewhere beyond the limits of experience? Reason has a presentiment of objects which possess a great interest for it. But when it follows the path of pure speculation, in order to approach them, they fly before it. Presumably it may look for better fortune in the only other path which still remains open to it, that of its *practical* employment.

I understand by a canon the sum-total of the *a priori* principles of the correct employment of certain faculties of knowledge. Thus general logic, in its analytic portion, is a canon for understanding and reason in general; but only in regard to their form; it abstracts from all content. The transcendental analytic has similarly been shown to be the canon of the pure *understanding*; for understanding alone is capable of true synthetic modes of knowledge *a priori*. But when no correct employment of a faculty of knowledge is possible there is no canon. Now all synthetic knowledge through pure *reason* in its speculative employment is, as has been shown by the proofs given, completely impossible. There is therefore no canon of its speculative employment; such employment is entirely dialectical. All transcendental logic is, in this respect, simply a discipline. Consequently, if there be any correct employment of pure reason, in which case there must be a canon of its employment, the canon will deal not with the speculative but with the *practical employment of reason*. This practical employment of reason we shall now proceed to investigate.

A 797
B 825

THE CANON OF PURE REASON

Section 1

THE ULTIMATE END OF THE PURE EMPLOYMENT OF OUR REASON

Reason is impelled by a tendency of its nature to go out beyond the field of its empirical employment, and to venture in a pure employment, by means of ideas alone, to the utmost limits of all knowledge, and not to be satisfied save through the completion of its course in [the apprehension of] a self-subsistent systematic whole. Is this endeavour the outcome merely of the speculative interests of reason? Must we not rather regard it as having its source exclusively in the practical interests of reason?

I shall, for the moment, leave aside all question as to the success which attends pure reason in its speculative exercise, and enquire only as to the problems the solution of which constitutes its ultimate aim, whether reached or not, and in respect of which all other aims are to be regarded only as means. These highest aims must, from the nature of reason, $\left\{\begin{array}{l}\text{A } 798\\ \text{B } 826\end{array}\right.$ have a certain unity, in order that they may, as thus unified, further that interest of humanity which is subordinate to no higher interest.

The ultimate aim to which the speculation of reason in its transcendental employment is directed concerns three objects: the freedom of the will, the immortality of the soul, and the existence of God. In respect of all three the merely speculative interest of reason is very small; and for its sake alone we should hardly have undertaken the labour of transcendental investigation—a labour so fatiguing in its endless wrestling with insuperable difficulties—since whatever discoveries might be made in regard to these matters, we should not be able to make use of them in any helpful manner *in concreto*, that is, in the study of nature. If the will be free, this can have a bearing only on the intelligible cause of our volition. For as regards the phenomena of its outward expressions, that is, of our actions, we must account for them—in accordance with a maxim which is inviolable, and which is so fundamental that without it we should not be able to employ reason in any empirical manner whatsoever—in the same manner as all other appearances of nature, namely, in conformity with unchangeable laws. If, again, we should be able to obtain insight into the spiritual nature of the soul, and therewith of its immortality, we could make no use of such insight in explaining either the appearances of this present life or the specific nature of a future $\left\{\begin{array}{l}\text{A } 799\\ \text{B } 827\end{array}\right.$ state. For our concept of an incorporeal nature is merely negative, and does not in the least extend our knowledge, yielding no sufficient material for inferences, save only such as are merely fictitious and cannot be sanctioned by philosophy. If, thirdly, the existence of a supreme intelligence be proved, by its means we might indeed render what is purposive in the constitution and ordering of the world comprehensible in a general sort of way, but we should not be in the least warranted in deriving from it any particular arrangement or disposition, or in boldly inferring any such, where it is not perceived. For it is a necessary rule of the speculative employment of reason, not to pass over natural causes, and, abandoning that in regard to which we can be instructed by experience, to deduce something which we know from something which entirely transcends all our [possible] knowledge. In short, these three propositions are for speculative reason always transcendent, and allow of no immanent employment—that is, employment in reference to objects of experience, and so in some manner really of service to us—but are in themselves, notwithstanding the very heavy labours which they impose upon our reason, entirely useless.

If, then, these three cardinal propositions are not in any way necessary for *knowledge*, and are yet strongly recommended by our reason, their importance, properly regarded, must concern only the *practical*.

A 800 }
B 828 }

By 'the practical' I mean everything that is possible through freedom. When, however, the conditions of the exercise of our free will are empirical, reason can have no other than a regulative employment in regard to it, and can serve only to effect unity in its empirical laws. Thus, for instance, in the precepts of prudence, the whole business of reason consists in uniting all the ends which are prescribed to us by our desires in the one single end, *happiness*, and in coordinating the means for attaining it. In this field, therefore, reason can supply none but *pragmatic* laws of free action, for the attainment of those ends which are commended to us by the senses; it cannot yield us laws that are pure and determined completely *a priori*. Laws of this latter type, pure practical laws, whose end is given through reason completely *a priori*, and which are prescribed to us not in an empirically conditioned but in an absolute manner, would be products of pure reason. Such are the *moral* laws; and these alone, therefore, belong to the practical employment of reason, and allow of a canon.

The whole equipment of reason, in the discipline which may be entitled pure philosophy, is in fact determined with a view to the three above-mentioned problems. These, however, themselves in turn refer us yet further, namely, to the problem *what we ought to do*, if the will is free, if there is a God and a future world. As this concerns our attitude to the supreme end, it is evident that the ultimate intention of nature in her wise provision for us has indeed, in the

A 801 }
B 829 }

constitution of our reason, been directed to moral interests alone.[1]

But we must be careful, in turning our attention to an object which is foreign[a] to transcendental philosophy, that we do not indulge in digressions to the detriment of the unity of the system, nor on the other hand, by saying too little on this new topic, fail in producing conviction through lack of clearness. I hope to avoid both dangers, by keeping as close as possible to the transcendental, and by leaving entirely aside any psychological, that is, empirical, factors that may perchance accompany it.

I must first remark that for the present I shall employ the concept of freedom in this practical sense only, leaving aside that other transcendental meaning which cannot be empirically made use of in explanation of appearances, but is itself $\begin{cases} \text{A 802} \\ \text{B 830} \end{cases}$ a problem for reason, as has been already shown. A will is purely *animal* (*arbitrium brutum*), which cannot be determined save through sensuous[2] impulses, that is, *pathologically*. A will which can be determined independently of sensuous impulses, and therefore through motives which are represented only by reason, is entitled *freewill* (*arbitrium liberum*), and everything which is bound up with this will, whether as ground or as consequence, is entitled *practical*. [The fact of] practical freedom can be proved through experience. For the human will is not determined by that alone which stimulates, that is, immediately affects the senses; we have the power to overcome the impressions on our faculty of sensuous desire, by calling up representations of what, in a more indirect manner, is useful or injurious. But these considerations, as to what is desirable in respect of our whole state, that is, as to what is good and useful, are based on reason. Reason therefore provides

[a] All practical concepts relate to objects of satisfaction or dissatisfaction, that is, of pleasure and pain, and therefore, at least indirectly, to the objects of our feelings. But as feeling is not a faculty whereby we represent things, but lies outside our whole faculty of knowledge, the elements of our judgments so far as they relate to pleasure or pain, that is, the elements of practical judgments, do not belong to transcendental philosophy, which is exclusively concerned with pure *a priori* modes of knowledge.

[1] [*nur aufs Moralische.*]   [2] [*sinnlichen.*]

laws which are imperatives, that is, *objective laws of freedom*, which tell us *what ought to happen*—although perhaps it never does happen—therein differing from *laws of nature*, which relate only to *that which happens*. These laws are therefore to be entitled practical laws.

Whether reason is not, in the actions through which it prescribes laws, itself again determined by other influences, and whether that which, in relation to sensuous impulses, is entitled freedom, may not, in relation to higher and more remote operating causes, be nature again, is a question which in the practical field does not concern us, since we are demanding of reason nothing but the *rule* of conduct; it is a merely speculative question, which we can leave aside so long as we are considering what ought or ought not to be done. While we thus through experience know practical freedom to be one of the causes in nature, namely, to be a causality of reason in the determination of the will, transcendental freedom demands the independence of this reason—in respect of its causality, in beginning a series of appearances—from all determining causes of the sensible world. Transcendental freedom is thus, as it would seem, contrary to the law of nature, and therefore to all possible experience; and so remains a problem. But this problem does not come within the province of reason in its practical employment; and we have therefore in a canon of pure reason to deal with only two questions, which relate to the practical interest of pure reason, and in regard to which a canon of its employment must be possible—Is there a God? and, Is there a future life? The question of transcendental freedom is a matter for speculative

knowledge only, and when we are dealing with the practical, we can leave it aside as being an issue with which we have no concern. Moreover, a quite sufficient discussion of it is to be found in the antinomy of pure reason.

THE CANON OF PURE REASON

Section 2

THE IDEAL OF THE HIGHEST GOOD, AS A DETERMINING GROUND OF THE ULTIMATE END OF PURE REASON

Reason, in its speculative employment, conducted us through the field of experience, and since it could not find complete satisfaction there, from thence to speculative ideas, which, however, in the end brought us back to experience. In so doing the ideas fulfilled their purpose, but in a manner which, though useful, is not in accordance with our expectation. One other line of enquiry still remains open to us: namely, whether pure reason may not also be met with in the practical sphere, and whether it may not there conduct us to ideas which reach to those highest ends of pure reason that we have just stated, and whether, therefore, reason may not be able to supply to us from the standpoint of its practical interest what it altogether refuses to supply in respect of its speculative interest.

All the interests of my reason, speculative as well as practical, combine in the three following questions:

    1. What can I know?   { A 805
    2. What ought I to do?   { B 833
    3. What may I hope?

The first question is merely speculative. We have, as I flatter myself, exhausted all the possible answers to it, and at last have found the answer with which reason must perforce content itself, and with which, so long as it takes no account of the practical, it has also good cause to be satisfied. But from the two great ends to which the whole endeavour of pure reason was really directed, we have remained just as far removed as if through love of ease we had declined this labour of enquiry at the very outset. So far, then, as knowledge is concerned, this much, at least, is certain and definitively established, that in respect of these two latter problems, knowledge is unattainable by us.

The second question is purely practical. As such it can

indeed come within the scope of pure reason, but even so is not transcendental but moral, and cannot, therefore, in and by itself, form a proper subject for treatment in this Critique.

The third question—If I do what I ought to do, what may I then hope?—is at once practical and theoretical, in such fashion that the practical serves only as a clue that leads us to the answer to the theoretical question, and when this is followed out, to the speculative question. For all *hoping* is directed to happiness, and stands in the same relation to the practical and the law of morality as *knowing and the law of nature* to the theoretical knowledge of things. The former arrives finally at the conclusion that *something is* (which determines the ultimate possible end) *because something ought to happen*; the latter, that *something is* (which operates as the supreme cause) *because something happens*

A 806
B 834

Happiness is the satisfaction of all our desires, *extensively*, in respect of their manifoldness, *intensively*, in respect of their degree, and *protensively*, in respect of their duration. The practical law, derived from the motive of *happiness*, I term pragmatic (rule of prudence), and that law, if there is such a law, which has no other motive than *worthiness of being happy*, I term moral (law of morality). The former advises us what we have to do if we wish to achieve happiness; the latter dictates to us how we must behave in order to deserve happiness. The former is based on empirical principles; for only by means of experience can I know what desires there are which call for satisfaction; or what those natural causes are which are capable of satisfying them. The latter takes no account of desires, and the natural means of satisfying them, and considers only the freedom of a rational being in general, and the necessary conditions under which alone this freedom can harmonise with a distribution of happiness that is made in accordance with principles. This latter law can therefore be based on mere ideas of pure reason, and known *a priori*.

A 807
B 835

I assume that there really are pure moral laws which determine completely *a priori* (without regard to empirical motives, that is, to happiness) what is and is not to be done, that is, which determine the employment of the freedom of a rational being in general; and that these laws command in an *absolute* manner (not merely hypothetically, on the supposition of other empirical ends), and are therefore in every respect necessary. I am justified in making this assumption, in that I can appeal not only to the proofs employed by the most enlightened moralists, but to the moral judgment of every man, in so far as he makes the effort to think such a law clearly.

Pure reason, then, contains, not indeed in its speculative employment, but in that practical employment which is also moral, principles of the *possibility of experience*, namely, of such actions as, in accordance with moral precepts, *might* be met with in the *history* of mankind. For since reason commands that such actions should take place, it must be possible for them to take place. Consequently, a special kind of systematic unity, namely the moral, must likewise be possible. We have indeed found that the systematic unity of nature cannot be proved *in accordance with speculative principles of reason*. For although reason does indeed have causality in respect of freedom in general, it does not have causality in respect of nature as a whole; and although moral principles of reason can indeed give rise to free actions, they cannot give rise to laws of nature. Accordingly it is in their practical, {A 808 / B 836} meaning thereby their moral, employment, that the principles of pure reason have objective reality.

I entitle the world a *moral world*, in so far as it may be in accordance with all moral laws; and this is what by means of the freedom of the rational being it *can be*, and what according to the necessary laws of morality it·*ought to be*. Owing to our here leaving out of account all conditions (ends) and even all the special difficulties to which morality is exposed (weakness or depravity of human nature), this world is so far thought as an intelligible world only. To this extent, therefore, it is a mere idea, though at the same time a practical idea, which really can have, as it also ought to have, an influence upon the sensible world, to bring that world, so far as may be possible, into conformity with the idea. The idea of a moral world has, therefore, objective reality, not as referring to an object of an intelligible intuition (we are quite unable to think any such object), but as referring to the sensible world, viewed, however, as being an object of pure reason in its practical employment, that is, as a *corpus mysticum* of the rational beings in it, so far as the free will of each being is, under moral laws, in complete systematic unity with itself and with the freedom of every other.

This is the answer to the first of the two questions of pure reason that concern its practical interest:—*Do that through which thou becomest worthy to be happy*. The second question is:—If I so behave as not to be unworthy of happiness, may I hope thereby to obtain happiness? In answering this question we have to consider whether the principles of pure reason, which prescribe the law *a priori*, likewise connect this hope necessarily with it.

I maintain that just as the moral principles are necessary according to reason in its *practical* employment, it is in the view of reason, in the field of its *theoretical* employment, no less necessary to assume that everyone has ground to hope for happiness in the measure in which he has rendered himself by his conduct worthy of it, and that the system of morality is therefore inseparably—though only in the idea of pure reason—bound up with that of happiness.

Now in an intelligible world, that is, in the moral world, in the concept of which we leave out of account all the hindrances to morality (the desires), such a system, in which happiness is bound up with and proportioned to morality, can be conceived as necessary, inasmuch as freedom, partly inspired and partly restricted by moral laws, would itself be the cause of general happiness, since rational beings, under the guidance of such principles, would themselves be the authors both of their own enduring well-being and of that of others. But such a system of self-rewarding morality is only an idea, the carrying out of which rests on the condition that *everyone* does what he ought, that is, that all the actions of rational beings take place just as if they had proceeded from a supreme will that comprehends in itself, or under itself, all private wills. But since the moral law remains binding for every one in the use of his freedom, even although others do not act in conformity with the law, neither the nature of the things of the world nor the causality of the actions themselves and their relation to morality determine how the consequences of these actions will be related to happiness. The alleged necessary connection of the hope of happiness with the necessary endeavour to render the self worthy of happiness cannot there-

A 809
B 837

A 810
B 838

fore be known through reason. It can be counted upon only if a *Supreme Reason*, that governs according to moral rules, be likewise posited as underlying nature as its cause.

The idea of such an intelligence in which the most perfect moral will, united with supreme blessedness, is the cause of all happiness in the world—so far as happiness stands in exact relation with morality, that is, with worthiness to be happy—I entitle the *ideal of the supreme good*. It is, therefore, only in the ideal of the supreme *original* good that pure reason can find the ground of this connection, which is necessary from the practical point of view, between the two elements of the supreme derivative good—the ground, namely, of an intelligible, that is, *moral* world. Now since we are necessarily constrained by reason to represent ourselves as belonging to such a world, while the senses present to us nothing but a world of appearances, we must assume that moral world to be a consequence of our conduct in the world of sense (in which no such connection between worthiness and happiness is exhibited), and therefore to be for us a future world. Thus God and a future life are two postulates which, according to the principles of pure reason, are inseparable from the obligation which that same reason imposes upon us. {A 811 / B 839

Morality, by itself, constitutes a system. Happiness, however, does not do so, save in so far as it is distributed in exact proportion to morality. But this is possible only in the intelligible world, under a wise Author and Ruler. Such a Ruler, together with life in such a world, which we must regard as a future world, reason finds itself constrained to assume; otherwise it would have to regard the moral laws as empty figments of the brain, since without this postulate the necessary consequence which it itself connects with these laws could not follow. Hence also everyone regards the moral laws as *commands*; and this the moral laws could not be if they did not connect *a priori* suitable consequences with their rules, and thus carry with them *promises* and *threats*. But this again they could not do, if they did not reside in a necessary being, as the supreme good, which alone can make such a purposive unity possible. {A 812 / B 840

Leibniz entitled the world, in so far as we take account only of the rational beings in it, and of their connection according to moral laws under the government of the supreme good, *the kingdom of grace*, distinguishing it from the *kingdom of nature*, in which these rational beings do indeed stand under moral laws, but expect no other consequences from their actions than such as follow in accordance with the course of nature in our world of sense. To view ourselves, therefore, as in the world of grace, where all happiness awaits us, except in so far as we ourselves limit our share in it through being unworthy of happiness, is, from the practical standpoint, a necessary idea of reason.

Practical laws, in so far as they are subjective grounds of actions, that is, subjective principles, are entitled *maxims* The *estimation* of morality, in regard to its purity and consequences, is effected in accordance with *ideas*, the *observance* of its laws in accordance with *maxims*.

It is necessary that the whole course of our life be subject to moral maxims; but it is impossible that this should happen unless reason connects with the moral law, which is a mere idea, an operative cause which determines for such conduct as is in accordance with the moral law an outcome, either in this or in another life, that is in exact conformity with our supreme ends. Thus without a God and without a world invisible to us now but hoped for, the glorious ideas of morality are indeed objects of approval and admiration, but not springs of purpose and action. For they do not fulfil in its completeness that end which is natural to every rational being and which is determined *a priori*, and rendered necessary, by that same pure reason.

A 813⎱
B 841⎰

Happiness, taken by itself, is, for our reason, far from being the complete good. Reason does not approve happiness (however inclination may desire it) except in so far as it is united with worthiness to be happy, that is, with moral conduct. Morality, taken by itself, and with it, the mere *worthiness* to be happy, is also far from being the complete good. To make the good complete, he who behaves in such a manner as not to be unworthy of happiness must be able to hope that he will participate in happiness. Even the reason that is free from all private purposes, should it put itself in the place of a being that had to distribute all happiness to others, cannot judge otherwise; for in the practical idea both elements are essentially

connected, though in such a manner that it is the moral disposition which conditions and makes possible the participation
in happiness, and not conversely the prospect of happiness
that makes possible the moral disposition. For in the latter
case the disposition would not be moral, and therefore would $\begin{cases} \text{A 814} \\ \text{B 842} \end{cases}$
not be worthy of complete happiness—happiness which in
the view of reason allows of no limitation save that which
arises from our own immoral conduct.

Happiness, therefore, in exact proportion with the morality
of the rational beings who are thereby rendered worthy of it,
alone constitutes the supreme good of that world wherein, in
accordance with the commands of a pure but practical reason,
we are under obligation to place ourselves. This world is indeed an intelligible world only, since the sensible world holds
out no promise that any such systematic unity of ends can
arise from the nature of things. Nor is the reality of this unity
based on anything else than the postulate of a supreme original good. In a supreme good, thus conceived, self-subsistent
reason, equipped with all the sufficiency of a supreme cause,
establishes, maintains, and completes the universal order of
things, according to the most perfect design[1]—an order which
in the world of sense is in large part concealed from us.

This moral theology has the peculiar advantage over
speculative theology that it inevitably leads to the concept of
a *sole*, *all-perfect*, and *rational* primordial being, to which
speculative theology does not, on objective grounds, even so
much as *point the way*, and as to the existence of which it is
still less capable of yielding any *conviction*. For neither in
transcendental nor in natural theology, however far reason
may carry us, do we find any considerable ground for assum-
ing only some one single being which we should be justi- $\begin{cases} \text{A 815} \\ \text{B 843} \end{cases}$
fied in placing prior to[2] all natural causes, and upon which
we might make them in all respects dependent. On the
other hand, if we consider from the point of view of moral
unity, as a necessary law of the world, what the cause must
be that can alone give to this law its appropriate effect, and
so for us obligatory force, we conclude that there must be
one sole supreme will, which comprehends all these laws in
itself. For how, under different wills, should we find complete

---

[1] [*Zweckmässigkeit.*]   [2] [Reading, with Wille, *vorzusetzen* for *vorsetzen.*]

unity of ends. This Divine Being must be omnipotent, in order that the whole of nature and its relation to morality in the world may be subject to his will; omniscient, that He may know our innermost sentiments and their moral worth; omnipresent, that He may be immediately at hand for the satisfying of every need which the highest good demands; eternal, that this harmony of nature and freedom may never fail, etc.

But this systematic unity of ends in this world of intelligences—a world which is indeed, as mere nature, a sensible world only, but which, as a system of freedom, can be entitled an intelligible, that is, a moral world (*regnum gratiae*)—leads inevitably also to the purposive unity of all things, which constitute this great whole, in accordance with universal laws of nature (just as the former unity is in accordance with universal and necessary laws of morality), and thus unites the practical with the speculative reason. The world must be represented as having originated from an idea if it is to be in harmony with that employment of reason without which we should indeed hold ourselves to be unworthy of reason, namely, with the moral employment—which is founded entirely on the idea of the supreme good. In this way all investigation of nature tends to take the form of a system of ends, and in its widest extension becomes a physico-theology. But this, as it has its source in the moral order, as a unity grounded in freedom's own essential nature, and not accidentally instituted through external commands, connects the purposiveness of nature with grounds which must be inseparably connected *a priori* with the inner possibility of things, and so leads to a *transcendental theology*—a theology which takes the ideal of supreme ontological perfection as a principle of systematic unity. And since all things have their origin in the absolute necessity of the one primordial being, that principle connects them in accordance with universal and necessary laws of nature.

What *use* can we make of our understanding, even in respect of experience, if we do not propose ends to ourselves? But the highest ends are those of morality, and these we can know only as they are given us by pure reason. But though provided with these, and employing them as a clue, we cannot make use of the knowledge of nature in any serviceable manner

A 816
B 844

in the building up of knowledge, unless nature has itself shown unity of design.[1] For without this unity we should our- {A 817 / B 845} selves have no reason, inasmuch as there would be no school for reason, and no fertilisation[2] through objects such as might afford materials for the necessary concepts. But the former purposive unity is necessary, and founded on the will's own essential nature, and this latter unity [of design in nature] which contains the condition of its application *in concreto*, must be so likewise. And thus the transcendental enlargement of our knowledge, as secured through reason, is not to be regarded as the cause, but merely as the effect of the practical purposiveness which pure reason imposes upon us.

Accordingly we find, in the history of human reason, that until the moral concepts were sufficiently purified and determined, and until the systematic unity of their ends was understood in accordance with these concepts and from necessary principles, the knowledge of nature, and even a quite considerable development of reason in many other sciences, could give rise only to crude and incoherent concepts of the Deity, or as sometimes happened resulted in an astonishing indifference in regard to all such matters. A greater preoccupation with moral ideas, which was rendered necessary by the extraordinarily pure moral law of our religion, made reason more acutely aware of its object, through the interest which it was compelled to take in it. And this came about, independently of any influence exercised by more extended views of nature or by correct and reliable transcendental insight (for that has always been lacking). It was the moral ideas that gave {A 818 / B 846} rise to that concept of the Divine Being which we now hold to be correct—and we so regard it not because speculative reason convinces us of its correctness, but because it completely harmonises with the moral principles of reason. Thus it is always only to pure reason, though only in its practical employment, that we must finally ascribe the merit of having connected with our highest interest a knowledge which reason can think only, and cannot establish, and of having thereby shown it to be, not indeed a demonstrated dogma, but a postulate which is absolutely necessary in view of what are reason's own most essential ends.

---

[1] [*zweckmässige Einheit.*]   [2] [*Kultur.*]

But when practical reason has reached this goal, namely, the concept of a sole primordial being as the supreme good, it must not presume to think that it has raised itself above all empirical conditions of its application, and has attained to an immediate knowledge of new objects, and can therefore[1] start from this concept, and can deduce from it the moral laws themselves. For it is these very laws that have led us, in virtue of their *inner* practical necessity, to the postulate of a self-sufficient cause, or of a wise Ruler of the world, in order that through such agency effect may be given to them. We may not, therefore, in reversal of such procedure, regard them as accidental and as derived from the mere will of the Ruler,

A 819
B 847

especially as we have no conception of such a will, except as formed in accordance with these laws. So far, then, as practical reason has the right to serve as our guide, we shall not look upon actions as obligatory because they are the commands of God, but shall regard them as divine commands because we have an inward obligation to them. We shall study freedom according to the purposive unity that is determined in accordance with the principles of reason, and shall believe ourselves to be acting in conformity with the divine will in so far only as we hold sacred the moral law which reason teaches us from the nature of the actions themselves; and we shall believe that we can serve that will only by furthering what is best in the world, alike in ourselves and in others. Moral theology is thus of immanent use only. It enables us to fulfil our vocation in this present world by showing us how to adapt ourselves to the system of all ends, and by warning us against the fanaticism, and indeed the impiety, of abandoning the guidance of a morally legislative reason in the right conduct of our lives, in order to derive guidance directly from the idea of the Supreme Being. For we should then be making a transcendent employment of moral theology; and that,[2] like a transcendent use of pure speculation, must pervert and frustrate the ultimate ends of reason.

[1] [Reading, with Hartenstein, *nun* for *um*.]
[2] [Reading, with Grillo, *der aber* for *aber*.]

THE CANON OF PURE REASON

Section 3

OPINING, KNOWING, AND BELIEVING

The holding of a thing to be true is an occurrence in our understanding which, though it may rest on objective grounds, also requires subjective causes in the mind of the individual who makes the judgment. If the judgment is valid for everyone, provided only he is in possession of reason, its ground is objectively sufficient, and the holding of it to be true is entitled *conviction*. If it has its ground only in the special character of the subject, it is entitled *persuasion*.

Persuasion is a mere illusion, because the ground of the judgment, which lies solely in the subject, is regarded as objective. Such a judgment has only private validity, and the holding of it to be true does not allow of being communicated. But truth depends upon agreement with the object, and in respect of it the judgments of each and every understanding must therefore be in agreement with each other (*consentientia uni tertio, consentiunt inter se*). The touchstone whereby we decide whether our holding a thing to be true is conviction or mere persuasion is therefore external, namely, the possibility of communicating it and of finding it to be valid for all human reason. For there is then at least a presumption that the ground of the agreement of all judgments with each other, notwithstanding the differing characters of individuals, rests upon the common ground, namely, upon the object, and that it is for this reason that they are all in agreement with the object—the truth of the judgment being thereby proved.

So long, therefore, as the subject views the judgment merely as an appearance of his mind, persuasion cannot be subjectively distinguished from conviction. The experiment, however, whereby we test upon the understanding of others whether those grounds of the judgment which are valid for us have the same effect on the reason of others as on our own, is a means, although only a subjective means, not indeed of producing conviction, but of detecting any merely private validity in the judgment, that is, anything in it which is mere persuasion.

If, in addition, we can specify the subjective *causes* of the judgment, which we have taken as being its objective *grounds*, and can thus explain the deceptive judgment as an event in our mind, and can do so without having to take account of the character of the object, we expose the illusion and are no longer deceived by it, although always still in some degree liable to come under its influence, in so far as the subjective cause of the illusion is inherent in our nature.

A 822
B 850
I cannot *assert* anything, that is, declare it to be a judgment necessarily valid for everyone, save as it gives rise to conviction. Persuasion I can hold to on my own account, if it so pleases me, but I cannot, and ought not, to profess to impose it as binding on anyone but myself.

The holding of a thing to be true, or the subjective validity of the judgment, in its relation to conviction (which is at the same time objectively valid), has the following three degrees:[1] *opining*, *believing*, and *knowing*. *Opining* is such holding of a judgment as is consciously insufficient, not only objectively, but also subjectively. If our holding of the judgment be only subjectively sufficient, and is at the same time taken as being objectively insufficient, we have what is termed *believing*. Lastly, when the holding of a thing to be true is sufficient both subjectively and objectively, it is *knowledge*. The subjective sufficiency is termed *conviction* (for myself), the objective sufficiency is termed *certainty* (for everyone). There is no call for me to spend further time on the explanation of such easily understood terms.

I must never presume to *opine*, without *knowing at least something* by means of which the judgment, in itself merely problematic, secures connection with truth, a connection which, although not complete, is yet more than arbitrary fiction. Moreover, the law of such a connection must be certain. For if, in respect of this law also, I have nothing but opinion, it is all merely a play of the imagination, without the least relation to truth. Again, *opining* is not in any way permissible in judging by means of pure reason. For since such

A 823
B 851
judging is not based on grounds of experience, but being in

[1] [*Stufen*.]

every case necessary has all to be arrived at *a priori*, the principle of the connection requires universality and necessity, and therefore complete certainty; otherwise we should have no guidance as to truth. Hence it is absurd to have an opinion in pure mathematics; either we must know, or we must abstain from all acts of judgment. It is so likewise in the case of the principles of morality, since we must not venture upon an action on the mere opinion that it is *allowed*, but must know it to be so.

In the transcendental employment of reason, on the other hand, while opining is doubtless too weak a term to be applicable, the term knowing is too strong. In the merely speculative sphere we cannot therefore make any judgments whatsoever. For the subjective grounds upon which we may hold something to be true, such as those which are able to produce belief, are not permissible in speculative questions, inasmuch as they do not hold independently of all empirical support, and do not allow of being communicated in equal measure to others.

But it is only from a *practical point of view* that the theoretically insufficient holding of a thing to be true can be termed believing. This practical point of view is either in reference to *skill* or in reference to *morality*, the former being concerned with optional and contingent ends, the latter with ends that are absolutely necessary.

Once an end is accepted, the conditions of its attainment are hypothetically necessary. This necessity is subjectively, but still only comparatively, sufficient, if I know of no other $\left\{ \begin{matrix} \text{A 824} \\ \text{B 852} \end{matrix} \right.$ conditions under which the end can be attained. On the other hand, it is sufficient, absolutely and for everyone, if I know with certainty that no one can have knowledge of any other conditions which lead to the proposed end. In the former case my assumption and the holding of certain conditions to be true is a merely contingent belief; in the latter case it is a necessary belief.[1] The physician must do something for a patient in danger, but does not know the nature of his illness. He observes the symptoms, and if he can find no more likely alternative, judges it to be a case of phthisis. Now even in his own estimation his belief is contingent only; another observer

---

[1] [*Glaube*. This is also Kant's term for 'faith' (cf. above pp. 31, 296).]

might perhaps come to a sounder conclusion. Such contingent belief, which yet forms the ground for the actual employment of means to certain actions, I entitle *pragmatic belief*.

The usual touchstone, whether that which someone asserts is merely his persuasion—or at least his subjective conviction, that is, his firm belief—is *betting*. It often happens that someone propounds his views with such positive and uncompromising assurance that he seems to have entirely set aside all thought of possible error. A bet disconcerts him. Sometimes it turns out that he has a conviction which can be estimated at a value of one ducat, but not of ten. For he is very willing to venture one ducat, but when it is a question of ten he becomes aware, as he had not previously been, that it may very well be that he is in error. If, in a given case, we represent ourselves as staking the happiness of our whole life, the triumphant tone of our judgment is greatly abated; we become extremely diffident, and discover for the first time that our belief does not reach so far. Thus pragmatic belief always exists in some specific degree, which, according to differences in the interests at stake, may be large or may be small.

But in many cases, when we are dealing with an object about which nothing can be done by us, and in regard to which our judgment is therefore purely theoretical, we can conceive and picture to ourselves an attitude[1] for which we regard ourselves as having sufficient grounds, while yet there is no existing means of arriving at certainty in the matter. Thus even in purely theoretical judgments there is an *analogon of practical* judgments, to the mental entertaining of which the term '*belief*' is appropriate, and which we may entitle *doctrinal belief*. I should be ready to stake my all on the contention—were it possible by means of any experience to settle the question—that at least one of the planets which we see is inhabited. Hence I say that it is not merely opinion, but a strong belief, on the correctness of which I should be prepared to run great risks, that other worlds are inhabited.

Now we must admit that the doctrine of the existence of God belongs to doctrinal belief. For as regards theoretical knowledge of the world, I can *cite* nothing which necessarily presupposes this thought as the condition of my explanations

A 825
B 853

A 826
B 854

---

[1] [*eine Unternehmung.*]

of the appearances exhibited by the world, but rather am bound so to employ my reason as if everything were mere nature. Purposive unity is, however, so important a condition of the application of reason to nature that I cannot ignore it, especially as experience supplies me so richly with examples of it. But I know no other condition under which this unity can supply me with guidance in the investigation of nature, save only the postulate that a supreme intelligence has ordered all things in accordance with the wisest ends. Consequently, as a condition of what is indeed a contingent, but still not unimportant purpose, namely, to have guidance in the investigation of nature, we must postulate a wise Author of the world. Moreover, the outcome of my attempts [in explanation of nature] so frequently confirms the usefulness of this postulate, while nothing decisive can be cited against it, that I am saying much too little if I proceed to declare that I hold it merely as an opinion. Even in this theoretical relation it can be said that I firmly believe in God. This belief is not, therefore, strictly speaking, practical; it must be entitled a doctrinal belief, to which the *theology* of nature (physico-theology) must always necessarily give rise. In view of the magnificent equipment of our human nature, and the shortness of life so ill-suited to the full exercise of our powers, we can find in this same divine wisdom a no less sufficient ground for a doctrinal belief in the future life of the human soul. {A 827 / B 855}

In such cases the expression of belief is, from the *objective* point of view, an expression of modesty, and yet at the same time, from the *subjective* point of view, an expression of the firmness of our confidence. Were I even to go the length of describing the merely theoretical holding of the belief as an hypothesis which I am justified in assuming, I should thereby be pledging myself to have a more adequate concept of the character of a cause of the world and of the character of another world than I am really in a position to supply. For if I assume anything, even merely as an hypothesis, I must at least know so much of its properties that I require to assume, *not its concept*, but *only its existence*. The term 'belief' refers only to the guidance which an idea gives me, and to its subjective influence in that furthering of the activities of my reason which confirms me in the idea, and which

yet does so without my being in a position to give a speculative account of it.

But the merely doctrinal belief is somewhat lacking in
stability; we often lose hold of it, owing to the speculative
difficulties which we encounter, although in the end we
always inevitably return to it.

It is quite otherwise with *moral belief*. For here it is absolutely necessary that something must happen, namely, that I
must in all points conform to the moral law. The end is here
irrefragably established, and according to such insight as I
can have, there is only one possible condition under which this
end can connect with all other ends, and thereby have practical validity, namely, that there be a God and a future world.
I also know with complete certainty that no one can be acquainted with any other conditions which lead[1] to the same
unity of ends under the moral law. Since, therefore, the moral
precept is at the same time my maxim (reason prescribing that
it should be so), I inevitably believe in the existence of God
and in a future life, and I am certain that nothing can shake
this belief, since my moral principles would thereby be themselves overthrown, and I cannot disclaim them without becoming abhorrent in my own eyes.

Thus even after reason has failed in all its ambitious attempts to pass beyond the limits of all experience, there is
still enough left to satisfy us, so far as our practical standpoint is concerned. No one, indeed, will be able to boast
that he *knows* that there is a God, and a future life; if he
knows this, he is the very man for whom I have long [and
vainly] sought. All knowledge, if it concerns an object of
mere reason, can be communicated; and I might therefore
hope that under his instruction my own knowledge would be
extended in this wonderful fashion. No, my conviction is not
logical, but *moral* certainty; and since it rests on subjective
grounds (of the moral sentiment), I must not even say, 'It is
morally certain that there is a God, etc.', but 'I am morally
certain, etc.' In other words, belief in a God and in another
world is so interwoven with my moral sentiment that as there
is little danger of my losing the latter, there is equally little
cause for fear that the former can ever be taken from me.

[1] [Reading, with Grillo, *führen* for *führe*.]

The only point that may seem questionable is the basing of this rational belief on the assumption of moral sentiments. If we leave these aside, and take a man who is completely indifferent with regard to moral laws, the question propounded by reason then becomes merely a problem for speculation, and can, indeed, be supported by strong grounds of analogy, but not by such as must compel the most stubborn scepticism to give way.[a] But in these questions no man is free from all $\begin{cases} \text{A 830} \\ \text{B 858} \end{cases}$ interest. For although, through lack of good sentiments, he may be cut off from moral interest, still even in this case enough remains to make him *fear* the existence of a God and a future life. Nothing more is required for this than that he at least cannot pretend that there is any *certainty* that there is *no* such being and *no* such life. Since that would have to be proved by mere reason, and therefore apodeictically, he would have to prove the impossibility of both, which assuredly no one can reasonably undertake to do. This may therefore serve as *negative* belief, which may not, indeed, give rise to morality and good sentiments, but may still give rise to an analogon of these, namely, a powerful check upon the outbreak of evil sentiments.

But, it will be said, is this all that pure reason achieves in opening up prospects beyond the limits of experience? Nothing more than two articles of belief? Surely the common understanding could have achieved as much, without appeal- $\begin{cases} \text{A 831} \\ \text{B 859} \end{cases}$ ing to philosophers for counsel in the matter

I shall not here dwell upon the service which philosophy has done to human reason through the laborious efforts of its criticism, granting even that in the end it should turn out to be merely negative; something more will be said on this point in the next section. But I may at once reply: Do you really require that a mode of knowledge which concerns all men

---

[a] The human mind (as, I likewise believe, must necessarily be the case with every rational being) takes a natural interest in morality, $\begin{cases} \text{A 830} \\ \text{B 858} \end{cases}$ although this interest is not undivided and practically preponderant. If we confirm and increase this interest, we shall find reason very teachable and in itself more enlightened as regards the uniting of the speculative with the practical interest. But if we do not take care that we first make men good, at least in some measure good, we shall never make honest believers of them.

should transcend the common understanding, and should only be revealed to you by philosophers? Precisely what you find fault with is the best confirmation of the correctness of the above assertions. For we have thereby revealed to us, what could not at the start have been foreseen, namely, that in matters which concern all men without distinction nature is not guilty of any partial distribution of her gifts, and that in regard to the essential ends of human nature the highest philosophy cannot advance further than is possible under the guidance which nature has bestowed even upon the most ordinary[1] understanding.

[1] [*gemeinsten.*]

CHAPTER III

THE ARCHITECTONIC OF PURE REASON

By an architectonic I understand the art of constructing systems. As systematic unity is what first raises ordinary knowledge to the rank of science, that is, makes a system out of a mere aggregate of knowledge, architectonic is the doctrine of the scientific in our knowledge, and therefore necessarily forms part of the doctrine of method.

In accordance with reason's legislative prescriptions, our diverse modes of knowledge must not be permitted to be a mere rhapsody, but must form a system. Only so can they further the essential ends of reason. By a system I understand the unity of the manifold modes of knowledge under one idea. This idea is the concept provided by reason—of the form of a whole—in so far as the concept determines a priori not only the scope of its manifold content, but also the positions which the parts occupy relatively to one another. The scientific concept of reason contains, therefore, the end and the form of that whole which is congruent with this requirement. The unity of the end to which all the parts relate and in the idea of which they all stand in relation to one another, makes it possible for us to determine from our knowledge of the other parts whether any part be missing, and to prevent any arbitrary addition, or $\begin{Bmatrix} \text{A } 833 \\ \text{B } 861 \end{Bmatrix}$ in respect of its completeness any indeterminateness that does not conform to the limits which are thus determined a priori. The whole is thus an organised unity (articulatio), and not an aggregate (coacervatio). It may grow from within (per intussusceptionem), but not by external addition (per appositionem). It is thus like an animal body, the growth of which is not by the addition of a new member, but by the rendering of each member, without change of proportion, stronger and more effective for its purposes.

The idea requires for its realisation a *schema*, that is, a constituent[1] manifold and an order of its parts, both of which must be determined *a priori* from the principle defined by its end. The schema, which is not devised in accordance with an idea, that is, in terms of the ultimate aim of reason, but empirically in accordance with purposes that are contingently occasioned (the number of which cannot be foreseen) yields *technical* unity; whereas the schema which originates from an idea (in which reason propounds the ends *a priori*, and does not wait for them to be empirically given) serves as the basis of *architectonic* unity. Now that which we call science, the schema of which must contain the outline (*monogramma*) and the division of the whole into parts, in conformity with the idea, that is, *a priori*, and in so doing must distinguish it with certainty and according to principles from all other wholes, is not formed in technical fashion, in view of the similarity of its manifold constituents or of the contingent use of our knowledge *in concreto* for all sorts of optional external ends, but in architectonic fashion, in view of the affinity of its parts and of their derivation from a single supreme and inner end, through which the whole is first made possible.

A 834
B 862

No one attempts to establish a science unless he has an idea upon which to base it. But in the working out of the science the schema, nay even the definition which, at the start, he first gave of the science, is very seldom adequate to his idea. For this idea lies hidden in reason, like a germ in which the parts are still undeveloped and barely recognisable even under microscopic observation. Consequently, since sciences are devised from the point of view of a certain universal interest, we must not explain and determine them according to the description which their founder gives of them, but in conformity with the idea which, out of the natural unity of the parts that we have assembled, we find to be grounded in reason itself. For we shall then find that its founder, and often even his latest successors, are groping for an idea which they have never succeeded in making clear to themselves, and that

[1] [*wesentliche.*]

consequently they have not been in a position to determine the proper content, the articulation (systematic unity), and limits of the science.

It is unfortunate that only after we have spent much time in the collection of materials in somewhat random fashion at the suggestion of an idea lying hidden in our minds, and after we have, indeed, over a long period assembled the materials in a merely technical manner, does it first become possible for {A 835 / B 863} us to discern the idea in a clearer light, and to devise a whole architectonically in accordance with the ends of reason. Systems seem to be formed in the manner of lowly organisms,[1] through a *generatio aequivoca* from the mere confluence of assembled concepts, at first imperfect, and only gradually attaining to completeness, although they one and all have had their schema, as the original germ, in the sheer[2] self-development of reason. Hence, not only is each system articulated in accordance with an idea, but they are one and all organically united in a system of human knowledge, as members of one whole, and so as admitting of an architectonic of all human knowledge, which, at the present time, in view of the great amount of material that has been collected, or which can be obtained from the ruins of ancient systems, is not only possible, but would not indeed be difficult. We shall content ourselves here with the completion of our task, namely, merely to outline the *architectonic* of all knowledge arising from *pure reason*; and in doing so we shall begin from the point at which the common root of our faculty of knowledge divides and throws out two stems, one of which is *reason*. By reason I here understand the whole higher faculty of knowledge, and am therefore contrasting the rational with the empirical.

If I abstract from all the content of knowledge, objectively regarded, then all knowledge, subjectively regarded, is either {A 836 / B 864} historical or rational. Historical knowledge is *cognitio ex datis*; rational knowledge is *cognitio ex principiis*. However a mode of knowledge may originally be given, it is still, in relation to the individual who possesses it, simply historical, if he knows only so much of it as has been given to him from outside (and this in the form in which it has been given to him), whether through immediate experience or narration, or (as in the case

---

[1] [*wie Gewürme.*]   [2] [*bloss.*]

of general knowledge) through instruction. Anyone, therefore, who has *learnt* (in the strict sense of that term) a system of philosophy, such as that of Wolff, although he may have all its principles, explanations, and proofs, together with the formal divisions of the whole body of doctrine, in his head, and, so to speak, at his fingers' ends, has no more than a complete *historical* knowledge of the Wolffian philosophy. He knows and judges only what has been given him. If we dispute a definition, he does not know whence to obtain another. He has formed his mind on another's, and the imitative faculty is not itself productive. In other words, his knowledge has not in him arisen *out* of reason, and although, objectively considered, it is indeed knowledge due to reason, it is yet, in its subjective character, merely historical. He has grasped and kept; that is, he has learnt well, and is merely a plaster-cast of a living man. Modes of rational knowledge which are rational objectively (that is, which can have their first origin solely in human reason) can be so entitled subjectively also, only when they have been derived from universal sources of reason, that is, from principles—the sources from which there can also arise criticism, nay, even the rejection of what has been learnt.

A 837⎫
B 865⎭

All knowledge arising out of reason is derived either from concepts or from the construction of concepts. The former is called philosophical, the latter mathematical. I have already treated of the fundamental difference between these two modes of knowledge in the first chapter [of this Transcendental Doctrine of Method]. Knowledge [as we have just noted] can be objectively philosophical, and yet subjectively historical, as is the case with most novices, and with all those who have never looked beyond their School, and who remain novices all their lives. But it is noteworthy that mathematical knowledge, in its subjective character, and precisely as it has been learned, can also be regarded as knowledge arising out of reason, and that there is therefore in regard to mathematical knowledge no such distinction as we have drawn in the case of philosophical knowledge. This is due to the fact that the sources of knowledge, from which alone the teacher can derive his knowledge, lie nowhere but in the essential and genuine principles of reason, and consequently cannot be acquired by the novice from any other source, and cannot be disputed; and this, in turn, is owing to the fact that the employment of reason is here *in concreto* only, although likewise *a priori*, namely, in intuition which is pure, and which precisely on that account is infallible,[1] excluding all illusion and error. Mathematics, therefore, alone of all the sciences (*a priori*) arising from reason, can be learned; philosophy can never be learned, save only in historical fashion; as regards what concerns reason, we can at most learn to *philosophise*.

Philosophy is the system of all philosophical knowledge. {A 838 / B 866} If we are to understand by it the archetype for the estimation of all attempts at philosophising, and if this archetype[2] is to serve for the estimation of each subjective philosophy, the structure of which is often so diverse and liable to alteration, it must be taken objectively. Thus regarded, philosophy is a mere idea of a possible science which nowhere exists *in concreto*, but to which, by many different paths, we endeavour to approximate, until the one true path, overgrown by the products of sensibility, has at last been discovered, and the image, hitherto so abortive, has achieved likeness to the archetype, so far as this is granted to [mortal] man. Till then we cannot learn philosophy; for where is it, who is in possession of it, and how shall we recognise it? We can only learn to philosophise, that is, to exercise the talent of reason, in accordance with its universal principles, on certain actually existing attempts at philosophy, always, however, reserving the right of reason to investigate, to confirm, or to reject these principles in their very sources.

Hitherto the concept of philosophy has been a merely scholastic concept—a concept of a system of knowledge which is sought solely in its character as a science, and which has therefore in view only the systematic unity appropriate to science, and consequently no more than the *logical* perfection of knowledge. But there is likewise another concept of philosophy, a *conceptus cosmicus*, which has always formed the real basis of the term 'philosophy', especially when it has been as it were personified and its archetype represented in the ideal *philo-* {A 839 / B 867} *sopher*. On this view, philosophy is the science of the relation of all knowledge to the essential ends of human reason

---

[1] [*fehlerfreien*.]   [2] [Reading, with Rosenkranz, *welches* for *welche*.]

(*teleologia rationis humanae*), and the philosopher is not an artificer in the field of reason, but himself the lawgiver of human reason. In this sense of the term it would be very vainglorious to entitle oneself a philosopher, and to pretend to have equalled the pattern which exists in the idea alone.

The mathematician, the natural philosopher, and the logician, however successful the two former may have been in their advances in the field of rational knowledge, and the two latter more especially in philosophical knowledge, are yet only artificers in the field of reason. There is a teacher, [conceived] in the ideal, who sets them their tasks, and employs them as instruments, to further the essential ends of human reason. Him alone we must call philosopher; but as he nowhere exists, while the idea of his legislation is to be found in that reason with which every human being is endowed, we shall keep entirely to the latter, determining more precisely what philosophy prescribes as regards systematic unity, in accordance with this cosmical concept,[a] from the standpoint of its essential ends.

A 840
B 868

Essential ends are not as such the highest ends; in view of the demand of reason for complete systematic unity, only one of them can be so described. Essential ends are therefore either the ultimate end or subordinate ends which are necessarily connected with the former as means. The former is no other than the whole vocation of man, and the philosophy which deals with it is entitled moral philosophy. On account of this superiority which moral philosophy has over all other occupations of reason, the ancients in their use of the term 'philosopher' always meant, more especially, the *moralist*; and even at the present day we are led by a certain analogy to entitle anyone a philosopher who appears to exhibit self-control under the guidance of reason, however limited his knowledge may be.

The legislation of human reason (philosophy) has two objects, nature and freedom, and therefore contains not only

---

[a] By 'cosmical concept' [*Weltbegriff*] is here meant the concept which relates to that in which everyone necessarily has an interest; and accordingly if a science is to be regarded merely as one of the disciplines designed in view of certain optionally chosen ends, I must determine it in conformity with *scholastic concepts*.

the law of nature, but also the moral law, presenting them at first in two distinct systems, but ultimately in one single philosophical system. The philosophy of nature deals with all *that is*, the philosophy of morals with that which *ought to be*.

All philosophy is either knowledge arising out of pure reason, or knowledge obtained by reason from empirical principles. The former is termed pure, the latter empirical philosophy.

The philosophy of pure reason is either a *propaedeutic* {A 841, B 869} (preparation), which investigates the faculty of reason in respect of all its pure *a priori* knowledge, and is entitled *criticism*,[1] or secondly, it is the system of pure reason, that is, the science which exhibits in systematic connection the whole body (true as well as illusory) of philosophical knowledge arising out of pure reason, and which is entitled *metaphysics*. The title 'metaphysics' may also, however, be given to the whole of pure philosophy, inclusive of criticism, and so as comprehending the investigation of all that can ever be known *a priori* as well as the exposition of that which constitutes a system of the pure philosophical modes of knowledge of this type—in distinction, therefore, from all empirical and from all mathematical employment of reason.

Metaphysics is divided into that of the *speculative* and that of the *practical* employment of pure reason, and is therefore either *metaphysics of nature* or *metaphysics of morals*. The former contains all the principles of pure reason that are derived from mere concepts (therefore excluding mathematics), and employed in the *theoretical* knowledge of all things; the latter, the principles which in *a priori* fashion determine and make necessary *all our actions*.[2] Now morality is the only code of laws applying to our actions which can be derived completely *a priori* from principles. Accordingly, the metaphysics of morals is really pure moral philosophy, with no underlying basis of anthropology or of other empirical {A 842, B 870} conditions. The term 'metaphysics', in its *strict*[3] sense, is commonly reserved for the metaphysics of speculative reason. But as pure moral philosophy really forms part of this special

---

[1] [*Kritik.*] [2] [*das Tun und Lassen.*]
[3] [Reading, with the 4th edition, *in eigenen Verstande* for *im engeren Verstande.*]

branch of human and philosophical knowledge derived from pure reason, we shall retain for it the title 'metaphysics'. We are not, however, at present concerned with it, and may therefore leave it aside.

It is of the utmost importance to *isolate* the various modes of knowledge according as they differ in kind and in origin, and to secure that they be not confounded owing to the fact that usually, in our employment of them, they are combined. What the chemist does in the analysis of substances, and the mathematician in his special disciplines, is in still greater degree incumbent upon the philosopher, that he may be able to determine with certainty the part which belongs to each special kind of knowledge in the diversified employment of the understanding and its special value and influence. Human reason, since it first began to think, or rather to reflect, has never been able to dispense with a metaphysics; but also has never been able to obtain it in a form sufficiently free from all foreign elements. The idea of such a science is as old as speculative human reason; and what rational being does not speculate, either in scholastic or in popular fashion? It must be admitted, however, that the two elements of our knowledge—that which is in our power[1] completely *a priori*, and that which is obtainable only *a posteriori* from experience—have never been very clearly distinguished, not even by professional thinkers, and that they have therefore failed to bring about the delimitation of a special kind of knowledge, and thereby the true idea of the science which has preoccupied human reason so long and so greatly. When metaphysics was declared to be the science of the first principles of human knowledge, the intention was not to mark out a quite special kind of knowledge, but only a certain precedence in respect of generality, which was not sufficient to distinguish such knowledge from the empirical. For among empirical principles we can distinguish some that are more general, and so higher in rank than others; but where in such a series of subordinated members—a series in which we do not distinguish what is completely *a priori* from what is known only *a posteriori*—are we to draw the line which distinguishes the highest or *first* members from the lower subordinate members? What should we say, if in the

A 843
B 871

---

[1] [*Gewalt.*]

reckoning of time we could distinguish the epochs of the world only by dividing them into the first centuries and those that follow? We should ask: Does the fifth, the tenth century, etc., belong with the first centuries? So in like manner I ask: Does the concept of the extended belong to metaphysics? You answer, Yes. Then, that of body too? Yes. And that of $\left\{\begin{matrix} A\ 844 \\ B\ 872 \end{matrix}\right.$ fluid body? You now become perplexed; for at this rate everything will belong to metaphysics. It is evident, therefore, that the mere degree of subordination (of the particular[1] under the general) cannot determine the limits of a science; in the case under consideration, only complete difference of kind and of origin will suffice. But the fundamental idea of metaphysics was obscured on yet another side, owing to its exhibiting, as *a priori* knowledge, a certain similarity to mathematics. Certainly they are related, in so far as they both have an *a priori* origin; but when we bear in mind the difference between philosophical and mathematical knowledge, namely, that the one is derived from concepts, whereas in the other we arrive at *a priori* judgments only through the construction of concepts, we have to recognise a decided difference of kind, which has indeed always been in a manner felt but could never be defined by means of any clear criteria. Thus it has come about that since philosophers failed in the task of developing even the idea of their science, they could have no determinate end or secure guidance in the elaboration of it, and, accordingly, in this arbitrarily conceived enterprise, ignorant as they were of the path to be taken, they have always been at odds with one another as regards the discoveries which each claimed to have made on his own separate path, with the result that their science has been brought into contempt, first among outsiders, and finally even among themselves.

All pure *a priori* knowledge, owing to the special faculty $\left\{\begin{matrix} A\ 845 \\ B\ 873 \end{matrix}\right.$ of knowledge in which alone it can originate, has in itself a peculiar unity; and metaphysics is the philosophy which has as its task the statement of that knowledge in this systematic unity. Its speculative part, which has especially appropriated this name, namely, what we entitle *metaphysics of nature*, and which considers everything in so far as *it is* (not that which

---

[1] [Reading, with Erdmann, *des Besondren* for *das Besondere*.]

ought to be) by means of *a priori* concepts, is divided in the following manner.

Metaphysics, in the narrower meaning of the term, consists of *transcendental philosophy* and *physiology* of pure reason. The former treats only of the understanding and of reason, in a system of concepts and principles which relate to objects in general but take no account of objects that *may be given* (*Ontologia*); the latter treats of *nature*, that is, of the sum of *given* objects (whether given to the senses, or, if we will, to some other kind of intuition) and is therefore *physiology*—although only *rationalis*. The employment of reason in this rational study of nature is either physical or hyperphysical, or, in more adequate terms, is either *immanent* or *transcendent*. The former is concerned with such knowledge of nature as can be applied in experience (*in concreto*), the latter with that connection of objects of experience which transcends all experience. This *transcendent* physiology has as its object either an *inner* connection or an *outer* connection, both, however, transcending possible experience. As dealing with an inner connection it is the physiology of nature as a whole, that is, the *transcendental knowledge of the world*; as dealing with an outer connection, it is the physiology of the relation of nature as a whole to a being above nature, that is to say, it is the *transcendental knowledge of God*.

A 846 }
B 874 }

Immanent physiology, on the other hand, views nature as the sum of all objects of the senses, and therefore just as it is given us, but solely in accordance with *a priori* conditions, under which alone it can ever be given us. There are only two kinds of such objects. 1. Those of the outer senses, and so their sum, *corporeal nature*. 2. The object of inner sense, the soul, and in accordance with our fundamental concepts of it, *thinking nature*. The metaphysics of corporeal nature is entitled *physics*; and as it must contain only the principles of an *a priori* knowledge of it, *rational physics*. The metaphysics of thinking nature is entitled *psychology*, and on the same ground is to be understood as being only the *rational knowledge* of it.

The whole system of metaphysics thus consists of four main parts: (1) ontology; (2) rational physiology; (3) rational cosmology; (4) rational theology. The second part, namely, the doctrine of nature as developed by pure reason, contains ${\scriptstyle\left\{\begin{array}{l}\text{A 847}\\\text{B 875}\end{array}\right.}$ two divisions, *physica rationalis*^a and *psychologia rationalis*.

The originative[1] idea of a philosophy of pure reason itself prescribes this division, which is therefore *architectonic*, in accordance with the essential ends of reason, and not merely *technical*, in accordance with accidentally observed similarities, and so instituted as it were at haphazard. Accordingly the division is also unchangeable and of legislative authority. There are, however, some points which may well seem doubtful, and may weaken our conviction as to the legitimacy of its claims.

First of all, how can I expect to have knowledge *a priori* (and therefore a metaphysics) of objects in so far as they are given to our senses, that is, given in an *a posteriori* manner? And how is it possible to know the nature of things and to arrive at a rational physiology according to principles ${\scriptstyle\left\{\begin{array}{l}\text{A 848}\\\text{B 876}\end{array}\right.}$ *a priori*? The answer is this: we take nothing more from experience than is required to *give* us an object of outer or of inner sense. The object of outer sense we obtain through the mere concept of matter (impenetrable, lifeless extension), the object of inner sense through the concept of a thinking being (in the empirical inner representation, 'I think'). As to the rest, in the whole metaphysical treatment of these objects, we must entirely dispense with all empirical principles which profess to add to these concepts any other more special experience, with a view to our passing further judgments upon the objects.

Secondly, how are we to regard *empirical psychology*,

^a I must not be taken as meaning thereby what is commonly called *physica generalis*; the latter is rather mathematics than philosophy of nature. The metaphysics of nature is quite distinct from mathematics. It is very far from enlarging our knowledge in the fruitful manner of mathematics, but still is very important as yielding a criticism of the pure knowledge of understanding in its application to nature. For lack of it, even mathematicians, holding to certain common concepts, which though common are yet in fact metaphysical, have unconsciously encumbered their doctrine of nature with hypotheses which vanish upon criticism of the principles involved, without, however, doing the least injury to the employment of mathematics—employment which is quite indispensable in this field.

[1] [*ursprüngliche.*]

which has always claimed its place in metaphysics, and from which in our times such great things have been expected for the advancement of metaphysics, the hope of succeeding by *a priori* methods having been abandoned. I answer that it belongs where the proper (empirical) doctrine of nature belongs, namely, by the side of *applied* philosophy, the *a priori* principles of which are contained in pure philosophy; it is therefore so far connected with applied philosophy, though not to be confounded with it. Empirical psychology is thus completely banished from the domain of metaphysics; it is indeed already completely excluded by the very idea of the latter science. In conformity, however, with scholastic usage we must allow it some sort of a place (although as an episode only) in metaphysics, and this from economical motives, because it is not yet so rich as to be able to form a subject of study by itself, and yet is too important to be entirely excluded and forced to settle elsewhere, in a neighbourhood that might well prove much less congenial than that of metaphysics. Though it is but a stranger it has long been accepted as a member of the household, and we allow it to stay for some time longer, until it is in a position to set up an establishment of its own in a complete anthropology, the pendant to the empirical doctrine of nature.

A 849
B 877

Such, then, in general, is the idea of metaphysics. At first more was expected from metaphysics than could reasonably be demanded, and for some time it diverted itself with pleasant anticipations. But these hopes having proved deceptive, it has now fallen into general disrepute. The argument of our Critique, taken as a whole, must have sufficiently convinced the reader that although metaphysics cannot be the foundation of religion, it must always continue to be a bulwark of it, and that human reason, being by its very nature dialectical, can never dispense with such a science, which curbs it, and by a scientific and completely convincing self-knowledge, prevents the devastations of which a lawless speculative reason would otherwise quite inevitably be guilty in the field of morals as well as in that of religion. We can therefore be sure that however cold or contemptuously critical may be the attitude of those who judge a science not by its nature but by its accidental effects, we shall always return to metaphysics as to a beloved one with whom we have had a quarrel. For here we are

B 878
A 850

concerned with essential ends—ends with which metaphysics must ceaselessly occupy itself, either in striving for genuine insight into them, or in refuting those who profess already to have attained it.

Metaphysics, alike of nature and of morals, and especially that criticism of our adventurous and self-reliant reason which serves as an introduction or propaedeutic to metaphysics, alone properly constitutes what may be entitled philosophy, in the strict sense of the term. Its sole preoccupation is wisdom; and it seeks it by the path of science, which, once it has been trodden, can never be overgrown, and permits of no wandering. Mathematics, natural science, even our empirical knowledge, have a high value as means, for the most part, to contingent ends, but also, in the ultimate outcome, to ends that are necessary and essential to humanity. This latter service, however, they can discharge only as they are aided by a knowledge through reason from pure concepts, which, however we may choose to entitle it, is really nothing but metaphysics.

For the same reason metaphysics is also the full and complete development[1] of human reason. Quite apart from its influence, as science, in connection with certain specific ends, $\left\{\begin{array}{l} \text{A 851} \\ \text{B 879} \end{array}\right.$ it is an indispensable discipline. For in dealing with reason it treats of those elements and highest maxims which must form the basis of the very *possibility* of some sciences, and of the *use* of all. That, as mere speculation, it serves rather to prevent errors than to extend knowledge, does not detract from its value. On the contrary this gives it dignity and authority, through that censorship which secures general order and harmony, and indeed the well-being of the scientific commonwealth, preventing those who labour courageously and fruitfully on its behalf from losing sight of the supreme end, the happiness of all mankind.

---

[1] [*die Vollendung aller Kultur.*]

A 852} THE TRANSCENDENTAL DOCTRINE OF METHOD
B 880}

CHAPTER IV

THE HISTORY OF PURE REASON

THIS title stands here only in order to indicate one remaining
division of the system, which future workers must complete.
I content myself with casting a cursory glance, from a purely
transcendental point of view, namely, that of the nature of
pure reason, on the works of those who have laboured in this
field—a glance which reveals [many stately] structures, but in
ruins only.

It is a very notable fact, although it could not have been
otherwise, that in the infancy of philosophy men began where
we should incline to end, namely, with the knowledge of God,
occupying themselves with the hope, or rather indeed with
the specific nature, of another world. However gross the
religious concepts generated by the ancient practices which
still persisted in each community from an earlier more
barbarous state, this did not prevent the more enlightened
members from devoting themselves to free investigation of
these matters; and they easily discerned that there could be
no better ground[1] or more dependable way of pleasing the invisible power that governs the world, and so of being happy
A 853} in another world at least, than by living the good life. Ac-
B 881} cordingly theology and morals were the two motives, or rather
the two points of reference, in all those abstract enquiries of
reason to which men came to devote themselves. It was chiefly,
however, the former that step by step committed the purely
speculative reason to those labours which afterwards became
so renowned under the name of metaphysics.

1 [Reading, with Rosenkranz, *grundlichere* for *grundliche*.]

666

I shall not here attempt to distinguish the periods of history in which this or that change in metaphysics came about, but shall only give a cursory sketch of the various ideas which gave rise to the chief revolutions [in metaphysical theory]. And here I find that there are three issues in regard to which the most noteworthy changes have taken place in the course of the resulting controversies.

1 *In respect of the object* of all our 'knowledge through reason', some have been mere *sensualists*, others mere *intellectualists*. *Epicurus* may be regarded as the outstanding philosopher among the former, and *Plato* among the latter. The distinction between the two schools, subtle as it is, dates from the earliest times; and the two positions have ever since been maintained in unbroken continuity. Those of the former school maintained that reality is to be found solely in the objects of the senses, and that all else is fiction; those of the latter school, on the other hand, declared that in the senses there is nothing but illusion, and that only {A 854 / B 882} the understanding knows what is true. The former did not indeed deny reality to the concepts of the understanding; but this reality was for them merely *logical*, whereas for the others it was *mystical*. The former conceded *intellectual concepts*, but admitted sensible objects only. The latter required that true objects should be *purely intelligible*, and maintained that by means of the pure understanding we have an *intuition* that is unaccompanied by the senses—the senses, in their view, serving only to confuse the understanding.

2. *In respect of the origin* of the modes of 'knowledge through pure reason', the question is as to whether they are derived from experience, or whether in independence of experience they have their origin in reason. *Aristotle* may be regarded as the chief of the *empiricists*, and *Plato* as the chief of the *noologists*. *Locke*, who in modern times followed Aristotle, and *Leibniz*, who followed Plato (although in considerable disagreement with his mystical system), have not been able to bring this conflict to any definitive conclusion. However we may regard Epicurus, he was at least much more consistent in this sensual system than Aristotle and Locke, inasmuch as he never sought to pass by inference beyond the limits of experience. This is especially true as regards Locke,

who, after having derived all concepts and principles from experience, goes so far in the use of them as to assert that we
A 855⎫
B 883⎭ can prove the existence of God and the immortality of the soul with the same conclusiveness as any mathematical proposition—though both lie entirely outside the limits of possible experience.

3. *In respect of method.*—If anything is to receive the title of method, it must be a procedure in accordance with principles. We may divide the methods now prevailing in this field of enquiry into the *naturalistic* and the *scientific*. The *naturalist* of pure reason adopts as his principle that through common reason, without science, that is, through what he calls sound reason, he is able, in regard to those most sublime questions which form the problem of metaphysics, to achieve more than is possible through speculation. Thus he is virtually asserting that we can determine the size and distance of the moon with greater certainty by the naked eye than by mathematical devices. This is mere misology, reduced to principles; and what is most absurd of all, the neglect of all artificial means is eulogised as a special *method* of extending our knowledge. For as regards those who are naturalists from *lack* of more insight, they cannot rightly be blamed. They follow common reason, without boasting of their ignorance as a method which contains the secret how we are to fetch truth from the deep well of Democritus. *Quod sapio, satis est mihi; non ego curo, esse quod Arcesilas aerumnosique*
A 856⎫
B 884⎭ *Solones*[a] is the motto with which they may lead a cheerful and praiseworthy life, not troubling themselves about science, nor by their interference bringing it into confusion.

As regards those who adopt a *scientific* method, they have the choice of proceeding either *dogmatically* or *sceptically*; but in any case they are under obligation to proceed *systematically*. I may cite the celebrated Wolff as a representative of the former mode of procedure, and David Hume as a representative of the latter, and may then, conformably with my present purpose, leave all others unnamed. The *critical* path alone is still open. If the reader has had the courtesy and patience to accompany me along this path, he may now judge for himself whether, if he cares to lend his aid in making this

[a] Persius [*Sat.* iii 78-79].

path into a high-road, it may not be possible to achieve before the end of the present century what many centuries have
not been able to accomplish; namely, to secure for human
reason complete satisfaction in regard to that with which it
has all along so eagerly occupied itself, though hitherto
in vain.

INDEX

Absolute, 78, 317 18. *See* Unconditioned

Accidents, and substance, 214-16, 333, 389, 403, 405-6; the accidental, 262, 390

Action (*Handlung*), as derivative concept, 115, 228; empirical criterion of substance, 229

Actuality (*Wirklichkeit, Realität*), category of, 185, 239, 242-4, 249-51, 252 n., 350. *See* Reality

Aesthetic, Transcendental, 65-91; meaning of term, 66, 93; alterations in second edition, 34; results of, 244, 266, 407

Affection, intuitions rest on, 105; of the self by itself, 87-8, 166, 168 n.

Affinity, 139-40, 145 ff., 488 n., 542. *See* Association

Algebra, 579, 590

Alteration (*Veränderung*), 115, 216-18, 230 ff., 255, 405-6, 413, 415 ff. *See* Change

Amphiboly, meaning of term, 282

Analogies of Experience, 208-38; meaning of term, 211

Analysis, 14, 47, 60-61, 111-12; all analysis presupposes synthesis, 152

Analytic and synthetic judgments, 48 ff., 70, 75, 76, 85-6, 155, 157, 189-194, 199, 274-5, 284, 363, 369-70, 444, 447, 504 ff., 530, 580 ff. *See* Synthetic *a priori* judgments

Analytic and synthetic methods, 119, 325 n., 374-5

Analytic unity of apperception, 154 and n.

Analytic, Transcendental, 102-296; content of, 98, 100, 103, 176-7, 466

Ancient philosophy, in general, 1, 9, 99, 215, 254 n., 516

Anthropology, 474

Anthropomorphism, 531, 566, 568

Anticipations of Perception, 201-8; meaning of expression, 202

Antinomies, 297-570; meaning of term, 328

Apagogical proofs, 625 ff.

Apodeictic judgments, 70, 75, 110

Appearance (*Erscheinung*), in general, 65, 124 ff., 143-4, 201, 470, 494; as opposed to things-in-themselves, 24, 82 ff., 172-3, 219-20, 230, 259, 265 ff., 278 ff., 282 ff., 346 ff., 351 ff., 356 ff., 381 ff., 440, 441, 444 ff., 447 ff., 453 ff., 457, 460, 466 ff., 482 ff., 485 ff., 494; as opposed to illusion, 88-9, 440

Apperception, 127, 472; transcendental unity of, 135-61, 166, 168 ff., 209 ff., 237, 335 ff., 362 ff., 369 ff., 376, 377 ff.; empirical apperception, 136, 141, 153, 158; analytic unity of, 154 and n.; apperception distinguished from inner sense, 136, 166, 168 ff., 365 ff., 368 ff. *See* 'I think'

Apprehension, 144, 209, 224; synthesis of, 131-2, 170-71, 173, 233-4; is always successive, 213, 219

A priori, in general, 11, 18 ff., 22 ff., 42-8, 58 ff., 149, 195, 210, 605-6; meaning of term, 43, 188; concepts, 45, 581, 583, *see* Understanding, pure concepts of; synthetic judgments, 50 ff., 70, 76, 80, 85 ff., 91, 237-8, 243, 251, 253, 265, 273 ff., 353, 363, 370, 402, 529, 545 ff., 580 ff., 589, 608, 609-10, 621; *a priori* concepts presupposed in all experience, 42, 45, 126, 133-50, 170-71, 174, 193, 219, 223, 225-6; *a priori* character of mathematics, 52, 68, 70-71, 85-6, 259-60, 577 ff.; forms of intuition are *a priori*, 66, 68, 70 ff., 74 ff., 81, 170-71; *a priori* knowledge in logic, 94 ff., 102, 179; how *a*

THE END